To Hilary a...
with very b...
fro...
David.
September 2018.

From Hackney to Horsham

a schoolmaster's life

by

David Arnold

Grosvenor House
Publishing Limited

The right of David Arnold to be identified as the author of this
work has been asserted in accordance with Section 78
of the Copyright, Designs and Patents Act 1988

The book cover picture is copyright to David Arnold

This book is published by
Grosvenor House Publishing Ltd
Link House
140 The Broadway, Tolworth, Surrey, KT6 7HT.
www.grosvenorhousepublishing.co.uk

A CIP record for this book
is available from the British Library

ISBN 978-1-78623-156-7

For Cathy

◇◇◇◇◇◇◇◇◇◇◇◇◇◇◇◇◇◇◇◇◇◇

who read the whole thing and offered substantial

criticisms, most of which I accepted and acted on.

I am grateful to her for that and much else as well.

Contents

◇◇◇◇◇◇◇◇◇◇◇◇◇◇◇◇◇◇◇◇◇

VIII. KGV (1976-83)

IX. Collyer's (1983-92)

X. The FEFC Years (1992-2000)

Illustrations

THE ARNOLD FAMILY

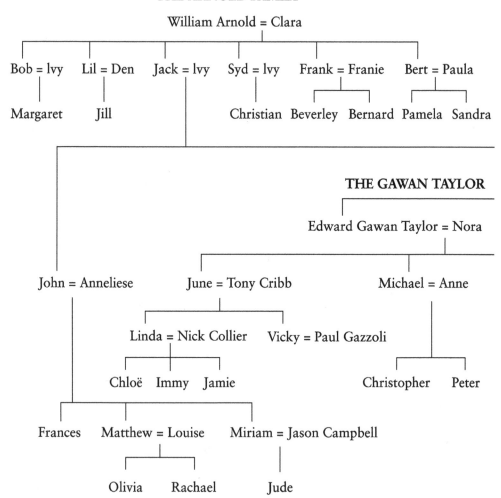

William Arnold = Clara

Bob = Ivy   Lil = Den   Jack = Ivy   Syd = Ivy   Frank = Franie   Bert = Paula

Margaret   Jill   Christian   Beverley   Bernard   Pamela   Sandra

THE GAWAN TAYLOR

Edward Gawan Taylor = Nora

John = Anneliese   June = Tony Cribb   Michael = Anne

Linda = Nick Collier   Vicky = Paul Gazzoli

Chloë   Immy   Jamie   Christopher   Peter

Frances   Matthew = Louise   Miriam = Jason Campbell

Olivia   Rachael   Jude

Table.

THE ROBERTS FAMILY

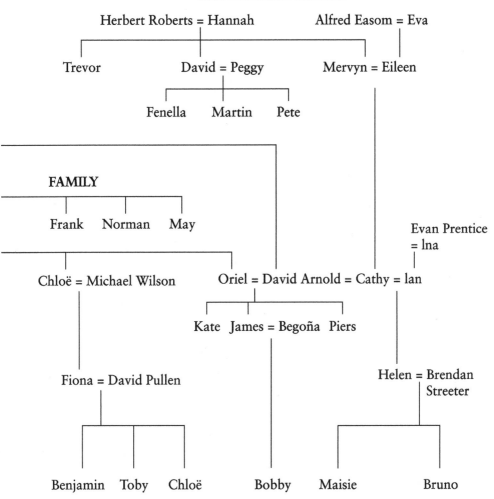

Herbert Roberts = Hannah   Alfred Easom = Eva

Trevor   David = Peggy   Mervyn = Eileen

Fenella   Martin   Pete

FAMILY

Frank   Norman   May

Evan Prentice = lna

Chloë = Michael Wilson   Oriel = David Arnold = Cathy = lan

Kate   James = Begoña   Piers

Fiona = David Pullen

Helen = Brendan Streeter

Benjamin   Toby   Chloë   Bobby   Maisie   Bruno

Childhood
(1933–1944)

1. Beginnings

◇◇◇◇◇◇◇◇◇◇◇◇◇◇◇◇◇◇◇◇◇◇◇◇◇◇◇◇◇◇◇◇◇◇◇

On 24th October 1933 Mrs Violet Kray of Stene Street in Hackney was delivered of two healthy baby boys, the twins Reggie and Ronnie, who eventually acquired fame and notoriety after engaging vigorously in crime for about twenty years and then in their mid-thirties were sent to prison. Ronnie died in prison in 1995 and Reggie five years later, a few weeks after being released. On the morning of 1st November 1933, a week after the Kray twins were born, my mother, Mrs Ivy Arnold, of Laura Place, nearby and also in Hackney, was similarly delivered of twins, John and David, in the Salvation Army hospital in the Lower Clapton Road.

Before we were two years old we moved just over five miles to the North-east, across the Hackney marshes and Epping Forest, to Woodford Bridge, where John and I grew up in respectable obscurity. But I have sometimes imagined swapping places with the Krays and have hoped that, if we had stayed in Hackney and set out to organise the crime there, we would have managed it more discreetly and more effectively. I have also wondered if Reggie and Ronnie, with a home life and an education more like ours, might have led worthy and respectable lives, perhaps one as a clergyman and the other a schoolmaster.

My grandfather, William Arnold, had been a prosperous farrier in London towards the end of the nineteenth century. That is, he had made a good living from shoeing horses at a time when there were a lot of horses to be shod, and as a young man he met and married the daughter of the coachman of the Earl of Rosebery. Archibald Primrose, 5th Earl of Rosebery, had by then, before the age of fifty, achieved his threefold ambition of marrying an American heiress, becoming prime minister (1894-5) and winning the Derby (twice during the eighteen months that he was prime minister). He had a London house (noblemen in those days had houses rather than homes) in Hanover Square, and it was from that house that my grandparents were married in 1896.

In the early years of the twentieth century they had six sons and four daughters. One of the boys and three of the girls died young. The six children who survived to adulthood (Bob, Lil, Jack, Sid, Frank and Bert – in that order) all married and had either one or two children. By the 1930s, when their children were born, it seemed that you could have a better life and give your children a better life if you only had one or two, and by then it was possible to avoid having more than one or two.

The first three boys all married girls called Ivy, the name of a clinging vine which was a popular symbol of femininity in the early twentieth century. Bob and Bob's Ivy had a daughter called Margaret, and they were the only ones who lived on the far side of London, at Hayes in Middlesex. Jack (my father, John Stanley Arnold) and Jack's Ivy had twin boys, the elder of which was my brother John. We were the oldest of the cousins. Sid and Sid's Ivy had a son called Christian, who was eight years younger than us. Frank and Franie had a daughter, Beverley, or Bev, blonde and beautiful, and later a son called Bernard. Bert and Paula had two girls, Pamela and Sandra, or Pam and Sand, both dark-haired and pretty, taking after their mother, who was exotically Jewish. Lil, who was the second child to be born and whose husband was called Den, had a daughter called Jill, and she, Christian and Sandra were all the same age. Beverley and Pamela were a bit older. Margaret was only about eighteen months younger than John and me.

While my father and his brothers and sister were all small children the family lived for a while in a three storey house in the Holloway Road in North London. But my grandfather was no longer a prosperous farrier. After being kicked by a horse he took to drinking too much. There were too many children, and trade was poor as motor vehicles replaced the horse in much of London. My Auntie Lil, who outlived all her brothers and eventually died at the age of 101 in 2006, recalled towards the end of her life how their landlord had offered to sell my grandmother the house for £100, but she had replied that she had too many responsibilities already and couldn't take on a debt as large as that. It would probably be worth a couple of million now, nearly a hundred years later, in 2017.

Some time between the wars they moved to Islington, to a house in Sonning Street, immediately to the north-east of Pentonville Prison. The road survived the Blitz of 1940 but disappeared when the whole area was redeveloped in the 1960s. Back at the time of the First World War the boys all slept in the same bed, two at one end and three at the other, and they all went to school at St James's Church of England elementary school in Highbury. There my father, born in 1906, a year after Lil, learnt the five Rs, Reading, Writing and Arithmetic, Right and Wrong, sang in the choir and played in the school football team, for which he borrowed a pair of his mother's boots.

He left school at what was then the school leaving age of thirteen, and many years later, when he was away in the army, my mother showed me his school leaving report which said what an admirable and clever little boy he was, what an asset to the choir and football team, and ended with the words 'He will make a first-rate workman.' His first job was as a chaff-cutter. But his education continued in the Boy Scouts ('The Boy Scouts', he said to me once, 'is the poor boy's public school.'), and I still have his copy of the *Hackney Scout Song Book* and a photograph of him in his scout uniform.

It was through the scout movement that he somehow encountered my mother. She, Ivy Ireland, thus having the extraordinarily economical initials I.I., was also born in 1906. By contrast with my father's family, she was an only child and the illegitimate daughter of a young woman who was a cook in service in a large house in Barnsbury, a prosperous part of Islington before it fell on hard

5

My father as a young man. My mother playing the part of Titania in a school production of 'A Midsummer Night's Dream.'

times and long before it was revived and re-gentrified and became prosperous again.

In terms of the moral climate of the time my grandmother was fortunate to be allowed to keep her job, but she was not allowed to keep her baby with her, so my mother was brought up by her Aunt Nell, who saw her as a child of sin and regularly reminded her of that, and by her Uncle Ernie, a kindly, quiet jeweller who worked for a pittance in Hatton Gardens, fitting into gold and platinum settings jewels worth more than he earned in a year.

My mother always had a sense of insecurity. On the one hand she knew she ought never to have been conceived, still less born, and it was not till I was at university that she brought herself to tell me of her illegitimacy. ('What does it matter, Mum?' I said. 'It wasn't your fault.' But it clearly mattered to her.) On the other hand, she felt that she had somehow been cheated in life. From time to time as a child she had been able to visit her mother in Barnsbury. On one of those visits the lady of the house came down to the kitchen,

6

declared that so beautiful a child belonged in the drawing room rather than downstairs, and took her up to be admired by her fashionable friends. The memory remained with my mother, who combined a crippling sense of worthlessness with the feeling that she had been destined for something better and that her position in life as a housewife in a small house in a London suburb, with a husband and two small children, was somehow a mistake.

At the Barnsbury Central School a teacher devoted to both Shakespeare and my mother gave her all the best parts in her numerous productions, so my mother as a teenager played Titania in *A Midsummer Night's Dream*, Viola in *Twelfth Night* and Portia in *The Merchant of Venice*. The manager of the travelling *Ben Greet Theatre Company* offered her a job on the strength of one of her school performances, and all her life she would from time to time regret that she hadn't accepted it and had what she thought would have been a glamorous life as an actress. Instead she learnt shorthand and typing and got a job in a shipping firm in the city. Her mother died when she was eighteen, and she never knew her father.

Meanwhile my father was working in the factory of a small perfumery firm called *Breidenbach's* in Hackney. He was 5 foot 11 inches tall, handsome, and with dark hair which went grey during the war, while he was still in his thirties, and all his life he retained a relatively youthful figure and appearance. My mother, by contrast, was as a young woman slight, pretty and blonde, and only 5 foot 4 inches in height, but as she grew older put on weight. By the time they were out of their teens they wanted to get married, but though they saved what they could, they knew that one necessary consequence of marriage was that my mother would have to give up her job, since at the time it was felt unfair for a woman who had a man to keep her to deprive another girl of a job. So they put marriage off for two or three years while they tried to save some money, until at last, in early December of 1929, when they were both 23, they were married and moved into a flat in Laura Place, off the Lower Clapton Road in Hackney.

More than seventy years later, in 2002, Richard Chartres, the then Bishop of London, and the only man in the Church of England, my brother John said, who 'sounds like God, looks like God and very probably is God', preached at a service at St Paul's Cathedral to commemorate the founding of Christ's Hospital 450 years earlier. Afterwards, at lunch in the Guildhall, John, who by then had been the Dean of Durham for about the last dozen years, introduced me to him. He enquired about our origins, and when I mentioned Laura Place, he replied, 'Ah! I know Laura Place. I was at a meeting with the Metropolitan Commissioner of Police last night and Laura Place was on the agenda. It has been taken over by the Triad gangs.'

But seventy years earlier Laura Place had been a respectable road in a peaceful working class area. As it happens, John and I did not live there for the first six months of our lives. Our mother suffered from what is now called post-natal depression. So I went to be looked after by my grandmother in Sonning Street in Islington for six months, though any memories of her and my grandfather date from later. I remember her in the back yard behind the house with the mangle and its large wooden rollers, and I remember my grandfather throwing a penny to me out of the window and across the railings which prevented anyone from falling down to the basement. But they both died while I was still very young; and necessarily I have no recollection of either of my mother's parents.

Meanwhile John was cared for by some friends of my parents, Connie and Hugh Lazenby, who lived nearby in Powerscroft Road. Connie was a large and motherly nurse with no children of her own. Hugh, or Hughie, who had been born at the turn of the century, had joined the Royal Navy as a stoker in 1916, when he was only sixteen years old, and within a few weeks had found himself in the boiler-room of a battle cruiser in the Battle of Jutland. 'Is it usually as noisy as this?' he was reputed to have asked.

For the six months that our mother was ill, our father coped with work, a wife who was desperately unhappy in hospital, and with two new-born babies, one with friends and one with his parents in

Islington. He walked for miles each day from home to work, to his parents' house, to the hospital, to Powerscroft Road and home again, saving the cost of bus fares. Then by the early summer of 1934 my mother was well enough to come home.

Once she was home she applied herself effectively to being a loving wife and mother and a good housekeeper. She hugged her children and surrounded them with warmth and affection. She shopped carefully, cooked well and cleaned conscientiously. Both she and my father had seen enough of dirt and squalor to believe that 'Cleanliness is next to Godliness', and they had seen enough of drunkenness and its consequences to avoid having any alcoholic liquor in the house. It wasn't something they spoke about, and they would have a drink with other members of the family at Christmas time. But generally they avoided it, just as they avoided playing cards and any form of gambling, and they never entered a pub.

The one serious problem they had while we were still living at Laura Place was that John contracted poliomyelitis, which in those days everyone called infantile paralysis. He was looked after in the German Hospital in Dalston Lane, which was less than a mile from where we lived. Back in 1845, by an extraordinary act of philanthropy, that hospital had been founded principally to care for the large German community in the East End of London, but right from the start, more than a century before the founding of the National Health Service, it had provided free treatment, care and even arrangements for convalescence, for the poor of whatever nationality who lived in the area.

It was staffed largely by German nuns who had remained in Hackney throughout the First World War caring for the sick. That in itself was remarkable. It was also remarkable that they had been allowed to. It was there, in 1935, that a Doktor Winkler saved John from being what at that time was called a cripple. Not only was the treatment free. They also arranged for him to convalesce at the Lord Mayor Treloar Cripple's Home, Hospital and College at Alton in Hampshire. He was away in all for eighteen months, and by the time he came home we had moved to Woodford Bridge. I am told that I sat disconsolately in my high chair saying 'Johnny gone', and not understanding why he was gone.

I remember quite clearly that when he was back he had to wear a splint, and at night in the bed we shared there was a hard and uncomfortable board which stuck out sideways from the splint to stop him from turning over. Fortunately the damage to his muscles was slight, and by the time we were in our teens he could beat me over 100 or 220 yards.

The Doktor Winkler who had looked after John so well was, my parents told us later, an enthusiastic member of the Nazi Party, which had relatively recently come to power in Germany, and he spoke of the great achievements and potential benefits to mankind of the Third Reich. He returned to Germany before the Second World War began.

The nurses, most of them German nuns, took no interest in politics and stayed in Hackney when the war began to continue looking after their patients. At the end of May 1940, as the German army drove down towards Dunkirk, they were suddenly arrested and taken to Holloway prison. In August, at the height of the Battle of Britain, they were interned on the Isle of Man. The hospital staggered on with a skeleton staff and survived the Blitz and both the doodlebugs and the V2s, but in 1948, with the founding of the National Health Service, it lost its independent status. In the 1980s it was turned into flats.

Meanwhile John, like so many Londoners before him, benefited from the care the German nurses had provided, and in his case also from the care of the enthusiastic Nazi Doktor Winkler.

2. Waltham Road

◇◇◇◇◇◇◇◇◇◇◇◇◇◇◇◇◇◇◇◇◇◇◇◇◇◇◇◇◇◇◇◇◇◇◇◇◇◇

My parents' marriage, early in December 1929, was just six weeks after the Wall Street Crash of late October, whose repercussions were felt around the world. The following year, when *Breidenbach's* was taken over by *Eugene Rimmel*, my father was relieved to keep his job, but his pay was reduced from three pounds and five shillings a week (£3.25 in decimal currency) to just £3, and, of course, my mother was now no longer earning. But they lived frugally, continued to save, and in 1935, by which time they were both twenty-nine and my father had been working for sixteen years, they had saved enough to put down a deposit of £30 on a newly-built, end-of-terrace house costing £485 in the village of Woodford Bridge in Essex.

My parents were the first of their generation in the family to have children, and they were also the first to buy a house on a mortgage. The £3 a week which my father earned was a long way short of wealth, but it was not poverty either, and we lived quite comfortably through the 1930s on £156 a year – all the more because it was a deflationary period, with money gradually increasing in value and buying more.

Woodford Bridge was in the valley of the River Roding. The next stop on the railway line, travelling South-west towards London, was South Woodford, in an area which had a London postcode, E18, and Woodford Bridge, though an Essex village, was also a London suburb. Both Woodford Bridge and South Woodford are now parts of the Greater London Borough of Redbridge.

A short walk away were the oaks and beeches and hornbeams of Epping Forest, and beyond the ditch at the end of our garden was open marshland which flooded every winter, but where, for most of the year, the horses which pulled the carts of the local

11

tradesmen grazed freely. Immediately beyond the marsh and across the river was a gas works with two large gas holders, and beyond that was Ray Lodge Elementary School, where John and I started in the infants department at the beginning of November 1938, when we reached the age of five in the middle of the Autumn Term.

It was only about seven miles by bicycle to the factory where our father now worked for *Delavelles*, another perfumery firm, this time in Orsman Road, Hoxton, backing on to the Grand Union Canal, and still earning £3 a week. He cycled there six days a week for five and a half years (but only for the mornings on Saturdays) until he joined the army in January 1941. He bought boxes and bottles and bottle tops and labels and could calculate the cost of seven gross at eleven pence three farthings a dozen in his head. He had a range of self-taught arithmetical devices which were useful in his job. It is possible, for example, to multiply numbers by eleven by adding the integers together and putting the answer in the middle. Take, for example, 23 and 71 and 48. The answers are 253, 781 and, slightly more complicated, 528. He enjoyed passing on such things to his twin sons.

Meanwhile, from where we lived in Woodford, steam trains of the L.N.E.R. (the London North Eastern Railway) ran to Liverpool Street in the city, the hub of the British Empire, only eight miles away, and six miles south of us were the Royal Albert and King George V docks, half way between the Isle of Dogs to the west and the point east of that where the River Roding emptied into the Thames.

From Woodford Station you could walk down Snakes Lane, past Ray Lodge School, turn left over a bridge across the River Roding, and into Woodford Bridge. The first shop on the left was a green-grocer's and the last before you turned into Waltham Road was *Roberts, Wet, Dried and Fried, Fishmongers*. On the right-hand side of Waltham Road the houses looked relatively old, and until recently they had looked out over the marsh to the River Roding. But now there were two newly built terraces of houses facing them, five houses in each, and ours was No.9, at the end of the first terrace. Next to us, in No.7, were the Foggs. Across the passage-way between the two terraces, at No.11, were Mr and Mrs Davis, who let us play in their garden and could be relied on for a cup of sugar or anything else if we ran out. Further along was Mrs Bassenthwaite, a large competent woman who ran things like the local W.V.S., the Women's Voluntary Service, though that must have been later, during the war.

Beyond the Bassenthwaites were the Waites, who had a grown-up daughter. It used to puzzle me that the Co-op milkman used to leave his horse and cart outside the Waites's house for quite a long while some mornings, and my parents wouldn't tell me why. I dis-approved of the milkman because when I went to the door to pay him and give him our Co-op number (808464) he used to call me 'Dave.' He was a communist and wore a hammer and sickle badge in his lapel, and I decided that I disapproved of communism because communists were the sort of people who called you 'Dave' when your real name was 'David.' But there was an advan-tage to his leaving his horse and cart outside the Waites's house. The horse quite often left a pile of manure on the road and I was able to go out with my bucket and spade and put the horse manure around our tomato plants.

The last house before a turning left down to the marsh, shortly before the right-hand turning up Stoneycroft Road, belonged to Mr and Mrs Plant. Mr Plant worked as an engine driver on the railways, something which was generally seen as rather prestig-ious, and Mrs Plant was someone who could always be relied on to help her neighbours in a range of different ways. If a young woman was having a baby, she would help with the delivery. If someone had died, she would lay out the body. Between them she and Mrs Bassenthwaite seemed to be able to do everything that needed doing to keep the surrounding area functioning.

No-one in the road had a car, and none of the houses was built with a garage. You either went by foot or by the No.10 bus, which ran all the way from Woodford Bridge to Victoria Station in the West End, or you could go by train to Liverpool Street Station in the City. The only person I knew who had a car was Doctor Roberts, the local GP, and even during the war, when petrol was unavailable to most people, he was still allowed to have a petrol ration in order to be able to visit his patients. He charged five shillings a visit, but when John was seriously ill and he thought we could not afford it, he waived the fee.

We lived for twenty years at 9, Waltham Road, Woodford Bridge, Essex. The house was typical of many built in the London suburbs at that time. Downstairs there was a front room with a piano, and at the back was the living room, with a so-called back-boiler behind the fireplace, so that one had hot water in winter but not in the summer. In summer, if you wanted hot water, you had to boil it up in a kettle on the gas stove or in the gas boiler in the kitchen. In that boiler my mother did the regular weekly wash each Monday and I still have hanging on the wall of my garage the washboard that she used. Beyond the entrance hall was the kitchen and beyond that the garden. In summer the washing was hung on a line in the garden. In winter it was hung on a line diagonally across the living room.

Upstairs were two double bedrooms. My parents slept in a double bed in the one at the front. John and I slept in a double bed in the one at the back. There was also a small single, spare bedroom, which for many years was unused, a separate bathroom and a separate lavatory. We had electric light in every room and my mother had an electric iron of which she was particularly proud. In the living room we had a wireless on which it was possible to listen to *Children's Hour* and in particular to *Stories for Younger Listeners*.

For more than twenty years of my life 9, Waltham Road was my home. To my parents it was also the fruit of years of conscientious hard work. You needed to do 'a fair day's work for a fair day's pay', and if you did, this was the reward. On the piano in the front room my mother could play almost any tune by ear, and she and our father would sing a wide range of music, he a baritone and she a soprano. We also had a wind-up gramophone, on which John and I would, time and again, play each of the few records in the house. The best of them and the most played was an English version of Schubert's setting of Goethe's poem, *The Erl-King*, which had on the other side a setting by Tchaikovsky of Count Alexey Tolstoy's poem, *Don Juan's Serenade*, both of which our father could sing.

Two of the pictures on the wall were reproductions of portraits by Greuze and Romney. Each had been bought by my mother from the woman in the flat below us in Laura Place for the price of a pint of porter. The Greuze was a picture of an idyllically beautiful and wistful listening girl; the Romney was a portrait of Emma, Lady Hamilton, the mistress of Lord Nelson. But I was not told that she was Nelson's mistress.

There were relatively few books in the house, so we read everything there was, from Enid Blyton's *The Enchanted Wood* (a book which, contrary to the popular view of Enid Blyton's work, did an immense amount to stir my youthful imagination) to *The World Pictorial Gazeteer*, *Lamb's Tales from Shakespeare*, a number of Shakespeare's plays (mainly the ones my mother had acted in as a teen-ager) and Oliver Goldsmith's *The Vicar of Wakefield*. When I went away to school at Christ's Hospital at the age of ten, my first form master, Teddy Edwards, was surprised by my knowledge of and liking for Shakespeare and astonished that I had read *The Vicar of Wakefield*. But I had simply read anything in the house.

Every year the marsh flooded and the bus conductors called out 'Woodford-under-water' when they reached our bus stop. Epping Forest, which went on for ever, was at its nearest point not much more than a mile's walk away. Half-way up the hill in the direction of Chigwell was a smithy, where most of the trade still consisted of shoeing horses. At the top of the hill was St Paul's Church, and across the green the No 10 bus began its journey from Woodford Bridge via the Mile End Road to Victoria Station, crossing the river to the south of the Thames at London Bridge and back again to the north side of the river over Westminster Bridge.

Because we lived in Waltham Road for twenty years, early memories are mixed with later ones and with oft-repeated stories, so it is difficult to sort them out. Inevitably we spent far more time with our mother than with our father, because so much of the time he was away at work, and later in the army, but when we were small we looked forward each day to the time when he got back and would pick us up in turn and rub each of us against the stubbly bristles on his chin. He had a natural gift for playing with children, kicking a ball about or whatever, so that on Saturday afternoons other children in the road would sometimes call at No.9 to ask if Mr Arnold was coming out to play.

On our second birthday, when John was still away in hospital, my father brought to see me a girl called Violet Gostling who was eighteen at the time and worked in the same factory as he did. John and I called her Auntie Gossie and she had a considerable influence on our lives. She would give us Enid Blyton's *Sunny Stories* and a three-penny piece and take us for walks in Epping Forest. Later she would take us to the Regent's Park Open Air Theatre and the Old Vic, to the People's Palace in the Mile End Road to hear Bach's *Christmas Oratorio*, to a Prom at the Albert Hall to be introduced to Delius, or to an opera at Sadler's Wells, and to the Kingsley Hall in Bow to see where Gandhi had stayed during his visit to England in 1931.

While she was still quite young she became a Labour councillor and for decades was involved in the provision of good libraries, schools, arts festivals and such-like in the Leytonstone area, and at ninety she was rewarded with an MBE. She always lived in the same house in Cheneys Road, Leytonstone, where she had been born, and when she was ninety-six and I was eighty, seventy-eight years after we first met, I could from time to time drive up from Horsham, through the Blackwall Tunnel, through what used to be docklands and the East End, up the A12 to the Green Man

16

roundabout and from there to Cheneys Road, where everything was much the same, except that the gas mantle had been replaced by electric light and I called her Gossie rather than Auntie Gossie. Sadly in 2014, just after her 97th birthday, she died.

Sometimes, on a Saturday afternoon, our father would take us to see Leyton Orient playing football, and one Saturday after the Second World War, when Stanley Matthews was playing for Blackpool and they came south to play against Tottenham Hotspurs, we went with him to see Matthews playing brilliantly on the right wing, but marked by a young and similarly good Spurs left back called Alf Ramsey, who was later to go on to be the manager of the England team which won the World Cup in 1966.

On Sundays John and I often got up before our parents and took them a cup of tea. Apparently, on the morning of Sunday 16th March 1939 we went in with their tea and a copy of their regular Sunday newspaper, *Reynolds News*, and John, at the age of five, read the headline and told them that the Germans had marched into Czechoslovakia. That summer we went to Southend on a paddle steamer, the *Golden Eagle*, which used to ply up and down the Thames from London to Southend and back, taking Londoners on day trips. We enjoyed it so much that on another occasion we all got up early, my parents bought two cheap day-return work-man's tickets to Southend and back on the train, and John and I were able to travel free.

Later still, in the summer of 1939, we went for a week on our first family holiday, to Littlehampton on the Sussex coast. There I managed to fall into the round pond, after which my parents re-clothed me in Woolworth's for half-a-crown (twelve and a half pence in decimal currency): 6d. (or two and a half new pence) for a shirt, another 6d. for shorts, 1/- (or 5p.) for a pair of plimsolls, and finally another 6d. for an elastic belt with a snake clasp, which I loved. It was our last family holiday for a long while, because once the war began it was no longer possible to go down to the coast.

Both John and I look back on our childhood with pleasure and with gratitude to our parents. They loved each other, and John and I grew up listening to them singing duets from the musical, *Lilac Time*, based on Schubert's music, while my mother played the tunes on the piano by ear. Their affection for each other and for us was so much a part of the atmosphere of our growing up that it came as a surprise later to discover that not all couples were so devoted.

3. Evacuation, the Battle of Britain and the Blitz

When the war came it was clear even to a child that no-one wanted it. There was a sense of apprehension, and grown-ups with worried expressions talked about 'the last war.' On 3rd September 1939, the day war began, when we were still five years old but would be six in two months time, our mother went with John and me to Ray Lodge School to deliver us to the convoy of red, London, double-decker buses which was waiting to take all the children in the school to be evacuated.

I had a sort of rucksack on my back, made by my mother the previous evening out of a cloth bag and a pair of my father's braces, and containing my clothes. Over one shoulder was slung a bag with sandwiches and some water for the journey. Over the other was slung my gas mask. I knew that if the Germans attacked us, all I had to do was put the gas mask on and then I would be safe. So I was well equipped for the journey. Round my neck was a luggage label with my name and address, and like all the other children I was holding the toy bucket and spade I had been told to bring. My bucket had a Mickey Mouse pattern on it, which gave the impression that we were off to the sea-side, but really it was for peeing in on the journey.

I was given a little boy with dark curly hair to look after on the journey. He was only three, and for the first time in my life I felt a sense of responsibility for someone else. The bus took us eastwards through Essex to Heybridge near Maldon, where the River Blackwater empties into the North Sea, but we never got to the sea because the coast was banned to civilians. At Heybridge the local people turned out to welcome the busloads of London refugees and offer them a bed for the night, while the local WVS (the

Women's Voluntary Service) worked out what to do with us afterwards. An old lady (at least she seemed old, though she was probably younger than I am now) collected John and me and took us back to her cottage. It was decorated with pictures and china and seemed to me the most beautiful house I had ever seen.

The next day we were moved to the Heybridge Mill House, which was a delight. There were lots of rooms and a large garden which had the River Blackwater running one side of it and the mill stream the other. John and I revelled in it. Many years later I saw an advertisement for it in *The Week* under a heading *Best properties on the market which have been in the same family for a hundred years*, and wrote to the owners to thank them for their family's hospitality seventy years earlier. The outcome was that Bunny Farnell-Watson, who grew up there in the 1960s, invited John and me and our wives to lunch there together with her husband Peter and her sister Nettie, and we enjoyed walking with them round the garden we had not been in since September 1939.

Their Aunt Mary, who had been eighteen at the time, still remembered our evacuation there more than seventy years later. But sadly back in 1939 we only stayed at the Mill House for two or three weeks. The authorities decided that a garden with a river on one side and a mill stream on the other was not safe for five year old refugees. So we were moved again, this time to a cobbler's house, where we played among the rolls of leather in the workshop behind the house where he mended shoes. The smell of leather still reminds me of evacuation.

We continued to go to school. The Heybridge infants' school lent us their building for half of each day. Sometimes they had school in the morning and then had the afternoon off while we went to school. Sometimes it was the other way round, and I believe that that arrangement continued for two years, from the start of the war until the autumn term of 1941. But John and I did not stay there that long. In May 1940 the Germans struck in the West, and in June they drove the British army into the sea at Dunkirk.

The *Golden Eagle,* on which we had gone on our daytrip to Southend the previous year, left the Thames Estuary for the first time in its life and did two and a half trips to Dunkirk. It was sunk on the third one, and paddle steamers never again plied up and down the Thames. France collapsed. A German invasion of England seemed imminent, and to my parents it didn't make sense to leave their children near the Essex coast waiting for the Germans to arrive. So we came back to Woodford in July, just in time for the Battle of Britain.

With an imminent threat of German bombing, someone issued us with sheets of corrugated iron with curved ends which could be turned into an Anderson Shelter, and John and I, with our toy spades, helped our father dig the hole at the end of the garden to put it in. It was well dug in, with the top almost level with the ground, and with two large metal water tanks full of earth in front of the entrance to avoid direct blast. At that stage the only furniture in it was what was called a put-you-up, a collapsible sofa-bed, and our mother and father slept at one end with John and me at the other.

We got used to the wail of the air raid siren, which sent us down to the shelter, and to the long continuous sound of the all-clear, which let us out again, and once the raids were over I used to go out to find particularly interestingly shaped pieces of shrapnel for my growing collection, while eventually most houses in the road had at least one brass incendiary bomb case as a decoration on the mantelpiece. Years later, when I was away at school, my mother threw my shrapnel collection away, thinking it macabre. I felt angry and betrayed and found it difficult to forgive. Even today I can still remember the shapes of some of my carefully chosen pieces.

At first the raids came mostly by day. There was a certain excitement about it when you were a child, and it wasn't particularly frightening. After all, the bombs usually fell some distance away, and it was fascinating to have a front row seat at a small part of what was later called the Battle of Britain, and my memory of the late summer of 1940 is of idyllic days of sunshine and broad blue skies with aeroplanes making vapour trails and fighting each other.

While we collected blackberries to make a summer pudding or played in the grass, there was a different world overhead. Dornier and Junker bombers, accompanied by Messerschmitt fighters, were shot at by Hurricanes and Spitfires from the North Weald aerodrome. I had my Daily Mirror spotter's book and became an expert at aircraft recognition. I got used to the rationing system, and would line up my sweets on the sideboard and discuss with my mother what to do with the week's egg. I carried my identity card and learnt the number (DCEB1614), so that I could recite it, together with my name and address, if I got lost.

In September, as the Battle of Britain ended, the Blitz began. There were raids almost every night for months, until May 1941, when Hitler withdrew his aircraft in preparation for the German attack on Russia in June, on the anniversary of the fall of France. Every night searchlights criss-crossed the blackness looking for enemy aircraft, while the Ack-Ack, or anti-aircraft, guns on the Wanstead flats kept up a barrage of noise, though probably seldom hitting anything, and the barrage balloons at Chigwell, just up the road, kept the enemy aircraft flying high for fear of hitting the wires which the balloons were holding up.

When Silvertown, down by the docks, was bombed early in the Blitz, a man who worked in the same factory as my father had his house destroyed, and my parents had him and his wife come and share our Anderson shelter. Now the two women slept at one end of the put-you-up, John and I at the other end, and the two men got what sleep they could, sitting up alongside. The only thing I remember about our visitors is that the woman used to tickle my feet, and I thought she shouldn't – especially as she was a visitor. Incendiary bombs seemed to do more damage than high explosives, and one night we all stood outside the shelter and watched London on fire.

Only occasionally did bombs land anywhere near us, and I was struck by the fact that the gas holders behind our house, which seemed to me an obvious target, were never hit. John thought the Germans deliberately left them because they were good land-marks. I thought that their aim was not very good, and sometimes it seemed that they just wanted to unload their bombs and make for home. The bombs had to land somewhere and when one of them hit our mains water supply nearby, John and I spent hours going to and from the fire hydrant with buckets and filling the bath so that water was always available at home.

The whole nation was adjusting to war. It was no longer the 'phoney war' of September 1939 to May 1940, but a real fighting war which was apparently going to go on until we won. My own understanding of it at that stage was limited to the idea that the Germans were bad and came from a big country which was attacking us, who were good and lived on an island. Apparently the Germans had caused a lot of trouble in 'the last war', and now they were doing it again. At the same time the Russians, who were also bad, were attacking Finland, which was another little country like us and whose people had bravely held off the attacker in the winter of 1939-40.

The war seemed to involve everyone. Our next-door neighbour, Mr Fogg, who in civilian life was a butcher, was now a corporal in the Duke of Cornwall's Light Infantry. Dad's friend, our Uncle Hughie, was back in the Royal Navy as a Chief Petty Officer Stoker on *HMS Dido*, an M Class cruiser. Our own MP, Mr Churchill, now the prime minister, had said that we all needed to work together for victory, and there were even things that children could do. We needed, for example, to grow as much of our own food as possible, so that merchant seamen didn't have to bring it from overseas. So again we got out our spades and we grew tomatoes and spinach in the back garden and potatoes and beans and cabbages and leeks on the allotment which we acquired at the end of the road. After each meal we conscientiously took any left-overs or potato peelings along to the pig-swill bin at the end of the road. Apparently pigs would eat anything and needed fattening up.

Meanwhile the marsh behind us was being transformed. It appears to have been the most convenient place for dumping all the detritus from the air raids on the East End of London and the docks, and the way into the dumping ground was along Waltham Road. In those days Waltham Road was fairly short, and immediately after No.19, where Mr and Mrs Plant lived, was the turning on the left down to the marsh, shortly before the gates at the end of the road into the allotments.

Day after day lorries would dump the waste from the East End factories that had been bombed, and day after day John and I and any other children who had come back from evacuation would play among the debris, rushing off home if the air raid warning went. We did not have to go to school, because our school was officially still evacuated, and we sometimes wore rather strange American clothes, such as dungarees, which had come over in *Bundles for Britain* and had been distributed by the members of the Women's Voluntary Service.

Meanwhile, all through the autumn of 1940 my father continued to cycle from Woodford along the Lee Bridge Road to work in Hoxton, and day after day he must have seen more and more destruction as in the second half of 1940 Hoxton was virtually destroyed. You only have to walk through Hoxton today, in the twenty-first century, and you can see the post-war blocks of council flats, built on the areas which were flattened, vastly outnumbering the relatively few pre-war houses, to realise how massive was the devastation in that area of London.

The German bombers could use both the Thames and the Grand Union Canal to guide them to the areas where innumerable small factories were concentrated and then wreak destruction on both the factories and the housing. If you walk a couple of miles west of Hoxton to Bloomsbury, you can similarly see just where the

German bombs fell, because again there is a mixture of pre-war housing and post-war council flats. But in the case of Bloomsbury the elegant nineteenth century terraces greatly outnumber the blocks of unattractive council flats scattered among them where the bombs fell.

By Christmas of 1940 Britain had been standing alone in Europe for six months. More and more men were needed in the army, and in January 1941 the conscription system reached men of thirty-four, which was our father's age. He was to join the Royal Artillery, and before he left, while John and I were still in bed together, he gave us what I still regard as the best explanation I have ever heard of why Great Britain fought the Second World War. 'You know, boys,' he said, 'that I've got to go off and join the army. I don't want to be a soldier, but you know the way I always get up in the morning and make Mummy a cup of tea. Well, the Germans want to come here and stop us doing that sort of thing. So we've all got to go and stop them. Be good boys, look after Mummy while I'm away and I'll come back and see you as often as I can.' And off he went.

4. War in Wales and Woodford

The next time we saw him he was in uniform, 1766149 Gunner J. S. Arnold, and on his cap-badge was the first Latin I ever came across: UBIQUE QUO FAS ET GLORIA DUCUNT (*Everywhere where Right and Glory lead*), the motto of the Royal Artillery. Before long he was a lance-bombardier, with one stripe, then a bombardier, with two, in charge of a searchlight site on the north-east corner of Wales, by the village of Pen-y-ffordd, looking out over the Dee estuary and across the Wirral to Liverpool. He and his men slept in tents in a field, with pick-axe handles as their only weapons. They were waiting for two searchlights, a Lewis machine gun and a number of Lee Enfield rifles.

Before any of these arrived nearly seven hundred German bombers flew up the Irish Sea and for the first seven nights of May 1941 destroyed large parts of Liverpool, including the docks. It was the largest-scale destruction of anywhere in England other than London throughout the war. The men of the Pen-y-ffordd searchlight site could only watch Liverpool burning, just as we had watched London and the London docks burning six months earlier.

Pen-y-ffordd was a mining village. The men who lived there were almost all called Jones and were also almost all miners at the Point-of-Ayr colliery, where they used to walk anything up to five miles underground to get to the coal face. During the day their wives pumped up water with the pump at the end of the village street, heated it up, and then scrubbed their husbands' backs in a tin tub in the kitchen when they got back. It was a close community, and once the searchlight site was established, the parents sent their children to get a soldier. Blodwen and Gwenda Jones, two little girls about nine or ten years old, collected my father, who thereafter always had a home where he could get a cup of tea and sometimes a hot bath.

Sometime in the summer of 1941 my mother and John and I went up there for a holiday. How they fitted us in I can neither remember nor imagine. We helped collect water at the pump, and I learnt my first words of another spoken language: *Bore da!* and *Nos da!* (Good morning, Good night) and *Iechyd da!* (pronounced Yackeedar), which meant something approximating to 'Good health' and was widely and casually used. *Un, dau, tri, pedwar, pump* (pronounced pimp) were 1,2,3,4,5 and *Cymru am byth!* was 'Wales for ever!'

I also spent quite a lot of time at the searchlight site. By then, just as some young children are experts on dinosaurs, I was an expert on searchlights and on aircraft recognition. My father, when home on leave, had explained in detail how a searchlight works, how one could get either a broad beam or a narrow one, and he had explained how a Lewis gun and a Lee Enfield rifle worked. I could tell the difference between a Junkers 86 and a Junkers 88, and I could recognise a Dornier or a Heinkel, and a Messerschmitt 109 or 110.

Similarly I could recognise a Blenheim, a Wellington or a Lancaster, and, of course, the Hurricane, which had dominated the skies around us during the Battle of Britain, and that most beautiful and effective of any fighter aircraft yet made, the Vickers Supermarine Spitfire. 'What more can I do for the Luftwaffe?' Goering once asked one of his leading fighter commanders, Gallandt, who replied, 'Give me a squadron of Spitfires.'

It never occurred to me that we might lose the war. I had a map showing the world in Mercator's projection, which makes Canada look vast and the countries on the equator rather small. The British Empire was all coloured pink and the seas were blue. That was all ours and it seemed stupid of the Germans to think they could beat us. Anyway, the grown-ups told me that the British always won in the end, and although Great Britain was standing alone in Europe against Nazi Germany, we had the comfort of seeing soldiers and airmen with shoulder flashes saying Canada, Poland, Norway, France, and so on. It gave an impression of solidarity.

It was confusing in the middle of 1941 to find that the Russians were now on our side. I had thought that they were bad like the Germans, and were attacking the Finns while the Germans were attacking us. Another puzzle was what the Americans were up to. I knew that they were good, for I wore the clothes they sent over in *Bundles for Britain* and I ate the spam and dried egg and dried bananas which they also sent over to us, but for some reason they weren't doing any fighting. It somehow tidied things up when the Japanese attacked Pearl Harbour in December 1941 and brought them into the war. The Russians and the Americans might not be as good at fighting as the British, but clearly it would help to have them both on our side.

During 1941 air-raids had become intermittent. Increasingly we didn't bother to carry our gas mask cases, and we quite often slept indoors rather than in the Anderson Shelter, and that in turn meant that quite often, if a raid came during the night, we would sit in the cupboard under the stairs rather than go out in the cold and wet to the shelter at the end of the garden. Staircases were the places that survived best when houses were bombed.

Even if the bombing was random, it made an awful lot of noise, and the anti-aircraft guns made even more. Once, when we were sitting under the stairs and a stick of bombs approached, my mother crouched lower and lower as each bomb exploded, and then hurt herself quite badly as she shot up and hit her head on the staircase as the last one went beyond us.

The rationing system meant that food that was scarce was distributed fairly, and since throughout the war bread and potatoes were never rationed, we never went hungry. But we spent a lot of time queuing for things in short supply, and my mother had to decide how to use our 'points.' Various items required a given number of 'points' coupons, and she had to decide whether to spend them on biscuits and sugar for regular consumption or on a tin of spam from America for a special treat at the week-end. Sometimes, relying on my blue eyes and curly blonde hair, she would send me to the butcher's shop to ask if I could have a bit of suet, and the women in our road regularly complained about the lack of those bits of meat which were not rationed (pigs' trotters and ox tail, for example) but somehow were never available either.

Our school was officially still evacuated. So until the autumn of 1941 we were very largely free to play all over the now vast rubbish dump built up on the marsh and to investigate the extraordinary variety of materials from the bombed out factories of the East End. One day, when I was on my father's bike, pretending that I was in an aeroplane in the Battle of Britain, I was shot down by a boy who lobbed a brick at my front wheel. I baled out, grabbed for some support as I fell and ripped my hand on barbed wire. 'Look Mum!' I said, as I came in the kitchen door pulling back a flap of loose skin. She promptly fainted and needed to be revived before she could walk up the road with me to Claybury Hospital, which in those days was referred to as a lunatic asylum, and which now, because of the war, had an accident and emergency department. They stitched me up and I still have two faint scars on my right hand – my nearest approach to war wounds.

As a child I got into a number of fights, but I only remember one, and that is because of the issue over which we fought. Father Christmas had always visited us at Christmastime and filled our stockings with good things. But a boy of whom I have no other recollection asserted that Father Christmas did not exist. Since my mother had assured me that he did, it seemed that her honour was being impugned, so I fought and got home dirty and bloody but quite proud of myself and confident that my mother would be pleased that I had fought on her behalf. 'Oh, you stupid boy!' she said, 'Fancy fighting over a silly thing like that! That John never gets himself into stupid fights.' As she said that, I realised I had been wrong about Father Christmas. What is more, I had been fighting without right on my side, and I was growing up in a world in which it seemed to matter a great deal to be right when engaged in conflict.

She was also right that John did not get into fights like that. He was of an amiable and emollient nature. We spent an immense amount of time together, and despite that, or perhaps because of it, we never quarrelled with each other and we valued each other's company. I always recognised that, as the older brother (even if only by twenty-five minutes) he had a natural seniority. I never challenged it, but on the other hand he never abused his position. He seldom caused offence to anyone and was naturally concilia-tory in his manner. I was more likely to upset someone, whether our mother or another boy, and if there was trouble around, I tended to steer into it, while John usually managed to avoid it. Later in life I had to learn to avoid being aggressive or unnecessar-ily confrontational; John, on the other hand, had to learn to stand firm when circumstances required it – and he did.

Occasionally those serving overseas, such as Uncle Hughie, came home on leave. By then he had served on a considerable number of warships, at first the cruiser *HMS Dido*, and later the *Boadicea*, a destroyer, and then the *Flamingo* and the *Hasty*, both of which were both corvettes. The reason for the relatively large number of ships was that they kept being sunk. He was torpedoed four times and, surprisingly for someone down in the engine-room, survived each occasion, as well as the bombing of the *Boadicea* back in Portsmouth Harbour. He had exchanged leave dates with the other chief petty officer stoker, who lived in the north. The ship was blown up while Hughie was at home. A bomb went down the funnel and exploded, killing everyone in the boiler-room. He always felt a sense of guilt at surviving that.

There was no school to go to in Woodford Bridge, so although small groups of children would meet from time to time in some-one's house and practise reading or arithmetic, for more than a year, from the fall of France in June 1940 until the beginning of the autumn term of 1941, we did not have any formal schooling. I never learnt the multiplication tables, often thought to be part of the staple diet of the elementary school curriculum, and got away with it because there are all sorts of devices one can find for working out such things as 6 x 8. It's the same as four lots of twelve, which I did know, or two lots of twenty-four. Even now, in retirement, I still multiply in that way.

At home our mother read us poetry: Thomas Campbell's *Lord Ullin's Daughter*, for example, which I still know by heart, Matthew Arnold's *The Forsaken Merman*, and *The Highwayman* by Alfred Noyes. Almost always it was something emotional and with a story to it. We would also read through some of Shakespeare's plays (*Twelfth Night*, *As You Like it* or *The Merchant of Venice*) sometimes sitting under the staircase or else in the Anderson shelter, and most weeks John Purkis, a boy whom I had first met in a sand-pit before the war, would lend us *The Beano* and *The Dandy*, comics which during the war came out on alternate weeks to save paper, and he would borrow Enid Blyton's *Sunny Stories* from us. Invasion was no longer a threat, and bombing was less of a threat than it had been.

With our mother in the middle of the war. John is on the right of the page – on her left.

For someone who had been inclined to be dependent on our father for any small jobs such as changing a light bulb or finding her purse when she had mislaid it, our mother was extraordinarily competent during the war when our father was away. She did whatever was immediately necessary and also planned ahead, so that, for example, she always cooked half a hundredweight of marmalade each year in one go – that being just enough, since half a hundredweight was 56 pounds, to provide one pot a week throughout the year, with a few extra for special times such as Christmas or Easter. She would also go out on her bike into the Essex countryside visiting farms to see if she could get some eggs, and once came home bruised and dirty after diving into a ditch to avoid the gunfire from an attacking Messerschmitt.

From time to time our father came home on leave and once he brought a rabbit which he had shot with a .303 Lee Enfield rifle to supplement our meat ration. On another occasion he had compassionate leave to go to the funeral of his mother, whom I had seldom seen since the beginning of the war, because travelling from Woodford to Islington, though only five or six miles in a direct line, was relatively difficult by public transport. I was sorry not to go to the funeral, but it was, mistakenly I think, not seen as suitable for a small child. Nor, of course, had I been to the funeral of my grandfather, who had died before the war.

Towards the end of the war, just as our father was leaving to go back to his unit, he gave my mother a big hug and kissed her good-bye. There was, of course, nothing remarkable about that. What was memorable to me was that as we watched him walk off down the road, she said to me, 'Oh, your Dad does love me', and I wondered why she said that rather than telling me how much she loved him. Similarly, she would pick me up and give me a hug, saying, 'You do love your Mummy, don't you?' Yes I did, but it helped to make me aware of her inbuilt insecurity – and I noticed that when my father got back from the army, she reverted to being unable to change a light bulb and needed him to find her purse if she mislaid it.

She wanted a safe, secure world with her husband and her two sons, and resented anything which interfered with that. So far as I could tell her attitude to the war was that Hitler had made her life difficult, and although she often complained about her lot, she reacted instinctively against anything which disturbed it. After the war she took a job as secretary to Sylvia Pankhurst, the former suffragette leader, who lived up the hill in Woodford Green. When Miss Pankhurst invited her to go with her to Ethiopia, she could have gone with all expenses paid. She declined because she did not want to leave her husband and children, who were eleven or twelve at the time and perfectly capable of looking after themselves. 'You foolish girl', said Miss Pankhurst. 'You could have come with me and eaten off the emperor's gold plate.'

If our cousin Beverley was playing hockey nearby and called in, or if my father's youngest brother, Bert, called in with his wife, Paula, and their two little girls, Pam and Sand, she would apparently be pleased to see them, but as soon as they were gone would collapse exhausted, saying, 'Oh! Thank God they've gone!' Once, many years later, my father was driving us all back from London and we were near Bethnal Green, where Frank and Franie lived with Bev. My father suggested calling in to see them. 'Oh, they won't want to see us', said my mother. 'Right-o' replied my father and drove on. 'I bet they would', I said, 'and anyway, I'd like to see Bev.' John said nothing. That is a fairly good example of the way each of us was likely to behave. My mother expected her feelings and preferences to be given priority. I was difficult. John avoided trouble. Our father was a good conscientious husband, trying to look after his wife and give her what she wanted.

Some time later I asked my father why he always let her get away with things. His answer was clear and unequivocal. 'She's my wife.' He had promised to love and cherish her when they got married, and he was determined to go on doing so. Much later in life, when she suffered from severe depression, the psychiatrist at the Maudesley Hospital who had been treating her suggested to my father that he had been colluding with her self-obsessed behaviour. He was devastated, telling me what had been said, as near to tears as I had ever seen him. I tried to reassure him. I had all my life watched him trying to be as good a husband as he always was a good father.

5. Ray Lodge and Doodlebugs

In September 1941 Ray Lodge opened again and then, at the age of seven, it was time for us to move up from the infants, most of which we had missed, to what we called 'the Big Boys.' The entrance, with *Boys* carved into the stone, was at one end of the large Victorian building which stood behind an asphalt playground, which in turn was behind the large iron railings along Snakes Lane. At the other end of the building was the entrance for *Girls*. They entered and left the building at a different time from us, and although they used the same playground, they used it at different times, and we lost almost all contact with girls for years – in my case for ten years or more.

We were in a class of 56, with all the desks arranged in straight lines. We did arithmetic every morning and we wrote a composition every Tuesday afternoon. We did spelling bees, so that I learnt to spell the names of flowers such as antirrhinum, phlox, aubrieta (not aubretia!) and rhododendron. Those who were good little boys eventually became milk monitors or ink monitors, with small brass pots with very long thin spouts for pouring ink into inkwells. I think it was at this point in my life that I thought I would like to be a teacher, but I found long division difficult and wondered if I would ever be good enough at it to be allowed to be a teacher.

In later years I have seen pictures of elementary school classrooms of that time, much like ours, with serious-looking boys sitting in straight rows with their hands on the desk, and I have thought how misleading such pictures are. They give an impression of oppressed and deprived working class children, ruthlessly disciplined. What one needs to bear in mind when looking at such pictures is that the children were sitting there precisely in order to have their picture taken. It was a special occasion, so of course they looked conscientiously serious. Many of us thoroughly enjoyed school, and we liked the teachers. I cannot remember disliking any of my teachers, and although Mr Moss, the headmaster, had a cane, I cannot ever remember him using it.

We enjoyed the work we did and we trotted home at lunch-time, and again at the end of afternoon school, to tell our mother what we had done. We enjoyed the company of the other boys, played conkers and 'It' and hopscotch in the playground, and marbles in the gutter on the way home. We sang cheerfully together, '*Oh, Hitler's got a bunion and a face like a Spanish onion, and a nose like a squashed tomato, and feet like sardines.*' We asked anyone who might not already know the answer the question, 'Why does Hitler wear braces with swastikas on them?', and the answer was, 'To keep his trousers up.' We patriotically chalked dot, dot, dot, dash (Morse code for V for Victory) on any available wall.

Something none of us knew about at the time was radar, the discovery which enabled British air crew to, in a sense, 'see in the dark.' Nor did the Germans know about it, and to deceive them into accepting a different explanation the information was leaked that British pilots were fed carrots to enable them to see in the dark. The Germans believed it and started to feed carrots to *Luftwaffe* pilots. We believed it too, and the greengrocer's shop, which was the last shop on the right before the bridge over the River Roding on the way to school in Snakes Lane, sold large scrubbed carrots for a penny each to children on the way to school. I preferred to buy a pound of carrots, with the mud still on them, for a penny ha'penny (just over half of 1p. in modern money) and scrub them clean at home. It was far better value.

There was a small group of six boys who regularly were at the top of our class. John Purkis usually came top, together with my brother, and after them came Eric Savory, John Revell, Arthur Brown and me. In 1943 two places became available at Christ's Hospital, a London school for the poor which had somehow moved to Sussex. These two places were for anyone who happened to live in Woodford, so all six of us took a competitive examination, as a result of which John Arnold and John Purkis got the places and left at the age of nine, a year before the other four of us.

During 1944 large numbers of American soldiers arrived, getting ready for the invasion of Europe, and night after night our bombers could be heard flying eastwards to bomb German cities. Some time that summer, shortly after the Allied troops had landed in Normandy, some of us took what was then still known as the scholarship examination for the local grammar schools. The so-called 11+, which followed from the 1944 Education Act, did not arrive until 1947. Four of us won scholarships. Eric Savory went to Chigwell School and from there to London University. John Revell went to the Wanstead High School and also to London University. Arthur Brown went to the Buckhurst Hill County High School and from there to the Royal Naval College, Dartmouth.

I didn't have to choose which grammar school to go to, because by then, between taking the scholarship examination and getting the result, I had got a place at Christ's Hospital. At that time there was what was called an Almoners' Nominees' Examination. The almoners of the hospital, who formed the Council responsible for the school, were entitled to nominate children to take the hospital's own scholarship examination, and my mother spent a lot of time and ink writing to various almoners to try to persuade them to let me take the examination.

A Dr Hall, who was a Mathematics fellow of Trinity College, Cambridge, an almoner of the hospital and himself an Old Blue (that being the term for a former pupil of Christ's Hospital), nominated me. So I got the opportunity to demonstrate my ability to do sums, write essays and even answer the questions on what was called an intelligence test, and I did it to such good effect that they gave me a place, to start in September 1944. I remember only two things about the exam. One is that on the History paper I was able to get in my favourite piece of historical information: that Alfred, King of the West Saxons, agreed the Treaty of Wedmore in

878 with Guthrum the Dane, dividing England along the line of Watling Street, with the Danelaw to the North-east and the territory he ruled to the South-west. The other is that the intelligence test required us to draw a circle and put a cross in it. It seemed a very strange requirement.

During that year, when John was away at Christ's Hospital and I was still at home, I would sometimes go on my own to South Woodford to the Plaza cinema, where, together with a number of other children, I would stand outside and accost any man or woman approaching the ticket kiosk and, holding out my sixpence, say 'Would you take me in, Mister?' It did not occur to us or to our parents that that was in any way to risk harm. We knew that the Germans and the Japanese intended us harm. It was unthinkable that any of our own people would be anything but friendly and helpful. Nor were they.

By then the war was coming towards an end. The first half of the war had been about avoiding defeat. The second half had brought a shift of emphasis towards looking forward to victory. But in June 1944, the same month that Anglo-American forces landed on the beaches of Normandy, there was a reintensification of air raids, this time with the new German secret weapons: the V1, or doodlebug, or flying bomb, and later the V2, or rocket.

One of the only two occasions I can remember being frightened during the war was when the V1, or doodlebug, attacks started. I was playing in a neighbour's garden. The air-raid warning had gone, but we had got a bit blasé about it by then, there was no gunfire and my ears were accustomed to the drone of an aeroplane overhead. The fear came from the fact that the noise suddenly stopped. There was silence, and I had no idea what was going to happen next. I ran round in a circle about three times, jumped over the fence into the ditch at the bottom of the garden, and waited there until the doodlebug landed and exploded a mile or more away.

The next day we found out what they were. In a strange way they were only mildly threatening. You could even feel quite fond of them. They chugged across the sky until they ran out of fuel and then they curved down in a semi-circle and exploded. But they clearly weren't aiming deliberately at you, and the chances of getting a direct hit were negligible. It did, however, mean that we had to revert to living in the Anderson Shelter again.

By now our father was a troop sergeant (one rank above a sergeant and one below company sergeant major) and he explained to me when home on leave the difference between anti-aircraft fire against bombers early in the war and against V1s, or doodlebugs, in 1944. Early in the war Junkers and Dornier bombers had turned left and right and up and down and varied their speed at the same time, and it was almost impossible to hit them. All anti-aircraft fire could do was make it more difficult for them to have a straight and easy bombing run up to their target.

With our father when he was home on leave, some time near the end of the war. This time John is on the left.

Doodlebugs, on the other hand, flew in a straight line at a steady speed. You could shoot them down with a Bofors gun by checking their direction and calculating where they would be when your shell exploded. It was difficult to miss. Then you looked for the next one. Meanwhile fighter aircraft of the R.A.F. were shooting them down as they approached the coast or turning them round by lifting a wing, so that they came down somewhere in the North Sea. Probably no more than ten per cent of the doodlebugs launched on the continent ever reached the London area.

All the same, a large number did, and we got all the more of them because the newspapers deceived the Germans by reporting massive V1 attacks South of London, thus causing them to adjust their aim further North towards us. It was in the summer of 1944, when John was home from Christ's Hospital on holiday and our father was home on leave that one landed and exploded just behind us. We had all been asleep in the Anderson shelter. Wartime gets you into the habit of sleeping through a lot of noise. But this shook everything and woke us up, and the noise was shattering. It sounded as if the whole road was falling down. We crawled out of the shelter expecting to see devastation, but instead everything looked normal.

What had happened was that the bomb had blown most of the windows out all along the road, and a lot of tiles, shaken loose on the roof, had come sliding down and crashed onto the concrete behind. That produced enough noise to give the impression that a whole town was collapsing. It was something of a relief to see that so little damage had been done, and my main reaction on seeing slivers of glass sticking into my bed indoors, and in particular into my pillow, was that it had made it worthwhile spending so many cold and uncomfortable nights in the Anderson shelter. Once the dust had settled we all gathered in Mrs Bassenthwaite's house, just down the road at No 15. She put on a large kettle and we all drank cups of tea, feeling rather proud to be British.

The event which most frightened me happened on a peaceful morning towards the end of the war. Out of the window of my mother's bedroom I saw a girl who was few years older than me running round in the road and screaming. My mother told me that her father had just been killed, and it left me with a complicated mixture of emotions - relief that it wasn't my own father, fear that it could be, and a vague sense of apprehension. I was getting older.

As I grew older I followed the news and the course of the campaigns with ever closer interest. The war dominated our lives. We got to know the newsreaders on the BBC Home Service, such as Alvar Lidell, and to recognise their voices: 'This is the six o'clock news, and this is Alvar Lidell reading it.' Inevitably the newspapers and much of adult conversation centred on the war. I could scarcely remember life before the war. The horses on the marsh, the day trip to Southend on the *Golden Eagle* and another by train, the holiday in Littlehampton and starting in the infants' department at Ray Lodge were almost the only memories that must have been pre-war.

Eventually I began to wonder what peace would be like. Somehow I associated the idea of peace with bananas, for I had seen pictures of them and looked forward to tasting one. But I had got used to the taste of dried bananas, which I liked, and in the event, when the war was over, I decided that fresh bananas had a disappointingly bland taste by comparison. John and I discussed with each other what news there could possibly be once the war was over. Would it, for example, be about how much milk the cows were producing or how many eggs the chickens were laying? We could not imagine what the papers would have to write about if there was no war. In the end we realised that we would just have to wait and see.

From September 1944 we were both away at Christ's Hospital and on 1st November 1944 we reached our eleventh birthday. Our father was still away in the army, and would be until the summer of 1946; our mother was working for Sylvia Pankhurst. When we came home for the Christmas holidays we usually got our own lunch at home, but on Fridays our mother would leave us sixpence to go to *Roberts, Wet, Dried and Fried, Fishmonger* on the corner of the road. 'Two tuppennies and two h'aporths, please, Mrs Roberts' we would say and get two large pieces of fried cod in batter and two portions of chips – all for five pence, with a penny left over to buy liquorice.

Since there were twelve pence to the shilling and twenty shillings to the pound in old money (£.s.d.), tuppence-ha'penny was roughly equivalent to 1p. in decimal currency, so the price of a piece of fish and chips, now about £10, has increased by roughly a thousand times over sixty years. But it is the money which has declined in value rather than the fish and chips getting more expensive. Over the same period houses have similarly increased in price a thousand times, say from £485 to £485,000.

We still had to put up with the doodlebugs that got past our fighters and anti-aircraft guns, and now we were also threatened by V2s, or rockets, Hitler's other secret weapon. Instead of chugging gently across the sky as the doodlebugs did, they were propelled from the continent high into the air and then came down at an immense speed, faster than sound, to explode on impact. I remember them less well, perhaps because there were simply far fewer of them. What I do remember is that when you heard one coming you knew it hadn't hit you. Because they travelled faster than sound, you heard the explosion first and only after that could you hear the whine of their approach. It may be that I missed most of them because in September of 1944 I had gone away to school at Christ's Hospital in Sussex.

The war in Europe ended on 8th May 1945 with the unconditional surrender of Germany. Exactly a month later King George VI wrote a letter to every boy and girl still at school to say that we had 'shared in the hardships and dangers of total war' and 'shared no less in the triumph...' I kept it and still have it.

Christ's Hospital
(1944–1952)

6. The Religious, Royal and Ancient Foundation

◇◇◇◇◇◇◇◇◇◇◇◇◇◇◇◇◇◇◇◇◇◇◇◇◇◇◇◇◇◇

Christ's Hospital was a charitable institution founded in the middle of the sixteenth century to provide for 'fatherless children and other poore men's children.' It admitted its first children in 1552 and the following year received a royal charter from the young King Edward VI shortly before his death at the age of fifteen. The children were provided with 'meate, drink and cloths', and soon with 'virtuous education' as well. Those of us who were educated there in the middle of the twentieth century were encouraged to believe that the young king signed the charter of Christ's Hospital on his deathbed, saying 'I thank God that he hath given me breath this long to do this good work', and promptly expired.

The hospital's endowments were vast and immensely valuable, largely because it owned so much land in the City of London, and by the beginning of the twentieth century, when the London site was too constrained for the school's purposes, its very considerable assets made it possible to build a grand new school for boys on a site near Horsham in the north of West Sussex and at the same time a Christ's Hospital Girls' School in Hertford. Income from investments and from property sustained the two schools separately through most of the twentieth century and enabled them to continue the charitable purpose of caring for children in need and giving them a first-rate education.

The essential requirement for a child's entry was that his or her parents should have a low enough income not to be able to afford to pay fees. There were various means of entry; the one thing they all had in common was that the child's parents should have a low income. If their income increased they were asked to contribute something according to their means, and in the year 1951-52, by which time the cost of educating a child at Christ's Hospital was just over £200 a year, my parents were expected to contribute £12 for the two of us. When we left at the end of that year, both with open awards to Oxbridge colleges, the school gave each of us £100 for clothing, on the assumption that any child of the hospital going up to Oxford or Cambridge would need to buy some clothes in place of our school uniform, and they also gave each of us another £20 for books.

While at school we had worn a school uniform which had hardly changed since the hospital was founded: a long blue coat down to the ground, with silver buttons and a loose girdle (or belt) resting somewhere between the hips and the knees, grey knee breeches, also with silver buttons, yellow stockings (or socks) and black shoes. Under the coat we wore a white shirt with no buttons, but with a pair of bands, such as were once worn by Protestant preachers, attached to it and hanging over the front of the coat. Part of the uniform was that we wore no headgear. That may seem a strange point to make in the twenty-first century when hardly anyone wears a hat or cap, but in the 1940s almost everyone did. Working men wore a flat cap, City gents wore a bowler hat, military uniforms and school uniforms almost always included some form of headgear. So the absence of any headgear was part of the Christ's Hospital uniform.

John had gone there in September of 1943 at the age of nine and had spent a year in one of the two preparatory houses. Now we were both going to join one of the fourteen senior houses in each of which there lived fifty boys aged from ten, as we were, to eighteen, the age we were when we left in 1952. At the beginning of the Michaelmas (or Autumn) Term of 1944 my mother went with John and me on the No 10 bus all the way from Woodford Bridge to Victoria Station on the western side of central London to see us off on the special train which, as at the beginning of every term, took a few hundred London boys down to the site of Christ's Hospital in Sussex, 'ringed with downs and woodlands fair.'

*With John, who is standing, when we were
fourteen and at Christ's Hospital.*

When we arrived we marched (It was the beginning of a lot of marching) up to the Avenue which reached from east to west on either side of the main school buildings, which were around a large quadrangle with a statue of King Edward VI in the middle. The dining hall was on the north side of the quadrangle; Big School, flanked by two classroom blocks, faced it to the south; chapel and one line of cloisters were on the west side; the old science building and another line of cloisters were on the east. Beyond the quadrangle, stretching out to both east and west was the Avenue, on the south side of which were a few houses for senior members of the teaching staff. On the north side were sixteen boarding houses, eight at each end of the Avenue. Ours had the rather strange name of Barnes A.

Downstairs at the front was a dayroom for forty-eight boys, as well as two studies at the end of the dayroom for the two most senior boys in the house – the house captain and his deputy. The furniture was four large tables, two lengthways and two across, each with four benches. The eight most senior boys other than the house monitors sat at the top table. Then there were twelve boys to each of the other tables, and four small tables around the room, one for each of the four house monitors who presided over the dayroom and maintained order. Downstairs at the back of the house were the changing rooms, the washrooms and the lavatories.

On the first floor was the senior dormitory, with twelve beds on each side and a cubicle for the house captain, and with the so-called lav ends at either end. The second floor was the same, with the cubicle for the deputy house captain in charge of the junior boys. The beds had iron frames and boards, on which were placed horse-hair mattresses and a horse-hair bolster. When the beds were made up they were 'poled' with a long wooden pole which reached from one bed to another to ensure that the bolsters were in a perfectly straight line. In the mornings, until they were made up, the mattress was arched on top of the boards, with the bolster underneath it, and the blankets and sheets were folded into a perfect square.

The day began at 7a.m., when the Big School bell rang fifty times, and by the time it stopped we had to be standing at the end of our beds holding our handkerchiefs. Noses were blown by numbers, and then, after we had washed and dressed, we stripped and stacked our beds. At 7.25 we lined up outside in height order and in two lines, numbered off from the right, formed fours, turned right when ordered to do so, and marched to breakfast in the Dining Hall. Grace before Meat was said from a pulpit by one of the senior boys, or Grecians, and was also said every day at lunch and tea-time: *Give us thankful hearts, O Lord God, for the table which Thou hast spread for us. Bless Thy good creatures to our use, and us to Thy service, for Jesus Christ's sake, Amen.*

We ate our breakfast, cleared everything away, according to our variously allotted 'trades', and then, after breakfast as well as after lunch and tea, stood for Grace after Meat: *Blessed Lord, we yield Thee hearty praise and thanksgiving for our founder and benefactors, by whose charitable benevolence Thou hast refreshed our bodies at this time. So season and refresh our souls with Thy heavenly spirit that we may defend Thy Church, the King and all the Royal Family, for the sake of Jesus Christ, Our Lord, Amen.* Then we walked back to the house to go to the lavatory, make our beds and get our books ready for school.

Before school we lined up again to march to chapel. Marching in fours, we had to get into just two lines in order to go through the door of chapel, as we did when entering the dining hall. When entering the dining hall the order to 'form two deep' was shouted. When entering chapel it was given by the raising and lowering of the arm by the monitor in charge of chapel parade, so as not to disturb those already inside and assumed to be at prayer.

Once the short chapel service was over we walked back to our houses, collected our books and went to lessons, which lasted through the morning until 12.15, with a break of half an hour in the middle of the morning. Every break, except on Saturdays, we changed into games clothes, did PT (Physical Training) under the direction of the house monitors, then washed, got dressed again and went back into school. The three-quarters of an hour from 12.15 until 1.00 was free time. After that we marched to lunch and returned to the house to check the notice-board for our afternoon activities. Usually in the autumn that was either training for or playing rugby football, and when that was over we went back into school at 4.30 until tea at 6.00.

From 6.30 until 7.15 we did our house 'trades' - such things as sweeping the floors, cleaning the changing-rooms, and, while the war was still on, putting up the black-out boards. We then cleaned our coats and shoes for inspection by a monitor, and sat in our allotted places in the dayroom by 7.15 for fifteen minutes of quiet reading. At 7.30 one of the monitors called 'Books away', and that marked the beginning of the first session of Prep (Preparation, or what in most day schools is called homework). That was followed by house prayers conducted by house monitors, after which the younger boys went up to the junior dormitory to get washed, inspected for cleanliness by the matron and go to bed, while the older boys returned to their Prep until their bedtime an hour later.

Of course there were variations. Sundays were entirely different, with chapel services, letter-writing and a free afternoon. Wednesdays and Saturdays were half holidays, with time in the late afternoon for various voluntary activities, and on Saturdays there was no PT in the middle of the morning. Nor was there Prep on Saturday evenings. Instead we would march to Big School carrying a blanket each, because there was no heating, to watch a film or go to a concert. On summer afternoons school shifted to the beginning rather than the end of the afternoon, and we then played cricket interminably.

The housemaster, Mr Burleigh, was a nice, kindly, elderly man who had retired before the war and come back during the war to teach science and run the house during the day and act as an Air Raid Warden for at least part of the night. On Sunday afternoons he would take new boys for a walk and each evening he would come to the junior dormitory to wish them a good night. But he had little idea of what was going on in the house most of the while.

The house captain, Jim Lewis, was a good, conscientious and high-minded young man who was serving in the Home Guard and preparing to join the army at the end of the school year to fight the Japanese. None of us, of course, knew that the war would suddenly end with the dropping of the atom bombs in August 1945. He, like many thousands of other young men, instead of going off to fight and die over the eighteen months or two years which the Joint Chiefs of Staff calculated would be needed to defeat the Japanese, simply did eighteen months of National Service in peacetime and had the rest of his life to live in freedom. He spent most of it as a missionary. He had apparently been imported into Barnes A as house captain because it was perceived to need some external influence. But the house had developed its own barbaric customs during the relative anarchy of the war years and there was a limit to how much difference one eighteen year old boy could make.

My first few months at Christ's Hospital, starting in September 1944, were the last months of the war in Europe. We still had blackout boards on the windows in the evenings, but there were no longer any air raids in Sussex. British and American forces had landed in Normandy in June. The Russians were advancing from the East, and as the war continued I followed it in detail on the map: the Rundstedt Offensive, the crossing of the Rhine, and so on.

When Victory in Europe came on 8th May 1945, it was no surprise, but it was still an occasion for great rejoicing. The whole school went to the top of Sharpenhurst, a hill just the other side of the railway line on the way to the village of Itchingfield, and there we had a bonfire on which we burnt the Squanderbug, a cartoon character who wasted things and thus damaged the war effort, and also effigies of Hitler and Goering.

Victory in Europe was followed by the ending of the coalition government and the calling of a general election. Devoted though

I was to Winston Churchill, I had no doubt that this was the opportunity for a Labour government to build a better future, and I was astonished to find that many of the boys and, I suspected, quite a number of the masters, were hoping for a Conservative victory.

The results were declared on 26th July, just before the end of term, and when a boy called Bernard Levin, later a distinguished journalist, celebrated the Labour victory by hanging a red flag out of one of the windows of his house, he was beaten by his housemaster, Derek McNutt. McNutt had invented what are known as cryptic crosswords and under the name of *Ximenes* he for many years compiled crossword puzzles for *The Observer*, and years later Bernard Levin joined him on *The Observer* as a colleague.

Some seventy years later, when I went to the funeral of his son-in-law, John Page, another Christ's Hospital master whom I had known well, I met Derek McNutt's widow, by then an old lady in her nineties, and spoke to her about his teaching me. She told me that his favourite of all the thousands of crossword clues he had devised was 'He ought to keep the classroom in order' and the answer was an anagram of 'the classroom': 'SCHOOLMASTER.' It has an elegant simplicity and seems to me worthy to go with my two other favourite clues. One is 'Zero squared is cubed (3 letters)', to which the answer is OXO. The other is HIJKLMNO (five letters), to which the answer is WATER.

When the war was over, in Europe in May and then against Japan in August, John and I still had seven more years to go at Christ's Hospital, and throughout those years we regularly travelled at the beginning of each term on the No. 10 bus, from Woodford Bridge to Victoria Station, along the Leytonstone High Road and the Mile End Road, and then back at the end of term, wearing our school uniform without embarrassment and even with a sense of pride.

7. School Life

Christ's Hospital was above all an academic institution, a 'Religious, Royal and Ancient Foundation', where Godliness and Good Learning were promoted. Quite a large part of the day was spent in lessons, and unlike my elementary school, in which we had stayed in the same classroom all day, we went to different classrooms for different subjects. English and History might be taught by the same master in the same room, but German or French were on another floor, Geography was in a separate building, and so were Mathematics and Science. The really distinctive thing about the Christ's Hospital curriculum for new boys was that we all had to learn Ancient Greek. In many grammar schools throughout the country new boys learnt Latin, but Christ's Hospital was one of very few schools (perhaps the only one) where all new boys learnt at least the rudiments of Greek.

I felt a sense of privilege in doing so. I liked the mysterious letters: $\alpha, \beta, \gamma, \delta$ and so on, down to $\varphi, \chi, \psi, \omega$. I discovered that the Greek language had grammar, with words ending differently, depending, for example, on whether they were the subject or the object of a sentence, or whether they were the first, second, or third person, singular or plural, of a verb, and whether they were in the present, future, imperfect, perfect or pluperfect tense. The complications fascinated me, even if I found it difficult to disentangle all the various endings.

After a couple of years, when I was asked what I wanted to do in the future, I answered 'History' and was told that in that case I had better start learning Latin. So I started Latin at the age of twelve, in a class in which a substantial number of the boys were going on to win classics or modern languages scholarships to Oxford or Cambridge. After only two years, and at the age of fourteen, I took School Certificate Latin and failed it. Many boys going through a standard preparatory school and public school course would have started it at the age of seven or eight and taken it at School Certificate another seven or eight years later at fifteen or sixteen. I did not know that at the time and just thought that I was not very good at it.

Another large part of the day was spent on organised games, and I soon found myself learning to play rugby football and again feeling privileged to do so. That rugby football was superior to soccer was impressed on us, and I enjoyed the rough and tumble of it. Because I was quite large for my age and not particularly skilful I found myself playing in the middle of the scrum, and because I continued to enjoy it and played it enthusiastically, by the beginning of my fourth year in the school, in the Great Erasmus, the form in which we took School Certificate, I was playing as a second row forward in the school under-fourteen team (You had to be under fourteen on 1st September, and I was not fourteen until 1st November).

I was less enthusiastic about time spent in the house (whether in the dayroom, the junior changing room or the junior dormitory), where the life of a new boy was spent in an atmosphere in which relatively harsh official discipline was combined with a continuing unofficial threat of brutality. Anyone who believes that the point of a boarding school education is to harden up the young would have been well satisfied. My own view, which developed clearly and consciously at an early stage, was that it was important to avoid being hardened and essential to have a fixed determination not to give future generations the treatment we had had.

The discipline, such as it was, was enforced by house monitors. Minor misdemeanours (being the last boy on parade or having uncombed hair) were punished with 'quick changes' (change into games clothes, report, change back into uniform and report again) and anything seen as more serious, such as 'insolence', was punished with a 'mile' (the same as quick changes, but with a run of a mile before changing back into uniform). Failure to do the punishments quickly enough resulted in further punishments, and some boys spent a large part of their spare time working off punishments. There were no official beatings by boys, as happened in many boarding schools at that time and for many years afterwards, so the punishments were no more than an irritating intrusion into one's spare time – but I resented them none the less.

Far more unpleasant was the casual bullying by those boys in the middle age range, around thirteen or fourteen, who made up for their lack of academic or sporting distinction by brutalising new boys. For no better reason than that a little boy was in their way as he walked past they would pull his head down by the hair and 'foch' him several times, hitting with cupped hand on the back of the neck, keeping him still and aiming to get a loud sound as the hand hit the neck. Up in the dormitory, when no house monitors were present, a little boy might be made to stand with loosely tied pyjama trousers while older and larger boys tried to hit them down using the girdle, or belt, worn around the uniform blue coat. There was no particular villain, no Flashman who stood out from the rest. There was just a continuing atmosphere of insecurity and anarchy.

Since I was a stroppy little boy with a confident view of right and wrong, who would not keep his mouth shut and accept this sort of thing meekly, I more than once found myself held upside down with my head in the lavatory bowl as the chain was pulled to clean my mouth out. I was, I suppose, treated no worse than most others, and I had the advantage of having the companionship of a twin brother and of another boy, Barry Lendon, who was in the same year as us. But it must have been unspeakable for a ten year old who was alone and without friends. The occasional boy who left early, judged to be 'unsuited to a boarding environment', had usually been the victim of extended and excessive treatment of this sort.

One example I came across when we had a reunion in 2002, fifty years after I left the school. The boy in question had left after only two years in the school, in the summer of 1944, just before I arrived, after being badly bullied. He went to another school, left, got a job, joined the Gloucestershire Regiment for his National Service, was posted to Korea, captured by the Chinese at the battle of the Imjin in April 1951, and then spent three years in captivity in China, with even worse treatment than he had known at school, before being released in 1954 in the exchange of prisoners which followed on from the ceasefire in 1953. Why he came back to a reunion in the early twenty-first century I could scarcely understand – perhaps to demonstrate that he had survived.

My own solution to the unpleasantness of life in the house was to join anything which provided an excuse for being out of the house: the School Band, the Scouts, the Christian Union, the Debating Society, the Chess Club, and the Boxing Club. In our first term John and I went up to the Music School and asked if we could join the band. He was given a clarinet; I was given a French horn. The band master gave us basic instruction on how to get a noise out of each instrument, on the appropriate fingering for the various notes, and on the relative lengths of breve, semi-breve, minim, crochet, quaver and semi-quaver. From then on we went up to the Music School regularly at the end of morning school at 12.15, and we gradually picked up more about how to play our instruments, and in our last year at school John was the band captain and I was the leading, if not especially good, horn player.

We also joined the school Scout Troop, the 1st Christ's Hospital, and found ourselves in the Kingfisher patrol whose patrol leader was a boy called Derek Baker. He taught me to tie reef knots and clove hitches, how to splice two pieces of rope together, and how to build a structure with wood and rope using square lashings and diagonal lashings. I got used to pitching a tent and digging a trench round it to keep out the rain. I learnt how to light a fire and cook in the open, and above all I enjoyed the luxury, afforded only to members of the scout troop, of occasionally going off with another boy at a week-end in the summer with a hike tent on top of a ruc-sack and with an axe and cooking utensils slung below, wearing scout uniform and carrying a stave, and being able to walk through the Sussex countryside, sleep out and eat only what one could carry and cook oneself.

When Derek became the troop leader, I took over as the patrol leader of the Kingfisher patrol. When he left school I took over as the troop leader. Derek, who had been a History specialist, known at Christ's Hospital as a History Grecian, left to do his National Service in the Royal Corps of Signals, went up to Oxford with a scholarship to Oriel College, became a schoolmaster and then a lecturer at Edinburgh University, and in 1979 returned to Christ's Hospital as Head Master.

Another organisation which I joined and which influenced me was the Christian Union. It was entirely unofficial and operated within the context of an avowedly Christian school in which everyone went to chapel every morning and everyone attended house prayers in the evenings. It had the merit of being run by senior boys like Jim Lewis, who proclaimed the importance of living in accordance with Christian principles in a society which often seemed only to pay lip service to those principles and in which many boys neglected them or acted in a manner entirely contrary to them.

On the other hand, the speakers at the Christian Union were usually young men from some such organisation as the Inter-Varsity Fellowship with cheerful abbreviated and monosyllabic Christian names (Bill, Dick, Tom and so on) who seemed to me as I grew older excessively sure that it was important to have a personal Pauline conversion, that intercessory prayer would result in divine intervention, and that if you gave your life to Jesus and encouraged others to do the same, all sorts of benefits would accrue to you both in this world and the next. It was the style and excessive self-confidence which bothered me, but in their own way they unintentionally encouraged me to think critically.

The Debating Society meanwhile consciously encouraged critical and structured thought. Whereas in the Christian Union it seemed that there was a clear line one was expected to accept and any dissent was viewed with sorrow and suspicion, in the Debating Society the whole object of debating was to construct arguments and challenge the opinions of others. Two senior boys who were particularly good at it were Bryan Magee and Richard Cavendish, both in the same house as me and both History Grecians, and I remember with pleasure hearing Bryan speaking on the motion that 'this house shares with Caesar his preference for fat men.'

My ambition from a fairly early age was to become a History Grecian like them, and I also sought to emulate them in the Debating Society. It was unrealistic to expect to get anywhere near speaking as well in public as Bryan Magee, who went on to be President of the Oxford Union, a presenter of programmes about philosophy on television, and Labour Member of Parliament for Leyton. But I made a practice of attending and speaking regularly, and before I left school was elected a member of the Debating Society committee. I learnt enough to be able to run debating societies when I became a schoolmaster.

The Chess Club was an organisation which took me into other houses, something which was usually discouraged, and I enjoyed it enough to go on playing when I no longer had any particular need to escape from my own house. I continued to play spasmodically through much of my life and taught my sons, who both became good enough chess players to beat me. Many years later my younger son and I would sometimes play our way through the moves of the famous match played in a box at the Paris Opera House in 1858 between the world champion, Paul Morphy, and two talented amateurs, the Duke of Brunswick and Count Isouard.

Finally I made my way to the Boxing Club in an era in which boxing was a perfectly acceptable school sport. Barry Lendon was particularly good at it. He was a naturally talented boxer, upright and with a swift left jab and powerful right hook. When engaged in competitive boxing we fought against other boys in the same weight range as ourselves (8 stone 7lbs to 9 stone, for example) and I remember being glad in our second year in the school, the Little Erasmus year, that Barry, though about my height, was too light for me to have to fight him. Without him as an opponent I won my weight. But he was growing, so the following year I had to fight him and was soundly beaten. Fortunately he went on growing and the year after that he was too heavy for me to fight and I was able to win my weight again.

By then I was regularly fighting in school matches, and whereas within Christ's Hospital I won more matches than I lost, in matches against other schools I lost more often than I won. What is more, as I got heavier, being hit on the side of the jaw hurt a lot more than it had a couple of years earlier. I was never knocked out, nor did I ever knock anyone else out, but three one and a half minute rounds, which sounds trivial by comparison with what professional fighters do, could be exhausting.

When I was fifteen, boxing at 10 stone to 10 stone 7lbs, I lost in the final of the West Sussex schoolboys' boxing championship, and that was my last fight. Barry carried on, getting bigger and stronger and more experienced, and two years later, by which time he was house captain and playing in both the 1st XV and the 1st XI, he also won the national heavyweight Amateur Boxing Association championship.

The School Band, the Scout Troop, the Christian Union, the Debating Society, the Chess Club and the Boxing Club all had their various influences on me. So did the CCF, which we had to join when we reached the age of thirteen, and in which we learnt about the Lee Enfield rifle and the Bren gun, and practised foot drill, which had been an important tactical device in the eighteenth century and had somehow survived as part of basic military training a century and a half later. We went on to learn more and more: setting a compass for a night march and how to give orders for a platoon attack, for example. I was gradually promoted and by my last year was one of the two senior boys in the CCF, sergeant-major in A Company, whose company commander was John Page, a housemaster whose war had been spent in Burma.

Playing the French Horn in the band led on to playing in the school orchestra, which had rather more interesting parts for the horn than did the band, and then when my voice broke it led on to singing bass, first in the Big School Choir, which had fifty or sixty basses, next in the Chapel Choir, which had only about a dozen, then in the Madrigal Choir, which had only four, and finally even to singing the occasional solo. The band, the orchestra and singing, scouting and military training, Christianity, whether in chapel or the CU, debating, chess, boxing and rugby football, with school work thrown in, and even learning to cope with life in the house, were all in their own ways helping to prepare me for the future.

The Christ's Hospital band, in which I was playing the French horn, marching through the City of London at the head of the whole school on the way back from a service at St Sepulchre's Church and from tea at the Mansion House on St Matthew's Day, 21st September, a couple of years after the war. We are just entering Newgate Street form Cheapside. The bomb damage done about seven years earlier has at least been tidied up. That area is now Paternoster Square.

8. Pongo

◇◇◇◇◇◇◇◇◇◇◇◇◇◇◇◇◇◇◇◇◇◇◇◇◇◇

When we started at Christ's Hospital we were given one choice about the curriculum. It was about which modern language to learn: French or German. In the twenty-first century it may seem surprising that out of about a hundred and twenty boys more than a hundred of us opted for German. But Germany had dominated our lives. To most of us at the age of ten or eleven France was just one of the many European countries which had been defeated in 1940 and had disappeared into relative obscurity. After giving us a choice, the Modern Languages department found it difficult to make up one French set. The rest of us were divided at random into four German sets.

As it happens the set I was in was taken by an elderly man who was one of those employed to try to keep things going during the war. Perhaps he knew some German, but he had no idea how to teach or how to maintain order in a class of unruly small boys used to tight discipline and willing to break free when given the opportunity. We learnt little or nothing, and in the examination at the end of the year we all performed worse than any of those in the other sets. So the next year, when there was a top, second, third and bottom set German set, we were all in the bottom set, and that, perhaps inevitably, was taken by the same incompetent master who was supposed to have taught us in the first year. We had another year of learning virtually nothing in German lessons.

At the beginning of my third school year, in September 1946, with the war now a year over, men who had been fighting their way across the Western Desert and the Lüneburg Heath, or through the jungles of Burma, were returning to their peace-time occupations. Those elderly and infirm, and in some cases incompetent, members of the teaching staff of Christ's Hospital who had tried to fill in during the extended emergency of wartime, were able to retire. The new men, returning from the armed forces and used to military discipline, generally expected high standards, and Mr Johnstone, who took over our German set at the beginning of the Lower Fourth year, plunged into the syllabus where we should have been, expected me to know something of German modal verbs, found that I didn't, and put me into detention to learn them.

My new housemaster, Eric Littlefield, wanted to know why. He also was recently back from the war and had taken over the house some time in 1946. He had served in the RAF and was generally known as 'Pongo', partly because of the bouncy, springy step with which he walked, but also because he had at some point referred to soldiers as 'Pongos', the standard RAF slang for those who fought on foot. The name somehow fitted and it stuck. He had been a squadron leader, but instead of flying, he had, as a fluent German speaker, spent most of the war interrogating German airmen who had been shot down and were prisoners-of-war.

He applied much the same technique to the interrogation of schoolboys who appeared to be guilty of some misdemeanour. I remember a school friend, Bob Finch, telling me much later in life how he still felt frissons of fear whenever he came near the school as he remembered such interrogations. After ten or fifteen minutes of standing in silence while Pongo smoked and stared at him, he would, he said, have confessed to anything.

When Pongo sent for me to find out why I had been put in detention, I told him that Mr Johnstone thought that my ignorance of modal verbs was an indication of indolence, but it wasn't. I had no idea what they were and had spent two years not being taught German, when I would really have loved to be able to learn it. 'Do you mean that?' he asked. 'Yes sir', I replied. 'Very well then', he said, 'Come along here after tea at 6.30 and we'll start.' So I did.

I did the detention, of course, but day after day I had a few minutes of individual tuition in German, going off afterwards to learn whatever we had dealt with: the definite article, pronouns, word order, the prepositions which always take the dative (*Beimitnachausseitvonzu*), learnt as they were one word and an extended expletive, and also all those which always take the accusative (*Durchfürgegenohneumwider*), also learnt as if they were another even more vindictive and extended expletive.

The outcome was that I was moved up to the second set for the fourth, or Great Erasmus, year, got a distinction in School Certificate, went on to take German at Higher Certificate, continued to read German, used German regularly during much of my National Service, and even taught it briefly when I was first a schoolmaster.

One of the first times I encountered Pongo as someone other than as a teacher or figure of authority was late in the Summer Term of 1946, when Barry Lendon, aged thirteen, and John and I, both aged twelve, were walking down the Avenue after lunch on a Sunday and his Wolsey motor car, one of those 1930s cars with a running board, stopped alongside us. Pongo and another housemaster, Colin Tod, who taught me to box, asked us if we would like a trip down to the coast. So we jumped into the car and he drove us down to Worthing. It was the first time we had seen the sea since before the war. It was also memorable as the first time in my life that I had ever been in a motor car.

It was at just that same time, in July 1946, nearly a year after the end of the war, that the government introduced bread rationing. The war had left Great Britain in a difficult economic position. Overseas assets had been sold off to pay for the war. We were deeply in debt to the U.S.A., and wartime posters such as *Dig for Victory* were now replaced by posters proclaiming *Export or Die*. Somehow we had to pay for the food eaten by a population of about fifty million people, and the introduction of bread rationing in the summer of 1946 was followed by the long, cold winter of 1946-7 and by potato rationing as well.

In a school of 830 growing boys, in which bread and potatoes were the basis of our diet, it produced a problem which was made worse by the way in which senior boys dealt with it – at least in our house. Thick slices of bread were cut for the most senior boys and thin ones for the juniors. Any left over went to the most senior boys. Similarly, large potatoes were distributed to the seniors and small ones to the juniors. The school food at that time was bad enough. The last meal of the day, tea at 6.00p.m., was no more than bread and jam or, on a good day, a sausage, but at least we had been able to fill ourselves up with, for example, bread and salt. But now it was not only that the quality of the food was poor; the quantity was seriously inadequate as well.

In the winter of 1946-7 John, Barry Lendon and I were in our third year in the school, still relatively junior, but old enough to recognise serious unfairness when we saw it and hungry enough to do something about it. Between us we wrote a petition to the housemaster asking for fair shares in the distribution of bread and potatoes, and then we got most, perhaps all, of the juniors to sign it. It worked, and Pongo got the house monitors to ensure that portions were fairly distributed.

Many years later, when John was a young clergyman staying at the monastery of Taizé, he told me that he had a strange sensation which reminded him of school. It puzzled him, and only after a few days did he realise that the strange sensation was hunger. Even more years later, when I taught the French Revolution and later the Russian Revolutions as special subjects at A level, I was not surprised to find how important bread shortages and bread riots were in the development of those revolutions.

The three of us were in the slightly strange position that year that, being young for the forms we were in, we were still in the lower half of the house and in the junior dormitory, but needed to stay up for second Prep. One warm summer evening, when all the senior boys were allowed to sit out on the grass at the front before going to bed, we took it into our heads to fill all the basins in the lav. end with water and then throw the water down on those below. Not surprisingly it caused an uproar.

The housemaster came out to see what was going on just as we got rid of the last of our ammunition. He came upstairs and said, 'Down in my study.' Once we got there he then said, 'Youngest first' and gave each of us six stokes of the cane. That was it. No more was said. It was the only time that any of us was beaten officially, and although later as a schoolmaster I always opposed corporal punishment, at the time it seemed to me a quick and simple way of dealing with the problem. We did not hold it against Pongo. Nor did he ever say another word about our foolish behaviour.

In the autumn of 1947 we entered what was called the Great Erasmus year, the year in which some centuries earlier the children of Christ's Hospital had studied the greater *Colloquies* of Desiderius Erasmus, having studied his lesser *Colloquies* two years earlier in the Little Erasmus. Now it was the year in which we took School Certificate, the predecessor of O levels and GCSE, and then, in the summer holidays of 1948, with School Certificate behind us, Pongo took John, Barry and me on a delightful week's holiday, learning to sail on the Norfolk Broads on a 26 foot Bermudan sloop, *Perfect Lady 4*, from Potter Heigham.

The following year he arranged for me to spend the Easter holidays with a German family in Munich. *Herr Bundesbahnoberrat Curtius* (Mr Federal Railway Senior Official Curtius) was, despite the change from the Third Reich to the German Federal Republic, still generally referred to by his former title of *Herr Oberreichsbahnrat Curtius* (Mr Senior Imperial Railway Official Curtius), and his wife was *Frau Oberreichsbahnrätin*. They were a gentle, pleasant and hospitable couple with two teen-age children, Renate and Carli, who were good company and made me welcome.

It was only much later that I realised that during the war Herr Curtius must have been in charge of the rail transport in and out of the Dachau concentration camp. He was in the same position as large numbers of others. Many, perhaps most, Germans were in some way involved in the logistics of the concentration camps and the Final Solution of the Jewish Question, as it was euphemistically called, but they were not necessarily enthusiastic members of the Nazi Party, and sometimes, partly because it was a mistake to ask questions, they did not appreciate the significance of what they were doing. When they knew more, after the war, they were often profoundly ashamed.

I went there with a solid grounding in eighteenth century German literature and addressed Frau Curtius as *Gnädige Frau* ('Honourable lady'), which would have been correct two hundred years earlier. I also used phrases such as *Mich dünkt* ('Methinks') lifted straight out of Schiller. It was now time to learn some colloquial German. It was a pleasure to find that a grammatically complex sentence such as *Das hätt' ich gern tun können* ('I would very much have liked to have been able to do that') could slide easily off the tongue without any thought of transferring past participles into infinitives.

We visited the *Englischer Garten* (laid out in the manner of an English park, so at that stage of my life I did not understand why it was called a garden) and the *Haus Deutscher Kunst* - the Museum of German Art. I was surprised to find that Renate and Carli, who were Protestants from Prussia living in Catholic Bavaria, had never been inside the Catholic cathedral, the *Frauenkirche*. But then I reflected that I had been past the Tower of London innumerable times but had never been in.

We visited *Schloss Neuschwanstein*, the inspiration for Walt Disney's fairy tale castle, as well as *Herrenchiemsee* and *Schloss Linderhof*, all built by King Ludwig II of Bavaria in the late nineteenth century, and *Ettal Kloster*, where I encountered baroque architecture and decoration for the first time. Until then it had never crossed my mind that a church could be built in any other style than what is called Gothic or neo-Gothic. I thought I had never seen any church interior so beautiful.

One day Carli took me on his scooter to visit the farm to which he had been evacuated when the Americans were bombing Munich by day and the British were bombing it by night. The farmer's

66

wife was delighted to see him again, sat us both down in the farm
kitchen and gave each of us a plate of four fried eggs. For as long
as I could remember I had only ever had one egg a week, so this
was a whole month's ration at one meal – and eggs were still
rationed back in England. It was the first time that I had occasion
to think that the price paid by Great Britain for winning the war
was losing the peace.

I probably thought little at that time about how much I owed to
Pongo. He had rescued me from a disastrous situation with the
learning of German, he introduced me to German literature and
culture, he taught me to sail, and he gave me a complete set of all
the novels of Jane Austen, which I read with pleasure as a teenager
and re-read with even greater pleasure fifty years later in retirement. He was not an easy man, he was not popular, and many
boys counted themselves unfortunate to have been in his house.
But by the way he ran the house he taught me the importance of
the maintenance of good order in an educational environment.

Freedom is a noble ideal, and one has good reason to give thanks
for the privilege of living in a society in which people are free to
live their own lives, while allowing others freedom as well. But
Liberty can easily disintegrate into Anarchy, and the best Liberal
political philosophers knew that it is only possible to have
Freedom within the Rule of Law. Barnes A had been brutal and
anarchical during the war. Some fairly tough assertion of authority was needed to turn it into a society in which boys were
expected to treat each other at least decently, and preferably with
some understanding and kindness, so that all could be free to
engage in purposeful activity.

9. 'Daddy' Roberts

<><><><><><><><><><><><><><><><><><><><><><><><><><><><>

The Honourable David Roberts, son of the first Baron Clwyd (pronounced Kloo-id) and Head of the History Department at Christ's Hospital, was known to the boys either as DSR or as 'Daddy' Roberts, probably because, unlike most of the masters, he was married and had three children. He was also a remarkable schoolmaster.

Some time in the early 1970s, when teaching at Stowe, I asked Bob Heller, previously the Economics Editor of the *Observer* and by then Editor of *Management Today*, to speak to my Historical Society. He had been a History Grecian at Christ's Hospital a few years before me, and as we walked round the grounds of Stowe and reminisced, he told me that after School Certificate he had set out to be a modern linguist. Some time later he decided that that was a mistake and asked David Roberts if he could switch to studying History.

There were only four terms before he would need to take the Cambridge scholarship examination. David asked him a few questions, agreed to take him on, and set him his first essay: 'Explain the significance of Giotto in the development of European Civilisation.' He then sent him away to read about it and write the essay. Bob said that it never occurred to him that there was anything in the least unusual about that as an introduction to the study of History in what in most schools would be called the Sixth Form, and it was the beginning of a life-long love of painting.

Christ's Hospital had no 'Sixth Form.' Most boys left school at the age of sixteen for jobs in the City of London. Those who were thought capable of getting scholarships to Oxford or Cambridge were put through School Certificate as young as possible and stayed on to prepare for the college examinations. The cleverest boys were expected to specialise in Greek and Latin. It was accepted that some, rather strangely, would study Mathematics or Science. It was even accepted that some would study modern rather than classical languages. But there always remained a core of difficult and perverse boys who wanted to study History. Some, like Bryan Magee, were not particularly attached to History itself, but were determined to be taught by David Roberts. Others, like me, thought History the most interesting of all the subjects we were studying and hoped he would accept us.

School policy appeared to be opposed to such aspirations. There were Classical Grecians, Maths Grecians, Science Grecians and Modern Languages Grecians. Those who wished to study History were first labelled Deputy Geography Grecians, even though they did no Geography, and later Modern Grecians – anything but History. But David had a long established record of his pupils getting open scholarships to Oxford and Cambridge colleges (an average of three a year for twenty-five years), which was well known to the boys, and those who did so always thought of themselves as History Grecians – and were perceived as such by the next generation. There was more pride in being a History Grecian than in winning one's colours at rugby football or cricket.

My introduction to that small select group was different from Bob Heller's. I had taken School Certificate at fourteen and was still fourteen when the new school year began. When I saw David Roberts at the beginning of term he gave me a book on medieval history whose first chapter was on the rise of the Carolingian Empire and whose second chapter was on the fall of the Carolingian Empire, told me to write an essay explaining the rise and fall of the Carolingian Empire and bring it to him at the end of the week. From then on, for the next four years, I went on writing essays for him and having them marked and criticised, and that was how I was taught.

I was also studying German and English Literature and sometimes what was called 'Divinity', which for a long stretch of time amounted to listening to a detailed exposition of the Headmaster's views on the *Book of Job*. For all of those subjects I would go along to a classroom to be enlightened on whatever we were studying. But throughout my last four years at school I never sat in a classroom to be taught History. I simply read, made notes, thought, wrote, and then faced criticism of what I had written.

The difference between Bob Heller's induction into that system and mine was that he, with four terms to go until his Cambridge scholarship exam, was plunged directly into Giotto's influence on European civilisation, while I, with three years and a term before I needed to face the Oxford examination system, was allowed to put my toes gently in the water and tackle a relatively easy question. In both cases David Roberts, with that unerring instinct he seemed to possess for what a boy could cope with at any time, gave us a piece of work to do, left us to get on with it, and then marked it and went through it with us, revealing where we had gone astray and how we could improve.

As time went by the reading matter was weightier and the questions less simple: J. J. Jusserand on *Wayfaring Life in the Middle Ages* and the essay title, 'Most of those on the roads in the fourteenth century were up to no good.' Discuss ; or Jakob Burckhardt on *The Civilisation of the Renaissance in Italy* and Clive Bell on *Civilisation*, and the question, 'Was anything reborn in the Renaissance?' David Roberts would read each essay, mark it with a system of Greek letters, plus and minus signs and question marks, and return it with appropriately acerbic comments and questions, both in writing and orally.

The mark β?α meant that the essay was good sound work, with perhaps (that was the force of the question mark) just a touch of something first class (α) about it. One then strived to get βα or even αβ on the next essay. The whole process, including the subsequent questioning, was designed to get us to think for ourselves. 'What do you mean by 'cold logic', mister?' Then, 'What's cold about logic?' And finally, and devastatingly, 'What is logic?' I never used the again so long as I was at school. I took care to go away and find out what logic was. It was characteristic of David Roberts that he did not tell me. He provoked me to find out for myself.

Quite apart from getting me to write essays on medieval history, he would give me a range of books to read on apparently entirely unrelated topics (Milton's *Areopagitica*, Voltaire's *Candide*, for example, Samuel Butler's *Erewhon*, Lytton Strachey's *Eminent Victorians*, Bertrand Russell's *Authority and the Individual*, and T.S Eliot's *Notes Towards a Definition of Culture*) and a range of essays to write on topics which he thought would challenge me: 'Music hath charms to sooth the savage breast.' Discuss, or 'Make out the strongest case you can either for or against Christianity.'

One day, when I returned Orwell's recently published *Animal Farm*, which he had lent me, he asked me, 'What did you make of that, mister?' My reply was something like, 'I thought it was a really good story, Sir.' He looked at me quizzically, rubbing his finger along the side of his nose, and said nothing. As a schoolmaster many years later I could not have resisted the temptation, if one of my pupils had said that, to explain its relevance to the Russian Revolution. But David Roberts was determined not to teach us things. His mission was to get us to think and find things out for ourselves. Some years later I saw the connection.

Not only did he not tell us what to think. He seldom told us what to do, or not to do – so seldom that I can remember the one occasion when he did. As he came into the History Grecians' room one day, I removed my feet from a bookshelf. He made it very clear very quickly that my feet should not have been there, whether or not he was in the room. That is not what bookshelves were for. Precisely because it was so unusual for him to say anything of the sort (in an environment in which we were used to having everything we should do and should not do dictated to us by someone in authority, so that in our minds we wrote off the various injunctions) I took his admonition to heart and if ever again tempted to mistreat a bookshelf in that way for the rest of my life, I remembered his rebuke and desisted.

On another occasion, when I had made some casually dismissive remark about modern art, he beckoned me and walked silently with me to the School Library, where he removed from the shelf the Phaidon Press volume on Picasso. He opened it at the beginning, so that I could see some examples of how good a landscape painter Picasso was as a very young man, and then he turned the pages slowly and selectively, so that I could get some idea of Picasso's development as an artist. Not a word was said until he replaced the book on the shelf. I said, 'Thank you, Sir', and we parted.

Later on, one day when I was visiting his house to go through an essay and had just stepped over Peter, his youngest child, playing in the hall, I expressed my admiration for a picture hanging on the wall of his study. It was a painting of a ploughed field, with the ploughman and his horse disappearing towards the woodland in the distance. He took it off the wall, handed it to me and told me I could keep it in my study until the end of the year.

The only poetry David Roberts ever gave me to read was by a former History Grecian, Keith Douglas, whose *Collected Poems* were published in 1951, the year before I left school. Keith Douglas had been born in 1920. At Christ's Hospital we had been taught by several of the same masters, played in the same position in the 1st XV, won the same history prize and afterwards went on to the same university. But a few weeks before I arrived at the school in 1944 at the age of ten, and four days after the Normandy landings, he climbed out of his tank and was killed by a shell splinter. He was twenty-four. In 1952 I sat weeping in my study over his poetry.

Half a century after Keith Douglas was killed I went to find his grave and found it in the small military cemetery at Tilly-sur-Seulles, north of Caen, plot no.1, row E, grave no.2. The inscription on the tombstone is *'These things' he loved. He died in their defence.* 'These things' is a reference to the passage which was always read in the Christ's Hospital chapel on Founder's Day. It is in the fourth chapter of the letter to the Philippians, where St Paul writes: 'Finally, brethren, whatsoever things are true, whatsoever things are honest, whatsoever things are just, whatsoever things are pure, whatsoever things are lovely, whatsoever things are of good report; if there be any virtue, and if there be any praise, think on these things.'

The biography of Keith Douglas by Desmond Graham, published in 1974, describes the large tempura picture of African soldiers at bayonet practice which Douglas painted in 1937 and which hung in his study during his last year at school. He left it with David and Peggy Roberts, and after Peggy died in 2010, having been a widow for more than half a century, their younger son, Pete, gave it to me, so at one time I had a biography of Keith Douglas in my study, his *Selected Poems* in the kitchen, which then housed all my poetry books, his remarkable account of desert warfare, *From Alamein to Zem Zem*, in the sitting room, and the painting in the conservatory.

David Roberts's aim was not so much to teach us History as to educate us, and I have heard it said more than once that Christ's Hospital's History Grecians often performed better in the Oxbridge scholarship General Paper than they did in English or European History. His influence on many lives was profound. Bryan Magee, in his *Confessions of a Philosopher*, published in 1997, describes him as possessing 'what could almost be called a genius for teaching.'

In my case I acquired a lifelong interest in history and in what one might call the world of ideas, and though I could not teach a large number of A level candidates the way he taught his History Grecians, the impact of his method was that I always gave my pupils a reading list and an essay to write on any topic we tackled before I ever discussed it with them or taught them anything about it in class. Secondly, it was largely because of the books he gave me to read by people such as A.S.Neil, the founder of the progressive school Summerhill, that I came to believe that education could be a more human and humane business than had been the case for most of my own experience. Thirdly, the experience of visiting No.3, The Avenue, with my essays showed me that it was possible to combine teaching with family life in a house which had pictures on the walls, rugs on the floor and books everywhere. Those three things together led me to see life as a schoolmaster as an attractive example of the Good Life. More than sixty years later I remain grateful to him.

10. M.T.C.

◇◇◇◇◇◇◇◇◇◇◇◇◇◇◇◇◇◇◇◇◇

The other member of staff who shared with David Roberts the teaching of the History specialists was Michael Cherniavsky, who arrived at the school in the autumn of 1948, just after I had taken School Certificate. At the time he was twenty-eight, a large man with a powerful, jutting jaw, whose soft voice, with its slight lisp, and gentle manner were at odds with his appearance. He was the eldest son of the celebrated Ukrainian Jewish 'cellist, Mischel Cherniavsky, who had played before Tsar Nicholas II but left Russia at the time of the revolution of 1905.

Michael had been born in Buenos Aires, but was educated at Westminster School, where in his teens he was one of the founders of an anti-Fascist group called 'the United Front of Progressive Forces', commonly known as Uffpuff. From Westminster he won the top history scholarship, the Brackenbury, to Balliol College, Oxford, and went up in the autumn of 1938, when he was eighteen.

His tutor at Balliol was the distinguished medievalist, Richard Southern, and when, a year later, the Second World War began, they both left Oxford to join the army. Michael, because his surname was Cherniavsky, was put in the Pioneer Corps, which provided the army with manual labour, and almost anyone with a foreign name was placed in it. Ironically it probably had the highest average IQ of any corps or regiment in the army. Later on he was able to transfer to the Education Corps.

At the end of the war he was a sergeant producing a newspaper for the 4th Line of Communications sub-area of the British Army of the Rhine, which had just provided the logistical support for the Potsdam Conference of 17th July – 2nd August 1945. I still have a copy he gave me of the special edition he produced on 8th

August to mark the conference. On the back page it mentions that a 'new type of bomb' had been employed in a raid on Hiroshima two days earlier. The Japanese Osaka radio had apparently announced that a number of trains had been cancelled in the Prefecture of Hiroshima and in a later broadcast it described the damage caused by the bomb as 'considerable.'

Once Michael was demobbed he returned to Oxford and went to see his tutor, who had also just returned. Southern, with casual insouciance, ignoring the interruption into academic life of six years of warfare, referred back to Michael's last essay and set him another. After getting a First and then a brief spell of teaching at the Newcastle-under-Lyme High School in Staffordshire, he arrived at Christ's Hospital at the beginning of the Autumn Term of 1948, just as I returned from the Summer holidays after taking School Certificate, to be what at Christ's Hospital was very peculiarly called a probationary deputy Grecian and start on the course leading to the Higher School Certificate.

Like David Roberts, Michael Cherniavsky never taught me in a classroom; like David he gave me books to read and set me essays to write; and like David he marked the essays, commented on them, and then gave me another topic to tackle. Throughout four years the two of them got me to read widely, think for myself and write. They were a formidable combination, and while David's responses to my work were often challenging, sending me off to think for myself or re-think what I had been writing about, Michael was more likely to suggest, for example, that while I had dealt fully with two out of three important issues, I had neglected the third. He would then go on to explain why that was arguably the most important.

There was a similar difference in the titles of the essays they set. David Roberts would put to me a wide-ranging quotation, such as that '*In the fifteenth century the young nation states of Europe stand forth with the mark of their future destiny on their brow*' and get me to comment on it. Michael, by contrast, would ask something deceptively specific and simple: *Account for the anarchy of King Stephen's reign* or *What was great about Magna Carta?*

When getting me to write about the causes of the anarchy he was not only getting me to understand that particular topic. He was also providing a valuable introduction to how historians, especially when writing at different times, can have widely differing opinions about the same thing. He got me to look at the comment by Walter Map, a chronicler writing in the twelfth century, only a generation after the events he is describing, that Stephen was a *vir armorum industria praeclarus, ad cetera fere ydiota* ('a man outstanding in the pursuit of arms, but for the rest, almost an idiot'). He got me to read *Geoffrey de Mandeville* by the nineteenth century historian J.H.Round, who argued that it was the conditions of the accession, with both Henry I's daughter, Matilda, and his nephew, Stephen of Blois, as candidates for the throne, that explain the outbreak of anarchy. Thirdly, he got me to read Sir Frank Stenton's Ford Lectures of 1929, *The First Century of English Feudalism 1066-1166*, in which Stenton sees the over-centralisation of Henry I's reign as leading to an inevitable reaction.

It impressed on me not only how very different can be the explanations provided by historians writing at different times, but also the need to look beyond their differing views to what had actually happened in order to understand an issue better. I also began to grope towards a recognition that historical explanations are always going to be provisional, dependent not only on the time at which they are written, but also conditioned in the case of every writer by a whole range of assumptions and attitudes of which he or she may or may not be aware.

When getting me to consider *Magna Carta* Michael revealed the value of looking at a document in detail. 'The Great Charter' has traditionally been held up as the foundation stone of English liberty, and its most quoted clause is the promise that 'no freeman shall be captured or imprisoned or disseised...except by the lawful judgement of his peers or by the law of the land.'

But the revisionist view, which first emerged in the seventeenth century, is that the charter was imposed on the king by a group of self-interested barons who did little or nothing for the rest of the people. They required the removal from office of a large number of the king's favourites, they required, for example, the removal of the fish-weirs by which the king deprived them of fish, and they required that widows should not be forced to marry or be married off to someone of lower social status.

There are some fairly simple conclusions one can come to after looking in detail at the charter. First, it was a 'great charter' simply because it was big. Secondly, it is not a foundation document for nineteenth century liberal democracy. Thirdly, it placed quite reasonable limits on the arbitrary abuse of power by the king. It is only by looking at it in detail that one can move closer to understanding its place in early thirteenth century history and, indeed, its place in the context of the gradual development of the English constitution.

One issue in medieval history which Michael and I both found interesting but over which we disagreed was the conflict between Empire and Papacy or, on a smaller scale in England, between the King and the Archbishop of Canterbury. Michael, though an avowed atheist, sympathised with Pope Gregory VII rather than with the Emperor Henry IV, and with Archbishop Thomas Becket rather than with King Henry II. My sympathies, though I counted myself a Christian, were more with the emperor and the king. After all, they needed to rule their territories and could not afford to have a separate state within the state, exempt from the laws which applied to everyone else.

That was an issue we talked about some thirty years after I had left Christ's Hospital, as we walked round the grounds of Stowe School, where I was by then the Head of History, and to which I had invited Michael to come and talk to my Historical Society. It was a summer when he was in England on leave from the

University of Waterloo in Canada, where he was now teaching, and was spending that Summer Term at Radley College, where another former History Grecian, Dennis Silk, was the Warden.

Michael had a particular talent for mixing the teaching of history with philosophy. 'Philosophy' is a word meaning 'the love of wisdom', and history can be seen as a branch of philosophy - 'philosophy teaching by examples.' He might be returning an essay on the Norman Conquest and commenting on the difference between 'conquest' and 'colonisation', and then, as if the question had just struck him, he would ask, 'If you throw a stone at the front of a railway engine approaching you at speed, and the stone bounces back, does it stop when it hits the engine?', and then, 'Does the train stop?' Or he might ask, 'If you are walking along the corridor of a moving train towards the back of the train, are you going forwards or backwards?' Of course, a lot depends on how you are using words, and he got me used to saying, and thinking, 'It depends on what you mean by...'

He puzzled me once by asking, 'Is this a fair question?' I could not think of any answer that made sense. His solution was, 'If this is a fair answer, then it is a fair question.' Another of his problems I enjoyed was what he called 'the pseudo-paradox of the barber': 'In a certain village the barber shaves all those and only those who do not shave themselves. Does the barber shave himself?' Michael's contention was that this was not a true paradox, because the premise was a compound statement in which the two halves could not both be true. But if you took the question to be 'Does the barber shave-himself-or-not-shave-himself?', then the answer was 'Yes.'

His cast of mind led him to think up an alternative to the sentence which is sometimes used to illustrate the difficult relationship between spelling and pronunciation in the English language: *I thought the rough and dough-faced ploughboy coughed and hiccoughed his way through Scarborough.* Michael produced a sentence which reproduces the same eight sounds but with a different spelling in each case. He suggests that, in place of the unpolished, sickly country lad, we should imagine a surly tourist from the North American West: *The untaught, gruff and po-faced cowboy hiccupped his way thru Edinburgh.*

He passed on to me his interest in historiography, the study of the study of history, by getting me to read books such as *History: Its Purpose and Method* by the Dutch historian G.J.Renier, and it was while reading that that I was struck by Renier's comment on an example he uses of when Robinson Crusoe finds a footprint in the sand and wonders if it could possibly be his own. It was, of course, Man Friday's, and Robinson Crusoe realises that it is not his own when he tries his own foot in it. Renier points out that 'by applying experimental verification he was constrained to discard that comforting hypothesis.' I realised that what he meant was that Robinson Crusoe tried his foot in the print and found that it did not fit. Of course he was a Dutchman writing in English and perhaps should be forgiven for his verbosity. But I have used that example any number of times when trying to persuade teen-agers to write simply - to have clear in their mind what it is they want to say, and then say it as simply and clearly as possible.

Another significant moment in my historical education came when I was reading a book Michael had lent me about the twelfth century schoolman, Peter Abelard. It brought me as near as I have ever come to what might be seen as the equivalent of a religious conversion. I had got up early one summer morning and gone outside to read. I sat with my back to a fence behind my boarding house, looking out over a field in which Friesian cattle were grazing. I read some words which summed up Abelard's approach to philosophy and theology: 'By doubting we are led to inquire and by inquiry we perceive the truth.'

That struck me forcibly as the key to an understanding of life, the universe and everything. With time I modified my view. Doubting and inquiry were no guarantee of finding truth, but all my life I retained the view that at the very least they could help us to recognise nonsense when we hear it or read it. At the time it was a revelation and its influence on me was powerful and lasting.

In my last year at school, with a History scholarship to Oxford behind me, Michael sent me off for the Easter holidays to read Plato's *Republic* and Karl Popper's *The Open Society and its Enemies,* with an essay to write commenting on the proposition that 'Plato raises some fundamental problems in political theory, but his answers are not always satisfactory.' Again, he had judged well what would influence me.

Four years later, in 1956, he succeeded David Roberts as Senior History Master at Christ's Hospital, and continued in that position until 1966, when he went to teach at the University of Waterloo in Canada. He retired in 1983, and returned to Horsham at the same time that I arrived there as Principal of Collyer's, by then a sixth form college, and he continued to give me books which he thought would be good for me – such as David Hackett Fischer's *Historians' Fallacies – Toward a Logic of Historical Thought.* In 1992 he was seriously ill in the Horsham Hospital, just across the road from where I worked, and I was able to go and sit with him a number of times before he died.

11. Grecian

◇◇◇◇◇◇◇◇◇◇◇◇◇◇◇◇◇◇◇◇◇◇◇◇◇◇◇◇◇◇◇

The policy of Christ's Hospital in the middle of the twentieth century was that most boys should leave school one or two years after reaching the school leaving age, which at the time was fifteen. Every year many of them were advised to go into the City and get a job in insurance, banking or shipping, and many did that. Some stayed at school long enough to take Higher Certificate two years after School Certificate. A minority stayed on longer, either to prepare for the Oxford and Cambridge scholarship examinations or with the intention of going to the Royal Military Academy, Sandhurst, or with a view to becoming a doctor and training at one of the London teaching hospitals.

The Headmaster, Henry Lael Oswald Flecker, brother of the poet James Elroy Flecker, seemed to assume that no child of the hospital could possibly afford to go up to either of the universities (there were only two in his mind) as a gentleman commoner. So the school's connection with the City provided employment each year for dozens of teenagers who were judged not bright enough to win a college scholarship to either Oxford or Cambridge, and who did not aspire to join the army or become a doctor. This was at a time when state scholarships and county scholarships made generous provision for many of those who went up as commoners, and indeed for even more who went to other universities. But Flecker had not adjusted his mind to that, so any number of boys who could have gone to university did not do so.

Those of us who took Higher Certificate took two main subjects and one subsidiary subject, so John took French and German as his main subjects, with English as a subsidiary subject, while I took History and German and the same subsidiary subject. That was a slightly unusual combination, and the only other person in my year doing it was John Whitehead. He was rather more than a year older than me and in a house at the other end of the Avenue. But we met when playing rugby football, we played chess together (and he won), we went cross-country running together (and he was faster than me), and we met in school, in particular in German and English lessons. We became good friends.

But in 1950, at the end of the summer in which we took Higher Certificate, he, like so many others, was told that it was time for him to leave, so during my last two years at school he was already doing his National Service in the army. Like many Old Blues, as former pupils of Christ's Hospital were known, he was advised to go into the City, but he was determined to go to university and by his own efforts managed to get a place at Hertford College, Oxford, to read Modern Languages. Many years later, when he was Sir John Whitehead, GCMG (Knight Grand Cross of the Order of St Michael and St George) and Her Majesty's ambassador in Tokyo, he met the parents of one of his daughter's school friends. The father, it turned out, was another Old Blue and had, like John, been required to leave at seventeen as someone seen as unsuitable material for an Oxbridge scholarship. That was Sir Ian Trethowen, who was by then the Director General of the BBC. Both had felt 'I'll show them', and they had.

While John Whitehead and Derek Baker went off to the Royal Corps of Signals, I buckled down to two more years of writing history essays, translating German, reading English lyric poetry, playing rugby football, singing madrigals, playing the French horn, and filling a number of those roles which naturally fell to a conscientious schoolboy in a school from which so many left early that the number of those at the top from which to choose for such roles was limited. Thus I eventually found myself troop leader of the scout troop, sergeant-major in the CCF (the Combined Cadet Force), editor of the school magazine, a member of the debating society committee, singing a bass solo in a performance of Purcell and Dryden's dramatic opera, *King Arthur*, and playing the horn part in the *Nocturne* from Mendelssohn's *Incidental music to A Midsummer Night's Dream*. It was all very enjoyable.

The cast of King Arthur, *a dramatic opera by Purcell and Dryden, performed in our last year at school. John, a tenor and one of the three priests who sacrificed to Woden, is standing at the far right-hand end of the top line. I sang the bass part of Grimbald, an evil spirit, and am standing second from the left in the middle row, holding the horned mask I wore for the part.*

With Higher Certificate behind us at the age of sixteen both John and I qualified to be Grecians, but not till our seventeenth birthday did we get our new coats with large buttons, floppy velvet cuffs and velvet collar. John was a Modern Languages Grecian and I was a History Grecian. At the end of the Summer Term of 1951 there was a History Grecians' examination. It was marked by Billy Pantin, the medievalist fellow of Oriel College, Oxford. One of the questions was 'Why was there so much agrarian unrest in England in the late fourteenth century?' I was delighted and wrote a detailed explanation of the causes of the peasants' revolt of 1381, confident that it was a first-rate answer. It wasn't, and I learnt a salutary

The Christ's Hospital 1st XV in 1951.
I am seated at the right-hand end of the middle row.

lesson about the importance of answering the precise question set. Despite that and on the strength of the rest of my work Billy Pantin offered me a place at Oriel College, with an invitation to take their scholarship examination the following January.

Back in the early part of the autumn term of 1950, while still sixteen, I had been selected to play in the 1st XV for a couple of matches. But I was too young and not good enough, so I was demoted to the 2nd XV, where we had a splendid season, winning all our matches. The school usually won its rugger matches. We were not necessarily particularly talented sportsmen, but we were very fit and we were trained from an early age to play in a disciplined manner. We were also more successful than most schools at seven-a-side rugby football and in April 1951 Christ's Hospital won the public schools seven-a side tournament at the Old Deer Park near Richmond, after two years in which the Christ's Hospital team had gone to eight periods of extra time against

Taunton School. One year, in the semi-final, Taunton won and an exhausted Taunton team was then beaten by Stoneyhurst in the final. The next year Christ's Hospital won and an exhausted Christ's Hospital team was beaten by Stoneyhurst in the next round. So it was a particular pleasure to beat Stoneyhurst in the final in 1951. I was watching rather than playing, but over the years I had played regularly in the school under-14s team (at that stage I was big for my age), for the colts (under-16s), for the 2nd XV and then, in my last year, for the 1st XV. Throughout that time I only once ever played in a game that we lost.

Back in September 1944 Barry Lendon, John and I had been the three youngest and most junior boys in the house. Seven years on, in September 1951, we were the oldest and most senior. Barry was the house captain. All three of us were Grecians. At that stage of life I suppose I would have thought of my main interests as rugby football, medieval history and singing madrigals. But the experience of exercising authority over other boys, whether as a house monitor, or as an NCO in the CCF, or as the troop leader in the scouts, combined with the reading I was doing, whether about political theory, Christianity or education, led to the development of my views on how authority should be exercised and how people should behave towards each other in society.

I would not have gone as far as Rousseau, or even Robespierre (not that I knew about either of them at the time), in believing that people in a state of nature would behave well and that they only behaved badly when corrupted by the world around them. But I certainly came to believe that there was a case for trying to create a pleasant and co-operative society by treating people well rather than seeking to control them by threats of disciplinary sanctions. So about a year and a half before I left school I decided that I would not punish anyone, and for the rest of my time at school I sought to maintain order, whether as a house monitor or as a school monitor, whether in the CCF or in the scout troop, by asking younger boys politely to do, or not do, something. I believed that courtesy, reason, persuasion and example should suffice. Perhaps surprisingly that approach worked. But with hindsight I can see that a large part of the reason it worked, and far more than I realised at the time, was because it was in the context of a strict disciplinary system which provided a base from which one could afford the luxury of being polite and amiable.

The same applied in the army. One could give an order in a pleasant tone of voice, as if making a request, and it would be promptly obeyed. There was an assumption that orders must be obeyed, however politely put, and that the consequences of disobedience would be serious. Years later it took some weeks of being a schoolmaster in a perfectly pleasant but less ruthless environment to appreciate that not all schoolboys would react co-operatively to a polite request. Some would. Others would go their own way unless they knew that some sanction would be the consequence of disobedience. I had to face the fact that what I took to be an amiable approach would be perceived by some of them as weakness, and though I continued to dislike punishment and always believed in the desirability of seeking to achieve high standards of behaviour and work without punishment, I eventually recognised that punishment, if it was needed, should not be avoided.

Another way in which my attitude changed in the later part of my time at school was in my view of Mathematics and Science. It had not in the least bothered me to give up Science at the age of twelve and I was pleased to put Mathematics behind me once I had taken School Certificate at fourteen. We had been required to perform all sorts of mathematical operations, such as solving simple and quadratic equations, but I had no idea why anyone should wish to know how to do that, other than in order to be able to pass the Mathematics examination in School Certificate. The one aspect of Mathematics I found interesting was Geometry, but by the time I was beginning to take an interest in it, it was already time to give the subject up.

In my last year before leaving school the school decided to introduce 'Science for Non-Scientists' for senior boys studying such things as Classics, Modern Languages and History. There were three modules. The first was about Electricity, which failed to capture my imagination. The second was on Astronomy, which I found enthralling, discovering that the sun was so far away that the distance had to be measured by the speed of light, and that, while the sun was eight or nine light minutes away, the next nearest star was four light years away, and that there were other stars a thousand light years away. It cut the earth and its affairs down to size. The third module was on Genetics, and that had a transforming effect on my attitude to History. Issues of human motivation could never be the same if one saw them in the context of the way human beings and their behaviour was at least influenced, if not determined, by their genetic make-up.

Meanwhile, although my main area of study was History, I was still reading German plays, poetry and *Novellen*, and I was still going to English lessons and finding that I could enjoy T.S.Eliot as well as Keats. Once, when I wrote an essay for Edward Malins, the Head of English, about *Civilisation*, I explained, not very originally, that I saw it as a state of society in which a cultured and intellectual élite would appreciate the arts, conversing as they dined with each other about drama, the visual arts, music, philosophical ideas and so on, and able to do so because their society was sustained by the work of a slave class.

When he returned my essay, congratulating me on my sensitive and perceptive view of civilisation, he was shocked to find that, while I had described what I took civilisation to be, I had not been making any comment on how far such a society should be seen as either moral or desirable, and as it happens my own view was that it was profoundly immoral. I did not believe that the exploitation of a slave class by a self-centred and self-indulgent élite could be justified. It resulted in something of a row. He was clearly disappointed in what seemed to him, and probably was, a somewhat priggish attitude.

Shortly afterwards David Roberts, who was a great friend of Edward Malins, said to me, looking at me quizzically as he rubbed his finger along the side of his nose, 'You're a very serious-minded young man, aren't you?' I was not sure whether to take it as a compliment or a criticism. But yes, I was a serious-minded young man, developing my own ideas about such things as how schools should be run, how personal relationships should work and how society should operate.

In the summer holidays of 1951, immediately before our last year at school, John and I were away from home most of the while. First of all there was the CCF (or Combined Cadet Force) camp, at which we practised a range of basic military activities which would turn out to be quite useful when we joined the army - all the more so because the Christ's Hospital CCF was very efficiently run by men who had fought in the war and knew what they were doing.

Shortly after that, by contrast, we went to a madrigal camp down by the river Arun at Pulborough. The school madrigal choir spent a week going round Sussex villages giving madrigal concerts. John and I were both members of the madrigal choir (he was a tenor, while I was a bass), and the camping skills we had picked up in the scouts were of particular value when it poured with rain and we were able to keep everyone dry, digging trenches round the tents and managing to cook under an awning in the rain.

We had also, rather surprisingly, been invited by the headmaster to spend a week with him and his family at the Fleckers' country home in Dorset. We travelled there on the former Great Western Railway, changed at Maiden Newton, watched the driver and his fireman on the little local train cook their bacon and eggs on a spade in the fire which drove the engine, and then climbed aboard and set off via Toller Fratrum and Toller Porcorum down to Askerswell to stay in the Fleckers' house under Eggardon hill, the site of the first iron age settlement I ever saw.

During the day John and I would go off with the Fleckers' two teenage daughters, Philippa and Nicky, to visit Eggardon Hill or Golden Cap on the Dorset coast. They were attractive girls and delightful company, objects of desire to many of the boys in the school, but understandably seen as inaccessible because they were their father's daughters. In the evening Henry Lael Oswald Flecker would emerge from his study and over supper tell us his latest thoughts on the *Book of Job*. It was very unlike our own home life.

Because of that visit I got to know Philippa sufficiently well to be able to spend quite a bit of time in my last summer term playing tennis with her. In those days the only tennis courts in the school were for the use of masters and their families rather than for the boys, so one could only play tennis by invitation. Being bad at cricket turned out to have the bonus that I was able to play tennis on the masters' courts if Philippa invited me. We would quite often play in the evenings during Prep. Then I would dash back to the house and have a quick, cold bath before taking house prayers and reading the next instalment of, for example, *The Book of Ruth* or *Ecclesiastes*. But that was towards the end of my last school year, and for the moment, as the Autumn Term of 1951 began, it was time to get down to work in preparation for the Oxbridge examinations.

12. Last Year at School

As the new school year began John was now the house captain and I his deputy. He had been much impressed by a comment by Flecker that the best form of government devised by man was probably benevolent oligarchy, so long as you were one of the benevolent oligarchs, and he aimed to run the house in that way, with the two of us and the other four house monitors forming the oligarchical group who would consult and co-operate in the business of good government. It was probably rather good experience for him for later life. That is the manner in which the Dean and chapter run a cathedral, and he was to spend twenty-three years of his life as a Dean of a cathedral - eleven of them at Rochester and twelve at Durham.

I, on the other hand, had gradually acquired a belief in the virtues of what I was eventually inclined to call 'consultative autocracy' - a system in which individuals were expected to make their own decisions within their own area of responsibility, but preferably after consulting others involved about any issue on which a decision needed to be made.

In the Autumn Term we were both much engaged in preparation for the Oxbridge examinations. At that time both the Oxford and Cambridge colleges were divided for the purpose of scholarship examinations into three rotating groups, with their examinations in December, January and March, and with the candidates spending nearly a week in the college of their choice, taking examinations, going to interviews and either being captivated by their first experience of Oxford, as I was, or finding that it was not to their taste. The system gave candidates three opportunities to try for a scholarship at different colleges, so David Roberts suggested that I should have a trial run at Pembroke in December 1951. I filled in the appropriate application form, and was able to answer 'No' to whether or not I wanted a place if I failed to get a scholarship, because I was already assured of a place at Oriel.

On Saturday 8th December 1951, the day before I was due to go home on my way to Oxford on the Monday, we had the last away rugby match of the season and returned in triumph in time to get bathed and changed in time for another away match – this time dancing at St Catherine's, Bramley. It was the first dance I had ever been to, though we had all been instructed in the basic steps of the waltz, the quick-step, and the fox-trot, carrying a chair for a partner.

I was more apprehensive than before climbing into the boxing ring or waiting for the kick-off of a rugger match, and the apprehension increased, though mixed with a determination to overcome my nerves, when I saw across the room what seemed to me the prettiest girl I had ever seen in my life. She had dark hair and sparkling eyes and was wearing a short, white dress with a wide skirt such as might have been worn by a fairy on a Christmas Tree (most of the girls were wearing long dresses), and she was smiling a wicked smile as if pleased with herself for having just made some acerbic comment. I knew I must try to dance with her and manoeuvred to do so. When I did, I found her company and her personality as captivating as her appearance, and I was entranced by her smile.

Her name was Oriel, the name of the college where I had already been offered a place. She was a twin, but neither of our twins was at the dance – in John's case because a couple of days earlier he had gone up to Cambridge to take the modern languages scholarship examination at Sidney Sussex College. Oriel knew of Sidney Sussex because both of her uncles, Frank and Norman Gawan Taylor, had been there just before the First World War. Both were killed in the war, one on the Somme and one on patrol near Ypres. Her own father had been a classical scholar at Pembroke College, Oxford, from 1908 until 1912, and that, of course, was where I was going in a couple of days.

92

She was sixteen, in her school certificate year, and seemed to me entirely adorable. She wanted to be an actress. We had enough in common to make conversation easy and she promised to keep the last waltz for me. In those days we were required to keep changing partners between groups of dances, and that made the last waltz all the more important. We danced to *Destiny* and *Charmaine*, played by Mantovani and his orchestra, exchanged addresses and telephone numbers, and the world never seemed the same again. The next day I went home. My father told me later that after I had left for Oxford my mother said that I didn't seem my normal self. He had replied, 'I expect he's fallen in love.'

At Oxford we took a whole series of examinations: English History, European History, a General Paper, a translation paper (I did the German well, the Latin badly, couldn't cope with the Greek, but had a go at the French because, although I had not learnt any French, it was full of words like *democracie*, *égalité*, *constitution* and so on, which made it more or less intelligible), and then there was an extended essay. There was no choice of subject. We had three hours to think about and write about *Enthusiasm*.

I spent an hour planning what to say and then set out to tell them that enthusiasm was very desirable when applied to unimportant things, such as stamp collecting and team games, but was very dangerous when applied to anything important like religion or politics. With teen-age presumption I formulated a somewhat pretentious general principle along the lines that the value of enthusiasm is in inverse ratio to the importance of that to which it is applied, drew a diagram to illustrate what I was getting at, and sought to demonstrate the truth of my proposition by reference to a range of varied examples.

There were several individual interviews. One was with the Economics fellow, Neville Ward-Perkins, who asked if I had studied any economic history. 'I'm afraid not', I replied. We then spent the rest of the interview talking about the medieval wool trade and how the Frescobaldi family bought the wool crop of the

Cistercian monasteries of Yorkshire before the sheep had even been sheared – what is now called trading in 'futures'. 'But you haven't done any economic history?' he asked with an amiable smile as I departed.

The scholarship arrangements reached a climax with an interview in the Senior Common Room with the whole fellowship of the college gathered together to elect that year's scholars. I assumed that they all knew everything. But of course one was a mathematician, another a classicist, another a physicist and so on. Probably the only one who knew anything about medieval history was Tommy Parker, a fellow of University College who had been imported for the occasion between the retirement of one don and the election of his successor. Parker necessarily led the questioning and after a short while said, 'Mr Arnold. In your essay on the Investiture Contest you suggest that the problem could have been resolved if bishops had divested themselves of their temporal responsibilities and confined themselves to their spiritual duties.' 'Yes', I replied, wondering what was coming. 'Did you realise that one of the popes had suggested that solution?' 'No', I answered, with a sinking feeling. 'Could you think which one it might have been?' 'Might it', I replied hesitantly, desperately trying to think of the name of any pope of about that time, 'might it have been Paschal II?' 'Yes, indeed', he said, and the murmur of surprise and appreciation around the room gave me the feeling that I might at that moment have got my scholarship.

Just over a week later, on the Saturday after the school term had ended, I was due to play in the trials for the Eastern Counties Schoolboys' Rugby Football Team. As I was tying up my boots before going out onto the field, I was told that there was a telephone call for me. It was my father ringing to say that the school had telephoned with the news that I had got the top scholarship at Pembroke. So I went out onto the field, played as well as ever I had, and was selected to play right wing forward in the Eastern Counties' team. In a period of a fortnight I had met the girl I was going to marry, got a scholarship to Oxford and been selected to play for the Eastern Counties. It was a good Christmas present. I spent that Christmas reading George Orwell's *1984*. I started it on Christmas Day, found it horrifying, couldn't put it down, and finished it on Boxing Day.

John meanwhile had won an exhibition (the word for a minor scholarship) to Sidney Sussex College, Cambridge. Our parents had good reason to be pleased – and our father was. Had he been born a generation later he would no doubt have done much the same, and he was pleased for us. For our mother it was more of a problem. Before getting married she had had a job as a secretary in a shipping firm in the City but had had to give it up on getting married. In a time of high unemployment it was thought improper for a woman to have a job when she had a man to keep her. She had taken immense trouble to get us into Christ's Hospital and she was happy for us to stay on at school to take Higher Certificate. But ideally at that point we would, like so many Old Blues, have got a job in banking or insurance or shipping in the City, have worn dark suits and white shirts, carried a brief case and an umbrella, and commuted each day from Woodford to Liverpool Street and back, and perhaps eventually, but not too soon, married a local girl. Oxford and Cambridge were a step too far, and she was understandably worried that it would cut us off from her and that she would lose us.

What is more, university was still some way off. First we had two more terms at school, and after that there would be two years of National Service. A couple of years earlier it would have made sense to leave school at Christmas and do eighteen months in the army before going up to university. But the Korean War had begun in June 1950, British forces were extended throughout the world, and National Service had been extended to two years. So there seemed nothing to be gained from leaving early. Some years later, when I was a schoolmaster, and while the Oxford and Cambridge colleges still set their own scholarship examinations, my pupils would stay on for what was referred to as the 'seventh term', and then leave and do something else for a few months before going up to university the next autumn. It never occurred to us to do so. We stayed on, still writing essays, reading voraciously, playing cricket (or in my case tennis), and presiding over the younger boys for whom we were responsible, before going off to do our two years' military service.

Oriel had sent me a card wishing me well in the Oxford exams, and in December of 1951 we began a correspondence which was to last until we got married in 1959, each of us writing at least once a month. Thus in February 1952 I wrote to her commenting on the sad death of the king, George VI. In March she replied telling me about her latest lacrosse match in the St Catherine's team (she played right defence and they won 11-6) and about winning the house lacrosse championship. Any feelings towards each other were implied and inferred rather than explicit. Over time the letters became more intimate, but for years neither of us ever mentioned anyone else we went out with, and only at about the time we got engaged did we exchange memories about that.

Meeting was difficult. For neither of us was it easy to get away from school, and to do so at the same time as each other was a real problem. But one beautiful day in the summer of 1952 I joined the geographers from Christ's Hospital on a trip to Guildford, on the pretext that I wanted to see a modern Gothic cathedral still under construction, and Oriel told her form teacher that she had a dentist's appointment (she was a good enough girl that her form teacher didn't hesitate to believe her) and we took a boat out on the River Wey – with me wearing my long blue coat and yellow stockings and Oriel wearing her school blazer. It was idyllic and at the end of the afternoon we were all the more eager to meet again.

She, of course, was taking School Certificate that summer, and in June wrote with delight to say that her exams were over, that she had been playing tennis all the morning, and that now she was lying on a rug in the garden, reading *Gone with the Wind* and eating chocolates. Then in July she wrote about the thrill of appearing on stage in a school performance of *As You Like It*, asked if I could get over to Shalford one Saturday, and gave me instructions for how to get there from Christ's Hospital by taking the train to Bramley and going on by bus. As it happens it was not possible for me to get away and to Shalford during term time, but shortly before the end of term there was a dance to which we were able to invite our own partners, and Philippa was a good enough friend to invite Oriel to stay with her in the headmaster's house. Oriel came and lent delight and a romantic haze to my last weekend at school.

Term ended with a leaving service at which the headmaster read us the charge: '*I charge you never to forget the great benefits that you have received in this place, and in time to come, according to your means, to do all that you can to enable others to enjoy the same advantages; and remember that you carry with you, wherever you go, the good name of Christ's Hospital. May God Almighty bless you in your ways and keep you in the knowledge of his love.*'

I was given a copy of the *Revised Standard Version* of the Bible (not the most attractive translation, so it remains relatively unthumbed) and a similarly leather-bound copy of the *Book of Common Prayer*, which has survived fairly regular use for some sixty-five years. I had been at Christ's Hospital for eight years, from the age of ten until the age of eighteen. The first four were difficult; it often felt that it was a matter of surviving them. The next four were increasingly enjoyable, and I left with a genuine and lasting sense of gratitude for the benefits I had received there.

The Army
(1952–1954)

13. Aldershot

On 4ᵗʰ September 1952 John and I both set off to join the Royal
Army Service Corps at North Camp, Farnborough, with advice
from my father to beware of small NCOs (non-commissioned
officers - sergeants and corporals) and from my mother to beware
of girls who wore black underwear (I wondered how you discovered what colour their underwear was).

For the next two months I was 22712269 Private D.J.Arnold. In
the first fortnight we drilled and did basic weapons training while
the army authorities decided what to do with us. John, with his
Modern Languages exhibition to Cambridge, was transferred
to the Intelligence Corps to spend most of the next two years
learning Russian. Most of us learnt to drive three-ton trucks.
Some were separated off to be clerks or storemen. Forty of us
were designated as P.O.C.s (potential officer cadets) and sent to
Buller Barracks (built shortly after the Boer War and named after
General Sir Redvers Buller) to prepare for W.O.S.B. (pronounced
Wosby, with the letters standing for War Office Selection Board)
which determined whether or not you were judged to be suitable
for training as an officer.

Rumour had it that Buller Barracks had been condemned as
unsuitable for human habitation some time between the wars, and
it certainly had that feel about it. The daily routine started early
and ended late. There was foot drill before breakfast, and during
the morning we would learn fieldcraft and have weapons training
with the Lee Enfield rifle, the Bren gun, which you fired lying
down, and the Sten gun, which you fired from the hip. We were
introduced to other weapons as well, and when it came to a flame-
thrower, complete with a back-pack for the fuel, I made the mistake
of asking if they weren't contrary to the Geneva Convention. 'Oh!
We've a right one 'ere', said the corporal instructing us, and I

learnt to keep my mouth shut under such circumstances. All the same, I was young and foolish enough to volunteer to go through a large building filled with tear gas, and I emerged unable to open my eyes for some time.

One afternoon we would go for a route march in full kit, with boots and gaiters, large pack on the back, small pack in front, wearing a steel helmet, and carrying a rifle, whose bayonet was strapped to the belt. On another afternoon we would be firing our rifles on the range, and the next day we might have to cross an assault course, and then do it again against time, divided into teams and helping each other over difficult obstacles. In the evenings it was time to clean one's boots and equipment and make sure that every item of clothing was lined up, labelled and squared off, ready for inspection the next morning.

The regime was deliberately harsh and while some believed that our sexual appetites were reduced by having bromide put in the tea, I suspected that we were simply exhausted. By the time we faced the preliminary Unit Selection Board, more than half of the original forty P.O.C.s had dropped out voluntarily and gone off to Willems Barracks to train as clerks. Of the eighteen who faced U.S.B. eleven passed and went on to W.O.S.B., nine passed that, and eight of us completed our training as officer cadets and were commissioned six months after first joining the army.

November and December were spent at Mons O.C.T.U. (Officer Cadet Training Unit) in Aldershot with others from the gunners (the Royal Artillery), the sappers (the Royal Engineers), the Royal Armoured Corps, and a number of smaller corps, while the infantry trained at Eaton Hall, somewhere in the north. We now wore a white disc under our cap badges to indicate the peculiar rank of Officer Cadet.

Its peculiarity is well illustrated by the memorable words of the Company Sergeant Major on my arrival at Mons: 'Mr Arnold Sir, while you are 'ere, I call you 'Sir' and you call me 'Sir'. The only difference is that you mean it. Do you understand me – Sir?' To which the answer, standing rigidly to attention, was 'Yes, Sir!' From time to time, if, for example, my turnout was less than immaculate, there would be an exchange such as this: 'Mr Arnold Sir, you are an 'orrible, idle, manky man. What are you?' The answer, again rigidly at attention, with not a flicker of an eyelash, was 'I am an 'orrible, idle, manky man, Sir', with the final 'Sir' shouted.

A group of officer cadets in training at Aldershot early in 1953.
I am seated, third from the right.

After Christmas those of us in the R.A.S.C., known to others by various names such as *Ali Sloper's Cavalry* (pre-dating the addition of 'Royal' to the name) or even as the *Rubbish and Shit Collectors,* returned to Buller barracks just down the road for what was referred to as our Special to Arm Training. Transport was overwhelmingly the main business of the R.A.S.C., most of which was later reorganised as the Royal Corps of Transport before becoming the Royal Logistics Corps, embracing a wider range of services.

We learnt to drive a Bedford three-ton truck, taking turns, half-a-dozen at a time, to drive and then be jolted in the back, learning to double de-clutch (i.e. de-clutch to shift out of fourth gear, re-engage the clutch and rev up while in neutral, and then de-clutch again to shift into third, preferably having revved up to the right amount so as not to grate the gears as you did it). After a few hours we were assumed to be competent drivers. We learnt quite a lot about the engines of trucks, and I could draw a meticulous diagrammatic electrical circuit and an equally meticulous servo braking system, even though I had little idea what they were and would not have been able to find what I had drawn inside a vehicle.

The R.A.S.C. was not only concerned with vehicular transport. We also learnt about the storage of jerry cans (the very efficient petrol containers which had been used by the Germans, the 'Jerries', in the Western Desert and were then adopted by the British), about mule transport (how to calculate the fodder needed to shift a gun a given distance over the Himalayas, and how much would be needed to feed the mules carrying the fodder), about camel transport (I only remember a song which explained that 'the sexual life of the camel is stranger than ever you'd think'), about canary platoons (needed for providing warning to sappers about gas in mines), and about air dispatch (pushing supplies out of aircraft over Malaya – preferably without falling out). One thing we did not get round to was the transportation of tanks, which, as it happens, was the activity which was to occupy me for most of my National Service.

However extraordinary it might seem to learn about mule and camel transport and about canary platoons and air dispatch, I soon came to be convinced that the role of supply and transport was genuinely of immense importance for the successful conduct of war. General Bill Slim, when writing after the Second World War about the fighting in Burma and reflecting on how to maintain a large force across the Chindwin once the river had been crossed, wrote that 'the answer, as almost always in war...depended on supply and transport.' And Marlborough's success at Blenheim had depended at least in some measure on having new boots from Northampton available for his men half way across Europe.

The quality of instruction, whether at Mons or at Buller, was high. An NCO whose job was to teach you something always knew that he first needed to tell you what he was going to teach you, then that he had to teach you it, and finally that he had to tell you what he had taught you. It was useful training for a future schoolmaster. So was the military insistence on asking 'Any questions?' before going on to something else.

It was also useful to find out about mnemonics, or useful ways of memorising things, and now I suppose that my favourite mnemonic is the one for remembering how to spell 'mnemonic': *My Nurse Educated Me One Night In Carshalton*. But in the army I learnt, and for the rest of my life would never be able to forget, *GRIT* and *It Is Most Awfully Important*.

Fortunately I never had to make use of either of them other than in training, but I could see the value of having them firmly embedded in one's consciousness in a crisis. *GRIT* was the sequence for fire orders: Group (e.g. Bren group); Range (e.g. 300 – yards is assumed); Indication (e.g. Half right, door of barn); Type (e.g. Rapid); Fire. If you miss out any one of those instructions, things will go wrong.

It Is Most Awfully Important was the mnemonic for remembering how to give the order for a platoon attack, and regardless of whether one was a gunner, a sapper, or in command of a transport platoon, one had to know how to act as an infantryman:

It: Information (e.g. Enemy sniper in the copse half right.)

Is: Intention (e.g. C Platoon will attack and kill the enemy.)

Most: Method (e.g. Right flanking. Bren group stay here. Rifle group, prepare to follow me.)

Awfully: Administration (e.g. Keep all equipment with you. Fix bayonets now.)

Important: Intercommunication (e.g. Short blasts on the whistle for rapid fire by the Bren group.)

Before we finished our training we were given the opportunity to express a preference about where we were to be posted. The choices, as I recall them, and in the order in which I put them, were:

B.A.O.R (i.e. The British Army of the Rhine, which meant Germany) and *B.T.A. (i.e. British Troops in Austria).* We still had an occupation zone in both, and particularly after studying German for Higher Certificate I liked the idea of going there.

Far East Land Forces, which probably meant Korea, where we were at war, but could have been Malaya, where British forces were fighting Chinese Communists in the jungle. Part of me was tempted by the idea of taking part in a real war, but the other part told me that if I came back blind or maimed or shell-shocked, it would have been foolish to have made it my first choice. So I put it second.

Middle East Land Forces. The occasional lucky person might get a posting to serve in the Arab Legion in Jordan with Glubb Pasha, Lieutenant-General Sir John Bagot Glubb, who led, trained and commanded Jordan's Arab Legion between 1939 and 1956, but for most of those in the Middle East it was a matter of sitting for days on end in a tent or hut in the Suez canal zone, which we still occupied, but where our troops were vulnerable to being shot if they strayed, because the Egyptians wanted to be rid of us. Those I knew from school who had been stationed there warned that it was unutterably boring.

Home. Whatever the attractions of home, it was going to be the last choice for almost all of us. Why waste an opportunity to see another part of the world while young by hanging around at home?

Because we might go anywhere and the destination had not yet been settled they pumped us full of injections, inoculations and vaccinations on every part of one's arm (drill the next day was agony), and then they gave us a colour blindness test. We filed past four sheets of paper on which there were coloured dots in the *Pointilliste* style. The person two in front of me said *73, 9, 16, 24*. The person immediately in front of me said *73, 9, 16, 24*. I saw only an indistinguishable jumble of dots on each page and had the awful feeling that, if I failed the test, I might spend the rest of my National Service cleaning latrines. So I said 73, 9, 16, 24 and discovered as I passed the test that I was colour blind.

Shortly before we passed out (i.e. completed our course) I found that I had got my first choice and was to be posted to 119 Heavy Transport Company in the Corps Troops Column of the British Army of the Rhine, and was to report to Catterick Barracks in *Bielefeld, Nord Rhein Westph*alen. In March 1953 we were commissioned, marched past to the tune of *Wait for the Waggon*, the rather appropriate regimental march of the R.A.S.C., dating from the Boer War, and we received our commissions.

Mine, on a smart scroll of paper, began: *Elizabeth the Second by the Grace of God of Great Britain, Ireland and the British Dominions beyond the Seas, Defender of the Faith, To Our Trusty and well beloved David James Arnold Greeting! We, reposing especial Trust and Confidence in your Loyalty, Courage, and good Conduct, do by these Presents Constitute and Appoint you to be an Officer in Our Land Forces from the Fourteenth day of March 1953....*It was beautifully written, in copperplate handwriting, and it seemed worth keeping – just like my letter from the king at the end of the war.

As a private soldier and an Officer Cadet my pay had been four shillings a day - 20p. in decimal currency. That added up to £1.8s.0d. a week, but with only 25 shillings paid out on pay parade, because three shillings were deducted each week in case of barrack damages. That now went up by more than three times to thirteen shillings and sixpence a day, or just over £20 a month, paid into a new bank account at Cox and King's in Pall Mall, who provided bank accounts for all new officers with names beginning A – M (Those with surnames beginning N – Z had their accounts with Coutts).

I had been transformed from a schoolboy, 'creeping like snail unwillingly to school', into some sort of a soldier, and though not 'full of strange oaths and bearded like the pard', I was ready to join the British Army of the Rhine in its task of occupying the British zone of Germany.

14. Train crash

◇◇◇◇◇◇◇◇◇◇◇◇◇◇◇◇◇◇◇◇◇◇◇◇◇◇◇◇◇◇◇◇◇◇◇

Before reporting for duty in Germany there was time to go home on leave for a couple of weeks. In those days, when almost all young men did National Service, soldiers travelled home on leave in uniform and officers travelled first class and in service dress, with a shiny leather Sam Browne belt and a peaked cap. So I found myself walking down Snakes Lane in my brand new uniform, past Ray Lodge School, left over the River Roding into Woodford Bridge, where I had lived for eighteen of my nineteen and a half years, hoping that I would not meet any of my contemporaries from elementary school, with the obligation to exchange salutes.

All was well. Once I was home I could change into civilian clothes, go to the corner of the road and buy fish and chips, and feel like a normal civilian for a brief while. It was good to see my parents again, but at the top of my priorities was seeing Oriel, who had left school at the beginning of the Easter holidays and was due to start at R.A.D.A., the Royal Academy of Dramatic Art, in April of 1953, just as I was off to Germany.

We had met a couple of times during the summer holidays before I joined the army. I travelled over from Woodford all the way to Shalford, outside Guildford, on what at the time seemed a very long and complicated journey via Waterloo Station, which I had never used before. It provided the opportunity to meet Oriel's parents, Nora and Teddy, who had spent his working life in the Indian Civil Service.

While Teddy was still up at Oxford he took the examination for entry into the I.C.S. and after coming down in 1912, spent the next two years learning enough Hindi and Guajarati and Urdu to be able to get by and training for his job as an Assistant Collector. He sailed for India in the summer of July 1914, the month in

109

which the British Chancellor of the Exchequer, Lloyd George, said that 'in the field of international relations the sky has never seemed more blue.' By the time he got there England was at war and his whole career, during both the wars of 1914-18 and 1939-45, and of course the years in between, was spent in India, ending when he was the Commissioner for Bombay and in 1943 had to come back to England for an operation on one of his eyes.

My visits to Shalford also provided an opportunity to meet Oriel's twin sister, Chloë, who looked very similar, though they were not identical twins, and also their elder sister June. June was twenty-one, had trained as a ballet dancer, was now appearing in a musical called *Blue for a Boy*, and seemed extraordinarily grown up and sophisticated. Their brother Michael, who was the same age as me and had been at school at Cranleigh, was away at the time as a cadet on the *Worcester*, a merchant service training vessel.

In August, when Oriel got her School Certificate results, it turned out that she had done well in everything except Biology, which she had failed because she had refused to dissect a frog – something which I saw as entirely to her credit. But when she wrote to tell me about it, she seemed less interested in the examination results than in describing a very attractive plumber who was doing some work in their house and who, she said, had fought at Arnhem and looked like a mixture of Lord Byron and Rupert of the Rhine.

Apart from my visits to Shalford, we met once by chance. John and I went to see a performance in the West End of Ibsen's *Hedda Gabler*, and Oriel, by now very keen on the theatre, was taken to see the same performance by an elderly friend of the family who, when we met in the interval, clearly suspected me and Oriel of having planned the meeting beforehand. It was all the more embarrassing because we could not very well protest our innocence when no-one had actually accused us of anything. We were both too embarrassed to enjoy the meeting.

In September, by which time I was in the army, Oriel wrote to me as 22712269 Private D.J.Arnold at Blenheim Barracks, wondering how I looked in army uniform and if I would be able to get over to Shalford from Aldershot some time. I did, but not till nearly three months later, on week-end leave from Mons. At some point she wrote to tell me that she had got a prize for doing well at School Certificate, and also that she and Chloë were both going to try to get scholarships to R.A.D.A. In the event they were both successful and went there together.

Nowadays, in the early 21st century, almost all girls leaving St Catherine's, Bramley, would be going on to university. Not so in the 1950s. It was so unusual then that only one girl in her year did, and meanwhile the number of places for girls at Oxford and Cambridge was so limited that girls had to reach roughly the same standard as a male scholar in order to get a place. One consequence was that the women's colleges performed outstandingly well in Finals, only to lose that pre-eminence when the first men's colleges went mixed and many of the best female applicants deserted to them, with the effect that within a few years the women's colleges had slid from the top to the bottom of the league tables.

Later Oriel mildly regretted not having spent three years reading English Literature, but at the time she was entirely sure that what she wanted to do was act. So she stayed on at school in the Lower Sixth until it was time to go to R.A.D.A., and meanwhile felt pleased with herself when she was made a School Prefect and Head of House. She felt particularly grown up when her house-mistress invited her in to talk over house affairs and offered her both a drink and a cigarette.

Then, about three days before I was due to leave for Germany and shortly before she was due to start at R.A.D.A., we had one of those infrequent but emotionally intense meetings which were characteristic of our relationship for some years. We were very young, very inexperienced with the opposite sex, had met only about half a dozen times in the last year or so since we had first met, and still knew each other relatively little. Holding hands was erotically charged. Kissing would have been one move too far.

We met for a few hours in London, had a meal together, and then I saw her off at Waterloo on the train to Guildford, before catching the Northern Line train to Tottenham Court Road and changing onto the Central Line train to Woodford.

A few years after the war the steam trains which had taken us to Liverpool Street all through my childhood had been replaced by trains powered by electricity. To the north-east the line went all the way to Epping. In London, when travelling west, it went beyond Liverpool Street, through the City, and on via the West End out to Ealing Broadway, though I would seldom have gone further west than Marble Arch. It was no longer the London North Eastern Railway but the Central Line of the London Underground – still called the Underground even when it got into Essex and travelled above ground.

At Tottenham Court Road I deliberately got into the front part of the second carriage of the Central Line train, because that was convenient for getting out at Woodford Station. But the train was crowded, so I couldn't get a seat. I stood in the section where the doors slide open and shut, leaning my back on the glass partition beyond which was the front one third of the carriage. I took out of my pocket the copy of *The Decline and Fall of the Romantic Ideal* by F.L.Lucas which I had started reading at the beginning of my leave, and I was reading it as the train rattled north-east from the City, through Mile End, Bethnal Green and Stratford and on towards Leyton.

Without any warning, somewhere underground between Stratford and Leyton, the train ran into the back of a stationary train in front, and in a couple of seconds the front third of the second carriage, the one I was in, was crushed into a couple of yards. Everyone in that section of the carriage was killed. It was the worst underground disaster that had ever happened.

The first carriage was intact. It was stronger than the others because it was the engine carriage. But at the time we only knew that the train had suddenly stopped and that all the lights had gone out. I had dropped my book and bent down to pick it up. My hand groped and slipped on blood and brains. There was very little screaming. Most of the people in the crowded and crushed front third of the carriage were already dead. The others did not yet know what had happened. Then in the silence we heard another train approaching – louder and louder, and more and more frightening, until it shot past on the next track.

Shortly afterwards someone above ground realised what had happened and shut off all the power. The emergency services started cutting their way through. It was a long job, because all the carriages were concertinaed together – though no-one was killed other than in the front section of the second carriage. So for the next two hours I stood holding up the top half of the body of a young man who was sticking out of the crushed wreckage and was entirely conscious, although the lower half of his body was trapped. He was called Alan Connor and was a few years older than me. He gave me his wife's telephone number to ring as soon as I got out, so that I could tell her why he had not arrived home at his normal time.

When at last I emerged from under ground there were cameramen taking photographs and journalists wanting to know what it had been like. There was a bus to ferry those who wanted transport to the next station. I telephoned Alan Connor's wife, told her that he was hurt and that the bottom half of his body was still trapped, but I hoped that he would be alright. I then caught the bus to Leyton and the train on to Woodford. I ran all the way down Snakes Lane home to tell my mother and father that I was alright. But they had not heard the news, so they were not in the least worried. They knew I had gone to see Oriel and had no idea when I would be back.

A couple of days later a representative of the railway or their insurer came to see me to ask what compensation I would like. It seemed obscene. I was glad to be alive. But in the end I let them

113

pay the few shillings that it cost to send my sports jacket to the cleaners. I went to see Alan Connor in hospital in Stratford on my way to Germany. He was in bed with any number of tubes attached to him and was able to talk. But his body had been crushed from the waist down and he died a few days later.

I caught the train to Liverpool Street, from there to Harwich, and thence by boat to the Hook of Holland, and on by train through Holland and into Germany. When I got to the officers' mess in Catterick Barracks, Bielefeld, I saw my picture on the back page of the *Daily Mirror*, taken as I emerged from the underground. But no-one in the mess recognised it as me and I avoided mentioning it. For the next fifty years I never travelled in the second carriage of any train. I still have not read the rest of *The Decline and Fall of the Romantic Ideal.*

15. Blueland versus Redland

119 Heavy Company was in the Corps Troops Column of the British Army of the Rhine. An army might have three or four corps, but BAOR had only one, 1 Corps, whose area was co-terminous with that of the army, which was the British zone of occupation in the north of Germany. 1 Corps (and, indeed, BAOR) was made up of three armoured divisions and one infantry division and numbered about 80,000 men in all. Also stationed in the British zone was 2nd Tactical Air Force, or 2TAF.

There was an Army Troops Column, which contained units such as tank transporters or bridging companies which might be deployed anywhere in the British zone, i.e. in the army area. Then in the Corps Troops Column there were the units such as 119 Heavy Company, whose vehicles might also be deployed anywhere in the British zone, in this case in the corps area. But most transport companies were in divisional columns in their own divisional areas, so all the soldiers of those companies would wear the desert rat shoulder flash of 7th Armoured Division, the black bull on a yellow background of 11th Armoured Division, the white mailed fist on a black background of 6th Armoured Division, or the crossed keys of 2nd Infantry Division. The shoulder flash for those of us in the Corps Troops Column was a white spear on a red, diamond shaped lozenge.

Facing us across the eastern border of the British zone were some hundreds of divisions of the Red Army. Despite the Korean War, the so-called Cold War was not yet at its worst, but relations between East and West were frosty. Although Churchill, Roosevelt and Stalin had agreed at the Yalta Conference in February 1945 to establish a united 'democratic' post-war Germany, which would be temporarily divided into zones of occupation, they had carefully avoided asking each other what they meant by 'democratic', and the division between the Russian zone in the East and the three Western zones was clearly not temporary.

Distrust and disagreements among the former allies resulted in 1949 in the formation of the German Federal Republic in the American, British and French zones and the proclamation of a German Democratic Republic in the Russian zone. In 1945 the Russians had moved Poland over. They had incorporated the eastern part of it into the USSR and at the same time had transferred to Poland the German territories east of the rivers Oder and Neisse, with whole populations being driven out of their homelands and fleeing as refugees to the West. Berlin, which in 1939 had been nearer the western than the eastern border of Germany, was now nearer to the eastern than the western border of the Russian zone, the DDR, which we usually called East Germany and which the Germans understandably spoke of as *Mitteldeutschland*.

The Russians did not only have vast conventional forces in their zone of Germany. They had even more divisions in the other East European countries they had occupied: Poland, Czechoslovakia, Hungary, Bulgaria and Roumania. Their conventional forces were vastly greater than ours – perhaps a hundred times greater. But we had the great strategic advantage that from November 1953 V-bombers carrying atom bombs were in the air day and night and potential Russian aggression was frustrated by the fact that they could not yet deploy any nuclear weapons.

How many soldiers of BAOR understood that I do not know, but what was clear was that, although BAOR units spent their time training for a war in which the opposing sides were Blueland and Redland, no-one seriously expected us to have to fight the Russians. There was an 'iron curtain' between East and West, literally as well as metaphorically. If you got near the border there were signs saying *Hier verlassen Sie die Britische Zone* ('This is where you leave the British zone') before you encountered the barbed wire which cut us off from the Russian zone. Crossing was not a realistic option - neither for us nor for the Red Army.

We were based in Catterick Barracks, Bielefeld, which had been built for the German army to a far higher specification than any barracks I had encountered back in England and, like all other barracks in the British zone of Germany, had been re-named as if we were in Yorkshire or Surrey or Argyllshire. The accommodation, which looked like particularly well-built council flats, was arranged around a central square, and in the middle was a vast statue of a naked Arian youth, kneeling as he pulled back the string of a bow. It was altogether more grand and militaristic than suited us. We were a National Service army made up of conscripted civilians – both officers and men. The number of professional soldiers in 119 Company, officers, NCOs and drivers, could be numbered on the fingers of two hands.

When I took command of C Platoon the only man in the platoon who was a regular was my sergeant. He was 28, had joined the army ten years earlier, had taken part in the final advance of 21 Group across the Lüneburg Heath in 1945, and had stayed on. So he was a veteran. Over the next three months I would often find myself saying, 'What would you do now, sergeant?' He would tell me, and I would reply, 'Righto! Carry on, sergeant.' The outcome would show whether or not he was right, and it was a helpful way to learn one's trade.

There were about 45 men in the platoon and at nineteen I was the second oldest. Apart from half-a dozen in the platoon headquarters group, such as a clerk and the driver of our 15cwt utility truck, there were three sections, each with a corporal and lance-corporal, who rode motor cycles, and ten drivers, each in charge of a truck and trailer. Besides that there were two or three others, such as the occasional private soldier who had failed his driving test back in England. When one inspected their clothing, equipment and other possessions in the barrack room, the reading matter ranged from Graham Greene or Agatha Christie to the *Beano* and the *Dandy*.

We were equipped with diesel-fuelled, air-cooled, ten-ton Magirus Deutz trucks, each with an eight-ton trailer, which had been

117

handed to the British army as part of reparations. They had been designed to travel at high speed on the Autobahn and had relatively thin tyres with a fine tread, but quite inappropriately we used them to move ammunition, fuel and food along the muddy tracks of the *Teutoburger Wald* as we played our part in the mock battles of the exercise season.

The first time I took my platoon into the forest to our designated location for provisioning our forward troops, we sited each truck carefully, camouflaged them even more carefully with our camouflage netting, and dug slit trenches around the site. When my sergeant had marked where a slit trench should go, I would take a spade or entrenching tool and do the first bit of digging. It was not a style which commended itself to all my fellow officers, but it suited me and, I hope, my platoon.

But neither our slit trenches nor our camouflage netting could save us from enemy attack. RAF meteors (from Redland) flew over the next day and sent a message to say that they had shot us up and destroyed the whole platoon. They offered to show me their photographs of our position. When I saw them I protested that there was nothing to be seen in the photographs other than trees. Then they showed me the previous day's photograph. The difference was striking. A whole series of spaced out darker patches in the later photos showed clearly that something had moved into the area during the night. Nothing more was needed to convince me of a modern army's need for air superiority.

Then it rained and the wheels of my trucks stuck in the mud. REME (the Royal Electrical and Mechanical Engineers) sent a Scammel recovery vehicle to get us out, but the wire cable used for winching the trucks out started sawing the trees down while the trucks stayed put. In the end I solved the problem by walking down to a nearby farm and negotiating with a German farmer to bring two massive cart-horses to rescue our trucks in return for a substantial quantity of 'compo' rations. The horses heaved the trucks out one by one until they could slither down the forest track to firm ground.

I spoke to the farmer in what is called *Hochdeutsch* (High German). He replied in the local dialect, *Plattdeutsch*, and I found that many of his words were nearer to English than to the sort of German I had learnt. Where I spoke of *Wasser*, with the W pronounced like a V, he spoke of *Watter*, with the W pronounced in the English fashion. Where I spoke of *Milch*, he spoke of *Melk*.

Being able to speak German was clearly an advantage, and later in the summer I was seconded to a bridging company because a lot of the transportation of bridge parts for a crossing of the River Weser was being done by German service units, manned almost entirely by Germans who had served in the war. I sat in a truck all night getting requests for parts from the sappers building the bridge, arranging the necessary movements, and marking off what had been done so far by shifting plastic pegs from one side of the truck to another, rather in the manner of someone constructing a school timetable.

In the end every peg was moved, so I thought I might as well go and see how our bridge was getting on. Dawn was just breaking, the bridge had only just been completed, and as I arrived the first of our Centurion tanks were crossing towards the East. Out of the trees, across the river, a hundred yards away came three Meteor jet fighter aircraft and swept across our position. A few minutes later they rang up to say that they had taken out our bridge and the column of tanks waiting to cross. The point about the need for air superiority was again forcibly made.

Meanwhile the former German officers with whom I had been speaking during the night had persuaded me that our practice of travelling in convoy with thirty yards space between one truck and another was profoundly misguided unless one had overwhelming air superiority – in which case there was no need for the thirty yards distance. Without air superiority, they said, you had to let each driver use his own initiative. He needed to know where he had to go, and then he had to get there as best he could, taking cover whenever enemy aircraft appeared.

119

It seemed like sound common sense and unanswerable, and it was the first step in persuading me that the conventional British view of German militarism, with men obeying orders like automata and moving to an inflexible timetable, was seriously mistaken. Much of German military success came from a long tradition of training troops at all levels to use their own initiative and, in particular, be prepared to take over at a higher level if one's superior were to be killed. Thus, for example, a *Feldwebel*, or sergeant, was expected, if necessary, to be able to take command of a platoon, and often did.

I was fortunate that a large part of my first three months in Germany was spent out on exercise engaged in mock battles. I thoroughly enjoyed it and felt that I learnt quite a lot. In the first place it seemed to me that I learnt quite a lot about how the battles of the relatively recent past had been fought. Secondly I concluded that what I had learnt might well be largely irrelevant in any future war. But it had been an enjoyable experience, for there were no real bullets flying around.

The time spent back in barracks in Bielefeld was less enjoyable. Most of what we were doing was tedious. We engaged in entirely unmemorable activities such as cleaning vehicles and equipment, going out on convoy with each truck thirty yards from the next, putting what was called 'scrim' into camouflage netting, or practising drill as we prepared to advance in review order and fire a salute on 2nd June 1953, the day of the new queen's coronation.

The most senior officer I encountered while in Germany was a colonel, who inspected 119 Company and, when he came to my platoon, told me that I was improperly dressed, since I was wearing a King George VI cap badge rather than a Queen Elizabeth one, and told me to change it. I reflected that I was unlikely to see him again and kept my old cap badge. It saw me through my National Service and service in the Army Emergency Reserve without further comment and it is still on my now more than sixty year old cap upstairs in a cupboard. Back in Bielefeld in 1953 most of the drivers were finding the daily routine boring and wished they were home. I understood their frustration.

16. From Bielefeld to Fallingbostel

Sometimes a Rhine Army order disrupted our regular rather boring routine at Catterick Barracks, Bielefeld. One such order required that every member of a transport platoon should sign for and take responsibility for a vehicle. In C Platoon we had a private soldier who had previously served a term of Borstal training and had failed his driving test before being posted to Germany. Vehicles frightened him, at least when in the driving seat, but he was happy to have a job cleaning the latrines, and the other members of the platoon were happy to be excused such tasks.

I asked the O.C. (the officer commanding the company) if an exception could be made. He, understandably (though at the time I thought it entirely unreasonable) made the point that he was not going to authorise disobedience to an army order. So I had to instruct the young man, whose name I have forgotten, to sign for and, at least in theory, take responsibility for a truck. I assured him that he would not have to drive it. I warned him that disobeying an order could have serious consequences. But he could not be persuaded.

I had to charge him under section 40 of the Army Act with 'disobedience, with intent to show wilful defiance, of the lawful command of a superior officer.' He was incarcerated in the guard room, where he took off his clothes, caused mayhem and refused to do anything he was told. He was court-martialled, imprisoned, and after serving a prison term was dishonourably discharged.

If I had been older and more experienced I would either have ignored the original order, without saying anything, or would have put a forged signature on the vehicle documents. No-one would have noticed. As it was, the O.C. was cross with me and C Platoon lost a valuable latrine orderly. It was a useful lesson.

Another Rhine Army order required that all trucks should have their radiators emptied of water each evening and be refilled each morning. The idea was to save money on the cost of anti-freeze by ensuring that there was no water in the radiators overnight to freeze and burst them. To ensure that this was done efficiently platoon commanders were required to keep a record of the emptying of the radiators of every vehicle in the platoon each evening and of the refilling of them each morning.

It was no problem for me. All the trucks in the company, except for each platoon's small 15cwt truck, were air cooled. So were the motor bikes. So the only record we kept was of the regular emptying and refilling of the 15cwt truck. Unfortunately the O.C. decided to check on my platoon and found that I appeared to have disregarded a clear Rhine Army order. He was furious and in front of my platoon sergeant and platoon clerk demanded an explanation.

The explanation, of course, was that our trucks did not have radiators which could be filled or emptied. It became obvious to everyone present that the O.C. did not know how the trucks in his own company worked. It improved neither his temper nor my relationship with him.

I was pleased to hear shortly afterwards, in July 1953, that I was to be posted to another unit, 312 Tank Transporter Company, and could make a new start with a new O.C. The War Office had just changed its policy on the training of newly commissioned regular R.A.S.C. officers and wanted them to have their first experience of command in a standard British transport platoon. That meant moving National Service officers out of such platoons when it was possible to do so.

Thus I found myself posted to be a member of the small British Supervisory Element in a unit which was unusual in that it was predominantly Polish. The British element was the O.C., an amiable Catholic Irishman called Major McCabe, the 2 i/c, who was a captain nearing the end of the period of his short service commission, four platoon commanders and four platoon sergeants.

312 Tank Transporter Company was one of only two tank transporter units in the whole of the British Army of the Rhine and I liked to think it was given the number '312' to deceive the Russians into thinking that we had more than two. Both of the transporter companies were Polish and both were what were called 'working units.' That is, unlike most of the units in BAOR, which were engaged in training, these were units which had been formed to do the job of shifting tanks and self-propelled guns around, so that cavalry and artillery regiments could engage in their training on the heath or on the ranges without damaging either the vehicles' tracks, which had a limited range, or the roads around their barracks.

We were stationed in a very large former German army barracks, renamed Campbell Barracks by the British, just outside the small town of Fallingbostel on the Lüneburg Heath - north of Hannover and south of Hamburg. The overwhelming majority of the members of the unit were Poles who had, ever since the end of the war, been 'displaced persons', without a country of their own. They were technically civilians, but they wore British battledress died blue, together with British army boots, as well as belts and gaiters blancoed yellow.

Our transporters were Diamond T tractors, which had seen service in the Second World War, and they pulled Rogers trailers, which had thirty-two wheels and had been built to carry far smaller tanks, Shermans and Churchills for example, rather than the fifty ton Centurions which were now in service in BAOR. Loading them was a precarious business, and when a Centurion went up the ramp onto a trailer, it crashed down and overlapped the edge on either side by about a foot. I was surprised that the National Service troopers driving the tanks were so capable of managing what looked to me an almost impossible task.

We shared Campbell Barracks with two cavalry regiments, the Queen's Bays and the Seventh Hussars, both of which were in 7th Armoured Division and so wore the desert rat shoulder flash. The Queen's Bays were due to go to Korea, where the war had begun nearly three years earlier, and in July 1953, the month in which I arrived in Fallingbostel, I was invited to a farewell cocktail party in their mess.

In the middle of it the adjutant came in, tapped on the table to attract everyone's attention, and announced that 'Colonel Jim' would like to have a word. The colonel apologised for interrupting and explained that he had just had the disappointing news that their posting to Korea had been cancelled. Apparently a cease-fire had just been signed and the regiment would no longer have the opportunity of going to the Far East to win new battle honours.

Perhaps I do not remember accurately, but at the time I wondered if I was the only person in the room who was delighted to hear the news of the cease-fire. The immediate consequence was that the Queen's Bays stayed in Fallingbostel and I had the pleasure of working with them throughout the time I was there.

As a member of the British Supervisory Element I was ostensibly a platoon commander (again it was C Platoon), but the real commander was Superintendent Szczepan Oleszczuk (if you pronounce SZCZ as SHCH it is no longer so difficult to pronounce), who was assisted by two foremen (the equivalent of sergeants) and six charge hands (corporals). Then there were thirty-six drivers, two for each of our eighteen tank transporters. Four platoons with eighteen transporters each gave the company a total of seventy-two transporters, and that was just the right number for carrying a regiment of Centurion tanks.

On the afternoon that I took over the platoon Oleszczuk lined up eighteen small glasses in two rows of nine, so that I could follow the Polish tradition of drinking my way into the platoon. 'Nasdrovye, Panie Porucznyke' he said (literally, 'To your health,

Mr Lieutenant), sinking his vodka. '*Nasdrovye, Panie Oleszczuk*' I replied, sinking mine – and so on down the line. '*Vodka*' is a rather delightful Russian word, the diminutive of '*voda*.' '*Voda*' means water and has the stress on the second syllable. '*Vodka*', or 'little water', shifts the stress to the first syllable and so sounds quite different.

It was a far stronger drink than anything I was used to, and by the time I had knocked back nine glasses I knew that I had taken in quite a lot of alcohol. So I walked back to the English mess (*na casina Angielskiego*), took off my clothes, went to bed and slept for fifteen hours until woken up by my batman. I felt fine, and as soon as I was dressed walked down to the vehicle park to see the transporters starting up.

The Poles all spoke German, some well and some badly, and the language we communicated in was a form of basic German, with some Polish syntax and with some English and some Polish words mixed in. It seemed to me polite to learn a bit of Polish. So as I came into the platoon office in the morning I would say, '*Djien dobre panstwo*', and they would reply either '*Djien dobre Panie Porucznyke*' or 'Good morning Mr Lieutenant'. But mostly we spoke German.

The British officers of the unit shared their mess with other R.A.S.C. officers in more conventional transport units and with the Royal Electrical and Mechanical Engineer officers who mended and kept running the trucks of the R.A.S.C., the tanks of the cavalry regiments and the self-propelled guns of the Royal Horse Artillery, which between them made up the main striking power of Seventh Armoured Division.

The two cavalry regiments which shared Campbell Barracks with us each had its own rather up-market mess, and it was rumoured that a cavalry subaltern's monthly mess bill was usually rather more than his pay. I, on the other hand, saved about £200 out of the £300 or so that I earned in the eighteen months of service after

I was commissioned. After all, we were provided with free board and lodging and clothing.

When I went home on Christmas leave at the end of 1953, I shared a carriage on the train from Harwich to Liverpool Street with a cavalry subaltern who was going up to Worcester College, Oxford, in a few months' time, when I would be heading for Pembroke. We spoke in the manner and tone of voice characteristic of young army officers. He was going home to Chelsea. I was going to Woodford Bridge. As soon as I got home I changed into civilian clothes, and as it was a Friday and no-one else was in the house at the time, I went along the road to the Roberts's fish shop to get some fried fish and chips. Mrs Roberts asked how I was getting on in the army. I told her it wasn't too bad and we chatted for a while. As I walked home I reflected that I had slipped without thinking into the accent and way of speaking of an Essex suburb. The difference from how I had been speaking a few hours earlier was marginal. A foreigner might not notice. But it was real nonetheless.

I took home ham, butter and various other things which were all freely available in Germany, to help brighten up the grey, post-war austerity of Britain, where they were still rationed. I also bought my mother a dinner service of elegant German bone china, white with a thin gold decoration. But she was disappointed. After years when one could only buy white earthenware, she would have liked lavishly decorated Crown Derby or Royal Worcester cups and plates, which were still being produced in England but were for export only – to Germany, for example.

On Christmas Day I did the washing up after lunch, made a cup of tea and was taking it through when I heard the air raid warning go. My immediate reaction was that the Russians had chosen Christmas Day to attack, so I was surprised to find my parents entirely unconcerned in the living room. The explanation was that my father had just switched on the wireless to listen to the new queen's Christmas message and the BBC was providing an historical run-through beforehand. My father happened to have switched on when they reached 1940 and it was a recording of a 1940 air raid warning siren that I had heard.

John meanwhile was learning Russian, paid as a sergeant, wearing civilian clothes, and on the same course as Michael Frayn and Alan Bennett in Newmarket. They had all been required to get to A level standard in six months, anyone who dropped behind had been removed from the course, and they were now expected to speak Russian all day. When I went to visit John, he had to get permission to speak to me in English. At the end of their year at Newmarket their commanding officer commented that they might not be a serious threat to the Russians, but they had produced the best revue among all the forces of the North Atlantic Treaty Organisation.

17. The Poles

◇◇◇◇◇◇◇◇◇◇◇◇◇◇◇◇◇◇◇◇◇◇◇◇◇◇◇◇◇◇◇◇

A few weeks after I had arrived in Fallingbostel the second-in-command of 312 Tank Transporter Unit, a short service captain who had stayed on after the war, reached the end of his term of service and I found myself appointed to be the new 2 i/c. So I signed for the service revolver, its holster and the six rounds of ammunition which I needed each month when my driver, Jablonski, took me in our *Volkswagen* to Hannover to collect the considerable sum in *Deutschmarks* which was the pay of all the employees of the unit – all of them, from driver upwards, paid more than I earned as a National Service subaltern. On one visit Jablonski pointed out to me that if we drove down to the American zone and disappeared we could live in luxury for the rest of our lives. His calculation may have been correct, but I was intending to go up to Oxford in a few months' time and, as he explained, it was, of course, only a joke.

My job was largely to act as liaison between British units that wanted our services, such as the Queen's Bays and the Seventh Hussars, and the Polish platoon superintendents whose drivers and transporters did the work. Sometimes only a couple of transporters were needed, sometimes a platoon, and sometimes the whole company. We took pride in being able to get all seventy-two transporters on the road when needed, and Major McCabe was pleased to be able to stay back in camp and leave me to get out on the road with the transporters. I loved it.

As I recall it, the sun was usually shining and in August 1953, just after I had arrived, and again in 1954, just before I left, the heather was in bloom all over the Lüneburg Heath. One morning I got up before dawn to move the Queen's Bays out onto the heath, spent about eighteen hours on the job, got back to the mess for three hours sleep, and then spent another eighteen hours moving the Seventh Hussars, before crashing into bed, exhausted but satisfied, and sleeping until nearly lunchtime the next day. Sometimes it was less enjoyable, when travelling on a motor-bike in winter at temperatures far below zero.

Some of the Poles, who made up the bulk of the unit, had served with the allied forces in the west during the Second World War. One of them, Bererzanski, had served in the Austro-Hungarian army on the Carpathian front in the First World War. Others had been in German prisoner-of-war camps, some in labour camps, and some had fought in the Polish resistance, the Polish Home Army. Two had very unwillingly served in the German army, because they had lived in that part of Poland which had been designated part of Germany and they had been sent their call-up papers like any German.

One of them described himself to me as *des ersten königlichen, Preussischen Fallschirmjägerregiment, vom Führer ernannte Obergefreiter Cieslar* ('Cieslar, designated by the Führer as a corporal in the 1st Prussian parachute regiment'). Now he was a charge hand, or corporal, in C Platoon, which was my platoon when I first arrived. All of them were 'displaced persons', *staatenlos*, living in Germany because the Russians, one of the enemies who had attacked them in September 1939, were still occupying their homeland.

Some of those I knew best were anxious that I should acquire an understanding of three issues which were of immense importance to them. The first related to the way in which the Second World War had begun. I knew, of course, that Great Britain had gone to war in September 1939 when Germany attacked Poland. What I did not know until then was that the Germans and the Russians had reached a secret agreement on 23rd August 1939 (the Molotov-Ribbentrop Pact) to divide Eastern Europe between them, with the dividing line running through the middle of Poland.

A week later, on 1st September, the *Alemmanni*, the Germans, attacked from the west, and a fortnight after that, when all the

Polish forces were committed in the west, the allies of the *Alemmanni*, the *Russki,* attacked from the east and were able to take almost the whole Polish army captive. Later on, after the Germans had failed to invade Great Britain and had turned against their former ally, Russia, large numbers of Poles, held as prisoners-of-war by the Russians for nearly two years, were allowed to leave the USSR through Persia, or Iran, and they made up the bulk of General Anders's Army, the Polish army which was the third largest allied force in the west during the Second World War. Only the American and British armies were larger.

The second issue the Poles were keen I should understand was the Katyn massacre. I had never heard of it, but once heard of, it could never be forgotten. In the early summer of 1941, before the Germans turned against their former ally and attacked the USSR, the NKVD, the Russian security police, took all the members of the Polish officer corps, whom they had been holding in captivity separately from the rest of the Polish army, and one by one tied their hands behind their backs, took them out and killed them with a shot to the back of the head. They then buried them in mass graves in the forest of Katyn, near Smolensk. By then Stalin had decided to kill anyone who could be seen as a member of the Polish ruling class and the NKVD killed more than 20,000: government officials, landowners and university lecturers, for example, as well as army officers.

In April of 1943 the invading Germans discovered and dug up the mass graves and proclaimed to the world what they had discovered. The Russians blamed the Germans (it must have been the *Gestapo* or the S.S., the *Schutzstaffel*, they said), and since by now the Russians were allies of the British, the Russian version was accepted by the British government and Germans were even accused of the atrocity at the Nuremberg trials after the war. But the Poles knew when it had happened (every diary found on the bodies of the dead men came to an end at the same time in the early summer of 1941, while they were in the hands of the Russians), and those who told me about it wanted the truth to be known.

They held no brief for the Germans, but the truth was quite simply that it was a Bolshevik atrocity rather than a Nazi one. Sadly our Russian allies committed atrocities comparable with those of the Nazis, and as far as the Poles were concerned they were equally objectionable. It was only in 1990, as the Soviet empire was collapsing, that the Russians at last acknowledged the truth. After I had retired, and in the early twenty-first century, I went to see the film of *Katyn* in the Renoir cinema in Bloomsbury and sat weeping in my seat.

The German atrocities were similarly appalling. It was as a child of eleven that I saw with horror the pictures of the inmates of the concentration camp at Belsen when it was liberated. Back in 1945, as a child, it seemed to me that I had encountered evil, even at some distance removed, for the first time in my life. Belsen was relatively near Fallingbostel, and one day when out on the heath one of the platoon sergeants asked me if I had ever seen the Belsen concentration camp. I hadn't. So we slung our legs over our motor-bikes and drove there.

There was mound after mound covering the dead bodies which had been bull-dozed into mass graves by British troops in 1945. Each was now covered in grass and had an inscription: *Hier liegen 5,000 tot* (Hear lie 5,000 dead) or *Hier liegen 10,000 tot* (Hear lie 10,000 dead). The figures were clearly very approximate. In the middle of the camp was an obelisk with the words, in English, German and Hebrew: *To the memory of 500,000 Jews, slaughtered in this place at the hands of the murderous Nazis.*

The third issue on which the Poles were keen to put me right was about the situation at the end of the war. By then the Russians had been the allies of the British for nearly four years and were in control of Poland. 'You think you won the war', the Poles would say to me. 'We know we lost it.' That was the reason they were in Fallingbostel as displaced persons. One of their two enemies, the Russians, had been occupying their country since the end of the war and they had no intention of going back until the Red Army

131

withdrew. It was to be a long wait – nearly another forty years, by which time many of them were dead.

When we took all seventy-two transporters out to move a cavalry regiment, I would go on my motor-bike, usually wearing the working clothes known as denims, and one day shortly after dawn I particularly enjoyed a brief conversation with a major of the Queen's Bays. Our vehicles were moving into position, and I had just called out to a platoon superintendant, '*Czy jest wszystko w porzientko, Panie Susmarski*' (Is everything in order Mr Susmarski?), when a major who had just arrived, seeing that I appeared to be in charge and was speaking Polish, said to me diffidently and politely, *Entschuldigen Sie mir. Sprechen Sie Deutsch?* ('Excuse me. Do you speak German?'). I was able to reply, 'Well, yes. As a matter of fact I do, but I'm quite happy to speak in English.' I was able to assure him that we would load and transport their tanks in whatever order suited him, and I could see him looking at my uniform and wondering about my nationality and rank. But he was too polite to ask.

The Queen's Bays were a pleasure to work with. They had the casual, relaxed self-assurance characteristic of the cavalry and always gave the impression that they were confident that they could rely on us to get them wherever they were going on time and with everything in order.

Not so 4RHR, the 4th Royal Horse Artillery. The horse artillery, who needed their self-propelled guns moved as much as the Queen's Bays and the 7th Hussars needed their Centurion tanks moved, were far more obviously efficient. They had white lines drawn on their parade ground and officers whose hair was cut short, as indeed was mine, but quite unlike that of subalterns of the Queen's Bays, whose hair curled over their collars, so that they looked as if they would have been more at home in a lady's boudoir than in a tank. While a major of the Queen's Bays might say to me, 'That's terribly good of you. Do carry on', and come over at the end of the journey to say, 'Thank you so much', a major of 4RHA once tried to take over and determine the route and decide the speed at which we should travel to get to their destination earlier than originally planned.

I had to insist that Rogers trailers, loaded with self-propelled guns and pulled by Diamond T tractors left over from the Second World War, must not go faster than 10m.p.h. and that we had to stop for a break for ten minutes within every period of two hours and check the tyres. He found that irritatingly frustrating and wanted to override my arrangements. I told him that I would only do what he wanted if he put the order in writing, acknowledging that what he was requiring was in contravention of standard Rhine Army orders. He declined. But I felt vulnerable and insecure, standing stiffly to attention and telling a major the terms on which I was prepared to obey him. When I got back to camp and reported what had happened to Major McCabe, it was a relief that he rang the 4RHA HQ to demand and get an apology.

Not all the Polish drivers were as meticulous as I was about obeying Rhine Army orders. On one occasion four of our drivers had to go on a round trip of more than four hundred miles all the way to the base camp at München-Gladbach to collect two Centurion tanks which had been repaired and bring them back to Fallingbostel. They were anxious to be home as soon as possible and on a long down-hill stretch of the *Autobahn* slipped into neutral. The general officer commanding the British Army of the Rhine was being driven at about 60 m.p.h. in his Opel staff car and was overtaken by two tank transporters, each carrying a 50 ton Centurion tank. A message arrived at 312 Tank Transporter Unit. Major McCabe sent for me. I sent for Superintendent Susmarski. He had the drivers brought before the Chief Superintendent, who dismissed them, and an account of the disciplinary action taken then went all the way back up the chain of command to Rhine Army Headquarters.

We were an unusual unit in various ways. On ordinary working days British troops stopped for a morning break with hot sweet tea and a sticky bun. We had rye bread with garlic sausage and tea with a slice of lemon. If I was in the town of Fallingbostel with other British subalterns and British troops passed us, they would march past with shoulders back and saluting smartly to a count of five: 'up, two, three, four, down.' If Polish members of 312 unit passed by and saw me across the road, they would grin amiably and wave, calling out, '*Djien dobre, Panye Porucznyke*', and I would wave back.

Our working hours were unusual and very varied, and we took time off to celebrate a range of Roman Catholic feast days: the Annunciation of the Blessed Virgin Mary, her Immaculate Conception and her Bodily Assumption, and Corpus Christi Day. Because Poland had been conquered and dismembered so many times, we also celebrated what appeared to me to be an extraordinary number of Polish Independence Days. On such occasions we always had a parade in the morning and the senior Polish officer would make a speech in which I picked up words of approval, such as *Catholicki* and *Polski*, and words which clearly registered disapproval, such as *Alemanni* and *Ruski*.

Then we would all go to Mass and after that to a party which was likely to last ten or twelve hours. The Poles brought the food as well as vodka and a German drink called *Kirschwasser*; the British brought gin and cointreau. What the four drinks had in common was that they were transparent, and the Poles appeared to believe that a combination of vigorous dancing and keeping to transparent alcoholic drinks would ensure that one was fit for work the next day. It seemed to work, and for the rest of my life, although I have never drunk much, I would always choose gin rather than any other spirit and cointreau rather than any other liqueur, and while others might choose ham or salami or sliced beef in a supermarket, I would opt for *zywiecki* – Polish garlic sausage.

18. Kleine

Most members of 312 Tank Transporter Unit were the Poles, who operated the unit with little interference from the British Supervisory Element. But the administrative staff in headquarters were mostly German, though Frau Lust, the Chief Clerk, or *Oberangestellterin*, came from Lithuania (*Bin gar keine Russin, stamm' aus Litauen, echt deutsch*). Her deputy, Gertrud Musik, was a pretty girl in her twenties from East Prussia who, with her mother, had fled West as the Russians advanced in 1944. Because of her small size and youthful appearance she was known as '*Kleine*', or 'little'un'.

At about the same time that I took over as 2 i/c Frau Lust left and Gertrud Musik, or *Kleine*, was promoted to be the *Fräulein Oberangestellterin* (or Chief Clerk) and, as a consequence, my secretary. We worked closely together. She managed the office excellently well in a cheerful manner which brightened the place up. She had a delightful personality and an attractive, rather Slav appearance, and before long we were spending quite a lot of time together in the evenings as well as during working hours.

I enjoyed exploring the Lüneburg Heath with her as if I were a civilian, rather than in a military vehicle or on a motor-bike. I enjoyed going to the Fallingbostel cinema with her to see German films rather than to the camp cinema to see Hollywood films, and so long as they were German films, with their own film stars, such as O.W. Fischer or Renate Mannhardt, I found I could follow the German quite well. What I found difficult, to the point of impossible, was when British films had the sound dubbed into German. Then I would see Dirk Bogart with his mouth moving as if speaking English, but with the sound coming out in unintelligible German.

With *Kleine* I was able to fraternise with Germans far more than was usual for members of the occupying army and to discover things hidden from most of the British. There was a Herr Müller in charge of the German civilian workers in the camp - the mess waiters, the cleaners and so on. He was perceived by my fellow officers to have a particularly brutal manner in dealing with his subordinates. Typically he was described as 'a right Nazi'. On the other hand Herr Neupert, who worked as a clerk for the Queen's Bays, was seen as pleasant and charming. So he was, and *Kleine* introduced me to him because he wished to improve his English with a view to emigrating to Australia.

I spent several evenings with him, tidying up his pronunciation and his grammar and introducing him to English colloquialisms. Eventually we got to know each other well and he told me that one of the problems about being accepted in Australia was that he had served as an officer with the *WaffenSS* during the war, and he showed me where, in the manner of the *SS*, his blood group was tattooed on his arm. He also told me that Herr Müller had been imprisoned in a Nazi concentration camp throughout the war because he had been a member of the Social Democratic Party.

I could pass for a German so long as I didn't say too much, and once when I was with *Kleine* and a group of young Germans, I saw my fellows from a German viewpoint. A couple of officers from my mess walked past on the other side of the road. *Kinderwagenschieber!* said one of the young German men contemptuously, and my immediate reaction was one of resentment. But then I felt a warm glow of satisfaction. Yes, we were 'pram-pushers.' The Germans had provoked a war, and as a result, and years later, we were still constrained to spend two years of our lives in the army. But at heart we remained civilians. I avoided commenting.

Kleine told me about growing up on her parents' estate in East Prussia during the war. For years it was entirely peaceful. Any fighting was hundreds of miles away, whether in the east or the west. No bombers came anywhere near. The news of German military successes came over the wireless, there was no shortage of anything, and the only direct impact of the war was the absence of her father, together with many others, in the army.

Then everything changed. In 1944 the Russians were advancing and East Prussia was the first part of Germany that they reached. *Kleine* and her mother got ready to escape westwards. Before they left her uncle came to say an emotional goodbye and told her that, whatever happened, there was something she should try to remember. 'Try', he said, 'to remember that the *Führer* is not necessarily always right. Try to remember that the party is not necessarily always right.' And with that he kissed them goodbye and went off with his shotgun to die defending the Fatherland from the advancing Russians.

One week-end we went to Hamburg together and in the evening went to a night club on the notorious *Rieperbahn*. The floor show consisted of pretty but rather depressed-looking young women parading past in fur coats. At some point they all opened their coats to show that they were wearing nothing underneath. It was not in the least titillating but, on the contrary, rather sad. *So was hat in der Hitlerzeit nicht vorkommen können*, said *Kleine* ('That wouldn't have been possible in the Hitler period'), and for the first time in my life I registered that there was a price to be paid for liberty.

Another week-end we spent in Goslar, a particularly beautiful small town near the border of the Russian zone, and while there I had my only experience of fearing that the Germans might be about to rise against the occupying forces. I had gone out on my own, when around the corner came a platoon of German soldiers in the field-grey uniforms which I knew well from innumerable war films. They were marching three abreast with guns slung over their shoulders. I gave thanks that I was in civilian clothes and walked on as if unconcerned.

137

Kleine, the *Fräulein Oberangestellterin*

When I got back I asked *Kleine* what on earth was going on. 'Adenauer's army', she replied dismissively (Konrad Adenauer was the head of government, or Chancellor, of the Federal Republic): '*die Grenzepolizei*' - the border police. 'But why are they wearing field grey uniforms?' I should have known the answer. The uniforms were left over from the war, and so cost little or nothing.

I was able to go on local leave to Munich, which was in the American zone, and visit the Curtius family, whom I had last seen when I was fifteen, and on the way the train stopped at Frankfurt station. I realised how different was the manner of the American occupation from ours. I saw an American soldier with a can of lager in one hand and a German girl on the other arm. At first I was shocked. When British troops walked out in the evenings they wore belt and gaiters and marched rather than walked; fraternising with the locals was discouraged and it certainly needed to be discreet. But before long I had decided that it was probably a better way of occupying the country of a former enemy. The behaviour of the armies in the various zones reflected how far the Germans' former enemies had suffered during the war. The Russians were brutal. The French were hostile. The British were correct. The Americans were relaxed.

From time to time I went on leave back to England. Early in 1954 John was posted to Bodmin in Cornwall for a course in military Russian, learning such things as the Russian line of battle, the names of bits of equipment and brief biographies of their various generals. So early that summer, when he had a week's leave, I arranged my own leave for the same time and made out my travel pass to Bodmin.

We spent a week cycling round Cornwall together. Then, scruffy and unshaven, I said good-bye to John and climbed into a first class carriage, from which a porter understandably tried to eject me. I should, of course, have been wearing uniform, but I showed him my first class railway pass and he seemed to accept that I must have been engaged in some important military activity.

Later still, when John's course at Bodmin was finished, he took and passed WOSB, went to Mons Officer Cadet Training Unit back in Aldershot, and was commissioned three or four days before he was due to end his National Service. He reported to the Intelligence Corps Headquarters at Maresfield. There the adjutant wondered what to do with him, considered the problem, and then told him to go and have a good lunch in the Officers' Mess, 'a very good lunch', and come back and collect his demobilisation papers. So he left the army a couple of days early and was able to meet me at Liverpool Street Station on 4ᵗʰ September, when I arrived back from Germany.

In the event he never, of course, needed to use his Russian as an interrogator or interpreter during the Cold War. But many years later when he was the Dean of Rochester, the choir master found it useful for ensuring the good behaviour of choristers to tell them that the Dean had served in the Intelligence Corps and was a trained interrogator. The last part of that, of course, was not true, but it was a useful devise for keeping choristers in order.

Later still, when John was engaged in conversations on behalf of the Church of England with representatives of the Russian Orthodox Church, one of his opposite numbers was a Russian, Gregor Gregorievich, who had learnt English in the Red Army at just the same time that John was learning Russian during his National Service. Now they were using the languages they had learnt in the army not for the Cold War but in the service of the Prince of Peace.

At some point in the summer of 1954 Field Marshall Kesselring came to Fallingbostel to recuperate after being released from the prison where he had been sent after the Nüremberg trials. Fallingbostel, long before the Germans had built a large army camp outside the town, had been known as *Luftundkneippkurort Fallingbostel* ('Air and curing by the methods of Doctor Kneipp place Fallingbostel'), just as the next nearest town, Walsrode, was *HermannLönsstadt Walsrode*, taking its name from the Romantic poet of the Lüneburg Heath, and Germans came to Fallingbostel to take the waters.

That was why Kesselring came in the summer of 1954. In honour of his visit the town laid on a concert to which I went with *Kleine*. The town hall was decorated with large red flags with black Maltese crosses (but no swastikas), the band played, the mayor welcomed Kesselring and spoke with emotion about our comrades-in-arms still in captivity in the East, and I reflected that it was Kesselring who had been in command of the bombers which had attacked London in the Blitz.

We all sang the German national anthem. At the time it was illegal to sing the traditional words, *Deutschland, Deutschland Über Alles* ('Germany, Germany over all'). They were expected to sing about unity, justice and freedom (*Einigkeit und Recht und Freiheit*). But we all stood to attention and sang the traditional words and I trusted that no-one would realise that I was English.

At the time I did not feel particularly sympathetic to the German soldiers who were still prisoners in Russia. But shortly afterwards I reflected that the war had been over for nine years and those prisoners might have been in captivity from my age until nearly thirty with no prospect of release. Fortunately, at just that time, in the thaw after the death of Stalin, most of the prisoners who had survived, though they were a small minority, were released and straggled home.

The time was approaching for me to leave the army. The emotional and physical attachment to *Kleine* intensified as the summer drew on, and by August I didn't want to leave. I enjoyed the job. I was attached to many of the Poles I had been working with. Above all I didn't want to leave *Kleine*. Both of us knew that I was going to return to England and go to university, but shortly before I left we had been together to see *Madame Butterfly* at the opera house in Hannover, so I could not help but feel a bit like Lieutenant Pinkerton.

On 3rd September 1954, fifteen years to the day since the war had begun when I was only five, I now, at the age of twenty, with two years' military service behind me, caught the train westwards across Germany and Holland, reading Graham Greene's *The Power and the Glory*. I caught the boat from the Hook of Holland to Harwich and met John in London the next day, before going to Borden in Hampshire to be demobbed and go home.

Some years later, when the newspapers on the continent were full of news about shortages in England (I cannot remember the particular circumstances) *Kleine*, now married to Hartwig Serchinger and with a little boy called Reinhardt, sent a food parcel to sustain me through the apparent crisis. Later still, when Oriel and I had three small children, we arranged to meet Herr and Frau Serchinger and Reinhardt in Cornwall, where we were all on holiday. It was nearly twenty years since I had left Germany and I had not yet been back, and it was about another twenty years after that before I saw Germany again.

19. The Army Emergency Reserve and after

On 4th September 1954 I completed my two years of full-time National Service. But that was not the end of my military obligations. All through the rest of the 1950s, while at university and while teaching at Clifton College, I went off every summer to the depot of the Army Emergency Reserve transport column, at Sandy near Bedford, to engage for a fortnight in some sort of training.

It was a particularly well-paid holiday job. I was paid for the fortnight as a full lieutenant (promotion was pretty well automatic eighteen months after being commissioned, so I got my second pip a few days after completing my full-time service); we got an annual lump-sum payment (I think it was £30) of 'bounty', which was related to our obligations as part of the reserve; and to that was added clothing and travel allowances. The total of pay, 'bounty' and allowances was rather more than £60, or about the amount of a student grant for two months, for what was in a way a fortnight's holiday.

It was a complete change from life as an undergraduate. Usually we spent most of the fortnight engaged in some sort of imitation battle, ensuring the supply of food, fuel and ammunition to troops pretending to fight their way across East Anglia or the Salisbury Plain. The reserve column, like a divisional transport column, was divided up into a number of companies, each with four platoons of three-ton trucks. But the reserve column was unusual in that it also had an independent transport platoon, unattached to any company or other formation, and I found myself its platoon commander.

Maybe it was the consequence of having a name beginning with A, which could result in being the first choice for peeling potatoes or for extra guard duty, but now perhaps gave me command of the independent transport platoon. There were sometimes surprising consequences, such as being on the opposite side from the rest of the column in a mock battle and being able to drive unmolested through enemy lines because my trucks were marked up with the same insignia as the rest of the column.

I think it was in the summer of 1958 that we spent the fortnight engaged in an imaginary war fought with what were described as 'tactical nuclear devices.' An infantry major gave a lecture in which he suggested that the use by the enemy of nuclear devices within the divisional area could result in widespread temporary blindness, which in turn could lead to 'some lowering of morale.' I shuddered and remained uncertain ever afterwards about whether or not he really understood the significance of what he was saying.

We started our mock battle on the Suffolk coast. The assumption was that Lowestoft and Felixstowe had both been destroyed by atomic 'devices', and one of the first things all the subalterns of the column had to do was go through a large barn in which was a miniature model of Lowestoft containing a number of radioactive sources. We each carried a Geiger counter and had to measure and map the extent of radiation in the various areas of the town. The idea that the radioactivity to which we were exposed could be dangerous did not occur to anyone at the time.

Shortly afterwards, both Lowestoft and Felixstowe having been destroyed by the enemy, we loaded our trucks on the Suffolk beaches from amphibious vehicles, and I made my way westwards, laagering the platoon up in cover during the day and travelling as fast as possible by night. I was given a map reference somewhere in the Salisbury Plain and arrived there just when I was required to do so and in time for a beautiful sunrise on a summer's day in August.

We got our trucks into position ready to unload, pleased that we had got to the right place at the right time. Then, about a hundred

144

yards away, there was a tremendous explosion and a vast mush-room cloud rose into the sky. The sappers had been at some pains to build an imitation atomic explosion, and we were at the epicen-tre. So as far as the battle was concerned we were all dead. We spent the rest of the day sunbathing.

As it happens, that was the end of my career in the reserve. Shortly afterwards the AER was reorganised. It was referred to, at least temporarily, as the 'Ever-Readies', the amount of bounty was sub-stantially increased, and it was to be made up entirely of volunteers, who had to be prepared to go anywhere and do anything at any time. It was not an appropriate commitment if teen-agers were going to have to rely on me to teach them their O level and A level courses.

We were given four choices: apply to join the 'Ever-Readies'; transfer to the Territorial Army; be listed on the Regular Army Reserve of Officers; or resign one's commission. I resigned my commission. If they should ever want me back, I thought, I could go back as a private soldier or as a driver.

During the later years of my time in the AER I was also in the Clifton College CCF, or Combined Cadet Force, in which I ran a demonstration platoon made up of senior boys who had not been promoted to be NCOs. This was still the era when every boy in the school was expected to be in the CCF, and if the boys were expected to be in the CCF, then I felt that I should as well. But as a mere National Service soldier I felt very much an amateur. Most of the officers in the Clifton CCF, like those who had run the CCF at Christ's Hospital when I was a boy, had fought in the Second World War.

When I left Clifton in 1960, I finished as a CCF officer at just the same time as I left the Army Emergency Reserve. So it seemed as if any connection with the army had come to an end. It was also a peak time of the movement for unilateral nuclear disarmament. Those who supported CND, the campaign for nuclear disarmament, argued that Great Britain should give up its so-called independent nuclear deterrent unilaterally rather than after international negotiations, and expressed their attitude succinctly in the slogan, 'Better Red than Dead.'

My own view was that I wanted to be neither Red nor Dead. I no more wanted the Red Army in England in the 1960s than a German invasion in the 1940s, and I hoped it was possible to avoid it and still stay alive. The immediate price for that was the Mutually Assured Destruction (or MAD) of nuclear deterrence. That might avoid war for half a century (it did) or even a hundred years, but it was difficult to see it as a solution for five hundred or a thousand years.

By the time I joined the staff of Stowe in 1967 things had changed significantly. The war had been over for more than twenty years. It was no longer compulsory for boys to join the CCF. Men who had served in the war had now given perhaps twenty years service to the CCF and felt that was enough. I had no wish to join, and some members of staff who now served in the CCF had not even done National Service. If there were to be another war, we hoped that it would be a limited one which could be fought by professional soldiers rather than by a nation of conscripts.

Once I was a headmaster I found that I needed to go from time to time to a conference about careers in the armed services, just as I sometimes went to university conferences, and there I was much impressed by the way in which the army and the other services trained their young officers, ensuring that they got a range of different experiences, moving, for example, from command of a platoon at home to a small arms course, to command of a platoon overseas, to a job as *aide-de-camp* to a general, then on promotion to a post as an adjutant or 2i/c of a company, and so on.

It seemed to me that there was a case for trying to do something similar with teachers, perhaps with a greater element of choice than in the army. A typical career would normally start with a junior teaching post. Then, after a few years in his or her first post, the teacher might move to be an administrative officer with a local authority, from that to be a head of department in another school, then on to be a subject inspector or a deputy head, and so on.

Of course there would need to be some flexibility and it would need to take account of the talents of each individual, but it would help to avoid the problem of first-rate people staying happily in the same job for years, without getting any broader experience, while a far less able colleague might be driven by circumstances to seek promotion and rise from one job to another until appointed to a senior post for which entirely unfitted by temperament and lack of ability, though apparently well suited to it by experience.

Rather surprisingly, and just before my fiftieth birthday, I found myself the Commanding Officer of a CCF unit. At the College of Richard Collyer in Horsham, where I had just taken over as Principal, there was, very unusually for a sixth form college, a CCF contingent. Its members were very largely boys, and some girls, from the local 11-16 comprehensive schools, but the Officer Commanding, Peter Pointer, was a Physics teacher at Collyer's, and the NCOs were students there.

Back in the summer of 1939, when Collyer's was a grammar school some four hundred years old, the then Head of the History Department, A.N.Willson, had started an OTC (Officer Training Corps), which flourished for more than half a century. He continued as the Officer Commanding (the headmaster was *ex officio* the C.O., or Commanding Officer) until eventually Peter Pointer succeeded him, and in 1989, when we celebrated the fiftieth anniversary of the founding of the college CCF, Peter Pointer was still in command – only the second O.C. over a period of fifty years. I was the fourth C.O.

Because of the way the English educational system had developed since the Second World War, almost all CCFs were in independent schools. The name 'Officer Training Corps' had been changed as a sop to changing fashion, but the reality was that virtually every independent school had a CCF, while hardly any schools or colleges maintained by local education authorities had one. Collyer's was unusual and could even be viewed with suspicion as not being suitably adjusted to a changed world in which only socially superior schools which charged fees were expected to provide the sort of training which prepared a young man or woman for a career as an officer in one of the armed forces.

Because I was the principal of Collyer's I found myself representing the maintained sector of education on the Joint Services Cadet Committee, which met once a year at the Duke of York's barracks in Chelsea to talk over the state of the various cadet formations in the country. The occasional general, admiral and air marshal would take a couple of hours off to discuss with three or four headmasters how cadet corps should best occupy their time, and they were always immensely polite and treated us as if we were honorary generals or admirals. Then we would have a very good lunch and go home.

The First Gulf War of 1990 provided the one significant potential involvement of Collyer's in an armed conflict. When Saddam Hussein, the dictator of Iraq, invaded Kuweit in August of 1990, there was serious concern that he would use chemical and biological weapons against British troops. He was known to have used such weapons against the Iranians and against some of his own people with devastating effect.

Preparations were made for the possibility of massive casualties and for an overflow from hospital ships arriving at Portsmouth to hospitals in the south-east, and even for the possibility of an overflow from Horsham Hospital across the road to Collyer's, where I had to calculate how many beds we could take in the college hall and in the sports hall, and draw up a list of parents who might be called upon to drive the parents, wives and girl-friends of wounded servicemen to come to see them. In the event the number of British casualties could be numbered on the fingers of two hands, and they were all the consequence of what was called 'friendly fire', when an American gunship fired by mistake on a British troop carrier.

I had reason to reflect on how lucky I and others of my generation had been. We had been too young for the Second World War. Few of us had seen any fighting during National Service, and later, when Great Britain was involved in wars such as the Falklands War of 1982, they were fought far away by professional soldiers, sailors and airmen and impinged very little on the lives of civilians back home. We had cause to be grateful, and when British troops occupying Iraq after the Second Gulf War of 2003 were being blown up by I.E.D.s, or improvised explosive devices, I had particular cause to be thankful that occupying Germany fifty years earlier had been so much easier.

Oxford (1954–1957)

20. Freshman

◇◇◇◇◇◇◇◇◇◇◇◇◇◇◇◇◇◇◇◇◇◇◇◇◇◇◇◇◇◇◇◇

In the autumn of 1954 I went up to Oxford. Pembroke was a small college (only Corpus Christi was smaller), and while its two quadrangles were very attractive, the outer walls were dark with grime, so that the college was sometimes called 'the coal-scuttle of Christ Church', which stood just across the road, very big and grand.

The number of freshmen was between sixty and seventy, and about half of us had just finished our National Service. At that time there was still an assumption among politicians that it was the divinely ordained duty of the British to police the world. I had only been as far as Germany. My brother, learning Russian to fight the Cold War, had been no further than Bodmin and Cambridge, to which he had now returned for his first year as an undergraduate, reading a combination of French, German and Russian for the Modern Languages Tripos. Of young men among our contemporaries whom I knew, one had served in the King's African Rifles, fighting the Kikuyu in Kenya, another in the Arab Legion with Glubb Pasha in Jordan, another with the Ghurkas, and yet another had seen action in Korea.

The other half of the freshmen at Pembroke had arrived straight from school and most of them had National Service to look forward to after completing their BA, or Bachelor of Arts, course. It was, by the way, a BA course whatever subject you were reading. Oxford undergraduates reading Physics or Biochemistry or Engineering all received a Bachelor of Arts degree at the end of their course.

Eight of us were scholars. As a matter of college policy all eight of the first year scholars lived on the staircase in the Old Master's Lodgings now known as the Doctor Johnson staircase in honour of that distinguished alumnus of the college. We sat on our own scholars' table for dinner in hall each evening, and I believe that the intention was that we should educate each other. To some extent we did. Peter Prescott, the other History scholar of my year, David Speller, an opera-loving medic, and Robin Ellis, who was reading Law, would talk over the meal about Truth or the infallibility of the pope, and so on, and afterwards we would continue the discussion over coffee back in the Old Master's Lodgings. Peter was a Roman Catholic and Robin the son of an Anglican clergyman.

Our rooms were spacious and comfortable, but without any washing facilities. To wash or bathe one had to go down the stair-case, across a small yard, through an arch into the chapel quad, across that to another archway and into the old quad, at the far end of which was yet another archway, and beyond that the yard in which the washrooms were situated – now the site of a splendid library.

We were required to attend chapel at least three days a week and our names were ticked off by the head porter, Mr Ponsford. If we wanted our shoes cleaned we left them outside our rooms, and an elderly 'scout', Hector, cleaned them for us. On our first day there was a notice in the porch requesting that all freshmen should be in the hall at ten o'clock the following morning. Once we were there, all conscientiously wearing our gowns, the Dean, Bobby Heuston, the Law don, came in to say, 'Good morning, gentle-men! Welcome! If you want to get a good degree while you are at this university, don't fall in love and don't get converted. I think that's all I have to say to you. Thank you!' And out he swept.

Many years later, when I was a sixth form college principal, I used each year to expand on that excellent advice to my new students. Falling in love and getting converted were, in their own ways, two of the best things in life, so long as you fell in love with the right person and it was reciprocated, and so long as you were converted to something that made sense. But both used up an awful lot of time and emotional energy. So, I would suggest, avoid them while you are engaged on your A level course. Leave it till you can afford the time. I am not sure that many of them took my advice, any more than we took Bobby Heuston's advice.

As Dean he was responsible for discipline. It was not a very onerous task. Most of us had been used to far more rigid discipline than that imposed by the college, but we did have to be in by midnight and we were not allowed to walk on the grass in the quad. If one did, and was seen to do so, the penalty usually imposed was a fine of half a mark. A mark was a medieval coin which was two-thirds of a pound of silver, or thirteen shillings and four pence (i.e. two-thirds of the total number of pennies in a pound – 240). Thus half a mark was six shillings and eight pence. In those days we naturally thought in pounds, shillings and pence. The calculation was not difficult, and the penalty, while not exorbitant, was enough to dissuade one from walking on the grass.

After two terms we had to take an examination known as Prelims, and preparation for that included reading two set books. One was Bede's *Ecclesiastical History of the English People,* which we had to read in the original, so that everyone needed to know at least a little medieval Latin. The other, which almost everyone studied, was de Tocqueville's *L'Ancien Régime.* But four of us out of the three hundred and eighty or so Oxford undergraduates in that year reading History opted for German rather than French and tackled Bismarck's *Gedanken und Erinerungen* (his 'Thoughts and Recollections') about his career.

Because it was such an unusual thing to be doing I was sent off to St Anthony's College in North Oxford to be taught by a young Czech called Zbyněk Zeman, who had left Czechoslovakia in 1948 at the age of nineteen, at the time of the Communist coup, and had skied across the mountains to freedom and a history degree course in England. Now he was working for his D.Phil. Oxford, being the oldest English university, used the medieval Latin word order, *Doctor Philosophiae,* and awarded D. Phils for its doctorates, whereas Cambridge and other later universities used the classical word order, *Philosophiae Doctor*, and so awarded PhDs. An exception was the University of Sussex, which was founded in 1961 but wanted to be like Oxford and awarded D. Phils.

Dr Zeman went on to be a specialist in modern East European History. He put up with me writing about Bismarck, but late nineteenth century European history was something about which, at that time, I knew little and understood less, and with hindsight I shudder to think of the rubbish I must have written. Later, as a schoolmaster, I found it a fascinating period and a joy to teach, and ideally I would have chosen that period of European history when working for Finals, but at the time I was fairly strongly committed to the idea of specialising in medieval history to the exclusion of all else.

My tutor, Colin Morris, who was the college chaplain as well as the medieval history don, seemed at first acquaintance to be a middle-aged man with an elderly manner. The first essay he set me involved discussing a quotation from Bede: *'Those who came over were of the three most powerful people of Germany - that is, Angles, Saxons and Jutes.'* It was about the Anglo-Saxon invasions after the departure of the last Roman legions from Britain in the early fifth century in an attempt to save Rome from the Goths, and it was a pleasure to get away from '406 inspections' (I had for months inspected one tank transporter a day), ration returns and vehicle accident reports and get back to reading and to writing essays.

Shortly afterwards, when I arrived for a tutorial, Colin was on his knees by an oil fire and said to me, 'Do come in, David. Sit down. I am just adjusting my oil fire with a copy of the *Apocrypha*. It is not canonical scripture, but I find it remarkably effective for adjusting my oil fire.' But as he got older he seemed to get younger. By my last year, when we lived on the same staircase, he was often visited by his girlfriend, Brenda, and shortly afterwards they were married. By the time he retired nearly forty years on, as Professor of Medieval History at the University of Southampton, and I went to his retirement party, we seemed more or less the same age.

While in the morning I tried to decide such things as where the Jutes had come from (not Jutland), in the afternoons I felt I should engage in some strenuous physical activity, and the outcome was that before long I was spending every afternoon except Sundays rowing in an VIII on the river. I never went to more than one or two lectures in a week, because lectures intruded on the time available for the real work of reading and writing, and that was limited if one spent each afternoon on the river and wanted some time with one's friends. I always went to dinner in hall in the evening, and afterwards would sit and talk until it was time for me to go to bed at 9.30. Some of my friends would start their day's work then, would carry on until about three in the morning, not get up until it was nearly time for lunch, and spend the afternoon punting on a different part of the river from that on which I was training in a college VIII.

I joined the Camden Society, the college historical society, which was named after William Camden, the great sixteenth century antiquarian who had had his schooling at Christ's Hospital and then been an alumnus of Broadgates Hall, which was Pembroke's name before it was re-founded in the early seventeenth century. At that point it was named in honour of William Herbert, Earl of Pembroke, but the king, King James I, was thought of as the founder and his salvation from the papist powder plot of 1605 was celebrated each year on 5th November with a special service in chapel and the flying of the college flag from the tower. Three times a term the members of the Camden Society would read papers to each other and discuss them, or else invite a distinguished guest, usually one of the university dons, to speak to us.

Because I had enjoyed debating at school I joined the Oxford Union, but I only spoke in one debate before deciding that the emotional energy required for regular involvement was more than I could readily muster and the time more than I could spare. What is more, the Union was a university rather than a college institution, and already by the end of my first term I was conscious that I was content to be living, metaphorically as well as literally, in the college rather than in the university.

Money was not a problem. One could live comfortably on a state scholarship of £365 a year, and in principle I got the full grant because my parents' income was relatively low, but it was reduced by £100 a year to take account of the value of my college scholarship. My income was supplemented in four other ways. There was the £100 for clothing and £20 for books which Christ's Hospital had given me. I also had rather more than £200 saved up from my army pay during the eighteen months when I was an officer. Besides that I used to get about £60 each summer for a fortnight's service with the Army Emergency Reserve. Finally, my parents provided me with food and lodging during the vacations, which, considering that they might reasonably have expected me to be contributing something to the household expenses by then, was very generous. What with all of that, it was possible to live pretty comfortably in college for three years.

Term at Oxford was always frantic, with two essays and two tutorials a week, every afternoon except Sundays on the river, and little time for reading other than that directly related to the immediate task. The long summer vacation of three months was meant to be a time for reading widely and preparing for the work to come, but I had to fit in my two weeks with the Reserve and, as it happens, this particular summer I was off to France for a month. At the start of August I set off to Tours.

21. *Le mois d'août*

<><><><><><><><><><><><><><><><><><><><><><><><><><><><>

The reason I was off to France for the month of August 1955 was that my tutor, Colin Morris, had suggested that I use part of the vacation to learn some French, if only to be able to read Rousseau's *Du Contrat Social* in the original, since it was one of the set books for the Political Theory paper in Finals and we had to answer questions on passages set in the original French. Colin had kindly arranged for me to have a grant to spend the month of August at the University of Poitiers in Tours on an elementary French course. By then I would have done my two weeks reserve training in July and there would be all of September to get some reading done before the next academic year began in October. Oriel, who had finished at RADA at the end of 1954, was now away on the North Wales coast in her first summer season acting as juvenile lead at the Galleon Theatre, Prestatyn.

When I arrived in Tours I stayed in a house with five or six other students of various nationalities. The only other one of us with a British passport was a girl from Trinidad called Kemlin Ching, or Kim, who was an ethnic mix of Chinese, Afro-Caribbean, Anglo-Saxon and Native American. She was an attractive and intelligent girl who was spending three years at Queen Mary College, London, on a Commonwealth scholarship. The others thought it strange that she, whom they perceived to be one of the oppressed people of the British Empire, and I, who was one of the oppressors, should get on well together, apparently on equal terms.

We showed them our British passports. We explained that we were both British, she British and Trinidadian and I British and English, and that as British citizens we were both entitled to travel and live anywhere within the bounds of the British Commonwealth of Nations. She, as it happens, was living in England, in London. I could go to Trinidad if I wanted to. The others clearly all felt that there was a catch in it, and with hindsight one can see that they had a point. But in the 1950s immigration was not yet a political issue and Kim and I were both proud of the absence of any restrictions. We remained good friends. She returned to Trinidad after completing her studies in London and taught Spanish at the University of the West Indies.

When I arrived at the university buildings in Tours with a view to learning some French, there were dozens of young people milling around, far more girls than young men, all in summer clothing, so that the impression was of a holiday or festival rather than of serious hard work – and in those days girls wore summer dresses rather than jeans and tee-shirts. I saw one particularly good-looking, dark-haired girl, young, but already with a voluptuous figure, probably from some Mediterranean country such as Spain, and chose to ask her in very simple French if she knew the way to the place where I needed to sign on.

She did, and it immediately became apparent that she was not from Spain or Greece. She was from Surbiton and her name was Deirdre. She said that she would show me the way, and then, after I had signed on, she said she would look out for me at morning break. When break-time came there seemed no particular reason for either of us to return to the hot and sultry classrooms. There were plenty of cafes where one could sit outside in the street, and there was also the riverside of the Loire to discover. So we took ourselves off.

I had never before been anywhere with such a large number of attractive young women, other than the entrance hall of RADA in Gower Street. I was used to all-male or predominantly male communities, which had their own virtues and sometimes operated all the more effectively because of the absence of female distractions. In Tours in August 1955 I found the predominantly female atmosphere very appealing. There was, or at any rate there appeared to me to be, an amiable eroticism in the air.

160

Young women of many different nationalities, away from home, were looking, if not for love, at least for appreciation and affection. A Norwegian girl taught me to say *Jeg elsker deg* (I love you) 'just in case you need it later.' An Italian girl was immensely appreciative of the fact that I knew a sentence of Italian, *E pericoloso sporghersi dal finistrino* ('It is dangerous to lean out of the little window'), which I had learnt from a European railway carriage alongside the more abrupt German, *Nicht hinauslehnen* (Not out to lean!). So she taught me to pronounce it correctly.

But it was Deirdre with whom I spent more time than with anyone else. She was younger than many of the others who had enrolled at Tours that summer. Unlike most of them, she was still at school, but she now had the opportunity to mix with others as a young adult and she had the confidence which comes to girls who know they are attractive. She seized the opportunity avidly. We saw each other most days, visited a number of the chateaux of the Loire, went on a coach trip to Mont St Michel, and were in regular close contact. The emotional and physical contact increased, and each had an effect on the other. The weather was hot. The Loire valley was beautiful.

Deirdre on holiday... and back home in Surbiton.

Deirdre had discovered what neither of us would openly have referred to as sex, and both of us found it exciting and enjoyable. She clearly wanted more. So did I, but at the same time I was anxious not to get so carried away that we did something one or both of us would regret. We enjoyed time spent in the company of other young people, with Italians singing extracts from opera and Norwegians complaining about how the Swedes had allowed the Germans to invade them in 1940.

I suppose I learnt enough French to get by orally at a very elementary level and enough to be able to read and understand Rousseau with the help of an English translation. Back in the house where I was staying I enjoyed the company of Kim, with whom I could talk much as I did with friends back in Oxford. But above all I enjoyed that month because of Deirdre.

Then the month came to an end and we all went home, Kim to a college hostel in Cavendish Square in London, Deirdre to Surbiton, and I to Woodford Bridge. During September I no doubt got some reading done. I saw Deirdre once or twice and Kim as well. At some point I rowed bow in a coxless four, persuaded by Derek Baker, a friend from school who was now Captain of Boats at Oriel College, to join him and two other Oriel men to get the boat to London. We rowed for most of two days, with an overnight stop in Reading, and as I was bow I had to steer with my feet as well as row, perpetually looking over my shoulder, and thus we brought the boat all the way from Oxford to Putney.

Quite a lot of time at home was spent with John, comparing notes on Oxford and Cambridge and on the difference between studying Modern Languages and History. John was studying original material, reading the novels, plays and poems of great German, French and Russian writers. But it was fiction. My own reading was far more concerned with reality, with the study of what had really happened and why. But my reading was mostly of secondary sources. Which was the more valuable? If philosophy was the love of wisdom and history was philosophy teaching by the examples of times past, the study of literature was philosophy teaching through the creative imaginations of great men – and sometimes women.

Some time in the early autumn, when Oriel had finished her summer season as the juvenile lead with the Prestatyn Repertory Company, I was able to meet her again in London. I had always gone on writing to her each month and a couple of weeks later would get a reply from her. In my letters I told her about life at Oxford and about such things as my army reserve training and the course I went on in Tours. But I did not mention Deirdre any more than I had ever mentioned *Kleine*. Oriel and I met only briefly before I returned to my second year at Oxford, but it was enough to establish that I had never got over the feelings which had overwhelmed me when I first met her. Each time I met her I felt more in love and knew that when it was possible I would want to marry her.

Meanwhile Deirdre was back at school in Surbiton, where she lived with her father and elder sister, her mother having died some years earlier. She wrote frequently and fluently, seeking to retain or recapture the romance and emotion of our month in Tours. She poured out her feelings and her erotic fantasies, her longing to feel my hands on her and her yearning to be a slave girl held captive for my enjoyment, and I found it both flattering and a bit worrying. I was very fond of her, but not in love.

I found Deirdre immensely, intensely attractive, but did not imagine or expect a future together. Possibly the difference of about five years in our ages, which would have been so trivial a few years later, made an equal relationship difficult, and I certainly did not want a relationship in which I was expected to be a dominant male subduing a subservient female – not that she was naturally subservient!

In December, when she was at the end of her first term as head girl of her grammar school, she invited me to their school dance. There was possibly an element of wanting the prestige among her contemporaries of having an Oxford undergraduate as her boy-friend and partner, but there was also the memory of how close we had been in France and the hope, and even expectation, that that would continue and grow.

I went to stay for the week-end of the dance, and found when I arrived that her father was away on business and that her sister was away ice-skating in a show on ice. So once the dance was over, we had the house and the night to ourselves. We were free to do whatever we liked. But it was still the 1950s, and despite the intensity of the physical feelings, the social and religious rules of the society I had grown up in and a sense of responsibility towards a girl of whom I was genuinely fond meant that I was going to avoid 'going all the way.'

I think it felt to her like rejection. At the very least it meant that I was not so overwhelmed by passion for her that I could not restrain my desire. I did not deal with it well, and effectively it ended the relationship. At the end of that school year she went abroad to work as an *au pair* in what is now called a 'gap year', before going to university. I never heard from her again.

I had found Deirdre intensely attractive, but there was something quite different about my feelings for Oriel which went beyond physical attraction and affection, powerful though those feelings were, to include admiration, devotion, delight in her company and the wish to be with her. Some time later, by which time we were engaged and I was showing Oriel a photograph of Deirdre, her father came into the room, looked at the photo and said that, if I had a chance of going out with a girl like that, he really couldn't see why I was spending my time with his daughter. Oriel was cheerfully unconcerned. She was perhaps the most fundamentally secure person I ever met, she knew I loved her, and quite rightly assumed that I would go on loving her.

22. The Pembroke Boat Club

For most of the last ten years before going up to Oxford at the age of twenty I had trained for and played rugby football in the autumn. Even during my first months in the army I had played rugby football. The one exception was my second year in the army, when I was out in Germany and during the rugby season was shifting Centurion tanks around the Lüneburg Heath. But already at twenty I was past my prime. I was simply not big enough to be an effective forward in an adult game, nor fast enough to be an effective half-back or three-quarter.

In my last year at school, when we played against Tonbridge, the only time they had scored was when a very large forward called Marques, whom I was marking, caught the ball in the lineout and pushed his way over the line without my being able to stop him. The following year, when in the army, I was given a trial for the RASC team and found myself marking another very large forward called Currie, and I had the feeling that, if I touched the ball, he might pick me up and break me. It was clear to the selectors and also to me that I was out of my class. A few years later Currie and Marques were regularly playing together both for Harlequins and for England as the two second-row forwards.

All the same, when I went up to Oxford it seemed worth investigating the possibility of playing for the college, whose very successful XV needed a scrum half. I had a go, but I was not a scrum half, and I had to accept that my rugby days were over, except for the occasional Old Blues' team during the vacations and later, as a schoolmaster both at Clifton and at Stowe, in an annual masters' match against the school, until I was over forty and went off to be a headmaster.

I thought I would try rowing, and it turned out to be a sport that suited me. I lacked the skill to be even competent at cricket, and my tennis and squash were social rather than athletic accomplishments.

But I had been reasonably successful in my teens at rugby football, boxing and cross-country running, all of which required a certain amount of brute force and determination, and rowing fell into that category. I particularly liked the way in which eight men had to co-ordinate their actions and move as one. It was in some ways similar to foot drill. Soon I was rowing in the college second boat, preparing for the races at the end of the Michaelmas Term known as 'Torpids.'

Those of us who were new to rowing had to learn how to balance the long, thin, very unstable boat, while coordinating arms and legs to act together to transfer as much thrust as possible along the oar into the water, and besides that to do it in concert with the other members of the crew. We worked at it every afternoon, hammering up and down the river and preparing for the very peculiar Oxford style of racing known as 'bumps.'

In Oxford, where the Thames is known as the Isis, the river is too narrow for boats to race side by side. Consequently the boats are drawn up in line, one after the other, in groups of thirteen, in the order in which they finished the races the previous year. Each group of thirteen boats is known as a division, and in each division the boats are lined up at the start of a race with a length and a half between each of them. The various races start at half hourly intervals. A gun is fired to indicate that there is a minute to go to the start of a race, and at the sound of the starting gun a minute later all the crews drive off together, each boat trying to catch and bump into the one in front of it, while at the same time seeking to avoid being bumped from behind.

When one boat bumps another, both pull over to the side and the next day they change places. That carries on for four days. The boat which ends the day at the top of its division changes places with the boat at the bottom of the next division up. It is possible to go up or down each day. Torpids, at the end of the Michaelmas Term are less prestigious than the Summer Eights, because each college lacks those of its oarsmen who are part of the university squad in training for the Varsity Boat Race between Oxford and Cambridge – both the 'Blue' boats and the second crews, known as Isis (Oxford) and Goldie (Cambridge). Summer Eights' Weeks culminates with the most successful college crew either rowing over or bumping the boat ahead of it to become Head of the River at the top of the first division, as Pembroke did nearly sixty years later in 2013. Back in 1955 we were way below that.

As my first year went by I found that more and more of my time was spent on the river, and we were reasonably successful in Torpids. In the Hilary (or Winter) Term at the beginning of 1955 I was promoted to row in the college's long-distance VIII. Then, after that I was selected to row at bow in the 1st VIII in the Trinity (or Summer) Term. Bow is at the front of the boat, furthest from the cox, and is usually one of the lighter members of the crew (I was not much more than eleven stone), while the heaviest oarsmen are in the middle.

For the week before the Trinity Term the whole of the 1st VIII stayed at the Little Angel Inn in Henley and hammered up and down the river morning and afternoon. Chris Davidge, the Olympic oarsman who was coaching us, believed that 'mileage makes champions', so we covered a lot of miles, paddling, which is a euphemism for rowing quite hard, and paddling slow, which still required maximum effort while the oar was in the water but involved coming forward to the next stroke slowly and concentrating on balance. Every so often we would do a spurt of rowing for a short distance and manage to get in as many as forty strokes to the minute. It was exhausting, even when fit.

Peter Prescott, the other History scholar of my year, had rowed for Windsor Grammar School before coming up, and he was also in the 1st VIII. The most immediately obvious thing about him was that he was a strikingly good-looking young man, and he also had the self-deprecating diffidence which is seen as characteristic of the sort of aristocratic young men portrayed in late twentieth-century films by the actor Hugh Grant.

Peter had in fact grown up on a council estate in Windsor and gone to the Windsor Grammar School, from which he had come straight up to Oxford. The fact that he had been a member of the Eton

167

Excelsior Rowing Club in Windsor and wore their badge on his blazer led to a rumour that he was an Old Etonian who preferred a scholarship at Pembroke to a place across the road at Christ Church. His gentle and amused dismissal of such an idea seemed to some a confirmation of its truth. We enjoyed each other's company and remained friends until his sudden and unexpected death in 2005 at the age of sixty-nine, after which I spoke about his life at his memorial service at St James's Church, Piccadilly.

I read the famous passage about Love from St Paul's first letter to the Christians at Corinth and spoke about him as someone who had grown up a Roman Catholic and, while he was sometimes turned away from the church by being required to give assent to propositions he knew perfectly well were not true, had never been diverted from continuing to seek further understanding, however elusive it might be, as he travelled hopefully towards the destination he had now reached.

During our first two terms Peter and I talked in Hall on the schol-ars' table with David Speller and Robin Ellis about such matters as the Roman Catholic doctrine of the infallibility of the Pope or the nature of Truth. In the Trinity Term, once we were back in Oxford after our training week in Henley, we were moved away from the scholars' table in Hall to eat steaks and be fattened up on a special 1st VIII table. Much of the talk around us was of clearing our puddles and the height of the work above the water, but we had each other for company and could continue to discuss grand metaphysical matters.

Although we were both reading History and went to many tutorials together, our interests in History were very different. When we came to choose a special subject to study for Finals, I devoted myself to St Bernard and early Cistercian monasticism, while Peter was more concerned with finance and such things as drainage policy during the premiership of Sir Robert Peel. So our conversation was sometimes about the differences between medieval and modern history, though also about such matters as the nature of Faith and how to avoid irrelevant digressions in argument.

We were still covering a lot of miles on the water each afternoon, and we followed a strict training regime: no smoking, no drinking and bed at 9.30. I didn't smoke anyway, it was no hardship not to drink alcohol, which was unbelievably expensive by comparison with the prices in the mess in Germany, but if I was to go to bed at 9.30, get my work done and have some time to spend with my friends, I needed to establish a daily routine.

The outcome was that I regularly got up at 5.30, made myself a cup of coffee, worked for a couple of hours till 7.45, trekked to the bathhouse to get washed and shaved, went to chapel at 8.10 for the very brief daily service of Matins, went to breakfast ten minutes later, and reckoned to do three hours' work between 9.00 and 1.00, with about an hour off for a walk round Christ Church meadows or, once or twice a week, a lecture on something recommended by my tutor.

The Pembroke 1st VIII of 1955. I am standing at the far right. Peter Prescott is seated at the far left.

While I went off to bed at 9.30 each evening, some of my friends would start their day's work then, would carry on until about three in the morning, not get up until it was nearly time for lunch, and spend the afternoon punting on the river. While they punted, Peter and I and the rest of the 1st VIII continued our preparations for Eights' Week. In the event we went down two places. We rowed over on the first day, were bumped on the second and third, and struggled to avoid being bumped again on the last day. It was very dispiriting. Of course in all sports someone has to lose if someone else is going to win. But it is more enjoyable to be on the winning side.

It was with that fairly recent experience of being bumped twice in Eights Week that I went off to Tours for the month of August, and when I returned to Oxford at the beginning of my second year, I did not want to go through further weeks of training. My intention was to give up rowing. But Roy Chivers, the new Captain of Boats, wanted me to take over as Secretary of Boats. At first I declined. He tried to persuade me, and at length we agreed that I would do it so long as I could row in the 2nd VIII, which I thought would be less time-consuming.

Peter Prescott felt much as I did and agreed to join me. I asked Bill Dorey, who had stroked a successful 1st VIII a couple of years before and was now doing a D.Phil., to join us as well, and we ended up with four 1st VIII colours in the back of the second VIII: Tongyoi Tongyai, a Siamese prince, as cox, Bill as stroke, me at seven and Peter at six. It made a good start in building a strong 2nd VIII. We went on to win our oars in Eights Week of 1956 by making a bump every day, ending up as the second highest 2nd VIII on the river, and with most of the other members of the crew going on to row in the Pembroke 1st VIII the following year. More than sixty years later the oar is still hanging in our conservatory.

In the event I spent far more time than I had intended on the affairs of the Boat Club. As secretary I needed to arrange which boats took to the river at which times, coached by whom, and

The Pembroke 2ⁿᵈ VIII making a bump in 1956. I am third from the right, rowing at seven. Peter Prescott, at six, is behind me.

with any necessary adjustments in the crews to take account of illness or decisions by the coaches about who should row in which position in the boat, and I needed to put up a notice every day in the Porter's Lodge, indicating that information.

We had five boats regularly on the river for six afternoons a week, and also what was called the Schools Eight, for rowing veterans in their Finals year, who trained far less frequently. I needed to ensure that each boat always had a coach, and in practice I spent part of most afternoons coaching one of the VIIIs, as well as part of every afternoon training in the 2ⁿᵈ VIII. It was enjoyable, but both exhausting and time-consuming.

171

23. College Life and the JCR

In October 1955, a few weeks after my month in Tours, I was back in Pembroke. In those days all of the college's undergraduates except the scholars spent the first year in digs, but all had the second year in college before going into digs again for the third and final year. There was a ballot for rooms, and because I came out fairly high in the ballot I had a very attractive new room, between the old quad and the chapel quad, right in the middle of the college, with its adjacent bedroom abutting what had once been Broadgates Hall, and with a medieval wall. It had the disadvantage that it was in such a good position that it was very convenient for friends wanting, for example, to listen to *The Goons* after hall or leave their gowns somewhere until they needed them later.

Even acquaintances would sometimes park something there till later. One day someone whom I knew only slightly from the Boat Club left his girlfriend for an hour or so while he went off to a tutorial. Under the circumstances I could scarcely just get on with my work. Anyway, she wanted to talk about her discontent with the way she felt he was treating her. Half an hour later she was explaining to me that she had a bra which unfastened at the front. At that stage of my life I did not even know that most bras fastened at the back, and I failed to take advantage of the information.

If I was to spend as much time as I did on the river each afternoon, as well as organizing the Boat Club, I needed to maintain the regular daily routine that I had established the previous year. So I kept to the practice I had established in my first year of getting up early to work. I reckoned that, with two hours' work before breakfast and three during the morning, I could reasonably reckon on having finished my work for the day by lunch-time.

Social life was above all a matter of time spent with friends in college. It might include testing David Speller on names of parts of the body drawn at random from a hat (as a medic, and unlike the rest of us, he was subjected to numerous tests). It might be a matter of indulging in port, raisins and nuts with Martin Henry, another historian of my year, while reading each other poems we particularly liked. It could be finding out from Dick Lugar, an American over on a Rhodes scholarship, why, unlike almost all other Americans in the university, he was a Republican rather than a Democrat.

There came a time during our second year when Peter and I both needed to learn something about what was referred to as early modern history, the Tudors and Stuarts, and we were sent off each week to Trinity College to an early modern specialist to learn how Queen Elizabeth 'ruled much by faction and party as her own great judgement advised.' We skated rapidly over several centuries and I drew the conclusion that more or less all of the history of the early modern period was to be understood as a matter of the manipulation of factions. My main memory is of walking up to Trinity with Peter, with both of us wearing the rather unusual combination of a scholar's gown with a white and cerise Pembroke 1st VIII scarf.

The reason we were farmed out to Trinity was that, of the two history dons in Pembroke, one, Colin Morris, was a medievalist and inevitably the one I knew well, while the other, Piers Mackesy, was a modern historian. Later on, when I had to study some relatively modern history, I got to know Piers better, though Peter, whose special subject was *Financial and Social policy under Sir Robert Peel*, and Martin Henry, whose special subject was *The French Revolution*, always knew him far better.

He was the son of the Major-General Mackesy who had commanded the British forces sent to Narvik in April 1940. Narvik was the port in the north of Norway from which the Germans transported the Swedish iron ore which they needed for building tanks and warships, and Churchill, as First Lord of the Admiralty early in the war, devised a scheme for landing a brigade at Narvik, crossing the mountains into Sweden and carrying on into Finland where they would help the Finns against the Russians. Fortunately the Russo-Finnish Winter War ended in March 1940, before Great Britain could get herself involved in violating the neutrality of both Norway and Sweden and fighting Soviet Russia at the same time as Nazi Germany.

But the iron ore was still important, and Britain began mining Norway's coastal waters on 8th April, while Hitler launched an attack on Scandinavia the next day. Demark fell without fighting. Sweden allowed the Germans through, and the German army moved swiftly to occupy various strategically significant parts of Norway, such as Narvik. By now the British transport vessels, which had been loaded on the assumption of being able to land without opposition, were approaching Narvik, with the men separated from their weapons and the weapons separated from the ammunition.

The Germans were in prepared positions ready to defend the harbour with machine guns, while the British had no landing craft and would have had to try to wade ashore from open boats through freezing water along a long sloping beach in daylight or, at best, during the brief April twilight. Mackesy could see that a frontal assault was impracticable. With four foot of snow on the ground all around, a flank attack was not yet practicable either, so he ordered the British forces to withdraw.

For understandable political reasons Churchill had wanted a success in Scandinavia. Instead the Narvik episode was an ignominious failure. Mackesy was made the scapegoat, and a month later Churchill was prime minister. He was, of course, a great wartime prime minister, and among the qualities needed to fulfill that role successfully was a measure of ruthlessness. Mackesy was one of the first victims of that ruthlessness.

During my second year at Pembroke Dick Lugar, who was later to be one of the senators for Indiana and Chairman of the United States Senate Foreign Affairs Committee, suggested that I might succeed him as President of the JCR - the Junior Common Room. It was a position to which the successful candidate was elected by the transferable vote system, with all the candidates numbered by each voter in order of preference. In those days no politics were involved. It was very much a domestic position, representing the undergraduates of the college, who were the electors, to the Senior Common Room, usually represented by the Bursar.

In a small college and with a room right in the middle, I was probably known to most of the undergraduates. As a scholar I was generally acceptable to the intellectuals, and as Secretary of Boats was similarly acceptable to the 'hearties.' As an Old Blue, a former pupil of a notable charitable institution, I fitted in comfortably somewhere between those who had been to a public school and those who had been to a grammar school. So, being all things to all men, a regular chapel-goer but neither an Anglo-Catholic nor an Evangelical, I won, ahead on the first count, and with an overall majority on the third.

One consequence was that I had three years in college. Most of my contemporaries had only the second year in college. I was in for the first year because I was a scholar, for the second because we all were, and for the third because I was President of the Junior Common Room. For that year I wanted a bit more privacy and deliberately chose a room on the top floor of what was then called the Besse Building in the far north-west corner of the college, so that visitors would not call in casually. Now it is staircase 11 in the North Quad.

During the Trinity (or Summer) Term of my second year, i.e. in 1956, I was very busy. I had just taken over as President of the JCR and was heavily engaged in negotiations with the college Bursar (eventually successfully) for a college bar under the hall. As Chairman of the Camden Society I was organising a programme of speakers, both internal and external. As Secretary of Boats I was making all the day to day arrangements of the Boat Club, as well as both rowing and coaching in preparation for Eights Week. Eights Week was also the time for the Pembroke Summer Dance. Once again Oriel couldn't come, this time because she was now the juvenile lead in a sixteen week summer season at Morecombe. I needed to find another partner, and it was Kim rather than Deirdre whom I invited instead.

During 1956 a problem relating to the Suez Canal developed and gradually built up to a crisis in the autumn. Great Britain, which had occupied Egypt since 1882, largely in order to secure the route through the Suez Canal to India, had at last in 1955 withdrawn from Suez and handed the Canal Zone back to Egypt, then ruled by Colonel Nasser. International politics involving the USA and the USSR as well as the building of the Aswan High Dam led to a secret deal between the British, French and Israeli governments for Israel to attack Egypt.

In October, by which time the next academic year had begun in Oxford, Israel attacked. While Israel's army still had two hundred miles to advance before reaching the canal, the British government issued an ultimatum to both sides, requiring them to retire to ten miles either side of the canal, and then launched an invasion of Egypt. The Russians threatened Great Britain with a nuclear strike, the Americans withdrew financial support, and with both of the world's super-powers opposing the adventure, the British troops, which had been militarily successful, were ignominiously withdrawn. The Russians, who at the same time had their own crisis in Hungary and had withdrawn from Budapest, took advantage of the fact that the eyes of the world were on Suez, to move their tanks back in.

I was strongly opposed to the invasion of Suez and wrote to my MP to ask him to do what he could do to stop it and, since I lived in the Woodford constituency, got a printed card in reply saying, 'Sir Winston Churchill has received your communication which is

With Kim at the Pembroke Summer Dance in 1956.
In those days it was customary for those with 1st VIII
colours to wear their blazer with a black tie for the occasion.

receiving his attention.' Sadly, I lost the card. But at the time I was faced for the first time in my life with a personal crisis of conscience.

I was the commander of the Independent Transport Platoon of the Army Emergency Reserve Column and in no way a pacifist. While I recognized that it would not have made sense for Great Britain to have tried to oppose the Red Army in Hungary, if that had been British policy, I would not have hesitated to go. Suez was another matter. I did not expect to be called up to go to the Middle East, but I thought it likely that I would be required to take the Independent Transport Platoon of the Reserve Column to somewhere such as the London docks in order to free others to go to Suez.

I decided that I would refuse to go. But then the Russians moved their forces back into Budapest, and I asked myself what I would have done if I had been a subaltern in the Red Army required to go to Hungary. The answer is that I would have obeyed my orders. The consequences of not doing so in the U.S.S.R. would have been entirely different from anything one might have expected in England. Thus the nature of the moral conflict going on inside me changed. In the event I did not receive my call-up papers, so nothing happened that directly concerned me. But it helped to educate me in the complexities of moral issues.

At that time I was the President of the J.C.R. at Pembroke (having a term earlier taken over from Dick Lugar) and was asked to go to a meeting of J.C.R. Presidents to consider taking some joint action. One group wanted to send a letter to the Prime Minister and to *The Times* expressing the common opposition of Oxford undergraduates to the Suez operation. Susie Greenwood (of Somerville I think, and daughter of the distinguished Labour politician, Arthur Greenwood, who had been in the war cabinet in 1940) was one of the main advocates of doing that. On the other side was a rather laid-back, aristocratic young man (possibly from Worcester College) who had done his National Service in the

Canal Zone and felt that it was about time that we gave the 'Gyppos' a good bashing.

My own position, while sympathizing personally with Susie Greenwood, was that it would make no sense for me to presume to speak on behalf of Pembroke. The college was divided down the middle, and I would not have liked to have to guess whether more were in favour of the government's action or against it. As it happens much the same was true of most of the J.C.R. presidents. Nothing got decided, not because anyone won the argument but because, while there was an immense amount of passionate feeling on both sides, there was no possibility of reaching agreement.

It was now my last year and I was no longer spending every afternoon on the river, so there was time to enjoy visiting the quadrangles and gardens of the other colleges. I had in the past regularly walked through Tom Quad, just across the road in Christ Church, on my way to the river, and then through Christ Church Meadows. Now, sometimes alone but more usually with a friend, I would go exploring the gardens of other colleges. The gardens of St John's, Merton and Wadham were particularly beautiful, and Addison's Walk in Magdalen was a delight.

I visited the various college chapels as well and was much struck by the memorial in the ante-chapel of New College which read, 'In memory of the men from this college, who, coming from a foreign land, entered into the inheritance of this place and, returning, fought and died for their county in the war 1914-1918: Prinz Wolrad-Friedrich zu Waldeck-Pyrmont, Freiherr Wilhelm von Sell, Erwin Beit von Speyer.' Warden Spooner had had it put up just after the First World War and had faced considerable opposition. It seemed to me that it was to his eternal credit.

The regular routine of reading, making notes, writing essays in a rush just before a tutorial, and even going to the occasional lecture, kept me busy. There was the occasional outing in the Schools VIII. There was time to walk round Christ Church Meadows with friends and drink coffee with them after Hall in the evenings. At times I even gave some serious thought to what I was studying, and regularly once a month I wrote to Oriel and once a month she wrote back to me.

24. Oriel and the theatre

◇◇

For five years, from when we met in December 1951 until the end of 1956, Oriel and I met relatively seldom. We wrote regularly, each writing once a month throughout those five years, but from the day in March 1953, when we met in London before I was involved in a train crash, our lives diverged and meeting was difficult. I went out to Germany a few days later, and apart from occasional home leave I was away for the next year and a half. Meanwhile Oriel and Chloë, who had both won scholarships to R.A.D.A., the Royal Academy of Dramatic Art in central London, left school after only two terms in the sixth form and started at R.A.D.A. in April 1953. They were still only seventeen, and while they found a flat in the Cromwell Road in South Kensington to live in during the week, they usually went home to Shalford at the week-ends.

When in Germany I wrote to tell her about ten ton trucks and then about the Poles and tank transporters, and I told her that I missed her. But I never mentioned *Kleine*. She wrote back (at one time to BAOR 30, Poland, which the army post office dealt with efficiently), told me about her lessons at RADA, but only mentioned as acquaintances some of the young men who were at RADA with her, such as Albert Finney, Brian Bedford, Frank Findlay, John Stride and Peter O'Toole, who played the White Rabbit in a production of *Alice in Wonderland* in which she was Alice. I still have a copy of the programme.

When I came home on leave from the army I was able to see her briefly in London, and when I went to meet her at RADA, as I waited for her in the RADA entrance hall in Gower Street, I watched a procession of strikingly beautiful young women going past. Then, when Oriel arrived, we went to a nearby cafe, where she ordered two portions of chips, at sixpence each, and we ate them with free bread and butter, tomato juice, vinegar and salt. She was adjusting to life as a drama student, living cheaply and loving it.

She was still at RADA when I finished my military service and went up to Oxford, but it was no easier to meet regularly during the next three years than it had been during the previous two while I was in the army. As her course at RADA came to an end in December 1954 she wrote to tell me that she was one of those chosen to act in the prestigious Kendal Competition. She had the part she wanted of Pauline in *The Constant Nymph*. It went well and immediately afterwards her name appeared on the notice board with her performance rated as 'highly commended.'

Shortly afterwards she got a letter from a theatrical manager and agent who had seen it to arrange an appointment with her, she saw a complimentary reference to her performance in *The Stage*, and she was offered a job, which she accepted, at the Guildford theatre as an ASM (Assistant Stage Manager), painting and building scenery and acting small parts.

'Isn't life great?', she wrote, and ended her letter, 'Much love, Oriel (STAR) Gawan Taylor.' She sent me a copy of the very glamorous photograph of herself which she sent round to repertory theatres when looking for a job, and that has hung in my study ever since, and I also still have on my desk a photograph of her in the Guildford theatre playing the part of Lady McDuff's small son in a production of *Macbeth*.

By then I was at the end of my first term at Oxford and missing female companionship. I had spent eight years in the virtually all-male environment of Christ's Hospital and had found my emotional life transformed by meeting Oriel. I had spent the next two years in the largely all-male environment of the army, though with the immense good fortune to have been able both to work and spend free time with *Kleine* for more than a year.

Oriel at RADA in 1953. This is the picture she sent to repertory companies when applying for a position as a juvenile lead.

Then I went up to another all-male environment in Pembroke, spending much of the time when not working out on the river rowing. I enjoyed the conversation and companionship of my friends at Pembroke and I enjoyed rowing. But I was aware that I had left *Kleine* behind in Germany, and I was aware that Oriel was living a separate life far away. I missed her, and that affected my relationship with Deirdre.

The one particularly attractive girl I met in my first year was the very blonde and very bright Valerie Paget, who was reading History at LMH, or Lady Margaret Hall, and used to go to the same lectures as me. But she already had an established boyfriend, Colin St Johnston, who was still doing his National Service and would come up to Oxford the following year, and whom she later married.

All the same it was a pleasure to be able from time to time to be able to cycle up to LMH after the afternoon's exertions on the river for a cup of tea and female companionship. Valerie was later the Head of History at the Frances Holland School in London and then at Westminster School, and I kept in touch with her and Colin over the next half century and saw them again recently more than sixty years after we first met. When in 2016 I finished writing the first draft of a book on *Education and Politics, a history of unintended consequences and the case for change*, she was one of the three people who read it through, provided useful comments and encouraged me to go ahead.

Oriel's job as an ASM at Guildford was a useful start in the theatre, but she wanted to be a juvenile lead in a repertory company and in the spring of 1955 she auditioned for and got the job of juvenile lead for the coming summer season at the Galleon Theatre in Prestatyn, which was why she was away in North Wales while I spent the month of August 1955 in France.

Juvenile leads are the young men and women who play what are usually the main parts in a play. A summer season was hard work. It lasted sixteen weeks, and plays ran for one week each, from Wednesday to Tuesday, so as to catch the holiday makers at both ends of the week. There was a dress rehearsal on Wednesday morning and the first public performance was that evening. It was followed by six more evening performances.

While that play was performed in the evenings, the first act of the following week's play was read through on the Thursday morning and rehearsed on Friday. The second act was read through on Saturday morning and rehearsed on Sunday. The same was done with the third act on Monday and Tuesday. Dress rehearsal was on Wednesday morning - and so on for sixteen weeks. The afternoons were free, but that was the only time available for learning the lines, and if one was the juvenile lead and usually on stage for most of the play, there were a lot of lines to learn.

The first time that she played the part of a young married woman she realised that she needed a wedding ring and went into Prestatyn to the shops to get one as cheaply as possible. She asked the advice of a shop assistant in Woolworths, who said that the only thing they had like that was a brass curtain ring. 'Oh, that's alright,' said Oriel, 'I only need it for a week', and then the shock on the shop assistant's face caused her to realise the implications of what she had said.

Once the summer season was over and after a week or two of resting (a rest really was necessary) Oriel would get a temporary job, such as working as a waitress at Dickens and Jones, until it was time for the Guildford pantomime. Work in pantomime was at the opposite end of the spectrum from a summer season. It lasted nearly as long, but Oriel would get a job as, for example, a slave girl in *Ali Baba and the Forty Thieves*, and each night would climb into (and eventually out of) a large earthenware jar, and each night say just one line. It was profoundly boring.

Then she would go back to being a waitress at Dickens and Jones, join the Dundee Theatre Company, for example, for a small part in a radio play, and appear with Chloë as decoration in a television show.   At one time she and Chloë were photographed together for an advert for Toni home perms which appeared in magazines and newspapers all over the country with the question, 'Which twin has the Toni?' The answer is that it was Oriel.

I wrote to tell her what I was doing at Oxford; she would reply two weeks later with what she was doing in the theatre. When we did meet we carried on, if those are the right words, where we had left off.   There was no commitment to a future together, but certainly on my side there was the hope that that would one day be possible.

In 1956, when it was time for another summer season, she took over as the juvenile lead in the Morecombe Repertory Company, where an actress called Thora Hird, who was playing the character parts, took Oriel under her wing and looked after her. Nearly half a century later, after a long and successful theatrical career, Thora eventually died in 2003 at the age of 91. At the time, when she was already quite often playing elderly character parts, she was still in her early forties.

Oriel was more than twenty years younger, still learning a new part every week while at the same time playing the one learnt and rehearsed the previous week, and she was beginning to wonder how much longer she wanted to go on living in digs with little money, no normal social life and little prospect of anything else. She had an audition for the part of Alice in a projected film of *Alice in Wonderland*, but nothing came of it. She began to think of quitting the theatre.

A few months later, on New Year's Eve 1956, I was able to take her to the Chelsea Arts Ball at the Albert Hall. The Old Blues' Rugby Football Club had the rather strange privilege of providing bouncers for the ball each year. Wearing a pair of slacks and a rugger shirt we patrolled the occasion, politely asking anyone who took a drink or a cigarette onto the dance floor to move to the

*This advertisement appeared regularly in the mid-1950s
in magazines such as Woman and Woman's Own.
The caption underneath explains that 'Oriel, on the right,
has the Toni', which was a lotion used for putting
waves into straight hair.*

side, and then, if they were difficult (most were not in the least difficult), half-a-dozen of us would pick them up and tip them out of one of the doors to the waiting police. But trouble was infrequent and any one of us with a partner was able to spend the night with her rather than on patrol.

By now I was 23 and Oriel was 21. Chloë had gone home for the New Year, but Oriel had stayed on at their flat in the Cromwell Road in order to go to the ball. With short hair, a very short green tabard over her slight figure, and fishnet tights on her very striking legs, she made an entirely implausible Robin Hood or Peter Pan, but was immensely feminine and attractive. We were five years older than when we had first met, still relatively inexperienced, but not as inexperienced as three years earlier. Dancing together that night was memorable and intensely erotic. She leant back, felt the effect she was having on me, and enjoyed it.

The way she moved intensified the pleasure and the pain, and she smiled a wicked smile, confident that I was hers. I understood what had been meant by some wag who said that dancing in those days was 'the vertical equivalent of the horizontal desire.' When the ball was over the trains were no longer (or not yet) running. So we went back to her flat, I desperate to make love to her and she apparently feeling much the same. But we both knew that to 'go the whole way', as it was called at the time, could lead to pregnancy, shame and practical consequences that we were in no position to deal with. So we managed to avoid that while discovering more about each other, both physically and emotionally.

We were fortunate that circumstances had conspired to keep us apart for most of the previous five years. If we had been able to see each other regularly, there was the danger that the relationship would have burnt hotter and hotter, at a time when neither of us was in a position to get married. Then something would have gone wrong. As it was, the infrequency of our meetings prevented things from developing too far too fast and getting out of hand.

Oriel was still acting, with offers from theatre managers which she would have welcomed immediately after leaving R.A.D.A., but she no longer had the same enthusiasm for life in repertory theatre that she had had back then, and both of us wanted to try to see more of each other. She did a secretarial course and got a job in London.

25. Finals

◇◇◇◇◇◇◇◇◇◇◇◇◇◇◇◇◇◇◇◇◇◇◇

Before the end of my second year I had opted for the special subject on *St Bernard,* which was taken by a small group of about half-a-dozen, including Henry Mayr-Harting, who had been born in Prague, came to England aged three in 1939 on the *Kindertransport,* was educated at Douai, a Benedictine monastery, and thirty years after we took Finals in 1957 became Oxford's Regius Professor of Ecclesiastical History. There was a lot of reading to do, in Latin as well as in English, about early Cistercian monasticism. So for part of the long vacation of 1956 I stayed up in Oxford in digs, lived cheaply on dried dates, bread and butter, Danish blue cheese and coffee, did a lot of reading, and went for walks with Peter Glazebrook, a friend in the next year who was reading Law.

One weekend Peter took me down to Belmont Abbey, where he had been at school, to stay in the monastery for a few days and get a flavour of Benedictine monastic life. I found it fascinating. At all meals there was silence as they listened conscientiously to a biography of St Ignatius Loyola. I learnt how to ask with signs for bread or water or cheese, and I listened to a discussion in which there were widely differing views about belief in the Blessed Virgin Mary as the Mediatrix of all Graces and whether or not the Pope was likely to proclaim that to be infallibly true and belief in it a requirement for salvation.

I also had to fit in my two weeks of reserve training, and besides that I went to a camp on the Yorkshire moors with some Pembroke friends and a group of Borstal boys, and then went back with them to spend a few days living as an inmate of a Borstal institution. It was a bit like being in training in the army, and though an attempt was obviously being made to provide them with education, so that they could earn their living after coming out without resorting to crime, a term of Borstal training was for at least eighteen months, and some of them understandably resented the fact that those who had committed a crime with them, but were a few months older and counted as adults, got away with perhaps a six month sentence.

Several of them explained how they had come to be in Borstal. One had been in a pub one evening, when a squaddie had called him 'a silly bastard.' 'Don't you call me that', he had replied. 'Call me that and I'll lay you out.' 'Come off it, you silly bastard', answered the squaddie. So he hit him and broke his jaw. The reason he reacted so violently, he explained to me, was that he was an illegitimate child and he hated being called a bastard. What was more, the thing he minded most about being in Borstal was that it had upset his mother, who was the person he loved most in all the world. I reflected that few of my Oxford friends would have spoken so openly about loving their mother. Education can inhibit the expression of strong feelings.

Another of them, who was clearly very bright, had been arrested and convicted for smuggling watches into England from the Channel Islands. The great problem for him about being incarcerated for so long was that he already had a girlfriend whom he wanted to marry. I met her later, when he had finished his term of Borstal training. I took them out to a meal and later went to lunch with them in their flat in South London. He had a job, and they seemed determined to live their lives with him avoiding crime and thus the danger of being separated again if he should have to go to prison. For a while I thought of the possibility of teaching in Borstals, but it would have involved joining the prison service, and the thought did not last long.

Later that summer I stayed for a couple of weeks with Martin Henry and his mother, Aileen, and step-father, Duncan Watson, at their house in Teddington. We spent some hours each day reading: I read about St Bernard and the Cistercians, and he about the French Revolution. At other times we went out, and one evening went to see the film *Sink the Bismarck* at the Odeon cinema in

Twickenham. At that time there were trolley buses in Twickenham and Martin suggested that instead of getting off at the bus stop we should wait until the bus had to stop at the traffic lights opposite the cinema.

As we approached, the traffic lights changed, the bus accelerated (and trolley buses had remarkable acceleration), and Martin, who had spent his National Service in the parachute section of the Royal Corps of Signals, did a splendid parachutist's jump. I tried to emulate him and crashed on the pavement with torn trousers and a bleeding knee. But the trousers staunched the blood, we saw the film, no permanent damage was done, and I hope I learnt not to be quite so casually foolhardy in future.

During the long vacation as a whole I got quite a lot of reading done on the *St Bernard* special subject, and that paid off when it came to Finals. I did far too little reading on early modern and on modern English History, and that resulted in a relatively poor performance in those papers in Finals. The value of the reading on St Bernard went beyond preparation for an examination. There were two elements in his thought which had a lasting influence on me.

The first was the idea that contemplation should issue in action. Of course Bernard believed it was important for monks to pray, but he also believed that their prayer and their contemplation of the divine will should eventually have its outcome in action. It was no good to seek to contact God and tell Him what He ought to think and what He ought to do. There was, however, some point in holding up problems before God, seeking to understand the divine will, and then taking action to try to do what one understood to be God's will.

The second aspect of his thinking which influenced me was the advice he was reputed to have given to young men undertaking the responsibilities of an abbot. It was characteristic of the Cistercian Order that a monastic house such as Clairvaux would found daughter houses. Bernard might send a young man off across the sea to find 'a place of horror and vast solitude', such as Fountains or Rievaulx, both in Yorkshire, where a new Cistercian monastery could grow. One can imagine a young twelfth century monk, sent off with half-a-dozen companions to do that, wondering how on earth he would cope with the responsibilities of an abbot. Bernard's advice was threefold: notice everything; correct a little; cherish the brethren. It still seems to me better guidance than any twentieth century management advice that I have encountered.

Later in the year I had to decide what I wanted to do the following year. One possibility was to start a research degree and I toyed with the possibility (improbable though it sounds) of starting a B.Litt. on the financial transactions of Aaron the Jew of Lincoln in the early thirteenth century with the Cistercian monasteries in Yorkshire and the Frescobaldi banking family of Florence, who were buying up wool futures. But at the same time I was aware that I was now twenty-three and that my father had started work, earning his living, ten years younger than that. What is more, I wanted to get married, and that would be difficult if trying to live on a research grant.

I decided to look for a job and only take the idea of research further if I didn't find a job I liked before the end of the academic year. Since I was intending to be a schoolmaster it might have seemed sensible to do a teacher training course and acquire the Oxford Dip. Ed. qualification, but at the time there was no requirement to have such a qualification, and it was widely, though mistakenly, assumed that an educated man did not need any guidance in how to teach. It was also assumed that the main reason for staying on for another year would be, for example, to stand for a position such as President or Treasurer of the Union, or aim to get a Blue, or act in a production of OUDS, the Oxford University Dramatic Society.

I answered advertisements from Westminster School and Clifton College and was invited for interview at both on successive days.

Westminster was my preferred choice, largely because it was in London. I had always thought of myself as a Londoner, and it would be closer to Oriel. But I had the feeling that they were looking for an oarsman rather than an historian (and in the event they appointed someone with a Rowing Blue), whereas Clifton seemed to be above all looking for an historian. The journey westwards was not as long as I had feared, and the whole area of Clifton around the college was very attractive. So when I didn't hear from Westminster I was glad to get a telegram from Clifton offering me the post there.

While I was getting ready to enter the world of work, even if it was still in an educational institution, Peter Prescott, who had come straight up to Oxford, was preparing to do his National Service. We now went to fewer tutorials together than before, since I was specialising in medieval history while he concentrated on the nineteenth century. But we rowed together in what was called the Schools VIII and he, a Roman Catholic, took me to tea at the Catholic Chaplaincy, where I met Monsignor Ronny Knox, who at the time was translating the autobiography of St Thérèse of Lisieux and is one of the few relatively famous people I have ever met. He talked to me about the problems of translation and spoke to me with a twinkle in his eye about how very difficult it was for a celibate English priest to get under the skin of a young French virgin.

When Peter went down he spent two years in the Royal Artillery, had a brief shot at the world of business in the early 1960s, and then found his niche and his wife with the British Council. An early tour in Paris was followed by postings which included trips to Ulan Bator in Mongolia and to Uzbekistan, and eventually by a distinguished career which culminated in presiding over the British Council's operations in Australia, based in Sydney, and then back to Paris in full charge, with a magnificent house in which to live and entertain, before returning to London in 1990 to run the Arts Division, his last post before retirement.

194

Inevitably we saw each other seldom while he was overseas, but early in the twenty-first century, when we were both retired, it was possible to meet more often, and on a walk along a canal in Warwickshire, when we were staying with Martin and Margaret Henry and had gone with them to hear Britten's *War Requiem* in Coventry Cathedral, he reminisced about rowing on the Thames one evening during one of the Oxford vacations. The Eton Excelsior VIII turned into the home reach and they rowed down a shaft of light with the huge red ball of the sun resting on the horizon behind them. There was no wind. The timing and rhythm of the oars seemed perfect. The boat ran steady and free and the moment seemed timeless. Half a century later he still remembered 'the magic evening when we rowed down the setting sun.' It was a pleasure to be able to spend time with old university friends in that way when we had been separated for so long by the varying demands of our careers.

During my last term in Oxford, and during the Eights Week of 1957 when I was rowing in the Pembroke Schools VIII, Oriel came to the Summer Dance and she enhanced my last days at Oxford just as she had enhanced my last days at Christ's Hospital. She also brought her father to visit his old college. From 1908 until 1912 Edward Gawan Taylor had been a Classics scholar of Pembroke, where his tutor was H. L. Drake, who was still living in the college rooms known as the Almshouses during my time at Pembroke, and regularly dined in Hall.

I took Teddy to see his former tutor. It was the first time he had been back since before the First World War, principally because his career, through both wars and in the years between, had been in India. The two of them reminisced about Teddy's contemporaries. If I understood them correctly, the only survivors of the 1914-18 War from those who matriculated in 1908 were Teddy himself and Mr Justice Finnemore, with whom he had shared rooms when they were undergraduates. As they went through the names there was a grim litany of Ypres, Gallipoli, Neuve Chapelle, the Somme, Paschendaele and so on.

The three years at Oxford all led up to Finals in the last Trinity Term. Those of us who read History took ten three hour papers in less than a week: three on English History, two on European History, two on our Special Subject, one on documents related to a period of Constitutional History, one on Political Theory, and a General Paper. To get a First, not that I thought that at all likely, one needed to get marks with an alpha in them in eight of the ten papers. I got five.

Colin Morris wrote to give me the marks, adding that the examiners had commented, 'We tried some re-reading on Arnold to see whether he might not come up and be vivaed for a First, but it did not succeed enough to give him a run. All the same, his Second is better than a formal II.' So shortly after term was over I went up to Oxford, as did everyone else who had taken Finals, for a viva – that is a *viva voce*, or oral, examination. Mine was effectively a formal one, even if my Second was 'better than a formal II.'

I got back to London in time to take Oriel to the theatre to see *Salad Days*, a delightfully lighthearted musical which had just moved from the Bristol Old Vic to the Vaudeville Theatre in The Strand, and then I had to prepare for the beginning of term at Clifton.

Clifton (1957–1960)

26. Clifton College

◇◇◇◇◇◇◇◇◇◇◇◇◇◇◇◇◇◇◇◇◇◇◇◇◇◇◇◇◇◇◇◇◇◇◇◇

Clifton College was one of a large number of schools founded in the 1860s to meet the increasing demand for the education of the sons of the middle classes. The first Headmaster of Clifton, J.C. Percival, who had been a master under Thomas Arnold at Rugby, started the tradition of Clifton headmasters leaving written advice for future members of staff, and I was particularly struck by the advice of a far later headmaster, H.D.P.Lee, who had been head of Clifton from 1948 until 1954 and was now Headmaster of Winchester College, 'that we should all remember the force of example. Boys will judge a master by what he is and does as much as by what he says.'

Percival's successor from 1879 until 1890 was Canon J.M.Wilson, who also left behind him some particularly wise advice: 'Masters need to be reminded that in every boy before them is a very large unalterable element; and no worrying or severity will affect the unalterable.' So, he concluded, teachers had no right to make miserable those whom they were unable to make good. He quoted Goethe: *So wie Gott sie uns gab, so muss man sie haben und lieben* ('We have to accept them and love them just as God gave them to us').

His advice soaked into me and became part of my way of thinking. Some forty years later, when writing something directed at members of staff in a sixth form college, I suggested that our aim should be 'to get them on our side against a fault instead of siding with the fault against us.' Only some years later did I realise that I had been quoting J.M.Wilson almost word for word. Back in the nineteenth century he had written: 'Get the boy on your side against his fault, and not on the side of the fault against you.'

It was also J.M.Wilson who influenced me to believe in the importance of teachers engaging in some academic work of their own.

'No Master can long maintain his stimulative power unless he is seriously studying some subject for himself', he wrote, 'It is the only way to maintain intellectual thoroughness.' In the 1950s that was a well-established tradition at Clifton, and while I was there I counted eighteen members of staff who had already published something, whether a book on medieval European history, a treatise on *Light*, or a series of French text books.

The Headmaster when I was there was N.G.L.Hammond, a Cambridge academic, whose detailed knowledge of classical Greece had led to his being recruited in 1940, when he was thirty-two, to the S.O.E. (the Special Operations Executive) to serve behind German lines in Greece. After the war, now with a DSO and the Greek Order of the Phoenix, he returned to academic life and became the Senior Tutor of Clare College, Cambridge. When he became the Headmaster of Clifton in 1954 he was engaged in writing a large-scale *History of Greece to 322 BC*, and later he was Professor of Greek at Bristol University from 1962 until his retirement in 1973.

The school was built in a particularly attractive part of Bristol, between the Downs and the Clifton Gorge, and on my first afternoon there I walked up towards the gorge and came round the corner to see the astonishing sight of the Clifton Suspension Bridge, built by Isambard Kingdom Brunel and completed in 1864, just two years after the foundation of the school.

One of the most famous of Old Cliftonians was Sir Henry Newbolt, who in 1892 wrote the poem *Vitaï Lampada*, which I already knew because my father had learnt it by heart to recite at a Hackney Scout Jamboree and had recited it to me much later. The first verse begins: *There's a breathless hush in the Close tonight. Ten to make and the match to win* - and it ends: *But his captain's hand on his shoulder smote. 'Play up! Play up! And play the game!'* The Close referred to is the Clifton College Close where W.G.Grace scored a number of centuries for Gloucestershire, and where John Cleese was a 1st XI fast bowler while I was a master there.

It is surveyed by a statue of another Old Cliftonian, Field Marshal Earl Haig. Once, when there were lines of trenches dug across the Close in order to improve the drainage, Martin Scott, the Head of History, commented to me caustically, though perhaps unfairly, that that was about the nearest Haig had ever got to the trenches.

Something which distinguished Clifton from other public schools was that it had a boarding house for Orthodox Jewish boys. For clever boys from prosperous Orthodox Jewish families Clifton was the one boarding school in England where they could have the experience of an English public school but also keep the Sabbath (from sunset each Friday until sunset on Saturday) – not working during that time and not going into lessons on Saturday morning. Most were clever boys who easily made up the work they missed, and many of the cleverest of the boys doing A level History were Jewish. Polack's House, like all the others, was named after its first housemaster.

In my second year, ten years after the proclamation of the Republic of Israel in May 1948, I gave a talk to the sixth form boys of Polack's House on the Kingdom of Jerusalem, which had been founded when the crusaders took Jerusalem in 1098. To survive, I suggested, it had needed to hold all the land from the sea to the desert, it had needed support, both men and material, from Western Europe, and it had needed the neighbouring Arab states to be disunited. But in 1187, when a Kurdish general, Saladin, united the neighbouring Muslim states, the forces of the Kingdom of Jerusalem were defeated at the battle of the Horns of Hattin. As a significant power in the Middle East it had lasted not quite ninety years.

My contention was that Israel was faced with similar problems. It was smaller than the Kingdom of Jerusalem had been. It needed support from both Europe and the USA, and above all it needed its neighbours to remain disunited. Yet in February of that very year, 1958, Gamal Abdul Nasser, the President of Egypt who had emerged triumphant from the Suez Crisis of 1956, was able to unite Egypt and Syria as the United Arab Republic (the union only lasted until 1961) and threaten the existence of Israel. If Israel was to survive as long as the Kingdom of Jerusalem had, it had not quite another eighty years to go. It was the first of many talks which I gave to sixth-formers over the next forty years about how the past can illuminate the problems of the present.

In my first year I was the form master of 42C and, like all other form masters, was to teach them Latin, English Language and Literature, History, Old Testament and New Testament. That occupied half the week, and in the other half of the week I taught sixth form History, and, with a change in my programme because the Head of Modern Languages had died suddenly in the summer, German to a group in the penultimate year of their O level course.

It was a tough programme for a new teacher. I could manage the German with very little preparation, enjoyed teaching the grammar, and particularly enjoyed introducing them to the poetry of Rainer Maria Rilke. I taught English, both Language and Literature, with virtually no preparation. Teaching the sixth form a period of European History which was new to me was hard work but enjoyable. Teaching the history of the kingdoms of Israel and Judah to a fourth form, when I started knowing nothing, was difficult – even though it was only once a week. Latin was almost every day, and I struggled to keep one page ahead as we worked through a text book, for which, fortunately, I had a crib – i.e. a separate book which had all the Latin exercises correctly translated.

I found discipline difficult with my fourth form. They were neither particularly bright nor particularly dull, and when I knew what I was doing they were reasonably attentive and well behaved. When I was only half in control of the material I was teaching, they got bored, I knew I had lost their attention, and they drifted into misbehaviour. It was a salutary lesson. Discipline had been so rigorous and clear-cut both at Christ's Hospital and in the army that I had never thought of it as a problem. Now I had to work out for myself how to cope. There was little guidance from senior colleagues. The assumption was that one just picked these things up.

Being a schoolmaster in a school such as Clifton was not simply a matter of teaching. The range of activities was vast, and any new and reasonably energetic member of staff soon found himself acquiring a number of responsibilities. I joined John McKeown, the master in charge of rowing, in coaching boats on the river. I took over the Rover Crew, a self-selecting group of the most senior boys in the school, with whom it was possible at the weekends to engage in outdoor activities such as climbing the Clifton Gorge, camping and building an aerial runway.

I joined the CCF (the Combined Cadet Force) and ran a demonstration platoon made up of sixth form boys who were not NCOs. I took over the 'Q' Club, a debating and play-reading society for junior boys (i.e. those aged thirteen to fifteen), which was named after Sir Arthur Quiller-Couch, another Old Cliftonian. I was the master in charge of Fives, taking Fives teams to away matches. It was very time-consuming, especially in the midst of trying to distinguish between final and consecutive clauses before the next Latin lesson. Later I decided that there should be a scientific principle that any new teacher will find that responsibilities expand up to the point of his declining competence.

I sang each week with the Clifton Choral Society under the excellent Director of Music, Evan Prentice, and we rehearsed for the Christmas Concert, at which we sang the school song with a mixture of embarrassment and enthusiasm. Each verse is followed by a chorus which begins with the words *We'll honour yet the school we knew, the best school of all,* and ends *They were great days and jolly days at the best school of all.* The words had been written by Sir Henry Newbolt and they were set to music by Sir Hubert Parry. Few schools can have a school song with so resounding a combination of words and music.

We also rehearsed the Brahms *Requiem* and sang it in English at the splendid St Mary Redcliffe Church the following March.

It was too near the end of the war for us to sing *Ein Deutsches Requiem* in the original German. I later learned that Evan had been a glider pilot in the war – a job in which it was in the nature of things that any flight was one way only. You only got another flight if somehow you managed to land, deliver your load of paratroopers, make it back to England and get another glider.

Some years later, after I had left Clifton, Evan was appointed to a lectureship in Music at Bristol University and, when moving house, went up onto the roof to remove the television ariel. His wife, Ina, went out and called to ask if he would like a cup of coffee. He stepped back and fell to his death, leaving Ina a widow for over forty years and his children, Alison and Ian, orphaned.

During my first year I lived in a small but convenient bed-sitter in Worcester Crescent at the far end of the Close, with a very pleasant family called Meade-King. The school provided all my meals in the refectory of the masters' common room and kept me busy most of the while with teaching and with all the other various activities, so my expenses were few.

My pay in my first year was £700. The starting point on the salary scale was £675 and went up by annual £25 increments to £1000. I was started on the second point of the scale to allow for two years spent in the army. Clifton had its own rather extraordinary system for paying its staff. Everyone, from the headmaster down, was given £100 at the beginning of each term. Then, at the end of each term, each member of staff received one third of his annual salary minus the £100 provided at the start of term.

By the end of my second term I reckoned I had saved enough to buy an engagement ring, and also believed that I could at last ask Oriel to marry me, confident that I was earning enough to keep us both.

27. Engagement

After the Eights Week Summer Dance in my last term at Oxford Oriel and I had agreed that we should see more of each other in future, even if I was in Bristol and she in London, and now we started to make sure of that. She had had enough of the exhausting business of acting in repertory theatre, had completed a secretarial course, found herself a job as a secretary, and had rented a bed-sitter in Hogarth Street near Earls Court Underground Station, only four stops along the Inner Circle line from Paddington, where the trains from Bristol came in.

Because of the way my timetable and other responsibilities were arranged I was able to get away at lunch-time on Thursdays, and every other Thursday would cycle downhill to Temple Meads Station in the centre of Bristol, get a half-day return ticket to London for 16/6 (sixteen shillings and sixpence, or eighty-two and a half pence in decimal currency), arrive in London some time after 4 o'clock, and meet Oriel as she came home from work.

We always had a meal in a nearby Indian restaurant, one of very few Indian restaurants in England in the 1950s. Then we had a couple of hours back at her bed-sitter before I had to leave to catch the train back to Bristol. If I caught a train from Paddington at about 9.30, I would get into Temple Meads before midnight, but then had a long cycle ride uphill all the way back to Clifton. The cycle ride back took four or five times as long as the ride downhill earlier in the day.

Not only were we meeting more frequently than ever in the past; we were also writing more frequently - at least once a week in the autumn of 1957. We had both always kept all the letters we sent each other, and we continued to do so, so that more than half a century later, after they had sat in a box in the loft and gone from one house to another, it was possible to re-read them and catch a glimpse of ourselves back in the mid-twentieth century.

Sometimes the letters were long. In the middle of my first Autumn Term at Clifton I wrote a particularly long one, starting by telling her about the Bristol Old Vic, about the merits of Terence Rattigan as a playwright and about John Gielgud acting in one of Rattigan's play, *The Browning Version*. I went on to describe getting a letter from a girl I had known a little at Oxford, a rather attractive, half-French, fellow-historian from Somerville College, who had written to tell me that she had given up her plan to go to the USA after Finals and get a job as a long-distance lorry driver, and instead was now doing a secretarial course and living in South Kensington.

I wrote about going caving in the Mendips with two colleagues and a group of new boys. I described my landlady, Lavender Meade-King, and her small daughter Sarah, who brought me the post in the mornings. I described talking in the evenings with Alister Cox, a classicist who had joined the staff at the same time as me, and how we puzzled over whether or not it was possible to hear a clock stop chiming.

I went on to write about imagining being with Oriel in her room in Earls Court, and I quoted *The Song of Solomon* ('How fair and how pleasant art thou, O love, for delights!') and poetry by Sir Charles Sedley ('All that in woman is adored in thy dear self I find'). I wrote of the difficulty of dragging myself away from thoughts of her so that I could bring the letter to a close. But close it I eventually did, after twenty-two pages.

In her reply she agreed with me about Rattigan and went on to describe what a pleasure it had been to meet him when he came backstage to congratulate her after she had been acting in one of his plays, *The Sleeping Prince*. She had played the part of the young actress who, in the era before the First World War, had captivated a foreign prince. It was the part played in the film by Marilyn Monroe, while the prince was played by Lawrence Olivier.

She then went on, 'I studied your bit of news about the rather attractive, half-French Oxford girl, but I'm not jealous yet' and told me about her new job as secretary to a married man who was the managing director of a mailing company, good-looking, about thirty-five years old and flirtatious. He was apparently already asking her to go out to dinner with him. She also wondered if being a schoolmaster would make me different. 'I hope you're terribly bossy and push me around. I need it, because I'm getting terribly spoilt.'

Sometimes the letters were very short. In one I simply said that I was already half an hour late for supper after being delayed down at the river mending a boat, but I just wanted to tell her again that I loved her and would post the letter, brief as it was, on the way to the masters' refectory. There were, of course, no mobile 'phones in those days, and neither Oriel nor I had a 'phone in our room.

Early in the Easter holidays of 1958, when Oriel was at home in Orchard Road in Shalford with her parents, I went there with the firm intention of asking her to marry me. We went for a walk, which should have provided a good opportunity for a romantic proposal, but before long it started to rain, and the shortest way back, if we were not to be soaked, was over the railway footbridge near Shalford Station.

I did not want to leave proposing till another day (after all, we had known each other for more than six years, and now at last I was in a position to propose), nor did I want to ask her at her home when we would not be alone, so just short of the footbridge I rather abruptly asked her to stop and then asked her to marry me.

'Just a moment', she said. But there was little time for thought, for the rain was getting steadily stronger, so a moment later she said 'Yes', and then we ran the rest of the way back, arriving at Brook Cottage rather bedraggled.

I went to see Teddy, who expressed himself delighted, but explained that, living on an Indian Civil Service pension, he was not in a position to provide Oriel with a dowry. I assured him that it was simply his daughter that I wanted and that I thought of dowries as something that had happened centuries ago in the mists of history. Teddy called Nora. 'Tea-pot! Come and hear Osie's news.'

Once her mother had also approved of our plans, Oriel and I decided to go up to London together as soon as possible to choose an engagement ring. We spent a couple of days looking at rings with a central emerald and a diamond on either side, and eventually found one which seemed perfect in a jeweller's shop in the Burlington Arcade off Piccadilly.

Once we were engaged the rate at which we wrote to each other increased further. Over the fifteen months of our engagement we wrote to each other on average every other day. To anyone other than the writer and the recipient, the letters would seem boringly repetitive, with their protestations of love and complaints at being apart. One of my letters rather typically began, 'My darling, I love you, and as I was walking back to my room thinking how wonderful life is and how wonderful you are, I decided that I must write and tell you.'

It goes on like that for a couple of pages before ending, 'You are too wonderful, and I am lost in love, desire and adoration.' Her reply was less dramatic but typical of her. It began, 'Thank you for that lovely letter. I love getting the post on Monday mornings', and she went on to tell me that one of her friends had given her the secret of a successful marriage ('Marriage is a matter of give and take, darling. If he won't give you all you want, take it'), before ending, 'I love you, I miss you, and so I shall go to bed and think about you until I fall asleep.'

I was entranced by her casual and cheerful light-heartedness and the way she delighted in people and incidents around her, all of which she had been used to sharing with Chloë and now would share with me as well. She told me of a girl sitting next to her on

208

the tube reading one of my letters over her shoulder. 'So when I needed to turn the page over,' wrote Oriel, 'I took off my left glove so that she could see my engagement ring.'

She and Chloë were invited to go to Manchester for a personal appearance as the Toni twins. She was to wave a bottle of Toni perm and sing, 'It's odour free, it's frizz free. It makes the boys all look at me.' Chloe was to look sad and sing, 'Oh sister dear, I envy you. I wish I had a Toni too.' They were not sure whether to be disappointed or relieved when nothing came of it.

We looked forward to going on holiday to Salcombe in Devon, where the Meade-Kings had invited us to spend a week with them at their holiday cottage. 'Just think', she wrote, 'In a week we'll be in Devon together. What fun!' Then she reflected that if we had got married soon after we met, 'we could have four children by now, and she even speculated on what their names might have been. She enjoyed words and their associations. 'Isn't 'bride' a beautiful word?' she wrote. 'To think that in another nine months I shall be your bride!'

Throughout our engagement she wrote to me about what she was reading. She had first discovered Browning at school. Now she was reading his dramatic monologues and she introduced me to them. Her favourite was *My Last Duchess*, in which a wicked old Duke of Ferrara describes to a visiting envoy how and why he had his last duchess killed. Later I learn it by heart and still know it.

Oriel wrote about Alan Paton's *Cry, the Beloved Country* and Evelyn Waugh's *Decline and Fall*, which a friend had given her when he heard that she was marrying a schoolmaster, and Stanley Kauffmann's *The Philanderer*, which had caused a sensation when its publication in England by Secker and Warburg in 1953 led to the prosecution (and acquittal) of Frederic Warburg for obscenity in 1954.

She read *Anna Karenina,* and I, foolishly, was rather cross with her because she had no sympathy for Karenin. She went on to

War and Peace and decided that, although it was a work of genius, it did not match *Anna Karenina*, because Tolstoy drifted away into boring reflections on Freemasonry and History. I was and am still inclined to agree with her. She was horrified by Golding's *The Lord of the Flies* and wanted to know why I said it could only have been written by a schoolmaster. She was moved by the letters of Heloise and Abelard and by *The Diary of Anne Frank*.

We found time to go to the theatre together to see Peter O'Toole in Shaw's *Man and Superman* at the Bristol Old Vic and in the holidays went to see John Osborne's plays, *Look Back in Anger* and *The Entertainer,* as well as *The Long and the Tall and the Short* by Willis Hall, at the Royal Court in London. We felt rather daring when we went to a production of *Lysistrata* by Aristophanes, since the play was all about the women of Athens ending the Peloponnesian War by withholding sex from their husbands until in the end the men of both Athens and Sparta were so sexually desperate that they agreed a peace treaty and their women returned to them.

Oriel wrote to me about being invited to the Sandown Races by her boss and declining to go. I replied rather stuffily that I felt there was something wrong with a married man taking an attractive secretary to the races in office time. Later, when we were together, she said that she thought she might go out to dinner with him one evening ('After all, he is rather attractive.') and my reaction was, 'But he's over thirty!' At the time that seemed impossibly old.

I loved being with Oriel, I loved getting her letters, and I enjoyed the time when Sarah Meade-King, bringing the post, told me that she thought my fiancée was really very silly because she had written two letters on the same day and sent them by the same post. Nearly sixty years later, when writing this, and thirty-five years after her death, I went through all those letters, both hers and mine, and remembered how much they had meant to us. But I also realised how little they would mean to anyone else, so I destroyed them.

210

28. Dakyns House

When I got back to Clifton at the end of the Easter Holidays of 1958, after getting engaged, one of the first people to speak to me was Yngve Lidell, the housemaster of Dakyns House. Yngve was the younger brother of the BBC newsreader Alvar Lidell, whom I remembered from the war ('This is the six o'clock news and this is Alvar Lidell reading it'). Their names came from having had a Norwegian mother, and they were bi-lingual in English and Norwegian.

Yngve had joined the staff of Clifton in the 1930s, served as a young officer in the school OTC, or Officers' Training Corps, volunteered for military service as war approached in 1939, and filled in a form on which he noted that he could speak Norwegian. Then he returned to teaching Maths until March of 1940, when the school porter arrived at his classroom with a telegram instructing him to report to London in uniform the next day.

From London he was sent by train to the north of Scotland. There, still wearing his Clifton College OTC cap badge and shoulder flashes, he joined a Royal Navy ship, set to sea, and eventually found himself off the coast of Norway in the far North, near Narvik. But the Germans had got there first. So his ship sailed away again. By now he was in the army, in which he served with distinction, and at the end of the war he was a colonel and had been awarded the DSO (the Distinguished Service Order).

He returned to Clifton to the job he was doing before the war as a house tutor, or under-housemaster, and teaching Maths. Before long he was appointed by Desmond Lee, then Headmaster of Clifton and later Head of Winchester, to be the housemaster of Dakyns House, and now he asked me to join him in Dakyns as his house tutor the following September.

I was pleased to be asked and would have liked to be able to accept immediately. But there was a problem. It was a job for a bachelor, living in. I explained to Yngve that I had just got engaged and he suggested that I talk to Oriel to see if she would agree to my being a house tutor for just one year. It would mean putting the wedding off from the time we had planned, April 1959, until the beginning of August. We had first met back in December 1951, so in the light of that waiting an extra three and a half months did not seem too great a sacrifice. Oriel agreed.

The following September I found myself living in Dakyns House and looking after the boys' pocket money. I kept a lot of change in my pocket, as well as a notebook in which I recorded when they asked for a shilling or half-a-crown. I coached house teams in the afternoons, took house prayers in the evenings, and produced end-of-term entertainments.

It continued to be possible to go to London every other Thursday, and although there must have been some variation in what we did each fortnight, the way I remember it is that Oriel and I met when she got back from work, went to the local Indian restaurant, ate poppadums and a curry, followed by lychees and coffee, and then went back to her bed-sitter in Hogarth Street in Earls Court for an hour or two before I had to set off on the return journey.

Once we were engaged Oriel regularly went to see my parents, which I could seldom, if ever, do during term time, though I still lived with them during the school holidays. Shortly before Christmas in 1958 they gave her an expensive cut glass bowl. She took it with her to an office Christmas party on her way home, enjoyed the party, drank rather more than she was used to, and consequently dropped it and smashed it on the way to the station. For the next few years, whenever my parents came to see us, we had to think up excuses for why it was not out on the table.

One pleasure of life in Dakyns was that on most Saturday evenings Yngve would invite boys with an interest in music to come along to his very large sitting room, where he would play a wide range of records, introducing each one with a brief comment. What made it unusual was that he encouraged the boys to bring a book along, so on most Saturdays I would go along as well and either read a book or mark essays, while being introduced to the music of Sibelius or Delius or Grieg.

Yngve was a wise and kindly man, for whom I came to have a high regard, but he could also seem stern and forbidding to teenagers, so it should not have seemed surprising when the house prefects came to see me, rather than going straight to the housemaster, to say that they were worried about the extent of homosexuality in the house. I volunteered to have a word with Yngve, assuring them that he was someone I trusted entirely and pointing out that I could do nothing without appearing to be trying to usurp his authority. So I went to see Yngve, and he in turn suggested that I should bring them along to see him and encourage them to talk to him.

They agreed with some trepidation and, when it came to the point, found it difficult to say anything very explicitly, but conveyed that they were worried. 'Well', he said, 'do you mean buggery or just mutual masturbation?' One of them had the courage to ask, 'What's buggery sir?' Without batting an eyelid Yngve replied: 'The insertion of the erect male member into the anus of another person.' 'Oh, no sir!' they said, 'Nothing like that.' 'Good!' replied Yngve. 'In that case I don't suppose you've much to bother about.'

'Oh, thank you sir', they said, and went away much relieved. To that I should add that I was particularly glad that one of the boys had had the courage to ask what buggery was. At the age of twenty-five and engaged to be married, I didn't know until Yngve told them. I also wondered how many housemasters would have dealt with the issue so well. I enjoyed being his house tutor and I valued working with him and learning from him.

213

I told Oriel about the house (she was interested to hear that both Michael Redgrave and Trevor Howard had been boys in Dakyns), about winning the house rugger cup, about practising for the school singing competition and about planning an end-of-term entertainment. I told her about reading Edgar Allan Poe to the youngest boys in the house and finding that at the age of twelve or thirteen they decided that they would prefer *Winnie the Pooh*.

She looked forward to seeing my room and hoped she could be there while boys were coming in and out and she could watch me being stern with them. 'Oh darling, what fun!' Yngve invited her to come and stay for a long week-end, and in the event she came to a rehearsal by some junior boys of the melodrama I was producing for the end-of-term entertainment and gave the sort of professional advice which transformed it from something mediocre into something we could be proud of.

We continued to write about a whole range of things. In October of 1958 she told me of Chloë's distress at breaking up with a boyfriend whose company she enjoyed but whom she did not find at all attractive. He had fallen desperately in love with her and was bitter about her rejection of him when he wanted to take the relationship further. I wrote back: 'Poor Chloë! The trouble really is that she's too attractive. That adoring, come-hither, soft and dewy-eyed look of hers attracts men to her like moths to a candle. But you should tell her that she would be in a far worse position if she kept falling in love with men who were not in the least attracted by her.'

Chloë and Oriel had been were similar enough in appearance to do the *Which twin has the Toni?* advertisement, but they were not identical twins, and to anyone who knew them there was no possibility of mistaking one for the other. By comparison with Oriel, Chloë, by a few minutes the elder of the two, seemed to me dreamy, soft and wilting. I could quite see why she attracted large numbers of adoring young men around her, though it was less clear why she sometimes seemed dreamily unaware of their attentions. Oriel, by comparison, was altogether more acerbic and assured in her manner.

Later that same month I was commenting in one of my letters on events in the wider world: 'And now there's a new pope - called John XXIII of all things! There was a John XXIII back in 1410-15, but he had previously been a pirate in the Mediterranean, led a band of mercenary soldiers in Italy, lived in Rome with his brother's wife, and reputedly ravished two hundred other women, including married ladies and nuns. So I suppose they may prefer to forget him. Anyway, there were two others at the time claiming to be the true pope, so now they will probably say that the previous John XXIII was not really a pope at all but only an anti-pope.' That is indeed what happened, and the new John XXIII was a significantly more attractive figure than the previous one.

Oriel liked to imagine that other girls found me attractive, while at the same time knowing that I was hers and that they couldn't have me. 'I enjoy being jealous and possessive', she wrote, 'so long as I don't need to be' and went on, 'You must write and tell me that you miss me and that you like me in my new trousers and that you think I'm pretty, and you must be stern with the boys and not too friendly with any girls.'

Once, in the flurry of correspondence, I got a letter to an old boyfriend of hers from the theatre. He had written to her to say that he would be in London and wondered if they could meet. She replied saying she would be pleased to see him, but, I was pleased to see, explained that she could not invite him to her room because the electric fire was so inadequate, and suggested somewhere else to meet. By mistake she put it in an envelope addressed to me. I cannot remember if at the same time she sent a letter intended for me to him.

John, meanwhile, was still in Cambridge. For a year while in the army he had been learning Russian at Cambridge, based just up the road in Newmarket. Then, during the three years when I was at Oxford, he was at Sidney Sussex College, Cambridge, reading Modern Languages (a combination of German, French and Russian) and ended up with a First. By then he had decided to become a clergyman, so he stayed on in Cambridge for yet another three years, took another degree, this time in Theology, and worked for the General Ordination Certificate at Westcott House.

At times he would talk about his course, and I remember hearing two particularly wise pieces of advice for young men starting off as curates, from John Hapgood, the Vice-Principal of Westcott, who was later Archbishop of York. He recommended distinguishing between those temptations one should stand and fight and those from which one should run away. Sexual temptations, he suggested, are in the second category. If you stand and fight them, it is all the more enjoyable when you give in. The second piece of advice was a warning to avoid pious young women who might see a curate as less dangerous and threatening than most men, but nevertheless, somehow still a man.

As the summer of 1959 drew on and our wedding drew near Oriel wrote about imagining me dragging her about and throwing her onto a bed – though in reality she would never for a moment have stood for my treating her like that. Then she wrote that she was 'in such a state that I'd like to make you hate me and fight me, and then, if you didn't kiss me better, I'd kill you. I hate you and I love you.' Neither she nor I knew at the time that she was quoting Catullus (*Odi et amo*), and she ended the letter with a 'Grr' and a 'Sss'. She had a talent for adopting the persona of a cat, whether flirting or fighting - and could even evoke it in writing.

29. Getting married

During the two years between coming down from Oxford in the summer of 1957 and getting married on 1st August 1959 I got to know Oriel's family increasingly well. Teddy, who had been born in October 1889, was 68 when we got engaged, but had already been retired from the Indian Civil Service for fifteen years as a result of a detached retina, which had needed surgery back in England in 1943.

He was the eldest of the three sons of a judge in Cumberland, had won a classics scholarship to Pembroke College, Oxford, and had gone up in 1908 to read *Literae Humaniores*, or Mods and Greats, the peculiar Oxford name for its Classics course. While at Oxford he ran for the university, getting his Blue running against Cambridge, winning the three-mile race in under fifteen minutes, and becoming President of the Oxford University Athletics Club.

In 1912, after completing the four year degree course, he was successful in the open competition for entry to the Indian Civil Service and then had a couple of years of probation and preparation before sailing for India. He was invited to run in the 1912 Stockholm Olympics, but the Olympics lacked the prestige they have today, so, busy with his preparations for India, he turned down the invitation – something he regretted later.

Some time later Pandit Jawaharlal Nehru, the first prime minister of an independent India, remembered the description of the Holy Roman Empire by Lord Bryce as 'neither holy nor Roman nor an empire' and rather unkindly said of the ICS that it was 'neither Indian nor civil nor a service.' But in the early twentieth century it was an impressive organisation in which about a thousand Englishmen, the 'heaven-born', ruled an empire which embraced the territories which today are India, Pakistan, Bangla Desh (East

Bengal), Myanmar (Burma), Sri Lanka (Ceylon), and South Yemen, where was situated the important staging and coaling station of Aden.

Teddy sailed for India in July of 1914. The Austrian Arch-duke Franz Ferdinand, heir to the throne of the Austro-Hungarian Empire, had been assassinated at the end of the previous month. But there was trouble in the Balkans every summer without it necessarily leading to catastrophe, so there was no widespread expectation of war, as there was twenty-five years later. Nevertheless, while Teddy was en route to India (and it was a long sea voyage in those days), the First World War began. By the time he arrived there the British Expeditionary Force was in action on the continent of Europe.

Teddy's two younger brothers, Frank and Norman, were both up at Sidney Sussex College, Cambridge. They went in turn from Cambridge into the army and were commissioned in the York and Lancaster Regiment. Frank was killed on the Somme in July of 1916. Norman was killed on patrol near Ypres in April 1917. There were three sisters as well. One married a clergyman. The other two remained unmarried. The only one of Teddy's siblings whom I met, Auntie May, had worked for a while as a secretary to Lloyd George, and when she died, shortly after Oriel and I were married, she left Oriel £500 and a rather beautiful oak rug chest.

Teddy survived the First World War because he was, in Kipling's words, 'quartered safe out here' in India, but he lived for more than another half century regretting the loss of his two younger brothers. Oriel, who seldom went to church, always made a point of going on Remembrance Sunday to remember the two uncles she had never known.

The titles, or ranks, by which members of the Indian Civil Service were designated, were based on the taxation system. Thus at first Teddy was an Assistant Collector (of Taxes), though the job also involved a whole range of other functions, such as acting as a

magistrate and even as a big game hunter when a man-eating tiger
was loose in his area (I still have the tiger skin). Later he was a
Collector, and eventually the Commissioner in what was then
Bombay.

When he had been out in India for about fifteen years, he came
back to England on a long six month leave, quite deliberately
looking for a wife, and that was when he met an Edinburgh girl,
Nora, who was twelve years younger than himself and living in
Chelsea. After a few months they were married and then, out in
India, their first child, June, was born in 1931. Michael followed
in the spring of 1934, and then in July 1935 the twins, Chloë and
Oriel, were born in Karachi, on the south coast of what is now
Pakistan.

As small children they lived in Ahmadabad, going up to Srinagar
in Kashmir in the hot weather, and then they moved to Bombay
and lived in what was effectively a palace with the extraordinary
but delightfully English name of *Sea View*, with two or three
dozen servants, including *punka wallahs,* whose job was to pull
the cords which moved large fans to keep some air circulating
through the house.

For part of the time in her childhood Oriel would play in the compound with Chloë and with the servants' children, Anji, Gunpat,
Jagiar and so on, and for another part of the time she would be in
the main house where English government officials and Indian
members of the Congress Party visited. It was remembered in the
family that when a senior member of the ICS, Sir Humphrey Gibb,
arrived at the house while her parents were still upstairs, Oriel as a
small child, trying to emulate her mother as a good hostess,
greeted him with the words, 'Good evening, Gibb. Would you like
a gin?'

Teddy spent the whole of his working life in India. At one time a
young man called Moraji Desai worked for him in the civil service.
Then Desai became an influential figure in the independence

movement, and later, when the time came for the English members of the ICS to help with preparing the country for independence, Teddy found himself working for Moraji Desai, who was eventually the fourth prime minister of India, from 1977 until 1979 - long after Teddy had left India.

In retirement Teddy still remembered with unhappiness the problem he faced repeatedly as demands for independence grew and riots threatened. It was if and when to call out the military to maintain order. If he called them out before anyone was killed, it was an over-reaction. If he left it until a riot had become serious, he had not acted early enough. He continued in retirement to worry about it, always uncertain about whether or not he had made the right decisions. His last years in India were not the happiest.

A fortnight before Oriel and I got married my cousin Beverley married John West, whom she had met while they were in their teens and he was playing for the Tottenham Hotspurs A team. He seemed to have a promising future as a footballer before him, though it was before the days when successful footballers earned wealth beyond the dreams of avarice, but it was cut short by a knee injury, so he learnt the trade of an upholsterer and then ran a successful upholstery business.

Their wedding in Bethnal Green, or rather the party afterwards, introduced Oriel to a previously unknown world. We all sang 'Knees up Mother Brown', danced the Hokey Cokey and did the Lambeth Walk. Oriel danced with the milkman in his braces and thought it the best party she had ever been to.

When it was time for our own wedding, in the parish church in Shalford on 1st August 1959, John was my best man. Sadly Chloë could not be a bridesmaid because she was away in Jordan as a Foreign Office secretary, so June, only recently married herself, was a matron-of-honour. Oriel's brother Michael, home from the sea, was one of the ushers and my cousin Christian, in his Christ's Hospital uniform, and with one year to go at school before going up to Cambridge to read Classics, was the other usher.

*With Oriel on our wedding day, 1st August 1959, standing
outside the church of St Mary the Virgin, Shalford.*

A group wedding photograph, with, from the left, my cousin Christian, who acted as an usher and had one year still to go at Christ's Hospital, my father and my mother, the groom and the bride, my brother John, who was best man, Oriel's mother and father, her sister June and June's husband, Tony Cribb.

The reception was in a marquee in the garden of Brook Cottage, and afterwards Oriel and I went off in my father's Ford Popular, which he kindly lent to us for a couple of weeks, to spend our first night as a married couple in a hotel in Marlborough and the next week on the north Cornish coast at Trebarwith Sands.

A fortnight after our own wedding we went to the wedding in Wargrave of an old school friend, Bob Finch, and his fiancée, Sue, as we drove back from Bristol to return the Ford Popular to my father. Bob had read Chemistry at Reading University, where he met Sue, who was reading English Literature and was astonished at how Bob could spot the biblical allusions in the works of literature she was studying. It was not that he was particularly religious. It was that he had been soaked in Bible readings at chapel in the

*Leaving the reception at Brook Cottage, Orchard Road,
Shalford, a few hours after our wedding.*

mornings and at house prayers in the evenings, through eight years at Christ's Hospital.

He went on to teach Chemistry at Hurstpierpoint and Uppingham, but then spent most of his career as the education liaison officer for I.C.I. in the days when the Imperial Chemical Industry was one of the largest and most successful businesses in the country, and wrote entertaining articles for the back page of the T.E.S., *The Times Educational Supplement.* I remember one about parents boasting of their children's achievements in Christmas letters until one year Pandora isn't mentioned and one is left to guess if she has been expelled or is pregnant or on drugs. The article ended with the advice of a French philosopher: 'Be modest. It is the kind of pride least likely to offend.'

In Clifton Oriel and I had found a cheap basement flat to rent in Worrall Road, under the Downs, and very shortly after settling in I was off to do my fortnight's Army Emergency Reserve training – as it happens, for the last time. The evening I got back Oriel provided me with roast beef and Yorkshire pudding, the next evening with an Indian curry, and the one after that with a Chinese meal. She had spent much of the previous fortnight practising cooking and had learnt a lot in a short while.

She had also been out to find herself a job with a secretarial agency doing temporary work. Our aim was to save as much as possible during the year with a view to buying our own house, so we spent as little as possible and saved all we could. Our one occasional indulgence was to go to a Chinese restaurant we had discovered near the top of Park Street in central Bristol.

Sometimes we spent the evening with friends, such as Alister Cox, with whom I had spent a lot of time in my first year before we both went off to be house tutors, he to School House and I to Dakyns. As bachelors we had often eaten breakfast, lunch and dinner together in the masters' refectory and talked interminably about life, the universe and everything. Now he was engaged to a girl called Janet, while I was newly married to Oriel.

We also saw quite a lot of Gilly and John McKeown, a young married couple who were particularly welcoming and helpful to Oriel. John was already the housemaster of North Town House and I knew him mainly because he ran the Clifton Boat Club and I helped him with the coaching. He stayed at Clifton throughout his career and I became godfather to their elder son, Simon. We always kept in touch, and still, after sixty years, with Oriel long dead and John more recently dead, I still go to Bristol from time to time to see Gilly.

Back in 1959 I found that I loved married life. For the previous fifteen years, since the age of ten, I had lived largely in institutions: eight years at Christ's Hospital, two in the army, three at Pembroke and two at Clifton. I had slept on my own, eaten meals communally, and most of the while been quite happy. But I had long sensed that there was something better. Now Oriel and I could sit on a sofa together in the evening, eat a simple meal of bread and liver sausage with a mug of instant coffee, spend the night together, and wake up looking forward to the next day and night.

30. Changing jobs

In the mid-1950s John was reading Modern Languages at Cambridge, I was reading History at Oxford, Oriel's elder sister June, who had trained as a ballet dancer, was dancing in musicals, her brother Michael was a junior officer on the Orient line, and Oriel, after eighteen months at RADA, was acting in rep. Chloë, who had gone to RADA with Oriel, had left early and eventually, after doing a secretarial course, had joined the Foreign Office. She and Oriel remained close, sharing with each other thoughts, hopes and fears they would not easily have shared with others, but once Chloë was posted to Amman, the capital of Jordan, and then to Singapore, they were separated for months at a time and missed each other.

June by then had had enough of bar exercises and touring and decided to join the WRNS (the Women's Royal Naval Service), in which before long she was commissioned and had a job touring girls' schools talking about a career in the WRNS, pronounced 'Wrens'. Then, at about the time that Oriel and I got engaged, she met a young officer of the Royal Electrical and Mechanical Engineers called Tony Cribb, who had read Engineering at Imperial College, London, joined the army for his National Service, and while doing his National Service had transferred to the regular army.

Tony had served in the Korean War and suffered a breakdown after some particularly horrific experiences after the Chinese crossed the Yalu River. But now he appeared to be entirely recovered, and in July 1958 the *Daily Telegraph* recorded the engagement of Captain Anthony Cribb REME to Third Officer June Gawan Taylor WRNS. They got married shortly afterwards, with both Chloë and Oriel as June's bridesmaids.

Their brother Michael had given up his relatively easy job as a junior officer on the Orient Line and was the mate on a cable-laying ship in the Atlantic. It was a hard life but well paid, and with the money he made he was able to come ashore and work for his Master's Certificate. He met and married a girl called Anne, and shortly afterwards commanded a ship for the first and only time in his life when he took a new tug with a skeleton crew on a one way trip out to Australia.

He arrived in Sydney to newspaper headlines about his voyage, because somewhere in the middle of the Pacific he had run into a typhoon, and the newspapers were celebrating the survival of this small boat which had been right at the centre of the storm. Anne joined him in Australia and he found a job in Sydney as an assistant harbour master. He worked first of all part-time and later full time at an Economics degree course, got a First, and then worked for the Treasury of the Commonwealth of Australia. He and Anne settled in Canberra, and ever afterwards visited England every few years to keep in touch with friends and family.

It was during my last year at Oxford that Oriel decided that she had had enough of the theatre. Like Chloe she did a secretarial course, after which she rented a bed-sitter in Earls Court and found a job as a secretary. Once we were engaged she quite often used to go to South Woodford to see my parents, got on with them increasingly well and enjoyed her visits. My father had always liked her and before long my mother found that they had a never-ending supply of things to talk about: books, plays, poetry and the foibles of men.

In my second year at Clifton, while I was the house tutor in Dakyns House and at the same time engaged to Oriel, my teaching programme was very different from my first year. It included a lot more sixth form history. I was now the form master of the second year of the History Sixth and was teaching an A level special subject on *The reign of Henry II* – something central to my special interest in the twelfth century. That was the aspect of teaching I found most worthwhile and it was where I felt that my future lay.

The headmaster was not so sure. Nor, apparently, were John Thorn, the Head of History when I was appointed, and his successor, Martin Scott, who had shared the sixth form teaching of history at Clifton with him for about the last ten years and probably saw me as an inadequate substitute for John, who shortly afterwards became the Headmaster of Repton School and then the Headmaster of Winchester College, with Martin as his Second Master, responsible for the scholars' house.

I was somewhat overawed by both of them and never had a close personal or working relationship with either. Nor did I know the headmaster at all well. One way or another the three of them decided (though who really made the decision I never knew) that my future at Clifton should be as a form master rather than as a sixth form history specialist, and the headmaster assured me that in another ten or twelve years, assuming everything went well, I could expect to be a housemaster.

I suppose I had created the problem for myself. As a house tutor who coached house rugby teams and school boats on the river, ran the Rover crew, was the master in charge of Rugby Fives, served in the CCF and ran the 'Q' society, I looked more like a future housemaster than a future head of the history department.

It was not what I wanted to do. I found teaching medieval history to A level students very satisfying. I was increasingly interested in teaching them how to organise their thoughts and write good history essays. Teaching Latin to fourteen year olds, on the other hand, was something I would do conscientiously while I had to but would be pleased to abandon as soon as possible.

With every year I remained as a form master my credentials as an academic historian would be eroded. I was going to have to look for another job before I got stuck firmly in a rut where I had no wish to remain. I liked Clifton and would have been happy to stay as a history specialist, but I did not want to spend years as a form master and I had no aspiration to be a housemaster.

I got into the habit of looking in the T.E.S. (the Times Educational Supplement) to see what jobs were available. As a married man I was no longer a suitable candidate for the sort of job I had applied for at Westminster and at Clifton when first looking for one. I considered applying to be a lecturer in medieval history at the recently founded Keele University, or to be a lecturer in military history at the Royal Military Academy, Sandhurst, but in the event applied to neither. I still thought of myself as essentially a schoolmaster and perhaps, I thought, I might be well enough qualified and have sufficient experience for it to be reasonable to apply for a job as head of a history department in a grammar school. So I did.

One advantage I had when looking for another job while I was at Clifton was that all of our A level candidates who had taken History in the summer of 1959 had done best in the Special Subject paper on *The Reign of Henry II*, which was what I had taught them. They took three papers, English History, European History and a special subject, and in those days, instead of getting a grade, we were given their marks for each paper. Every one of them got his highest mark for the special subject, and that was something Nick Hammond made a point of commenting on when writing me a reference.

Shortly afterwards I was encouraged to be offered the post of Head of History at King Edward VI School, Bath, but though it was a very attractive direct grant grammar school in a beautiful town, it was very small and I would have been teaching history to all the classes from the age of eleven upwards. So I turned it down. At about the same time I applied to and was interviewed for the post of Head of History at two larger grammar schools, the Priory School, Shrewsbury, and Marling School, Stroud, at both of which I was interviewed and in both cases was disappointed not to be appointed.

After that I applied to Quintin School, a voluntary controlled grammar school in St John's Wood, London. Meanwhile, out of the blue a letter arrived from Desmond Lee, the former headmaster of

Clifton and John Thorn's predecessor as headmaster of Winchester, asking if I would like to be considered for a post as a form master at Winchester. I think Yngve must have written to him to tell him that I was looking for another job. It was tempting, simply because Winchester was reputed to be such a particularly good school, but it faced me with the problem that I was intending to leave Clifton precisely because I wanted to be a history specialist rather than a form master. Before either he or I had to make up our minds I was offered the post at Quintin School and accepted it. So now Oriel and I needed to think about where to live and see if we could buy a house of our own.

It was at that time, in the summer of 1960, as we were getting ready to leave Clifton and move to London, that John met a young German girl at a youth conference in Lausanne. Anneliese had been born in 1934 in the small German town of Eisleben, Martin Luther's birthplace, where her father was a schoolmaster. During the war he served as an infantry officer on the Eastern Front and was killed in the Ukraine in 1944 by a grenade splinter.

After the war Anneliese and her mother, whom she called *Mutti*, and who was to be a widow for the next fifty years, found themselves in the Russian zone of occupation, later the German Democratic Republic, *das Deutsche Demokratische Republik*, or *DDR*. As the daughter of someone who had been both an army officer and a schoolmaster, she was not deemed suitable for any further education, which was for workers and the children of workers. So she had to become a worker and spent the next seven or eight years as a children's nurse.

In her early twenties, either because the administration of the *DDR* was not efficient enough to register and remember that she was unsuitable, or because she had now qualified as a worker, she was able to go to the University of Halle, where she opted to study Musicology, partly because she enjoyed music, but principally because it was the least political of the subjects open to her and thus the least likely to get her into trouble.

Nevertheless, when she joined a student Christian organisation she did get into trouble. She was arrested and questioned, and although she was only imprisoned overnight, it was sufficiently frightening that shortly afterwards she and her mother decided to try to get to the West. It was illegal to do so, but in 1960, the year before the Berlin Wall was built to keep East German citizens in, it was easier to get out than it was to be for nearly the next thirty years until the wall was eventually pulled down in 1989.

Anneliese and her mother left everything at home as if they were intending to come home after a day's shopping trip in Berlin. Even Anneliese's wristwatch was left at the mender. Once in the Russian sector of Berlin it was possible to walk across to West Berlin, and there Anneliese was able to enrol to continue her Musicology studies at the University of Berlin – not the ancient Humboldt University, which was in the Russian sector, but at the new, so-called Free University of Berlin.

It happened that in the summer of 1960 a European youth conference for Christian students was planned to take place at Lausanne in Switzerland, and representatives were expected from all the East European countries, with the exception of Albania. But the day before the East German representatives were due to leave, their permission to travel was withdrawn, and so, since Anneliese had only recently arrived in the West, she was asked to take their place.

At the conference she met John, who had just finished his training for the ministry at Cambridge and was at Lausanne as an interpreter before being ordained deacon and taking up his first job as a curate. On returning from Lausanne he was off to the north to the parish of Holy Trinity, Millhouses, in Sheffield. Millhouses in Sheffield sounded to me, as a southerner, as if it would be entirely foreign territory, with factories and mills and smoke and clogs, so it was something of a surprise to discover later, when I visited him there, that it was a very prosperous, leafy suburb of Sheffield, with beautiful countryside only a short walk away.

There he spent one year as a deacon and two further years after being ordained priest in 1961. Meanwhile Anneliese and her mother had moved to Hamburg. She and John were only able to meet infrequently, but in 1963, as John was coming to the end of his curacy, they got married. By then I had been at Quintin School and Oriel and I had been living at Strawberry Hill in Twickenham for three years.

31. Married life

◇◇◇◇◇◇◇◇◇◇◇◇◇◇◇◇◇◇◇◇◇◇◇◇◇◇◇◇◇◇◇◇

It is sometimes suggested that a good basis on which to build a happy and successful married life is a shared background, with the same religion, a similar attitude to politics, and shared interests and activities. That may be so as a general principle. It was not so with us. We were different in almost every way – not dramatically so, but enough for us to notice it and find it interesting.

Oriel's background was that of the relatively prosperous ruling class of the Indian Empire, with her parents now living comfortably in retirement in the village of Shalford just south of Guildford. Each of the four children had been to an independent school. June was now an officer in the WRNS. The twins had both been to RADA. Michael had served as a junior officer on the Orient Line.

I, by contrast, had been born in Hackney and grown up in a working class suburb of north-east London, from which I had gone on to Christ's Hospital, the army and Oxford. My parents were now living in South Woodford, one stop on the train nearer central London than where I had grown up, and my father now drove by car to work rather than cycling. Both he and my mother retained the assumptions of what was once thought of as the aspirational working class.

Oriel and I regularly visited both my parents and hers. The most obvious difference was that when we went to South Woodford we slept in a double bed, while when we went to Shalford we were put in the room which Oriel and Chloë had shared as teenagers, with two single beds. Although we slept in just one of them, we always rumpled up the other so that it looked as if it had been slept in. Even though we were married, it did not seem proper for it to be obvious that we had slept together in a single bed.

Oriel spoke in the manner of a well brought up Surrey suburban girl, with perhaps just a touch of the Raj about her speech – something which was noticed by the speech coach at RADA. I generally spoke in the manner of someone who had been through an independent school, an officers' mess and an Oxford college. But just as Oriel retained a touch of the Raj in her speech, I still had something of the London suburbs about mine.

Oriel noticed that the glottal stop so characteristic of the speech of Londoners still survived when I spoke of Mr A(t)lee or Mr Bu(t)ler. She tried to get me to pronounce the T, but At-lee and But-ler sound wrong. What is needed is to make a 'tl' sound in the middle of the word, as in 'cattle', neither omitting the T nor sounding the T and the L separately.

While she sometimes corrected my pronunciation, I sometimes corrected her grammar. She might, for example, say, 'He took Chloë and I to the cinema', using the nominative of the personal pronoun instead of the accusative for the object of the sentence. That is, she should have said 'me' rather than 'I', and would certainly not have said, 'He took I to the cinema.'

It is the sort of mistake that is quite commonly made by BBC presenters half a century later – though I doubt if BBC presenters would have got it wrong in the middle of the twentieth century. We both found this sort of thing interesting. It never caused the least friction between us, and we both had the sense to correct each other in private rather than in public.

At the beginning of October 1959, just two months after we got married and were living in Clifton, there was a general election. Bristol North-west was a safe Conservative seat and our votes were not going to make any difference. But it helped to highlight our political differences.

Oriel understandably admired the prime minister, Harold Macmillan, who appeared to have established peace abroad and prosperity at home in the years since the Suez Crisis of 1956. She saw the leaders of the Conservative Party as people who would necessarily understand the economy and most other things better than Labour politicians, and it seemed to her entirely natural to vote Conservative.

I, on the other hand, had grown up in an environment in which the Tories were blamed both for the depression in the 1930s and for the policy of appeasing Nazi Germany and Fascist Italy. I assumed that God and his angels were on the side of the poor and the oppressed and that a Labour government would produce a more just and equal society. The post-war Labour government had already established a National Health Service and brought the railways, the coal mines and iron and steel production into public ownership. Another Labour government, I believed, would continue the process of building a better world in which the taxation system would be used to redistribute wealth from the rich to the poor.

We recognised that our votes would cancel each other out, but as it happens Oriel did not have the chance to vote because, having only just moved to Bristol, her name was not on the electoral roll. We solved the problem by agreeing that I would go along and vote Liberal, thus achieving the effect of cancelling out each other's vote.

Our attitudes to religion diverged in a rather different way. I was overtly both Christian and a member of the Church of England. I found the accounts given in the gospels of Jesus's birth, life, and teaching, and of his death and resurrection, immensely impressive. Similarly I was impressed by the beauty of some (though not all) of the Old Testament and by the view of life given in the translations, or paraphrases, by J.B.Phillips of St Paul's letters.

As a teenager I had heard an impressive talk by a Franciscan friar on prayer, in which he suggested using the word ACTS as a mnemonic for remembering Adoration, Confession, Thanksgiving and Supplication as the four main aspects of prayer, and I had got into the habit of trying to pray each day, and was aware of some of the difficulties and problems associated with an attempt to pray. Meanwhile, much of the historical work in which I had specialised (the *St Bernard* special subject, for example) assumed a Christian society. I regularly attended church on Sundays. At Christ's Hospital, at Pembroke, and then at Clifton, I was used to starting each day with a chapel service.

Oriel, by contrast, simply found church services and what she had heard of as Christianity neither interesting nor helpful. She was, like me, a member of the Church of England, and she was sympathetic to a view of things in which goodwill towards all men (and women) was important and discrimination against minorities objectionable. But she could see little or no point in church services and thought it an amiable eccentricity on my part that I went off to Holy Communion on Sunday mornings. She had no objection to coming with me on a special occasion such as Remembrance Sunday, but on many special occasions, such as Christmas or Easter, she needed to stay at home and get the lunch.

All these issues, our social backgrounds and our views of politics and religion, never caused difficulties between us. Indeed, they were among the many things we enjoyed talking to each other about – and we did a lot of talking. We did not have a television set until 1967, eight years after we got married. Nor did we have a car until shortly before that time, or a record player until some years later. The evenings were above all a time for talking together, going out to a meal with friends, or having friends to dinner with us.

Nor was there ever a problem over where we should live and what job I should do, largely because Oriel so generously went along with whatever I wanted to do as far as my work was concerned. We enjoyed house-hunting together once we were in a position to buy a house of our own and found it easy to agree on what we did and did not like. And once we had our own house, in Strawberry Hill in Twickenham, near the Thames and half way between

Richmond and Teddington, Oriel devoted herself to looking after me and the house and before long to caring for our children as well.

By the time we had been married for seven years we had had our own house for six of them, and we had three children. Life was both busy and enjoyable. The one thing that sometimes caused trouble between us was that life was so busy that I did not always find time to re-paint the kitchen or the outside of the house when Oriel felt it needed doing. She would conscientiously clean the house, but there is a limit to how much good cleaning will do when what is needed is a coat of paint or new wallpaper.

I would frequently protest my devotion to her, and I always had the time and inclination to make love. But she sometimes felt that protestations of devotion and evidence of sexual desire were an inadequate substitute for getting out a blowlamp, stripping off the old paint, preparing the surfaces and brightening them up with a new coat of magnolia. There was I reading a life of Lord Curzon and making notes on the Lloyd George coalition government when, if I really cared about her as much as I said I did, I would be wielding a paintbrush.

If she exploded with anger I was devastated and anxious to do anything I could to put things right again. But while we were both still in our twenties neither of us knew how best to resolve things. We were both shaken. She did not want her anger to be seen as an irrational outburst to be soothed by renewed protestations of love and willingness to do whatever I had failed to do earlier. I could think of no alternative.

Eventually the clouds would blow over. She would quite suddenly forgive me. Somehow it was always clear when that was so, and the reconciliation was accompanied by a decision never to have a row like that again. At its worst, and when it first happened, the row lasted about two weeks. As time went by we both got better at resolving things quicker. By the time we had been married ten years a row might last a couple of days rather than a couple of weeks. By the time we had been married twenty years it might last no more than a couple of hours or even minutes. The process of reconciliation was much the same, but we understood the problem and each other well enough to get through it quicker, and I was also anxious to avoid creating the problem which generated the row in the first place.

It was probably the fact that things could go wrong in that way that caused me as a young man to reflect on the nature of love and marriage. In 1960, during our first year of marriage, I was much impressed by C.S.Lewis's book, *The Four Loves*, in which he explained that the ancient Greeks had four separate words to distinguish different aspects of Love: *storge* (two syllables and a hard G), for devotion such as that of parents to their children; *philia*, for close friendship; *eros*, for sexual passion; and finally *agape* (again a hard G, and this time three syllables), which is sometimes translated as 'compassion' or 'charity.'

But the more I thought about it, the more I appreciated the English use of just one word to convey that whole range of those emotions, leaving the context to make the meaning plain. Family attachments, friendship, erotic love, and compassion don't necessarily have clear dividing lines between them. All can be intermingled in one person's attachment to another, and that is a characteristic of marriage when it is working well.

I had somehow come to realise by then that the approach to marriage in the area of the western world where we lived was very different from the way it was arranged in many eastern societies. We assumed that two young people would meet, find each other attractive, fall madly in love, decide that they wanted to spend the rest of their lives together, get married, and then ideally stay together, have children and live in loving companionship until they were parted by the death of one or other of them. Sadly that early love would sometimes fade and die, one or the other would leave, and they would even get divorced.

Many Asian marriages often came about in an entirely different way. The parents of young people would try to find a suitable wife or husband for their own child, reach a provisional agreement with another couple, and if the parents were sensible, they would arrange for the young people to meet and afterwards express an opinion about their putative spouse. Then, if all parties were agreed (sometimes, sadly, even if the girl protested) a marriage would be arranged and the two young people were committed to each other for life. Ideally they would grow to love each other and eventually aim to arrange a similarly happy marriage for their own children.

What seemed to me clear was that in both traditions the same two elements were needed for a happy marriage: emotional attachment and commitment. Both are necessary, and when one fails the other is all the more necessary. Western marriages sometimes go wrong because, when the emotional attachment fades, it is not reinforced by commitment. Eastern marriages sometimes fail because the emotional attachment never develops. Oriel and I were fortunate that the combination of emotional attachment and commitment kept us together until she died.

Quintin (1960–1967)

32. Quintin School

Quintin School, like Clifton College, was the product of that zeal for educational improvement which was widespread in the second half of the nineteenth century. Quintin Hogg, an Old Etonian businessman and philanthropist, founded the Polytechnic Day School in Regent Street in the heart of London in 1886, sixteen years after the introduction of universal elementary education, and sixteen years before the government got involved in secondary education.

He founded it with the clear intention of providing good modern education for the sons of the prosperous middle class families who lived in the residential area around Upper Regent Street. There were to be three divisions in the school, providing between them an extraordinarily progressive curriculum, which would still have looked progressive a century later.

The 'Professional Division' had a curriculum which included English and Mathematics, Classical and Modern Languages, the Humanities and Science. In the 'Commercial Division' English was accompanied by shorthand rather than literature, Mathematics by book-keeping rather than algebra and geometry, and the Humanities by modern, but not classical, languages. In the 'Industrial Division' English and Science were important, but there was a further shift towards such subjects as mechanical drawing, applied art, carpentry and metal turning.

The fees were moderate: only £2.12s.6d a term, or roughly £2.62 in decimal currency, when the school was first founded, and above all it appealed to members of the mercantile middle class living in central London who either could not afford to or did not want to send their sons to one of the new public boarding schools.

It also appealed to the many foreign diplomats living in central London who had no wish to send their sons away to school, and to prosperous immigrants who similarly wanted to keep their sons at home among their own people. There were still many sons of foreign diplomats and recent immigrants among the school's population of the middle of the twentieth century.

The Polytechnic Day School flourished and developed in the early twentieth century. Then on the morning of 1st September 1939, the day Germany attacked Poland, the whole school gathered in the hall, sang 'O God, our help in ages past', and walked down the road to Oxford Circus Station, from which they travelled by underground to Ealing Broadway at the end of the Central Line. From there they went by Great Western train to Somerset, and after a few weeks of chaos the Headmaster, Dr Worsnop, arranged for them to settle in Minehead and share the building of the Minehead County Grammar School - each school using it for half a day for the rest of the war.

That worked well, but when the school returned to London at the end of the war, another problem arose. The Regent Street Polytechnic, on its way to becoming the University of Westminster, was now using the building in Regent Street all through the day, and there was no room for the Day School. It needed buildings of its own, but land and property were very expensive in central London, so the solution was for the London County Council to provide both a site and a building. The name was changed to *The Quintin School* and planning began to find a suitable site, design a new school and build it.

The years of austerity after the Second World War made that difficult. So for a decade the school was spread around a variety of buildings in Soho, and Quintin boys wearing green blazers with red braid might be seen walking from one lesson to another anywhere between Regent Street and the Charing Cross Road.

The sixth form boys I first taught at Quintin had all spent their early years at school in Soho, and they told me of how, in the late

244

1940s, shortly after the change of name, a boy taking a scholar-ship examination at Oxford was asked by a don where Quintin School was. 'Well sir', he is reputed to have replied, 'You know the Windmill Theatre....' The Windmill was notorious for its public displays of young women in nude tableaux, which were permitted by the Lord Chancellor, who was responsible for public decency, so long as the young women did not move. It was also famous as the one theatre in London to stay open throughout the Blitz, and its slogan was *We never closed*. Some of the Quintin classrooms were just across the road.

Eventually a site for a new building was found, just north of St John's Wood station, between the Finchley Road and Marlborough Place, where the school's main entrance was to be, and in 1956 the staff and pupils moved into the new premises. Because the new buildings had been provided by the London County Council the official status of the school changed from 'voluntary aided' to 'voluntary controlled', a change which most people would neither have noticed nor understood. Few would have seen it as signifi-cant. The only immediate practical consequence was that there was now a majority of local authority governors on the Governing Body instead of a majority of foundation governors. Ten years later that was to be immensely significant.

The headmaster from September 1937 onwards was Dr Worsnop, who had come from a post as Senior Lecturer in Physics at King's College, London. He led the staff and pupils through the wilder-ness for seventeen years, down to Minehead in September 1939, when a German attack threatened, back at the end of the war to temporary premises scattered around Soho, and at last in September 1956 into the promised land of St John's Wood. He was the headmaster for two years in Regent Street before the war and for another two in St John's Wood before he retired. But it was the seventeen years in between which were the truly remarkable achievement.

When he retired in 1958 his successor was A. J. Holt, a nice man and a competent administrator, who suffered from having a

Staffordshire accent, something which was amusingly 'northern' to London schoolboys and tended to distance him from them and even from the teaching staff. In 1960 he appointed me to be the Head of the History Department, and it was under him that I worked for nearly seven years, from September 1960 until April 1967.

When I arrived I was only twenty-six and looked younger. The sixth form, unlike the junior boys in their green blazers with red trimmings, wore black blazers and grey trousers, and on my first day I arrived early wearing a dark blue blazer and grey trousers. The caretaker, seeing me walking casually into the school, called out to me that I should know perfectly well that boys were not allowed in at that time. I had to reassure him that I was a new member of staff, and afterwards I was more inclined to wear a sports jacket.

My form during my first year was made up of Fifth Form boys who had chosen to specialise in Arts subjects. There were thirty-four of them, which was not uncommon in grammar schools at the time, and it was perfectly possible to cope with that many O level candidates in one group because they were mostly talented and intelligent youngsters who wanted to do well and were prepared to work hard.

The cosmopolitan tradition of the Polytechnic Day School still survived, and the roll call of my form began: Balyuzi, Bhattacharyya, Boereboom, Brandt, Cahn, Cohen, Collins – and even with Collins one had not yet reached an English boy, for Collins was Kilburn Irish. Balyuzi was the son of an Iranian diplomat, Bhattacharyya's father imported and sold Indian rugs, Boereboom's father was a Dutch pastry chef, and Brandt, Cahn and Cohen were all three the sons of German Jewish immigrants who had fled Nazi Germany for England in the 1930s.

The *Eagle* comic flourished at that time, and one of the characters regularly featured was Jeff Arnold, one of the *Riders of the Range*, so to my form, though not, I think, to the rest of the school, I was known as Jeff, and before long, whenever we passed each other anywhere in the school's corridors, we would aim to see who was faster on the draw with an imaginary six-shooter.

Towards the end of the year, on a day when I had told them I would be late because I had to collect some books for them, I opened my classroom door to find that each of the room's seventeen tables had two chairs on top with the legs pointing towards the door. Kneeling behind each chair was a boy with a handkerchief over his head. They all opened fire with thirty-four imaginary machine guns, and I collapsed dead on the floor, the books scattered around me, reflecting as I lay there that the Headmaster or any such person as a visiting H.M.I. would not readily understand the situation. A couple of minutes later we were all purposefully engaged in the teaching and learning of history.

My predecessor as Head of History at Quintin School (the definite article in the name was soon dropped) was Bernard Seaman, a former pupil of the Polytechnic Day School who is better known as L.C.B.Seaman, the author of *Vienna to Versailles*, a brilliant interpretive account of international relations from the end of the Napoleonic Wars until the end of the First World War, and later of *Post-Victorian Britain, Victorian England* and *A New History of England 410-1975*.

After leaving school in 1930 he went up to Cambridge, and in 1947 he returned to what was now Quintin School as Head of History. At a time when A.J.P.Taylor was giving impressive historical lectures on television, a member of staff at Quintin asked in the Common Room who was this chap, A.J.P.Taylor. The answer came immediately from another colleague: 'A sort of poor man's L.C.B.Seaman.' I felt that it was a privilege to take over from him in 1960.

Inevitably much of what I taught in my first year was determined by the plans he had already made, by the work the pupils had done in the previous year, and by the books they had. The A level candidates needed to prepare for three papers – on English History, European History, and a Special Subject. Those starting in the Upper Sixth had already studied seventeenth century English History, nineteenth and early twentieth century European History, and some had started reading about their proposed special subject, *The French Revolution*.

As for those starting in the Lower Sixth, it made sense that they should tackle the same courses. I needed to adjust myself to what they needed to study rather than attempt a radical change of syllabus to suit my own historical preferences. Much the same applied to the teaching of the O level course.

The syllabus the Fifth Form boys were tackling at O level was *English History 1865-1955* and *European History 1871-1954*. Most of them wanted to do well, many would go on to study History at A level, and some would read it at university. There were two things they had to do in the examination. The most important was the writing of essays. Essentially they needed to learn to write about ten paragraphs in half an hour, setting out their opinions in a rational sequence, providing factual evidence to support those opinions, and providing both an appropriate introduction and a clear conclusion. It is worthwhile for anyone to learn how to do that, and it can be valuable throughout life as a way of organising one's thoughts.

The second thing they had to learn was how to '*Write short notes on four of the following.*' That was the format of the first question in all O level History papers in those days, and for that I told them that they needed to make use of Rudyard Kipling's 'six honest serving men' from the *Just So Stories*, whose names were 'What and Why and When and How and Where and Who', and also answer the question, 'What is its historical significance?'

If there were twenty marks for an essay, there would be five for each of the short notes, and I would give a maximum of three for good factual answers, while reserving two for what they said about its historical significance. The topic would only have been set if it had some significance, and they needed to think about what it was. The main problem, which I needed to hide from them as I worked away to learn more, was that my own knowledge of nineteenth and twentieth century history was very limited. I needed to work hard to keep just ahead of them.

33. Strawberry Hill

◇◇

The chaplain at Quintin School was a gentle and pleasant clergy-man called Parkinson who taught history to some of the junior forms. He was the brother of the Parkinson who made a name for himself with Parkinson's Law ('that work expands to fill the time available for its completion') and the Peter Principle ('that in any hierarchical institution men are promoted to the level of their own incompetence'), and he lived in Strawberry Hill, an area of Twickenham by the Thames, a mile downstream from Teddington Lock and nearly two miles upstream from Richmond Bridge. He recommended it as a pleasant place to live, with an easy journey by train, on the North London Electric Line, to South Hampstead.

We took his advice and found an attractive end-of-terrace house in Michelham Gardens, a small road off Strawberry Vale. Behind it were the grounds of Strawberry Hill House, and only about a hundred yards from the end of the road was Radnor Gardens, a small park which ran alongside the Thames. In ten minutes I could walk up Tower Hill to Strawberry Hill Station, where I reg-ularly caught the train to work. If Oriel and I wanted a short walk, it was scarcely any distance before we were watching the ducks and the water go by in Radnor Gardens. Bushy Park was only a mile and a half away, and a walk round both sides of the Thames, with Teddington Lock at one end and Richmond Bridge at the other, was about five miles.

Our house cost £3,750. Half a century later, when a similar house in the road has just sold for nearly £700,000, that seems a ludi-crously low price. My parents, however, who had paid £485 for their house in 1935 and had only just finished paying off their mortgage, were concerned that I would have 'a millstone round my neck' for untold years while trying to pay off a loan of nearly £3,000. The reason that the loan was under £3,000 was that

Oriel's Auntie May had left her £500 when she had died and that we had managed to save another £300 since getting engaged two and a half years earlier.

As it happens the monthly repayments were £19.5.0 a month (£19.25 in decimal currency) out of an annual salary, before tax, of £1,180, so it was quite a lot less than a quarter of my take-home pay, and far less than we would have had to pay in rent for a comparable property. What is more, it was appreciating in value by far more per month than our mortgage repayments – though we did not realise that at the time.

While we were looking for a house and going through the process of buying 34 Michelham Gardens, we stayed with my parents and only moved into our new house in October. By then Oriel was pregnant. She had decided the previous summer that she wanted a child and conceived almost at once. She suffered relatively little from morning sickness as we trudged round looking at houses, and once we had moved in she turned her mind energetically to decorating the house (we began with magnolia paint everywhere) and getting it ready for our first child.

The baby was born in St Luke's Hospital, Guildford, on 11th April 1961. I spent the day digging the garden in Oriel's parents' house in Shalford and told myself that I was not really worried. It seemed to me a fairly long labour, about eighteen hours, but I was assured that everything was straightforward and entirely normal, with no complications. We had wanted a daughter first and got one. We named her Katharine Helen but usually called her Kate.

By then I was in the middle of my first year at Quintin School, and during the week I regularly left home at 8.15 in the morning to catch the 8.30 train from Strawberry Hill. I left school promptly at the end of the school day at 4.00 p.m. and used to get home at 5.15, except when the North London Electric line train missed the connection at Richmond, when I would have a cup of tea and a piece of bread pudding (price 4d.) on Richmond Station and get home at 5.30.

I had a lot of work to do. My knowledge of the French Revolution and of subsequent nineteenth and twentieth century European history was negligible, and my knowledge of English history in the seventeenth century was not a lot better. But a degree in History is intended to be a preparation for subsequent study of the subject, whatever the period and whatever area of the world, and the great advantage I had was that I was naturally interested in what was facing me. The great disadvantage was the lack of adequate time, especially when moving home and preparing for a new baby.

The biggest challenge appeared to be the teaching of *The French Revolution* as an A level special subject. But I remembered that that was precisely what my friend Martin Henry had studied for his special subject at Oxford. So I contacted him and he sent me all his notes and essays, which were immensely helpful. The essay titles alone were an indication of what topics to tackle.

For international relations in the nineteenth century I found that Bernard Seaman's *Vienna to Versailles* was the most interesting and illuminating book on the subject, and I was able to master the internal affairs of the various European powers bit by bit, at least for the purpose of teaching A level candidates, as I read and tried to get my thoughts organised.

There were plenty of useful books on seventeenth century English history, and anyway I was already of the opinion that my job was not so much to cram my pupils full of facts (useful though facts are) but rather to teach them how to study History, how to use the *Contents* and the *Index* of a book, think about the title of any essay they were set, plan the essay, and set out their thoughts persuasively paragraph by paragraph. That being so, it was essential to set my pupils essays to write, regularly, week after week – and if they had to write essays, I needed to mark the essays and guide them about how to improve their performance.

The result was that I had a lot of marking to do: an essay a week for each member of my Upper Sixth, for each member of my

Lower Sixth, for each member of my form, and for the boys in a second History set in the O level year, made up of those who had opted out of Chemistry. It was the one period in my life when I commuted any significant distance to work, and it turned out to be extraordinarily convenient for keeping up-to-date with marking. I made myself a rule that I would always mark essays on the morning journey to work, and on the return journey in the afternoon I either continued with the marking or rested, doing nothing.

Throughout the years I was at Quintin School I never allowed myself to do anything other than that until I was home, and in the event I got a large part of my marking done by keeping to that regular daily schedule. Working through thirty-four essays by the members of my form could take up to two days of journeys to and from work each week – and then there was another O level set, as well as the essays of the Lower Sixth and the Upper Sixth.

Oriel and I agreed that it would be good to have a boy when we had another child, and early in September 1963, nearly two and a half years after Kate had been born, we had a son. This time the labour was only a few hours. Oriel woke in the early hours of 9th September with contractions which gradually became more frequent until at 7.00 a.m. she asked me to ring the midwife, a Mrs Higgins, who lived nearby.

There was no answer, so I rang the reserve midwife. She said that Mrs Higgins should be back from her holiday by now and I should try again. I did. This time Mrs Higgins did answer the 'phone and explained that she had just opened the front door on arriving back from her holiday and wondered if she had time to have her breakfast or if she really was needed immediately.

I said I would ask Oriel, who gasped, 'Tell her to come at once', so by ten past seven Mrs Higgins had arrived. She sent me to boil a kettle and get her bag from her car, and by twenty past seven the baby was born. I watched Mrs Higgins check that the umbilical cord was not round his neck and then, after he had slithered out, she held him upside down and he gasped and started breathing. Till then it had never occurred to me to wonder how babies kept alive in the womb and how they could switch from life in the womb to the very different life outside it. It still seems a wonder to me.

Oriel had recently been reading Margaret Irwin's historical novel, *The Proud Servant*, about James Graham, the first Marquess of Montrose in the mid-seventeenth century, and had decided that James would be a good name for our son. Since Edward was her father's name, he was called James Edward Arnold, although during his childhood he was usually known as Jamie.

When our next child was born, less than two years later, we thought it was time to have another girl and had agreed to call her Rosalind. As for boys' names, I was inclined to go for something Norman, such as Richard or Geoffrey, while she preferred Hugo or Toby. The problem remained unresolved while we waited for a girl and it only became urgent when a boy was born.

Once again the issue was determined by a book. I was reading *The War for America* by my former tutor, Piers Mackesy, about how naval warfare had influenced the outcome of the American War of Independence and I read Oriel a particularly good paragraph. 'That's good', she said, 'Who wrote that?' 'Piers Mackesy', I replied. 'That's a good name', she responded, 'What about that?' So the baby was called Piers, and since my father's name was John, he was Piers John Arnold, though during his childhood he was usually called Pip. Oriel was quite keen to have all her children before her thirtieth birthday, and Piers was born on 1st July 1965, a fortnight before Oriel was thirty on 16th.

So the seven years we lived at Strawberry Hill were dominated by babies, by washing and wringing out nappies (by hand, because it was some years before we had a washing machine) and by children learning to walk and talk. Each of the children was different. If you picked Kate up, she wriggled; holding Jamie was like holding a floppy cushion; Pip clung like a limpet.

I was always home in time for the children's bath time and bed time. It was one of the benefits of a London grammar school, to which both pupils and members of staff often commuted considerable distances, that most of the activities other than academic work usually took place in the lunch hour, on Thursday afternoons, the designated games afternoon, and on Saturday mornings. Most afternoons few of us stayed at school more than a few minutes after 4.00 p.m.

I started a Debating Society which met on alternate Tuesday lunch hours, with a committee meeting on the Tuesdays in between to plan the next debate. On Thursday afternoons I always joined John Price, the Head of Classics, in coaching boats on the river at Chiswick, where there were the Polytechnic games fields and the Quintin Boathouse - the one which is used each year by the Oxford crew at the end of the boat race from Putney to Mortlake. Moored on the other side of the river was *The Quintinian*, the school's Sea Scout boat, which had the distinction that it had been across to Dunkirk in 1940 and had survived.

From Chiswick it was an easy journey home on Thursday afternoons, and I also went there regularly on Saturday mornings to coach our crews, usually cycling along the towpath, but from time to time, when someone was away ill, getting in the boat and rowing. Other than that and my Tuesday lunch hours with the Debating Society I confined my school activities to the teaching of history to the O level and A level groups and to the relatively light task of organising the affairs of the history department, in which the subject was taught in the junior forms by the headmaster, the chaplain and the head of the economics department.

The fact that I was regularly coaching boats on the river on Saturday mornings did not save me from an angry dressing down one Monday morning in the middle of my first term, when I arrived at the Common Room to be faced by the member of staff who organised a rota for his colleagues to share in the supervision of boys training for or playing football at the games fields at Chiswick each Saturday morning.

I had failed to turn up. I had not even bothered to read the notice. The reason, of course, was that I had spent all that Saturday morning, like every other one, cycling up and down the towpath coaching the 2nd VIII. It was an impeccable excuse, and the point was effectively made that I was more than fulfilling the norm for involvement in what were referred to as 'out of school activities.'

34. Teaching and Writing

A year's hard work at Quintin School while living at Strawberry Hill enabled me to sort out my thoughts on the various aspects of the new history syllabuses I was teaching. By the end of the year I could explain the difference between the *Girondins* and the *Jacobins*, between the Treaty of San Stefano and the Congress of Berlin, and between Arthur Balfour and Stanley Baldwin.

I had also made a good start on breaking up the various aspects of modern history into their component parts for my O level pupils. If we were looking at international relations before the First World War, I would divide it into separate topics: the British policy of 'Splendid Isolation', the development of 'The Triple Entente', the German policy of *Weltpolitik*, colonial rivalry, events in the Balkans, even the Italian policy of *sacro egoismo*, and finally the events of the summer of 1914 which led to the outbreak of war.

Similarly it made sense when dealing with British domestic history to look separately at the Liberal, Conservative and Labour parties, at Irish Home Rule, the Trade Union movement, or the Boer War, rather than jumbling them up together. Plenty of books mingled them together. What was needed was something which dealt with one topic at a time.

I found that it was worth devising various ways in which my pupils could make sure of remembering such things as the dates which provide a framework for what one is studying. When studying international relations before the First World War it can be useful to remember that crises happened alternately in Morocco and Bosnia every three years. In 1905 there was the first Moroccan crisis, in 1908 the Bosnian crisis, in 1911 the second Moroccan crisis, and in 1914 the assassination of the Arch-Duke Franz Ferdinand at Sarajevo in Bosnia, which led to the outbreak of the

First World War. There are pitfalls with this approach, however. I remember that a quite clever boy asked me why there was no crisis in Morocco in 1917.

Similarly it is useful when studying the stages by which the power of Nazi Germany expanded in the 1930s to remember a succession of six dates: *March 1935; March 1936; March and September 1938; March and September 1939.* Get the framework right and it is relatively easy to fill in the detail in between. To begin with one may have to remember the sequence of events which fit the dates: Re-armament, the Rhineland, the *Anschluss*, the Sudetenland, the rest of Czechoslovakia, the invasion of Poland. But the history of German expansion does not make sense in any other order, and eventually a schoolboy doing his revision may only need to memorise the sequence M35/ M36/ M&S38/ M&S39 to have an adequate framework within which to explain what happened, and how.

Historical issues are very different when observed at the age of fifteen from the way they appear a few years later, and some are difficult for teenagers to grasp because of the circumstances in which they are living. In the sixties there were frequent strikes in which trade unions were demanding better pay and conditions for their members. It was difficult for a teenage schoolboy to adjust his mind to a time in which miners were going on strike not for better pay and conditions but to avoid having their pay reduced and their hours of work extended.

That was the issue which precipitated the General Strike. In 1925 Winston Churchill, as Chancellor of the Exchequer, had returned Great Britain to the gold standard in such a way that British exports were now 10% more expensive, and the only way the coal owners could make a profit was by paying their workers less or getting them to work longer hours, or both. The miners' slogan when they went on strike was 'Not a penny off the pay. Not a minute on the day.' The difficulty when teaching about that was to get boys to avoid saying that the miners wanted better pay and conditions.

The Head Boy of the school in my first year was David Akers, who was in the Upper Sixth studying *The French Revolution* as a special subject with the help provided by Martin Henry's work at university. He lent me the notes he had made on the O level course when being taught by Bernard Seaman and I found them a better introduction to modern British and European history than the text books we were using. They were also immensely useful for deciding just which topics to teach, what essays to set and so on, since Seaman was the Chief Examiner for the London University Examinations Board.

I was, of course, in the middle of getting to know several different periods of history, while at the same time all my teaching was to examination groups. So I was very grateful both to David Akers and to Bernard Seaman, as well as Martin Henry. What with the French Revolution, seventeenth century English history and nineteenth century European history all needing to be taught at A level, while at the same time I taught modern English and European history to two O level sets, and everything for the first time, it was hard work. But it was also fascinating and felt very worthwhile.

If possible I wanted my pupils to find it as fascinating and worthwhile as I did myself and read and find out for themselves about the period they were studying. Some did. One year, in which I had entirely omitted to teach anything about the Spanish Civil War, simply because of limitations of time, a boy told me after taking O level that he had written about Guernica. He had been able to tell the examiners about the bombing of the Basque town of Guernica in April 1937 by the German Condor Squadron, about the painting by Picasso, and even something of Guernica's medieval past. I was delighted.

Early in 1962, when I was in my second year at Quintin School, a young man called Nicolas McDowell called in as a representative of the publishing firm *Edward Arnold* (no relation, despite the name) to show members of staff the various books which they published. I explained to him why their books on modern history did not suit me and said that I was looking for a book which combined British and European history for the period my students were studying rather than two books which covered a great tract of material we did not need and dealt only perfunctorily, if at all, with more modern history.

About three weeks later I had a letter from J. A. T. Morgan, the senior partner at *Edward Arnold*, referring to my conversation with Nicolas McDowell and asking if I would like to join him for lunch at the Oxford and Cambridge Club. I was pleased to do so (it was the first time I had been to a London club) and we had a long talk about what sort of book was needed. He suggested that I should go away and write two or three short chapters of the sort I had described, and that I should then let him see them. The outcome was that we agreed to go ahead with a book on British and European history.

As time went by, and because some O level syllabuses now included world history, the book I was writing expanded to embrace the rest of the world, and it ended up as seventy-five chapters, an average of five pages long, arranged in sections of about half-a-dozen chapters, and with forty simple sketch maps and twelve diagrams. For three years I produced roughly one chapter a fortnight. Oriel typed them, told me when something was not clear or appeared to be superfluous, and where necessary she typed them again.

Books in those days were produced in multiples of thirty-two pages, and this book was 416 pages long: eight preliminary pages for such things as the title and the *Contents*, 385 pages of text, and twenty-three pages at the end for appendices and indices. It was intended as a practical manual of instruction - a simple introduction to something complicated, and it dealt with British, European, and eventually World history as well, in one book, with seventy-five short chapters, each dealing with a separate topic. Every chapter could be read in isolation, and although each of the various sections of the book contained about six closely related topics, the chapters could be read in almost any order that was convenient.

The maps and diagrams were designed to illustrate specific points made in the text. Thus, for example, if one wanted to illustrate the so-called 'Triple Entente', it was possible to draw Great Britain as a triangle, France as a square and Russia as a large oval, with thick continuous lines joining France and Russia in the Dual Alliance of 1893 and dotted lines joining Britain to France in the *entente cordiale* of 1904 and Britain to Russia in the *entente* of 1907.

The appendices provided information to which the reader might want easy access: the names and dates of various heads of state, for example, and the results of British general elections. There were cross-references when something mentioned at one point was dealt with more fully elsewhere. There were brief biographical notes in an *Index of Persons,* so that no-one mentioned in the text disappeared into oblivion. The book was, of course, written with modern O level syllabuses in mind, but it was also intended to be a useful guide for anyone starting to explore the history of these years and wanting a straightforward account of what happened and a simple explanation of why things happened the way they did.

The finished material went off to the publisher in the summer of 1965 and a hardback version of the book appeared in print in the summer of 1966 at the price of 14/6d - or between 72 and 73 pence in decimal currency. I was to get 10% of the published price (almost 1/6d) for each copy sold, and over the years the price and the royalties kept going up, as well as the sales. An annual cheque rising in value progressively over the years from about three hundred pounds to about three thousand was a useful supplement to a schoolmaster's income.

Five text books aimed at the O level market were reviewed in *The Times Literary Supplement* on 14th April 1967. The anonymous reviewer left mine till last, and then wrote that 'one must admire the manner in which Mr Arnold has dealt with the mosaic of events in *Britain, Europe and the World, 1870-1955.*' He went on to write approvingly of the maps and diagrams and of the general index and the index of persons, and he ended by saying that it was 'a remarkable book – practical, lucid, original in treatment, and possessing a breadth of vision unusual in the average text-book.' He commented approvingly on the selection and arrangement of topics, and then added that 'the author intersperses from time to time a certain wisdom in his general observations.' He quoted this as an example: 'Depending on the time and place from which one views the years 1870 to 1955 they may appear primarily as a time when European imperialism stimulated the emergence of the Afro-Asian peoples, as a time when revolutionary Socialism began to transform the world, as a time of immense technological advance, or as a time when aggressive Nationalism began to give way to internationalism.' He finished by quoting the final sentence of the book: 'Men themselves are moulded by circumstances, but by their reactions to circumstances men make history.'

I was rather pleased while still in my early thirties with the image it seemed to present of an elderly historian dispensing wisdom along with practical guidance, and the review must have helped the book's sales. It went on selling well and being reprinted, and when in 1973 I produced a second edition covering the years 1871 – 1971, that sold even better, so that by the time *Edward Arnold* was bought up by *Hodder and Stoughton* in 1987, the book had sold 120,000 copies, or an average of about 6,000 a year for twenty years.

Hodder and Stoughton never reprinted it. It was, I think, characteristic of publishing houses which bought up their competitors that they fairly casually discarded many of the books on the previous competitor's list as they calculated how to maximize their profits. My book was one of the casualties of that process, and once the few remaining copies from the fifteenth and last printing had been sold, it went out of stock. It had had a good run, and if they had wanted to keep it going, I would probably have needed to find time to produce a third edition. As it happens, I would by then have found it difficult to find the time for that.

35. Friends and Family

One of the pleasures of living in Strawberry Hill was that we had friends who had a widely varied range of jobs: one was an official with the water board, one a civil servant at the Home Office, another was a businessman working for Gillette, yet another a Physics lecturer at University College, London, and another was a mathematician who worked on what are called 'war games' at the Admiralty Research Laboratory in Bushy Park. As was usual in those days, the wives stayed at home, looking after the house and the children.

We became members of a baby-sitting circle based on the road we lived in, Michelham Gardens. When we went out there was always someone we could rely on to come in and be available in case one of the children should wake up. Similarly, we would baby-sit for them. I was usually happy to be the one who went out to do the baby-sitting, because our neighbours all had television sets, which we did not, and although I always took my marking with me, I found it difficult to resist the temptation to sit and watch television programmes, drink coffee and eat chocolate biscuits.

34 Michelham Gardens was an attractive house for a busy young married couple with small children. The grounds of Strawberry Hill were immediately behind us; there was a small front garden with a laburnum tree; and there was a larger back garden, mostly grass, where I built a sandpit for the children to play in with old bricks bought for £1 a hundred from a demolition site.

There was also a shed made out of an old war-time Anderson shelter. At Kate's fifth birthday party I told a child that I had lived in something like that during the war. She replied, 'Where did your Mummy keep her washing machine?' It made me remember my mother's boiler and the wash-board which I now have hanging in my garage.

Kate was a pretty little girl, who learnt to talk early, far earlier than her brothers, and attracted a lot of attention, which caused us to glow with pride. She was always pleased to go with Oriel or me, or both, to watch the ducks in Radnor Gardens, and once she could walk she seemed pleased to come to church with me on those Sundays when we were not visiting either Oriel's parents or mine.

We quite often visited both of them. My parents were now living in South Woodford, on the North-east side of London, while we were in the South-west, and Oriel's parents were still in Shalford, a village near Guildford. In both cases we had to make the journey using public transport, and in both cases it was a considerable undertaking, with small children and without a car. We only acquired a car towards the end of our time at Strawberry Hill, when my father rather generously sold me his Ford Anglia for £200.

Oriel saw a lot of Aileen Watson, Martin Henry's mother, who was living in Teddington with her second husband, Duncan Watson, in the house where I had stayed with them when an undergraduate. Aileen did a lot to help Oriel and she and Chloë became Kate's godmothers, while Yngve Lidell became the godfather. We quite frequently went to dinner with Aileen and Duncan and got used to dinner parties at which wine flowed freely and conversation about politics and international affairs was vigorous.

Duncan, later Sir Duncan Watson, who had been a colonial officer in Cyprus before and during the Second World War, was now working at the Foreign Office attempting to create a workable Central African Federation out of Zambia, Southern Rhodesia and Nyasaland. He had read Mods and Greats at New College, Oxford, and was devoted to the idea that the Roman Empire provided a model for the English to emulate as they sought to extend the *pax Britannica* to those parts of the world fortunate enough to be in the British Empire.

From the autumn of 1963 onwards it was also possible at times to see John and Anneliese. It had been difficult to see much of John

264

during the previous three years, partly because I was so busy both at school and at home, partly because Twickenham and Sheffield are a long way apart, and partly because John, during his curacy, was increasingly involved in the Ecumenical Movement, attending the conference of the World Council of Churches at Delhi in 1961 as a translator, for example, and afterwards working for the Conference of European Churches.

During 1962-3 John combined his curacy not only with work for the Ecumenical Movement, but also with a Research Fellowship at Sheffield University, working on the writings of Dostoevsky. That turned out to be particularly worthwhile when the Bishop of Winchester was trying to persuade a reluctant Southampton University to appoint a chaplain. It was only when he was able to provide them with someone who could teach Russian Literature as well that they agreed to do so. So immediately after getting married John moved from his curacy in Sheffield to be the chaplain of Southampton University and teach Russian Literature. It was there that we sometimes visited them.

The move to England was in some ways difficult for Anneliese. Memories of the war were still vivid and the wounds were raw. So while both my parents tried to be polite, they were not instinctively welcoming. One peculiar side-effect was that Oriel, of whom my mother had at first been suspicious because she came from a different class background, was now everything a daughter-in-law could ideally be. She shone with the merit of not being German.

It was, however, difficult to resent or dislike Anneliese for long, and they came round to accepting her, then loving her, and even to recognising that someone of her generation, who had lost her father in the war and later been interrogated by the *Stasi*, the East German police, simply for being a member of a student Christian organisation, should not be blamed for evils for which she was in no way responsible. In 1964 Anneliese and John had a daughter, Frances, in 1965 a son, Matthew, who was born shortly after

Piers, and then it was another seven years before their second daughter, Miriam, was born.

While I could from time to time see John, Oriel seldom saw Chloë and missed being able to share thoughts and experiences with her, as they had for so many years. Although Chloë returned to England after only two years in Amman, before long she was sent on her next posting, this time to Singapore, where she met a captain in the Argyll and Sutherland Highlanders, Michael Wilson, who persuaded her to marry him. Then, after only a couple of years of married life Chloë was diagnosed with breast cancer. She had an operation, a mastectomy, to remove her left breast, and after that, apparently recovered, she went out to Brunei, where Michael was now serving with the forces of the Sultan of Brunei.

In May of 1966 she had a baby daughter, Fiona, a year younger than June's second daughter, Vicky, and Oriel's second son, Piers. But before the end of the year Chloë's cancer had recurred and was spreading through her body. She was brought back to England to the King Edward VII Hospital for Officers in Millbank, next to the Tate Gallery, and there she died. I visited her in hospital and was allowed to take her out to lunch next door at the Tate Gallery. She was pale, slim and ethereally beautiful. I was aware of men looking admiringly at her and enviously at me, while both she and I knew that death was only a matter of weeks away. She died not long afterwards, still only thirty-two.

We would also go to see June and Tony Cribb, who had been working for some years now as the REME liaison officer on the *Blue Streak* missile, Britain's projected independent nuclear deterrent. His job was to ensure that when anything went wrong, the appropriate part could be accessed and mended by REME artificers. Then in 1960 the British Prime Minister, Harold Macmillan, met the American President, John F. Kennedy, and agreed to scrap *Blue Streak* and buy the American *Polaris* missile instead.

For Tony that was a personal tragedy. He had put years of his life into *Blue Streak*, and just when all the work appeared to be paying off and the project was coming to fruition, it was cancelled. It felt to him as if he had completely wasted some of the best years of his life and he found it difficult to come to terms with it. He was an intelligent and sensitive man who had managed to combine his work in the army with writing amusing articles for *Punch*. Now he did not know what to do with his life and I remember walking along the Thames with him near Richmond as he wondered if he should leave the army and become a schoolmaster.

With a new baby, Linda, born in 1960, the same year that *Blue Streak* was cancelled, it was difficult to make a complete change and he carried on, but without the same zeal for his work, and he eventually suffered a recurrence of the serious stress problem that had first affected him after 200,000 Chinese 'volunteers' crossed the Yalu River in the Korean War, throwing the United Nations Forces into disarray. He and June had a second daughter, Vicky, born in May 1965, shortly before Piers, but sadly, while Vicky was too small to remember, Tony died, choking on the medication which was intended to cure him of the continuing stress problem.

Meanwhile Kate had gone to nursery school, where they reported that she did not seem very keen to mix with the other children. We were mildly surprised, but thought little of it. She was still a great pleasure to us at home, and Oriel spent a lot of time helping her to learn to cut things out, which she found difficult, and helping her to colour things in, which she found much easier and enjoyed. Eventually she went on to the local primary school, and Oriel would push the pram there with Kate walking on one side and Jamie trotting along on the other.

We were surprised at a parents' evening to be asked if Kate had difficulty with her hearing, and were relieved to find when she was tested that her hearing was fine. But the teacher was then looking for another explanation of why Kate so often did not seem to hear what was being said and spent so much time looking out of the window. We asked Kate, and the only answer we got was that she thought what they were doing at school was 'silly.'

With hindsight I suppose we should have taken her to a child psychologist to have some tests done and see if he (or she) could discover anything wrong. But at the time it did not seem particularly significant and we failed to follow it up.

We had crammed a lot into the period of nearly seven years when we were living at Strawberry Hill and I was working at Quintin School. Oriel had had three babies by the time we moved in August 1967, and by then Kate was six, Jamie was just coming up to his fourth birthday and Pip was one – too young to remember ever having lived at Strawberry Hill. Over the three years from 1962 to 1965 I had written a text book, sometimes with children climbing over me, Oriel had read it, criticised it and typed it, and very often, after I had taken account of her criticisms, re-typed it.

Whether she was ironing or typing, she was always surrounded by small children, and sometimes she would climb into the children's playpen with either her iron or her typewriter to get some peace, while the children played outside it. We went out to dinner with friends and had them to dinner with us. If the house needed painting, we did it ourselves – inside and out. We went shopping together and we played with the children together. I read stories to the children at bedtime. Oriel made up stories to tell them.

We were, of course, living in the 1960s. We had no idea then that they were the Swinging Sixties and that we were living in what was later called 'the permissive society.' In any case, no-one ever let us join it. Oriel, however, had just the right figure for wearing mini-skirts and looked wonderful in them, as she did in short dresses or denim shorts or her '*matelot* pants' - trousers with flared bottoms and with diagonal lemon and pink and orange and red stripes. Having been brought up in the forties and fifties, she wondered how proper it was to be wearing a mini-skirt or denim shorts or psychedelic trousers once she was a mother. But I loved it, and she still looked young enough that when she answered the door to a Conservative canvasser at the time of the 1964 election, he asked her if her mother was at home.

The previous year I had encountered one of the less attractive aspects of life in London in the 1960s. On a day when there were protests in Grosvenor Square against the state visit of the King and Queen of Greece, one of the boys in my form, who lived in the *Edward Arnold* building in Maddox Street, because his father was the caretaker there, was returning home from playing tennis. He was seized by the police and bundled into a police van, and later was required to sign for his possessions. But a brick had been added to them, so he refused.

One of the *Edward Arnold* directors and I both had to put some effort into explaining his innocence and why, when arrested, he was walking towards his home with a tennis racquet. Eventually he was released without charge. The sergeant who had arrested him hit the headlines a few years later when convicted of engineering false arrests on a large scale. Until that incident I had not believed that such things happened.

I would sometimes get out of the underground train at Oxford Street to go to *Edward Arnolds*. If, walking down Regent Street, I had gone left instead of right, I would have found myself in Carnaby Street, the fashion Mecca of the Sixties, but at the time I had no idea that Carnaby Street even existed, and I only heard of it much later when people were talking about the Swinging Sixties. I did notice that in Regent Street there always seemed to be any number of long, slim girls looking gorgeous in their mini-skirts, and I was glad to be going home to the one of my own.

36. QK

In 1965, the same year that Piers was born and in which I finished writing *Britain, Europe and the World 1870-1955*, Anthony Crosland, the Secretary of State for Education in the Labour government which had taken office in 1964 with a majority of only four, sent a circular (Circular 10 of 1965) to all local education authorities requesting them to submit proposals for the reorganisation of secondary education on comprehensive lines.

It was just over twenty years since the 1944 Education Act, which was widely hailed as a great reform – understandably, since before the Second World War only 2% of all English children received free secondary education, and now, at least in theory, and from 1947 onwards, free secondary education was to be available to every child in the country.   Less understandably it has continued to be widely regarded as a great reform, despite being based on the peculiar assumption that children could be neatly divided into three categories (those suited to a grammar school education, those suited to a technical education, and those whose lack of ability suited them to neither) and subsequently directed to whichever sort of school was judged by education officers to be best suited to them.

The way in which the Act was implemented was arguably even more of a disgrace than the theoretical assumptions on which it was built. In the austerity of the post-war years too few grammar school places were provided, few technical schools were built, and most children were directed to the new 'secondary modern' schools, where they were provided with a low level of precisely the sort of curriculum to which they had been judged unsuited, often in run-down buildings which had previously housed the senior sections of the old elementary schools. It was, in a sense, a fraud on a national scale, and all the more of a disgrace because parents were given no choice, unless they had the money to opt out of the 'state' system and pay for a place in an independent school.

It was a time bomb waiting to explode, and it only needed one generation to grow up and demand that their children should not be humiliated as they had been. That generation grew up with the vast majority of them having been given the impression at the age of eleven that they were failures, and in many cases they went through life, even if they were successful at running their own business, believing that they were in some sense stupid. No wonder there was a demand for 'comprehensive' schools, which would educate all children together.

Reactions of local education authorities to Crosland's circular 10/65 varied widely. Under the legislation in force at the time the Secretary of State had no power to constrain local authorities to reorganise on comprehensive lines, and some, such as Buckinghamshire, were determined not to do so and retained their grammar schools into the twenty-first century. Others, such as the Inner London Education Authority, which had been formed in 1965 with responsibility for education in the twelve Inner London boroughs, grasped the idea of having comprehensive schools with zeal. Its members seemed to believe that by adopting a 'comprehensive' policy they would automatically be creating a system in which all children would have equal opportunities, every child would benefit from going to a comprehensive school, and society would be transformed for the better.

The reality was entirely different. This was partly because most proponents of comprehensive education were moved by enthusiasm for a noble ideal but had not done any practical calculations about how schools work, had mistakenly assumed that secondary schools must necessarily cover the age range 11 – 18, and as a result created schools which were too big, and often ill-disciplined, with sixth forms which were too small to operate effectively.

There was a further problem, which was particularly acute in London, that local politicians had no authority to make changes to public schools, private schools, 'direct grant' grammar schools or 'voluntary aided' grammar schools. In creating their comprehensive schools they could only reorganise schools on whose governing bodies they had a majority of governors. They had none on the governing bodies of public and private schools and only a minority on the governing bodies of 'direct grant' and 'voluntary aided' grammar schools.

The status of Quintin School had changed from 'voluntary aided' to 'voluntary controlled' because of its need for new buildings after the Second World War. That made no difference at all to the way the school was run so long as the London County Council was the local education authority, but it became immensely important in 1965, when the Inner London Education Authority (the I.L.E.A.), was formed and adopted its policy of comprehensive reorganisation. Here was a grammar school which it did have the power to reorganise.

The I.L.E.A. plunged into comprehensive re-organisation with irresponsible enthusiasm. Its creation of comprehensive schools covering the age range 11 -18 led to disaster in the immediate future and did immense and often irreparable damage to the education of a generation or more of young Londoners.

The problem for Quintin School was that it was planned to make it part of a comprehensive school in an area in which some of the boys living there would go to leading public schools such as Westminster and St Paul's, to minor public schools such as Highgate or Mill Hill, to 'direct grant' grammar schools such as City of London and Latymer Upper, and to two nearby 'voluntary aided' grammar schools: William Ellis in Hampstead, to the North-east, and St Marylebone Grammar School, not much more than a mile away, to the South.

What is more, less than three miles to the South-west of Quintin School was Holland Park Comprehensive, purpose-built in 1958 as the flagship of the comprehensive movement, 'the Socialist

Eton', set down in the middle of an area which had the highest average house prices in the whole of England, and where Labour cabinet ministers could demonstrate their Socialist credentials by sending their children to a comprehensive school and where for thirteen years Caroline Benn, wife of the Labour politician Tony Benn, was Chair of Governors.

As soon as the education officers of the I.L.E.A. revealed their plans, it was clear that, coming at the end of a pecking order of independent schools, 'direct grant' grammar schools, 'voluntary aided' grammar schools and a purpose-built and fashionable comprehensive school, Quintin School and Kynaston School, just up the road on the same site, were to be re-organised as what would in practice be a secondary modern school under another name. It was an ideological decision which took little or no account of the practical problems likely to result from it.

No doubt the local politicians of the I.L.E.A. were frustrated by the legal framework within which they had to operate, but even within that framework they could have made more sensible arrangements. Kynaston School, named after the second President of the Regent Street Polytechnic, had a natural connection with Quintin School, and it might have made sense to make it a Junior High School, covering the age range eleven to fourteen, and to have made Quintin a Senior High School doing O and A level courses. Alternatively, if the politicians had had sufficient vision, they might have made them into Junior and Senior Technical Schools. But to pretend that the combination of the two of them was a comprehensive school at a time when there were so many selective schools nearby was to plunge them into a disaster from which it would take decades to recover.

These problems could be foreseen. There were others which emerged later, such as the difficulty some grammar school teachers faced when trying to cope with the bottom stream in the Fourth Form of a comprehensive school or the difficulty some secondary modern teachers had in coping with bright former grammar school boys. But for the moment the obvious problems were enough. Officers of the I.L.E.A. came to Quintin School and explained the plans of their political masters, but they had nothing in the least reassuring to tell us in response to our questions.

I was the first of the heads of department to leave. I looked at the advertisements in the *Times Educational Supplement,* saw one for a Head of History at Stowe School, applied and was invited for interview. Oriel and I drove up there, and as we drove up the Grand Avenue from Buckingham we got our first glimpse of what must be the most beautiful school in the country. We met the then head of department, who was leaving to join the diplomatic service. We met the headmaster, Bob Drayson, got on well with him as we walked round the grounds, and as we were having a cup of tea before leaving, he offered me the job and I accepted – to start in April 1967.

Six other heads of department left Quintin over the next eighteen months: the Head of English to an independent Roman Catholic monastic school, the Head of Modern Languages to a lectureship at Glasgow University, the Heads of Mathematics and Biology to posts in university education departments, and the Head of Physics to a Canadian independent school. Thus over a period of eighteen months six heads of department were lost, not just to Quintin School but to the 'state' sector of education – three to independent schools and three to universities.

The Head of Economics was appointed as Deputy Head in a comprehensive school. By September 1968, the beginning of Quintin School's last academic year before officially becoming Quintin Kynaston School, all seven of us had gone. The three other heads of major departments, Classics, Geography and Chemistry, were all nearing retirement and had to stay and cope as best they could.

A.J.Holt had been a competent, if uninspiring, head of a good grammar school, and he had the administrative skills needed to manage the re-organisation of Quintin and Kynaston as one school. But there was no way in which he was going to be able to cope with the human problems which would inevitably face him. Nevertheless, he was appointed as the first head of the new Quintin Kynaston School which opened in September 1969, and by then things were already falling apart. He struggled on with ever increasing problems until in 1972 he had a nervous breakdown and had to retire early. At about the same time his very effective Deputy at Quintin, Dickie Weedon, who became Deputy Head of QK, as it was now usually called, had a heart attack and died.

My successor as Head of History, Michael Barcroft, came from Gordonstoun, where he had been teaching Prince Charles. He took over for the summer term of 1967, stayed three more years and left in 1970 to be the headmaster of a school in Peterborough. So the post of Head of History was once again advertised.

This time one of the applicants was David Akers, whom I had taught in my first year at Quintin and who had left in 1961 to go up to Cambridge to read History. While at Cambridge he got a Football Blue as well as his History degree and in 1965 he started teaching at the Brighton, Hove and Sussex Boys' Grammar School. By 1970 he was well qualified for the post of head of department at his old school and was invited for interview.

Many years later, when we were both retired and sitting in my garden having lunch, he told me how John Price, the Head of Classics, with whom I had shared the coaching of the school VIIIs on the river, had taken hold of him when he went to QK for interview, pulled him into a side room and asked him what he was doing. He was warned of the danger to his future career if he accepted the post, so he returned to Brighton, where eventually he became the head of the history department, was still there when it changed into a sixth form college, and where he stayed until he retired.

A couple of years after I had left Quintin, while the school was going through its transformation to comprehensive status but before its official designation as Quintin Kynaston School, I visited it to see old friends such as John Price. As I walked up to the main entrance from Marlborough Hill, I saw that the rose beds on either side had been trampled down. Inside the door to the passageway which led to the school office and the headmaster's study was locked. The library was boarded up. There was graffiti on the walls and there were surly-looking boys in the corridors. It was a sad change from the school I remembered.

Things got worse. When the two schools amalgamated, Kynaston and Quintin boys rather extraordinarily continued to wear their distinctively different uniforms and Kynaston boys jeered at 'Quintin queers' in their green blazers with red trimmings, while Quintin boys hit back at the 'Kynaston cunts', using language not significantly worse than that of the Secretary of State who had helped to put them in this position.

Some years later, when I walked past QK on the way to visit a friend who lived in St John's Wood, I saw that the whole site had been enclosed within a tall metal barrier, as if a prisoner-of-war camp had been set down in the middle of the expensive and exclusive residential area of St John's Wood. Whether it was to keep the pupils in or everyone else out was not clear.

Holt's successor, Peter Mitchell, took over when things could scarcely have been worse and stayed for eleven years. Failing schools do not need a super-head to come in for a year, 'turn things round' with a lot of money and a lot of noise, and then move on elsewhere. They need someone who will stay long enough to live with the consequences of his (or her) own decisions. Peter Mitchell did that, and it was under him that the school started to recover and in 1976 admitted girls for the first time. He stayed until 1983.

The difficult process of regeneration and transformation which began with him continued under three more heads, and by the end of the century sufficient progress had been made that in 2001 it was designated a Specialist Technology College, rather ironically taking it back to the progressive educational ideas which had distinguished it a hundred years earlier, and the following year a new dynamic female head teacher, Jo Shuter, was appointed and lauded as a 'superhead'.

The next year the prime minister, Tony Blair, chose QK as the place from which to launch the Children's Services Green Paper and in 2004 an OFSTED report described the school as 'excellent.' In 2007 Jo Shuter received an award as 'Headteacher of the Year in a Secondary School', and in 2008, the year in which another OFSTED report described QK as 'an outstanding school, exceptionally well led by its inspirational headteacher', she was awarded a CBE. In 2011, by which time her annual salary was £170,000, it became a Community Academy, responsible only to parliament. It must have seemed as if all things were possible.

Less than a year later allegations were made of financial impropriety. Jo Shuter described them as 'malicious and vindictive', but there was enough substance in them for the governing body to arrange for an investigation and suspend her pending its outcome. The investigation by the Education Funding Agency led to a report published in May 2013. The only clearly illegal acts were two instances of claiming travel expenses more than once from different organisations, but it also showed that, since QK had become an academy, more than £3,000 had been spent on flowers and £7,000 on taxis, including trips to some of London's leading restaurants, that one overnight meeting of the 'Senior Leadership Team' in a hotel had cost over £8,000 and that another £7,000 had been spent on the head's fiftieth birthday party. Seven members of her family had been employed at the school, including her mother and her children. The report recommended that resources should not be spent on arranging aspects of the head teacher's personal life, 'such as booking family holidays, organising rental of her Turkish villa and lunch and dinner engagements.'

Somehow a particularly good teacher and someone lauded as an outstanding headteacher had been seduced into a culture of self-indulgence paid for by claiming expenses in a manner characteristic of the worst elements of political and business life. Before long she found her position untenable and resigned, saying that her eleven years as head of QK had been 'a source of pride and happiness.' Perhaps there had been a bit too much pride and happiness.

In 2015 QK was rebuilt on a different part of the same site at a cost of many millions of pounds as the government spared no expense in its bid to rescue London comprehensive schools from failure, but Ofsted was now judging it to be 'inadequate' and those rich enough to live nearby sent their children to independent schools. I realised that before I went to Quintin I had taught boys at Clifton who lived in that immediate area, and that after I had left I had taught boys at Stowe who lived there. But throughout the seven years I was at Quintin, even though then it was a grammar school, I had never taught any boys who lived in the immediate surroundings.

Stowe (1967–1976)

37. From JF to RQD

◇◇◇

My first staff meeting at Stowe was in April 1967, the day before the Summer Term began. After I was welcomed the next item on the agenda was an explanation of the precautions which needed to be taken to protect the school beagle pack from the outbreak of foot and mouth disease which was affecting the cattle in Northamptonshire and was now moving south into Buckinghamshire. The next item on the agenda was about whether or not it was acceptable for shotguns to be kept in their studies by those boys who had been given permission to shoot over a neighbouring farmer's land. I do not remember the outcome in those days before Health and Safety legislation would have settled the issue unequivocally, but I do remember being aware that I had come to a very different environment from that I was used to.

The main school building was the grand house in the north of Buckinghamshire which had been the home of the Dukes of Buckingham and Chandos, and the names of the famous families associated with the house (Bruce, Temple, Grenville, Chandos, Cobham, Grafton, Walpole, Chatham and Lyttelton) were commemorated in the names of the school houses. But the family's fortunes declined in the nineteenth century, in 1889 the last Duke of Buckingham died without a male heir, and his daughter's only son was killed in the First World War. The family had to pay two lots of death duties and soon everything was sold. The furniture, pictures, statues and ornaments were scattered far and wide – and sometimes not so far. I remember having my hair cut in Buckingham in a small barber's shop whose far wall was entirely covered by a vast gilt mirror which had been bought in the great sale of 1921.

In 1922 a group of men who had formed a committee with the express intention of establishing a new public school to be among

281

'the first six in the country', acquired Stowe House, with 750 acres of landscaped gardens together with temples and monuments, for £34,500. Then, either with brilliant judgement or with extraordinary good fortune, or both, they appointed a remarkable young man to be the first headmaster.

J.F.Roxburgh (he was always known by his initials, and I still do not know his first name nearly half a century after first going to Stowe) was a housemaster at Lancing College when he was appointed, and early in 1923, before the school opened, he spoke publicly of the sort of school it was to be, saying that 'every boy who goes out from Stowe will know beauty when he sees it all the rest of his life.' He saw it as important that Stoics should appreciate the beauty of the house and grounds, and later said that he had found that 'boys respond much more quickly to beautiful surroundings than they are usually given credit for.'

Stowe, though a new foundation, had a number of inter-related advantages. First, and most obviously, was its setting in Stowe House and its landscaped gardens, and the splendour of the approach along the straight mile-long tree-lined Grand Avenue, which was generously presented to Stowe in 1924 by a number of Old Etonians.

The next advantage was Roxburgh. When he died in 1954, Lord Annan, an old boy of the school, said of him that 'in the history of education he will go down as one who added another great school to the country; in the history of the public schools he will stand out as the man most responsible after the First World War for civilising their outlook and enlarging their substance; and in the history of Stowe he was the man who fused the spirit of the past with the present and made us feel that we were heirs of the rulers and poets of England who two centuries ago sauntered on these lawns.'

Another advantage that Stowe had over other public schools was that it had a very different ethos from that in which learning to tackle low in rugby football and play a straight bat in cricket were seen as the ideal way to form character and turn boys into gentle-men. After the horrors of the First World War many mothers wanted a more civilised educational environment for their sons.

Stowe, with J.F.Roxburgh as headmaster, was ideally suited to provide the sort of education they wanted, in which academic work, art, drama and music could flourish alongside individual sporting activities and team games in a relaxed environment which had something of the flavour of a country club. To that environment Roxburgh was able to attract a number of remarkable masters. The English Tutor, for example, during most of the thirties was T.H. White, who regularly hunted with the Grafton and was well known later as the author of *The Sword in the Stone*. At the same time the Director of Music was Dr Leslie Huggins, who went off to war, won the Military Cross, and returned to Stowe to produce numerous superb concerts. Like T.H.White he regularly rode to hounds, and he eventually became the Master of the Grafton Hunt.

Under Roxburgh Stowe rose to eminence. He quite deliberately set out to attract the sons of the English aristocracy, such as the Duke of Wellington and the Viscount Maitland, both of whom were killed in the Second World War, and also foreign royalty, such as the Russian Prince Galitzine and Prince Rainier of Monaco. When I was teaching there in the late 1960s and early 70s I asked a boy called James Methuen-Campbell, who had just joined my History Sixth, what his father did. 'Well, Sir', he replied, 'Sometimes he's a lavatory attendant and sometimes he's a car park attendant, but most of the while he doesn't really do anything.' Not knowing quite how to respond, I asked him his address. The answer was 'Methuen Castle, Sir.'

During those years I taught boys from the grouse moors of Scotland, the political fastnesses of Northern Ireland and the tax havens of the Channel Islands, as well as from India, Germany and the United States of America, and if I taught boys called Russell or Shackleton or von Schleicher, as I did, the first would be a relative of the Duke of Bedford, the second of the great explorer, and the third of the former German Chancellor whom Hitler had murdered in the Night of the Long Knives.

Almost every boy who entered Stowe from its beginnings in 1923 was eligible for front line combat in the Second World War, and two hundred and seventy of them, approximately one in seven, were killed. I remember showing visitors the war memorial, and hearing them express horror at the devastation wrought by the First World War. I had to explain that this was not the war of 1914-18. Stowe had not yet been founded then. They were all victims of the war of 1939-45. They came from the sort of background in which it was natural for them to become infantry platoon commanders, fighter pilots or tank commanders. Between them they won 242 decorations, including two VCs, 28 DSOs, 22 DSCs, eleven MCs and 46 DFCs.

Roxburgh had known personally every boy who had been through the school; it was part of his distinctive style of headmastering. He had met their parents as well. Now, on average about once a week, he found himself writing to those parents to express his sorrow at the death of their son. It took its toll on him, and by the end of the war he was generally perceived to be an old man, no longer his flamboyant former self, but gallantly keeping things going until at last, in 1949, he retired.

His successor, Eric Reynolds, was a former Rugby housemaster of considerable charm and ability. But he suffered from the fact that he was not Roxburgh, he had a serious climbing accident two years after he had taken up the post, and as the years went by Old Stoics complained that the school was no longer what it had been. The governors decided to ask Reynolds to retire early and decided to find someone vigorous and forceful to replace him.

They got what they were looking for. Donald Crichton-Miller, an international rugby football player who was reputed to have transformed both Taunton School and Fettes College in Edinburgh, was appointed in 1958 with an impressive record as a reforming headmaster behind him. Several members of staff were required to leave, some housemasters were removed from their houses, and he made a whole range of changes, including bringing the beagle pack to Stowe and making the arrangements for a school golf course.

But there was a high price to pay. Roxburgh had led by charm, example and goodwill. Many members of staff complained that Crichton-Miller, by contrast, was a tyrant. On the other hand, a number of younger members of staff greatly admired him, so by the end of four years the staff were bitterly divided. All except two of the housemasters said that they would resign unless he went. Sixteen other members of staff said that they would resign if he did. The governors dithered but eventually decided to require Crichton-Miller to go.

In 1964, after getting rid of two headmasters early in just over five years, they had to look for a new headmaster. They were extraordinarily fortunate to find Bob Drayson. Robert Quested Drayson, or RQD, had gone up to Cambridge in 1938 to read Modern Languages and was just twenty when the Second World War began. He joined the Royal Navy and served in motor torpedo boats. As the officer commanding MTB 236 he took station in October 1942 in a flotilla on its way to intercept a German auxiliary cruiser, *Komet*, which was attempting to slip through the Channel to attack British merchant shipping and supply U-boats.

The *Komet* was, as it happens, commanded by the former first officer of the *Graf Spee*, who, after the scuttling of the *Graf Spee* at Montevideo, had made his way back to Germany via neutral countries, including finally the U.S.A. That night Drayson somehow lost contact with the rest of the flotilla, was unable to re-establish contact, and was concerned about the trouble he would be in when he eventually got back to port. But he knew the designated rendezvous off Barfleur and made his way there.

As he arrived shortly after midnight he found that he was cut off from the rest of the flotilla by the *Komet*, which had powerful enough guns to keep its attackers well out of the range. He approached from the other side, reached point-blank range (perhaps about a quarter of a mile), fired off two torpedoes, turned and sped away as fast as possible. The *Komet* exploded and sank with all its crew.

The debris, as it came down, damaged the steering gear of MTB236, now about half a mile away. In Portsmouth his girlfriend Rachel, later his wife, was serving as a Wren in the Women's Royal Naval Service. She had been plotting the movement of ships involved, was concerned for his welfare and was greatly relieved when he arrived back safely. Shortly afterwards he was awarded the Distinguished Service Cross for his 'great skill and bravery.'

With the war over he returned to Cambridge, read History for Part II of the Tripos, won a hockey Blue, had a trial for England, and then in his late twenties started out on a career as a schoolmaster, while still a relatively young man became the headmaster of a small school in Surrey, Reed's School, Cobham, and in a few years doubled its size.

On the strength of his achievements there he was recommended to the governors of Stowe, who were impressed by what they heard, invited him to consider the headship of Stowe, and appointed him. He arrived in April 1964 when he was forty-five, and retired in the summer of 1979. I arrived at Stowe as History Tutor in April 1967, just three years after his arrival, and left in the summer of 1976, just three years before he retired. So I had the pleasure of working for him for nearly ten years in the middle of his headship.

Bob Drayson had a number of advantages when he took over. First was the fact that the governors had required two headmasters to retire early within the previous six years. They could not very well do the same again. Secondly, while Eric Reynolds had had the disadvantage of not being Roxburgh, Bob Drayson had the advantage of not being Crichton-Miller. One outcome of the divisions of the final years of Crichton-Miller's time was that a substantial number of the staff had decided to move on, so Bob Drayson had a third great advantage of being able to make a significant number of new appointments.

In particular he was able to transform the academic leadership of the school by making external appointments of new tutors to almost all the nine academic sides. When I arrived in April 1967 there were only two tutors who had been on the staff for any considerable time. One was Brian Stephan, the very able tutor of the Classics and English Side, who had been recruited by Roxburgh in 1944. The other was John Hunt, the Geography Tutor, who shortly afterwards left to be the Head Master of Roedean. Apart from them and Peter Longhurst, who had arrived two terms before me from King George V School, Southport, as Economics Tutor, the others, those responsible for Modern Languages, Mathematics, Physics, Chemistry and Biology, were all a year or two younger than me (I was thirty-three), and all were recent appointments. It was a healthy position from which to develop the academic aspect of the school and improve the quality of the teaching and learning.

A fourth advantage from which Bob Drayson benefited was the very effective recruitment of pupils done by Donald Crichton-Miller in his contacts with prep. schools. In Bob's first full school year, 1964-5, a very respectable six open Oxbridge awards were won, the 1st XV was undefeated, as were the squash and athletics teams, the 1st hockey and cricket teams lost only one match each, and the golf team won the Micklem trophy, the public schools' golf championship. Whatever the traumas within the staff, they had not significantly affected the school's performance or its reputation and attraction for both parents and their sons.

Finally, Bob Drayson's greatest advantage was his own personality and ability. He was in some ways a simple man, still a brisk naval officer inclined to speak in clichés and open to the accusation that he had no clear educational ideas. He used the words 'curriculum', 'syllabus' and 'timetable' as if they were synonyms. But he knew what he believed in and what he wanted from his staff and he conveyed it clearly and consistently by what he did as well as by what he said.

He had a firm evangelical Christian faith, which gave him a clear view of right and wrong, but at the same time he had no interest whatsoever in theology. He expected the boys to work hard, play hard, wear their hair short ('short' in those days meant clear of the collar) and their shoes clean. If I had said to him that short hair or clean shoes could, in a way, be seen as sacraments, as "outward and visible signs of inward invisible grace", he would have replied, "I'm sure you're right about that" – and later would have said cheerfully to one of my senior colleagues, "Don't understand half of what he says, but I'm sure it makes sense."

He had no interest in educational or curricular theory. He expected members of staff to prepare their lessons, turn up punctually at their classrooms, teach, set work, mark it conscientiously, and engage vigorously in what he thought of as 'out-of-school activities.' At a staff meeting in the Aurelian Room he referred to running a good school, and Jo Bain, the housemaster of Chandos, said from the back of the room, "It depends on what you mean by 'a good school', Headmaster." Drayson, without a moment's hesitation, replied, "I'm sure we all know what we mean by that" and moved on to the next item.

We did all know what he meant and how he expected us in our different ways to co-operate in achieving it. At another staff meeting one of our colleagues expressed concern about an increase in litter and suggested that it resulted from having too few litter bins. "I'm sure you're right about that", Drayson immediately replied, "I think we'll make you master-in-charge of litter bins." It was characteristic of his style. It produced a laugh, but it also provided a good solution to the problem by delegating it to someone who could be relied on to deal with it.

Decisions were made primarily through a continuing process of delegation. Housemasters were left to run their own houses, tutors ran their own departments, and members of staff in charge of all the various activities made their own arrangements for whatever they were responsible for. It worked well for the fifteen years during which he led Stowe, and he handed over a flourishing school to his successor.

Many years later I heard of an American college principal being chosen for some accolade by his fellow principals. He was asked the secret of his success and answered, "You do your own job; you don't do anyone else's." He would not get involved in decisions about car parking; that was someone else's job. But when a colleague was caught *in flagrante dilecto* with a student, he was the person who needed to dismiss him; it was not something to leave to a personnel department. That view of things reminded me of Bob Drayson.

38. *Et in Arcadia ego*

◇◇

The words *et in Arcadia ego* (literally 'and in Arcady I') are a quotation from Virgil and suggest something like, 'Here am I, a mere mortal, in the idyllic fields of Arcady.' It is the title of a painting by Nicolas Poussin (1594-1665), now in the Louvre, of idealised shepherds of classical antiquity, living in a Utopian garden paradise, surrounded by beauty and perpetual summer, but gathered round a tomb. The grounds of Stowe in summer are the nearest thing I know to the pastoral idyll of Arcady.

The opening words of psalm 84, *Templa quam dilecta* ('How lovely are thy temples!'), were the motto of the Temple family, and the profusion of temples and other monuments in the grounds of Stowe form an extended pun on the family name. The great architectural historian, Sir Nikolaus Pevsner, described Stowe as the most perfect combination of architecture and landscape gardening in the country.

During the nineteenth century, as the fortunes and the political influence of the Dukes of Buckingham declined, the trees grew and the house was saved from being up-dated in the then fashionable Gothic style, because there was too little money to maintain well what already existed, let alone change it. So the greatest gem of eighteenth century architecture and landscape gardening matured and by the early twentieth century was becoming overgrown.

In 1988, twelve years after I had left, a businessman, who knew nothing of Stowe before he came with his family to picnic in the grounds, was so moved by the experience that shortly afterwards he called on the Chairman of the National Trust and promised £2,000,000 towards the vast task of restoration. Since then the National Trust has spent many more millions of pounds on restoration work of the thirty-eight garden buildings, with just one of them on its own, the Temple of Concord and Victory, costing £2,000,000.

Twenty years earlier I had arrived at Stowe to live as a sort of temporary bachelor, at least during the week, and I shared a flat with the then unmarried school chaplain, Peter Hancock, at the top of Chatham House, with a sitting room looking out over the landscaped gardens down to the Eleven Acre Lake and the Temple of Venus. Peter gave me a copy of the book, *Mistress Masham's Repose*, by T.H. White, the English Tutor in the 1930s, in which the little people from Lilliput, who had been brought back to England, escape and live on an island in the grounds of the palace of Malplaquet, where they meet Maria, a young girl who lives in the great house.

Malplaquet, placed in Northamptonshire, is of course Stowe in Buckinghamshire, and in 1967 one could still find the remains of the boathouse from which Maria set off across the lake when she first makes contact with the little people, though the *Rotundo* in which they live is in real life in a quite different part of the estate, housing a golden statue of the goddess Venus. Meanwhile on the island where the little people lived there is in real life a monument to the playwright William Congreve. Not far away there is a small hermitage, which had at one time in the eighteenth century housed a live hermit, and even nearer there is a pebble alcove. The grounds of Stowe were full of things like that. Quite a few were overgrown, and it was a joy finding them and finding out about them.

Bob Drayson had undertaken to provide Oriel and me with a school house, and there was even some choice of which house to have. But it would not be available until just before the start of the next school year in September 1967. So I was provided with free board and lodging for the summer term, while Oriel and the children stayed at home in Strawberry Hill until we could move into a school house near the end of the summer holidays.

As it happens I was, just for that one term, by an extraordinary stroke of good fortune, the one member of staff with no teaching to do on Saturday mornings, nor did I have any other commitment throughout the week-end. So every Friday afternoon, when lessons ended at 3.30 p.m., I could get into my car, drive back to Strawberry Hill, and be home by about five o'clock. Then I had two days and nights at home when I could help Oriel with the children and make up for the previous five days of separation from them all. After supper on Sundays I would get back in my car and return to Stowe.

During the week I taught two sets in their final A level year, all vigorously revising for their examinations, and two sets of boys in the first year of their A level course, studying seventeenth century English History and getting ready to tackle *The Age of Cromwell* as their special subject the following year. Unlike the position when I started at Quintin School, I was already reasonably well acquainted with the material I was teaching and had the luxury of a term in which to get better acquainted with the department and the school and to start planning for the future.

During the afternoons of my first term at Stowe, when all the boys were engaged in cricket or some other activity, I could not escape umpiring cricket matches by coaching boats on the river, because Stowe did not have a river, and I did not fancy supervising swimming. So I took over as master in charge of archery. At that stage my role was minimal, partly because archery only took place one afternoon a week and partly because the coaching was done by an excellent archer who drove over from Stoke Mandeville Hospital.

He was a paraplegic with immensely powerful chest and arms, and I learnt from him how to string a bow, notch an arrow onto the string with the cock feather pointing outwards, use the nose, lips and mouth as the back sight, and aim and loose an arrow. I took to it with enthusiasm. Before long I was practising alongside the boys who had opted to do archery. Soon afterwards I was joining in teaching them.

I also enjoyed taking visitors round the buildings and the grounds. My old friend David Speller, working at the Radcliffe Hospital in

Oxford at the time, impressed me by spotting a *Laburnocytisus Adamii* in the grounds – a remarkable tree which, by virtue of clever grafting in the early nineteenth century by a French gardener, M. Adam, produced yellow, purple and pink blossoms simultaneously. He had looked it up beforehand in a book on the plants of Stowe.

In the main building it was worth stopping at the honours boards to let visitors spot the names of Old Stoics who had won Oxbridge scholarships and gone on to some distinction in politics or academic life. A name which they usually passed over without comment was that of C.R. Milne. When I drew it to their attention, they might mention A.A. Milne, but no-one, I think, ever realised until it was pointed out to them that this was Christopher Robin.

Anyone brought up on *Winnie-the-Pooh* and *The House at Pooh Corner* will remember the passage in the very last chapter when Christopher Robin goes up to Galleon's Lap with Pooh and tells him about some of the things he is going to have to do and know about. They include 'Kings and Queens and something called Factors, and a place called Europe ...and when Knights were knighted, and what comes from Brazil.' On the last page they go off together and we are told that 'in that enchanted place on the top of the Forest a little boy and his Bear will always be playing.'

What we are not told is that when Christopher Robin got to Stowe he did Factors and related things to such good effect that he won a Mathematics scholarship to Trinity College, Cambridge. He read Maths, Part I, then served in the Royal Engineers during the war, returned to Cambridge and read English Literature, Part II, after which he ran a bookshop in Dartmouth for most of his life. His time at Stowe was not always happy, for he was too well-known. On one occasion a visiting preacher got up into the pulpit and instead of taking his text from the Bible, began with the words, *Hush! Hush! Whisper who dares! Christopher Robin is saying his prayers.* Everyone laughed except the preacher, who did not understand what was so funny, and Christopher Robin, who did.

In the evenings I had supper in the masters' mess, which was a complex of rooms at the eastern end of the main building, including a sitting room with William Morris wallpaper and large sofas and armchairs, a dining room with pictures of how the grounds of Stowe were planned to look in the eighteenth century, and a separate area where we met during morning break for a cup of coffee and in the afternoon for tea. Breakfast for the bachelor staff was in the dining room of the masters' mess, lunch was with the boys in the main building, and supper back in the masters' mess.

This was the place where one was best able to get to know one's colleagues, not only the bachelors who lived in, but also married men, who were welcome to sign in for supper, which was free, whenever their duties kept them at school. Most evenings Jo Bain, the bachelor housemaster of Chandos House, who looked rather like everyone's image of Henry VIII, could be found propping up the mantelpiece in the sitting room before going in to eat, with a glass in one hand and a cigarette in the other, gossiping amiably about his colleagues.

One evening someone, I forget who it was, knowing that I was teaching about Oliver Cromwell, said something disparaging about the great man and Jo replied, "Well, my father's first wife's grandmother had a great aunt who said she had known Oliver Cromwell rather well when she was a child, and that he was a most amiable gentleman." Jo was not quite forty at the time, but he claimed to have been born when his father was 92, so it could just about have been possible. It was typical of him that during a staff meeting, when Bob Drayson had just said that "gossip is the bane of Stowe", Jo interrupted to say, "Haven't you got that the wrong way round, Headmaster?"

The Summer Term of 1967 passed with teaching, marking essays, exploring the grounds, discovering the pleasures of archery, enjoying the company of my colleagues, and every week-end going home to see Oriel and the children. Oriel made the arrangements for selling 34, Michelham Gardens and successfully sold it for two thousand pounds more than we had bought it for. She investigated local antique shops and bought at extraordinarily reasonable prices a number of pieces of furniture (chests of drawers, a tallboy, a grandfather clock) which were too big for most houses in suburban Twickenham but would do well in the large house we were to live in in the village of Dadford.

Towards the end of August we moved in to Ash Tree Cottage, paying a rent throughout the years we were there of £3 a week. It was just down the hill from Stowe across Farmer Davis's farm and within convenient walking distance. I could leave home a quarter of an hour before morning chapel each day, pick up my gown from my study and be in chapel in plenty of time. Dadford was the village which had been created when Lord Cobham had the village of Stowe dismantled and moved the villagers down the hill. Ash Tree Cottage was the house in which his steward had once lived, at the end of a short drive, with a large garden on one side of it and a large area we thought of as the wild wood on the other.

Beyond Ash Tree Cottage, at the end of a rather longer drive, was another school house, Vancouver Lodge, inhabited by Gillian and Charlie Macdonald and their three children. Charlie was an Old Stoic who had recently come from Haileybury to be the Chemistry Tutor. He had done his National Service in the Gurkhas and at one point a Saracen armoured car in which he was travelling turned over and crushed his ribs, which were only able to recover over six long months in hospital waiting for nature to take its slow course.

At university he met a girl of Huguenot descent called Gillian Digges la Touche, who, when she married him, thought that she would no longer have a problem with the spelling of her surname, only to find that the various ways of spelling 'Macdonald' presented most people with more of a problem than 'Digges La Touche.' Their children, Patrick, Harriet and Alastair, were much the same age as ours. Gillian and Oriel became great friends, Charlie stayed at Stowe for the rest of his career and retired as

Second Master, and now, fifty years after we first met, and with Oriel and Charlie both dead, I sometimes go back to Buckingham to see Gillian.

After all these years, with the grounds of Stowe now manicured by the National Trust and with the temples and other monuments carefully restored, I still see it as a sort of Arcady or Elysium. But back in the late sixties and early seventies Kate, Jamie and Pip, Patrick, Harriet and Alastair roamed and played in the area around our two houses in Dadford, in the wild wood and in what they called the conker range beyond, and in the twenty-first century and in middle age they look back nostalgically to our gardens, the village green, the wild wood and the conker range rather than to the landscaped garden of Stowe, as their idyllic childhood Arcadia.

*Three pictures of the children when young: on holiday
at the seaside, in a friend's garden, and in our own garden
at Ash Tree Cottage.*

39. History Tutor

◇◇◇◇◇◇◇◇◇◇◇◇◇◇◇◇◇◇◇◇◇◇◇◇◇◇◇◇◇◇◇◇◇◇◇◇◇◇

The job of being a tutor at Stowe was always seen primarily as a matter of being responsible for the care and guidance of a group of about a couple of dozen to thirty sixth form boys, who were assumed to specialise in the tutor's subject. When I arrived in April 1967 there were nine sides: No.1 was Classics and English, 2 Modern Languages, 3 History, 4 Geography, 5 Mathematics, 6 Physics, 7 Chemistry, 8 Biology and 9 Economics. In the History Side were about a dozen boys in the Lower Sixth, another dozen in the Upper Sixth, and in the Autumn Term anything up to half a dozen Oxbridge Candidates. In a typical year about thirty Stoics took A level History, with about half from Sides 1, 2, 4 and 9 and the other half from Side 3 itself.

The job of History Tutor was known to the outside world as Senior History Master and carried with it responsibility for running the History Department, but within the school the running of a department was always seen as a secondary responsibility. The main job was looking after the History Side and teaching A level and scholarship History. The History Side always had a certain prestige, many boys aspired to join it, and in the so-called 'slave market' at the beginning of each Autumn Term, when housemasters bargained with tutors about which boys they should take, I always had a good field of choice. It is a measure of the pre-eminence of the History Side that throughout the nine years and a term that I was at Stowe, there was only one year in which the head boy was in any other sixth form side, and he, David McDonough, who was in Peter Longhurst's Economics Side, was taking history as one of his A level subjects and was the secretary of my Debating Society.

That pre-eminence of the History Side had a long history. Brian Rees, the author of a history of Stowe, when commenting on

298

*History Tutor at Stowe in the late 1960s and
Oriel on holiday at about the same time.*

Roxburgh's early appointments, said: 'The most daring appointment was that of Martin McLaughlin as Head of History. Claiming descent from the O'Melaghlins, Kings of Meath in the Dark Ages, he supported the Fenians and the Easter Rising. He was oblivious of ordinary constraints and saved himself postage by writing O.H.M.S. across his mail. His technique for teaching was to make the most outrageous assertions which obliged his pupils to engage in research to show how unsound his views were. The results were phenomenal. Of Stowe's first twenty-four university awards half were in History, and Roxburgh added £50 to McLaughlin's salary by way of appreciation.'

Rather surprisingly McLaughlin left in 1933 for a predictably unsuccessful career in the Inspectorate, for which he was entirely unsuited, and his life moved from one disaster to another until in the early 1960s he was seen sleeping rough near Stowe, with newspaper under his coat to keep the cold out. Later still, in 1964, he was found in a similar condition in a country lane in Shropshire and was taken into hospital, where he died.

His place was taken in 1934 by another remarkable man, W. L. (Bill) McElwee (pronounced with the stress on the first syllable), who abandoned a promising university career (he had already published a *Life of the Emperor Charles V*) to be the History Tutor at Stowe. He held the post for the next thirty years, with a break for military service during the Second World War, when he served with the Argyll and Sutherland Highlanders, and in 1944 he won the MC during the invasion of Normandy.

Roxburgh wrote to him recollecting that when McElwee joined the army 'we both thought you would be a schoolmaster soldiering', but in reality, he went on, he was 'a soldier who did a bit of school-mastering before he joined.' Be that as it may, McElwee returned to be the History Tutor at Stowe, but left in 1964, at a time when many of his colleagues were also leaving in the wake of the dissensions caused by the Crichton-Miller affair. He became the Director of Studies at Sandhurst, where he wrote a very good book on the development of military technology *From Waterloo to Mons*.

While at Stowe McElwee gathered round him many of the brightest sixth form boys in the school, and the History Side was inclined to see itself as an élite. It was said that McElwee also gathered up members of the aristocracy (especially if they had a title) even if they were somewhat dim, but that the side maintained its intellectual pre-eminence because, as with David Roberts at Christ's Hospital, many of the cleverest boys wanted to be taught by him, and he welcomed them, even if their parents were in 'trade' - a term which I understood to include most of the professions.

Bill McElwee seems to have shared with Roxburgh the attitude which is now widely disliked and known as 'snobbery.' But as Brian Stephan, who only knew them after 1944, wisely pointed out, attitudes which made one uncomfortable in the late twentieth century might well not have caused the same resentment in the thirties, and 'those of us who were irritated by what we felt was Roxburgh's snobbery may ourselves be guilty of lacking historical perspective.'

The member of staff who shared most of the A level work with me was Brian Mead, who was about the same age as me, and whom I had first met, though without knowing his name, in the winter of 1951-52, when the Christ's Hospital and Taunton 1st XVs played against each other in Reading. I remember three things about the game: Taunton had a particularly good scrum half, the final score was 0 - 0, and after the game, in bitter weather, we had to wash in cold water. The particularly good scrum half was Brian Mead. On leaving school he did his National Service in the Royal Navy, read History at Pembroke College, Cambridge, and then came to Stowe, where he was now commanding the naval section of the CCF, was the master in charge of rugby football and had recently got married.

The other member of staff who also did some A level teaching was Chris Deacon. During the Second World War he had trained Spitfire pilots in Canada, and I remember his indignation when a Stoic, writing short notes on 'the Spitfire' in an internal examination, began his answer, 'The Spitfire was a German fighter aircraft of the Second World War.' Chris was another Cambridge historian, and like Brian Mead he always took an O level set as well as his A level work.

A fourth member of the department who regularly took an O level set throughout my time at Stowe was the Revd J.E.C. ('Jos') Nichol MC, MA. He was an Old Stoic and a Cambridge Rugby Blue who had joined the staff in 1959 as assistant chaplain and was soon a housemaster. He had served during the war in No. 2 Commando, much of the while in Jugoslavia, fighting alongside Marshal Tito, whom he used to visit each year for a reunion dinner.

One evening in the masters' mess a new, young master, David Temple, was showing some of us pictures of a recent holiday on the coast of Jugoslavia. When Jos Nichol came in he was called over to see if he recognised the area. He did. He even recognised a particular tree beside the coast road to which, he explained, he had tied a wire and taken off the head of a German motor-cyclist. I watched the expression on the face of David Temple as he heard this gentle, benevolent clergyman describe killing someone thirty years earlier.

As a young man Jos had, of course, lived with death as a frequent companion. A fellow Old Stoic in No.2 Commando was the Duke of Wellington, who was killed in Italy leading an assault behind German lines at Salerno, and I remember Jos telling me about the unit's chaplain, mortally wounded and dying in his arms. That was the point, he said, at which he had determined that, if he survived the war, he would himself become a clergyman. One of his sons was a member of my History Side shortly after I went to Stowe.

The Headmaster of Stowe in 1976 with the housemasters and tutors, several of whom are mentioned in the text. Bob Drayson is in the middle of the front row. I am at the far left and in the same row are Brian Mead at the right-hand end, Brian Stephan, the Senior Tutor, next to me, and George Clarke next to Bob Drayson, is three in from the right. In the second row the Revd J.E.C. ('Jos') Nichol, MC, MA is second in from the left and next to him is Charlie Macdonald. David Lennard is immediately behind Jos and Peter Longhurst is behind George Clarke.

Another of the housemasters, married with three children, was George Clarke, who was an expert on the history of Stowe House and the development of the gardens. He taught mainly A level English, but was always happy to teach local history to a Third Form History set, because that was something about which he was enthusiastic. He was a tall, good-looking, liberally minded man who ran his house in a relaxed manner, expecting boys to behave well rather than requiring them to do so. 'Public schools', he pointed out to me once, 'are not so much for the sons of gentlemen as the fathers of gentlemen', and he was the sort of person who had a civilising effect on boys in his care.

George telephoned me one day when Bob Drayson had found a boy who was a member of both George's House and my History Side swimming in the lake when he should have been working. 'Needs a beating', Bob had said in his usual brisk manner, and George, who never beat anyone, rang me to discuss what best to do. I suggested that I put the boy in detention, which would be something of a humiliation for a senior boy, and that would settle it. He could not reasonably be punished twice for one offence.

That, as it happens, was the argument Thomas Becket had used to Henry II about the punishment of criminous clerks. He had quoted St Jerome's commentary on the prophet Nahum: *non judicat Deus bis in idipsum* - 'God does not condemn someone twice for the same thing.' Not that we were likely to have to appeal to the authority of either Thomas Becket or St Jerome. Bob would certainly have expected appropriate action to dissuade boys from going swimming during a study period, but he would have been satisfied with an assurance that 'that has been dealt with, Headmaster.' He had the sense to leave such things to housemasters and tutors - especially if they agreed with each other.

As it happens, the headmaster was one of the other members of staff who taught a Third Form History set. He found it a useful way of getting to know new boys. The other was Peter Longhurst, who saw it as a relaxation from his main diet of A level Economics.

Between them Bob Drayson, George Clarke and Peter Longhurst covered the teaching of the Third Forms. Just what they did and how they did it must have varied immensely. That did not concern me. I simply wanted boys joining the school to learn something interesting about the historical significance of the environment around them. All three of them could be trusted to do that.

Like Bill McElwee I unashamedly encouraged the historians to see themselves as an intellectual élite, so long as that involved working hard and taking an interest in what one might call the things of the mind that went beyond the A level syllabus, and almost all the boys whom I was teaching aspired to go on to university, though one whom I only taught for one term when I arrived at Stowe in the Summer of 1967, did not. He was a bright boy who had done well at O level when fifteen and wanted to leave school and get on with his life. He very reluctantly stayed on in the Lower Sixth because the school leaving age was sixteen.

After marking a couple of his essays I suggested that he was making a mistake. 'Richard,' I said, 'your work is a bit chaotic, but all you have to do is impose a bit of order on your essays and there is no reason at all why you shouldn't go on to university.' But he declined to take my advice and went off to run his first project, the *Student* magazine, then sell records under the *Virgin* label, market *Mates* condoms, and eventually set up an airline and buy railways and an island in the Caribbean. I have sometimes thought that, if he had taken my advice, he might have disappeared into obscurity and spent his life in one of the honourable and poorly paid professions.

He was clearly an intelligent boy and towards the end of term I lent him my copy of *The Century of Revolution* by Christopher Hill, to give him a Marxist view of the seventeenth century. After he had left I realised that he still had it, so, since I needed it while working on *The Age of Cromwell* special subject, I sent him a postcard wishing him well and asking him to return the book. Not getting a reply, I called in at the school bookshop to pick up another copy. I took the best looking second-hand copy from the shelf, looked inside and found my name crossed out and Richard Branson's name written in, together with the second-hand price: 12/6. He had sold it at the end of term together with a pile of other books he no longer wanted. I thought it worth a letter from the headmaster rather just a note from me, so a letter duly went from Bob Drayson:

Dear Branson,

I understand from Mr Arnold that he wrote to you a week ago about a book he lent you called 'The Century of Revolution' by Christopher Hill, to ask if you would return it to him, but he has so far not had a reply from you. In the meantime he has discovered the book in question for sale, second-hand, in the Stowe Bookshop, with his name crossed out and yours written in above. I think you will agree that Mr Arnold expects an explanation from you for something which, not to put too fine a point on it, almost amounts to stealing. I feel sure that this was a mistake on your part, but you can understand that Mr Arnold is not at all pleased.

Apart from a letter of apology and an explanation, you should of course send him a cheque for 25/-, which is the cost of a new copy of the book in question.

Yours sincerely,
R.Q.Drayson.

I still have the carbon copy tucked inside the book. Unfortunately I do not have Richard Branson's reply, but it was memorable and went something like this:

My dear Drayson,

I'm so sorry about this misunderstanding over Mr Arnold's book. I'm afraid his card was at the bottom of a large pile of correspondence my secretary was dealing with. I enclose a cheque for 25/- to cover the cost of the book.

With very best wishes,   *Richard.*

As it happens, I knew that his secretary was his grandmother. 'He'll either be in prison or a millionaire by the time he's thirty', said Bob Drayson, and of course he was right.

Many years later, when my nephew, Matthew, was working for Virgin Atlantic, Richard Branson won a legal battle with British Airways and was awarded millions of pounds damages. The next day Matthew and every other employee of Virgin Airline got a letter from the boss, saying effectively, 'Well done! That was a team effort.' It was accompanied by a cheque for their share of the damages. I thought it immensely impressive, and what was particularly impressive was that everyone, from the top to the bottom, got the same amount. Many, perhaps most, teenage boys have done something as bad as selling someone else's book for its second-hand value. Not many employers have shared out millions of pounds equally among their employees when they had no need to do so.

40. The History Syllabus

One important difference between grammar schools and public schools was that, whereas boys usually entered the first form of a grammar school at the age of eleven, new boys usually arrived at public schools at the age of thirteen or fourteen. Most went into the Third Form (there was no First or Second Form) and spent one, two or three terms there before the two years leading to O level. Because of that variety there were, understandably, no very clear arrangements for what was taught in History classes in the Third Form. My experience of wandering round the grounds led me to decide that it would make sense to make use of the grounds, with all its temples, monuments and other objects of interest to devise for new boys a distinctive form of local history which could be spread over one, two or three terms.

From the South Front of the main building one could look out beyond the grass sweeping down to the Octagon Lake, across the Octagon to the Ionic pavilions and, in the distance, to the Corinthian Arch. To the left of that South Front vista was a Doric Arch, so the Doric Arch, the Ionic pavilions and the Corinthian Arch could act as an introduction to the three main orders of architecture of Greek antiquity. Through the Doric Arch there was a carefully contrived view of 'Stowe Castle' on the far horizon. It was an illusion. What one was seeing was a couple of cottages with small battlements on their roofs, giving the impression of a distant castle.

The Temple of Friendship, gutted by fire long ago and now a romantic ruin, was where Whig aristocrats, Cobham's cubs, used to meet in the eighteenth century to agree their political plans. Up the hill from the Palladian Bridge was an area designed to look like an idyllic English rural landscape, ideally decorated with sheep and cows and milkmaids, and with a Gothic Temple, certainly gothic in appearance, but scrupulously classical in design.

At the top of the hill was the Queen's Temple, with its floor inlaid with Roman mosaics and with the steps leading up to the entrance pitted with the marks of .22 ammunition from the time when the area just below it was used by the school's Officer Training Corps as a rifle range. Down the hill, the other side of the Palladian Bridge, were the Japanese gardens, beautifully laid out in the eighteenth century, but long overgrown and in the 1960s and 70s used by what was by then the school's Combined Cadet Force as an assault course.

The Oxford Avenue, which swept towards the school from the south-west, ran roughly along the line of the old Roman road to Towcester (or *Lactodorum*) where it met the main military highway running north-west from *Londinium* and *Verulamium* (St Albans) to *Deva* (or Chester). The ha-ha, which encircled the whole 750 acres of the home park, was built in the style of military fortifications at the time of the Marlborough wars, complete with bastions, which served no useful purpose around a peaceful park but were constructed that way because those who built them had been used to building military fortifications.

The old Anglo-Saxon village of Stowe had been removed by Earl Temple in the eighteenth century, and the villagers had been re-settled down the hill at Dadford, where Oriel and the children and I lived through most of the time that I taught at Stowe. All that remained of the original village was a thirteenth century church, carefully hidden by trees, but still the parish church for the inhabitants of the village of Dadford. Even a Whig aristocrat did not have the authority to demolish a church, even if he could demolish all the houses around it.

Beyond Stowe Church, and to the South-east of the main building, was an area known as the Elysian Fields. There was to be found the Temple of Ancient Virtue, which had once housed statues of

Homer, Lycurgus, Epaminondas and Socrates – those being seen by the Whig aristocrats who designed the grounds as the most illustrious poet, law-giver, general and philosopher of ancient times. Facing it across the River Styx was the Temple of British Worthies, with a dozen busts of those perceived by the Whigs to be the greatest men of British history, together with inscriptions setting out what had made them great.

Understandably it included Sir Isaac Newton, 'whom the God of Nature made to comprehend His work', and William Shakespeare, to whom was granted 'power beyond all other men to move, astonish and delight mankind.' It celebrated the so-called 'Glorious Revolution' of 1688-89 with a bust of William III, the Prince of Orange, who 'by a bold and generous enterprise, came to preserve the liberty and religion of Great Britain.' Perhaps more surprisingly it includes a bust of Edward, Prince of Wales, better known to history as the Black Prince, who is there because the outstanding achievement of his life was fighting and killing Frenchmen, thus endearing himself to the Francophobe Whigs.

The Temple of British Worthies alone could supply a mass of material for teaching, but there was also, for example, the Cobham Monument, the Wolfe Obelisk, the Grenville Pillar and Queen Caroline's Monument. On an island in the Octagon Lake is the memorial to the playwright William Congreve. The pediment has at the front a carving of the face of a pretty young girl, while on one side there is a representation of the face of a lascivious youth and on the other that of an elderly man with cuckold's horns on his head. It is inscribed with the words *vitae imitatio, consuetudinis speculum, comoedia* ('Comedy is the imitation of life and the mirror of custom'), and on top is a statue, made more than a century before Darwin's *Origin of Species by Natural Selection* was published, of a monkey looking at itself in a mirror.

All this could be used by those teaching the Third Forms. In the first place it was interesting in itself. Secondly, all of it helped to make the point that history is all around us. At Stowe it happened to be all around us in profusion.

Stowe historians. Each year we had a photograph taken of the members of the History Side by one or other of the various garden monuments. This one is from the early 1970s and was taken in front of the Rotunda, which now houses a gilded statue of Venus. Brian Mead and I are both sitting at the front.

During the Fourth Form year I expected my colleagues to cover an outline of British history from the Roman invasion in 60 AD, during the reign of the Emperor Claudius, up to the outbreak of the First World War in 1914, preferably devoting a reasonable amount of time to the millennium from the Roman invasion until the Norman Conquest. It is easy to neglect those early years, but it is worth reflecting that the period from the Claudian invasion until the withdrawal of the legions in 411 AD is exactly the same length of time (351 years) as that from the defeat of the Spanish Armada in 1588 until the outbreak in 1939 of the Second World War.

We are still very obviously living with the consequences of the Roman occupation. The Roman military highway running from London up to Chester is now the A5, and most of the best roads in England, at least until the nineteenth century, were the Roman ones. As late as the 1960s many grammar schools all over England were still expecting all the boys in their care to learn at least something of the language of the former conquering power. It was also worth noticing that the Anglo-Saxon division of the country into administrative districts called shires dated from the tenth century and lasted well into the twentieth, and in some cases beyond that. History is not about quaint romantic things in a lost past; it is about the relationship between the past and the present.

One danger with covering the whole sweep of English History over nearly two thousand years is that a teacher may go from one important event to another in a manner which seems to indicate that those events are part of a noble and inexorable movement towards the ideal of parliamentary democracy. That too often seems to be what politicians want of History teachers. It is not what pupils get when History is well taught. Ideally they develop a critical sense, learn how to organise their thoughts, acquire some understanding of how the past was both different from and similar to the world we live in today, and even develop the ability to recognise nonsense when they encounter it.

Once boys were in the Fourth Form I wanted them to learn how to write a simple essay. Ideally that would prepare them to do some good work by the time they started in the Fifth Form, during which they tackled the O level syllabus. At Stowe there were four O level sets in the Fifth Form and the syllabus in both English and European History was more or less the period covered by the book I had written on *Britain, Europe and the World, 1870 – 1955*. There was also a form called the Upper Fifth for those boys who were, unfortunately, sometimes referred to as 're-treads', whose relatively poor performance at O level (often because they had taken it when too young) required them to spend another year before going on to A level.

I decided that four of my colleagues would each take both a Fourth Form and Fifth Form set and that I would always take the Upper Fifth. That had a double advantage. It meant that those boys who had to spend a second year on an O level course never had the same master the second time round. It also meant that the Upper Fifth, who often needed some reassurance about their ability after their lack of success at O level, could see that they were regarded as important enough to be taught by the History Tutor, who was also the author of the text book they were using.

The syllabus for the A level course was very loosely determined by the Oxford and Cambridge Examinations Board and seemed to me admirable in its flexibility. All candidates took an English History paper which covered the whole range of English History. They were given a choice of about seventy to eighty questions, from which they needed to answer only four. They also took a European History paper, which similarly covered the whole range of European History, and again they were given a choice of about seventy to eighty questions and only had to answer four. That gave those teaching A level History a vast choice of what to teach. Each candidate also had to take a paper on a special subject, and there the choice was more limited. They had to answer three out of twelve questions.

At Stowe there were always two A level sets in both the Lower and Upper Sixth. I shared the teaching of each set with someone else, since I believed it was good for A level candidates to be taught by more than one person, if only to discover that there are different opinions about history and different approaches to it. Mostly the other person was Brian Mead, and while he taught what is known as early modern history (the Tudor and Stuart period in English history), I taught medieval history to one set in each year and recent history to the other.

One effect of this was that an A level examiner might be faced with an extraordinarily wide range of answers from the Stowe candidates. When I met George Holmes, a Fellow of St Catherine's College, Oxford, who was also the Chief Examiner for A level History for the Oxford and Cambridge Examinations Board, he asked me to explain how it was that his examiners might be faced with answers on, for example, Alfred and the Danes, King John and *Magna Carta*, the Dissolution of the Monasteries, the 'Eleven Years' Tyranny' of Charles I, Irish Home Rule and the 1930s policy of 'Appeasement' - and not necessarily in that order. It appeared all the more of a jumble because the A level candidates' papers were arranged in alphabetical order, mixing up those who had done medieval history with those who had done modern history.

As the History Tutor it was up to me to teach the A level special subject in the second year of the course. It soon seemed to me important not to be teaching the same topic to two different sets at the same time, so I would do a medieval special subject with one set and a more modern special subject with the other one. Eventually, after nineteen years as a schoolmaster, sixteen of them as head of a history department, first at Quintin and then at Stowe, I had taught eight different special subjects.

In chronological order there were three medieval ones, *The Crusades, The Norman Conquest* (both at Stowe) and *The Reign of Henry II* (at Clifton), two early modern ones, *The Reign of Henry VIII* and *The Age of Cromwell* (both at Stowe), and three modern ones, *The French Revolution* and *The Making of the Triple Alliance and the Triple Entente* (both at Quintin School) and *The Russian Revolution* (at Stowe). So my summer holidays were often largely spent in reading the next lot of books and documents.

I found the relationship between the English Civil War, the French Revolution and the Russian Revolution particularly interesting and would have liked to have found time to write a book comparing them. There were superficial similarities, such as that each of the rulers of the countries involved was married to a foreign princess from the country of a traditional enemy: Charles I and Henrietta Maria of France, Louis XVI and Marie Antoinette of the Hapsburg Empire, Nicholas II and the German princess Alix, who became the Tsarina Alexandra. There were also more fundamental similarities, such as that in each case trouble began at the top and shifted down the social scale until eventually a strong man seized power, eliminated enemies on both left and right, and established a form of government similar to but more efficient than that which had preceded the revolution. But time was limited and the only book I found time to write while at Stowe was a second edition of *Britain, Europe and the World*, bringing it up to 1971.

41. History in the Sixth Form

Some time around 1970, give or take a few years either way, I was introduced at a party to a young woman with the words, 'You really must meet Harriet. You're both teachers.' Uncertain of quite what the right response was to that, I said, 'Oh, what do you teach?' 'Children', she replied witheringly, 'and you?' 'History', I answered, knowing as I said it that I was putting my foot in it. 'Don't you think children are more important than any particular subject?' she asked. 'Probably,' I replied, 'but I find history more interesting.'

It was the end of a potentially beautiful friendship. Of course, part of the problem was that the verb 'to teach' takes a double accusative. You teach people, but you also teach something. She had to teach something to all the children in her primary school and I couldn't very well teach history unless there was someone for me to teach.

When I became a teacher it was History that I wanted to teach, and I was conscious that the word 'history' is used in two quite different ways, both of which were relevant to my wish to teach the subject. First, it means 'everything that happened in the past.' Secondly, it means 'the study of what happened in the past.' I quite enjoyed teaching students about what happened in the past, but I saw that as a secondary task and something of a self-indulgence. My principal job was to teach them how to study it. Another way of putting that is that my job was not so much to teach them History as to teach them how to think.

But if that is so, anyone can reasonably ask why one should particularly teach them History rather than, say, Physics. The answer is that it is largely a matter of preference. It did not especially interest me as a teenager to learn that 'when a body is wholly or

315

partially immersed in any fluid the body experiences an upthrust equal to the weight of the fluid displaced.' But it did interest me that Archimedes seems to have thought of that while lying in his bath and that he leapt up crying *Eureka* - 'I've got it.' That is a particularly striking example of a common experience. You grapple with a problem you cannot solve and in the end give up and go to bed or have a bath. Then, as you relax the answer comes to you. There we make contact with the experience of Archimedes centuries earlier.

From a relatively early age I found History particularly interesting. I prefer Archimedes to his principle and I prefer History to Physics. Similarly as a young man I preferred Brigitte Bardot to Grace Kelly, Mozart to Mahler and Keats to Milton. But that only leads on to the question of why one should prefer Brigitte Bardot, Mozart and Keats, and why anyone should prefer History to Physics. After all, Physics appears to have some practical value, and it is not clear that History does. Anyone can reasonably ask what point there is in knowing about the past, and especially the distant past.

The most helpful answer I can suggest involves looking at ourselves. Human beings are all interested in themselves and we are all born self-conscious and self-centred. That is, it is in the nature of human beings that they see the world from their own position outwards. Each of us is at the centre of our own universe, but despite this, or perhaps because of it, we want to understand something of our environment. Indeed, we need to. We need to be sure that the ground will not suddenly give way under our feet and that a fly will not turn into a crocodile and eat us. We need to have some idea of how people around us are likely to behave, and we need to understand how close relations and friends feel and think.

All such understanding depends on one's understanding of the past - largely, of course, on one's direct memories of the past. But where does one draw the line both in space and time? Do we want to understand our parents and children but not our aunts and uncles and nephews and nieces? Do we want to understand the English but not the Japanese? And can we understand English educational arrangements, our extraordinary legal system, or our parliamentary system without looking back to the distant past.

I am not suggesting that History should be studied as the development of present situations and institutions. I am merely suggesting that my own motive for studying History is essentially the same as the one which the Anglo-Saxon chronicler attributed to William the Conqueror when he had the Doomsday Survey made. He wanted, we are told, 'to know more about this realm of England, how it was peopled and with what kind of men.' It is this that really matters. I want to make the acquaintance of Archimedes in his bath and of William the Conqueror in his castle. I want to see the monastery of St Edmondsbury under Abbot Samson as what Carlyle called 'a real world of historic actuality' and not as 'a void infinite of grey haze with phantasms swimming in it.' I want to get to know the people of the past as intimately as possible.

Those who choose to study History rather than Mathematics have put behind them the pleasure of tackling a problem and getting the right answer. A mathematician can prove, granted certain axioms, that in any right-angled triangle the area of the square on the largest of the three sides is exactly equal to the areas of the squares on the other two sides added together. But we can never prove, for example, that those who start a rebellion will end up being destroyed as reactionary counter-revolutionaries – however likely that may seem.

What the historian can experience is the pleasure (if that is the right word) of getting better acquainted with Oliver Cromwell and Denzil Holles, with Robespierre and Danton, or with Trotsky and Zinoviev. As it happens, the last two of those pairs illustrate very effectively the general principle referred to above. They were destroyed as the revolutions they helped to generate overtook them. But Cromwell and Holles contradict it, and the career of Denzil Holles illustrates particularly well the unpredictability of historical developments.

Holles was one of the leaders of the opposition to Charles I before the English Civil War. He was one of the five members of parliament, Pym, Hampden, Holles, Haselrig and Strode, whom Charles I tried to arrest on 16th January 1642, thus helping to precipitate civil war. Back in 1629, when Charles wanted to dissolve Parliament, Holles held Speaker Finch down in the chair, saying as he did so, 'God's wounds, you shall sit until we please.' He then kept him there while three resolutions were passed by the House of Commons.

When the war began Holles was one of the first men to raise a regiment against the king. But by the time the war appeared to be won, power was increasingly in the hands of the leaders of the parliamentary army, who generally had a more extreme programme than Holles. So he now patched up what one of his former colleagues called 'an ungodly accommodation' with Queen Henrietta Maria. After the king's execution he went off into exile and in 1660, at the Restoration of King Charles II, he returned to England as the first Baron Holles to sit in judgement on his former revolutionary colleagues.

So the first point I am making is that history does not teach anyone the right answer to anything, but it may possibly provide some understanding or insight into the past and it may help you make the past part of your own experience. That is particularly so when you get round to studying elements of history in detail. History comes to life when you hear the learned and saintly Bishop Gilbert Foliot of London in the twelfth century commenting at Northampton on the archbishop of Canterbury, Thomas Becket, 'My dear fellow, the man was always a fool and always will be', or when you hear of the great Lord Curzon, former Viceroy of India and Foreign Secretary in the early 1920s, so totally out of touch with ordinary life that once, when in a hurry, he is said to have jumped onto a London bus saying to the conductor, 'To the Foreign Office, my man.' Such details prove nothing, but they enhance understanding.

318

In 1931, when the Labour Party suffered a devastating General Election defeat in most of the country, an extremist revolutionary splinter-group, the Independent Labour Party, or ILP, won four seats in Glasgow, and thousands of Glaswegian Socialists came to the station singing as they saw their MPs off to Westminster. They did not sing *The Red Flag* or *The Internationale*. Instead they sang the metrical versions of the psalms, and that helps to make intelligible the general comment that the Labour movement in Great Britain has its roots far less in Marxism than in Christianity, and in particular in the non-conformist Methodist and Baptist chapels in Wales and England and in the Presbyterian Kirk in Scotland.

All this is to do with History in the sense of it being what happened in the past. I am suggesting that getting to know various obscure corners of the past in detail can be interesting. But I suggested earlier that 'history' has another meaning, and that meaning is probably best approached by looking at the word's origins. *Historia* was a Greek word meaning 'search' or 'enquiry', so History in this sense involves a search or enquiry into the past, into why things happened the way they did and with what results. Similarly 'Natural History' implies a search or enquiry into Nature.

But once you have searched or enquired into an historical problem, you then need some way of communicating to others the outcome of your inquiry. You need not only an input system but also an output system, and that is why medieval scholars in the universities of Western Europe studied both Logic and Rhetoric. Logic is a means of systematic analysis of problems, while Rhetoric is a means of persuading others of conclusions already reached. Logic is input; Rhetoric is output. There was a lot to be said for including both in the curriculum, and the historian needs both to be able to study the past and to be able to communicate the results of his studies.

As it happens, the method of work of the historian is not and cannot be the method of Logic. Logic is deductive, as is Mathematics. With both of them you move from general principles to particular propositions, and since that was characteristic of medieval thought, it is understandable that there was not much historical work done during the Middle Ages - only descriptions of events in what are known as chronicles. But the great scientific revolution which got going in the seventeenth century involved a swing in fashion from deductive to inductive thought – to looking at evidence, fitting it together and drawing conclusions. That is what Sir Isaac Newton did when he looked at a spectrum of light broken up into separate colours by a prism and came to the conclusion that white light is the combination of all the different colours of the spectrum. What historians do is analogous to that. Historians have to look at evidence and draw conclusions from it. History is one of the many sciences brought into being by Man's willingness to think inductively - that is, to start with the evidence.

But History is not only a science. If it were, that would emphasise input to the exclusion of output and neglect communication with the reader, or what I earlier referred to as Rhetoric. The historian has got to be able to explain opinions and demonstrate that they fit the evidence, and I would suggest that the best physicists, chemists and biologists do that too. But they have the difficulty that they are very often using technical language and formulae which the average citizen finds difficult to follow. The historian should be able to express himself in a manner which is intelligible to anyone.

It is not necessarily easy. Shakespeare recognised the problem in his prologue to Henry V. 'Can this cockpit', he wrote, speaking of the Globe Theatre, 'hold the vasty fields of France, or may we cram within this wooden O the very casques that did affright the air at Agincourt?' In the event he made an impressive job of doing just that. But he was unusual and the rest of us need some guidance about how to cope. Partly it is a matter of keeping clear in one's mind just what one is seeking to explain or describe. 'Think, when we speak of horses, that you see them printing their proud hoofs i' th' receiving earth.' But very often it is not solid objects such as charging horses that you need to put across when writing history, but ideas or policies.

If you are trying to explain St Anselm's ontological argument for the existence of God or the convolutions of Bismarck's policy towards Austria-Hungary and Russia, you need to have a clear idea in your mind of the ontological argument or of Bismarck's policy, and if you keep it there and then write as simply as possible, you may be able to convey the gist of the ontological argument or Bismarck's policy to your reader.

No doubt the principles which apply to the study of History apply to most, even all, other subjects as well. You need to be interested in something, you need to work at it and you need to develop the capacity for explaining it. Above all, you have to learn to do it for yourself and not merely reproduce pages of other people's thoughts. Once, when Winston Churchill emerged from a long-distance bomber flight over the Atlantic and immediately gave a speech describing his meeting with the American President, Franklin D. Roosevelt, Roosevelt was astonished and asked how he was able to do it. The answer was, 'He rolls his own, Mr President.'

One of the pleasures of teaching sixth formers is that they are going through the gruelling though sometimes exciting process of adolescence, of changing from children into adults, and are at the stage of development when they can learn to roll their own. The study of history and of all other subjects should be part of a process of personal development, learning how much more there is to know and how impossible it is to know it all and understand it all.

I used to suggest to my A level historians at the beginning of their course that the two most important words written in the twentieth century were those which precede E.M.Forster's novel *Howards End*: 'Only connect.' At the start of the course that probably did not make sense to most of them. By the end I hope they saw the point. I also used to tell them that someone had once said that 'History teaches you nothing except that History teaches you nothing.' It is a valuable lesson to learn, but you have to go through the process of studying History in order to make sense of it.

42. Life as a schoolmaster

My working life was dominated by teaching history. I never had a formal departmental meeting. Instead, over a cup of coffee I would talk individually with Brian Mead, Chris Deacon, Jos Nichol and anyone else who taught history. We would talk about what they wanted to do and about what I wanted to achieve, and it proved remarkably easy to reach agreement. Because the range of what we taught and what sixth form historians studied was so diverse, it seemed important to me to develop a history library, in order that A level historians could read widely without incurring unreasonable expense. So I asked Bob Drayson for some money to start a history library. His reaction was typical of the way he did things: 'Would a thousand pounds do to begin with?' It would, and the result was the start of an invaluable and developing resource.

I started an Historical Society, which met three times a term on a Friday evening at Ash Tree Cottage, with Oriel providing coffee and chocolate biscuits, and addressed by outside speakers on a wide range of topics. Stowe was very conveniently placed, within easy reach of Oxford, Cambridge and London. I would show the visiting speakers round the grounds, an unending source of interest to historians, take him (or her) to a meal in the masters' mess, and then on to Dadford for the meeting, to stay overnight and be seen off after a leisurely breakfast by Oriel, while I had to be off promptly to teach the first two lessons on Saturday morning.

A schoolmaster's life in a school such as Stowe involved a range of other activities. In the autumn term Brian Mead would get me to take the under-14s rugby, in the winter term Stuart Morris, in charge of hockey, would get me to umpire (badly) junior hockey games, and in the summer I was increasingly involved in archery. In my second summer term the archery coach, who had been an excellent instructor, very sadly died, and the immediate assumption was that we would need to look for a new coach. I suggested to Bob Drayson that the money spent on paying a coach could now be better spent on equipment. I had picked up enough to be able to do the coaching. If I could have the money to buy targets, bows, arrows, strings, bracers, finger tabs, sights and a hut in which to store them, I would undertake to run an effective archery club myself. It was characteristic of Bob Drayson that he happily agreed.

Within a couple of years we not only had a large and flourishing archery club but also a very successful archery team. We had to travel some distance to find other schools with good archery teams to shoot against. Eton, at the other end of Buckinghamshire, was one, Haileybury another, and the others were Forest School in Wanstead and St Alban's Catholic Grammar School in Finchley. A visit to St Alban's Grammar School brought me as close as I have ever been in my life to the workings of MI5, which was investigating the Finchley Albanian Society on the suspicion that it was a Communist Party cell in North London in contact with the government of Albania. It was in fact the old boys' club of St Alban's Grammar School.

From 1970 to 1974 the Stowe archery team was undefeated, in 1975 we lost one match (against Haileybury) and in 1976, my last year, we were again undefeated. Brian Stephan, when writing *Stowe, Hearsay and Memory*, commented that 'the victories of the archery team had become almost monotonous in their regularity', and the *Illustrated History of Stowe School* includes a picture of the archery team standing in front of the Palladian Bridge. I always shot alongside the school team, and the members knew that they got their colours if and when they beat me in a match. One year, after I had been to a particularly good party the previous evening, every member of the team won his colours on the same day.

I learnt all sorts of historical and linguistic details related to archery. The Greek letter ψ (psi) is a picture of a bow and arrow.

*The Stowe archery team at the end of an undefeated
season in the early 1970s.*

The term 'rule of thumb' relates to making a rough check of whether a bow is too tightly or too loosely strung by placing one's fist on the belly of the bow with the thumb outstretched, ideally just touching the string. The once common description of unreliability as playing 'fast and loose' with someone's affections derives from the archery orders 'Loose', which means 'Fire', and 'Fast', which means 'Stop.' I also liked the idea that the German verb *schiessen* suggests an arrow sailing into the distance, whereas the T on the end of the English equivalent, the verb 'to shoot', suggests an arrow hitting its target.

The other activity I took on was debating. I had run a flourishing Debating Society at Quintin School and now did the same at Stowe. While archery took a lot of my time in the summer term, debating flourished in the autumn and winter terms and we packed up for the summer. I believed in having a formal structure for debating, and we always began the year by debating the motion 'that this house has no confidence in Her Majesty's government' and then anything from sharing with Caesar his preference for fat men to approving Edward Heath's decision to sack Enoch Powell from the shadow cabinet after the 'rivers of blood' speech in 1968. I wrote to Edward Heath to let him know that that motion had been carried by a substantial margin, and he replied that, as I could imagine, he had had a lot of correspondence on the issue; 'Yours was one of the nicest.'

Quite early in my time at Stowe I came to be concerned about a number of issues which I thought of as coming under the heading of 'academic administration'. The first was the issue of the form in which new boys were placed on arrival. Too many boys in the Upper Fifth, the so-called O level 're-treads', were quite clever but had been put through the O level course too young and needed to repeat the O level year before going on to A level. In a few cases they did well enough to stay on for the 'seventh term' to take the Oxbridge examinations and get a place at an Oxford or Cambridge college.

The case for putting a larger number of new boys in the Third Form seemed strong to me. Not everyone agreed. It was not the sort of issue which was of particular interest either to Bob Drayson or Brian Stephan. Bob's solution was to form a curriculum committee and make me chairman, with Charlie Macdonald, the Chemistry Tutor, and David Manly, the Modern Languages Tutor, as members. Then, when we reported with a unanimous and quite detailed recommendation on how to implement the change, he was entirely happy to approve our recommendation.

In the event the curriculum committee worked on a substantial number of issues, such as reorganising the options arrangements for O level and rearranging the A level subjects in four blocks of time instead of three, in order to increase the number of possible combinations. Sometimes we met together, and when we did we often co-opted David Lennard, who made the timetable, to help us with the practicalities of our proposals. Mostly we dealt with things by private conversations. Charlie Macdonald would go off to consult the scientists, David Manly would consult the linguists, and all of us would sound out the views of our colleagues and aim at an agreed solution.

David Lennard would work on the timetable implications and provide a clear indication of what was and what was not possible. Sometimes, after detailed negotiations which had gone on for a few weeks, we would meet during morning break to check if we could agree some draft minutes, and then the minutes would read, 'The curriculum committee met at 11.05 a.m. DJA, CPM, and DWM were present. They agreed to recommend the following:' Then there would be some pages of detailed recommendations, with a diagram if necessary to illustrate what was proposed, and the minutes would end, 'The meeting ended at 11.12 a.m.', followed by my signature and the date.

Another issue which concerned me was the regular loss of time on A level lessons by members of school teams who happened to be doing a subject in a block of time which included the two periods after morning break on Saturday. School teams often needed to leave by bus at break on Saturday to go to away matches. Someone who played in a rugby team in the autumn term, a hockey team in the winter term and a cricket team in the summer term was liable to miss a very substantial amount of A level teaching time, and with some subjects, where knowledge and understanding were cumulative, that could be a serious disadvantage.

I suggested via the curriculum committee that the solution was to have upper school lectures on Saturday mornings after break. It would, I believed, be good for the general education of the boys, and those playing in an away match would not miss part of their A level course. Bob Drayson's reaction was characteristic: 'I'm sure you're right about this. I think we'll make you master-in-charge of upper school lectures.' So from then on it was part of my job to invite lecturers on behalf of the headmaster (shadow cabinet ministers, generals, explorers and so on), meet them during Saturday morning break, preside over the lecture, show them round afterwards, take them for a drink with the headmaster before lunch, and see them off before I rushed off to referee a rugby match or coach my archers.

It was an enjoyable life, in an attractive environment, with congenial colleagues and boys who were usually a pleasure to teach. The main disadvantage was the lack of adequate time for everything that needed doing. I acquired responsibility for all matters to do with university entrance, and that involved finding time to go to admissions conferences at universities all over the country. I became the staff representative on the salaries sub-committee of the Governing Body – not a particularly onerous task, but occasionally taking quite a lot of time.

I regularly went with David Lennard each week to sing bass in the rehearsals of the large Stowe Choral Society and also to the rehearsals of a smaller group known as the Queen's Temple Singers. From time to time I would take the chapel service on Thursday, when a layman took over from the chaplain and spoke on whatever seemed to him important. When I did it I usually spoke about the meaning and significance of a hymn which the boys were used to singing – for example, A.H.Clough's hymn *Say not the struggle nought availeth*, which I saw as presenting the merits of St Paul's rather neglected theological virtue of Hope.

Usually the chaplain had to persuade his colleagues to take 'lay chapel' on a Thursday. But on one occasion I volunteered. The previous Saturday the school had had a visit from Sir Oswald Moseley, the controversial politician who had entered parliament as a Tory, defected to Labour, held a cabinet post under Ramsey Macdonald, resigned and formed the New Party, and been interned as a Nazi sympathizer during the war. Now in his seventies he was as controversial as ever.

In *Stowe, Hearsay and Memory* Brian Stephan described the visit of 'Oswald Mosley, whose reputation was such that he had to be guarded by two Smithfield porters, men built like barns. And such was the fiery eloquence of Mosley's right-wing diatribe in the Roxburgh Hall that David Arnold, that staunch upholder of tradition, felt impelled to mount the chapel pulpit to deliver an equally passionate, though less fiery, refutation of Mosley's doctrine.' Nearly forty years later, at an Old Stoic dinner, I found that there were Old Stoics who had never been taught by me at school but remembered me simply because of that one occasion.

At the end of each term, and on other occasions when he was making a speech at the Commemoration Dinner or at an Old Stoic Dinner, Bob Drayson used to ask members of staff for information which might be incorporated in his speech. I regularly gave him information about the archery team, the debating society, visiting lecturers, university entrance and so on, but such notes were ephemeral. I have a copy of only one, because it was sent by post six months after I had left Stowe in a letter shortly before I returned as a guest for the 1977 Commemoration Dinner:

Dear Bob,

In case you were thinking of things to say at the Commemoration Dinner, here is something which might be worth a mention. Of the secretaries of the Debating Society during the last decade two (Nigel Murray and David McDonough) have been chairman of the Oxford University Conservative Association, Andrew Kennon was one of the first two undergraduates ever to be appointed to be members of the Cambridge Senate, the Governing Body of Cambridge University, and Karan Thapar was last term's President of the Cambridge Union.

A couple of relatively minor points. I calculated when in Oxford recently that there are nine Old Stoics in residence at Pembroke, and a few days ago I saw Tim Lancaster on television in the Corpus Christi team which was narrowly beaten in University Challenge by Sidney Sussex, Cambridge.

I will look forward to seeing you on Monday.
Yours sincerely,   *David.*

328

One compensation for the high pressure of life during term was that we had longer holidays than those teaching in day schools, and at the end of the Summer Term Oriel and I would pack up our Ford Anglia and set off with the children to Camber Sands or Blue Dolphin Bay near Minehead or to Anglesey or Aldeburgh. The year we went to Aldeburgh we shared a house with Oriel's sister June and her daughters, Linda and Vicky. One day June stayed in to get the lunch while Oriel and I took the children out. Linda was about a year older than Kate, then came James, and finally Vicky and Piers, about the same age as each other – five children looking very similar and spread over roughly five years. Two elderly ladies looked at Oriel as we crossed the road and then looked disapprovingly at me, shaking their heads. 'Poor girl!' one of them said.

Sometimes during the term I needed to look after the children during the evening while Oriel went off to play readings, to help boys with their stage make-up or to take part in rehearsals for a school play. Both she and Liz Mead, Brian's wife, acted in more than one play. Perhaps the best was Jo Bain's production of *The Cherry Orchard,* in which he persuaded Oriel to play the part of Madame Ranevskaia - something she did superbly well. I watched with pride, while Brian Mead was able to have the same sense of pride at Liz's excellent performance in the part of Anya.

I first had the experience of teaching a girl in the early 1970s. Muir Temple, the housemaster of Grafton House, suggested to their daughter Nicola that she should live at home for the term in which she took the Cambridge entrance examination and be taught by me. She was a clever girl who had just got a grade A studying medieval history at Queen Anne's, Caversham, so I started by giving her a book on *Medieval Technology and Social Change* and asked her to write an essay on 'What was the importance of the stirrup in the development of medieval society?'

She produced it a few days later and I asked her to read it to me. As she did I listened and made notes. When she had finished I said, 'That was very good, Nicola.' It was. She was clearly going to be a good candidate, and she went on to get her place at Cambridge, but at that point, before she or I had said anything else, I noticed tears running down her cheek. It had all been too much of a strain, and I had to recognise that girls might sometimes be more sensitive than the boys I was used to teaching.

Girls arrived in the Stowe Sixth Form for the first time in the autumn of 1974. There were only six of them, and three took A level History. Their work was generally much the same as that of the boys. Its quality depended on the individual – not on gender. But there was a striking difference in how they completed university entrance application forms. I had been used to reading statements by members of my History Side about how they played stand-off half for the 1st XV, opened the batting for the 1st XI, played the trombone in the school orchestra and still had time for fencing and wine-tasting. But a girl called Nicola Hemsworth simply wrote 'Eventing and backgammon.'

I had never heard of eventing and asked her what it was. She told me. 'And backgammon?' 'Oh, that's what you do in the evenings after spending all day on dressage or cross-country.' She explained it all interestingly and in detail, so I suggested that she leave the form just as it was and wait to be asked about eventing and backgammon at interview. She left Stowe at the same time as I did, in her case for a university degree course in the History of Art. The next time I heard of her was when she appeared in *Vogue*, modelling in Japan.

43. Jesus College, Cambridge

In about 1970 the Council of Jesus College, Cambridge, decided that they would like to elect a number of schoolmasters as Fellow Commoners. It would be a good way of establishing closer contact with schools which would, they hoped, send them good candidates for admission as undergraduates. The college would provide free accommodation for a term, together with a meal on high table every evening. The school would need to give the member of staff a 'sabbatical term', while continuing to pay him. But there was disagreement about whether they should advertise opportunities for Fellow Commonerships or rely on personal contacts to find suitable schoolmasters from the sort of school from which they would wish to attract good candidates.

My friend Peter Glazebrook, whom I had known since the beginning of my second year at Pembroke, was a Fellow of the college, teaching Law, and was a member of the College Council. He argued for advertising publicly but lost the argument. Then when the members of Council were asked if any of them knew of suitable candidates, he suggested me. Stowe was seen as a very suitable school from which to elect a Fellow Commoner, so he was asked to put the idea to me, as something to be taken up at a time when the Headmaster of Stowe felt able to release me.

I put it to Bob Drayson and we eventually settled on the Lent Term of 1972. Meanwhile I had heard from another friend, Alister Cox, about a London University external and part-time Post-graduate Certificate of Education course, which he had just taken. We had been new schoolmasters at Clifton together, and he was now the Deputy Headmaster of the Arnold School, Blackpool, and would later go on to be the Headmaster of the Royal Grammar School, Newcastle-on-Tyne. He pointed out that this extra qualification added a further amount (£60 I think it was) to one's annual pay.

The PGCE course involved preparing for a number of papers on education and on subjects related to education, such as Psychology, Sociology and Statistics. It was not a course that appealed to me, but as I browsed through the London University brochure I found that they offered a two-year part-time Diploma in Education course, to provide a higher qualification to those who already had a PGCE, and that it was also open to candidates who did not have a PGCE but had a substantial number of years' teaching behind them.

It was a course which suited my interests. It involved taking two papers on the History of Education (one on education from ancient times to the Renaissance and one on everything since then) and two papers on educational theory (one on education in general and one on a particular subject). In my case the particular subject was, of course, History, and the sort of questions one had to answer (*Should historians make moral judgements?* or *Is it possible to write unbiased history?*) were just the sort of questions I had been setting and discussing with my scholarship candidates for years. Similarly, the questions likely to come up on the general education paper (*How can punishment be justified?* Or *Should you teach the child or the subject?*) were also about matters in which I was interested and to which I already ought to be able to provide a respectable answer. So most of my reading and work would need to be on the history of education – from Plato to the Plowden Report.

I had by then been teaching for fourteen years, with eleven of them as a head of department, so I wrote to explain that I had the opportunity of working full-time on the course during a sabbatical term at Cambridge, and I wondered if they would be prepared to let me squeeze the two-year part-time course into a few months of full-time work and let me take the examination the following summer. They agreed, so it gave me a clear purpose for my sabbatical term, and off to Cambridge I went in January 1972.

There was a bus which ran regularly between Oxford and Cambridge, stopping *en route* in the Buckingham market square and in the middle of Bedford, and throughout the Lent Term of 1972 Oriel would collect me each Saturday and then drive me down on Sunday afternoon to catch the bus, which got me in to the bus stop in Cambridge just in time to walk to college and pick up my gown in time for Hall. I could, of course, have stayed through the week-end, but in practice I always caught the bus back to Buckingham after breakfast every Saturday, except for one week-end when John was preaching in Cambridge and I stayed to see him and hear him preach. Oriel and the children would meet me in the Buckingham market square on Saturday mornings, and I then had rather more than twenty-four clear hours at home with them and saw more of them than I usually would in a normal week-end during term time.

It was a refreshing break. I always missed Oriel as soon as I went away and wrote two or three letters a week to tell her so, but the absence made meeting again at the week-end all the more of a pleasure. There were no essays to mark or tutees' parents to meet, and there was plenty of time to play football or chess with the children and watch television with them and read them a story. Also, bit by bit, I transformed a Victorian table which I had bought for £5 in a Buckingham junk shop. I planed it, rubbed it down with coarse sandpaper, then with medium sandpaper and finally with fine sandpaper, a bit each week-end, and after that I French polished it with button polish and cutting polish until it gleamed as if new. It was peculiarly satisfying because it was so unlike anything I usually did.

At Jesus I had breakfast in my own room and spent the morning reading and making notes on the history of education and on educational theory. After lunch I would go for a walk (sometimes Peter Glazebrook and I would walk up the river to Granchester and back; sometimes I would explore Cambridge and its colleges) and after some more reading it was time for Hall, where I dined remarkably well each evening on high table with a number of the fellows of the college and their guests, conversed about life, the universe and everything, and then moved to the Combination Room to continue the conversation while drinking port and eating fruit. Most of the fellows usually spent their evenings with their families or at work, but they would all dine in Hall on one or two evenings a week.

The college's medieval historian was Vivian Fisher. He had fought in the Battle of Monte Cassino in 1944, and that experience had influenced his view of conditions in England in the reign of King Stephen. The Peterborough chronicler had written of 'the nineteen long winters when Christ slept and his saints', and historians generally had assumed that throughout those years ordinary life had been virtually extinguished in that area. The Peterborough chronicler was, after all, a contemporary. But Vivian Fisher watched the Italian peasants going about their farming as British and German forces shelled each other over their heads across the valley below Monte Cassino, and he thought to himself that the position was probably much the same in East Anglia in the reign of King Stephen. However awful the depredations of Geoffrey de Mandeville's men were to the monks of Ely or Peterborough, the ordinary peasant would have just carried on tilling the soil.

At the time I was teaching *The Reign of Henry VIII* as a special subject to one of my Upper Sixth A level sets. A leading authority on Tudor England at that time was Geoffrey Elton, who had written on *The Tudor Revolution in Government*, asserting that there was a transformation in Henry VIII's reign both in royal control over the church and also over such things as taxation. The problem for me was that, after this great revolution in government, royal control over the church and over taxation looked to me much as it had been in the eleventh and twelfth centuries, which I was teaching at the same time to those Stoics specialising in medieval history.

'The trouble with Geoffrey', said Vivian Fisher, 'is that he thinks that just because they changed the labels on the doors, something else was going on inside the rooms.' Thus, when Henry VIII established *The Court of the Augmentations of the Revenues of the King's Crown,* he was really doing no more than employing more people to handle the extra income coming in from the dissolution of the monasteries. On the whole I preferred teaching special subjects in which something significant had happened, such as *The Norman Conquest* or *The French Revolution*, so the following year I dropped *The Reign of Henry VIII* for the modern historians at Stowe and started teaching *The Russian Revolution* instead.

At the end of a term which had been a refreshing change after a decade and a half of a working life dominated by teaching, marking essays and all the other activities and issues of school life, I was ready to return home, see how my A level candidates had been getting on in my absence, and prepare myself to do the same as them and revise for the examinations I had to take in the summer.

When the time came I went to stay with another friend, Christopher Holdsworth, who was a lecturer at University College, London, and later the Professor of Medieval History at the University of Exeter. I took the Diploma in Education examinations and as a result emerged with a further qualification which was probably a lot more useful to me than I realised at the time. It made me a properly qualified teacher in the eyes of anyone who, understandably, felt that the possession of a Master of Arts degree in History from Oxford University was no guarantee of knowing anything at all about education or of being able to teach.

The Oxford, or Cambridge, M.A. degree was all the more suspect because, unlike any other university, it was acquired by the peculiar system of keeping one's name on the college's books and paying the appropriate fee, which at that time was, I think, £17.10s.0d - £17.50 in decimal currency. The idea was that when one matriculated, which was a matter of joining the college as an undergraduate, one was in a sense setting out on a seven year apprenticeship, as one would with any other trade in the Middle Ages. After three years, and after taking the appropriate examinations, one became a bachelor of the arts of the university. Then, if one's name was still on the college's books, it was assumed that one was practising those arts, and after completing the seven years of apprenticeship, three as an undergraduate and four as a bachelor of arts, one at last became a master of the arts of the university, which ranged from Classics and History to Biochemistry and Engineering.

Other universities gave their scientists a B.Sc., and eventually, when they had done the appropriate work, an M.Sc. degree. In those days Oxford and Cambridge both stuck to giving them a B.A., and four years later, an M.A. degree. The merit of an Oxford degree in one of the humanities, Classics, Jurisprudence, History, English Literature or Modern Languages, was arguably that it could be seen as preparing its recipient for anything or nothing.

Back at the time when I graduated from Oxford it was quite usual for Oxford and Cambridge graduates to become schoolmasters, and there were many public schools and even more grammar schools in need of their services. During my term in Cambridge I met a college Tutor for Admissions who had been teaching Geography at his college for the last twenty years. He had, he said, always had about half a dozen undergraduates to teach each year, and in the late 1950s and early 60s probably three or four a year had gone into teaching. But while they were happy to go into grammar schools and public schools, they were a lot less inclined to spend their lives in comprehensive schools.

The effect had been a dramatic decline in the number going into teaching. In the last five years only one of his pupils had become a schoolmaster. What, I wondered, had they done instead? The answer was that most of them had gone into the City. A few years earlier the City had been an appropriate destination for those school leavers from a few select schools in the South of England who were not quite bright enough to go to university. Now it was where Oxbridge graduates went to make money instead of becoming teachers.

44. Looking for a headship

One of Her Majesty's Inspectors of Education visited Stowe only shortly after I had arrived. Before he left he suggested that I should stay for just another couple of years and then start looking for a headship. I assured him that that was really not the right course for me. I did not see myself as a headmaster. What I wanted to do was teach History. David Roberts and Michael Cherniavsky had had a considerable influence on me at school, and it was them I wanted to emulate rather than H.L.O.Flecker, who was still my image of what a headmaster was like. Flecker had been a tall and imposing man, presiding over Christ's Hospital in a manner which could leave no-one in doubt about who was in charge. But he had had relatively little direct impact on my life by comparison with David Roberts or Michael Cherniavsky, or indeed Eric Littlefield, and his whole personality and his manner were entirely different from my own.

I had, of course, served under two headmasters before coming to Stowe: N.G.L.Hammond at Clifton and A.J.Holt at Quintin School. Neither had particularly impressed me. Hammond was a distinguished academic with an impressive war record, but so far as I could tell (and I was very young and probably could not tell at all well) the school seemed to operate without him, while he was writing his *History of Greece to 322 B.C.* Holt was an efficient administrator who provided the framework within which Quintin School operated, but other than that he had little impact. They were very pale imitations of Flecker, and I had no wish to seek to emulate either them or him. So I settled down happily to my work as History Tutor and stayed at Stowe for nearly ten years.

As headmasters go Bob Drayson was an entirely different matter. I watched with admiration as he interviewed parents and their sons, left the husband feeling respected as a man of the world, the

337

mother feeling attractive, and the boy feeling understood. He had an impressive self-confidence in dealing with the most difficult of problems, and he did many things far better than I could ever expect to do. He lacked the grandeur of H.L.O.Flecker, but he knew what he believed in, the things he did he did well and with confidence, and he knew his own limitations and was prepared to delegate responsibilities to others, so that he could always find time for anyone with a problem to put to him, and he could always find time for a round of golf. He would check the timetables of those of his colleagues who played the game and telephone one of them before breakfast: 'You're free after break, I think? Good. See you on the first tee at 11.15.' Then at 11.15 he would play nine holes briskly and be back to meet prospective parents at mid-day.

The term in Cambridge, enjoyable though it was, probably had an unsettling effect on me, but I returned to a regular routine. Most days I got home in time to help with putting the children to bed and read them a story – *Winnie-the-Pooh*, all the *Narnia* books, *Watership Down*, *The Hobbit*, and then, because they had so much enjoyed *The Hobbit* and wanted more by Tolkein, we spent eighteen months reading through all three volumes of *The Lord of the Rings*.

But other things were changing. In the autumn of 1973 Charlie Macdonald took over as the housemaster of Lyttelton and a year later a house in the school grounds next to the Lyttelton housemaster's house, became available. The children were now twelve, ten and eight. For years they had enjoyed life in Dadford, roaming round the wild wood and the conker range with the Macdonald children, but they were now of an age when the tennis and squash courts at Stowe, the swimming pool and the lakes, on which it was possible to sail a small boat, were all becoming increasingly attractive. What is more, my study, my classroom and the history library, instead of being a quarter of an hour's walk away, would be a distance of only a couple of hundred yards, and the archery hut was about half-way between.

So we moved up to the school. I was enjoying my job and fairly soon completed the second edition of *Britain, Europe and the World*, which was published in 1973 and sold even better now that it was expanded to ninety chapters and covered the years 1871-1971. I would have been happy to carry on in much the same way for the next five or even ten years. But when I reached forty in November 1973 I reflected that I had been a head of a history department ever since I was twenty-six, and began to wonder if I really wanted to do much the same for another twenty years or more. I had no wish to be a housemaster, since I was more interested in both the teaching of history and in academic administration than in what I thought of as the domestic side of schoolmastering. I would have been glad to be the Senior Tutor, which at Stowe was the position in which one would be responsible for academic policy and its implementation, but there was no realistic prospect of that in the near future. So I started to think of looking for a headship.

I went to see Harry Judge, the very successful principal of Banbury School, who had dealt with the problem of organising a comprehensive school effectively by dividing it into separate units and presiding over a sort of federation. I had first met him after inviting him to speak to my Historical Society on *Louis XIV and Unlimited Monarchy*, and he subsequently got me to speak at a conference he was running on *History in the Sixth Form*. He and Mary had been to Stowe to visit us, we became good friends, and in particular I valued his advice. 'Why do you want to be a headmaster?' he asked. 'Frustration.' was my reply. I wanted to be at the end of the decision-making process rather than at the beginning. He encouraged me to go ahead and I decided to do so.

Next was the question of what sort of school to apply to. With my experience of teaching at Quintin School and the sort of responsibilities I had at Stowe I was probably best qualified for the headship of a grammar school, and from a personal point of view there was a lot to be said for that rather than an independent boarding school. In the first place, grammar schools had no problem with attracting pupils and they also appeared to be assured of regular and reliable funding. Secondly, the most serious disciplinary offences committed by teen-age boys in either a public school or a grammar school usually happen outside normal teaching time, and in a grammar school the boys were the responsibility of their parents in the evenings and at the week-ends. Finally, although I would expect to work hard, I liked the idea of getting back to a working week which, at least theoretically, finished at the end of the school day on Fridays and started again on Monday morning.

But the number of grammar schools was significantly fewer than ten years earlier – perhaps no more than a quarter. The movement in favour of comprehensive reorganisation had gained momentum and a majority in most of the country favoured it. So although I had no fixed view of what sort of school I should look for, at least I knew that everywhere things were changing and that my own experience did not make me a suitable candidate for the headship of a comprehensive school. I would have to give some serious thought to the various merits and demerits of the projected arrangements for the future of any school where I contemplated being the head.

I applied to Abingdon, a 'direct grant' grammar school just south of Oxford, and to King's School, Rochester, which was independent. I was not invited for interview at Abingdon, and at King's, Rochester, I went for interview but was not appointed. In both cases I knew those who were appointed. The heads of history at what were called 'the Rugby Group' of schools met each other once a term to discuss matters of common interest, so we all knew each other. It was Michael Parker, the head of history at Winchester, who was appointed to Abingdon, and Roy Ford, who had been the head of history at Uppingham when I first went to Stowe, but had now for some years been the headmaster of Southwell Minster School, who went to King's School, Rochester.

While some schools, or rather their governors, decided that they did not want me, there were others where, after visiting the school,

340

I decided against continuing with my application. William Ellis was a successful grammar school on the edge of Hampstead Heath. I had known it since my time at Quintin School and knew that it had escaped comprehensive reorganisation in the 1960s because it was 'voluntary aided.' Now, ten years later, its 'voluntary aided' status was no longer a defence against comprehensive reorganisation, discussions were in hand between the governors and the ILEA over how to manage that, and it was also in need of a new headmaster.

I applied, was invited for interview, and found that the plan for the future was to leave it much the same size as it was as a grammar school but turn it into a comprehensive school. In most areas that would not make sense, since a school that size would not be able to generate a reasonably sized sixth form. But with Hampstead being the sort of area it is, it could well have been possible to run a good school for those living in the neighbourhood, and with a flourishing sixth form.

It turned out, however, that the Inner London Education Authority was intending to revive the 11+ examination, divide children into categories (alphas, betas and gammas) and then bus them around London to ensure that each school had a fair share of able, middling and weaker children. It was ideological egalitarianism gone mad. I tried to explain the practical consequences which would necessarily flow from such a policy and was asked if I was still a serious candidate for the post. I replied that I did not see how anyone who understood about secondary education could be a serious candidate if that was really what they were going to do.

Harry Judge thought I had made a mistake. 'First get the job', he said. 'Then you can deal with the problem of the politicians' plans.' It was much the same advice that Lenin gave to his fellow Bolsheviks: 'First we must obtain power. Then we will think what to do with it.' He was probably right, and I would have loved to have taken Oriel and the children to Hampstead and lived in the headmaster's house on the edge of the heath. But at the time I was quite simply shocked by what seemed a foolish and potentially disastrous plan for the future.

By contrast King Edward VI School, Stourbridge, another 'voluntary aided' grammar school, seemed to have an excellent plan for the future. Those responsible for secondary education in Stourbridge had recognised that if they were not going to divide children by ability, they needed to divide them by age, and since the school leaving age was sixteen, that was a convenient point at which to do so. They had decided that King Edward VI School should be a sixth form college, providing for all the sixth form boys and girls in Stourbridge. It was as good a solution as I had come across to the comprehensive problem.

I went for interview there in a positive frame of mind, and found an excellent grammar school with the makings of a first-rate sixth form college, and in buildings which were well built, well cared for, and appropriate for their future purpose. But the journey by local train from Birmingham to Stourbridge was depressing, and the school, for all its merits, was situated on an inner ring road between an abattoir and a tannery factory. I felt I simply could not take Oriel and the children to live there, so I withdrew before the interviews in the afternoon. Harry again thought I was being too picky. If I had gone by car, he suggested, I would probably have appreciated the beautiful countryside to the west of Stourbridge and would have been pleased to live in one of the attractive nearby villages.

From a domestic point of view it would have been a pleasure to go to William Ellis, but from a professional point of view I had seen it as a bad mistake. King Edward VI School, Stourbridge, was precisely the other way round: it was a good grammar school with a good plan for the future, but it was not somewhere I wanted to live. What I needed, or wanted, was a good grammar school with a good plan for the future, situated somewhere where I would be pleased to take Oriel and the children to live.

K.G.V. (1976–1983)

45. Taking over at KGV

In 1920, three years before the foundation of Stowe, the burgesses of the County Borough of Southport on the coast of Lancashire, founded a new grammar school for boys in a building which had been a military hospital in the First World War. The first headmaster, George Millward, was appointed while still a serving officer with the Royal Engineers. There were six assistant masters and 110 boys. Middle class parents were happy to pay the fees of four guineas a term, and clever working class boys could win a free place in a scholarship examination at the age of ten.

A splendid new building was completed in 1926 and was opened by Edward Stanley, seventeenth Earl of Derby, friend of King George V, six times winner of the St. Leger and twice of the Derby, Secretary of State for War under three prime ministers, and ambassador in Paris immediately after the First World War. Because of his relationship with the king Lord Derby was able to confer the name of King George V on the school. It was a unique distinction in England, and one shared with one of the Royal Navy's greatest battleships, which took part in the sinking of the *Bismarck* in May 1941, and with one of the Great Western railway's most splendid engines, still preserved at the National Railway Museum in York.

In 1949, when George Millward retired after twenty-nine years in which the school developed and grew, his place was taken by Geoffrey Dixon, who came from being Head of the Science Department at the Royal Military Academy, Sandhurst, to lead the school through twenty-seven years of extraordinary stability, during which its high academic standards and reputation attracted able and dedicated men to the staff.

By the time the school celebrated its Golden Jubilee in 1970 public opinion towards grammar schools had changed significantly.

In 1920 a common attitude was that it was wonderful when a bricklayer's or bus-driver's son won a free place at a grammar school. A couple of decades later rather more people were suggesting that it was scandalous that so few bricklayers' or bus-drivers' sons got places at grammar schools. In the 1960s it was increasingly suggested that it was scandalous that grammar schools should be bastions of privilege for the clever, and there was a widespread demand for comprehensive schools. In 1965 there were still 1,285 grammar schools in England and Wales. By 1976, when Geoffrey Dixon retired, there were only 477, two of which were KGV and the Southport High School for Girls, and they were now due to be reorganised.

Local government reorganisation in 1975 had the effect that Southport was no longer a self-governing County Borough in Lancashire but an extremity of Merseyside, in the Metropolitan Borough of Sefton, and the new local education authority was faced with the problem that KGV needed rebuilding. Most of Southport was securely built on the sand bar running between the estuaries of the Ribble and the Mersey, and contrary to the impression given at the end of the seventh chapter of St Matthew's gospel, sand can be a sound foundation on which to build. But two miles inland the sand gave way to peat, which does not provide a firm foundation, and KGV had been built on peat. It had been built with three steps up to the front doors, but within eighteen months it was possible to walk straight in, and nearly thirty years later the whole school needed rebuilding.

By then it was impossible to get funding for a new grammar school building, so the Sefton council was going to have to face some form of comprehensive reorganisation. Fortunately there was enough experience of the problems produced by comprehensive reorganisation with 11-18 schools that it was planned to do it in a manner which made sense. The town's secondary modern schools and the Southport High School for Girls would be comprehensive schools covering the age range 11-16, while KGV would become a sixth form college. Once the decision was made, Geoffrey Dixon decided that sixty-three was an appropriate age at which to retire and let a new headmaster preside over the transformation of the boys' grammar school into a sixth form college which would also embrace the sixth form girls of Southport.

Thus in the spring of 1976 I found myself travelling to Southport by train to be interviewed for the post of headmaster of both the school and the projected college. I already knew something of both the school and the town, for the Economics Tutor at Stowe, Peter Longhurst, who had joined the school just before me, had come from teaching at KGV, and whenever anything happened at Stowe of which he disapproved, he would compare it unfavourably with this apparently idyllic school and town in the north, so that one wondered why he had ever left. After many years he left Stowe as well, and the last time I met him he was teaching at Eton. I wonder how many Etonians have heard from him of the merits of KGV.

After walking through Lord Street, which is possibly the most beautiful main street of any town in England, and booking in at the Scarisbrick Hotel, I went to the school, where the deputy headmaster, George Wakefield, showed me round. Knowing that I was an historian, he took me to see the history department, and there I met Chris Collier, the head of department, who was in the middle of teaching. I asked him what the class was doing and he explained that they were an O level group, studying modern history and using the standard text-book by Arnold. George asked me if there was any connection. The connection, of course, was that I had written it. It felt like a good omen.

That evening I rang Oriel to say that I had found the ideal place to work, live and bring up our children as teenagers, I had walked on the Southport beach and over the sand dunes into Birkdale and knew that I wanted to be the headmaster of King George V School, live in Birkdale and tackle the exciting project of transforming a very good grammar school into a similarly good sixth form college. I was looking forward to the interview the next day.

The next morning I turned up at the Southport Town Hall with five other candidates. Two were already headmasters, two were deputy heads, and the other was the Director of Studies at Manchester Grammar School. I got on well with Councillor Mrs Monk, the Chairman of the KGV Governing Body, and by then had had enough experience of being interviewed for headships to avoid some of the worst mistakes, such as giving the impression that I was soft on discipline. Then, asked by the Director of Education if I thought I could run a sixth form college on a staffing ratio of 14:1, I said I would rather do it on a ratio of 11:1 (I thought that 11, unlike 10 or 12, seemed to have a spurious precision about it). 14:1, I said, would be difficult but possible. I got the job.

It was a considerable advantage to me to have a background of independent and grammar schools. With a career at Clifton, Quintin and Stowe behind me, it would have been difficult to depict me as someone coming to destroy the academic traditions of KGV and turn it into a comprehensive at sixteen-plus. Instead I could publicly adopt the position that I was there to join with a carefully selected and first-rate staff in creating a college with high standards of scholarship, behaviour and dress, which could reasonably be described as elitist and exclusive. So long as that public image was maintained it would be possible to make the changes needed.

A lot of things were going to have to change, including in some ways my own attitudes. Early on I tried to reassure Miss Evans, the admirable and very successful headmistress of the Southport High School for Girls that I was in favour of a mixed sixth form, saying that I was sure the girls would have a civilising effect on the boys. She replied with a charming smile, but with just a touch of acerbity, that the girls were not there to civilise the boys but rather to enjoy an education which would develop their talents as fully as possible. She was, of course, right. It was a well-merited and (to me) influential rebuke.

I had the immense advantage of taking over from Geoffrey Dixon, who had run the school with exemplary efficiency, and I was fortunate in the staff I inherited from him. Five of them were Old

348

Headmaster of King George V School in the late 1970s.

Georgians, and three, George Wakefield, Bob Abram and Hubert Long, had between them spent more than a hundred years in the place, man and boy, and took pleasure in doing something different in their last few working years.

The school was divided into twelve houses for the purpose of providing for the care and discipline of the pupils. The housemasters, in keeping with a long-standing policy, were men who had been appointed as young men on scale 1 of the national salary scale, then had been promoted to scale 2 as they proved their worth, and eventually to scale 3 as housemasters. Each was responsible for about seventy boys, roughly ten boys to every year, and each of them knew all the boys in his own house.

Meanwhile the heads of department, again in keeping with a policy which Geoffrey had pursued successfully throughout his time at KGV, were mostly young men imported from other good grammar schools and appointed on scale 4. Chris Collier, the Head of History, had come from Manchester Grammar School, Peter Comfort, the Head of Geography, from Bury School, Peter Richardson, the Head of Physics, from Bristol Grammar School and Tony Fairburn, the Head of Chemistry, from Merchant Taylor's, Crosby.

Another great asset was my secretary, Jean Buck, who was only the second Head Master's secretary since the school had been founded. Her predecessor, Elizabeth Craig, had been appointed as a teen-ager in 1920 and had retired forty-two years later at the age of sixty. Jean had been Geoffrey Dixon's secretary for fourteen years when I arrived in 1976 and carried on for another six years until just a year before I left. She knew how the grammar school operated and could explain what Geoffrey Dixon would do next while politely wondering what I would like to do. I usually did what she told me.

Not only did I have the benefit of a first-rate Deputy Headmaster and a helpful and reliable secretary; I also had an excellent caretaker who had been appointed shortly before I arrived. Ken Miller had grown up in the Gorballs in Glasgow and had had little schooling. Still a teenager he joined the army when the Second World War began, served most of it in No.2 Commando, and was demobbed as a corporal in 1945. He married a fellow Glaswegian who had been on holiday to Southport and dreamt of living there one day.

Shortly after the war they went out to Northern Rhodesia, later Zambia, where Ken worked as a mine captain in the copper mines. When he retired and returned to the United Kingdom in the early 1970s, still in his fifties, he had made enough money to buy an attractive house in St Paul's Square in the middle of Southport. But it was too early in life for him to put his feet up and do nothing, so when he saw an advertisement in the local paper for the post of caretaker at King George V School, he applied and was appointed.

I was the beneficiary of the appointment. He took pride in looking after the buildings and would carry out quite substantial repairs himself. He organised the cleaning staff efficiently and supervised their work with cheerful confidence, pointing out anything that needed doing and praising good work. If I noticed that a fire extinguisher had come adrift and mentioned it to him, the answer, accompanied by a grin, would probably be, 'It's already done, Headmaster.' He found a wooden shield at the time that the old school building was being demolished and asked me the meaning of the Latin inscription: *Disce prodesse*. I said that, loosely translated, it meant something like, 'Learn to be of service.' So he cleaned it up, hung it in the cleaners' room, and we became probably the only school or college in the country whose cleaners had their own Latin motto.

The physical legacy from the past of a bust of King George V, a war memorial, and photographs of prefects and rugby football and cricket teams needed to be reconsidered before girls began to arrive in September 1979. King George V and the war memorial still seemed appropriate; the photographs did not. So instead both the classrooms and the corridors were decorated with well-framed, good quality reproductions of paintings, and from then on a walk through the college could be in a sense an introduction to the History of Art.

Another change was that as a sixth form college there was no longer a school uniform. Instead the boys were required to wear a sports jacket or blazer, plain dark trousers, leather shoes and a college tie. Similarly the girls were required to wear a plain skirt and jumper and a college brooch. In the second half of the summer term boys did not have to wear a jacket and girls could come to college in a summer dress. Forty years later it seems remarkable that any sixth form college was able to have dress regulations of that sort. At the time it worked well and the expectation of high standards of dress matched the expectation of high standards of work and behaviour.

Inevitably there were problems and even crises, and the most notable crisis I ever faced in twenty-three years as a head was in the so-called winter of discontent of 1978-79, when I had only been a headmaster for a couple of years. Stories are still told of disruption in Merseyside, of bodies left unburied, of garbage accumulating in the streets, and of threats of violence. At the point where N.U.P.E. (the National Union of Public Employees) called a one day strike of caretakers and cleaners, head teachers were told to decide whether or not to close their schools.

At KGV several members of staff told me why it was both sensible and right to close down until after the storm had blown over, and all over Merseyside secondary heads wiser and more experienced than I decided to close their schools. Indeed, every maintained secondary school in Merseyside except KGV closed.

I called a staff meeting during morning break the day before disaster was predicted and listened to the explanations of the staff representatives on the Governing Body about why we should close. First, they suggested, if there were N.U.P.E. picket lines outside, we ought not cross them. Secondly, female members of staff could be vulnerable to violence. Finally, if I closed the school, everyone would be paid as usual, while if I decided to keep it open, anyone unable to get in would lose a day's pay.

I knew enough about trade union law to be able to reply that walking past N.U.P.E. members outside the school did not constitute 'crossing picket lines', since we were not parties to the dispute. Nor did I expect normally law-abiding and helpful caretakers and cleaners to turn suddenly into violent thugs. The school should stay open and we should carry on with our normal work for the not very impressive reason that that was what we were paid to do. We should go on doing it unless prevented from doing so.

There was a pause. Then John Clough, Head of Classics and much respected by his colleagues, said, 'Well, we all think you're wrong, Headmaster. But if you've made your mind up, we'll be right behind you.' And they were. I would have liked to have hugged and thanked him, and did so rather more than thirty years later when we both went to the funeral of Bob Abram, George Wakefield's successor as Deputy Head.

Ken Miller brought me all the keys that might be needed and suggested that, while he needed to go on strike, I had better have his telephone number in case of a problem. In the event there were no N.U.P.E. pickets outside the next morning, and everything carried on as normal, except that it was George Wakefield rather than Ken who got the heating going, and both staff and pupils had to bring sandwiches for lunch.

The next day all the other secondary schools in Merseyside went back to work as well. It left me with a deepened appreciation of my colleagues and a sense of gratitude towards them. I also learnt that one of the most valuable things for strengthening one's position is the successful overcoming of a crisis.

46. Southport

◇◇◇◇◇◇◇◇◇◇◇◇◇◇◇◇◇◇◇◇◇◇◇◇◇◇◇◇◇◇◇

'We run this town', said John Rostron, the Chairman of the Old Georgians' Association, leaning back after a good dinner in the manner of a Mafia godfather. He was also my dentist, later he was a member of the Governing Body of King George V College, and later still, after I had left, Chairman of the Corporation, which was the new name for the Governing Body after 1992. He was right of course. When you needed a doctor, a solicitor, an accountant or an estate agent in Southport, he would probably turn out to be an Old Georgian.

I had experience of that on my second visit to Southport. It was Oriel's first, and we drove up from Stowe and eventually across the Moss, that vast, flat expanse of land which had once been an inland lake and which cuts Southport off from the rest of England. When we reached the school in the Scarisbrick New Road, we called in on Geoffrey Dixon in the study which was to be mine for the first half of my time in Southport. 'If you're looking for a house', he said, 'call in on John Duffy of Hatch and Fielding in the middle of Lord Street. He's an old boy of the school and he'll look after you.'

So we ate our sandwiches on the Promenade and drove all round the town to decide where we would like to live before going to see John Duffy. Southport reaches about ten miles along the coast, and until near the end of the eighteenth century there was nothing between the small village of Churchtown at the southern end of the Ribble estuary and the village of Birkdale about three miles away to the south-west. In both villages a few people made a living from fishing for cockles and other sea-food on the large shallow beaches reaching out to the west. Then, while the Norfolk coast on one side of England was being gradually eroded and Dunwich, once a great town, was being washed into the sea,

had just bought it. So he was now putting his present house on the market. It was in Weld Road, the road which runs down from Birkdale village to the beach, and he and his wife had lived in it for about the last twenty years as they brought up their family.

He rang his secretary to see if the particulars were yet ready. They were. The house was just where we wanted to live; it was just the size we wanted; the garden was an expanse of grass ideal for football or cricket; and the price was £19,850. 'I'll give Mary a ring,' he said, 'and you can go round and have cup of tea and have a look at it.' Half an hour later we said we were happy to pay the asking price, got back into the car and drove back to Stowe. We never regretted it and lived there happily throughout the years we were in Southport.

Meanwhile my friend Peter Glazebrook had written from Jesus College, Cambridge, to congratulate me on my appointment to KGV and said that he knew three things about Southport. One was that it had a good second-hand bookshop 'by appointment to King Peter II of Jugoslavia' – and in the twenty-first century that bookshop, Broadhurst's, is still there in Market Street, with a fire burning on the hearth and one's books done up in brown paper tied with string, though sadly the sign referring to King Peter II of Jugoslavia has long gone.

The second thing he knew was that little boys used to pick up golf balls lying around the Royal Birkdale golf course and that the secretary of the golf club had objected. This produced a court case which went to the High Court, and the judgement of the learned judge in the case (*Hibbert v McKiernan [1948] 2 K.B. 142*) was that, since the golf balls were lying on the ground rather than embedded in it, and since their owner could not be known, the person finding a ball rather than the Royal Birkdale Golf Club could rightfully take possession of it. If they had been embedded in the ground the legal position would have been different.

The third thing Peter knew was that the House of Lords had once made Esso pay a lot of money to the Southport Corporation to indemnify the burgesses the cost of cleaning up their lovely beaches after an Esso tanker had polluted them (*Esso v Southport Corporation [1956] A.C. 218*), and, he added, 'a jolly good thing too.'

Kate, who had not liked the local convent school which she had attended during our last years at Stowe, found the Ainsdale secondary school preferable, but she was never going to be enthusiastic about any school and was glad to leave two years later. At that point she was not at all clear about what she wanted to do next, but she talked it over with Oriel and decided to do a secretarial course at the Southport Technical College.

That proved to be a mistake, and after a couple of weeks she simply stopped turning up, but without telling us. The college eventually rang to ask where she was, and it turned out that she had been sitting in the library all day. She now said that what she was really interested in was Art, so I spoke to the Principal of the Southport College of Art and Design, who said he'd be pleased to take her on to do a year's foundation course. She could do a bit of painting and drawing, a bit of photography, a bit of textiles, a bit of sculpture and so on while making up her mind about the area in which she would like to specialise, or even, he suggested, since she had passed both English Literature and Art at O level, she might go on to take English and Art at A level with a view to going on to university to read Fine Art or Art History.

Meanwhile Jamie had started at Stowe in Brian Mead's house. Had I still been at Stowe I would only have had to pay a third of full fees, but there was no arrangement for any reduction if I left. 'We'll do it the other way round' said Bob Drayson, and that reduction of the fees by a third made it possible for Jamie to go to Stowe for the next three years. Fortunately, both from a financial and a domestic point of view, he was happy to leave in the summer of 1979, after taking O level, and start at King George V College at just the moment at which it became a sixth form college.

Our younger son, Piers, or Pip, was ten when I was appointed and was less than enthusiastic when he heard where we were moving. 'I'm not going to silly old slummy Southport', he said. 'I know about them. They're at the bottom of the Fourth Division and they're absolutely useless.' Worse was to come. They slid out of the bottom of the Fourth Division to be replaced by Wigan Athletic. But I sometimes reflected that Southport would have won almost any football competition if towns could only play their own residents. Almost all of the great Liverpool team of the late seventies lived in Birkdale, and Piers and James were proud to live near them.

Pip spent a couple of years at a Prep school in Birkdale, until in the summer of 1978, under the pseudonym of John Pearson, to avoid any possible accusations of sleaze and corruption if he were to be admitted, he took the thirteen-plus examination for late entrants to KGV. It was an examination which took place each year, testing the candidates in English, Mathematics and foreign languages, principally to give a second chance to boys who had failed the eleven-plus examination two years earlier but had done sufficiently well at their secondary school that it was thought that perhaps they should transfer to a grammar school. I asked George Wakefield if he would make all the arrangements that year, and left it to him to arrange who should mark the various papers and decide who should and who should not be admitted on the strength of the examination. Fortunately John Pearson did very well and joined the Fourth Form in September of 1978.

My mother and father came north to visit us and were impressed and pleased with what they found. It was characteristic of my father that as soon as he had arrived and had a cup of tea, he got out into the garden, took a broom and then a spade and got on with doing something useful. He also played football with the boys, and I remember his delight and laughter when, at the age of seventy, he was standing with his legs apart defending a makeshift goal in the garden and Pip, now eleven, slipped the ball between his legs and into the goal. He had always been good at playing with children, and it was a cause of regret to John and to me that the war took him away from home from when we were seven until we were twelve. In Birkdale he and I walked along the roads together and had a look in estate agents' windows to check the price of houses. He liked Birkdale Village, he liked the idea of being near us, and he began to consider seriously the idea of moving north.

47. Living in Birkdale

◇◇

We settled down to life in Birkdale. It had retained something of the atmosphere of a village, and Oriel enjoyed shopping at the village shops, which were a short walk away. In the other direction it was three-quarters of a mile down to the beach. There was something extraordinarily attractive about the beach, which stretched out to the horizon and gave the impression of being an entirely natural part of the world, untouched by man – though Janet Lawley, one of the vice-principals of KGV from 1978 onwards and a distinguished geographer, destroyed my illusion that the Birkdale beach had looked much the same ever since the world was young by telling me that the shoreline had changed significantly in relatively recent times as a consequence of the dredging of the Ribble estuary.

Every morning a string of race-horses led by Red Rum passed our house on the way down to the beach where they did their training. They lived round the corner behind what looked like a garage. Red Rum went on to be a local hero and won the Grand National for a third time while we lived there. Oriel even placed a bet on him after he had won the National twice and come second the next year, so when he won again, so did she. A few weeks later, when reading in a book by Susan Hill about someone called Kingsmill, she heard a reference on the wireless to a horse of that name running in a race later that day, placed a bet for the second time in her life and won again. Having grown up with a strong prejudice against betting, I was mildly worried that it would become a habit. It didn't, and with just two bets and two wins she retained an unbeaten record.

Just as my second year at KGV was beginning my father was briefly ill and suddenly and unexpectedly died. Apparently his kidneys had failed and that was rapidly followed by death.

He was only seventy-one, and it was a tragic loss. At his funeral on 16th September 1977 John spoke of him as a great man – 'great only in the ways in which it is possible for the powerless to be great.' He spoke of his strength and dependability, his absolute truthfulness, loyalty and probity, of his loving-kindness as a father and, above all, as a husband. He added this: "If he had a fault it lay in setting for himself too high a standard of service and conduct – in 'winding himself too high for mortal man beneath the sky'; and I mention this flaw, this little element of obstinacy and pride, both because a portrait must have some shadow in it, in order to be credible, and also because he loved the truth above all things and brought us up to speak it."

As faults go, it was a good one, and John went on to say that the most extraordinary thing about him was the extent of his self-giving, his dedication to the service of others and his determination not to be a nuisance or indeed the slightest burden to anyone. Strangely enough, he managed to combine that with a gaiety and joyfulness which could transform our lives when he came home from work and picked us up and rubbed us on his stubbly chin, or when, in the army, he came home on leave bringing gifts, such as a rabbit which he had shot with a .303 Lee Enfield rifle. He loved his brothers and his sister. He loved his sons. Above all he loved and looked after his wife and did his best to give her that sense of security which she so sadly lacked. I think it was from him that I learnt to see married love as a combination of emotion and commitment. The emotion, the falling in love, comes first (at least in our own culture); but it needs to be matched with commitment. Then, ideally, the two things interact. In this and in many other ways he was a model to emulate.

I was glad that he had lived long enough to see me as the headmaster of King George V School and I was sorry that he had not quite lived long enough to see John as Dean of Rochester – a position to which John was appointed in 1978, making him at that time the youngest dean in the Church of England. Back in 1963, three years after Oriel and I had moved to London, John completed his three years as a curate at Holy Trinity, Millhouses, in Sheffield, married Anneliese and became the chaplain of Southampton University. In 1969, a couple of years after we moved to Stowe, he was appointed to be the Secretary for the Board for Mission and Unity of the General Synod of the Church of England, working at Church House, Westminster. Then in 1978, two years after Oriel and I moved to Southport, he and Anneliese moved to Rochester, where they stayed for twelve years.

Like us they had three children, but while we had a daughter and then two sons, they had a daughter first, Frances, born less than a year after Jamie, then a son, Matthew, born just a few months after Pip, and seven years later another daughter, Miriam. We saw them intermittently, but most of the while we were at Strawberry Hill they were in Southampton, then while we were at Stowe they were in London, and through most of the time we were in Southport they were in Rochester.

When we first lived in Birkdale Kate was at school in Ainsdale, two stops away on the train, Jamie was far away at Stowe, where he acquired a taste for cross-country running and played squash for the school, and Pip was at Sunnymead, a preparatory school only five minutes walk away, where he appeared to flourish on a diet of Latin and French and cricket and football and chess.

Three years later things had changed. Kate by now had decided that she did not like the foundation course at the Southport College of Art. She wanted to spend her time painting and drawing and was not prepared to continue with the other things they expected her to do. So she got a job working as a nursing assistant at Greaves Hall, a hospital for handicapped children. Increasingly she did not like living at home either, especially if her mother expected her to keep her room tidy, and even more if I insisted that she should not be rude to her mother. She appeared to Oriel and me to be going through what is sometimes called 'a difficult patch' and when she was eighteen years old she decided that she would rather live her own life in a bed-sitter. We helped her to arrange that, and from then onwards she more and more lived her life separately from the rest of the family.

Jamie was gradually becoming James rather than Jamie, and after three years at Stowe and taking O level there, had been happy to come home and start an A level course at KGV in History, English and Maths, just as it became a sixth form college. Pip was gradually becoming Piers rather than Pip and was already in King George V School working towards taking O level in 1981. It is sometimes suggested that it is a mistake for children to attend a school where one of their parents is a teacher – worst of all if their father is the headmaster. That wasn't so for us, and they, like so many Old Georgians, remember the place with affection.

They easily learnt to distinguish between school (or college) life and home. At one time a member of staff sent Piers and his friend, Richard Elliott, to see me for missing Assembly. They were appropriately penitent, standing with heads bowed and saying 'Sorry, sir. No sir. I won't do it again,' and giving me an undertaking that they would turn up regularly for the rest of the year. But when I got home that evening the first words I heard were, 'Dad, don't you think that was ridiculous? Fancy sending me to send me to see you! He should have known that we'd both be embarrassed.'

The boys settled in happily. James carried on with his cross-country running and ran in the college team. Piers found that competition for a place in a school football or cricket team was tougher than it had been in his prep school, but played chess both for the school and later for the college – though never as well as their friend, Andrew Savage, about whom I once had to report in Assembly that he had defeated the Welsh women's champion in the semi-final of a recent chess championship, but in the final had lost to Nigel Short, a pupil at Bolton School who was on his way to becoming an International Grand Master.

At home Oriel, the two boys and I could all still give each other a good game, but increasingly it was Piers who won. We could also play each other at table tennis. We had a large basement, so we bought a full size table tennis table and regularly made use of it. We kicked a football around in the garden. I learnt to bowl a slow, good length and fairly straight ball as James and Piers practised their batting, and both of them joined the Birkdale tennis club.

At week-ends or during the holidays we could go walking in the Lake District or, more frequently, on the Howgill Fells near Sedburgh, where the school had a hostel, Long Rigg, in which we could stay, sharing it with parties of boys from the school. Once we managed to get to the top of all four hills which between them made up the Howgill Fells, starting by climbing Winder and going on to Crook, Knott and Sicker's Fell, before finding our way back exhausted to Long Rigg.

Oriel inherited from Geoffrey Dixon's wife, Nancy, responsibility for serving on the committee of the local branch of Guide Dogs for the Blind, and she did that conscientiously. She also started an informal play-reading society at KGV, which met after school and flourished, and she joined in with all the various events, barn dances, dinners and such-like, organised by the extraordinarily active committee of the KGV Parents' Association. On occasions like that I always looked at her with pride, and day by day I could go home to talk problems over with her and find that she put them in perspective. We went for walks around the local roads together, talked about everything and wondered whether we would retire where we were or perhaps move back south to somewhere near Guildford such as Shalford or Bramley.

While living in Birkdale we acquired a number of new friends, in particular George and Helen Bell, who moved there shortly after us when George came to take over the management of the Wayfarers' Arcade, the beautiful and (at least in the north-west) famous shopping arcade in Lord Street. George had been up at Pembroke just before me reading Law and he and Helen, who had been born and brought up in Edinburgh, had, like Oriel and me, got married in 1959. They also, like us, had a daughter, Susie, and then two sons, and they came to see me at KGV because they had to decide where their two boys, Robert and Duncan, should go to school, the most obvious alternative being Merchant Taylors', Crosby. I went home and told Oriel that I had met a very attractive couple whom I was sure she would like.

In the event they decided on KGV as their first choice for their boys, both of whom passed the appropriate entrance tests, and they bought a house just round the corner from us. George was a little older than me; Helen was a little younger than Oriel. We got to know them well and we would quite often go to dinner with each other. Duncan joined the school at the same time as Piers and they were in the same form. George eventually became one of the governors of King George V College. Helen became Oriel's closest friend.

Through them we got to know Jimmy and Pat Cape, a doctor and his wife who lived near us and were just a few years older. At a party in their house one New Year's Eve, as I was coming downstairs, I saw a picture of a Lancaster bomber. It was quite unlike any other picture in the house, so I asked Jimmy why he had a picture of a Lancaster on the staircase. 'I used to fly around in them a bit', he replied. 'Not for real?', I asked. 'Well', he answered, 'one and a half trips.' He had left school in the summer of 1944 at the age of seventeen and instead of going on to the medical training which was his long-term aim he had volunteered for the RAF, trained for service in Bomber Command, and started his first tour of duty in January 1945. On his second bombing raid over Germany his Lancaster was shot down and he spent the next three months in a prisoner-of-war camp. When they were freed, he and the other prisoners went to the administration block to get their papers and he showed me his, with his picture both full on and sideways, and underneath: *James Cape. Mediker Student.* 'Well', he said, 'I didn't want to tell them that I had only left school.' I reflected that he was just six years older than me and that I had been very fortunate not to have had that sort of experience.

George Wakefield, my Deputy Head at KGV, had not been so fortunate. George had been a boy at KGV and left school at the age of eighteen in the summer of 1939. He volunteered for military service but was told that for the moment he should go and do a crash two-year wartime degree course in English Literature at Liverpool University, while serving in the university's Officer Training Corps. In the summer of 1941, after completing his course, he eventually joined the army. Before long he was commissioned, and then he was posted to North Africa, arriving in time to take command of a platoon of the Durham Light Infantry when Eighth Army invaded Sicily.

After the war Montgomery wrote of his affection for and admiration of the DLI, singling out two actions which exemplified their determination and bravery. One of them was the fight in July 1943 for the Primosole Bridge, which spanned the River Simeto, barring the way to the Plain of Catania, south of Mount Etna and Messina. After a week or more of fighting up the east coast of Sicily, George was one of two platoon commanders of the DLI who, with ninety men, went upstream and forded the River Simeto during the night of 17th July with the aim of taking the bridge from the far side. They ran into fierce resistance. The Germans, seeing the Italians collapsing before Eighth Army's advance, had shifted two armoured divisions into the area. During the fighting George was hit in the knee by a shell splinter but carried on. Most of the men of the two platoons were killed. Only seven of the survivors were unwounded when eventually they were overwhelmed and captured.

George spent the rest of 1943 in a military hospital for prisoners-of-war. The shrapnel was easily removed but the wound was poisoned. An Italian doctor was going to amputate his leg, but a German doctor thought he could save it and did. Recovery was slow and he was never again able to bend his knee. After a year he was transferred to a prisoner-of-war camp, and then in February 1945 the Red Cross was able to have him repatriated. When he got back to Southport he limped up the road to see his old headmaster, George Millward, who suggested that, while he was deciding what to do with himself for the rest of his life, he could come and help out with some teaching at KGV. He did. He stayed on, and when he was twenty-nine became the Head of the English Department. By the time I arrived in 1976 he had been on the staff for over thirty years and was the Deputy Headmaster.

Throughout his life he never spoke about the battle for the Primosole Bridge to anyone, and it was only after his death that his son, John, researched the history of the Sicilian campaign, pieced together what had happened, and explained it in a book called *Dad's War*. I once, rather foolishly and frivolously, described George as perhaps the only Englishman in the Second World War who had managed to get himself captured by the Italians. He put his arm around my shoulder and said, 'Actually, David, it was the Hermann Goering Panzer Division.' To the best of my belief that was the nearest he ever came to speaking about it.

George Wakefield as a junior officer early in the war, from the front cover of Dad's War *by John Wakefield, and half a century later, in retirement.*

48. Reorganisation

We arrived in Southport in the hot summer of 1976, when the Open was being played at the Royal Birkdale Golf Club. We had to get sorted out in a new house and meanwhile I was heavily involved in my work. In the first place there was the ordinary day to day business of running of a large boys' grammar school. On top of that there was all the planning that was needed to create a new sixth form college. Three key things are needed in any educational institution once you know who its pupils (or students) are going to be. First you need a clear idea of an appropriate curriculum for them. Then you need the staffing to teach it. Finally you need suitable buildings in which the teaching and learning can take place.

Too often it happens the other way round. A school has its buildings which, whether good or bad, are permanent, and the opportunity for changing them, other than by doing a certain amount of internal reconfiguration, is negligible. The staffing is very often largely fixed as well. A new head teacher is likely to have to accept those who are already in place, and may be either fortunate or unfortunate in those who are inherited. The curriculum is in theory easier to change, but in practice it may well be decided very largely by what examinations the pupils are expected to take, by what the staff are accustomed to teaching and by what is possible in the buildings already in place. Changing almost anything may be difficult.

At King George V College there was an unusual opportunity to try to do those things in a rational sequence. The Conservative council of the Metropolitan Borough of Sefton, which had approved the school's change of status, required the new college to be restricted in size to 550 students, only a few more than the combined sixth forms of KGV and the Southport High School for Girls. This was because it was to be a grammar school at

369

sixteen-plus, proud of its grammar school past, and consciously aiming to be a model for academic sixth form colleges. The councillors were prepared to allow some expansion, but not so much as to alter the nature of the grammar school sixth form curriculum. We were to be an A level college providing traditional A level subjects and nothing else, other than the sort of sports and recreational activities traditionally associated with a grammar school.

I had to persuade the governors and the local education authority that students who were studying Maths and Science subjects at A level but had failed O level English Language in the Fifth Form, should not only be allowed to re-take it at KGV but should be required to do so. I wanted it to be college policy that they must continue with it until they passed. Similarly I insisted that we should require Arts students who had failed O level Maths to continue with it until they passed. It was not particularly difficult to convince the governors of that, but it was difficult to go beyond that. 'We don't want students coming here to take courses in origami and belly-dancing', said one of them. 'They can do that at the Tech.'

Nevertheless, before long they agreed to let me provide O level courses in a range of languages (French, German, Spanish, Latin and Ancient Greek) and also in a number of other O level subjects, such as Astronomy, Navigation, Economics and Geology, so long as those subjects were not on the curriculum of the 11-16 schools. I argued that I wanted all our students to take an O level subject during their first year, as well as studying for their A levels. The weaker ones would be re-taking either English or Maths. Meanwhile the stronger ones could well take an extra, and perhaps unusual, O level subject, and I wanted them to have passed it before filling in their university application forms.

It also became college policy that all the students should take A level General Studies. They were well qualified to do so, because the General Studies A level examination of the NUJMB, the

Northern Universities Joint Matriculation Board, was particularly well suited to students like ours who had had a broad academic curriculum up to O level. In the first year that statistics about examination performance were made public nationally there were more passes in that one subject at KGV than all the 'A' level passes in all the subjects taken in all of the comprehensive schools in the Metropolitan Borough of Manchester added together.

Getting the staffing right was more of a problem. The reorganisation of King George V School as a sixth form college was, of course, part of a wider reorganisation of secondary education throughout the bounds of the former County Borough of Southport, and you could not sensibly leave the staffing which had been appropriate for one system unaltered under another one. Substantial changes were needed.

We were fortunate that the reorganisation was largely in the capable hands of Mike Nichol, the Deputy Director of Education for the recently created Metropolitan Borough of Sefton, the northernmost borough of Merseyside. In Southport he was faced with changing the secondary provision from two grammar schools and five secondary modern schools into one sixth form college and five comprehensive schools, each with an age range of 11-16, and with amalgamating a boys' and a girls' secondary modern school next door to each other as one comprehensive school.

The first stage in the implementation of the plan for reorganisation was the appointment of the head teachers. My appointment as head of the sixth form college had, of course, already happened. Next Celia Evans, the headmistress of the Southport High School for Girls, was persuaded to stay on and see it through its transition into Greenbank High School, a girls' 11-16 comprehensive school. Then the heads of the secondary modern schools were able to apply for any of the comprehensive school headships, and when two were not appointed, the post was opened up to competition nationally, while they were found positions in other schools in the town as deputy heads.

That system was applied at all levels, and because of the knock-on effect, the number of senior posts in each school was increased. After me, the next appointment to KGV was of my deputy, and for that post George Wakefield was an obvious choice. Surprisingly the local authority had no record of his appointment, and it was as a result of that that I heard from George the story of how he came to join the staff back in 1945.

A proviso applying to all appointments to King George V College was that the candidate must have had recent sixth form experience. This meant that for many posts in the college there were likely to be candidates from both KGV and the Southport High School for Girls, and Mike Nichol, Celia Evans and I tried to resolve the problems which inevitably arose from that by seeing all members of staff at both of the schools and discussing with them what they wanted to do.

For KGV we aimed to create a staffing structure which would accommodate the members of staff we hoped to keep. Quite often we wanted to retain in the college both the High School head of department and the KGV one, so, for example, when John Clough from KGV became Director of Studies, Dorothy Hughes from the High School could be appointed Head of Classics. Similarly the appointment of the Head of Chemistry at KGV to a post responsible for Careers Advice left the Chemistry post open to the head of department at the High School.

In the case of English the head of department at KGV wanted that post in the college, while his opposite number at the High School thought it worth aiming to take charge of the library. I thought it would be better to have her as the head of the English Department, and I remembered how Clement Attlee had in 1945 disappointed the aspirations of Ernest Bevin to be Chancellor of the Exchequer and of Hugh Dalton to be Foreign Secretary, saying 'I think we'll do it the other way round.' I decided to do that with the Library and English Department appointments at KGV. The members of staff concerned were surprised, but they accepted it and in the event it worked well. So did the appointments operation as a whole, and most of those appointed to the college were satisfied.

Of course that left those who were not appointed. In many cases they were still needed at King George V School during the period of transition and several were promoted enough to encourage them to stay, especially as their promotion was accompanied by an assurance of a subsequent post at a no lower level in one of the comprehensive schools. Thus someone who had been appointed to KGV when it was a grammar school, stayed during the period of transition and then moved as a head of department to one of the town's comprehensive schools, might have on his *curriculum vitae* three years teaching in a boys' grammar school, three at a mixed sixth form college and a few years as a head of department at a mixed 11-16 comprehensive school. It could be a good start to a career.

Less satisfactory were the arrangements for the rebuilding of KGV, for the least impressive element in the Education Department of the Metropolitan Borough of Sefton was its Buildings Branch. KGV needed to be rebuilt because it was sinking into the peat, and permission had been granted on condition that it should no longer be a boys' grammar school. Buildings Branch got hold of regulations and specifications from the Department of Education for a replacement boys' school, planned it and started to have it built. There were no girls' toilets, and the sizes of the classrooms were all planned according to the specifications for a boys' secondary school. The school office, offices for senior members of staff and a large common room for other members of staff were all concentrated at one end of the building.

Fortunately the building work was at an early enough stage for me to seek some changes, and I contacted the Head of Buildings Branch. His reaction was that everything was being done properly and that the preferences of a newly appointed head teacher were irrelevant. Head teachers were ephemeral. He was building for the long term in accordance with specifications laid down nationally and after careful thought at Whitehall. There was no budging him.

I turned to Mike Nichol, who asked a number of pertinent questions. The point about the need for girls' toilets was clear. The issue of classroom sizes needed some thought. I explained why I thought it desirable to have small departmental offices scattered throughout the college rather than to concentrate all the staff in one corner, leaving the students entirely unsupervised in the rest of the college. He understood and set out to solve the problem.

Later we looked at the plans for Phase II of the college buildings. They presented an even worse problem. Although Buildings Branch had by now accepted that we needed to accommodate girls as well as boys, their plan for this building included an isolated upstairs area designated as a student common room, approached from one side only and with boys' toilets at the top of the stairs on one side and girls' toilets on the other.

No member of staff would have any reason to go there other than to check that everything was peaceful and orderly and then turn round and go away again. I wanted the common room in the middle of the building downstairs, next to the kitchen, and so arranged that both students and members of staff would naturally walk through it on their way from one place to another, and where, if they wished, they would go to have lunch in the middle of the day. All this was eventually achieved, but at the cost of untold hours of argument and explanation.

There was a stage at which we were working partly in the first of the new college buildings and partly in the old grammar school building, while alongside was a building site. The contractors began by driving piles thirty feet into the ground to get through the peat and establish a firm base for the building. They had detailed plans of all the services to the school building, so that they could avoid cutting through electricity cables or gas pipes, and they were meticulous in arranging their work in such a way as to cause minimum disturbance.

Then one afternoon all the lights in the new college building which we were already using went out and immediately afterwards water flooded not only over the grounds of the college but also over the Scarisbrick New Road, which became impassable. I tried to use the telephone, but the telephone was dead. It seemed that the gas supply had been cut as well; before long sewage was seeping into the flooding water. The explanation was that, although the contractors had detailed plans of the services to the school building and carefully avoided them, they had not been given a plan of the services to the first of the new college buildings and a mechanical digger had gone through everything. There was nothing anyone could do except pack up and go home. But by the next day things were already back to normal.

The process of reorganisation took years, as the last eleven-plus intake of 1977 worked its way through the school. There was no entry in 1978. At that stage Janet Lawley, who was later to be a very successful headmistress of Bury High School for Girls, arrived from Merchant Taylors', Crosby, as an extra vice-principal. Sex discrimination legislation had prevented us from advertising for a female deputy. Instead we explained in the advertisement that an extra deputy would be needed when the first girls entered the college to join the Head Master, the Vice-Master and the Senior Master on the Senior Management Team. Even then, two men applied. Then in 1979, when the change from grammar school to sixth form college officially took place, the first girls joined the college.

The school had begun its life with a staff of seven and ended it with a staff of 50. It grew from 110 boys in 1920 to 851 in 1977, the last year in which there was an 11-plus entry. In the last year of its existence as a school the sixth form numbered 267 and was larger than ever before, with eighty-six of the boys who left that year going on to degree courses. Throughout the life of the school it had retained the distinction of being the last school in the country to be named after a reigning monarch, and when it was transformed into a sixth form college, the name of King George V was retained.

In the summer of 1982 the very last grammar school boys, those who had joined the school in 1977, took O level, and almost all of them returned in September as students of the college, whose new buildings were now completed. The old school building, gradually subsiding into the peat, was being prepared for demolition. The period of transition was over. We had reached 'the broad sun-lit uplands' towards which we had been working for so long and I was looking forward to leading and developing the new college throughout the rest of the century. I was only the third headmaster, and my predecessors had been in post for twenty-nine and twenty-seven years respectively. So far I had only been there for six.

49. Good Order

◇◇◇◇◇◇◇◇◇◇◇◇◇◇◇◇◇◇◇◇◇◇◇◇◇◇◇◇◇◇◇◇◇◇◇◇

Discipline, or the establishment and maintenance of a well-ordered society in which good teaching and learning can take place, is understandably a matter of concern to school governing bodies, and especially when appointing a new head teacher. At the age of forty, when I first aspired to be a headmaster, I looked young for my age, had a cheerful and amiable manner, and was still only a head of department, with no obvious capacity for or experience of coping with difficult disciplinary problems. When first interviewed for a headship and asked about discipline my instinct was to stress the need to create a pleasant and purposeful environment in which both staff and pupils could be free to get on with their work, which is true enough but was not the answer needed.

I had to learn to say (and this is true as well) that in any society (a nation, a school or a family) people can only be free to get on with their work when living within the Rule of Law. Societies need rules, and rules need to be enforced if the society is to function properly. Staff and students in a school or college need to know what the rules are, members of staff need to know what decisions they are entitled to make, and they need to know that so long as they operate properly within the established system, they can expect unwavering support from the head.

The teaching staff all want an orderly and well-disciplined school, but understandably they vary in their views on how to achieve that. Less understandably they sometimes avoid facing the fact that many of the rules apply to them as well. Pupils are expected to turn up for their lessons at a designated place and time. The teacher should be there too, preferably before the pupils. In a well ordered school that is so. But the head and other senior members of staff need to be seen in the corridors before the beginning of morning school or in the staff common room at the end of morning break unless things are to become undesirably casual.

During my first week at KGV I asked my secretary to put up a notice in the staff common room saying that the headmaster would be grateful if all members of staff could let him have a copy of their personal timetable before leaving on Friday. At the weekend I looked through them. One was missing. It was the timetable of one of the heads of department. So on the Monday I sent him a note asking him to call at my study with it. When he arrived his manner was churlish and aggrieved. I asked him why I had not had it the previous Friday. 'Well', he said, 'You only said you would be grateful if we got them in. It wasn't clear that it was necessary.' 'John', I explained, 'When I say I should be grateful for something, that is intended as a polite way of saying that I require it to be done by the time indicated.' He never warmed to me, and he may have resented my appointment because one of the other candidates for my job had been a friend of his.

Some years later, when he was refereeing a 1st XV rugby football match, one of our forwards rushed into the scrum and broke his neck. John's reaction, holding him still while sending someone running down the road to the hospital for an ambulance, saved the boy from a lifetime of paralysis. After that I could have forgiven him anything. The boy was fortunate with the way it was dealt with and also with the fact that the Southport Promenade Hospital was the north-west centre for paraplegic cases. They welded three of the vertebrae in his neck together and within weeks he was able to do more or less anything other than play rugby football.

Rather surprisingly the issue on which the staff at KGV were most obviously divided when I arrived was discipline. That was all the more surprising because the school was so well-disciplined. Prefects could be relied on to maintain order – though on a wet day, when a large number of boys were confined during break in the hall, some of the perfects resorted to unofficial methods such as

378

putting badly behaved boys through a trap-door in the stage to cool off underneath.

To a new headmaster one of the most impressive things about KGV was its orderly nature and the extent to which housemasters and prefects knew what was going on and co-operated to check villainy. Housemasters kept a close eye on the behaviour of boys in their house, and there was a remarkably well-established understanding by the boys of the difference between 'sneaking' about another boy who had, for example, cheated in a test, and providing information to a prefect or member of staff about serious anti-social behaviour.

On one occasion the Head Boy of the school, Barry Klaasen, brought me an air rifle. It appeared that a Fourth Form boy (unnamed) had brought it in and put it on top of a cupboard, telling the other boys in the form that he had brought it 'to shoot the headmaster.' Another boy told a prefect, though without naming the culprit. The prefect collected the gun and gave it to the Head Boy, who brought it to me and asked what we should do next. I suggested that he give it to me and then do nothing other than wait to see if the owner complained of the loss. He never did. The air rifle lived in my loft, travelled from one house to another, and some twenty years later went to a dealer, together with a whole load of other accumulated possessions.

Another impressive thing about discipline at KGV was the institution of Saturday Morning Detention. It was the most powerful deterrent I encountered anywhere in more than forty years as a schoolmaster. It was seldom used, but any boy who had been given a Saturday Morning Detention might have to explain to his employer that he could not turn up for his Saturday morning job and then suffer the embarrassment of travelling through the town in his school uniform to spend two hours working under supervision and worrying that his whole future would be blighted. Once a senior boy who was hoping to go to Sandhurst had behaved disgracefully in some way I have forgotten. He offered as a plea in mitigation of his offence that 'I've been all through the school, sir, and never had a Saturday Morning.' It was a fair point, so I dealt with him leniently.

What divided the staff in their attitudes towards discipline was that some wanted a fixed tariff of clear-cut penalties for specified offences, while others believed that punishment was scarcely necessary so long as teachers with strong personalities and a sound knowledge of their subject got on sensibly with their job. My view was that they were more united than they realised. They shared a common belief that it was essential to have an orderly environment. Where they differed was over the appropriate strategy for achieving it, and my answer was that what was needed was what might be called a graduated response: start with a polite request, move on to firm insistence, then to minor sanctions and eventually to reporting to a housemaster, with more substantial sanctions culminating in Saturday Morning Detention, and finally on to the headmaster, with the prospect of suspension and even expulsion.

That was much the same view that had been taken by Geoffrey Dixon. It had worked in his time, and so far as I could see, it was still working. But with a new headmaster there were those who saw it as a good opportunity to shift things in the direction they favoured and the attitude of the new head needed to be made clear to them. So I produced a document headed *Some Thoughts on School Discipline* (something similar though in several respects different was needed for the sixth form college later) and distinguished between the appropriate responses to slovenly work, misbehaviour in the classroom, minor misdemeanours outside the classroom and serious moral or social offences.

Slovenly work is not primarily a disciplinary matter. A member of staff who requires a boy to do his work to a reasonable standard and produce it punctually is simply doing his job, and keeping a boy in after school in order to get the work done is not so much a punishment as a practical expedient.

Misbehaviour in class, unpunctuality and rudeness all need to be checked promptly and firmly. Members of staff need to be clear about the standards they expect, insist on adherence to those standards, and if possible ensure them without punishment. They should not be surprised if a boy misbehaves, and it should never be seen as an offence against themselves personally, but rather as an interruption in the proper work of the school. They should never let it make them angry, and they should be prepared, when necessary, to administer moderate punishments calmly and ruthlessly.

As for minor misdemeanours outside the classroom such as dropping litter, every member of staff is under an obligation to take action, even if only by requiring a boy to pick up the litter. They all need to enforce school regulations, because failure to do so imposes an unfair burden on one's colleagues and sometimes on the caretaking and cleaning staff.

The other category of offence was serious moral and social offences, such as bullying, stealing and vandalism. Such offences had to be reported, and either the boy's housemaster would deal with it or, eventually, I would. During my first term a fifth Form boy was found to have been systematically damaging the exercise books of younger boys in the express stream. I suspended him until the end of term, and found interesting the difference between the reaction of the local authority officer responsible for secondary education and the reaction of the boys in the school. When I reported the suspension to the local authority, I received a worried telephone call to say that they hoped this was not the beginning of a spate of suspensions. When I reported it to the school in Assembly, the boys cheered.

I indicated the disciplinary measures available to the staff and stressed that one form of sanction I would not tolerate was any form of physical violence. I had no wish to comment on the merits or demerits of corporal punishment, which was still widely used in schools at that time, but I disliked it myself and would find it very difficult to justify or excuse it to parents.

A couple of terms later one of my colleagues came to see me in distress. A particularly difficult boy had driven him mad, to the point at which he had lost his temper and hit him. The boy would, no doubt, go home and complain to his parents. I told him not to worry and reassured him that I was far more sympathetic to someone who, uncharacteristically, was driven to lose his temper and hit a boy, than to someone who beat a boy in cold blood. I rang the boy's father and we agreed that his son was very difficult and that it may have been good for him to discover that his behaviour had been unpleasant enough to drive a teacher to violence.

Some boys found it difficult to avoid trouble and even seemed to court it. One, Andrew Ray, was by far the tallest boy in his year, and that made him stand out. If he did anything wrong it was more noticeable than with other boys and he acquired something of a reputation. As the years went by he felt the need to play up to his reputation. I knew him moderately well because he was my daughter's boyfriend towards the end of his O level year, and on the last day of term he was due to come to supper with us. He was also a boy who was far better suited to a technical education than an academic one, and sensibly he was intending to go on to the Southport Technical College the following year.

On that last afternoon he brought his motor cycle to school and drove it into the building and down the Science corridor. He was apprehended and brought to see me. I took the view that it was a serious enough offence to justify expulsion, so I expelled him an hour or so before he was leaving anyway. That evening, as had already been arranged, he came to supper. Neither of us referred to the events of the afternoon, and we had an enjoyable meal together with the rest of the family. About a year later he set up a small lawn mower business, and for the next few years, until I left Southport, he always serviced and, when necessary, repaired my lawn mower.

Inevitably there were some problems with parents over disciplinary issues. Parents generally want good order in any educational establishment. Some proclaim their belief in strict, and even harsh, discipline, but they find that, when it is their own child who has contravened the rules, they want sensitivity and understanding rather than punishment. Most understand the problem well enough to accept that head teachers have to use their judgement, which will not always be the same as their own.

A few do not. A lecturer in Sociology at a Polytechnic sought to justify his son's behaviour when the boy saw the taking of an A level examination as an opportunity to flout the college's dress code. The boy suffered nothing worse than having to report to me properly dressed before being allowed into the examination hall. But the father complained to the local authority and threatened to go to the newspapers, asserting his son's right to take his A level examinations unharassed by college rules. But the boy had the sense to conform and his father did not press the issue any further.

Another father wanted to withdraw his daughter from a *Challenge of Industry Conference* at the end of her first year on the grounds that he disapproved of having a trade union official speaking at the conference. He pointed out that he was a management consultant and asserted her right not to go; I could not force her to, he said. I agreed. All our students were volunteers, but so long as they chose to stay at the college they had to accept its curricular requirements. She could leave if she wished to do so, but she could not just opt out of something her father disliked. The girl had to persuade her father to let her attend. I suspect that he was angry at having been made redundant and blamed union activity for the problems which had caused him to adopt the euphemism 'management consultant' rather than describe himself as unemployed.

Such problems were rare, and discipline was not a serious issue at King George V College. Most of the students wanted to do well at their A levels and wanted their parents and teachers to think well of them. Celia Evans was right, of course, that the girls who came to KGV were there to enjoy a good education rather than to civilise the boys, but all the same their presence did have a civilising effect. It was a well ordered society in which staff and students alike were engaged in worthwhile and purposeful activity, and it had a humane and civilised ethos. That owed something to the fact that half the staff and half the students were what I still thought of as the gentler sex.

50. Coping with Cuts

1976, the year in which I took over as headmaster of KGV, was the year in which the Labour government led by Jim Callaghan, with Denis Healey as Chancellor of the Exchequer, got into such financial difficulty that it needed a loan from the IMF, the International Monetary Fund. The IMF provided the money on the condition that the British government made substantial cuts in expenditure, and the subsequent requirement for savings reached most areas of local authority spending. Everything I did in the next few years, whether it was developing the new college or trying to maintain high standards in the grammar school as it was gradually phased out of existence, was done in the context of financial stringency and reduced funding.

The education department of the Metropolitan Borough of Sefton found itself required to make savings of 3%, which at first did not sound too bad. The Director of Education, Ken Robinson, called all the secondary heads of the borough together to explain the impact on our expenditure. There were some areas in which savings could not be made. First, the authority had entered into contracts, such as buildings contracts, which could not be broken. Secondly, the councillors had decided that they would not accept any change in staffing ratios, so pay expenditure, which was the largest element in the budget, would remain unchanged. Thirdly, they would not accept any reduction of what was known as 'capitation', the sum of money allocated to schools for books and equipment according to the number of pupils on roll. The effect of all this was that the 3% cut had to come out of the residual 15%, after contracts, pay expenditure and 'capitation' had been excluded from consideration. 3% is a relatively small reduction. £3 in every £15 is a big one. It meant a 20% cut in the total funding of those items being considered.

Ken Robinson had drawn up a list of everything which was in the 15% of the budget up for consideration: peripatetic music teachers, for example, foreign languages assistants, a youth club in Bootle at the southern end of the borough, and the building costs for the second phase of the new sixth form college being built on Southport. Somewhere about four-fifths of the way down the list a line was drawn. Everything above the line was, for the moment, saved. Everything below the line was scheduled too be axed – or at least reduced. We were encouraged to say what we wanted to save, but he made it a condition of recommending saving something that one should be prepared to say what should be cut instead. If you wanted to save a youth club in Bootle, would you find the money by making peripatetic music teachers redundant? If you wanted to keep peripatetic music teachers, were you prepared to dispense with foreign language assistants?

It was, of course, more complicated than that. You might dispense with the services of German and Spanish assistants but keep the French ones. You might not be able to cut out completely the second phase of the building of King George V College, but it was possible to reduce the size of the sports hall and reduce the provision for building materials, using a poorer quality of cement and cheaper bricks. It was also possible to cut out the cost of demolishing the old grammar school building and leave that until another time.

It was a very worthwhile meeting and a model, it seemed to me, of how to approach the problem of cutting costs to live within one's budget. For my own part, I would not have made either staffing ratios or 'capitation' sacrosanct. My preference would have been to have found a formula by which budgets could be delegated to individual schools, whose governing bodies would then have been responsible for determining a budget put to them by the head teacher, after consultation with the staff. All over the country, I discovered later, there were people drawing the same conclusion, but I did not know that at the time.

The good news I was able to take back to KGV was that the staffing ratio of 14:1 was not worsened. But it was already the toughest ratio for any sixth form college in the country, and since the average sixth form college staffing ratio at the time was under 10:1, some colleges with a staffing ratio well below the average had twice as many members of staff per student as KGV. At a staff meeting shortly afterwards a member of staff commented on what a difference it would make if only we could make just a few more appointments. I remembered how the Earl of Westmoreland in Shakespeare's *Henry V* had said on the eve of Agincourt, 'O that we now had here but one ten thousand of those men in England that do no work today!', and I replied in the words of Henry V: 'What's he that wishes so? My cousin Westmoreland? No, my fair cousin. If we are mark'd to die, we are enow to do our country loss; and if to live, the fewer men, the greater share of honor.' I expect a number of my colleagues wondered if I had gone mad. I left it to the English Department to explain it afterwards.

Meanwhile almost all the schools with which KGV had for years competed at cricket and rugby football, and also at trying to get the largest number of open awards to Oxbridge, were being threatened in a different way. The grammar schools in Blackburn, Bolton and Bury had all existed since the sixteenth century, Merchant Taylors' School down the coast in Crosby had been founded in 1620 by a member of the Merchant Taylors' Company, Arnold School in Blackpool, on the other side of the Ribble estuary, had been founded in 1896 and named after Dr Thomas Arnold, the headmaster of Rugby School, and King Edward VII School, Lytham, had been founded in 1908 by the Lytham Charity Foundation. Since 1926 they had all received a direct grant from the government in return for providing a percentage of free places, and once the 1944 Education Act was implemented, they all took a mixture of fee-paying pupils and others who received free places on the strength of a good performance in the eleven-plus examination. There were nearly two hundred such schools in the country, some for boys, some for girls and a few mixed.

A decade earlier the then Labour government had declared its aim 'to end selection at eleven plus and to eliminate separation in secondary education.' Now another Labour government wanted the governing bodies of 'direct grant' schools to consider with the local authority in which they were situated how best to co-operate with this development and reconstitute their schools as comprehensive schools.

As it happens, there was probably no grammar school in the country whose governors would have wanted the school to provide only for the children of the wealthy, nor did any of them want full independence such as was enjoyed by the public schools. They prided themselves on being engines of social mobility. But they also saw themselves as existing to educate children with 'some aptness for learning', from whatever social background they might come. They were concerned to maintain high academic standards, parental choice, a wide social mix, as many free places as possible and a sliding scale of payments according to income for the rest. That view of things was not reconcilable with a determination to 'end selection' and 'eliminate separation.'

Political dogma triumphed over common sense and in 1975 the Labour government which had come to power in 1974 announced its intention to phase out the direct grant. Since the direct grant schools were directly responsible for their own running costs, including pay expenditure and any building programme, the government was gambling that they would not have the financial strength to carry on as grammar schools without the support of the direct grant. It was a serious miscalculation.

Overwhelmingly the direct grant schools chose independence rather than be turned into what a Labour prime minister later referred to as 'a bog-standard comprehensive.' Thus a Labour government managed to create more than a hundred new independent boys' schools, as well as a large number of independent girls' schools, at the stroke of a pen. It was a very significant boost to the independent sector. Politicians had unintentionally gone one stage further towards creating a society in which the rich paid for their children to go to independent schools, while those on low or middle incomes had to put up with what their local authority provided, and particularly in inner-city areas there was a lot of dissatisfaction with what they did provide.

While the education departments of local education authorities were having their funding cut and were necessarily passing on the cuts to schools and colleges, the newly independent former direct grant schools increased their fees and launched appeals for funds with which to build new facilities. The effect was that before long a vast funding gap had opened between a former 'maintained' grammar school such as KGV, which was now a sixth form college, and all those surrounding former 'direct grant' grammar schools which were now independent. Up until 1976 the funding per student had been more or less the same. Twenty years later, when a sixth form college was receiving an annual grant of about £4,000 per student and it was illegal to charge parents anything, many independent day schools were charging fees of about £16,000 a year.

Nevertheless, the sixth form college system still had a number of substantial advantages. Not least were the obvious efficiencies of scale, and that in turn made it possible to provide a wider choice of A level subjects than was possible in most schools. But it was also the case that sixth form colleges attracted well-qualified, specialist staff. In a world in which the tenure of academic posts in universities was precarious, some young men and women would opt for a career teaching A level students, when they would not consider joining the staff of even a particularly good independent day school and having to teach the whole age range from eleven to eighteen.

A sixth form college such as KGV had to weather the prejudices of politicians on both left and right - those on the left who viewed such a college as a 'grammar school at 16+', managing somehow to subvert the comprehensive system which was intended to be the solution to all the nation's problems, and those on the right who viewed them with a mixture of fear and contempt, assuming that 'people like us' would send their children to independent schools but at the same time beginning to see sixth form colleges as a threat.

KGV emerged from reorganisation with a curriculum well adapted to the needs of the students, a staff well qualified to teach them, and buildings which provided a sound base within which that could happen. It also had a powerful developing ethos in which the encouragement of purposeful activity was combined with a light but effective system of supervision, good teaching, careful guidance about higher education, and a generally amiable atmosphere.

One consequence of its success was an ever increasing intake from independent schools: sixty-eight boys in the first four years, from schools which included Harrow and Rugby, Dauntsey's and Rossall, Ampleforth and Stoneyhurst, Millfield and Stowe, the one boy from Stowe being my own elder son, James. There was a similar influx of girls from perhaps less well known independent schools, and the numbers of both boys and girls were growing. Only two boys arrived from Merchant Taylors, Crosby, in 1980, but in 1983 there were ten.

During the 1980s the heads and the governing bodies of independent schools had good reason to worry about the success of sixth form colleges. Many were academically successful and they cost parents nothing. They were also increasing in number as one education authority after another realised that the development of sixth form colleges was the solution to many of the problems thrown up by comprehensive reorganisation. By the early 1990s there were a hundred and twenty of them, educating about a quarter of all the country's A level candidates.

But in 1992 the Conservative government of John Major, possibly quite unintentionally, checked the development of sixth form colleges and exerted on them sufficient financial pressure to reduce their numbers by a quarter. The government had decided to tackle the failings of English technical education, which was notoriously inadequate in the years after the school leaving age of sixteen and almost non-existent before that age. To do that it removed all technical colleges from local education authority control and created a new post-sixteen education sector presided over by a Further Education Funding Council.

When asked in parliament what would happen to sixth form colleges under the new dispensation, the minister, without thought or planning, said that they also would be in the new sector. Thus a hundred and twenty colleges, whose work was predominantly the provision of A level courses, were put into a sector which was directing its resources towards the improvement of technical education rather than towards A levels, and the funding of those colleges was massively reduced on the principle that economy would inexorably lead to efficiency and effectiveness.

Eventually a position was reached where a typical sixth form college would receive £4,000 a year for each of its students, while a comprehensive school which had been designated an academy might get as much as £8,000 for each of its pupils. Meanwhile a nearby independent day school could be charging £16,000 a year and an independent boarding school could be charging £32,000. All four of them, whether their income per pupil was £4,000, £8,000, £16,000 or £32,000, were doing the same job of educating teenagers up to A level. It was the sixth form college which was required to be 'efficient.'

No local education authority ever again founded one, because if it did, the college would immediately be removed from it and placed in the FEFC sector. The one hundred and twenty which were put into that sector were subjected to such financial and political pressure that their number reduced to ninety by the early twenty-first century. At that stage and for some years thereafter the academic performance of KGV was always among the top 10% of colleges, and even among the top 5%. But the financial and political pressure continued and after yet another quarter of a century it was being driven towards being the A level annexe of the local technical college. To anyone who had known it as a grammar school or as one of the leading academic sixth form colleges in the country it was immensely sad.

51. King George V College

◇◇

Oriel and I seldom celebrated our wedding anniversary because it was on 1st August, immediately after the end of the summer term, and we were always liable to be on our way with the children to a seaside holiday at somewhere such as Camber Sands or Aldeburgh or Minehead or Anglesey. But we had managed to celebrate the tenth anniversary in 1969 while at Stowe by driving over to Oxford to go to the cinema and see the film of *Who's Afraid of Virginia Wolfe.* We celebrated the twentieth, by which time we were living in Birkdale, by going out to dinner together at a Chinese restaurant in Southport. It was something we had not done since the children had been born, so when we told them what we intended Piers said, 'What about us?' But he had just had his fourteenth birthday a couple of weeks earlier, so we felt that they were old enough to be left alone while we went out together.

A month later, on 1st September 1979, King George V School officially changed into King George V College. The association with King George V had always been good for the prestige of the school and somehow seemed to suggest that we had friends in high places, though Peter Richardson, when Head of Physics, pointed out to me that some schools seemed to have friends in even higher places. He had answered the 'phone in the staff common room, saying 'King George V', and felt that he was being upstaged when the person at the other end of the line said, 'Christ the King here.' Christ the King was the name of the Roman Catholic comprehensive school in the town.

Ken Miller, the college's caretaker, suggested to me that we should mark the occasion by running the union flag up the flagpole. 'What a good idea!' I replied, 'Of course!' Much to my surprise a senior member of staff who had recently joined us from the Southport High School for Girls came to see me to express her concern. Did I realise that the union flag was flying over our building? She saw it as an emblem associated with right-wing racist thugs. I explained that I had grown up seeing it as a symbol of the defence of freedom against Nazi tyranny, and it was the flag under which colleagues of ours, such as the deputy headmaster and the caretaker, had fought so that she and I could live our lives in freedom. I hope she saw the point. I thought it sad that it needed to be explained.

Perhaps it was not so much that it was a symbol of right wing thugs as a symbol of an essentially male society. One could not get away from the fact that the name of the college, King George V, was male and that the headmaster and both of his predecessors were male as well. So were all the names on the war memorial, which clearly was more directly relevant to the history of KGV than to that of the High School, and listed the names of eighty Old Georgians, which was an average of four or five from each year group since the school's foundation.

It did had some relevance to the girls of that era as well, however. One day in the late 1970s a middle-aged woman, mother of a teenage boy, looked at it and pointed to the name Gerald Whelan. She said, 'I knew him. He was in Bomber Command. He was the boyfriend of my best friend at the High School. She cried all day at school when we got the news that he had been killed.' It brought home to me both how young were so many of those who were killed in the Second World War and also that each tragedy was not only the cutting short of a young life but also a loss for a mother, sister, wife or a schoolgirl who might still be remembering him with sadness fifty, sixty or seventy years later.

On the whole, and understandably, most Old Georgians deplored the change from grammar school to sixth form college and at the annual Old Georgians' Dinner, looking back with affection to their school and regretting its passing, they were disinclined to toast the college. But both school and college were popularly referred to as KGV, so we agreed that the toast should be 'KGV' and before long the change from school to college was generally accepted, even if not welcomed.

At times there were problems which arose from our being faced with regulations designed for comprehensive schools. At one time the government and the teachers' unions rather extraordinarily agreed with each other to specify the number of hours that a teacher could be expected to work under the direction of and in a place designated by the head teacher. They settled on 1265 hours a year, those hours to be spread reasonably over thirty-six weeks, on thirty-five of which teachers could be expected to teach pupils.

That did not make any provision for supervision during the lunch hour. So teachers in large comprehensive schools sometimes walked out for the duration of the lunch hour, leaving the head to supervise perhaps one and a half thousand teenagers, who might be perfectly well behaved when supervised, but were liable to be unspeakably awful if left day after day to their own devices. When representatives of the Secondary Heads Association went to meet the relevant minister and his civil servants to explain how unworkable this was, they were met with the response from a senior civil servant, 'But don't you have string quartets and that sort of thing in the lunch hour? We used to at Harrow.'

In the end local authorities tried to solve the problem by employing dinner ladies to supervise during the lunch hour, and this was an extra expense which had to come out of the education budget. It was an inappropriate arrangement in a sixth form college, and I was able to persuade the local authority that instead of paying dinner ladies, they should pay for free lunches for any members of staff prepared to supervise in the lunch hour. It was a good solution. It saved the local authority money; it gave members of staff a free lunch every day; and the supervision was both unobtrusive and effective.

There came a time when the Assistant Masters' and Mistresses' Association (AMMA), of which almost all members of staff at

KGV were members, required their members 'to withdraw their goodwill' by refusing to supervise during the lunch hour. Peter Richardson, now the Senior Tutor and also the AMMA representative, came to see me to suggest a solution. His members, he pointed out, could not be regarded as supervising the students if they paid for their lunches during the period when they were expected to 'withdraw their good will.' So for a fortnight those members of staff who wanted a cooked lunch paid for it. The students did not notice the difference. Everything continued as normal.

Another problem arose over the issue of admissions criteria. Under the old dispensation children at Roman Catholic primary schools in Southport had not taken the 11+ examination but had automatically gone on to the Catholic comprehensive school, Christ the King, and the question of transferring to the sixth form of either King George V School or the Southport High School for Girls had never arisen. Now it did.

In 1979, as KGV became a mixed sixth form college, a pupil at Christ the King asked for an application form for admission to KGV. The admissions staff provided the girl with an application form; she filled it in and then passed it on to her headmaster for him to provide a reference. He refused to do so and complained to the local authority. An officer of the l.e.a. then contacted me to say that I must not admit students from Christ the King School.

I replied that we were open to anyone living within the bounds of the former County Borough of Southport who met the academic criteria for admission. We would accept Muslims, Hindus, atheists and agnostics, as well as Christians of any denomination. I could not properly discriminate against someone on the grounds that she was a Roman Catholic. He insisted: Catholics had their own provision at Christ the King. I assured him that I would not seek to entice their students away; their headmaster could refuse to provide a reference; their priest could warn of the pains of Purgatory in the event of their going to a secular college. But if any got as far as applying, I would not turn them away because they were Roman Catholics.

In the event the problem went away. It was obvious to anyone that if the issue became public, the case for discrimination on grounds of religious denomination could not be upheld. So we simply carried on. Most pupils at Christ the King stayed where they were to take A level. A few came to KGV. Their headmaster continued to refuse to provide any of them with a reference. I assured their parents that that would not be held against them and they could write the reference instead.

It was only the second time in my life that I had been faced with what one might call an issue of conscience. The first was in 1956, when I was up at Oxford but still serving in the Army Emergency Reserve at the time of the Suez Crisis. On that occasion nothing happened that concerned me directly. The personal crisis, such as it was, was entirely in my mind. Now in 1979, twenty-three years later, the issue over admissions dissolved and faded away, unpublicised and unnoticed. I could only reflect that I was fortunate to have grown up and lived in a country where by my mid-forties those were the only crises of conscience I had ever encountered.

Yet another problem arose when the local authority produced guidelines relating to the supervision of children when not on school premises. A variety of incidents, some local and some further afield, had resulted in a decision that whenever children left school premises on any educational visit, they must be accompanied by at least one responsible adult of each sex, and the number of responsible adults (of both sexes) was increased by a specified formula to take account of any increase in the number of pupils.

The Head of Art at KGV quite often took an Art class to look at pictures in the Atkinson Gallery in Lord Street. I had recently gone one evening with all the members of an A level History set I was teaching to see the film *Nicholas and Alexandra*. The Geographers had recently taken groups of students on study visits to Dentdale and the Howgill Fells. Each case would have been a contravention of the new guidelines. The only let-out was that they were only guidelines rather than explicit instructions, so I could, and did, take responsibility for modifying them to take account of the life of a sixth form college. But it still meant that if anything went wrong there would not just be the problem itself but also the fact that the problem had happened in the context of my authorising contravention of the local authority's guidelines. There was no ideal solution. I could only tell the staff that we had to use our common sense and aim to act reasonably and 'in the manner of a wise and caring parent.'

Most of the while the staff simply carried on teaching and the students got on with their work. Most students aimed to do well at A level and go on to university. The transition to sixth form college was clearly a success, and visitors were often pleasantly surprised to find that high standards could be accompanied by a comfortable and relaxed environment in which staff and students alike were clearly all engaged in purposeful activity.

Some things were going to have to change, partly because of government policy and partly because society changes and nothing stays the same. When I left, in 1983, my immediate successor, Geraldine Evans, was anxious to make a new start. Far from wanting to emphasize continuity with the past, she felt that the time had come to broaden the curriculum to admit a wider range of students, to relax the clothing regulations, and to put more emphasis on gender equality and on ensuring that the female students understood the increasing opportunities opening up for women. As part of the process of escaping what she perceived to be the male dominated atmosphere of the past, the war memorial was removed, together with the pictures of her three male predecessors.

Sadly the merits of what she was trying to do were sometimes undervalued because her style was seen as unnecessarily aggressive. John Clough, the Director of Studies, rescued the war memorial and the pictures of her predecessors until they could be dug out again and replaced in a gentler climate, when Hilary Anslow took over in 1992. Hilary managed to combine an attractive personality with effectiveness and King George V College continued to develop and retained its position as one of the leading sixth form colleges in the country. She was awarded an O.B.E. for her part in that success and the college's A level performance was still consistently among the top ten (out of more than six hundred) post-16 colleges in the country.

The name of the college could still give the impression that we had friends in high places. Roger Mitchell, the Vice-Principal I appointed just before I left, described how he was discussing admissions with a family new to the area, when the door opened and a member of the office staff said, '*The Prince of Wales* on the 'phone.' 'Say I'll 'phone back on Monday', he replied. He knew that it was the Banqueting Manager of *The Prince of Wales* in Lord Street who was ringing to finalise the arrangements for a student end of term dance. His visitors looked impressed.

52. Crisis 1981

◇◇◇◇◇◇◇◇◇◇◇◇◇◇◇◇◇◇◇◇◇◇◇◇◇◇◇◇◇◇◇◇◇◇◇◇◇

By the end of the Summer Term of 1981 things were going well in the college. The long process of reorganisation was nearing its end. The very last eleven-plus intake, who had entered the school in September 1977, one year after I had arrived, were now the last surviving year of the old school and would be taking O level the following summer. We had decided to treat them as part of the college and whenever possible teach them in the new college buildings. The first intake of girls had just taken A level. We had completed the first year in which we had roughly equal numbers of boys and girls in the college. Things were settling down, and the staff celebrated the end of term with a buffet supper and a dance.

Oriel and I enjoyed the dance, but we needed to get away early the next morning. Oriel's elder sister, June, had had breast cancer and a mastectomy back in about 1970, three years after Chloë had died. She appeared to have made a good recovery, but now, after a remission of about ten years, it had returned and she was seriously ill. Oriel had already been down to stay with her and her daughters, Linda and Vicky, for a week. Now we both needed to get down to Shalford, just outside Guildford, where Oriel's mother, Nora, still lived and where June lived as well, in a different part of the village.

It also provided the opportunity for me to visit my mother, who was living in a retirement home in South Darenth in Kent, unhappy and unwell. Besides that I wanted to see my Uncle Hughie, who had survived two world wars serving in the Royal Navy (as a stoker when he joined up in 1916 and as a Chief Petty Officer Stoker by the time he left the navy for the second time thirty years later). Now a widower, he was living in Chatham in a home for former seamen.

Kate was by now twenty. Although she had abandoned the foundation course at the Southport College of Art and Design, she still enjoyed painting and drawing, and she was still working at her job as a care assistant looking after handicapped children at a hospital near Southport called Greaves Hall. Now she was no longer living at home she seemed to get on better with Oriel and me and with her brothers. Soon after the school holidays began she had some time off and that provided an opportunity for her to visit an old school friend from the days when we had lived at Stowe. So while Oriel and I went down to Shalford, we took Kate to stay for a while with her old school friend and Piers to stay with the Macdonalds at Stowe. James, meanwhile, in the middle of working for his A levels, opted to stay at home and look after himself.

Oriel and I got down to Shalford on the Friday evening and found June obviously very ill and Nora in distress. Linda, who had come down from Oxford with a Mathematics degree a year earlier and was just completing her first year of training as an accountant, was doing her best to look after them. Vicky, who was just a few weeks older than Piers, and had like him just taken O level, had been sent off on holiday in Dorset with a school friend whose father was a housemaster at Cranleigh. She understood that her mother was ill, but she did not yet know just how ill she was.

While Oriel spent the Saturday with Nora and June and Linda, I spent it working in June's garden. Then on the Sunday I drove to South Darenth in time for lunch with my mother. It was a difficult meal followed by a difficult afternoon. She was desperately unhappy (perhaps a psychiatrist would have diagnosed it as 'acute depression'), and while one of the elements in her unhappiness was that she saw so little of me, it was clearly impossible for her to enjoy my visit when I was there.

I stayed overnight in Rochester with John and Anneliese and then drove to Hughie's retirement home in Chatham, where there was a view over the Medway, with ships always coming and going, and where the corridors were decorated with ships' badges and the vast brass shell cases from the massive guns carried by battleships. I took Hughie out to lunch, and I recall that as we drove along he was shocked to see a union flag flying upside down. Six years later, at the time of the general election of 1987, by which time he had died, I thought of him when I saw the union flag upside down outside the office in Horsham of UKIP, the United Kingdom Independence Party. The irony of it appealed to me and I could not resist the impulse to go in and explain to them what was wrong. After dropping Hughie off back at his retirement home I went back to see my mother again and when I left wondered if there might be any other solution than the present one to the problem of where and how she could live when she was so unhappy and so demanding of attention and sympathy.

By the evening I was back in Shalford and as we were going to bed Oriel found a small lump in her left breast. She wondered if the fact that June was so near to death meant that she was over-sensitive to such things. I thought not and decided that when June's doctor, Ian Hatrick, came to see her the next day, I would get him to see Oriel as well. He did and said that, although there was no need to do anything immediately, it would be sensible to see our own doctor as soon as we got back to Southport. Meanwhile June was so unwell that it seemed necessary to arrange for her to go into a hospice and we went to visit the nearby Phyllis Tuckwell Hospice and arrange for them to take her in a week later.

The following morning, July 29th, the day of the wedding of Prince Charles and Lady Diana Spencer, June seemed well enough to get up and watch it on television. June, Oriel, Linda and I all watched it, and it was an immensely impressive occasion, but the contrast between that and the immediate reality around us was striking. I could feel little enthusiasm for it and at one stage commented that, although Diana might be very beautiful, she had, I understood, only got two O levels, and I wondered if she might turn out to be a rather boring companion for Prince Charles. The others under-standably thought that said more about me as a schoolmaster than about what qualified someone to be a suitable bride for the heir to the throne.

June's condition was getting worse and in the afternoon Linda rang the hospice and got them to agree that she could be taken in the next morning. Oriel and I drove back to Southport, collecting Kate and Piers on the way, and arrived home late. The first thing I did the next morning was fix an appointment for Oriel to see our doctor at 10.40 the following day. As it happens we had a long-standing arrangement for Yngve Lidell to come and see us and stay overnight. It was something he did pretty regularly once a year and it was always a pleasure to see him again. This year he was a particularly welcome distraction from our immediate troubles.

We saw Yngve off on his travels after breakfast at about 10.00 a.m. on Friday 31st July and just after he had gone the telephone went and it was Mrs Dundee, Nora's home help, ringing to say that Nora appeared to have had a stroke. Nora had not wanted Mrs Dundee to ring Oriel and had also told her not to ring the doctor. Oriel replied that that, whatever her mother said, Mrs Dundee should certainly ring the doctor and that she would come back down to Shalford later that day. We would ring after we had been to the doctor and would let her know when Oriel would be arriving.

We then went to see the doctor and I explained both the history of breast cancer in Oriel's family and also the immediate circum-stances. He rang up and arranged for Oriel to see a specialist immediately. We went to the hospital, where the specialist arranged for her to have a mammogram at another hospital the next Thursday, followed by an appointment with him the morning after. As soon as we got home I rang Mrs Dundee, who told me that Nora had now had another stroke, was unconscious, had been taken to hospital and was not expected to survive. We threw a few things into a suitcase and picked up something for Oriel to eat on the train, and then I drove her to Liverpool and saw her off on the 1.05 train from Lime Street Station.

When I got back I told the children about everything. They already knew enough for me to feel that it would be more worry-ing for them to be kept in the dark. However ill June was, and

Nora, and my own mother as well, the thing which concerned me most, of course, was the question of what was going to happen to Oriel. I tried to play it down to the children. After all, it might just be mastitis. It could be a benign growth, and even if it did turn out to be malignant, it might be possible to get rid of it in an entirely satisfactory fashion.

We had had reason to worry before and it had turned out alright. That could be so again this time. But until I knew something more I was going to go on imagining and fearing the worst, and at the same time I was imagining what Oriel was imagining and fearing, and all the while I was conscious that she was hundreds of miles away. I wanted to be with her, partly because she needed looking after at a time like this and partly just because I wanted to be with her and wanted her to be with me.

Once I had taken her to catch the train in Liverpool and then had spoken to the children, I needed to go into KGV. I hadn't been into work since the end of term a week earlier and there were things I had set in motion which were catching up on me. For example, it was essential to get letters off to the candidates for an Economics post inviting them for interview on Tuesday, and I needed to do the short-listing for one of the two Senior Tutor posts, now vacant because the current occupant, Veronica Morrell, was seriously ill and could not return to work. We needed a new Senior Tutor in place before the busy period in the later part of August when we would be dealing with the applications for admission in September.

The next day was our twenty-second wedding anniversary. Oriel spent part of the day with her mother in hospital and part of it at the hospice with June. Her mother was better than we had feared. She had recovered some use in her right arm and the doctors talked about the possibility of a complete recovery. June was a lot worse. On the Sunday Oriel was with her all day, and by two o'clock in the afternoon she was in such a bad way that the matron suggested to Linda that she should try to get Vicky back

403

before her mother died. So Linda drove down to Dorset, picked up Vicky and got back at 9.00 in the evening. They were able to talk with their mother before she went to sleep, and then they went outside to get some rest while Oriel sat with June. She was sitting with her in the early hours of Monday 3rd August when she died.

53. Cancer and remission

One of the things Linda was able to talk about with Vicky on the way back from Dorset was the question of where Vicky was going to live when their mother died. For all that Vicky had not said much, she had a fairly clear idea of what was happening and had already accepted what she guessed Oriel and I had in mind: that she should come and live with us. I had warned the Director of Studies at the end of term that we were likely to have another candidate to do English Literature, Latin and History, the first two of which were the same as Piers's subjects, and I rather hoped that Vicky and Piers could be in the same tutor group. They were. They were put in the tutor group of Dorothy Hughes, previously Head of Classics at the Southport High School for Girls and now Head of Classics at King George V College.

On the Tuesday I was in KGV appointing an Economist, short-listing for the second Senior Tutor post and dealing with accumulated correspondence. On the Wednesday Oriel returned to Southport, and on the Thursday morning we went to the Promenade Hospital for her to have a mammogram. Then on Friday morning we had an appointment with the consultant. He was an elderly man with a charming manner and a distinguished appearance who explained that he was retired but was standing in for his successor, who was on holiday. He examined Oriel and spoke about the mammogram, which he said showed nothing to be worried about.

He explained that he had had years of experience of examining women for signs of breast cancer, and if he cut open every young woman with a small growth such as Oriel had, half the women in Southport would have had surgery on their breasts. He was confident that she was going to be alright, but if she wanted extra reassurance, he would make an appointment for her to be seen near the end of the following week by his successor, Mr Thompson, who would be back by then. We were delighted. When we got home I put on the record of the tone poem *Also Sprach Zarathusra* by Richard Strauss and turned up the sound. Then we went out. Oriel needed a shirt to wear at June's funeral, so we bought one. We went to bed early.

The next day, Saturday, I was in KGV all day catching up on work so as to be able to go away for three days. On Sunday we drove down to Guildford with James and Piers, and in the middle of the day on Monday we all went to June's funeral. When everyone except the family had gone I had a talk with John about our mother's future. We were agreed that we had to look for some alternative, but we also knew that nothing was likely to solve the problem that she was desperately unhappy and was likely to go on being unhappy wherever she was and however well she was looked after.

Once John had gone I spent most of the rest of the day talking with Vicky, with whom, over the previous six years, I had exchanged remarkably few words. I knew Linda well and had always found her easy to get on with. Vicky meanwhile had kept herself to herself and I felt that I hardly knew her at all. But that evening we talked about the Vikings, the settlement of the Northmen in Gaul in the area which came to be known as Normandy, about their settlement in the area of Britain which came to be referred to as the Danelaw, and about the subsequent Norman Conquest of England. Vicky talked to me and I talked to her more than ever before, and ever afterwards we carried on easily from there.

On the Tuesday morning I went shopping with Oriel in Bramley, and in the afternoon we lay in the sun in the garden having a rest. It felt like a holiday. We were up at six o'clock the next morning to drive back to Southport, and I had to go into KGV in the afternoon to make sure I had everything ready for a meeting of the college's Governing Body the following afternoon. As it happens that clashed with Oriel's meeting with Mr Thompson, whose approach to the problem of the growth on her left breast was entirely different from that of his predecessor. He told her that the only way you could be sure that it was benign was to cut it out, look at it in the lab, and then either sew her up again or aim to remove as much tissue as possible to give her maximum security for the future.

The next day the A level results arrived at the college, and I needed to be there all the day. I stayed at home at the week-end and on Monday morning took Oriel into the Southport Infirmary in the Scarisbrick New Road on my way into college, which was a couple of hundred yards up the road. On the Tuesday morning she went into the operating theatre. I had been told that I could ring at eleven to see how things had gone. When I did, she was not yet back from the theatre. That, of course, was bad news. I rang again at noon. She was still not back. Clearly something had happened other than a small cut to check on a harmless growth. She was still unconscious when I called in on my way home, but when I went in with James and Piers that evening she was conscious and able to talk to us.

I was told that I could see Mr Thompson at 4.30 p.m. on Thursday. He appeared to be an efficient and straightforward man. He told me that the growth on Oriel's breast was aggressive and that the prognosis was not good. If he had got to it before it had reached the lymph glands there would have been a better chance of long-term survival. As it was it had reached the lymph glands and it was a matter of time before the cancer recurred. What is more, he explained, the X-rays they had taken had shown a shadow over Oriel's backbone. It might be the natural movement of the body, but it could also be cancer in that region, and in that case, he said, death could be a matter of days rather than weeks. I was shaken. All I could do was go home.

The next day it turned out that the shadow over her backbone had gone away, so there was no immediate threat to her life, but the long-term threat was still there. As it happens that day, Friday 21st August, was also the day that all the O level results arrived for the candidates seeking admission to the college. Apart from when visiting Oriel in hospital I was in college, where, from then on, there was perpetual activity in preparation for the beginning of term on Tuesday 1st September. Somehow I found time to visit a possible home for my mother near Leamington Spa. It was 145 miles from Southport, a distance such that I could sometimes drive down and get back in a day. I discussed it with John, but both of us felt dubious about it. There was no obvious good solution. Then on 12th September she died. Within a month and a half June and my mother had both died, Nora had had a stroke, and Oriel had been diagnosed with breast cancer and had a mastectomy.

Once Oriel had recovered from the operation to remove her left breast, she had to undergo a course of radiotherapy. The consultant radiologist, like the surgeon, indicated that the prognosis was not good. When I asked what that meant, he replied, 'Well, I'd be surprised – I'd be pleased if she's still alive in five years' time.' Oriel and I decided to make the most of the next five years.

People sometimes speak of fighting cancer. It is a misleading concept. Surgeons and doctors and nurses do the fighting. The patient lives his (or, in this case, her) life well or badly and, either way, with a threat always present. Oriel faced that threat with gallant and high-hearted courage, and both she and I enjoyed the next year. The threat of death ensured that we valued every day of life. She had to go for a check-up once a month and inevitably we felt apprehensive each time the next check-up approached. Then, when it was over and she was clear, we felt euphoric.

The children were growing up. Kate was twenty, James just eighteen, Piers and Vicky both sixteen. So we felt that we could go off on holiday together, just the two of us, for the first time since the children were born, and we decided to go to Paris. Oriel had spent the first eight years of her life in the Indian Empire, unable to come to England until towards the end of the war, once the U-boats had been defeated. She had never had a passport and the record of her birth had been lodged with the India Office, which no longer existed. Getting a passport nearly forty years later was difficult, but the Foreign and Commonwealth Office eventually found a record of the birth of twin (unnamed) girls to Mr and Mrs Gawan Taylor in Karachi in July of 1935. It was enough, and she got a passport.

We went to Paris in the Easter holidays of 1982, just as the Falklands War was beginning, and found it strange to be abroad reading in the French newspapers about the Task Force sailing for the South Atlantic. We stayed in a hotel about a hundred yards from the Louvre and visited the Louvre and Montmartre and the Champs Elysées and Versailles and Fontainebleau and the Louvre again and decided that next year we would go to Rome and then the year after that to Athens.

Meanwhile Oriel was preparing for a new sort of life. She had spent most of the last twenty years looking after children. Now Kate was living in Southport in a bed-sitter, sometimes coming home to use the washing machine and stay for an evening meal, and working at Greaves Hall. James would soon be off to university to read History. Piers would follow him to university before long, probably to read Classics, and Vicky would be going up at the same time, hoping to read Anglo-Saxon, Old Norse and Celtic. So Oriel was preparing for a life in which our children and Vicky would be visitors rather than permanent members of the household.

One thing she had always done well was make up stories to tell them. I read them books by C.S. Lewis, A.A. Milne and J.R.R.Tolkein. She made up her own stories. When the children were very young the stories were often about a little boy who was always getting into trouble. Later, as they got older, Oriel would tell them a longer story in instalments about three children, Helen, Edward and John (the middle names of our own children), who had exciting adventures from which they always emerged triumphant. Now she got the stories down in typescript and found an agent who was impressed by what she read and was keen to get them published.

Oriel had also been invited to become a magistrate and was sworn in as a Justice of the Peace shortly before we went on holiday to Paris. For some years she had been used to going to occasions at which someone would introduce her as 'Mr Arnold's wife.' Now we both enjoyed the experience of my accompanying her when she went to the swearing-in ceremony and of having me introduced to the presiding judge as 'Mrs Arnold's husband.'

Oriel at the time she became a magistrate in the spring of 1982, about six months before she died. The photograph was taken by the Southport Visiter (sic). Its name really was spelt like that – ever since a misprint on the first edition back in 1844.

At the beginning of the summer holidays of 1982 the house was full of visitors, with meals for up to a dozen at a time and extra beds squeezed in. The Macdonald children had come to stay with us. So had Linda, as well as Jean and Michael Hopwood, friends of Oriel's from when she was a teen-ager in Shalford. Besides that there was a French boy, Alain, who was on an exchange, visiting us before taking Piers back to France with him. Eventually they all left. The Macdonalds and the Hopwoods went home. James went off in one direction, Linda and Vicky in another, and only Piers and Alain were left. We drove them to Lime Street Station in Liverpool and saw them off en route to France.

Now there were just the two of us, and for a few minutes we looked forward to some time to ourselves in the early weeks of the summer holidays. We had thoroughly enjoyed the week or so after the end of term with numerous visitors, and once we had seen Piers and Alain off, we thought we would do a bit of shopping in the centre of Liverpool and stop for tea somewhere before driving home. But after a few minutes Oriel coughed, said she felt surprisingly tired, and asked if I would mind going straight home. Of course not! Home we went. That evening she rested, ate very little and as soon as possible went to bed.

54. The Last Chapter

By the morning Oriel was in considerable discomfort. She could not lie down any longer. Standing up was painful. Walking was difficult. Before long she could not sit or crawl or lie down without distress. The doctor came promptly, said it would be a good idea to get her into hospital, where they could do some tests, and anyway there was no reason why she should suffer pain and discomfort. He was confident that they could deal with that. An ambulance came and took her to the Southport General Infirmary.

He was absolutely right. They could and did get rid of the pain. What they could not do was save her life. The tests made it clear that she was suffering from what is called 'disseminated carcinoma.' That is, the cancer had spread all over her body and quite suddenly had taken over. For the next few weeks the doctors and nurses looked after her and kept her free from pain, drugging her heavily with morphine. They found her a separate room and I was able to visit her for hours on end. It was extraordinary. For the first two or three weeks she looked perfectly well. She could have been a young woman in hospital to have a baby. Reason and senses contradicted each other. She looked fine. She could talk rationally. But she knew and I knew that the cancer was killing her and that she would never leave the hospital alive.

The children came to visit her. So did her friends. At first she was interested in what everyone was doing and what the children's plans were for the future. She was sorry to be leaving me a widower and found it difficult to imagine me as an unmarried man. She went through all our friends and acquaintances and decided that the only one who would suit me as a wife was Helen Bell – though she recognised that that had the problem that Helen was already married to George. As it turned out, though I could

412

not see it at the time or for many months to come, she was right on both counts.

Gradually, as the end drew near, her interest in the world outside her room faded. I spent hours simply sitting with her and holding her hand. Two or three people suggested to me that I must find it very difficult to spend so long just sitting with her. Not so. It was all I wanted to do. I had a talk with a sympathetic and sensible young doctor about the appropriate way to care for her as the end drew near. We agreed that it was more important to save her from pain than stretch out her life for a few more days. He warned me that one consequence of increasing the dose of morphine could be that it would produce a significant personality change and I might be distressed if she started saying things unlike anything I would expect.

In the event that never happened, but on the afternoon of 12th September, the anniversary of my mother's death, she held my hand and said, 'It's wonderful. It's marvellous. It's almost ducal in its splendour. Tell Helen to get them to let me go now, out of the darkness and into the light.' Then she went to sleep. I went into college for a short while, just up the road, and signed a few letters. Then, after going home for something to eat, I returned to the hospital to sit with her. After a while it seemed that her breathing had stopped. I suddenly felt as if she was no longer there and instinctively said, 'Come back!' I told a nurse. She told a doctor, and that was it. Oriel had died. She was just forty-seven years old.

They asked me if I would like some sleeping tablets to get me through the coming night. I thanked them but declined. It had always seemed to me that drugs could be very useful for dealing with physical conditions, but I objected to the idea of giving them to the young to soften emotional distress, on the grounds that it inhibited growing up. Give a little boy a happy drug because his hamster had died and a few years later you might give him a similar drug because he had failed an examination and then because his mother had died, and he was liable to reach adulthood

413

with the emotional maturity of a small child. Be that as it may, I went home and told the children what they had been both fearing and expecting for some weeks, and then went to bed.

Shortly before dawn I slept for an hour or two. The only time in my life when I had gone through a whole night without any sleep was a year earlier after I was told that Oriel's death might be a matter of days away. Now I had had a year to get used to the idea that death was coming. Gratitude for the past we had had together was inextricably intermingled with the grief of losing her. Grief at loss is the price you pay for love. The more you have to be grateful for, the more you grieve.

I was asked if her death had shaken my Christian faith. Not at all. I knew perfectly well that we all have to die, and some die young while others live to an old age. Had I felt let down that my prayers for her recovery had not been answered? Not at all. Prayer does not inhibit the aggressiveness of cancer cells any more than it deflects bullets. We need to pray for the strength to cope with things, not that God will alter the Laws of Nature at our request. As it happens I had prayed for her recovery. 'Please God, just this one thing. I won't ask for anything else.' But I could not persuade myself that that was sensible. It was just an expression of my feelings.

It is difficult now, thirty-five years later, to explain that I felt at forty-eight that my life was finished. I did not for a moment consider doing anything to end my life. But Oriel had been at the centre of my emotional world for thirty years and now she was gone the main reason for living seemed to be over. It felt strange that life just continued. The main reason for carrying on was simply that there was no sensible alternative, and I also felt that, one way or another, the children would probably need me all the more now that their mother, or in Vicky's case her aunt, was no longer there. Friends provided practical help and emotional support. In particular Helen Bell made sure that we were well fed in the days after Oriel's death.

Meanwhile there was a sense in which it seemed to me as if my work had come to a natural end. The job of reorganisation of KGV was complete. The last eleven-plus intake of 1977 at both KGV and at the Southport High School for Girls had just taken O level in the summer of 1982 and most of them had entered the college a week and a half before Oriel died. Colleagues were sympathetic and helpful, as were friends outside the college. Small things mattered. Chris Collier, the Head of History, knocked on my door, put his head round it and simply said, 'David, I'm very sorry' and went away again.

One problem I became aware of was that, while many people were clearly aware that I was suffering, they were less aware of the pain felt by the children, each of whom was devastated – though in different ways. Kate carried on with her work at Greaves Hall and told no-one what had happened. The funeral happened to be on her day off, so once she was back at work she still just carried on. After about a fortnight, when she had just been on night duty, another girl arrived to relieve her, saying cheerfully, 'Hello Kate! Anyone died?' Kate collapsed. The sister found out what had happened and rang me at KGV to get me to come and collect her.

James found it impossible to say anything and lay for hours in silent misery on his bed. I sat and stroked his head but there was nothing I could say or do to console him, and it was twenty years before he ever spoke of his mother. Piers was able to weep and say how much he missed her. Vicky was stoical. She had lost her father when she was a small child and her mother a year ago. Now she had also lost the aunt with whom she was living. She immediately started to help with the shopping and the cooking and the cleaning, and continued to do so.

In some ways life just carried on as before. Term had begun a week and a half before Oriel's death and everything was going well enough in the college for the staff to get on perfectly well without me. But as it happens an appointment for someone to see me had been made some time before for what turned out to be the morning after Oriel died. A parent had needed to see me with his daughter about a problem with her course. So we met, the meeting went off perfectly well, and we found a good solution to the problem. Father and daughter left well satisfied. Later, when the father heard of the circumstances, he wrote to send his sympathy and thank me. But of course there was really nothing else I could do. One simply had to get on with normal life as if the world had not gone mad.

Late at night and early in the mornings were the worst times. I had to discipline myself to go to bed at a regular time, and within a few days I had established a regular morning routine. The alarm went just before 7.00 a.m. I was always out of bed by the time the sixth pip sounded on the wireless. Then I put on running kit and ran down Weld Road to the Birkdale beach and back again, a round trip of a mile and a half. After a shower, I got dressed and was ready to start the day. In the middle of the winter of 1982 – 83 it was hard work running down to the beach in the dark, into the salt and the sand carried by the wind from the sea. But coming back was easy; I was blown home.

In the middle of February 1983, five months after Oriel had died, I woke up one morning with the thought that my feet were cold. My second thought was that that was the first time since her death that my first thought had not been that she was not there. Perhaps it was a first sign of recovery, and I was thankful that I was so busy both at work and at home.

If Oriel had lived we might well have stayed in Southport until I retired, and even after that. But now I felt I had to make a new start. I looked in *The Times Educational Supplement* and at once saw three headships advertised – one at Cranleigh, an independent school, one at King Edward VI, Colchester, a surviving grammar school, and one at the College of Richard Collyer in Horsham, a former boys' grammar school and now a mixed sixth form college. I was quite well qualified to apply to any of them. I was still only forty-eight and had six years' experience as a headmaster behind me, though with what seemed to me the serious disadvantage that I was now a widower. I thought about it, decided that I really would not want to go to Cranleigh without a wife, and that, much as I liked the idea of a good grammar school, I had over the last six years become committed to the idea of the sixth form college as the only practicable solution to the problem of how to produce a good future for secondary education in the maintained sector. So I applied to Collyer's.

I was interviewed and appointed and now had to face getting ready to leave Southport. It was difficult. I had become attached to KGV and to my colleagues there, I very much liked Southport and Birkdale village and the vast expanse of Birkdale beach. During the summer, particularly after term had ended, I got more and more attached to Helen Bell and spent a lot of time with her. What had begun with sympathy on her part and gratitude on mine developed into a close mutual attachment, so that I was all the more sorry to be leaving Southport. But that was, I suppose, a good reason for moving rather than staying.

Vicky and Piers had both done well enough at A level to stay on for the seventh term to take the Oxbridge examinations. But while James and Piers both moved with me to Horsham, James *en route* to St David's University College, Lampeter, and Piers to

Helen Bell in my garden in Birkdale in the summer of 1983.

spend a term at Collyer's working for the Oxford entrance examination, Vicky stayed on at KGV and lived with Helen and George Bell as she worked for the Cambridge entrance examination. Kate was now working as a carer in a nursing home for elderly ladies and living in her house in Wright Street in the middle of Southport.

I had arrived at KGV in September 1976, and during the seven years I was there it was reorganised, re-staffed, rebuilt, re-furnished and re-equipped. Officially the change from boys' grammar school to mixed sixth form college happened in September 1979, when we had the first intake of girls from the Southport High School for Girls, and I wrote an article for the local newspaper in which I said that we had had to change the notice over the old gym door from *mens sana in corpore sano* (which I had assumed everyone knew meant *'a healthy mind in a healthy body'*) to *men's and women's sana in corpore sano*. My impression later was that I had amused no-one other than myself. Four years later, when I left, the process of reorganisation was complete, and the following September the college took its first intake of students from the town's 11-16 comprehensive schools.

Oriel and I had gone to Southport in the extraordinarily hot summer of 1976, when the Open was played at Royal Birkdale Golf Club. I left without her in the next extraordinarily hot summer of 1983, when the Open was again played at the Royal Birkdale Golf Club.

Collyer's (1983–1992)

55. Moving South.

Early in the Easter holiday of 1983, while still at KGV, I drove south to look for a house in Horsham. John was now the Dean of Rochester, about sixty miles north-east of Horsham, so I went to stay in the Deanery with him and Anneliese. One of the governors of Collyer's, a retired estate agent, had offered to help me find a house, and I was glad to have his help, but first I had to decide roughly where I wanted to live.

Easter is, of course, a particularly busy time for the clergy, but on the Saturday of Holy Week, immediately before the celebration of Easter Day, almost nothing happens in most churches and cathedrals throughout the country. So on that Saturday John kindly drove over to Horsham with me on reconnaissance. We looked round the town and I decided I would like to live somewhere to the north of Collyer's but within easy walking distance of the college. I rang and told the governor who had offered to help and he promised to get a number of houses lined up for viewing.

He was as good as his word. After Easter in Rochester I drove to Horsham by the late morning of Tuesday and was able to look over one house before he and his wife gave me lunch. We then visited five more in the afternoon and I chose the one I wanted. It was at the end of a small road called April Close, just across the main Warnham Road from what looked like a village green, with the Dog and Bacon pub the other side of it. The pub had originally been called 'The Dorking Beacon', and its sign had shown a dog dancing round the beacon, but in Sussex dialect it had become 'The Dog and Bacon' and the sign now showed a dog making off with a side of bacon.

I agreed to pay the asking price for the house in April Close. I think it was just over £60,000, and since I was selling the house in

Weld Road for not much more than £40,000, I needed to take out another mortgage. It was only five minutes' walk from Collyer's and another ten minutes or so across Horsham Park was what was thought of as the centre of the town - the Carfax, where North Street, South Street, West Street, Middle Street and East Street all met. Immediately north of the Carfax was Horsham Park, and immediately north of that was Collyer's.

Once I had decided on the house I wanted, I drove north-west for half an hour to Shalford, just the Horsham side of Guildford, and stayed with Michael and Jean Hopwood before setting off the next day back to Southport and my last term at KGV. I was increasingly conscious of what a change was facing me. I had lost Oriel. I was changing my job. I was now changing my house. I was leaving friends and colleagues to whom I was attached. Peggy Roberts, David Roberts's widow, with whom I had kept in touch since he had died in 1956, wrote to me when she heard that I was going to Horsham to say that her brother-in-law, Mervyn, David's younger brother, and his wife, Eileen, were living there, and I ought to meet them some time. But apart from that I knew no-one.

Collyer's, where I was taking over as Principal, had been founded under the terms of the will of a London Mercer who died in 1532, twenty years before the foundation of Christ's Hospital. He wanted the children at his school to be 'at no charge of their school hire', in return for which they were to say the De profundis, or Psalm 130, for his soul at the end of each day. Then for three and a half centuries it was a small grammar school in a Sussex market town with no more staff than the Master and his assistant, the Usher.

As a consequence of the growth of Horsham in the second half of the nineteenth century, largely as a result of the expansion of the railway system linking it to London, the school was rebuilt in 1893, and the 1920s saw it 'reorganised on modern public school lines', with the introduction of a house system, prefects, a school magazine, an Old Boys' Association, a school library, a chapel, Prize Giving and the annual celebration of Founder's Day. That was followed by thirty years from 1926 until 1956 of outstanding success during the headship of Philip Tharp, better known as P.A.T., a Cambridge classicist who came from teaching at Wellington College and whose period as headmaster was remembered half a century later as a Golden Age.

The Second World War was right in the middle of P.A.T.'s headship, and during it seventy-two Old Collyerians were killed – more than in the First World War because both Horsham and Collyer's had continued to grow in the years between the wars. A year after the end of the war in Europe, in the summer of 1946, Field Marshal Montgomery visited Collyer's to give away the prizes. P.A.T. had been able to get him to come because they had been in the same class at school at St Paul's.

Collyer's continued as what was known as a 'voluntary aided' grammar school. Its foundation, dominated by the Mercers' Company, was responsible for the buildings and the grounds, while the day to day running costs were paid by the West Sussex Local Education Authority. Then in 1975 a Labour government legislated to try to make the surviving grammar schools in England become comprehensives. Most became independent schools, but the West Sussex Director of Education, Roy Potter, came up with a clever scheme to persuade the governors of Collyer's to let it become a sixth form college.

He arranged for the West Sussex County Council to buy some of the school's land for £218,000 and then give the land back to the school. Thus the Collyer Foundation had £218,000 with which to pay 15% of the cost of new buildings, while the government, under the 'voluntary aided' arrangements, would pay the other 85%, and West Sussex acquired a sixth form college for a trivial sum. The change from boys' grammar school to mixed sixth form college officially took place at the beginning of September 1976, and its name was now 'The College of Richard Collyer in Horsham.' Locally it was still known simply as 'Collyer's.'

The headmaster, Derek Slynn, who had presided with distinction over the grammar school for seven years from 1969 until 1976, was now principal of the college for another seven years. In the summer of 1980 the last grammar school boys and girls took O level and entered the college, and that same year a grand new classroom block was completed. But shortly after that Derek began to suffer from ill-health and in 1983, at the age of sixty-three, he retired, fortunately able to live on in retirement for another quarter of a century. I arrived in September 1983 to take over from him.

During that summer Nora had died. By then she was eighty. Teddy had died ten years earlier and all three of her daughters had predeceased her, so she was living alone and despondent in Brook Cottage, which had once been bursting with life and hope for the future. My impression was that visits from her grandchildren, though welcome, only intensified the sense of loss.

One consequence of her death was that each of my three children acquired a legacy of about £11,000. I suggested that each of them should put a thousand pounds into a current account to use as and when they liked, put £5,000 each into property, and invest or save the other £5,000 as they chose. Kate was intending to stay in Southport, so I went house-hunting with her until she eventually chose an attractive, three bedroom, terraced house in Wright Street, in the middle of the town, on the market for £21,000. I encouraged her to put down a £5,000 deposit and take out a mortgage for £5,000 in order to get into the habit of paying a regular monthly amount.

Meanwhile each of the boys agreed to contribute £5,000 and treat it as an investment. They owned a quarter of the house each. Kate owned a half. I paid the extra £1,000, the various fees, and the cost of carpeting and furnishing it. Kate appeared to be well set up and could, if she chose, rent out a couple of rooms, decide for herself how much or little of the week she wanted to work, and seek to develop her undoubted gift for painting and drawing.

Linda, meanwhile, was living in Putney and training as an account-ant, and she had kindly taken on the task of selling Nora's house in Shalford. By the time I arrived in Horsham late in August all that remained for us to do was to go through the various contents, dividing them up between Linda and Vicky, Kate, James and Piers. In my new house I so far had no more than a camp bed, a deck chair, a garden table and whatever else had fitted in my car. The boys were due to arrive the next day, together with the removal men and our furniture.

I spent the afternoon and evening in Nora's house going through the contents with Linda and dividing them up. We decided to do it in age order, so we chose in the order Linda, Kate, James, Vicky, Piers. Linda chose for herself and Vicky. I chose for my three. We got through it quickly and amicably, I packed my car full with things which could be easily transported, we had a meal, cleaned and cleared, and late at night I set off back to Horsham with my car packed with small pieces of furniture and other objects.

As I drove into Horsham along the Guildford Road some time after midnight I noticed a police car behind me. I checked my speed, which was just under 30 m.p.h., and continued along the Bishopric, turned left into Albion Way and left again into Springfield Road. The police car stayed behind me. I drove up North Parade, turned right into Pondtail Road and right again into Ashleigh Road. At each turning the police car stayed with me. Finally I turned into April Close and drove to the end, where my house was.

The police car followed and pulled across the road. I got out and found two policemen wanting an explanation of what I was doing late at night, with the back of my car apparently full of loot. I told them, put my hand in my pocket and took out the keys to the house and invited them to come in and have a look. 'Ah!', said one of them, 'It's always a good sign, sir, when someone's got the keys to the house.' We parted with me thanking them and saying that I was glad to know that the police in the town I was moving to were so vigilant.

James, of course, came with me to Horsham in August of 1983, but after only a few weeks he was off to spend most of the next three years, from 1983 until 1986, at St David's, Lampeter, where week by week he wrote history essays and ran in the university cross-country team, which he ended up organising, writing out all his notices in both Welsh and English.

Piers came to Collyer's for just one term and was vigorously engaged in reading and translating Latin authors and writing proses as he prepared for the Oxford examinations. Then at the end of the Autumn Term James came back from Lampeter, Vicky arrived from Southport, and Linda joined us as well. We got the good news that Vicky had got a place at Newnham College, Cambridge, to read Anglo-Saxon, Old Norse and Celtic and that Piers had got a place at Pembroke College, Oxford, to read Mods and Greats, or Classics.

Godfrey Bond, the Mods tutor, who had taught me Latin for Historians nearly thirty years earlier, wrote to say that Piers's work in Latin in the entrance examination was the best of all the candidates applying to Pembroke that year and was of the standard that had been required in the past for a scholarship. But of course Piers was going to have to learn Greek if he was to make a success of reading Mods and Greats.

We had a celebratory Christmas dinner on Christmas Eve and then on Christmas Day all went over to Rochester to spend it with John and Anneliese, Frances, Matthew and Miriam. After that, one after the other, everyone went off in different directions. Linda went back to her flat in Putney and Vicky went to stay with her. James returned to Lampeter. Piers decided that he would spend the months before going up to Oxford travelling round Europe, covering as much ground as possible with a one month student rail card and then hitch-hiking through Italy and Greece. He took with him the old Parachute Regiment ruc-sac which I had bought in an army surplus store as a teenager to go camping with when I was a Boy Scout, and he weighed it down with books which he lugged all round Europe and as far as Crete.

He sent regular postcards with perceptive and often caustic comments about what he had seen. Shortly after crossing from Italy to Greece, and living largely on a diet of bananas, he was quite seriously ill and was picked up by some Greek soldiers, who took him to a Greek army hospital where he was looked after until he was fit and healthy again and they were able to discharge him - without requiring any payment. He was very fortunate.

He then crossed to Crete, where he walked down the Samarian Gorge to the sea - ten miles with a drop of 1,250 metres. From there it is usual to take a boat to the nearby village of Hora Sfakion, but he thought he would try walking round the coast. It was not a sensible decision. The south coast of Crete slopes steeply down to the sea and there is no way that one can walk it. So he found himself climbing the steep slopes until, many hours later, exhausted and with daylight gone, he eventually saw a light in the distance. When he got there he was welcomed and given food and drink and a bed for the night. What had made him so welcome, he realised, was his British Parachute Regiment ruc-sac. 'I hadn't even known what side they'd been on in the war, Dad' he said.

Once he had left for his travels around Europe I was, of course, on my own in the house in April Close. It was the first time since Oriel had died nearly a year and a half earlier in September of 1982, that I had lived entirely alone with no-one else to cook and clean for. I did not like it. Meanwhile I was finding my new job difficult.

56. First Impressions

Before my first term began at Collyer's I had looked at the college's A level results and been surprised that overall they were less good than I would have expected. In a couple of subjects, Chemistry and French, they were shockingly bad. A statement in *The West Sussex County Times* proclaimed with pride that the Collyer's A level pass rate was better than the national average, and so it was. The national average at that time was about 70%, with Collyer's just ahead of that. But a sixth form college, with the benefits which come from economies of scale and in the prosperous south-east of England, could reasonably be expected to perform significantly better than the national average. King George V College had an A level pass rate more than twenty percentage points above the national average.

It would need investigation, and unless the Chemistry and French results were an aberration, unlikely to be repeated, something would need doing about those departments as soon as possible. After all, if a college got a reputation for poor teaching and poor performance in those two subjects, and if potential students and their parents were aware of the problem, it could have a damaging effect on admissions not just in Chemistry and French but also in other subjects which normally went with them. Physics and Biology, for example, commonly went with Chemistry, and subjects such as English Literature and History would often be combined with French.

Nor was it just the A level results. A whole O level set of about twenty students had failed Economics. Something was wrong. On the day before the students arrived for the first day of the Autumn Term there was a full staff meeting. I introduced myself to the staff, said how glad I was to be joining them in a college with such a fine reputation, and said I'd be glad if each head of department would let me have a report by the end of the week on how their department had performed in that summer's examinations.

Then on the first day of term I went for a walk round with the senior of the two Vice-Principals, Roland Soper. He had been Colonel Soper at the end of the war and since then had written some very successful Biology text books. He had only one year to go before retiring in the summer of 1984, but during that year I found him an invaluable moral support in what turned out to be difficult circumstances.

On my first day as Principal he took me across the main quadrangle to the entrance to the main hall and turned left to an area where two classrooms had been knocked into one to form a student common room. Loud music was coming from a radio or record-player, and several youths, but no girls, were lounging about. I asked them if they would kindly turn the music off (they did) and told them that the common room was for the use of all students and not just for those who liked loud music. They should leave it off. That was met with surly and resentful looks.

Roland and I moved on and he guided me left again into another corridor. The first door on the right had an inset window painted black. I looked inside. The whole room was painted red and black. There were mattresses covered with rugs on the floor and joss sticks were burning on the window sills, filling the room with the scent of incense – but no students. It was, he explained without further comment, known as 'the red and black common room.' I decided to have the room locked until I decided what to do with it and asked Roland to arrange for the caretaker to come to see me.

I returned to my room in the old grammar school building, calling in on the boys' lavatories, where I was not pleased to see graffiti on the walls and found the smell of urine revolting. By now I was in a thoroughly critical mood and noticed that the skirting boards of the corridor leading to the school office and on to my room appeared to be coated with accumulated dirt. I avoided visiting the girls' lavatories until after the students had gone home at the end of the day. When I did I found that they were not much better than the boys', though they did not have the unpleasant smell.

Throughout that day members of staff were seeing new students and making provisional arrangements for which A level courses they should study and how their individual timetables should be made up. How far that process had progressed I was able to see at the end of the day. Meanwhile I looked at the post and found a number of letters from worried parents wanting to see me about how their son or daughter had performed in the A level examinations and about their prospects for university.

I asked my secretary, Enid Graves, to set up meetings with the parents who wanted to see me and to get from the tutors information about the students' expected performance, so that I would know what I was talking about when I met their parents. Enid was about a year older than me. She was clearly experienced in her job and efficient, she was smartly turned out, and she had an attractive personality which, combined with a certain natural presence, ensured that no-one would take any liberties with her. It was clear that she was going to be an asset.

The caretaker came to see me. I told him I was going to need his help, asked him to lock the red and black common room and said I would like his advice on how to turn it into a usable classroom. I said I wanted the graffiti in the lavatories cleaned off and the walls painted over. He protested that the students would only put more graffiti on the walls and asked what we would do then. I replied that the walls would need to be cleaned off again and, if necessary, re-painted again.

I then asked how the skirting boards came to be so caked with dirt. The explanation was that the cleaners had some cleaning material with which they mopped the floors. The dirt and the

430

cleaning material combined to stick against the skirting boards as they mopped from side to side and a thick layer gradually built up. I said I wanted the skirting boards cleaned. But that, he suggested, would show how badly they needed painting. Then we'll have them painted. But the cleaners, he protested, are cleaners – not painters and decorators. Then I shall have to find someone else to do the painting. By the time he left I realised that I had not managed to make an ally of the caretaker.

Once the new students had been deployed in their various teaching groups and the normal business of teaching had begun I took another walk round just after the beginning of the first period of the day and found a classroom full of students but with no teacher. I asked who they were waiting for and found him in the staff common room, where I pointed out as politely as possible that he had a class waiting for him. That was met with a cold response from others standing around. He went off to teach his class and I left as well, feeling distinctly unwelcome.

At KGV I had felt at home and had got used to students and members of staff, both teaching and support staff, being engaged in purposeful activity and many of them smiling and saying 'Good morning, headmaster!' as I walked down the corridors or into the staff or student common rooms. Here I felt like an unwelcome intruder. I could only remind myself that I had a very clear idea of what a successful sixth form college should be like, that Collyer's was in a good position to be an excellent college, and that it was my job to ensure that it became one.

I had left a newly-built college which the caretaker and his cleaners took pride in keeping meticulously clean. There were wooden lockers in the corridors, many with pots of flowers on them, and there were well-framed and attractive pictures on the walls. In the second half of the Summer Term the students were allowed to dress relatively casually. The boys were allowed to wear open neck shirts and were not required to wear a blazer or a sports jacket. The girls were allowed to wear summer frocks, and did.

No doubt that could not last, even in Southport. Society was changing and that level of expectation for student dress and appearance would come to be looked back on with amusement. But for the moment I could only regret the difference, recognising that the way students in Horsham (and some staff!) presented themselves was not an issue which could be tackled immediately when so much else needed doing, but also reminding myself that it was an issue which should not be neglected indefinitely.

I reflected that I had been very fortunate when I took over at King George V School back in 1976 as a new and inexperienced head. I would not have liked to try to cope at Collyer's if I had been as inexperienced as I was then. My predecessor at KGV, Geoffrey Dixon, was outstandingly efficient. His own subject was Physics and he had been running the school for twenty-seven years since he had arrived from Sandhurst in 1949, with teaching at Uppingham and war service before that. He expected and got high academic standards as well as high standards of behaviour and dress.

Geoffrey was seen as a cold, hard and taciturn man who kept control of the school firmly in his own hands. He was respected and even feared and was viewed with affection only with hindsight. His efficiency, his taciturnity and his centralised control of every aspect of school life all worked in my favour. His efficiency meant that the school continued to run with its customary effectiveness after he had had gone, leaving me with time to plan for its development into a sixth form college. His taciturnity meant that colleagues found me far more approachable, and on top of that they were generally pleased when they discovered that I was willing to delegate responsibility.

By contrast Derek Slynn was a charming, courteous and warm man, a connoisseur of wine, a member of the MCC who had played cricket for Oxford and for the Kent 2nd XI. He was also a gifted linguist with a wide range of languages at his disposal, including Russian and Chinese, and as a young man he had worked during the war at the British intelligence and code-breaking centre at Bletchley Park. His charm, courtesy and warmth, and his kindly and relaxed style, were missed by his colleagues, who were not inclined to welcome his successor with open arms, especially if he was critical of the examination results and the state of cleanliness of the lavatories.

Derek was, I am sure, sad to see the way Collyer's was going. During the period of transition after 1976, once Collyer's had been designated a sixth form college, he lived with the arrangements agreed between the Governing Body and the West Sussex education authority and tried to keep it as much as possible like the excellent grammar school it had been and aspired to make it the leading language centre in the south-east of England.

But he was unwell and he was trapped in arrangements for reorganisation which were seriously open to criticism. He still appointed prefects, he still provided the governors with lavish hospitality when they met at Collyer's, and he took pride in the annual inspection of the Combined Cadet Force, which was something which marked Collyer's out as different from most sixth form colleges and more like an independent school. Understandably he had some sympathy for those heads of department who regretted the passing of the former grammar school and felt that all they could do was put up with the new arrangements until they could retire. At least his own retirement came sooner rather than later, and they regretted his passing – all the more because what they had in his place was me.

Derek left me with three folders, one marked 'Immediate', the second 'Urgent', and the third 'Later.' It was kind and helpful of him, but with one issue after another needing to be dealt with in the first few days of term it was some time before I found a convenient opportunity to go through them. When I did I found that he had a good idea of what things needed doing immediately (but by then I had done them), and what else was urgent (but by then I had done them too) and, indeed, what were some of the issues which would need considering later.

433

It reminded me of a story I had heard of a newly appointed head-master who found that his predecessor had left him three envelopes – each to be opened only in the event of a crisis. After the first crisis he opened the first envelope. The note inside said, 'Blame your predecessor.' After the second crisis he opened the second envelope. The note inside said, 'Blame your Deputy.' After the third crisis he opened the third envelope. The note inside said, 'Prepare three envelopes.'

57. Perceptions

◇◇◇◇◇◇◇◇◇◇◇◇◇◇◇◇◇◇◇◇◇◇◇◇◇◇◇◇◇◇◇◇◇◇◇◇

In one form or another Collyer's had been providing education for the children of Horsham for four and a half centuries. One of the few pupils ever to have achieved some fame was Thomas Garnet, who had been executed, or martyred, in 1608 at the age of thirty-three. After his schooling at Collyer's he was one of the first pupils at the English Jesuit College founded at St Omer in France in 1593. He was active in the Catholic underground and after the Gunpowder Plot of 1605 was sent into exile. But he returned, was recognised, arrested and imprisoned, and in June 1608 he was executed as a traitor. In 1970 he was one of forty English martyrs canonised by Pope Paul VI and in the 1990s, when there were some sixteen Roman Catholic colleges in the post-sixteen education sector, I liked to point out to their principals that Collyer's was the only college in the sector to have a canonised Roman Catholic saint among its former pupils,

The only member of staff during those centuries who went on to a position of national, even international, importance was a certain John Pell, whom I first heard of when I had a letter from one of his descendants who was serving his time 'at Her Majesty's pleasure' at Ford Open Prison. He was investigating the career of his ancestor, John Pell, and wrote to say that he believed that Pell had at one time been the Usher at Collyer's. He wondered if I could tell him any more. So I set out to discover whatever I could.

As a young man of nineteen in the early seventeenth century John Pell had indeed for a few months been the Usher at Collyer's. By his early thirties he was Professor of Mathematics at Amsterdam, in his forties he was England's envoy to the Protestant Swiss cantons, and in his fifties he was one of the original Fellows of the Royal Society. I was particularly pleased to discover that he had invented the division sign. When writing a mathematical treatise in the seventeenth century it had been impossible to express mathematically one number divided by another other than by writing both numbers very small and cramming them into the same line, one on top of the other. Pell had the idea that it was possible to write the first number normal size, then write a dash with one dot above and one below, and follow that with the number by which the first one was to be divided. Thus came into existence the division sign, which has been used ever since.

Shortly after I had been appointed, some months earlier, Peter Longhurst, a former colleague at Stowe who had grown up on the south coast, wrote to me and described it as 'the best school in Sussex.' Later Roy Potter, the West Sussex Director of Education, described it as 'an outstanding example of the successful re-organisation of a grammar school as a sixth form college.' On the other hand the first person to whom I was introduced in Horsham as the new Principal of Collyer's said, 'Oh, you've got a job on your hands' and, on being asked why, went on, 'Well, it used to be a good grammar school, but if you go near the place now you'll see them all slobbing about in sweaty T-shirts and jeans - and that's just the staff.' It was an interesting alternative view.

I soon found that there were many people with some present or past connection with Collyer's who were anxious to tell me what was wrong. Two entirely different views emerged. The first went like this: 'Collyer's has failed to adjust to changing times. In all but name it has remained a grammar school. Its policy is to admit only the academic high-flyers and the staff have no use for any student who cannot do well at A level. The students are treated like children and permanently supervised to ensure full-time attendance, uniformity of dress and conformity of behaviour.'

The other view was this: 'Since becoming a sixth form college Collyer's has slid downhill rapidly. Academic standards have deteriorated, because the staff can only cope with former grammar school pupils. Children who did well in their 11-16 schools do badly at Collyer's. There is little control over attendance, students turn up late, miss lessons and are even away for whole days without anyone noticing. They drift in and out looking like punk rockers, tarts and louts. Smoking, drinking, litter and rudeness are all accepted as normal.'

These two descriptions were clearly incompatible and neither of them was fair, but it seemed to me something of a problem that two such contradictory but vivid pictures could be painted by different people at the same time. I tried to understand it. The local education authority, which was staffed by able and helpful officers, took an understandable pride in producing good results with low expenditure, and low expenditure was required by the Tory administration of West Sussex. But the price paid for this was that it was difficult to acknowledge that anything was less than admirable, and that in turn led to a tendency to sweep problems under the carpet.

The Governing Body met once a term for a brief meeting. It had retained a number of responsibilities, but it was not clear who was entitled to exercise them, and the consequence was that those with authority to act did not and anyone willing to act apparently lacked the authority to do so. The outcome was that trivia could be very time consuming and that matters which should have been dealt with swiftly were delayed for months and even years.

The internal organisation of the college was highly decentralised. Academic departments operated largely as autonomous units, and much the same was true of tutorial groups. The house system was in large measure a system for arranging organised games. There was no systematic decision-making system. Many individuals organised things well and many individual parts of the college worked well. But things which reached across the whole college tended to work badly. The system for evaluating student progress, for example, had slid into disrepute among both staff and students, and the timetable was no more than a rough guide to what might be happening.

The curriculum was limited and consisted principally of A level and O level courses. The A level results were poor, largely because too many students had been allowed to take courses which were too difficult for them, and in the more extreme cases quite simply because they had been badly or neglectfully taught. The O level results were even worse because this was the only alternative to A level, and too many O levels were taken by students who had failed everything at 16+ and went on to do the same at 17+.

In principle there was a wide range of General Studies courses, but in practice they were taken only by first year A level students and then only for two terms. It was the same with Recreational Activities. As with General Studies, students who had been in the college for a year were not required to take part. With both General Studies and Recreational Activities the silent message was conveyed that these aspects of the curriculum were unimportant.

The buildings looked impressive from outside and the grounds were well tended. Inside the accommodation was adequate but much space was wasted and there was a need to adapt the space to changed circumstances. Most of the old building was dirty and badly maintained and much of the new building was going the same way. There were more members of the teaching staff than could be justified by the number of students on roll. Some of the staff were probably already aware of that and conscious of the implication for the security of their jobs. What is more, the staffing was unbalanced in relation to the curriculum. Most notably there were three Classics masters but only two boys studying Latin, one of whom was my younger son, Piers, and he was only there for a term. There was also a woodwork master with no-one to teach.

At the same time there was no common view of how the college should be developing. Some of those left over from the grammar school took the view that a sixth form college was inevitably a third-rate institution with low standards and that all one could do was live with it until retirement. Some of those who had started their careers at Collyer's in the period of re-organisation took the view that the place was too much like a grammar school and that what was needed was to create an open and more 'democratic' society, with fewer restrictions and a friendly, co-operative atmosphere.

In a strange way those two groups colluded with each other. What was lacking was a significant number of senior members of staff with confidence that high standards could be maintained in a sixth form college and capable of giving effective guidance to their younger colleagues. On the other hand, many individual members of staff got on quietly and effectively with their own teaching, and once it was required of them, many were prepared to make a considerable effort to develop both the curriculum and the organisation of the college to improve the quality of education provided for the students.

Relations with the 11-16 schools in Horsham were poor. There was a legacy of ill-will remaining from re-organisation. The staff of the former girls' high school had not been considered for appointment to the sixth form college, apart from one who was made the second Vice-Principal. The two former secondary modern schools had had their sixth forms removed, and it was not at all clear that Collyer's could provide for their former pupils as well as they would have themselves. There was a wide-spread view at all three schools that Collyer's was unjustifiably exclusive and pleased with itself.

It seemed to me that the explanation of why Collyer's was perceived in two such different ways, on the one hand as excessively exclusive and elitist, and on the other as disgracefully ill disciplined and inadequate, was that there was a serious gap between the ideal and reality. The image projected from the top was of academic exclusiveness combined with an expectation of civilised behaviour from students who would all be dressed in a manner suitable for a formal place of work and most of whom would go on to university. The reality was varied academic standards achieved by generally pleasant students who were liable to withdraw their affection if required to do something they did not want to, most of whom were dressed casually and some scruffily, and many of whom did not go on to university. The reality was not especially bad, but it was a long way short of the proclaimed ideal.

'We don't want you taking in all those yobbos as they do at Haywards Heath', I was told by Christopher Buckle, the Chairman of the Governing Body, shortly after my arrival. Yet already the proportion of students with low academic qualifications on one year courses was higher at Collyer's than at Haywards Heath. Academic exclusiveness can be achieved by a small college in a large town. That had been the case in Southport. But Collyer's had been planned as a large college in a small town, without apparent awareness of the implications of that decision.

Anything which smacked of vocational training was eschewed. Typing was to be provided by an annexe in Horsham of Crawley Technical College. Practical Art courses would be provided by another annexe of yet another college, Worthing Art College, while Collyer's would teach Fine Art at A level. The curriculum at Collyer's was intended to be only A and O levels, and that aim of academic exclusiveness was objectionable to anyone who wanted to see the extension of the comprehensive principle to the 16-19 range.

More importantly, it was laughable to those who saw it as pretentiousness which bore little relationship to reality. The gap between academic pretensions, such as the number claimed on UCCA forms to be going on to university each year, and academic performance (the number really doing so) was worrying. The gap between the clothing regulations and the reality of what the students wore was ludicrous.

Collyer's was beginning to have the worst of both worlds. The ideals it proclaimed were too high to be taken seriously by the staff, let alone the students. The result was that the rules were ignored and the idea that they should be enforced was viewed with incredulity by many members of staff. Meanwhile, attitudes which were seen by some members of staff as progressive, liberal, caring and forward-looking, were perceived by those outside simply as an unimpressive inability to live up to the standards which the college proclaimed.

The central problem was how to close the gap between ideal and reality. There was no simple answer, and recognition of the problem raised more questions than it answered. In particular it raised the question of whether the ideal should be adjusted towards reality or the reality shifted towards the ideal. Sometimes one was necessary and sometimes the other. It was important to improve the reality, but it was also necessary to play down the glossy, superior, public image. Paradoxically, one way in which the college was going to improve its public image was by accepting a worse one.

There were some obvious dangers: of expecting general agreement among staff, officers of the authority and governors about desirable aims and objectives; of trying to do too much too quickly; of expecting too much too soon from individual members of staff; of neglecting to make use of latent but as yet untapped potential; of devoting so much attention to particularly difficult problems that one neglected too much else; of appearing excessively critical; and, worst of all in these particular circumstances, of giving the impression of being concerned only with surface appearances.

I made all these mistakes, and I was aware of the need for more patience than comes naturally to me. This was not a crisis to be tackled by dramatic solutions. It was a matter of turning a descending spiral into an ascending one, preferably with the co-operation of local education authority officers and members of the governing body and, most essentially, with the co-operation of both the teaching and support staff.

The curriculum needed to be extended to meet the needs of all the students. That in turn required the establishment of central control of the academic organisation, and academic standards needed to be improved. The staffing needed to be adjusted to meet the needs of the curriculum. If possible responsibilities needed to be spread out among members of staff, several of whom were in need of some broadening of their experience if they were to have a worthwhile career.

The college needed a decision-making process involving all the staff. It needed improved arrangements for the care and guidance of the students. It needed to develop a humane but effective disciplinary system. The buildings needed to be cleaner, better cared for and properly maintained, and both the buildings and the grounds needed some changes if they were to meet changing needs. If possible there would be some new building where those needs could not be satisfied by modifications to existing buildings.

I was not sure that I was the right person to manage all this. Above all I was aware that my natural inclination was towards delegation rather than centralised control, with each head of department, for example, responsible for his or her own department, and with minimum interference from the head. But I had a strong suspicion that I was going to need to exercise far more central control than either I or anyone at Collyer's was used to. It was not something I wanted to do, but I was going to have to face it.

58. Early Solutions

◇◇◇

As a general principle anyone taking charge of something should wait to see how it works before implementing significant changes. It does not do for a new head or principal to have a Platonic ideal of a school or college in mind and seek to create a replica of that ideal. One needs rather to adopt the Aristotelian approach of seeking to get to know it and understand it before trying to improve what already exists. Most particularly, if one has previous experience of headship, it is important not to impose the practices of one institution on another, as if one solution fits all problems.

Nevertheless, I closed the red and black common room on my first day, and by then I was already aware of the danger of some of our new students being placed on two year A level courses and on one year O level courses which were beyond them. Despite the Chairman of the Governors' comment about not taking in yobbos as they did at Haywards Heath, I had to face the fact that in practice we took any sixteen year olds from the Horsham area who wanted to come.

Some had failed nearly all their O levels at school, but their parents wanted them to go to a sixth form college in Horsham rather than to a technical college in Crawley. Such students needed courses on which they would stand a reasonable chance of success rather than ones on which they were doomed to failure. A student with an 'unclassified' result in O level Maths needed the new C.E.E. (Certificate of Extended Education) course or a basic Numeracy course rather than O level Economics. Once that was pointed out to them, most members of staff, most students and most parents could see the point. But it involved some fairly frantic work setting up the new courses in a matter of days, deciding who would teach them, and ensuring that each new student was provided with a sensible programme of study.

It was not only the new students who needed guidance about their future. Most of the second year students would be applying for admission to Higher Education courses, or else they would be looking for a job. The member of staff who had been responsible for everything to do with these matters was Brian Alner, who collapsed with nervous exhaustion two or three weeks into the term. His job was to advise the students about which universities they should apply to, and what course, and he was also responsible for giving them careers advice. He did no teaching, but was seen as the college expert on these matters and wrote every college reference for students applying to university and, indeed, any other references a student might need. No wonder he collapsed with nervous exhaustion!

A decade earlier I had been responsible at Stowe for all university entrance matters, but that had involved ensuring that my colleagues were up-to-date with new developments and, for example, that all housemasters and tutors kept to the prescribed dates for writing their parts of the references which accompanied each application. Advice on university matters was shared between the tutors. Charlie Macdonald, for example, would know far more than I about the various Chemistry courses available. David Manly, and later John Bennetts, would know more about Modern Languages courses. Then at KGV every member of staff was involved in the process and each tutor was responsible for drafting the reference for his or her students, making it personal, and doing the best they could for them within the bounds of honesty.

I selected two young men who had both been promoted to a higher pay scale than the basic one, though without any particular responsibility, and I told Jonathan Taylor, who taught English, that I wanted him to take charge of University Entrance, and Mark Rousseau, who taught History, that I wanted him to take charge of Careers Advice. They were both reluctant. Brian Alner, they pointed out, was an expert on these matters, while they knew nothing about them, and anyway they would not want to abandon the teaching of their own subject.

My answer was first of all, that they did not need to be experts. They needed to ensure that each of their colleagues became an expert on their own part of the system. Secondly, they would not be faced with any diminution in the teaching of their subjects. They would simply have extra work and responsibility to go with their promoted posts. Thirdly, it would be valuable experience for them of cross-college responsibility. In the event each of them did his job well. Mark Rousseau later went on to be an Education Officer in Gloucestershire. Jonathan Taylor was promoted further within the college and eventually became the Headmaster of Bootham School, an independent Quaker school in York.

They were not the only members of staff to have been promoted but without being given any particular responsibility. The very talented English Department led by Paul Clarke included not only Jonathan Taylor but also Sue Greenwood, David Sanderson and Martin Nichols, who all needed some responsibility to go with their promoted positions. So, while Paul moved to be one of the five Senior Tutors, each of whom took responsibility for half a dozen or more tutors and their tutor groups, and while Jonathan took charge of university entrance, Sue became Head of English, David took charge of the Library, and Martin became Head of Drama.

This did not happen all at once, but it illustrates the way in which responsibilities were spread around. Nor did things stay the same. Over the years there were many changes. Sue, for example, got married and went off to America. Penelope Maynard joined the English Department from Midhurst Grammar School and Richard Jacobs from Westminster School (He had acquired a left wing girl-friend who disapproved of his teaching in a leading independent school) and both of them were in turn Head of Department. Thirty years later Paul has just retired as Head of Adult Education, Penelope has retrained in her retirement for a new career as an actress, David had just retired as Director of Studies, Martin was Head of English before retiring, and Richard became the head of a department at the University of Brighton.

Only a few weeks after the beginning of my first term the caretaker was off sick and I decided that I needed to see some of the cleaners to find out more about how they operated. It was illuminating. They had no set hours and no clearly defined areas to clean. Each of them had a key to the college and they came in at various different times to do the cleaning. One of them, Sheila Planson, when asked about her hours, explained that if George, her husband, was free to help her in the evenings, they might get it done in half an hour or so. But sometimes they would go out in the evening and she would come in for an hour in the early morning. As for the area she cleaned, well that depended a bit on how far Mary had got.

I decided that first of all the college needed to be significantly cleaner, secondly that the cleaning operation needed to happen at a specified time of day, just after most of the students had gone home, that each cleaner should be responsible for a specified area, and thirdly, that the cleaners should not each have a key to the college, so as to be able to come in at any time, but instead should sign in when starting in a book kept by the caretaker, and should be signed off by him when their period of work was over and their area satisfactorily cleaned.

The caretaker warned me that most of the cleaners would not stand for this and would resign. He was right. He warned me that if, in a prosperous area like Horsham, we advertised for cleaners to work at a specified time at the rates of pay offered by the West Sussex County Council, there would be very few applicants. He was right again. So I decided to employ students. A rate of pay unacceptable to most adults was riches to A level students, and it was a particularly convenient part-time job. The college day finished at 4.00. They could do an hour's cleaning from 4.15 until 5.15, and go home with a sense of satisfaction at having earned some money for a straightforward job well done. Shortly afterwards a story about it appeared in the local newspaper and on local television, with pictures of our Oxbridge candidates armed with brooms and mops.

The second time we appeared in the news was when the paper was able to print what a journalist described to me as 'a warm, human story' about a mother and daughter. The daughter was taking the new C.E.E. Maths course and her mother, who wanted to train as a primary school teacher but had always found Maths difficult, wondered if she could join her daughter's class. The daughter asked the Head of Maths. He asked me and I agreed. The next week there was a picture in the West Sussex County Times of two blonde and photogenic young women, mother and daughter, both taking Maths at Collyer's in the same class. That small beginning was the start of Adult Education at Collyer's. It also, together with the story of students cleaning the college, made a start on giving Collyer's a more human public image.

One unexpected outcome of the change in the cleaning arrangements was that Sheila Planson was the only former cleaner to carry on. She approved of the new arrangements, and when there was a change of caretaker shortly afterwards, I took the opportunity of promoting her to a new position as 'cleaner-in-charge', and she did a very good job of supervising the work of the student cleaners. Some years later, when her husband, George, lost his job at Gatwick Airport during the recession, it was possible to appoint him to a post as odd job man in what by then was the Premises Department.

A small problem with a cleaner early in my first term turned out to be far more significant than anyone would have expected. She had come near to cutting off her index finger when closing a window in a new building. The windows all had catches which closed with a scissors motion, and it was clear when one inspected them that they could easily cut off any finger inserted in the circular piece on the catch. I gave instructions that they should all be wired up so that that could not happen.

I telephoned John Cobbett, the Area Education Officer, to ask what I should do about it. He explained that because Collyer's was a 'voluntary aided' college and the new building had been built and paid for under the 'voluntary aided' provisions, I should probably start by contacting the governor who was the Chairman of the Buildings Sub-Committee. I did. He took the problem to his sub-committee and reported to the Governing Body when it met later in the term. The governors decided to refer the problem to the college architect, who visited the college and made a number of drawings, of window catches, of windows with window catches attached to them, of the building, showing all the windows, and of the college with students walking past under as yet unplanted trees, under the windows with new window catches. He presented his drawings and his recommendations for new window catches to the Governing Body at its next meeting, the following term, and the matter was then referred to the Trustees of the Collyer Endowment, who would be meeting a few months later at Mercers' Hall.

What I learnt from this was that problems of this sort were not going to be dealt with by officers of the local authority, which was not responsible for them, nor by the Governing Body, which only met once a term and did not know what to do, nor by the Trustees, who were responsible but limited their view of their responsibilities to supervising the investments of the Collyer Endowment. I needed to find out how the 'voluntary aided' system worked.

By now most 'voluntary aided' grammar schools were independent schools, but twenty had become sixth form colleges and I had visited one of them, King Edward VI Stourbridge, only a few weeks before being appointed to King George V School Southport, and although I had not wanted to take Oriel and the children to live in Stourbridge, I had been impressed by the school and by the quality and care of its buildings and grounds. Clearly someone in Stourbridge knew how to operate the 'voluntary aided' system. Collyer's needed to bring its buildings up to the same standard.

When I contacted the appropriate department at County Hall in Chichester early in the New Year, 1984, I found that there were detailed rules about the responsibilities of the local authority and those of the college's Trustees. Essentially the Trustees were

responsible for the fabric of the building and the grounds, while
the local authority was responsible for internal decoration –
though not, for example, for the repainting of a room whose decoration had been ruined by the failure of the Trustees to repair the
roof. Exactly where the dividing line came between their responsibilities was not entirely clear, but with goodwill on both sides, he
said, it was perfectly possible to work the system.

I explained that there were several jobs which needed to be done
urgently. One of the most urgent was the gutting of the boys'
toilets in the old grammar school building, the replacement of the
floorboards which stank of urine, and the cladding of the walls
with tiles and mirrors rather than with plaster. 'What a pity!'
said the officer. He explained that he still had available several
thousand pounds of 'voluntary aided' money which in most years
would have been spent by then on jobs which needed doing on the
various voluntary aided Church of England primary schools in the
county. This year some thousands had not been spent and sadly it
would disappear at the end of the financial year.

I assured him that I would spend it. But there simply isn't time, he
pointed out, to put the jobs out to tender, decide on a contractor,
get the work done and the bills to County Hall in time for them to
be paid by the end of the financial year and the claims submitted
to the Department of Education. I assured him that I had everything in hand and that I would make sure he got everything he
needed in plenty of time to get the claims in to the D.E.S.

I got hold of a local builder, Peter Bland, who was an Old Collyerian,
and explained what needed doing and the constraints under which
we were operating. He understood, worked out what could be
done for the money available, and got on with it. I signed the cer-
tificates for the completion of the work and submitted them and
the bills to County Hall, and we were all well satisfied. I had
found a reliable local builder who could be relied on to do a good
job at a reasonable price, Peter was glad to have the work and the
prospect of more to come, and the officer at County Hall was glad

to have been able to spend that year's voluntary aided money. Even if the Trustees neglected this aspect of their responsibilities, I had found a way of making the system work and was able to use it to improve the care and maintenance of the college out of all recognition.

I allocated the relatively small sum of £1,500 out of the limited amount of the college funds over which I had direct control, to repairs and improvements. For every £1,500 we could get £10,000 worth of work done, because, so long as no repair cost more than £100 and no new work cost more than £500, the Department of Education would refund 85% of whatever had been spent and that money could then be recycled on further work.

Instead of submitting recommendations to the Governing Body, still less to the Trustees, I authorised all members of staff to let the college office have a simple form of request for a repair job or make a recommendation to the Vice-Principal for some new work. Then one of the secretaries in the office, Kath Scott, would arrange for the work to be done, pay the bills, submit claims to the D.E.S., and kept an account of money spent and received. Each term I included in my report to the Governing Body an account of what had been done, but whether the Trustees had any idea of what was happening I had no way of knowing, since throughout my sixteen years at Collyer's I was never invited to a meeting of the Trustees nor ever shown the minutes of their meetings. It did not matter. They got on with managing the investments. I got on with improving the fabric of the college.

59. New Life

At work I had more than enough to do. At home my life was empty. In the year after Oriel had died part of the emotional gap in my life had been filled with looking after the children – or at any rate looking after them had filled up the time. Once they had all gone (Kate still in Southport, James to Lampeter, Piers somewhere in Europe, and Vicky to live with Linda) I was all the more acutely aware of the loss of Oriel and at the same time of my separation from Helen Bell.

There was a strange difference between what felt like two different forms of bereavement. In the case of Oriel it was awful because it was so ruthlessly final. There was nothing I could possibly do about it, however much I wished to. In Helen's case it was awful because she was still fully and vigorously alive, and our separation was enforced by the fact that she was married and devoted to her husband. The separation was something which was in a sense a matter of choice rather than something imposed by an inexorable fate.

I could cope perfectly well with the day to day business of cooking and doing the housework. I would go by car to do large-scale shopping at a supermarket, getting half a dozen jars of marmalade at a time, half a dozen tins of rice pudding, and so on, and I would then arrange them in line in the cupboards to be worked through over the next few months. Meanwhile for ordinary everyday things there was a small shop just down the road which sold more or less everything and was open from dawn till dusk.

I quite often called in there to pick up a few things for immediate consumption and I was all the more conscious of how different life had become from only a few years earlier because, towards the end of my first term in Horsham, I saw an attractive young woman

451

in her early thirties shopping there with a small daughter who was, perhaps, four years old, and thought with envy of some lucky young man coming home to them at the end of the working day.

I still had the habit of getting up at 7.00 a.m. and going for a run. But instead of running down Weld Road to the beach and back, I now ran from April Close, cutting through Hawthorn Close to Ashleigh Road and on to Collyer's, through the college grounds and across to Horsham Park, where I did a circuit of the park and ran back home for a shower and breakfast. It was about two and a half miles in all and used to take me twenty minutes. Some mornings, as I ran through Hawthorn Close, I would notice the same young woman I had seen in the local shop, now standing with her small daughter outside their house. They were, though I did not know it at the time, waiting for the mother of one and grandmother of the other to pick them up in her car and take them to the nursery where one taught and the other was a pupil.

I was particularly aware of them because she was the only person I had seen since coming to Horsham whom I had observed with that peculiar sense which comes to a man when he sees an attractive girl whom he has never met, but knows he would like to know her better. I remembered first seeing Oriel across a dance floor and how I had concentrated on making sure that I could meet her and ask her to dance with me. I remembered, when Helen and George had come to see me at KGV about their sons' education, how I had gone home to tell Oriel that I had met someone I was sure she would like.

This was entirely different. I knew nothing about this young woman. She was clearly a lot younger than me. I assumed she was married. There was no reason why I should get to know her. But I still had that peculiar, almost detached, feeling that she was someone I would want if she were available. Without Oriel, without Helen, and without her, I felt all the more lonely, and meanwhile I was finding my new job very difficult.

In the middle of my first year at Collyer's, on 25ᵗʰ March 1984, the clocks went forward an hour to provide longer sunlit evenings for the next seven months. It was a welcome change and, I suppose, a sign that spring was on its way. But I failed to notice that the clocks were going forward until it was too late, missed going to the Holy Communion service at 8.00 a.m. in the parish church, and decided to go to Matins later in the morning instead.

It was a damp and overcast day with the rain drizzling down, and after the service, as I drove up the Causeway, I saw the young woman whom I had seen in the local shop or by her front door. She was walking up the Causeway from church, head bowed in the rain. So I stopped my red Ford Escort estate car and asked if she would like a lift home, explaining that I knew where she lived because I had sometimes seen her when I went for a run in the mornings. She looked me over. I was wearing a tweed sports jacket and was clearly coming from the church. She decided that I looked respectable enough for it to be worth risking getting in the car. Anyway, she had done a self-defence course recently and thought she would be able to cope, and besides that, the rain was increasingly unpleasant.

The conversation on the way back was brief and polite. We had both returned to Horsham the previous summer after some years away. I explained that I had known the town a bit when I had been at school at Christ's Hospital. 'Ah!' she said, 'My father used to teach there.' 'What was his name?' 'Roberts.' 'Oh! That must have been after my time', I said. After all, I knew she could not be the daughter of David Roberts, who had died back in 1956, because I knew not only his widow, Peggy, but also his three children, Fenella, Martin and Peter.

We reached her house. She thanked me, got out and gave her name: 'Catherine Prentice.' She later said that my reply was nothing more than a nod and a grunt, and that I drove off leaving her thinking that that was rather rude of me. What I recall is that I wondered briefly if she might be any relation of Evan Prentice, who had been the Director of Music at Clifton, where I had started teaching. But within a split second I had reflected that Prentice, like Roberts, is a fairly common name and, what is more, can be spelt in more than one way. So I had not asked.

About ten days later a card came through my letterbox saying she thought she had discovered who I was; her Aunt Peggy was staying with her parents; they were all coming round for a drink on Saturday evening; she was sure Peggy would be pleased to see me again and that her parents would be glad to meet me. I replied thanking her and turned up on the Saturday evening. It was a pleasure to see Peggy again. It was a pleasure to meet Eileen and Mervyn, David Roberts's younger brother. They were apologetic that they had not yet contacted me; they had thought I would be busy with a new job. I was apologetic that I had not contacted them – for the same reason. It was a particular pleasure to see their daughter again.

I found that she was separated from her husband and invited her out to dinner the following Saturday, the first day of the Easter

Cathy and her daughter, Helen, in the summer of 1983, a few months before we met. Cathy and me at the annual Pineapple Ball at Stowe shortly after we had met.

holidays. She asked me to help clear out her garage a few days later, and I worked out that her daughter, Helen, would be exactly four and a half shortly afterwards on 25th April. So I bought a fourth birthday card, carefully wrote in the half sign after the number 4, and had the pleasure of being the only person to give her a four and a half(th) birthday card. Catherine and I went out to dinner again and bit by bit learnt more about each other's past life.

She was thirty-three, seventeen years younger than me, born in Abergele on the north coast of Wales in December 1950. Her parents were both accomplished pianists and Mervyn was a good enough composer to rate an entry in Grove's *Dictionary of Music*. His father was the first Lord Clwyd, descended from a successful timber merchant and for many years Liberal Member of Parliament for a large area of North Wales, the neighbouring con-stituency to Lloyd George's constituency of Caernarvon Boroughs, until he was ennobled by Lloyd George in 1918. As it happens I had met him during my last year at school in 1952 and had trav-elled up to London with him on the train. I remembered him talking about attending the coronation of George VI and wearing baronial robes. Catherine remembered him from when she was a small child, but he had died when she was four, about four years after the death of his wife, the month after Catherine was born.

His wife, who was a girl called Hannah Caine when he married her and the very beautiful daughter of another MP, had been painted by George Clausen and her picture was hung in the Wallace Art Gallery in Liverpool. They had twin boys in 1900. The elder of them, Trevor, succeeded to the title in the 1950s, and it was the younger twin, David, who taught me at Christ's Hospital. The third of the brothers, Mervyn, who was born in 1906, the same year as both of my parents, was Catherine's father; and he and his wife, Eileen, had moved to Horsham in 1959, when Catherine was eight years old, to be near Peggy after David had died.

Catherine's maternal grandfather, Alfred Easom, had been born in Nottingham in 1890, got a science degree from London University in 1911 and taught for three years in London. Then the First World War broke out and before long he was commissioned in the Royal Flying Corps and was mentioned in dispatches before being forced down behind enemy lines early in 1916 and spending two and a half years in prisoner-of-war camps in circumstances which permanently damaged his health – though, of course, being brought down, which no doubt seemed a disaster at the time, was probably what saved his life.

After the war he joined the staff of Abergele Grammar School on the North Wales coast, got married and had a daughter, Eileen, in 1921, the year after he was appointed Senior Chemistry Master. He was serving again, in a training unit of the RAF, in the Second World War when he was over fifty, returned to Abergele Grammar School and was still teaching there when he died in September 1954, at the beginning of the term in which he was due to retire. Catherine, who was not quite four at the time, nevertheless remembered him, as well as his wife, her grandmother, who died in the mid-1950s, and her great-grandmother, who outlived most of her six children and died at the age of 102 in the mid-1960s.

As a child Catherine went to Parkfield School in Horsham, which no longer exists, and then was sent back to North Wales to be a boarder at Penrhos, an independent school for girls in Colwyn Bay. There she did particularly well in languages and since she had no wish to stay at school any longer than she needed to, went up to Bristol University to read Modern Languages (French and German) at the age of seventeen. She was only twenty when she came down from Bristol in 1971, whereas I, leaving school at eighteen and with two years' National Service between school and university, was nearly twenty-one when I went up to Oxford.

For a year after coming down Catherine worked in the Bristol University Medical Library and after that did a post-graduate Librarianship course at Manchester. A few years earlier, while on holiday in France the year before she went up to university, she had met a young man called Ian Prentice who was the son of the

Director of Music at Clifton College, Evan Prentice, and had been a boy in the school while I was teaching there. He went up to Bristol to read English. They fell in love, got married in 1974 after both had graduated and done their training, Ian as a schoolmaster and Catherine as a librarian, and at first they lived in Brighton and both worked in West Sussex. In 1976 they moved to Hitchin, when he got a job at Luton Sixth Form College and she a job as the Hitchin Children's Librarian.

Everything seemed fine until in 1979 Catherine became pregnant. Almost at once she felt a lack of support from her husband. That continued throughout her pregnancy and labour, and after the baby was born it seemed to her that he resented the child's arrival. He was an attractive young man, not yet ready to be a father and not yet ready to settle down. He needed to find out if the grass was greener on the other side of the hill. First that involved looking for yet another job, and he found one as a local authority education officer in Leicester. Secondly it involved looking for another girl, and before long he was moving from one girlfriend to another, eventually without even trying to hide what he was doing and saying that he needed his freedom.

Catherine spent an unhappy year and a half in Leicester. Ian was frequently away from home. She meanwhile was relying for support on the members of the local branch of the National Childbirth Trust, until in the summer of 1983 she felt she could stand it no longer. They agreed to separate and she moved back to Horsham to stay with her parents and look for a house where she could live with her daughter and find some part-time work. It was about six months after that that she and I met, in the middle of my first year at Collyer's, both of us bruised by recent experience.

60. Second Marriage

That was the position when we met. Both of us had taken something of an emotional hammering in the previous year of two. Cathy (I soon found that she was usually called 'Cathy' rather than 'Catherine') had got married sure that she and Ian would go on loving each other and that they would live together all their lives. Her self-confidence had taken a terrible knock when she found that Ian no longer saw her that way. She would even have forgiven and accepted his straying when their daughter was very young, but she could not accept a situation in which he was clearly looking for someone else and in which neither she nor their daughter was an important part of his life. She left, decided to cope on her own, and from now on viewed men warily and with suspicion.

I meanwhile was trying to adjust to being a widower. I thought it unlikely that I could find anyone unattached whom I could love and who would feel the same about me, so I was disciplining myself to live alone and reminding myself that I had coped perfectly well a quarter of a century earlier when I was a bachelor. But back then I had been living in hopeful expectation of marriage, and after that, married to Oriel for just over twenty-three years, I had turned into a married man.

Now I found that being a widower was nothing like being a bachelor. Instead it was a state of being a married man without his wife. I had twice spent a term as a sort of temporary bachelor – my first term at Stowe and, some six and a half years later, a term at Jesus College, Cambridge. But in both cases I was able to go home to Oriel at the weekends. Now I was trying to accept a life of solitude, with none of the close personal relationship and companionship which had both been for so long such a central and valuable part of my life.

I was delighted to find Cathy, and was both pleased and grateful that she was glad to spend time with me in the summer of 1984. We would often go out together, either just the two of us during the evening when her mother would baby-sit, or during the day with her daughter, Helen. I became more and more attached to her and, indeed, to her daughter as well, but it was difficult to believe that she could feel the same attachment to me that I felt to her, and it took me time to appreciate that our feelings were mutual.

Some time before the end of the summer holidays I asked her to marry me and she agreed. By that time she and Ian had agreed to divorce and once that was finalised we had no reason to wait. At the beginning of Half Term, on Saturday 19th October 1984, we were married in the registry office in the old town hall in Horsham, and the next day my brother conducted a service of blessing in St Peter's Chapel at the top of the Causeway. We had a reception for both our families at Cathy's parents' house and a wedding party for friends and colleagues at Collyer's.

I was always pleased to get home and see Cathy at the end of the working day. It was not that my second marriage was 'roses, roses all the way', but then, nor had the first one been. Oriel and I were young and inexperienced when we started married life together. I was three months short of twenty-six; she had just had her twenty-fourth birthday. We had to learn to live together. In many ways that was an enjoyable process; in some it was difficult. We had the enormous advantage that there was still a general assumption in society (and one that was shared by us) that marriage was for life, so if there were difficulties and disagreements, and of course there were, we knew that we had to work through them. The combination of mutual love and commitment is a powerful force for overcoming problems, and each reinforces the other.

Cathy and I were, of course, significantly older when we got married, or at any rate I was significantly older and she somewhat older. I was fifty and she was thirty-three. Both of us were bruised by recent experience, in my case by the death of Oriel not much more than two years earlier, so that the wound was still open and sore, and in her case by the breakdown of her first marriage, even more recently, which had been a terrible blow to her self-confidence.

The difference in age did not seem to matter much, and certainly the relationship between Cathy and me was not that of an older man as head of the household with a young and subservient wife.

With Cathy on our wedding day, 19th October 1984

It was far more equal. We loved each other and respected each other, and we both knew that we needed to look after each other. Each of us was old enough to be aware of the pain the other had suffered, and we were very glad to have found each other. Problems and difficulties never outweighed the love and mutual commitment.

I had the advantage of having a job which occupied my working hours. Cathy meanwhile had a five year old daughter to look after (Helen's fifth birthday was on 25th October, a few days after our wedding) but particularly after Helen went to school Cathy did not want to be at home all day. She had, of course, previously had a successful career as a librarian and had especially enjoyed being the Children's Librarian in Hitchin. But librarianship is a profession which almost always involves working on Saturdays, so it would have been difficult to go back to that.

For the moment she carried on with the part-time job teaching in a nursery school which she had already been doing when I first met her. She also trained with the National Childbirth Trust to provide evening courses on pregnancy, labour, childbirth, breast-feeding and so on to young women expecting a baby - and preferably their husbands came along too. But that was only an occasional evening occupation and was not a long-term solution to the question of what to do. We spent a lot of time talking over what she might do and what she did not want to do. She knew that she did not want more children. She knew that she did not want to stay at home, doing nothing but cleaning the house, looking after Helen and me, gardening, cooking meals and entertaining. She felt that she should be doing something else worthwhile with her life.

But what? I thought that with a degree in Modern Languages, with French as her main subject and German at her disposal as well, it would make sense to do a P.G.C.E. (Post-Graduate Certificate of Education) course, specialising in Modern Languages at secondary level. But she had only read Modern Languages at Bristol because she was good at languages at school and had done what her teachers told her to. With hindsight she would rather have studied Science subjects and applied for a place to read Veterinary Science. It was too late for that now.

In the end she decided to do a PG.C.E. course with a view to teaching the whole range of subjects to primary school children, and since Sussex University had a policy of taking on their P.G.C.E. course people who had worked at something else beforehand, she applied for a place on that course and started in the autumn of 1989. A year later, when she had nearly completed it, she found a job in a village under the South Downs, and for the next twelve years taught mostly seven and eight year olds at Storrington. After a few of those years she took charge of language work throughout the school, enjoyed what she was doing, and throughout her time there never even considered applying for another post.

Back in 1985, the year after we got married, Cathy and I had pooled our resources and bought a larger house, with a larger garden than either of us had previously had, in Wimblehurst Road, just five minutes walk away from Collyer's. The house had once belonged to a former Deputy Head of Collyer's, Bob Greenop. He had been a boy at the school, left at sixteen to take a job, joined the army in the First World War, was badly wounded, lost a leg and was told when he went back to the firm he had worked for that they had no jobs for cripples. He went to London University, got a degree in Chemistry, joined the staff of Collyer's in 1924 and stayed until he retired thirty years later, for the last eighteen of them as Deputy Head.

While we were in the process of buying the house in Wimblehurst Road I suggested to Cathy that it was time to put my house in April Close on the market. She replied that I should not do that quite yet, as she might have a buyer for me. Her mother and father were finding both the house and the garden in Worthing Road, where they had lived since 1959, rather too big for them. My house in April Close might suit them better. So in the event they bought 54, April Close from me and enjoyed living in it. Then, while Collyer's was five minutes' walk away from us in one direction, Cathy's parents were five minutes' walk the other way.

Sadly in July of 1990, when he was 83 and after living in April Close for five years, Mervyn died, just as Cathy's P.G.C.E. course was ending. Eileen was now a widow at the age of 69. She went on living in the same house, mostly on her own but eventually with a carer, for the next twenty years, always amiable, and regularly continuing to practice the Beethoven and Mozart sonatas and Chopin mazurkas that she had played all her adult life. She came to church with me on Sunday mornings until the strength of both her body and mind faded to the point that she needed nursing care in a home, where, half an hour's walk or ten minutes drive from us, Cathy regularly visited her three times a week and I went to see her on Sundays after church.

Back in the mid-1980s and early in our marriage one of the problems which Cathy had to face was that I was an Oxford graduate who had studied and taught History and was now a headmaster – even if the title of the job was 'Principal'. Her experience had been that most Oxford graduates were arrogant, most historians were boring and most headmasters were pompous. So I needed to try to avoid being arrogant, boring and pompous if our marriage was to flourish. At the same time she also suspected me of snobbery. I could not think that I had much to be snobbish about. But I was genuinely interested in class differences, and felt that one could not reasonably pretend that such differences did not exist.

I had grown up in an environment with working class assumptions, but those included the assumption by my parents that they should try to ensure that their sons could have a better life than theirs. I had been moulded by Christ's Hospital and had discovered in the army that officers in the cavalry were seen as socially superior to those in the transport corps in which I served – and that they probably thought of themselves as socially superior to most of the infantry as well. I had encountered at Oxford the division between those who came from public schools and those who came from grammar schools and had discerned any number of sub-divisions within those groups.

Before becoming a headmaster I had taught at Clifton (a middle class school, with a Jewish intellectual upper middle class element in Polack's House), at Quintin School (very cosmopolitan and also socially mixed) and at Stowe (generally upper middle class with a bit of aristocracy thrown in). Wherever I had been in fifty years of life I had encountered various forms of prejudice (for and against trade unions, for and against the police, for and against public schools, for and against grammar schools) and I had found both prejudice and class consciousness fascinating. They appeared to be integral to human nature and to all periods of history.

Almost every time I changed my job, the news provoked some expression of prejudice from people I counted as friends. My appointment to Clifton was greeted with the comment, 'But David, Clifton is a school which produces good chaps.' When I moved to Quintin School I was asked, 'Do you really want to teach butchers' sons?' When Quintin was threatened with re-organisation and I went back to the independent sector and to Stowe, I was asked, 'But don't you feel a bit of a traitor?' When I moved from Stowe to be the headmaster of King George V School in Southport, I was asked, 'How could you bear to leave such a beautiful place for the industrial North?' Only when I left KGV for Collyer's in West Sussex was there no comment of that sort. Instead George Wakefield, my former Deputy Headmaster, gave me a beautiful watercolour he had painted of Derwentwater and Skiddaw, with the inscription, 'David – a piece of the barbarous north, with love from June and George', and that, of course, was a comment by an intelligent and sensitive man on the world of prejudice in which we lived.

But my view was that an interest in such things did not of itself constitute snobbery, and Cathy gradually acclimatised herself to that, though with a lingering suspicion about me if, for example, I found it amusing that Alan Clark described Michael and Annabel Heseltine as 'the sort of people who bought their own furniture.' That comment, of course, told me more about Alan Clark than it did about Michael Heseltine, and I felt no sense of shame in buying my own furniture – even at IKEA. Cathy and I had to merge our own furniture – most of mine dark mahogany and most of hers light pine. But that worked well in our new house, which had been built at the turn of the nineteenth and twentieth centuries, and Cathy turned out to have a natural talent for internal decoration. She set out to make the house attractive, and I set out to do the same with the garden.

In a typical week I would work hard at Collyer's throughout the week, then on Friday evening we might well go out to a meal in Mr Li's Chinese restaurant, get to bed reasonably early, and after breakfast on Saturday I would get out in the garden and dig, cut or carry, wield a bow saw, felling axe, mowing machine, spade or fork, and perhaps, as the sun went down, light a bonfire which would burn all night - something which was acceptable to our neighbours, since it was lit after they had gone indoors and not while they were sitting in their own gardens. It was a refreshing change from what I was doing all the week. I would wake up on Sunday morning feeling re-invigorated, go to church in the middle of the morning, and afterwards feel ready to start preparing for the next week's work.

61. Redeployment

During my first week at Collyer's the Area Education Officer, John Cobbett, had come to see me about the problem that the number of teaching staff was significantly higher than it should have been. West Sussex allowed for a sixth-form student-staff ratio of 12:1 plus the principal, which was far more generous than at KGV where it had been 14:1, including the headmaster. So Collyer's, with nearly six hundred students, was entitled to forty-nine teachers other than the Principal. It had sixty. I was going to have to reduce that number by eleven over the coming year. The staff were not threatened with redundancy, but rather with redeployment to another sixth form college or to a comprehensive secondary school somewhere else in the county.

How the overstaffing of Collyer's had come about was not at first clear to me. Perhaps the local authority had failed to plan for the redeployment of members of staff employed to cover the period of transition from grammar school to sixth form college. But the last grammar school boys had taken O level three years earlier in 1980, so they had had plenty of time to deal with that. Perhaps they had not liked to face the problem while my predecessor was in post and had deliberately left it for his successor to deal with.

Eventually I worked out the reason. When Roy Potter, the Director of Education for West Sussex, was persuading the governors of Collyer's to agree to the change from grammar school to sixth form college, he promised them substantial new accommodation and in particular a large new building with numerous classrooms. Under the voluntary aided arrangements 85% of the cost would be provided by the Department of Education, and the Department of Education had to be persuaded of the need for a large new building.

That was achieved by pretending that student numbers were significantly higher than they really were. The way of doing that was to decide, for example, that all the students at the Crawley Technical College annexe in Horsham could, if they wished, take O level English and Mathematics at Collyer's, and then add them to the Collyer's roll. Few, if any, ever did, but at least in theory it boosted the Collyer's roll. Similarly all the students at a Worthing Art College annexe in Horsham were added in, for the same reason, though again few if any ever attended Collyer's.

This inflation of the college roll made it possible to get the building for a cost to the Collyer's Trustees of £45,000, 15% of the total cost of £300,000, but it also had the effect that my predecessor was allowed to appoint eleven more members of the teaching staff than the college would have been entitled to if the numbers had been accurate. That was the problem I was faced with a couple of weeks after taking up my post.

At the time of the negotiations it must have seemed a small price to pay for keeping Collyer's within the system, and if it smacks of dishonesty, one has to recognise that the English secondary education system had become so complicated that it was difficult to know what was acceptable and what was not. It may well have been that officials at the Department of Education were conniving at the deception.

My job was to get the number of teachers down to a staffing level appropriate to the number of students. I tried in a staff meeting to reassure the staff that the prospect of large-scale redeployment was not as bad as it seemed. It might encourage some of them to seek promotion elsewhere and the prospects for internal promotion were good, because I would need to make internal appointments rather than increasing the problem of overstaffing by making external appointments. I had, I explained to them, been through a similar process before, and I could say with confidence that things would turn out better than they feared. I could see that they clearly did not believe me.

In the event it did turn out better than they feared, but a number of them had good reason to feel that they had been badly treated. John Cobbett and I saw individually each member of staff scheduled for redeployment and explained why they had been designated. Often it was because of the principle of 'last in, first out' which the teachers' unions insisted on – though the unions always recognised that it had to be applied on a departmental basis rather than to the college as a whole.

That was the reason I had to give to a young woman called Margaret Jubb, who had joined the Collyer's staff a few weeks earlier with a first class degree in Modern Languages, and who replied that the day of our meeting was, as it happened, the anniversary of the day of her appointment. It seemed strange to her that she had ever been appointed. It did to me too, and I found it embarrassing. But she set out to look for another job and shortly afterwards was appointed to a lectureship at Aberdeen University.

Another member of the Modern Languages Department applied for and was appointed to a senior post in a comprehensive school and the Head of the Modern Languages Department came to me with the draft of an advertisement for another member of the department. I told him that the work would have to be rearranged within the department. For example, a group of four doing A level German could be amalgamated with another group of five doing the same subject at the same time with a different teacher, and that would produce a taught group size which would still be only nine. But, he protested, they had done different aspects of the course at different times and had studied different set books.

That, I told him, was a problem he would have to deal with within his department. He went away indicating that it was outrageous that the principal of the college, someone who had no understanding of the teaching of modern languages, should interfere in the internal workings of his department. From my point of view I had saved two out of the eleven posts that had to go.

In the case of the Classics Department one of the three classicists found promotion in another college, one was pleased to be able to take voluntary early retirement and spend his days on the golf course rather than in the classroom, and the third, Ed Tattersall, created a worthwhile job for himself. He proposed and then taught an increasingly popular A level course in Classical Civilisation. He taught Latin after the college day was over to volunteers from the local comprehensive schools, A level Greek in the lunch hour to the occasional particularly clever student who was prepared to put in the extra work involved, and a large class of O level English to students who had failed it at school and needed to repeat it. When one did the calculation of how many students each member of staff was teaching for how many periods of the week, he was more than earning his living.

When I arrived there were two Senior Teachers as well as the two Vice-principals. One of them, John Hamer, who had been Head of History for many years, had just been appointed to a post as one of Her Majesty's Inspectors of Education and was due to leave at the end of my first term. The other, Brian Alner, the Careers Master, had gone off sick with nervous exhaustion three weeks after I arrived. He assured me that it was nothing to do with me and I hoped that was true.

Either way, he was never well enough to come back, and the departure of two Senior Teachers made it possible to make at least one internal appointment at that level. Derek Slynn and Roland Soper both recommended Steve Gilham, a quiet, unassuming man who was Head of Geography and whom I hardly knew. I took their advice and never regretted it. Throughout my time at Collyer's Steve Gilham proved an invaluable aide, able to move from one responsibility to another as I delegated yet another issue to him in order to be able to move on to tackle something else.

With two Modern Linguists gone, two Classicists and two Senior Teachers, we were more than halfway to reducing the staffing of the college by eleven. As the year went another member of staff found promotion elsewhere, two were made redundant for reasons nothing to do with the problem of over-staffing, and the Woodwork master, with no-one to teach, and whose post therefore had to be made redundant, found himself a job outside teaching. That was ten posts lost, with no appointments to replace them.

I had been fortunate in the spread of subjects of those who were leaving. It had been necessary to create a record of what subjects members of staff could teach other than their own, so that not only did a Classisist teach an O level English class, but a Physicist could teach some Maths and a Geographer could teach some History while an Historian taught A level Politics. That meant that it was not necessary to exacerbate the staffing problem by making external appointments, and in the end the only member of staff who needed to be redeployed was a Physicist who was very happy with the job that John Cobbett found him at Haywards Heath Sixth Form College.

That whole problem had been the consequence of the way in which the West Sussex County Council was saved the millions of pounds it would have cost if they had needed to build a new school or college. Instead they had acquired a sixth form college at the trivial cost of the £218,000 paid for an area of playing field which was returned to the college, and the money went into the Collyer Endowment held by the Mercers' Company. The benefit to Collyer's, of course, was that it acquired a new classroom block and the promise of more new buildings. The benefit to the Mercers' Company was that it had avoided the costs which would have arisen if Collyer's had become independent.

The company was used to dealing with independent schools. Its members viewed the St Paul's schools with pride, they were spending a lot of money turning two other grammar schools, Abingdon and Dauntsey's, into independent schools, and it was possible that many of them looked down with scorn on any school funded out of the public purse. Early in my time as Principal a visit by the Master of the Mercers' Company, accompanied by his wife, did quite a lot to give that impression. As the Master's wife ate a good lunch she took the opportunity to explain to me what a splendidly charitable organisation the Mercers' Company was, emphasising that in all its charitable activities, whether almshouses for the elderly or the various schools in which it was involved, they ensured that their charity went to deserving people, such as those who sacrificed holidays abroad to pay the fees at St Paul's, rather than to those who 'sponged on the state.'

I was scrupulously polite. Neither her husband nor, I think, any member of the Mercers' Company would have been foolish enough to have expressed himself that way to the principal of a sixth form college, whose students all had parents who, from her point of view, were sponging on the state. But it gave an indication of how they might be thinking, even though it was they who had decided that Collyer's should stay within the local authority system rather than become independent.

The problem of overstaffing was not over at the end of my first year. As Collyer's had changed from boys' grammar school to mixed sixth form college it had year by year become less popular locally as a place to go to take A levels. Each year the number of applicants to join the college was smaller than the number leaving. By the autumn of 1984 the number of students was down to about 540, and since staffing was based on student numbers that meant a reduction of another four members of staff. In the autumn of 1985 there were only 504 students and a further staffing reduction of three.

That was the lowest point in the college's fortunes. By then things were visibly improving, whether the state of the buildings or the examination results, or in some subjects, particularly French and Chemistry, the quality of teaching – in both those departments as a result of staffing changes. From 1985 onwards student numbers increased year on year and Horsham became a net importer of students rather than an exporter. Instead of students escaping from Horsham to Reigate and Worthing and Haywards Heath, we were before long attracting students even from as far away as Kingston upon Thames, twenty miles to the North, and from Bognor Regis, twenty miles to the South-west. The growth of Horsham, as more and more houses were built, had a further impact, so that the average annual increase over the fourteen years from 1985 until I retired in 1999 was about fifty. By then the total number of students had doubled to approximately one thousand, two hundred. That trend continued, and in 2017 the number of students on roll was 2017.

62. Redundancy

◇◇◇

Back at the time of reorganisation Roy Potter had had to make a number of concessions on behalf of the West Sussex Education Authority in order to get the Governing Body of Collyer's to agree to the change from boys' grammar school to mixed sixth form college at a time when most voluntary aided grammar schools were opting for independence. One of those concessions was acceptance of the demand by the governors that Collyer's should keep all the staff of the boys' grammar school, rather than open up the staffing of the college to members of staff of the Horsham High School for Girls as well as to the staff of Collyer's.

The governors mistakenly assumed that by doing so they were looking after the interests of Collyer's, but the outcome was doubly unfortunate. First, it resulted in a staffing structure entirely unsuited to a sixth form college. It was not just that there were three Classicists with only two students to teach and a Woodwork master with no-one to teach. It was also that the staff were over-whelmingly male and that there was, understandably, long-lasting ill-feeling among the staff of the Horsham High School for Girls, who were excluded from the possibility of teaching in the college and had to adjust to an 11-16 mixed comprehensive school – with the one exception that a Biologist, Celia Jarratt, was appointed to be a female Vice-Principal at Collyer's.

Quite apart from the need to get staffing numbers down to conform to the staffing ratio of 12:1, I had several other staffing problems to be faced, many related to the insistence of the Governing Body on keeping the staff of the former boys' grammar school. The qualifications and experience of several members of staff did not match what needed to be taught, and there were some older heads of department, who may have been effective and successful teachers in the grammar school, who now took the

view that there was no way of maintaining the ethos and standards of a grammar school in one of these new-fangled sixth form
colleges. They saw the future as downhill all the way. They had
resigned themselves to living with it until retirement, but they
were not prepared to engage in the creation of a good sixth form
college.

The problem Collyer's faced was not a lack of talented and highly
motivated students in the area. It was that many talented and
highly motivated students were looking for somewhere else to
study for A level, and many parents of potential students were
increasingly aware that there was something seriously wrong at
Collyer's – in particular with the teaching of both French and
Chemistry. That manifested itself in understandable requests from
some parents that their son or daughter should not be taught by
the Head of the Modern Languages Department, and from others
that their son or daughter should not be taught by the former
Head of Chemistry.

The results in both of those subjects were poor, but the situations
were quite different. In the case of French the head of department,
who had been an inspiring teacher some years earlier, as I heard
from some of his former grammar school pupils, had gradually
cracked under the strain of the transition from grammar school to
sixth form college. He had come to believe that in a world of
declining standards no-one cared any longer about the distinction
between the *Past Historic* and the *Passé Composé*, or whether
adjective endings agreed with the noun they were describing in
number, case and gender (the A level examiners, of course, took a
very different view), so he had given up setting or marking homework. One day I went into his classroom and found him smoking.
Another day, as I walked along the corridor at the end of the lunch
hour, I found him propped up by two of his colleagues, who were
loyally trying to prevent him from falling over drunk in front of
the Principal. Parents wrote to me about the obscene language he
had used to their daughters and about the lack of homework.

I contacted the personnel department of the West Sussex education authority to suggest that we should try to arrange voluntary early retirement for a member of staff 'experiencing professional difficulties' and got the defensive response that there had never been a problem till now and it was something I should deal with without involving the authority in unnecessary expense. When I went on to explain just how bad the problem was, the response was one of shock and horror: this was a disciplinary matter which should be resolved by dismissal. That, of course, would have left him and his wife with neither pay nor pension until he reached the age of sixty, and it was not a solution I would consider. I prepared for a fight with the local authority. He had to go, but he should go in a manner which avoided either penury or public humiliation.

The first step was to have a meeting at which, I suggested, he should arrange to be accompanied by a union (or professional association) representative from outside the college. When the three of us met I started by commenting on problems of departmental organisation and teaching. Understandably he replied defensively. 'But it is not just that', I went on. 'I have had to require you not to smoke in your classroom, not to come in drunk at the end of the lunch hour, not to use obscene language...' At this point his association representative interrupted to say, 'I wonder, Principal, if I could have a few minutes alone with my member.'

Of course he could. Off they went to my secretary's room and ten minutes later the representative came back alone to ask me what sort of a deal I thought could be arranged. He wondered if I might consider redundancy and explained how that could work. Because it is the post rather than the person that is made redundant I would need to find some way of operating without a Head of Modern Languages. I realised that that gave me the opportunity to promote three current members of staff. So at the end of my first year Collyer's no longer had a Head of the Modern Languages Department. Instead it had a Head of French, a Head of Spanish and a Head of German. They were glad of their promotion, and I was relieved to have avoided a fight with the local authority and grateful to the professional association representative who had guided me to a good solution.

The case with Chemistry was entirely different. The teaching of the former Head of Chemistry was notoriously unintelligible to most students. One year four out of a group of nine students got the top grade; none got a B, C, D, E, or even an O; the other five all failed with the very bottom grade: F. He had been replaced as Head of the Chemistry Department two years before I arrived by a talented younger man, James King, who had previously been teaching part-time while trying to make a living making high quality furniture. The furniture was impressive, but it did not pay enough to live on, so he took on a full-time post as head of department, but with his predecessor still teaching some A level Chemistry.

Rather strangely his predecessor had been found another post as Head of Computer Science – still something relatively new in 1981. But since very few boys, and no girls, had opted to take Computer Science at either O or A level and be taught by him, he was still teaching Chemistry. Thus there were two problems instead of one. Again the solution was redundancy. The first decision I made about the curriculum was to abandon Computer Science at both O and A level. The small number of computers we had should not, I argued, be monopolised by a few specialists. Instead, our aim should be for every student and every member of staff to be computer literate in just the same way that previous generations had learnt to use pen and ink. Then, once Computer Science as an examination subject had been removed from the curriculum, it was possible to make the post of Head of Computer Science redundant and the person holding it had to go.

There was, of course, the complication that I would need someone in his place to teach Chemistry, and I could hardly advertise for a Chemist if he was being made redundant. As it happens, the senior Vice-Principal, Roland Soper, was retiring at the end of the year and in the case of the post of Vice-Principal it was possible to justify making an external appointment. The advertisement produced a large number of applicants from a wide range of subjects, and from among them I invited just five for interview. Each had a degree in Chemistry, and the one appointed, Peter Crees, proved to be an invaluable addition to the Chemistry Department, while at the same time, as Vice-Principal, running the tutorial system.

When he took the tutorial system over he arranged to have a tutor group of his own. I thought that inappropriate. One would not expect the second-in-command of a battalion to have a platoon of his own, I protested. But Peter insisted, arguing that it was the experience of having to do everything that he was requiring of the tutors which would enable him to run the system effectively. That fitted with my own view that I ought to do some teaching, so I gave in. Peter was very effective, and he continued to keep in touch with life at the chalk face by going on having a tutorial group of his own every year. He still had one when I retired fifteen years later.

A further problem was that there was a group of very keen, intelligent, but relatively inexperienced young members of staff whose communal view at its most extreme was that the past should be put behind us and forgotten. A new sixth form college, they believed, should be 'democratic', the students should be encouraged by the high quality of teaching to come to lessons, but they should not be upset by requirements such as regular attendance or punctuality. They spoke of 'a close and loving relationship' with the members of their tutor groups, and they did not wish that relationship to be damaged by restrictions on behaviour or regulations about clothing.

I told them that it was the job of the students' parents to have 'a close and loving relationship' with them. Members of staff were paid to teach the students, set them work and mark it critically and promptly, provide realistic assessments of performance and guidance about how to improve it, ensure that the students turned up regularly and punctually to their lessons, dressed in a manner which indicated both self-respect and respect for others, kept college regulations, such as that they should not smoke anywhere in or near the college, and did not scatter litter.

The response to this was that they did not wish to treat the students as children rather than as young adults. My reply was that they should most certainly treat the students as young adults rather than as children, but that meant that they should expect them to behave like responsible young adults. This was not a matter for discussion. We could discuss the details of the college regulations, and my own preference was to have as few as possible, with those we did have being both reasonable and realistic. But the general principle that regulations should be enforced and that they should enforce them, whether they liked them or not, was non-negotiable.

One response to this was that running the college in that way would turn students away. They were all past the school leaving age and were not obliged to come. Our numbers were already reducing year by year and potential future students would vote with their feet and go somewhere else. My reply was that in the long run students and their parents would vote with their feet against sloppy standards and in favour of high standards and high quality education. Anyone opting in should know that they were opting in to an institution which required from them high standards of both industry and behaviour.

This was viewed with caution by the idealistic young and with cynicism by a number of the older and disillusioned members of staff who should have been providing wise, professional guidance to the young. Change was not easy, and I frequently had cause to remember a comment of the American economist, J. K. Galbraith: 'Faced with the choice of changing one's mindset and proving that there is no need to do so, almost everyone gets on with the proof.' With one issue after another the objections followed a regular pattern. First, 'But we have always done it this way'; secondly, 'It isn't necessary'; thirdly, 'It's undemocratic'; fourthly, 'It will be too expensive'; and finally, 'It is the last straw which will break the camel's back.'

The most commonly asked question in staff meetings was, 'Are you sure you are right about this, Principal?', and it took time for them to get used to the answer, 'No, but like you, I am paid to do a job, and part of that job is making decisions of this sort – and that is the decision I have made.' With time they also got used to the idea that the same principle applied to the running of anything for which they were themselves responsible.

Fortunately there were many hard-working and well-qualified members of staff who usually said little in staff meetings and simply wanted to do a good job in circumstances in which they would be free to get on with teaching the students. Both grammar schools and sixth form colleges tend to attract well qualified staff. In grammar schools the sixth form work is sometimes the icing on the cake. In sixth form colleges it is the daily bread and butter, and a very healthy, staple diet it is. What is more, Horsham is a particularly pleasant town which naturally attracts good quality staff. Its attraction as a place to live was indicated by a national survey somewhere around the turn of the millennium which put it equal first with York as the most desirable town to live in in England.

So we had some natural advantages. Not least among those advantages were the students. The range of ability was wide. At one extreme were those who were clearly going to get the top A level grade in each of Maths, Further Maths and Physics, or in each of English Literature, French and History, and who opted to add to their programme of study an extra O level course such as Ancient Greek or, later, Russian Studies. At the other extreme were those who had failed to get any A-C grades at O level while at school and wanted to acquire enough qualifications either to start an A level course a year later or go on, with some success behind them, to a course at a technical college. Both usually came from homes where academic achievement was valued and where their parents had high hopes and aspirations for their future. The future was potentially bright.

63. Managing Change.

◇◇

A year after I took over at Collyer's I acquired a new Chairman of Governors. Rosemary Cowley was a county councillor who was a formidable politician when dealing with political matters and had been awarded the CBE (grander than an OBE and much grander than an MBE) for her services to the Tory Party in the South-East. But she was the sort of politician who could be entirely non-political when dealing with the affairs of a college and simply tried to do whatever she judged to be in its best interest. She was ten years older than me, had been at school when the Second World War began, at Penrhos in Colwyn Bay, the same school that Cathy went to, and then had moved with the school when it was evacuated to Chatsworth House, the Derbyshire home of the Dukes of Devonshire. By the end of the war she was the signals officer of 1st Airborne Division and afterwards married an Eighth Army officer who eventually retired as General Cowley to live in the Old Post Office in Nuthurst, near Horsham.

I was fortunate to have her as Chairman of the Collyer's Governing Body throughout the next fifteen years until I retired. She was quick-witted and efficient and was particularly good at conducting a meeting. If there were thirty items on the agenda of a meeting to be held at Mercers' Hall in the City of London starting at 11.00 a.m., she would start the meeting promptly at 11.00 and work through the agenda. I would have produced a number of notes for members of the Governing Body, asking one to propose item 7, for example, and another to second it. She, on reaching item 7, would look for the proposer and the seconder, avoid discussion if at all possible, get agreement and move on to item 8.

Of course discussion was sometimes necessary and inevitably there would sometimes be disagreements. The difference between her approach and mine was that I always went into the meeting knowing what I wanted the outcome to be of every item on the agenda, whereas she would take the feel of the meeting and would not waste time over something to which there was opposition. She never took a vote. Either there was agreement or she accepted that there was no agreement and moved on to the next item, always ensuring that the meeting ended promptly at 12.30 in time for sherry before lunch. As a system it usually worked pretty well.

Life in the college settled down to a regular routine. Our business, of course, was teaching and learning, so most of the while each day the teachers were engaged in teaching and the students, one hoped, were learning something of value. I taught a first year A level set each year, which kept me in touch with the normal work of my colleagues. I had to set work and mark it, even if on a smaller scale than any of them; I had to write reports at the right time and attend parents' evenings like any other member of staff. I instructed the office that when I was teaching I should only be disturbed in the most extreme of circumstances.

Some changes to the normal running of the college were made early on. We soon moved from having prefects, something which still survived from grammar school days, to having elected tutor group representatives, who between them formed the College Council and elected their own Chairman. At a very early stage I made it clear to the staff that the timetable was to be seen as prescriptive. They were expected to be with the group they were due to teach throughout the prescribed time and in the place designated on the timetable. A change could only be made with my authorisation.

I also insisted that the culture of encouraging students by unrealistic predictions of success should be replaced by honest assessments of their work, accompanied by kindly guidance about how to do it better. It was perfectly proper to tell a student in the middle of the first year that his or her work was not yet up to even a bare pass standard at A level, so long as that was accompanied by an explanation about what needed doing to improve and an assurance that

481

that was possible. This was viewed with scepticism and even dis-
belief by some, but gradually everyone got used to it.

Meanwhile there was some discussion among the staff about
when was the best time for us to write reports on the students. I
invited comments, read them with care and then at a staff meeting
suggested a possible solution. It included the proposal that reports
on the work of students in their second A level year should be
after their trial examinations – what in many schools are called
'Mocks.' 'Are you intending, Principal, to impose trial examinations on us without any consultation?' was the immediate
response.

I was taken aback. It had never occurred to me that there was any
sixth form in the country which did not give its students a trial run
at taking A level, and I said so. The resentment was clear. It was,
I was told, a matter which each department dealt with in its own
way. So I said I would meet with all the heads of department to
discuss it. I had a number of private conversations, some very
useful, about the real practical difficulties which arose from the
size and use of the various rooms we would need to use, and eventually there was a meeting of all the heads of department. By then
most agreed with what now looked inevitable. A few accepted the
change grudgingly.

We needed to make a number of improvements to the buildings.
The new classroom block had been built in accordance with an
architectural theory that one could maximize space by having no
corridors and instead anyone could walk through the classrooms,
even when in use, to get from one place to another. It was very
inconvenient, so we made use of the voluntary aided system to
change the configuration of the building, creating corridors to suit
our convenience.

The internal appearance of the buildings was transformed. James
King, the relatively new Head of Chemistry, set an example
by coming in during the holidays and repainting his laboratory.

The Chairman of Governors, Rosemary Cowley, found a few thousand pounds from the Collyer Endowment managed by the Trustees to re-furbish and re-furnish the Staff Common Room. Then, after the next Governors' Meeting, all the governors went upstairs to look at how effectively the money had been spent. Finding the room empty, one of them asked where all the staff were, and I was pleased to be able to reply, 'Teaching.'

Some governors complained that my own room looked run down and unbecoming for a college principal, with a large water stain on one of the walls, the broken remains of a nineteenth century dada rail, and the carpeting worn and torn. I said I was not prepared to have it re-decorated until the rest of the college had been tackled. But when at last it was done, I had it done well and in keeping with the age of the building, which dated from 1893. The fireplace was opened up to show the Victorian tiles, the 1930s cladding was removed from the door, and the room was redecorated with William Morris wallpaper, while at the same time it was re-furnished with a new desk and chair, book shelves and a couple of comfortable armchairs.

The problems arising from the interrelationships between the Governing Body, the Trustees of the Collyer Foundation, the Mercers' Company and the West Sussex Education Authority were by no means clear to me during my early years at Collyer's. What was clear was that the responsibility of the Trustees for making use of the voluntary aided system to look after the buildings had been seriously neglected, and that was because many of them were used to independent schools but had no idea of, and had never taken the trouble to find out, how the 'voluntary aided' system worked.

Although I had found a way of dealing with relatively small-scale repair and maintenance jobs and even a way to make minor improvements costing no more than £500, anything on a larger scale, which might be needed as the college increased in size, ran into obstacles. After the staff and governors had considered what was desirable, after plans had been drawn up and the Governing

Body had agreed them, the Trustees would say that the time was not right, though with no explanation of why the time was never right, leaving one with the suspicion that the Mercers' Company was so occupied with building works related to its other schools that it could not concern itself, at least for the moment, with the affairs of Collyer's. Sadly the whole system was altered before they learnt how to operate it effectively.

Within a year or so of arriving I was delegating large aspects of the running of the college to the four other members of the Senior Management Team. Celia Jarratt (CJ), one of the two Vice-Principals, looked after buildings and equipment; Peter Crees (PC), the other Vice-Principal, who took over in 1984 from Roland Soper, looked after personnel matters; Ray Smith (RAS), one of the two Senior Teachers, presided over the administration; and Steve Gilham (SRG), the other Senior Teacher, dealt with policies and planning. For convenience the affairs of the college could be divided into People and Paper, Thoughts and Things. Anyone with an issue which needed a decision from a senior member of staff, or who wanted to recommend some change, could decide who to go to so long as they remembered People (PC), Paper (RAS), Thoughts (SRG) and Things (CJ).

On many day to day matters the senior members of staff made their own decisions, though I liked them to tell me about anything of significance. We met regularly once a week to decide matters of policy in a Senior Management Team Meeting, and often those decisions were on matters we had discussed informally with each other during the week. But it was a firm principle that that the final decision on any matter of policy was made only at an SMT meeting, whose minutes recorded the decisions and were then published. I always wrote the minutes myself, and I recorded only the decisions – not the discussion leading up to them. Most items in the minutes began with the formula, 'It was agreed that....' Where we did not agree, they were recorded with the opening formula, 'The Principal decided that....' But I preferred to avoid that wherever possible and tried to adopt policies on which we could all agree.

*In my room at Collyer's in the 1990s and in one of
the livery halls of the City of London, just before
making an after dinner speech.*

At an early stage we settled on the practice of looking critically at
everything we did to see how to improve it. The admissions procedure, report writing, parents' evenings, the Founder's Day
Service, anything and everything could be viewed critically with a
view to improving it. Two American scholars writing on management theory had suggested a cycle which began with doing something, went on to reflecting on how it went, then consulting on
how to do it better, deciding what to do next, implementing the
decision, 'institutionalising' the decision, and finally evaluating
how things had gone. I decided that the way to turn the theory
into practice was that when reflecting, we should seek and
welcome criticism; when consulting, we should welcome advice;
when deciding what to do next, we should take responsibility;
when implementing the decision, we should expect to delegate to

others; and we should seek to 'institutionalise' whatever had been decided by checking on progress and encouraging those involved. The final stage, evaluation, should come as the process went full circle and was starting again.

This was set out in a college policy on how to improve things, with the various stages both listed and in diagrammatic form in a circle. The policy ended with the words: 'The various stages of this process will often overlap. That's alright. What is important is to be aware of the need for the process, apply it in an appropriate form to whatever we do, and keep it moving.' It proved to be a valuable device, keeping us alert to the continuing need to seek to improve things.

A few years after I went to Collyer's the West Sussex Education Authority decided that it was desirable for each of its schools (and colleges) to have a Development Plan. Development Plans became fashionable in the 1980s, and, like many such fashionable ideas, they had both merits and demerits. The merits could be seen in situations where a clear decision had been made and someone had to produce a plan for implementing the decision. Ideally the plan should say what needed to be done, who was going to do it, by when, and who was responsible for ensuring that it happened. The demerits could be seen in circumstances in which they produced aspiration rather than achievement, bureaucracy rather than creativity, and, worst of all, inflexibility rather than that openness of mind which is so often a pre-requisite for progress. Each of the faults was exemplified in Stalin's Five Year Plans, which were not a model to emulate. But centralised planning is frequently attractive to those at the centre of human organisations because it gives the illusion that everything can be controlled from the centre.

The alternative is to have a clear view of what one is aiming to achieve and a system for improving things. In the case of Collyer's our starting point was the assumption that the college existed to provide those who lived in the Horsham area with suitable post-16 courses and with the experience of success. The needs of the students were what should determine the curriculum, the curriculum should determine what staffing and accommodation were desirable, and the development of the college should be a matter of seeking to adjust the curriculum, the staffing and the buildings to the changing needs of the students. But of course the needs of the students were liable to vary from person to person and from year to year, so we always needed to retain a measure of flexibility so that our adjustments of the curriculum, the staffing and the buildings would be appropriate for achieving our aim.

To do that I believed it was desirable to engage the whole staff in what I thought of as piecemeal educational engineering, by which present policy and practice could always be modified. The best laid plans of senior members of staff would always be mutable. This did not involve an abdication of leadership by anyone in a position of authority, but it did involve a particular view of how leadership should be exercised. We needed, I suggested, a communal determination to go on planning the development of the college in whatever way seemed appropriate, always remembering the words of the old song which was revived by *The Fun Boy Three* when they got together with *Bananarama* in the early 1980s: "It's not what you do. It's the way that you do it."

It was also in those years, with Margaret Thatcher as prime minister, that there came to be a persistent emphasis on 'management', as if efficient management was the solution to all problems. So, with just a touch of tongue in cheek, I established three management principles to be applied at all levels in the college. One was *Ringi-sho*, a Japanese idea that, in a world in which it was fashionable to plan, implement, and then evaluate before starting again, one could get ahead of the competition by starting each stage before completing the previous one. The next was *Pareto Optimality*, which takes its name from the perceptive observation of the Italian economist, Luigi Pareto, that 80% of the evidence is enough to inform effective planning; time spent getting the last 20% would be better spent getting on with the planning. The final and most important of my three management principles I called *MMM*, which stood for *Medieval Monastic Management* and was based on the advice which St. Bernard of Clairvaux was reputed to have given in the twelfth century on how to be a good abbot: *Notice everything; correct a little; cherish the brethren.* My view was (and is) that no management theory of the twentieth century has ever bettered that. But it is easier to preach the ideal than to achieve it.

64. Settling Down.

Gradually we settled down to a regular routine of work. Towards the end of the 1980s a member of the Modern Languages Department, Leslie Gilchrist, who had studied Russian and French at university, suggested that we should provide a GCSE Russian course as an optional element in the programme of those students who were clearly going to get good grades at A level. The General Certificate of Secondary Education had recently replaced O level, and when the Curriculum Committee investigated the possibilities, they found a course in *Russian Studies* which led to a GCSE examination with two elements: unseen translation from Russian into English and Russian History.

Once it had been recommended and I had agreed to it, the Head of History was asked who would teach the History element. 'Well,' he was reputed to have said, 'He approved it, so he can teach it.' So after some thirty years of regularly teaching at least some A level History, I found myself instead teaching the History element of a GCSE Russian Studies course. We had five periods a week for the one year course and decided that three of them would be spent on Russian language and the other two on History. I already knew the occasional Russian phrase in its transliterated form, such as *hozhdenia v narod* ('the movement to the people'), but I realised that the students I would be teaching would learn the Cyrillic alphabet, of which I knew nothing, so I thought I would go along to Leslie's classes at the start of the course and at least learn the alphabet.

I found it fascinating. Leslie told me later that she was the daughter of a German-Jewish mother who had come to England as a child in the *Kindertransport* of 1939, been brought up by a Scottish family, and had put her German past behind her so effectively that Leslie only discovered her origins after her mother's

489

death. She and I shared the five periods. For three of them I sat in class with the students learning Russian, and then for two periods I turned myself back into a teacher and taught them Russian history. In the middle of the year Ray Smith, who was in charge of examination entries, asked me if he should include me as one of the candidates. 'Oh no!' I said, 'Don't do that.' But a couple of months later he said to me, 'By the way, I did enter you for GCSE Russian Studies.' So I decided I had better put in some hard work in order not to disgrace myself in the examination.

One element in the Russian History part of the examination was a piece of course work of one's own choosing. I decided to write something on *The Siege of Tsaritsyn* in the Russian Civil War of 1918-21. Tsaritsyn was the town which was later called Stalingrad to commemorate the part played by Stalin as the Bolshevik commissar sent there by Lenin during the Civil War to take responsibility for its defence, and which, since Stalin's posthumous fall from grace, has been called Volgograd. It was about forty years since I had taken School Certificate, the precursor of O level and GCSE, and about thirty years since I had come down from Oxford with a degree in History. Since then I had regularly taught History, so I ought to have been able to produce a respectable piece of coursework. Paul Smith, the Head of History, had to mark it and sent it off with the other scripts for moderation. Later he told me that he had given it 29 out of 30, but it had come back from the moderator with the mark moved up to 30. It was, to the best of my belief, the only time in my life that I ever got full marks in an examination paper.

Later, with a grade A in GCSE Russian Studies, I found myself the only member of staff with School Certificate and Higher Certificate (no-one else was old enough) and the only one with a GCSE qualification (no-one else was young enough!), and at the same time the only one with no O level or A level passes.

At the end of that year Leslie Gilchrist left, so if the *Russian Studies* course was to continue I was the only person available to

490

teach it. I found it a remarkably enjoyable experience. Having only just done the course, I knew what the difficulties were. I got through the early stages with a very bright group of students and then explained to them how difficult it is to get one's mind round the Russian past tense. Each Russian verb has only one past tense, it does not have any first, second or third person endings, either in the singular or the plural, but instead has a masculine, feminine, neuter or plural ending, and you have to decide from the context what English tense to use when translating it. 'I would have thought, Principal', said Meredith White, a clever girl on her way to Oxford, 'that that makes it rather simple.' She was right, of course, but it is still something which most English speakers find difficult to grasp. Sadly we were one of very few schools or colleges entering candidates for the *Russian Studies* course, and shortly afterwards it was cancelled.

Just because we developed our own ways of doing things did not mean that we were free from intervention from the local authority, and I was expected not only to have a Development Plan but also to make explicit the standards required of the staff. While I believed that example and occasional personal intervention were generally more useful than rules, I nevertheless set out five points which covered more or less everything I expected: set high standards for oneself; expect high standards of the students; set them a good example; when giving guidance to anyone, do it politely but firmly; respond to guidance positively and co- operatively.

We were also expected to have a policy for everything. I decided that every policy must be on one side of A4 paper, should indicate its aim, or aims, and prescribe the method for achieving it. We developed a file of policies and occasionally I wrote one myself. The college policy on smoking, long before smoking in public buildings became illegal, is typical. It had three aims: to discourage students from smoking at all; to ensure that they did not smoke anywhere in or in the vicinity of the college; and to encourage them to grasp the distinction between public and private behaviour.

The methods for achieving those aims were similarly threefold. Members of staff were expected to discourage students from smoking at all, but needed to recognise that we were unlikely to provide them with much new information and should avoid imposing high-minded advice to a point at which it was boringly repetitive. Achieving the second aim, of ensuring a pleasant, smoke-free and litter-free environment, was an altogether different matter. That was to be achieved by effective supervision, by the scrupulous recording of any breaches of the regulations and by the judicious use of progressively increased sanctions. The supervision had to be arranged by the Vice-Principal and the Senior Tutors. As for the third aim, I believed that the smoking issue could be useful for encouraging in our students an understanding of that distinction between private and public behaviour which is an essential ingredient of a happy and healthy society.

A pleasant smoke-free, litter-free environment mattered to our neighbours as well, and if any of our students stood around smoking in neighbouring roads, our neighbours were liable to telephone the college, and then someone would need to go out to deal with the offenders. One day a telephone call was put through to me from a resident of Angus Close, a road abutting the back of the college, saying that four students were making a nuisance of themselves, sitting on the pavement and smoking. I went round there immediately and found four young men in their teens who had no connection of any sort with the college.

As I approached, wearing my academic gown, they looked wary and suspicious. I explained about the telephone call, said I recognised that I had no authority over them, but pointed out that I tended to be blamed if it was thought that my students were smoking in the area, so I would be grateful if they could move somewhere else. They explained that three of them were unemployed (the other had a job as a cleaner at the local police station), and one, who was wearing a tee-shirt with the slogan *FUCK RACISM*, cut-off knee-length jeans, boots without laces, and rings in both ears and one nostril, told me that they were fed up with having nothing to do. We chatted for a minute or two about the nation-wide problem of unemployment, I said I had to be getting back, and they agreed to move on somewhere else.

The next day one of the office staff rang through to say that a rather strange young man was in Reception asking to see me. I told them to send him up and went out to meet him. It was the one who had spoken about being fed-up with nothing to do, rather more soberly dressed than the previous day but still with rings in his nose and ears. I asked him in, sat him in an armchair and asked what I could do for him. 'Can I come to your college?' he asked. 'I don't see why not', I replied. 'What qualifications have you got?' 'I haven't got any. Does that matter?' 'Not so long as you want to get some.'

Between us we worked out an appropriate course. He needed to get GCSE English and I assured him that he could do that if he wanted to. He insisted that he could not possibly do Maths and we settled on a basic Numeracy course. He also agreed to do the college's computer literacy course and opted for GCSE Technology and one other GCSE subject. He accepted that he would have to remove the rings from his nose and ears – at least during the college day.

I saw him the following summer when he collected his results. He had passed everything, and clearly what delighted him most was that he had got a Distinction in the Numeracy course. It delighted me too. I felt the same sort of sense of satisfaction that I had felt in the past when one of my pupils got an Oxbridge scholarship.

We had a meeting of all the teaching staff each week – for an hour after the end of the college day on Mondays. I always insisted that it was not a forum within which decisions would be taken, but an opportunity for senior members of staff to explain policy to their colleagues and for other members of staff to air their opinions. It was never entirely successful. Some members of staff wanted 'full, frank and open discussion' of more or less everything, some saw it as an opportunity to challenge the decisions made by the senior staff, and almost everyone wanted the meeting to last no longer than an hour. Those aims were incompatible, and over sixteen years I never felt that I got it right. I tried getting other members of the Senior Management Team to chair the meetings, but that was not obviously any more successful.

Once, a father brought his son to see me just after the boy had been arrested by the police. The boy's elder brother, on embarkation leave at the time of the First Gulf War in 1990, had persuaded him to join in raiding a bank in Crawley. They walked in with imitation weapons, got the bank staff to fill a holdall with money, and walked home. The next day the police called at their house and arrested them. Their father wondered if I would allow his foolish (rather than vicious) younger son to complete the course he was doing at Collyer's. I had no hesitation in agreeing and stressed to the boy that it was important that he should do as well as possible, because once he had completed the term of Borstal training which would be the necessary consequence of his crime, he would need some qualifications.

It was shortly after I had expelled a boy for the possession of illegal drugs, which a teacher of Sociology thought an excessive punishment, especially as the offence was committed out of college time at a week-end 'rave', after which the boy was arrested by the police. In a staff meeting the Sociology teacher wanted to know how I could justify allowing a bank robber to remain at the college, while expelling someone for what he saw as a less serious offence. The answer was that I was responsible for the welfare of all the students and judged anyone involved in the use and selling of illegal drugs, even outside the college, to be a potential danger to the other students, while I did not believe that there was any danger of the bank robber forming a Hole-in-the-Wall gang of our students to go round robbing banks. How most members of staff felt I do not know.

There were inevitably minor problems arising from local authority control. If they decided to upgrade all the asphalt playing fields in

West Sussex, it could be difficult to get agreement that our share of the funding should be used on rose bushes and shrubs instead. If all head teachers in West Sussex were required to inform their governors about new arrangements for paying for milk at morning break, it could be difficult keeping a straight face when doing so.

But in the late 1980s a new system of delegated funding was introduced, whereby the local authority handed over the funding of each secondary school to the head and the Governing Body. It was a valuable reform. As a general principle a head could deploy that funding in whatever way seemed best, so long as the budget was approved by the Governing Body, and could choose when to buy any services still offered by the local authority. The prospects for the future seemed good.

It was, of course, still necessary for the local authority to determine what level of resources to allocate to any particular school or college, and the level of funding varied from one year group to another, so every year each school completed what was called *Form 7 Schools*, giving an account of the number of pupils in each form in the school, and the names of the pupils. With that information the local authority could calculate the appropriate level of funding, and it was the responsibility of each head teacher to check all the information and confirm its accuracy before signing off the form.

One day I had a telephone call from John Cobbett to see what my reaction was to his discovery that one of the heads in the area, someone much revered and respected for running a good school, had apparently for years been falsifying *Form 7 Schools* by inventing a whole extra class of non-existent pupils, which had been working its way through the school, year by year. What, he asked, was my opinion of how to deal with the problem?

My response was that the head must go at the end of term, which fortunately was not far off, an early announcement needed to be made that it was for 'personal reasons', and arrangements needed to be made for a good send-off. That would then be followed by some years with no income before reaching retirement age and then a pension reduced by the reduction in years of service. The alternative would be to have the whole thing out in the open, with questions asked about how the local authority could have allowed such a thing to happen. The answer to that, of course, was that it had assumed, mistakenly as it turned out, that it was possible to rely on the honesty of all secondary head teachers. John Cobbett's view was the same as mine, but he had wanted to try it on someone else to see what response he got.

The following term we were both at a meeting at which the Director of Education, Dick Bunker, explained to all the secondary heads of West Sussex new arrangements for ensuring the accuracy of *Form 7 Schools*, with class teachers needing to guarantee the accuracy of the section about their own class. There was some indignation that this seemed to suggest that head teachers could not be trusted, but most accepted the point that, although of course their honesty was unquestioned, it was still worth having a system which demonstrably ensured that mistakes would not happen.

Sadly Collyer's was shortly afterwards removed from the authority of the West Sussex Education Authority, when in 1992 the government created the Further Education Funding Council and moved us into its orbit. John Cobbett, whose advice over many years as a local authority officer had been invaluable, was no longer available in that capacity, so instead he was recruited to be a member of the Governing Body.

The FEFC Years
(1992–2000)

65. Competition and Bureaucracy

◇◇

Back in 1976, when I was first the headmaster of King George V School, my job description indicated that I was responsible for the curriculum and for the conduct and discipline of the staff and pupils. That was it. Much was assumed. In those days it did not seem necessary to specify every aspect of a head teacher's responsibilities, nor the hours when it was necessary to be available for work. The job needed doing and one was appointed to get on and do it.

There was some scope for discussion of what was meant by 'the curriculum' and about what it should be. By then I took it to be the totality of the learning experiences which we deliberately provided. We should, I believed, seek to pass on to our pupils, or students, those ideas and skills which we judged to be of value. We should assist them to develop their potential for good - academic, personal and social. We should help them broaden their understanding, and at the same time we should guide them towards acquiring those qualifications which would enable them to progress further. If we taught them about Marxism or Christianity, that should not be with the intention of turning them into Marxists or Christians, but rather should be seen as introducing them to an aspect of our cultural inheritance which we believed was worth thinking about.

At the same time I took the view that activities which in many schools were described as 'out-of-school activities', or as 'extra-curricular activities', a Chess Club, for example, or a Debating Society or Table Tennis Club, together with football and netball, should be seen as part of the curriculum, or else we should not be providing them, and involvement of members of staff in such activities should be taken into account by head teachers when calculating their work load.

During the years in which I had been a schoolmaster there had been a number of public controversies about the nature of the sixth form curriculum. Should it aim to provide high quality specialised education or try to ensure a broad and balanced education for all? Should the emphasis be on academic education or on vocational training and the acquisition of skills? Should we be more concerned with educating our students or with ensuring that they were provided with useful and appropriate qualifications?

I had consistently taken the view that, although it was healthy to ask questions of this sort, the best answer to each of them was usually much the same as that given by Winnie-the-Pooh, wisest of bears, when Rabbit asked him if he would like honey or condensed milk with his bread. 'Both', Pooh had said, and then, so as not to seem greedy, he added, 'But don't bother about the bread, please.' That is, there could be elements of specialisation within a broad curriculum; there was no good reason why 'academic' and 'vocational' should be seen as antitheses rather than as complementary; it should be possible to acquire useful qualifications in the context of high quality education; but it was also worth making sure that any unnecessary, stodgy stuff was cleared away.

By the time John Major took over from Margaret Thatcher as prime minister towards the end of 1990 the government was taking a greater interest than in the past in what should be provided for students over the age of sixteen, and in 1992 it set up the Further Education Funding Council with the proclaimed intention of driving up standards in technical education for 16 – 19 year olds and increasing the number of students taking part. With apparently neither thought nor planning, though perhaps in order to give some intellectual respectability to this new sector, it decided to include the sixth form colleges, a hundred and twenty of them, in the new sector, together with more than five hundred technical colleges. At the same it wanted to cut public expenditure and assumed that a reduction in funding would lead to greater efficiency and to successful colleges taking over less successful ones, in the manner of successful businesses taking over weaker ones.

Now that the colleges were no longer under the authority of a local education authority but instead were expected to run their own affairs independently, each was required to produce a Strategic Plan and 'share' it with the FEFC, now in grand new and expensive buildings in Coventry. I did what was required and provided them with a strategic plan set out in nine sections dealing with *Student Numbers, the Curriculum, Staffing, Premises, Resources and Equipment, Student Guidance, Quality Assurance, Financial Health and Stability*, and finally *Flexibility*.

The FEFC responded with a telephone call asking if two of their officers could come to see me to talk over our Strategic Plan. I said they were welcome, so they drove down from Coventry and sat down in armchairs in my study and were provided with coffee and chocolate biscuits. The William Morris wallpaper, the book-shelves full of books on medieval history, and a large reproduction of the Wilton Diptych were not what they were used to in the office of a senior manager in the FEFC sector, and it turned out that what concerned them, or their masters in Coventry, was the inclusion of a section on *Flexibility* in my plan. With more than six hundred colleges in the sector, I was the only principal to have suggested a need for flexibility. It was very suspicious. Did I have a separate secret plan? Was the plan I had sent them intended to deceive? Was I trying to cover myself against the time when I launched my secret plan by including the section on *Flexibility*?

No, of course not. The plan I had sent them was an entirely straightforward account of how I intended the college to proceed. But 'the best-laid schemes o' mice an' men gang aft agley' and we needed to be prepared to cope with changes in government policy, changes in the level of funding, and so on. Circumstances can change. At some point we might need some tactical flexibility to achieve our strategic objectives. In my attitude to this I had been influenced many years earlier by reading General Bill Slim's book, *Defeat into Victory*, about the war in Burma. Towards the end of 1944, commanding 14th Army, he had planned to attack the Japanese forces and then cross the Irrawaddy River. But a new

Japanese commander decided to fight behind rather than in front of the Irrawaddy. So, wrote Slim, 'It was time for me to use a little of that flexibility of mind that I had so often urged on my subordinates.' A bit of flexibility of mind was, it seemed to me, similarly desirable in running a sixth form college in the 1990s, even though the problems facing me were on a relatively trivial scale.

We were planning to increase our student numbers, principally by having a reputation for good teaching and attracting a larger intake of A level students each year. But I was aware that large predatory technical colleges had their own strategies for expansion. Because of the way the FEFC's funding 'methodology' worked it could be in their interest to take over a smaller and financially vulnerable college, and they were putting out feelers to see where they might be able to strike. I suggested to the FEFC officers that they look out of the bay window of my study. Up the road to the left was the Business Studies annexe of Crawley Technical College, while to the right was the Art annexe of Northbrook, the technical college in Worthing.

It was still early days in the competitive struggle for survival which the government saw as an effective device for driving up standards. But eventually Crawley Technical College managed to swallow up Haywards Heath Sixth Form College, and Northbrook Technical College, with its back to the sea in Worthing, with Brighton on its eastern flank and Chichester on its western flank, made a vigorous bid to expand north and establish itself as a provider of A levels in Horsham. Although it failed and in the event did not get a single A level student in Horsham, the intention and the threat were real enough.

As it happens, at the time of this visit from officers of the FEFC, we were having some drainage work done on the college grounds, so I invited them to look at the trenches and told them that, while our Strategic Plan was precisely as I had set it out, our immediate tactical response to the threat from either side of us was to dig in and hold the line against what looked like a pincer movement encouraged by the FEFC's high command. They were not sure how far I was joking and how far I was serious. Surely we were not thinking in terms of having cadets of the Collyer's CCF manning the trenches! But I was entirely serious that we intended to survive.

Those running the FEFC continued to give the impression of being suspicious of Collyer's and early in 1996 that suspicion was given expression in a vigorous bout of auditing and inspection. They had required us to write strategic plans, accommodation strategies, three year financial forecasts, self-assessment reviews and so on. They required us to appoint internal and external auditors and meanwhile they set up their own audit department to audit our auditors. Everything needed to be evidenced, approved, monitored, validated, accredited, checked, inspected and audited to the point at which a straight-forward description of the various visitors to the college over a two month period, from the 8th January until 7th March, looks like material for comedy.

They checked what were called our 'achievement units' and audited our operation of Adult Education, our financial systems and the provision of management information. They inspected all eight of our curriculum areas and had external auditors 'validate' our ISRs, or Individual Student Records. Then an FEFC auditor and an FEFC audit manager audited the work of our auditors and checked on our management systems and an FEFC accountant accompanied by a finance officer looked at our three-year financial forecast and considered the financial health of the college. They audited our financial relationship with the local Training and Enterprise Council, Sussex Enterprise, and finally their inspectors looked at the full range of what were called the cross-curricular areas of the college.

Although we came out of it with a succession of reports that everything was in order and with high grades for almost everything that was graded, one could not help but get the impression that someone at the top was looking for trouble and expecting, even hoping, to find it. The extent and variety of paperwork required was extraordinary, the cost both in money and time ludicrous, and I came to believe that, if the extent of over-auditing and over-inspecting in the sector were generally known, it would be seen as a national scandal. What is more, things were getting worse, because the demand to audit everything was driving up the cost of auditors while our funding was being driven down.

If the extent of auditing by the FEFC was ludicrous, their bureaucracy sometimes seemed even worse, and one day I had a letter from their Head of Communications, which read like this:

'Dear Colleague,

We have found an error in the 'mode of attendance' column of table 2 of the press release on student numbers in the sector dated 23 January 1996. I am therefore enclosing an amended copy of the table.

I should be grateful if you would draw this amendment to the notice of any colleagues who may have received copies of the original release. Please accept my apologies for the error.'

So I replied as follows in language scrupulously copied from the FEFC:

'Dear Head of Communications,

I note that you have found an error in the 'mode of attendance' column of table 2 of the press release on student numbers in the sector dated 23rd January 1996 and acknowledge receipt of the amended copy of the table. I have drawn this amendment to the notice of those colleagues who had received copies of the original release.

The members of my Senior Management Team have jointly undertaken a Risk Analysis, considered the potential impact of the error on our ISR and DLE in the light of the February update and our Three-year Financial Forecast and our Self-Assessment Report.

They have reviewed our Strategic Plan and recommended modifications to our Operating Statement involving putting in place more robust performance indicators to ensure transparency in our Sensitivity Analysis.

I should now be glad to have your assurance that appropriate steps have been taken to ensure that such errors will not occur in future. You should alert the Research and Statistics Support Desk about the timetable of your Recovery Plan, and I should be glad if you would share with me your Action Plan and the Quality Assurance Procedures for ensuring recovery by 1st April.

Your apologies for the error in the press release dated 23rd January 1996 are accepted'.

To her credit the Head of Communications at the FEFC telephoned to say that she had enjoyed my reply and to ask if she could reproduce it in the FEFC's in-house staff newsletter. Fame at last!

66. Trustees and Governors

Collyer's was unusual in the Further Education Funding Council sector in that it was a former voluntary aided grammar school, which was now 'designated' as suitable for funding by the FEFC. Its Trustees owned the land and buildings but had no responsibility for running the college, while the Governors were responsible for governance but did not own the land or the buildings. I argued the case for combining the two bodies, but was told that it was unnecessary. So long as their responsibilities were set out clearly, any problems should be easily resolved. The Trustees held the land, buildings and any other assets in trust and were expected to maintain, develop, repair and insure them; the Governing Body was responsible for their effective and efficient use by the principal and his staff. Six of the nine Trustees were appointed by the Mercers' Company, which also appointed six of the nine Foundation Governors, and all except two of the Trustees were also members of the Governing Body. The Governors and the Trustees should have been able to talk to each other and reach agreement on virtually any issue. What was extraordinary was the extent to which they failed to do so.

It was clear that some sort of agreement between them was needed, but it was less clear what sort of agreement it should be. The legal position was uncertain. The Department of Education did not distinguish between trustees and governors and saw the decisions of one as binding the other. The FEFC, on the other hand, took the view that they were distinct and believed that it was necessary to have a lease agreement between them. Both were concerned lest the trustees should take and use public money but then decide to change their college into something quite different. Things had apparently gone badly wrong in two designated colleges, several governors had been removed and a report recommended having a 'defined procedure for the closure of designated colleges.'

Nearly three months later, at the FEFC conference at Birmingham in February 1995, I met Tim Boswell, then the Minister for Further and Higher Education. When he discovered which college I came from he said, 'Ah! You're one of these designated colleges we're going to have a close look at.' 'Yes', I answered, 'but the Scheme of Management for the Trustees of the Collyer Endowment requires the land and buildings to be used for the general educational purposes of the college within the FEFC sector.' 'Good!', he said, 'I see you've got the point.'

It was less clear that our Trustees understood the point, or that they realised the immediate damage to the college's financial position as a direct consequence of our being moved to the FEFC sector. They saw their responsibility as being above all to look after the Collyer Endowment, which was valued at about £300,000 in the early 1990s. That meant that its real worth had been about two million pounds, because under the voluntary aided arrangements the Trustees only had to pay 15% of the cost of any new building. An immediate effect of the move to the new sector was the loss of all the money which would have been the government's 85% contribution to new buildings. Sadly the time had never been quite right to get on with any significant building work before the government altered the system.

Because the Trustees had a limited sense of their responsibilities I had frequently found that I needed to act on their behalf, though without knowing anything of their intentions, without knowing when or where they met or what they discussed, and without ever seeing a copy of their agenda or their minutes. Once we were in the new sector it seemed to me that they needed to concentrate their attention on future capital works, so I found ways of cutting their regular annual expenditure on anything else to an annual grant of £5,000 to the Governors' Imprest Account– an account which I found very convenient for occasional expenses, and which another college principal understandably described as a slush fund. In each year that saved them £37,000, which was potentially valuable for future capital works. It seemed a useful first step towards a co-operative approach.

Within the college we developed an Accommodation Strategy which won the approval of the Governing Body, but the Governors then had to refer the plans to the Trustees. The Trustees in turn were guided by the Clerk to the Mercers' Company, who was used to dealing with independent schools, was unused to being accountable for public money, and spoke of the funds of the Collyer Endowment as if they were part of the munificence of the Mercers' Company, some of which it might donate if the time was right. So in the two years after the college entered the FEFC sector there were numerous Trustees' and Governors' meetings and various committee meetings, before at last agreement was reached on the Accommodation Strategy and on how it would be funded.

Then at the Governors' Meeting at Mercers' Hall in March 1995, just a month after I had met Tim Boswell and heard of the government's intention to have a close look at 'designated' colleges, one of the items on the agenda was the formal acceptance by the Governors of the mid-year update of the college's financial forecast – a complicated document which one could not reasonably expect them all to understand, but which required them to have a certain amount of trust in those of us who were working on their behalf.

One element in it was the funding of the Accommodation Strategy. The Governors had assured the Trustees that they would contribute £50,000 a year to the project for each of seven years, and I needed to budget for that. The Mercers' Company had undertaken to make at least two grants of £50,000 at specified times, though whether that was from the Collyer Endowment or from the Company itself was left unclear. They hoped, when the time was right, to make a third grant of another £50,000. The college accountant had produced a cashflow schedule, showing what was to be paid and when; the first £50,000 from the Governors had already been paid, and the Trustees had spent £44,000 of it on preliminary costs such as architects' fees.

Sadly on this occasion, and very unusually, Rosemary Cowley was unable to be there, so the chair was taken by the Vice-Chairman, a former Master of the Mercers' Company who was also the Chairman of the Collyer's Trustees. When we got to the item on the agenda about the financial forecasts the Master of the Mercers' Company for the year, also both a Trustee and a Governor, asked if the Clerk and the Treasurer of the Company could join the meeting. The acting Chairman agreed. They had produced their own very different funding schedule, in which they ignored the £44,000 already spent and made a number of changes in timings which had the effect of increasing the expenditure by the Governing Body in that financial year by an extra £94,000. It felt like an ambush, and they wanted the Governors to authorise these changes.

I explained that I could not hand over a further £94,000 of public money in the current financial year, and that the Governing Body could not responsibly authorise me to do so. The subsequent discussion was unpleasant. The Clerk to the Mercers' Company, as if speaking on behalf of the Trustees, questioned whether the Governing Body could be relied on to keep to its commitments. I said that of course it could and that the problem was the other way round. If the Governors had given in to the demand for an extra £94,000, they (and I) would subsequently have been criticised by the FEFC's auditors for financial mismanagement.

It was very uncomfortable. The demand for extra money was made without warning, with an implication of either incompetence or dishonesty or both, at a meeting and at a time when the Governing Body and I were guests of the Mercers' Company and our Chairman was away. The dispute was brought to a temporary conclusion by Roger Taylor, a Governor and Trustee who was also the Chief Executive of Sun Alliance, who proposed that further consideration of the financial forecast should be delegated to the Finance and General Purposes Committee of the Governing Body, who should have power to decide whether or not to approve it. By then it was time for lunch. None of the rest of the agenda could be dealt with and had to be put off for four months until the next meeting.

The problem was not one of incompetence in managing financial matters at Mercers' Hall. It was one of arrogance. They were used to dealing with the affairs of independent schools which were financially dependent on them, and they expected to be able to shift things around to suit their own convenience. They did not expect anyone to raise the issue of accountability for public money. Similarly, when our auditors indicated the need for a lease agreement between the Trustees and the Governing Body, the Clerk to the Mercers' Company dismissed the idea as 'unnecessary, misconceived and impracticable.' But he had no other solution to how to find a legally acceptable expression of the relationship.

He was used to deploying the vast financial resources of the Company, and he was used to telling the Court of Assistants, which was the governing body of the Company, what decisions it should take. He did not like to be crossed. In May, when the annual cheque for £5,000 from the Collyer Endowment to the Governors' Imprest Account did not arrive, the college bursar telephoned a finance officer at Mercers' Hall, who apologised and said he would get it to him as soon as possible. Later he rang back to say that the Clerk had told him not to pay it. I wrote to ask why, and the eventual explanation from an administrative officer at Mercers' Hall was that the Clerk felt that the payment was 'not appropriate now that Collyer's has changed status.' He had made the decision without authorisation, it was directly contrary to an arrangement agreed by the Trustees, and he had done it without telling us. It gave the impression of pique, but since the Trustees were too much in awe of the Clerk to tell him to meet their commitments, I had to budget for the matters it was spent on out of our recurrent funding from the FEFC.

Not only was the Clerk annoyed. The Master of the Company was as well. He did not like the Company's power to arrange things being challenged by a pedagogue referring to the authority of some government quango. I had the impression that the Master would have liked to have been able to get rid of me ('When is he due to retire?' he was quoted as saying), but in June I wrote a detailed and confidential account for the Governors and the Trustees of Collyer's of all that had gone wrong in the couple of years after we became a 'designated' college in April of 1993. It ran to forty-five pages plus four appendices, and it would have been immensely embarrassing to the Trustees and the Mercers' Company if it had been made public.

One other detail is worth recording. The Master suggested that the college's accommodation problems could all be solved by the adoption of a three session day. I then needed at short notice and at a time when much else needed to be done to produce a paper setting out what we were already doing about introducing a third session in the day to provide for adult education, while at the same time showing that it did not solve our accommodation problems. I recalled reading about how, when General Sir Alan Brooke and his staff were planning the invasion of Normandy in 1944, Winston Churchill had the bright idea of invading Portugal instead. For twenty-four hours Alan Brooke diverted all his resources to producing a case to show that it would not make sense to go through Portugal. It was time he could ill afford. In a very small way it felt analogous to that.

Towards the end of the report I suggested that the way the Trustees and the Clerk dealt with Collyer's needed to be changed, and I referred them to precepts laid down for the Egyptian Civil Service in the time of the Pharaohs and quoted by Sir Ernest Gowers in chapter 3 of his book *Plain Words*: '*Be courteous and tactful as well as honest and diligent. All your doings are publicly known, and must therefore be beyond complaint or criticism.*' They needed to consider how to exercise their powers in a way which would serve the college's best interests and also satisfy the requirement for public accountability. It was no doubt a difficult pill to swallow. I made a number of recommendations, all aimed at improving communications and ensuring clarity about who was authorised to decide what. It was a useful beginning and in later years things improved considerably - though probably most notably when the Clerk to the Mercers' Company and I both retired a few years later.

Rosemary Cowley, who, I believed, would never have allowed the fiasco at Mercers' Hall in March 1995 to have happened, understandably asked me why I had written the report without consulting her. The answer was that I knew that if I had consulted her, she would have felt obliged to tell me not to do it. I had not wanted to put either her or myself in that position.

67. *Quis inspectabit ipsos inspectores?*

◇◇

In nearly forty years as a schoolmaster, from 1957 until 1996, I had only twice met one of Her Majesty's Inspectors of Education. The first sat in on a lesson at Quintin School as I tried to explain the essentials of Marxism to an O level class before going on to teach about the Russian Revolution. He was flatteringly complimentary, describing it as a *tour de force*. The second came to Stowe, asked to see a copy of my departmental scheme of work, read it through, talked about it with me and then about broader curricular issues. Before he left he suggested that I should stay at Stowe for no more than another two or three years and then look for a headship. But at the time I had no intention of becoming a headmaster and in the event I stayed another seven or eight years.

The third inspector I met, a member of the FEFC Inspectorate rather than an HMI, came to Collyer's in 1995 to talk about a coming full inspection of the college. He began by asking me for the college's mission statement. I told him that the college had been founded for its scholars to say the *De Profundis* at the departing of the school each day for the soul of the founder, Richard Collyer, for that of his wife, Kateryn, and for all Christian souls. As it happens he was a Roman Catholic and saw the point, but he still wanted us to have a modern mission statement. Every college in the sector had to have one, he explained, so that we all knew what we were meant to be doing.

I drafted one, tried it out on the Senior Management Team, and eventually put it to the Governing Body: *The College of Richard Collyer exists to provide education for all those in the Horsham area who wish to continue their education beyond the years of compulsory schooling.* One governor suggested that we should add the word 'excellent': i.e. *provide excellent education...* I replied that that was implicit and that it would be mildly embarrassing to make it explicit. But most of the governors agreed with him. So that was what was settled on.

The inspector wanted to arrange for a couple of curricular areas to be inspected in the near future as a preliminary exercise before he and his colleagues inspected everything else and graded each area according to a five point scale. As it happens I had introduced a five point scale at King George V College twenty years earlier for assessing students' work and was now using it at Collyer's as well: 1 (outstanding); 2 (good); 3 (satisfactory); 4 (less than satisfactory); 5 (poor). The FEFC expressed it in more complicated language, but that was essentially what the grades amounted to.

We agreed to start with English and Mathematics, and the members of the English and Mathematics departments were all appropriately apprehensive until both were judged to be 'outstanding', at which point they were relieved and delighted, while the members of other departments were even more apprehensive, fearing that they would not do as well – all the more so since the number of 'outstanding' grades awarded throughout the sector was fewer than 10%. In the event every department was judged to be either 'outstanding' or 'good' and, whether that was a fair assessment or not, we had cause to be pleased. When the inspectors came to look at our 'cross-college provision', the one category which was only satisfactory was Quality Assurance. Rather peculiarly everything about the college was judged to be 'good' or 'outstanding' except the means by which we achieved it.

In June 1996, at a conference in Cambridge, the Chief Inspector spoke about Quality Assurance. He particularly wanted to make the point that there was very little correlation between student achievement and a college's funding. Colleges with low levels of funding sometimes produced good results, while the better funded sometimes did badly, so principals should not ascribe poor results to a lack of money. On the other hand, he claimed, there was a high correlation between student achievement and the grades awarded for cross-college issues such Quality Assurance. He spoke of a college which had raised its A level pass rate from 76% to 87% in two years by adopting a robust quality assurance system with students naming poor teachers and senior staff 'going in and in and in until they had got it right.' The suggestion was that if we could all adopt robust systems of that sort, student achievement would be ratcheted up so that England could once again compete in the real world with South Koreans and Malaysians.

He was making the fundamental mistake of assuming that correlation is the same thing as cause and effect, and there was a profound difference between my approach to education and that of the FEFC Inspectorate. The Chief Inspector was proclaiming the merit of a robust quality assurance system which would drive inadequate, indolent and untrustworthy teachers to do better. I believed that what was needed was to provide intelligent, highly motivated and reliable teachers with a structure which enabled them not only to teach well but also to monitor the progress of their students. The key to success, I believed, lay in caring about and concentrating on the individual student - not in devising systems for measuring mediocrity in order to ensure 'quality'. You do not fatten pigs by weighing them.

When I had gone to Collyer's in 1983 the A level pass rate had been only 71%. In the three years from 1984 to 1986 we moved it to 81%, and in the next three years, from 1987 to 1989, to over 90%. By 1996 it had been over 90% for over eight years. The statistics were a by-product of concern for each individual student. We guided them onto courses on which they stood a reasonable chance of success, while allowing a margin of error so that borderline candidates were not unreasonably deprived of an opportunity. We provided effective systems for monitoring progress. These included the grade record system on a scale of 1-5 for assessing students' work, joint reviews by tutor and student, internal examinations, parents' consultation evenings, absence slips and a system for following them up, a change of course procedure, a system for predicting A level grades, supervision arrangements, report slips on which any member of staff could report something to a student's tutor, and student record sheets.

None of this was of the least interest to the inspectorate. They did not look at the paperwork relating to these systems and they did not ask about it. They were not inspecting what we did. They were looking for something else which they did not find. That led to the problem that, while on the one hand they encountered high standards of teaching and learning, high levels of achievement, co-operative members of staff and well-behaved, hard-working students, on the other hand they did not find either the management or quality assurance systems favoured by the FEFC.

As it happens quality systems were fashionable at that time. They came from industry and were aimed at ensuring the reliable quality of bottles or door handles or widgets. The government seemed to assume that systems of that sort could be applied to educational institutions. Professor Ted Wragg of Exeter University, writing in the *Times Educational Supplement* in October 1994, pointed out how difficult it was to challenge this fashionable view of quality, with its emphasis on structures. 'If you do, then you run the risk of being accused of favouring the slipshod and the substandard.' So, since most of us are conformist, he suggested, we go along with it and set up quality assurance committees. 'As a result', he wrote, 'form takes precedence over content. I know of institutions that are bristling with quality assurance structures, that win medals and badges for them, but whose actual work is shoddy. There is an almost inverse relationship between the stridency with which institutions scream about *kwality* and the real quality of what goes on there. The top outfits are usually relaxed about it, and the naff ones keep telling you how much of it they have got.'

I took the view that the strength of the inspection system should lie in direct observation by the inspectors of lessons, meetings and other aspects of college life. They could look at something and then make a judgement on the merits and de-merits of what they saw. Their opinions, whether complimentary or critical, could then be helpful. But instead they had preconceived ideas about how a college should work, so instead of observing what we did and forming a judgement, they checked how far we conformed to the FEFC ideal.

At the June 1996 conference in Cambridge, after a talk from the Chief Inspector, I spoke about that problem, pointing out how the inspectors worked through a check-list to see if we had the documents and systems they expected, while taking little or no interest in seeing, still less understanding, what actually happened. The Chief Inspector, in the plain, blunt style characteristic of officers of the FEFC, replied that what I said was 'bunkum.' Principals, he suggested, often complain about grades because of hurt pride, and they ought to appreciate that the inspectors know what they are doing.

He had, whether deliberately or not, misunderstood what I was saying. I was not complaining about grades. On balance I thought that the inspectors had treated us generously. Nor was I complaining about the inspectors, who seemed to me to be mostly sensible and thoughtful people doing a good job in limited time and within the context of a defined system. I was criticising the system, which was too much like audit and too little like inspection, which should not have been a vast administrative exercise, with weeks to prepare the masses of paperwork they required to check on conformity, but rather should have required the inspectors to look at what was happening in the college and report on what was good and what was bad about what they had seen.

On health and safety matters, for example, the inspectors paid no attention to the sort of issues which would have concerned me, such as loose paving stones or insecure access to chemicals, but instead noted that the Health and Safety Committee reported to the Senior Management Team as a whole rather than specifically to me. On equal opportunities matters they had no interest in the fact that work had been done to accommodate a member of staff with multiple sclerosis by moving a Physics laboratory from the second floor to the ground floor to make wheelchair access easy. Instead they commented that the 'nature of existing buildings makes access to them difficult for users of wheelchairs', which was scarcely surprising since the college was built on a slope. Similarly, the appointment of a blind administrative assistant and the arrangements for her to use Braille were ignored, while they commented that there was 'no reference in the college's policy on equal opportunities to new appointments.' There was no pretence of inspecting what was done. It was quite simply an audit to check that our arrangements conformed to what the FEFC wanted.

A further problem was that the inspectorate operated on the principle that whatever you did, you always had to have systems for ensuring you did it better and for measuring the improvement. Two years earlier we had had a Further Maths set of ten students. They all completed the course, so the 'retention rate' was 100%. All ten got A grades in both Maths and Further Maths. I did not expect to see such results again. But for a measurable gain in performance I needed, for example, to find a larger number of further mathematicians and reduce teaching time in order to ensure cost effectiveness. What had been done had not been achieved by managers setting a target and requiring teachers to reach it. It had been achieved by the effective teaching of a particularly able group of students.

Judgements about quality, careful consideration of statistical evidence, and concentration on the learning needs of each individual student are all important. For certain practical purposes targets are useful as well. They have their proper place. But they should stay in their proper place. They are not a panacea. What was needed was an inspection system in which the inspectors concentrated on teaching and learning and on student achievement. Their reports needed to be shorter, setting out simply and clearly their opinions of what they saw, and they needed to open their minds to the possibility that high standards might be achieved by concentrating on the needs of students rather than on target-setting and on measuring everything.

Above all they needed to learn from good practice when they saw it, rather than seeking to clone every college into competent mediocrity. They needed to recognise that gentleness, diffidence and uncertainty can be valuable alternatives to robustness as routes to success, and that responsiveness at its best should be more a matter of responding to students' needs than their wishes. Teachers accumulate a variety of beliefs and attitudes during our lives, and we do not all have to believe the same things. For my own part I believed a number of things which were the opposite of the received wisdom at the FEFC: that when things went wrong it was more important to seek understanding than to look for someone to blame, that progress was more often achieved by co-operation than by competition, and that in educating the young one should emphasise the importance of obligations rather than rights.

In January 1996 the FEFC published a National Survey Report on colleges, and at a meeting of the seven sixth form college principals in Sussex a few days after its publication there was the same mixture of hilarity and cheerful solidarity in the face of a common enemy that I recalled as the reaction of adults to Nazi propaganda at the time of the Blitz. Sadly, the FEFC inspectorate was coming to be perceived as the thought police, and it was arguable that they themselves needed to be inspected. One could quite reasonably ask the question, 'Who will inspect the inspectors?'

68. *J'accuse*

◇◇◇◇◇◇◇◇◇◇◇◇◇◇◇◇◇◇◇◇◇◇◇◇◇◇◇

By 1997 I had publicly criticised the FEFC's excess of audit and bureaucracy and I had publicly criticised their inspection regime. Now it was time to criticise their so-called 'funding methodology', so in the spring of 1998 I wrote an article with the title *J'accuse*, borrowed from Emil Zola's famous article in Clemenceau's paper, *L'Aurore*, at the time of the Dreyfus scandal in nineteenth century France. I accused them of mismanaging the allocation of public money while at the same time operating a system which tended to encourage indolence among 16-19 year olds on a national scale. The article was first published in the college magazine *De Profundis*, which took its name from the opening words of the psalm which Richard Collyer wanted said at the departing of the school each day.

Later the article was printed separately and given a much wider circulation, with copies going to members of the Funding Council and to its officers, whose 'funding methodology' was, I suggested, so complicated that it hid both the large-scale misapplication of public funds and the financial pressure to have 16-19 year olds in England working for only half as many hours in the week as their contemporaries in Germany, France or Japan.

The bureaucrats who devised and operated the system were, I suggested, acting on behalf of an ideologically confused government which apparently could not see the paradox involved in what it was doing. On the one hand it claimed to want a free market in post-16 education, since in the manner of nineteenth century Liberals it saw the free market as the solution to all problems. On the other hand it wanted to be able to manipulate that market through a centralised bureaucracy, since in the manner of the commissars of the People's Republics of Eastern Europe it did not trust anyone – particularly teachers.

The complexities of the system were such that most members of the Funding Council and most of its officers probably did not understand the peculiar arrangements for which they were responsible, so if it was to be criticised effectively it was necessary to take a particular example, disentangle it from all the surrounding obfuscating complexities, show how what the FEFC actually did was quite different from what it claimed to be doing, and demonstrate how the particular example related to the operation as a whole.

I had written to the FEFC in June of 1997 explaining what was going wrong. For the purposes of the article I disguised the names of the colleges used as examples and also the name of the local authority involved, but all the information related to Collyer's and Haywards Heath, which, before the FEFC took over, were funded by the West Sussex local authority on the same basis, but over the next five years under the FEFC had increasingly different rates of funding until the discrepancy amounted to more than a quarter of a million pounds a year.

West Sussex had funded the two colleges at the same rate on the basis of the previous year's student numbers. Inevitably, and unavoidably, that meant that an increase in student numbers at Collyer's meant a temporary drop in the average level of funding per student. But the local authority always corrected that at the beginning of the next financial year in April, halfway through the academic year. At the same time a drop in student numbers at Haywards Heath necessarily meant that its average level of funding per student rose that year, and the local authority accepted that without requiring any reduction. In both cases the gain or loss only lasted a year, after which the colleges were back to the same base line, with the funding once again determined by the previous year's student numbers. It was a simple and sensible system with which we were all satisfied.

The FEFC proclaimed that it was a disgrace that levels of funding were so different from one local authority to another, and even within an authority, and they announced that their intention was to converge rates of funding gradually, year by year, until eventually there would be one national rate for all post-sixteen colleges. It was a noble ideal, but the practicalities were so badly handled that they achieved the opposite of their proclaimed intention. The gap in funding per student at Collyer's and at Haywards Heath grew wider each year until the discrepancy in overall funding was about £300 per student, or roughly £300,000 a year.

In the context of the sector as a whole £300,000 was arguably a trivial sum. But it was not an isolated case, and while the proclaimed policy was to get all colleges funded at the same rate, in practice some were funded at a rate two and a half times more than that of others doing more or less the same work. The scale on which they were getting it wrong was immense.

An important part of the explanation of how they could have got it so badly wrong was that they were trying to do two different things at the same time. On the one hand they were genuinely trying to find a way of converging levels of funding. On the other hand, and at the same time, they were having to cope with the government's regular annual reduction in the funding level for the whole sector, and living within the government's funding limits necessarily took precedence over converging the rates of funding of the various colleges.

A further reason for getting the funding arrangements for the sector so badly wrong was that they had devised what they rather pretentiously called a 'funding methodology', and they kept scrupulously to the rules they had themselves devised. If something was going wrong in some corner of the country, the officers of the FEFC could not use their judgement in order to put things right. They were bound by the rules of their 'funding methodology' and could only put right one particular problem by altering the whole system. But that in turn would throw up other problems.

I argued in my article that the FEFC could not be faulted on grounds of transparency. Those with eyes to see had been able to watch it going wrong and, to its credit, it had not hidden its own failures. Nor could it be faulted for lacking robustness. It had applied its mechanical systems indifferently to all alike and thus had managed to avoid the criticisms which would have arisen if its officers had used their judgement about particular cases. It had been outstandingly efficient in operating a fundamentally flawed and far too complicated system. But it had been far less effective than it should have been in producing convergence of college funding levels.

Efficiency is of course desirable, but it is not as important as effectiveness. It would be a serious flaw in the effectiveness of an infantry regiment if its only training for modern warfare was in eighteenth century foot drill, however efficiently and impressively that foot drill was carried out. That was the problem with the FEFC. It operated its funding system efficiently. But it was ineffective in achieving its proclaimed aim of producing convergence of the levels of funding of different colleges.

The Director of Funding and Strategy dismissed my criticism as if it were no more than a complaint that convergence was taking too long. He repeated the Council's commitment to achieving convergence and adding in typical FEFCspeak that they envisaged 'consulting the sector on the rationing mechanism to achieve the policy objective and related tariff issues, including the appropriate rate for franchised provision.' Either he had not understood the criticism I was making or more probably he preferred not to.

I replied with a letter to *Council News*, which fortunately had an independent editor for the *Letters* section who was pleased to publish it – indeed, insisted on doing so when an attempt was made to dissuade her. I explained how I had publicly criticised the funding methodology and how two separate but related mistakes in their system had over five years produced the opposite effect from their publicly proclaimed intention. I had not required an explanation of how it could happen. I knew the explanation. What I wanted was an acknowledgement that they had got it wrong and were working to put it right. 'Instead', I went on, 'The Director of Funding and Strategy chose to miss the point and treat my letter as yet another complaint that convergence was taking too long. That won't do. I have spent more than twenty years as a principal trying, not always successfully, to create an environment in which people can make mistakes and learn from them. Mistakes can be forgiven. Clinging obstinately to them is another matter. So is the deliberate misunderstanding of criticism when it is embarrassing to face it.'

It did not endear me to those operating the system, but I had only a year and a half to go until retirement and it was easier for me than for many other principals to risk offending them. The problem was handed on to an Assistant Director (Funding) who made a genuine attempt to understand what had gone wrong and what needed doing to put it right. Sensibly he got someone to produce all the factual information relating to the example I had given, but unfortunately the person who produced the figures got into a tangle which revealed with grim clarity how some of those serving the funding methodology simply could not find their own way through its Byzantine complexities, let alone guide anyone else.

The private correspondence continued, and because we were dealing with one particular example on which I had made myself a specialist I was able to disentangle the complexities, make clear what was obscure, and in one case switch the figures round, because they had applied each college's figures to the other one.

The eventual public reply in *Council News* from the Director of Funding and Strategy in February 1998, printed together with my delayed letter of the previous October, was this:

'I think we can agree that when the FEFC introduced a new system of funding, there were bound to be 'winners and losers.' (Yes, I could agree.)

The new system was successful in encouraging growth and was intended to achieve convergence of levels of funding. Again, there were 'winners and losers.' (Again I could agree.)

'*Convergence of funding has not been achieved as intended, so now the FEFC is adopting a new system to get convergence by 2000-01 and thus remove the perceived unfairness of colleges receiving different rates of funding for delivering the same level of activity.*' (Hurrah! That was what I had been arguing for all along.)

There was no explicit acknowledgement that I had been right in my criticism, and I could not know how far what I had pointed out had pushed them towards adopting the new system. But it was enough.

The other accusation I had levelled against the FEFC was that it penalised hard work and exerted financial pressure on colleges to have their students engage in what they called 'guided learning' for as little as thirteen and a half hours a week - i.e. the four and a half hours a week which the FEFC allocated for each of three A levels. If, for example, a student took four A levels, such as Maths, Further Maths, Physics and Chemistry, the funding allowed for the fourth A level was less than a third of that for the other three. That was clearly contrary to the FEFC's own proclaimed policy, that 'a student with the same attributes studying for the same qualifications should generate the same level of funding.'

I argued that the FEFC needed to adjust its funding arrangements to its own principles. It was not corrupt in the sense that it had told us some local authorities were, adjusting school budgets according to personal whim. It was scrupulously, high-mindedly and self-righteously correct. It was the 'sea-green incorruptible' of English education, and its servants, with their extraordinary ignorance of or disregard for high quality sixth form education (they were far more knowledgeable about technical education), ruthlessly misallocated funds, rebutted or ignored criticism, and used their pernicious 'methodology' to produce inadequate education for thousands of A level students unfortunate enough to suffer at their hands.

Shortly before I retired the Chief Executive of the FEFC spoke at a meeting in Brighton about the merits of the post-16 sector and I was able to challenge him over the problem that the FEFC's 'funding methodology' was encouraging indolence among English students by reducing the funding for anything beyond a bare three A levels to so low a level that colleges were being pressured to provide no more than that and, as a result, many sixth form college students were now at a disadvantage by comparison with those educated in good schools. He was clearly irritated, even annoyed, and his answer was that the task of the FEFC was to ensure a broad and balanced curriculum for all and to ensure that the available funding was distributed fairly and equally. It was, I suppose, the sort of answer I should have expected.

We needed, I believed, a relatively simple, national funding system which would be applicable to all post-16 full-time education, whether in schools or colleges, and one which would be aimed at ensuring a broad and balanced curriculum. What I did not say explicitly was that I also believed that it should be possible to devise a system which would be applicable to independent schools as much as to those funded by local authorities and by the FEFC. At the time that would have been a bridge too far and would have been scorned and opposed by politicians of all political parties – though each for different reasons.

A mildly entertaining comment emerged from this fracas. One of the officers of the FEFC expressed surprise that a college should have a magazine entirely devoted to funding issues. I had, after all, sent them my criticism published in *De Profundis*, the college magazine named after the opening words of Psalm 130, which Richard Collyer had asked should be said for his soul at the departing of the school each day: 'Out of the deep have I called unto thee, O Lord...' The officer of the FEFC knew enough Latin to mistranslate *De Profundis* as 'Concerning funding.'

69. A Day in the Life...

On a number of occasions during the twenty-three years that I was a headmaster or a principal I was asked if my time was now spent more on administration than on teaching. I found it a difficult question to answer, partly because I was never entirely sure what 'administration' was. No doubt someone did it, but it was not usually me. On the other hand, although far less of my time was spent on teaching than before, something or other filled the day. But what that was varied immensely.

As I dealt with one issue after another in my early years at Collyer's I soon found that there were others who could take them over from me, so I was glad to delegate more and more to a number of very helpful and talented colleagues. The division of responsibilities between two Vice-Principals, Celia Jarratt and Peter Crees, and two Senior Teachers, Ray Smith and Steve Gilham, worked well for some years. But eventually Celia retired and both Peter Crees and Ray Smith took advantage of a government scheme for voluntary early retirement. Both returned the next term to work part-time, Peter teaching A level Chemistry and Ray as the college's Examinations Secretary, and both still helped out with games. It kept them in touch with the college and although they were paid only on the basic scale, it provided them with a useful supplement to their pensions.

It also saved the college a considerable sum of money at a time when that was needed, because the most obvious and immediate impact of being placed in the new Further Education sector was a significant reduction in funding year on year. John Major's government had won the election of 1992 with a promise to cut taxes and take the fat out of the public sector, so while the fees of independent schools rose every year, the Further Education sector had its funding cut by 5% a year, while at the same time any pay rises were to come out of further 'efficiency gains.' In practice that made the rate of funding reduction 8% a year.

One consequence of that was that I decided to operate the college with only one Vice-Principal and share with Steve Gilham many of the responsibilities which had previously been spread among five of us. Fortunately much of the operation of the college was well bedded down by then and the change worked well. Steve was a quiet man who was very effective in a wide range of different ways. I found him invaluable. He ensured the efficient day-to-day running of the college, and by thoughtful planning for the future he guided me towards sensible decisions.

One consequence of the change in responsibilities was that I needed to be more directly involved in student discipline. For some years I had only been involved in disciplinary matters after a student had persisted in his (it was usually 'his' rather than 'her') wicked ways, and had graduated from action by his tutor to the relevant Senior Tutor and, if necessary, on to Peter Crees, who would then suggest that, if the problem were to re-occur, his only recourse would be to refer the student to the Principal, 'and you know what that will mean.' What it meant was suspension, and by the time a student was brought to me there was usually little else I could do other than suspend him. It did not happen very often, and now the Senior Tutors could give the final warning. That was usually enough and it was only infrequently that I had to suspend a student and very seldom that I had to expel one.

If one assumes that over twenty-three years as a headmaster or principal I had a fairly regular five-day working week for about forty-four weeks of the year (two weeks off at Christmas, two at Easter and four in the summer before the O and A level results arrived), that makes a total of more than 5,000 working days. They varied immensely. Some might be almost entirely devoted to the appointment of a new member of staff, some to a meeting of the Governing Body, most days I did some teaching and most days there was a meeting of some sort I needed to go to. But no one day was typical.

*With John, fifty years on from the photograph of us at
Christ's Hospital at the age of fourteen. Now he was the
Dean of Durham and I was the Principal of Collyer's
and approaching retirement.*

Nevertheless, one evening, when sitting in an Old Collyerians'
Committee Meeting, I decided to make a note of how I had spent
the day. Unusually there had been nothing at all in my diary for
that day, so I had hoped to get down to some planning for the following year. As I walked in to college that morning I found two
students smoking in the road outside the college, made a note of
their names and reported them to their tutors. I stopped to speak
to the groundsman, who told me that he had been calculating how
much money students could save if only they did not spend it on
drink and cigarettes. When I reached my room one of the tutors
was waiting to see me about a student in her tutor group whose
parents were away on a cruise and who, unknown to them, was
having an abortion. The tutor wanted to be sure that we were not
under a legal obligation to inform the parents. I assured her that
we were not.

My secretary brought in the post, which was relatively light that
day. There was the usual batch of papers both from the Department
of Education (its name frequently changed and just now it was the
Department of Education and Employment) and from the Further
Education Funding Council. I skimmed through them, decided that
there was nothing I needed to tackle myself, and on each wrote the
initials of the member of staff who would deal with it. There was a
letter requesting a reference for someone applying for another job,
and as I already had a copy of a previous reference I had written,
that was easily dealt with. There was another request for a reference for a colleague applying to be an A level examiner. That also
was easily dealt with, since it was no more than a matter of assuring the board that she was a suitable person.

A father who was concerned about a progress report on his son
had written asking to see me. I replied suggesting possible times
when we could meet and meanwhile sent his letter and a copy of
my reply on to the student's tutor with a request for more information. Another parent had written wondering why it was proposed to enter his daughter for AS rather than A level Economics.
I replied with reference to her performance in the trial

examinations, explained the options and the case for and against what was proposed.

Finally there was a reply after a long delay from a clergyman who had been invited to preach at the Founder's Day Service to say that he could not manage it. I decided that it was too late to invite anyone else and that I would preach the sermon myself. It was the only year I ever had to do that; usually one got a fairly prompt response. I went on to decide on a topic, choose the hymns and the readings and set out the format of the service sheet. I decided to preach on the story of the two men who went up to the Temple to pray and that I would cast a college principal in the role of the self-satisfied Pharisee and a rather grotty and unsatisfactory student in the role of the tax collector who cast down his eyes, saying 'God, be merciful to me, a sinner' and who, according to Jesus, went down to his house justified, or in a right relationship with God, rather than the other.

Towards the end of the morning, in Assembly with one of the five houses, I gave a recycled forty minute lecture on 'Words and Meaning.' I had first written it when I was at Stowe and had been asked by Dennis Silk, another former History Grecian at Christ's Hospital and now the Warden of Radley, to give a talk to his sixth form. I gave the same lecture five times that week – in Assembly with each house, one each day of the week. This was another consequence of the changes brought about by the FEFC. Instead of teaching an A level History set or a small group taking Russian Studies, I now gave a lecture five times a week, each time to over two hundred students.

What I spoke about ranged over Politics, Religion, Law, Morality, International Affairs (the background to the conflict in Bosnia, for example, or to the troubles in Israel and Palestine or in Northern Ireland) and more or less anything else. One topic was differing interpretations of the terms 'Classical' and 'Romantic', and this particular week it was a lecture on 'Words and Meaning.' I always stressed that I did not expect the students to believe everything I said, but I did expect them to ask themselves if what I said about one topic made sense in relation to what I said about another. That is, was what I said about Philosophy, for example, compatible with what I said about Religion? Because I was giving a lecture each day to more than two hundred students, my student/teacher contact time was very high - the highest in the college. But it would not have done to say so to any of my colleagues - all the more because I did not have to do any of the marking which they had, and which takes up such a large part of a teacher's time.

During the lunch hour a student came to see me about the problems she was having with Spanish. Her parents had telephoned me the previous day and I had suggested that she should come to see me. We agreed that even though it was half way through her first year, it would probably make sense for her to switch to Classical Civilisation instead. That would involve her in a lot of work to catch up on what she had missed, and I sent her off to talk to the Head of Classics, Ed Tattersall, and with her tutor. I wrote a note to the Head of Spanish. While I was doing that the Head of Maths came to see me to say that two of our students had reached the final of the National Mathematics Olympiad and he wondered if the college could pay for the cost of their travel to Exeter. I assured him that I could find the money from the Governors' Imprest Account.

During the afternoon one of the Senior Tutors came to see me with a report about a boy swearing at a member of staff during a football match, and we made arrangements for him to bring the boy to see me so that I could suspend him. Another Senior Tutor came to see me with a suggestion that another boy should be expelled for recurring absenteeism. I said I needed to see his record sheet and know what action had been taken so far by his tutor and the Senior Tutor. One of the tutors came to tell me about a boy in his tutor group who had just been told by a consultant ophthalmologist that he was gradually going blind. There was nothing I could do other than say that it was important that each member of staff who taught the boy should know about it – and any others likely

532

to come in contact with him. Then, during the last period of the college day, the Director of Studies called in to discuss what needed to be dealt with at the staff meeting the following Monday and who should do what.

Before the office staff went home I signed the letters which were to go off that evening, made myself a cup of tea, sat down in an arm-chair and did nothing for ten minutes. After that I turned my mind to starting to write the sermon I was going to preach on Founder's Day, and at 6.20 p.m., as on most other days, I left to walk home by 6.30. After supper I walked back again to go to the Old Collyerians' Committee Meeting, and while the members of the committee were discussing the proposed menu for the Annual Reunion Dinner (roast or croquette potatoes with the beef?), I jotted down some notes of what I had done all day and tucked them in a file, from which they emerged nearly twenty years later when I was writing this. It was not a typical day. Most days there would have been something in my diary before the day began. Most days there would have been fewer individual problems. Most days I would not have needed to go back into college for an evening meeting. But it does illustrate the point that a college principal's working life involves something other than teaching and administration.

70. Forty Years On.

◇◇◇

Some time in 1997 James King, who was only recently appointed Head of Chemistry when I arrived at Collyer's, was later one of the Senior Tutors, and finally, before he retired, was responsible for the effective operation of the tutorial system throughout the college, asked me to write something about my educational philosophy. He had some years earlier started the college magazine for governors and staff which was called *De Profundis*, the first two words of the psalm which the founder had asked should be said for his soul.

I had written a number of articles for *De Profundis*. One, of course, had been about the FEFC's 'funding methodology.' More often they were versions of talks I had given in Assembly on topics of current relevance, such as the background to the fighting in Bosnia, or the troubles in Northern Ireland or the conflict between Israel and the Palestinians. On matters such as these my aim was to give the students some idea of the past history, even the distant past history, of issues they would hear about on the *BBC News*. What they heard there was usually what had happened in the last day or two. I aimed to put that in the context of what had happened in the last few hundred years – even the last two or three thousand.

But now James had asked me to write about my 'educational philosophy,' and that appeared to me to be far more difficult. Philosophy is 'the love of wisdom', and it seemed to be implied that I should be able to produce some wise words about education. It was, after all, forty years on since I had started teaching, and just over twenty since I had become a headmaster, so I ought to have acquired some idea of what I was doing. But I still found the prospect difficult. I took the view that Education was a matter of passing on from one generation to the next whatever one

534

judged to be of value, and I recognised that that left the vast, intractable problem of deciding which things are of value, how valuable they are and who is going to do the choosing. In a school or college with an academic curriculum I would, for example, be inclined to include Keats's Odes, Euclidean Geometry, the periodic table, map-reading, chess, cricket, the Doctrine of the Trinity, an understanding of Marxism, and so on, but others might well disagree on every count. To that I could only reply that it is a matter of judgement. At first I felt that I had little more to add to that.

Then I remembered that some thirty years earlier I had read an essay by Arthur Koestler in which he had imagined an instrument which would break up patterns of human behaviour as a physicist breaks up a beam of light. Looking through this sociological spectroscope, he suggested, we would see a Commissar at the infrared end. 'The Commissar', he went on, 'believes in Change from Without. He believes that all the pests of humanity, including constipation and the Oedipus complex, can and will be cured by Revolution.....On the other end of the spectrum, where the waves become so short and of such high frequency that the eye no longer sees them, colourless, warmthless but all-penetrating, crouches the Yogi, melting away in the ultra-violet.' The Yogi, of course, believes in Change from Within. 'He believes that nothing can be improved by exterior organization and everything by the individual effort from within.'

Koestler had a poor view of both. He saw both as leading society down a slippery slope to disaster. 'One slope leads to the Inquisition and the Purges; the other to passive submission to bayoneting and raping....The Yogi and the Commissar may call it quits.' But that, though it raises interesting and important questions, was not what I was concerned with in this context. My interest was in the idea of the imaginary sociological spectroscope, which, it seemed to me, I could look through at a range of approaches to education.

In the article which emerged from this I suggested that we should imagine the ways in which schools operate spread out in a spectrum, like white light when it has gone through a prism. Then one could see all the varieties stretched out from one end of the spectrum to the other, gradually merging from ultra-violet to infra-red, and just as there are names for the different colours of the spectrum, even though they merge gradually from one to the other, so we could give names to the different modes of human interaction in schools. At the ultra-violet end, with behaviour at its highest and noblest, perhaps, there is *Spirituality*. Then, more achievable though still difficult, there is *Morality*. Next is *Legality*, and if even that cannot be achieved, schools may have to live with *Tyranny* or, even worse, at the infra-red end of the spectrum, they may fall into a state of *Anarchy*.

Spirituality, at the ultra-violet end of the spectrum, links all human souls to each other by invisible and undetectable high frequency waves generating light without heat. If only all men and women loved God with all their hearts, souls, minds and strength, if only they all loved their neighbours as themselves, if only they cared about Beauty, Truth, Liberty, Love, Loyalty, Equality, Forgiveness and so on, and if only they treated everyone and everything around them with understanding and generosity and devoted their lives to the care of others, the welfare of animals and the cultivation of Nature, there would be no need for any rules or any form of government. All would be perfection. But men are not angels. Nor, thank goodness (I suggested), are women. So Spirituality remained an unattainable ideal at the far ultra-violet end of the spectrum, and for many it is not even an ideal. Almost necessarily it involves some sort of concept of the Divine, and plenty of people see anything religious or spiritual as either mistaken or embarrassing or boring or irrelevant - or all four. But it would be sad if teen-agers went through their education without any glimpse of Spiriuality.

Morality is more widely seen as desirable, since it relates directly to human behaviour rather than to some ethereal, divine ideal. It is Man-centred rather than God-centred. It is more accessible and down to earth, and by now we are shifting into the indigo and blue areas of the spectrum. It provides a set of precepts for determining how Man (by which I mean human beings rather than Man as distinct from Woman) should live with Man, and how conflicts of interest should be resolved. The problem with this is that there is no universal agreement about Right and Wrong. Nor does an appeal to appreciate the difference between them produce universal agreement. People genuinely disagree with each other about moral issues, and there is no built-in provision in Morality for ensuring that the Good prevails and for enforcing Right as against Wrong. But it is essential that the young should be faced with at least considering such issues and that those who teach them should be seen to be concerned to behave well rather than badly.

Legality, or the Rule of Law, solves the problem about the way people disagree over moral issues in the sense that it establishes what is and is not permissible in a society, whether a nation or a school, and requires obedience to the rules, regardless of whether or not any particular individual agrees with them. Law cannot exist without provision for enforcing it, so Law can be seen as a matter of establishing convenient and enforceable rules to enable self-interested human beings to co-exist. It is not principally concerned with determining what is right and what is wrong. Much that is good is not required by law; much that is bad is perfectly legal. The law is concerned with social convenience. It is inconvenient if a car is driven on the right when the law requires drivers to keep to the left. It is particularly inconvenient if someone murders you. The former is clearly not intrinsically immoral (in some countries the law is quite different); the latter, arguably, is. By now we are in the solidly green, stable area in the middle of the spectrum where one wave follows steadily on another and produces warmth and a soft comfortable light, and we can expect a large measure of agreement about the desirability of maintaining the Rule of Law in a school. It is not necessary for everyone, whether teacher or taught, to approve of each rule, but it is necessary that there should be general assent to the proposition that rules should be obeyed and enforced.

Tyranny is what schools, like any other societies, end up with if they cannot achieve the Rule of Law. Somehow order has to be maintained and some authority has to maintain it. The British have for the last few centuries tried to find a way to be both bond and free, to have their cake and eat it, to have a government but be able to change it from time to time without needing to stand the members of the previous government against a wall and shoot them. It is a remarkable achievement and involves a paradox which would seem peculiar to most human beings in most of the world through most of human history. Far more commonly order has been maintained in the world by means which included less consensus and more brute force, and the more that happens the further we slide towards the relatively low frequency vibrations of the yellow and orange area of the spectrum where Tyranny triumphs, and the further we go the more we find heat rather than light. There is a natural temptation for head teachers to err in the direction of tyranny, for power notoriously tends to corrupt. It needs to be resisted, and heads need to find a way of ensuring order without becoming tyrannical.

Anarchy is located at the far infra-red end of the spectrum where the heat becomes unbearable and even the most brutal Tyranny has been unable to exercise effective control. Just like the other extreme end of the spectrum, it is characterised by an absence of authority and control. But whereas the cool ultra-violet of Spirituality offers at least the possibility of self-imposed order and in theory perfect human beings compete in caring for one another, the burning infra-red of Anarchy destroys all freedom as men and women jostle each other to get their snouts into the trough and eventually most of them cower in fear of the fist, the knife, the gun, or the hypodermic syringe. If Spirituality is an unrealistic and unattainable ideal, Anarchy can be an all too real reality. In schools it is the ultimate disaster.

'Co-operation and government', wrote John Ruskin, 'are in all things the law of life; competition and anarchy are the law of death.' When students emerge from their formal education into the world of work, most will find that they need to compete and some will find that they are working in an atmosphere of anarchy. They need during their teens to have had experience of something better. The task for anyone running a school or college is to shift things as far as possible towards the ultra-violet end of the spectrum and as far as possible away from the infra-red end, aiming to create a society in which teachers are free to teach and pupils are free to learn. A good school or college is likely to be rooted in the Rule of Law, with a measure of Morality informing every aspect of teaching, learning and the day-to-day life of the place, and with many aspects of the curriculum offering at least a glimpse of Spirituality. A bad school or college may well be characterised by Tyranny or, even worse, by Anarchy.

There is no clear dividing line between these different ways in which schools and colleges operate, but it is possible to get a sense that some work well and that others do not. 'Though no man can draw a stroke between the confines of day and night', said Edmund Burke, 'on the whole light and darkness are tolerably distinguishable.' That is true of the difference between good and bad schools and colleges. By the time I had been a schoolmaster for twenty or thirty years I was fairly confident that I could tell whether a school or college was 'good' or 'bad' within a few minutes of walking in. If in doubt, check on the state of the toilets. That can tell you more than you will learn from reading through any number of high-minded policies.

That was about the nearest I could come to anything which might be called an educational philosophy. It had emerged from the interaction between experience and reflection over forty years as a schoolmaster and from my own experiences at school before that. It was when I was a teenager that I decided that I wanted to be a schoolmaster. First, it looked an attractive life by comparison with the alternatives of a life on the railways, in the factories of East London or in banks in the City. Secondly, I found both the subject matter of History and the issue of how it could best be taught and learnt obsessively interesting. Thirdly, I was convinced that the educational process could be less brutal and should be less anarchic than some of the experiences I had had as a child.

In the event I enjoyed life as a schoolmaster, continued to find History fascinating, and continued to take the view that schools should be humane institutions. But my view of how that could and should be achieved shifted as circumstances changed around me. As a young man I thought it was principally a matter of teachers behaving well and setting a good example. As I grew older I became increasingly aware of the need for a well-structured, well-regulated, orderly society, if both teachers and pupils were to be free to engage in worthwhile and purposeful activity.

Of course harshness and cruelty are enemies of humanity, but I had come to believe that in the context of a school the main enemies one had to face were far more likely to be sloppiness and slovenliness. Where teachers were guilty of those faults they produced problems for themselves and for others and generated a need for greater sternness and strictness by their colleagues. I seldom saw much harm done by teachers who were consistently stern, strict or even tyrannical. I saw untold harm done both to individual pupils and to the ethos of an institution by teachers who were slovenly and negligent.

This produces the paradox that if you want a society in which teachers teach well and pupils learn effectively, and in which they can treat each other pleasantly, politely and with sympathetic understanding, then you need a secure base of order. You can only have Liberty within the Rule of Law. 'Tread softly', said Theodore Roosevelt, 'and carry a big stick', or, to quote a Latin adage of the fourth century attributed to Vegetius, *Si vis pacem, para bellum* – 'If you want peace, prepare for war.'

71. APVIC

◇◇◇◇◇◇◇◇◇◇◇◇◇◇◇◇◇◇◇◇◇◇◇◇

In the late 1970s the average size of school sixth form in England was 60, and in some parts of the country sixth forms were as small as sixteen or six. Even when there are as many as 60 pupils in a sixth form it is difficult to provide them with a reasonable range of courses without allocating disproportionate resources to them. After all, if there are thirty in each year, and if each year is divided neatly into one group of fifteen who are taught Maths, Physics and Chemistry and another group of fifteen taught English, History and French, that is a very limited range of subjects, and in practice things will never work out as neatly as that. So already in the 1970s some local authorities were starting to think of sixth form colleges as a possible solution to the problem of how to develop a comprehensive system which did not result in schools which were too large with sixth forms which were too small. Thus sixth form colleges came into existence, not because anyone had particularly advocated their creation, but rather as a solution to the problems thrown up by comprehensive reorganisation. If one was not to divide the young into different schools according to their perceived ability, it was necessary to divide them at some stage by age.

By 1975 so many sixth form colleges had been created, almost all out of former grammar schools, that there were enough for the Association of Sixth Form College Principals, or APVIC, to be created, and in 1976, after being appointed as headmaster of King George V School, Southport, I joined APVIC and went to its second summer conference shortly before taking up my new post. I found it a valuable source of support throughout the next twenty-three years.

We met each year for a conference, a couple of years in Cambridge, a couple in York, and so on, and had formal sessions, which were of some interest, and informal meetings, over breakfast or a drink in the evenings, which were very useful. Those who had already gone through the process of changing from grammar school to sixth form college could pass on the fruits of their experience to those who were facing similar problems. The best single piece of advice I was given was from an elderly principal approaching retirement who said to me, 'Always congratulate in writing and rebuke face to face.' It reminded me of a letter quoted by Sir Ernest Gowers in his book *The Complete Plain Words*. It had been sent by a Minister of Finance in the Egyptian Civil Service many thousands of years ago to a senior civil servant: 'Appolonius to Zeno, greeting. You did right to send the chickpeas to Memphis.' Either Zeno or his wife must have been sufficiently pleased with that tablet for it to survive and be found by an archaeologist in the twentieth century. It was advice I tried to follow, but I don't suppose I ever sent nearly as many congratulatory notes as I should have done; it is too easy to accept as normal much of the good work done by one's colleagues.

For many years politicians appeared to have little or no interest in sixth form colleges, and even after the decision to group them together with technical colleges in the sector funded by the FEFC, neither Secretaries of State for Education nor Ministers of State for Further and Higher Education seemed to know much about them. They would sometimes publicly proclaim the importance of the latest government initiative to 'drive up standards' in the sector, but it was sometimes clear that they did not know what they were talking about.

In the early 1990s John Patten, most remembered for his bouffant hair style and not to be confused with Chris Patten, was Secretary of State for Education under John Major. He spoke at an annual conference about the introduction of National Vocational Qualifications (or NVQs) and General National Vocational Qualifications (or GNVQs). 'The Prime Minister and myself', he said (his misuse of the reflexive pronoun causing a shudder among those with whom I was sitting), 'are entirely committed to NVQS and to GNVQS.' Unfortunately the secretary who had typed his speech for him had put a capital S in both cases, so that instead of saying 'NVQs and GNVQs' he had rattled off all the initials, including the Ss, making it clear that he did not know what he was talking about. Nor did he understand the laughter which followed.

One of the Ministers of State who coped best at an APVIC conference had only been moved from Agriculture a couple of weeks earlier and had clearly been briefed that the answer to most questions he would face was that the government was committed to giving parents choice, so that was how he responded to most questions. When given the opportunity to ask a question, I then explained that no comprehensive school in Horsham, whether boys', girls' or mixed, had a sixth form. Nor did we have a technical college or a city technology college or any other institution with a sixth form. My college, I explained, had a sort of monopoly of sixth form education in the town. What would the government be likely to do about that? He just grinned and said, 'Who's a lucky boy then?', which seemed to me as good an answer as it was possible to give.

At another summer conference the Chief Inspector spoke of simple arithmetical approaches which principals could use to improve things, and he held up King George V College in Southport as a shining example of a good college which did just that. As it happens I had introduced the very systems he was commending twenty years earlier, and I was pleased to hear from him that they were still in use. One was the grading system running from 1 to 5 which had been adopted by the FEFC for its inspectorate.

Another was the practice of comparing the average A level performance of a college's top 50 or 100 students with the performance of leading schools. I had done that ever since league tables of A level scores were first published, and a couple of years before had written to the *West Sussex County Times* to make the point that Westminster, St Paul's, Eton and Winchester were all very good, very selective and very expensive schools, and that they were the only schools in the country whose average A level score was marginally better than that of the top 50 Collyer's students (i.e. 30.1, or a bit better than AAA), and only 18 schools in the United Kingdom produced an average A level score higher than that of the top 100 Collyer's students (26 or ABB). Each was expensive and highly selective, and five of them had only 70 or 80 candidates.

A few years earlier John Rae, when Headmaster of Westminster School, had upset many of his fellow heads in the independent sector when he spoke of the disinclination of many independent schools to publish examination results, and he went on to say that 'one reason why they fear a league table is that there are parts of the country – West Sussex for example – where maintained schools get better exam results than the independent schools, despite the former's non-selective entry.' What he did not foresee was that when in 1992 the government did require the publication of examination results, it did so in such a way, by concentrating on averages, as to give the impression that selective schools were always better.

The annual APVIC conferences always made a pleasant break towards the end of the summer term, and in 1999, a couple of months before I retired, I spoke after dinner in the evening to say farewell on my own behalf and on behalf of Anne Smith of John Ruskin College, Croydon, and Sister Patricia of Loreto College, Manchester, who were retiring at the same time. I began by telling them how Rabbi Cohen, something of a celebrity at the time as an after-dinner speaker, had once begun by saying that he had been asked to be brief and circumspect. He went on, 'I can reassure you that I am only 5'4" and I have been.' I could not reassure them that I would be either brief or circumspect, but I would try.

It was the 24th such summer conference I had attended, the first in 1976 and this in 1999, and much had changed in that time. Some of the principals attending it had not even started teaching when I had been to my first of those conferences, and by 1999 I was one of relatively few principals in the FEFC sector surviving from the 80s and the only one surviving from the 70s. I had read Anne

Smith's articles in the *Times Educational Supplement* and had been in sympathy with her way of thinking. I had enjoyed Sister Patricia's company, so that when Cathy asked me on the 'phone if I had been out on the beer with the boys the previous evening, I was able to tell her that I had instead been to the cinema with a nun.

I commented on the excessive bureaucracy of the FEFC and on its mis-use of words, and I told them a story to illustrate how easily words can produce misunderstanding. An Australian fighter pilot who had fought in the Battle of Britain was interviewed on the BBC about his experiences. 'There we were', he said, 'stooging around at about 2,000 feet, and these two fuckers came at us out of the sun.' At that point the BBC interviewer interrupted him. 'I should explain', he said, 'for the benefit of younger listeners, that the Fokke Wulf was a German fighter aircraft of the Second World War.' The Australian fighter pilot replied, 'You're right there cobber, but these two fuckers were Messerschmitts'.

Before finishing I had more to say about the FEFC. I would not, I explained, have said it if its Chief Executive had still been there, because it would have been rude, but since he had left just before I began speaking, I thought I could happily comment behind his back on where he had diverged seriously from what I took to be good management principles – the principles of medieval monastic management that I had culled from St Bernard of Clairvaux:

First: *Notice everything.* Where things had gone scandalously wrong in a large further education college, the Chief Executive of the FEFC should have noticed it long before he did.

Second: *Correct a little.* He should have dealt with that particular problem rather than thinking up new auditing, accounting and reporting devices to apply to colleges which were not involved.

Third: *Cherish the brethren.* He should have been less concerned with apportioning blame and more concerned with praising what was good and looking after those who had made mistakes.

The next morning the conference ended with an Open Forum in which various principals spoke about current issues. High on the agenda, of course, was our relationship with the FEFC and its Chief Executive. He saw his job as working on behalf of the government to drive down funding and at the same time drive up standards. Ultimately he was responsible for the fact that, in a sector dominated by technical colleges, the funding was being directed more towards technical courses than towards A levels and that sixth form colleges were receiving far less funding per student than sixth forms in schools. Inevitably it did not make him popular with sixth form college principals.

As the meeting drew to a close one of my colleagues ended what he was saying with the comment that part of the trouble with the Chief Executive was that he was paranoid. I caught the eye of the chairman, who, knowing that I was retiring, said that he would give me the last word. 'Just because he's paranoid', I said, remembering Lionel Blue on *Thought for the Day*, 'doesn't mean that we're not out to get him.' They were my very last words as a member of APVIC.

The following year the Further Education Funding Council was abolished by the Learning and Skills Act of 2000. I would have liked to be able to claim some credit for its abolition, but so far as I know I had had no influence at all. I could at least, in my first year of retirement, be pleased that it was going, though it was difficult to feel confident that the Learning and Skills Council would be any better.

72. The Family

∞∞∞∞∞∞∞∞∞∞∞∞∞∞∞∞∞∞∞∞∞∞∞∞∞∞∞∞

From the time Cathy and I were married she was, of course, not only my wife and Helen's mother but also step-mother to my three children. When we first met, in the spring of 1984, Kate was still in Southport, James was away in his first year at St David's University College, Lampeter, and Piers had recently set off on his travels round Europe after spending one term at Collyer's. All three came to Horsham in time for our wedding. So did John and Anneliese, with their three children, Frances, Matthew and Miriam. So did June's daughters, Linda and Vicky.

Back in Southport Kate had met and shortly afterwards married one of my former pupils at King George V School, Andrew Savage, best known for his proficiency at chess, who had been a friend of both James and Piers. Once she was married and had gone to live with Andrew, she insisted that she wanted to sell the house we had bought in Wright Street. So we had it valued, James and Piers each increased their share from a quarter to a third, I bought the other third and for a few years we rented it out, before selling it and buying a flat in Islington instead.

Kate and Andrew were an ill-assorted couple. Kate was highly volatile; Andrew was quiet and reflective. If she wanted a row, he would go out for a walk turning a chess problem over in his head until, he hoped, she had calmed down. It was something of a continuing, even continuous, disaster for a few years until eventually they separated and Kate moved to London, saying that she wanted to be nearer to her family.

James seemed to enjoy his three years at Lampeter, and when he came down in 1986 he crossed the Atlantic to work in *Camp America* for a few weeks before travelling round the United States by *Greyhound* bus, from East to West and back again. On his return to England he worked briefly for the Department of Employment and then for a private car hire firm, liked neither, and answered an advertisement from *Berlitz*, who were looking for graduates to teach English in Spain.

It seemed a strange thing to do, because modern languages were what he had been least successful at school. At Stowe he had learnt French by the traditional drip-feed method and failed it at O level. At King George V College he had done a one year crash course in O level German and failed that as well. Fortunately he had not needed a modern language for entry to university because he had passed Latin. But that did not alter the fact that what he appeared to be least successful at was modern languages.

Nevertheless, once he got to Spain and was plunged into a Spanish-speaking world, within a few months he was speaking Spanish fluently, colloquially and in the manner of a native-born *Madrileño*. He worked first for *Berlitz*, then for the British Council, and then for many years for the *Universidad Alfonso Decimo, el Sabio* (the University of Alphonso X, The Wise), and it was clearly a job he thoroughly enjoyed. He came back home regularly every summer and every Christmas, but he liked Spain and liked life in Madrid and stayed there roughly twenty years.

Piers went up to Pembroke College, Oxford, in October 1984, exactly thirty years after me, though in his case to read the Classics course, officially known as the Honour School of *Literae Humaniores* and more commonly known as Mods and Greats. I always had the impression that he enjoyed Oxford and Pembroke less than I had. 'It's not what it was in your day', he once said. So far as I could tell the main differences were that the college was mixed rather than single sex and that the average age of under-graduates was younger. They had almost all come up straight from school.

Piers's tutor was Godfrey Bond, who had taught me some Latin for Historians in my first year, and with whom I walked along the river to the Trout on my last evening before going down. He was the successor of H. L. Drake, whom I remembered coming into Hall as an old man when I was an undergraduate, and who had taught Oriel's father back in 1908 when Teddy went up as a Classics scholar. Godfrey had succeeded Drake in 1950 and retired in 1992. Between them they taught classicists at Pembroke for most of the twentieth century.

By the time of Godfrey's retirement a classical education via the Honour School of *Literae Humaniores* no longer dominated the Oxford curriculum as it had in the past. Prime Ministers, such as Harold Wilson and Edward Heath, had read P.P.E. (Philosophy, Politics and Economics) instead of studying the literature, philosophy and history of the ancient world, and after Godfrey's retirement the college could no longer afford the luxury of a Mods tutor.

When he died in 1997 Piers and I went to his funeral together, and at it Godfrey's daughter, Catherine, recited A. E. Housman's poem that begins, 'Loveliest of trees, the cherry now is hung with bloom along the bough...' When she was a child Godfrey had offered her sixpence if she would learn it, but she never had. Now she had at last learnt it in order to say it at his funeral. It was strangely moving.

Piers, of course, had to learn Ancient Greek in order to tackle the Mods course, which was principally a matter of studying Greek and Roman Literature, and he did that very effectively, but he would probably have been well advised after that to have turned to a different subject, such as Oriental Languages, and learnt Arabic or Chinese. In the event he stayed with the traditional Oxford Classics course and in the second half, Greats, was studying Philosophy. It was not a subject he found at all congenial. The philosophy of the ancient Greeks was not too bad. 'Socrates and Plato and Aristotle came up with some pretty silly answers', he once said to me, 'but at least they asked the right questions.'

Modern philosophers irritated him, and it seemed to him that they too often concerned themselves with questions which were not worth asking. One evening he rang me up to say, "Would you believe it, Dad? The essay I've just been set is 'Can my yellow be your green?' " Later, when he had just taken Finals and we were having lunch together at the Trout and looking through the Moral Philosophy paper, he said to me, 'You know, Dad, the difference between you and me is that you find these issues fascinating and entertaining, whereas I find them entirely boring and trivial.' He was probably right – at any rate about the difference between us.

The oldest of the cousins, Linda, the elder daughter of Tony Cribb and Oriel's older sister, June, had gone to university young. Like Cathy she had gone up at seventeen. In her case it was to Wadham College, Oxford, where she not only read Mathematics but also took to the river. In her first year she rowed in the Wadham 1st VIII, which went Head of the River. In her second year she was Captain of Boats, and in her third year she rowed in the Blue Boat against Cambridge. Not only did she get her Blue; she was also in the winning crew. Then in the summer of 1980, after taking Finals, she won a gold medal in the double-sculls at the National Championships.

She went on to train as an accountant with the accountancy firm of Arthur Andersen and after a while met a young man called Nick Collier, whose father, I discovered, had played in the same Eastern Counties Schoolboys' Rugby Football team as me more than thirty years earlier. I thought to myself that anyone who was the son of such an excellent scrum half could not be all bad. Nick and Linda were married in 1989, went to live in Barnes, had three children, Chloë, Imogen and Jamie, and some years later also bought a large farmhouse at Walcott in North Norfolk, where we regularly visited them.

Vicky, Linda's younger sister, went up to Cambridge at the same time as Piers went up to Oxford and was one of the small, select band of ASNACs - those reading Anglo-Saxon, Old Norse and Celtic. She got a First, went on to do a Master's degree in Icelandic at University College, London, worked in publishing in both

London and Reykjavik, became the translator of choice for putting Icelandic literature into English (most notably the works of Sjón: *The Blue Fox*, *From the Mouth of the Whale* and *The Whispering Muse*), and taught Icelandic at both Cambridge University and University College, London.

Meanwhile, my brother John, who had become the Dean of Rochester in 1977, about a year after I had moved to Southport, and was, at 43, the youngest dean in the Church of England, stayed there until 1989, when Robert Runcie, then Archbishop of Canterbury, asked him to move to be Dean of Durham, saying, 'If I had been an ambitious man, that is the post in the Church of England to which I would have aspired.' I could see the point. Durham Cathedral must be one of the greatest buildings in the world, and the Deanery, which is attached to it, has public rooms into which one could almost fit a house, while also having smaller rooms tucked away which make it habitable by a family. It was a long way away from Horsham, but it was a very attractive place to visit and a good base for, for example, walking along Hadrian's Wall.

John and Anneliese's three children, Frances, Matthew and Miriam, were a bit younger than ours. By the time John moved to Durham Frances, who had read History at Royal Holloway College, London, was teaching at the Rochester High School for Girls, but she decided to retrain and did a course in Librarianship at Newcastle while living with her parents in the Deanery in Durham. Then for some years she ran the *Bede's World* educational centre in Jarrow, while also becoming a Reader at St Oswald's Church in Durham. Matthew, who spent his whole career in transport of one sort or another, was working for Virgin Airlines, scheduling the duties of the flight crews, and Miriam, who had been born a few years after the other two and was still at school when they moved to Durham, read Swedish and Dutch at University College, London, and while studying there lived in the International Lutheran Student Centre in Thanet Street in Bloomsbury.

We saw relatively little of Oriel's brother Michael and his wife, Anne, because they lived in Australia with their two sons, Christopher and Peter. But they were very good about visiting England regularly and at the end of a visit shortly after Oriel had died Anne left me perhaps the best present anyone ever gave me in all my life. On the day she left I found when I got back from work that there was a slow-cooker in the kitchen, with two chickens cooking away in it and a book of instructions propped up next to it. It proved to be invaluable during the period when I was without a wife and doing the cooking for the family.

Because we all lived busy lives we only occasionally saw Chloë's daughter, Fiona. She was another classicist, another one to do her degree at University College, London, and another to go into teaching. With June's two daughters and Michael's two sons, she brought the number of cousins my children had on Oriel's side of the family to five, and of course John's children gave them another three on my side.

Meanwhile Cathy's daughter Helen, who was ten in 1989 and was the only child of an only child, had no cousins. By the 1990s she was the only one living at home with us. She lived with us from the time we got married in 1984, a week before her fifth birthday, for the next sixteen years. She was at St Mary's Church of England Primary School in Horsham from 1985 until 1991, then for five years at Tanbridge House, the mixed 11-16 comprehensive school which had been formed from the former Horsham High School for Girls, and for the two years 1996-98 she was at Collyer's, where she coped well with the problem of being the Principal's step-daughter. So far as I know the only occasion when she made use of her relationship with me was one evening when she was in a pub with a Collyer's boy. A young member of staff who taught the boy came in to the bar and asked, 'Who's the tasty bit?', in the authentic accent of the 'dacent Protestant paple' of Northern Ireland. 'The tasty bit', said Helen, drawing herself up to her full height, 'is your Principal's step-daughter.'

From 1998 until 2001 she was at the Epsom College of Art and Design, part of Surrey University, doing a degree course in Fashion Promotion and Illustration, and even through most of the time that she was doing the degree course she lived at home with us. Once she had qualified she went to live and work in London. By then Kate was also living and working in London, James was living and working in Madrid, Piers was back in London, living in the flat we had bought in Islington and working as a crown prosecutor, Cathy was still teaching at Storrington, where she had started in 1990, and I was fairly recently retired.

73. Approaching Retirement.

From the spring of 1985 until January 1999, for nearly fourteen years, Cathy and I lived in the house in Wimblehurst Road, and throughout that time I was the Principal of Collyer's. From 1990 onwards, for the next twelve years, Cathy was teaching in Storrington, and until 2001 Helen was living with us. My children, on the other hand, were relatively seldom at home. Kate at first was living in Southport, and then, after separating from Andrew, was in London. James was with us during the vacations from St David's University College, Lampeter, and afterwards regularly came back at Christmas and for a few days each summer during the twenty years or so that he was in Spain. Of my children Piers was with us longest, during his Oxford vacations and throughout the year 1988-89 after he came down.

He had no idea what he wanted to do with his life and during that year did a variety of jobs in Horsham. He washed up in a restaurant and worked as an assistant caretaker. For some months he worked in a carbon filter factory, and that was enough to persuade him that he needed to get the sort of job that was available to an Oxford graduate, particularly if he could get himself some extra qualification. He applied to take what he described as a conversion course at the City University, London, to turn him from a classicist into a lawyer.

By then we had sold the house in Wright Street in Southport which had originally been bought for Kate, and with the proceeds we bought a flat near the Angel, Islington. I owned a half and James and Piers owned a quarter each. Now Piers was able to live there while working at the City University, then for the bar examinations, and afterwards doing what is known as a pupillage as a trainee barrister.

Shortly after being called to the bar he took a job with the Crown Prosecution Service and in the early 1990s returned to Oxford to live. The CPS office for the area was in Abingdon, but he appeared mostly in the Oxford Magistrates' Court, prosecuting the whole range of offences, from murder, which would be sent on to the Crown Court, to minor motoring offences, which were dealt with summarily. He seemed to take a dim view of the English legal system, of which he was now a part and which I had previously always seen as a model for the rest of the world to emulate. 'At least the French are concerned with Justice', he would say to me. 'They try to find out the truth about what really happened. We still operate a medieval system of trial by battle, only using words instead of swords.'

From the descriptions he gave of cases he prosecuted it sounded as if there were two *Triple Alliances* ranged against each other. On one side were the victims of crime, the police, and the lawyers of the CPS; on the other side were the criminals, the defence lawyers and the magistrates. Many of the Oxford magistrates were, he thought, 'middle-aged, middle-class, over-educated, under-intelligent, liberally-minded wives of Oxford dons', who believed that the police were all Fascists, the prosecuting lawyers not much better, and that the criminals were poor, misunderstood young men who needed sympathy rather than to be convicted of their crimes.

It seemed to him that the magistrates usually knew the defence lawyers by their first names and went to dinner with them. Meanwhile the defence lawyers kept crime going by such means as telling their clients the addresses of witnesses (after all, the English system was admirably open rather than secretive), so that they could sit in a car outside a witness's house looking threatening (but doing nothing which broke the law) until the witness was frightened enough to refuse to give evidence.

On one occasion, when a burglar was caught red-handed in a North Oxford house and remanded in custody, the family whose house he had broken into got anonymous threatening letters pointing out that they knew where the wife worked and where their children went to school and speculating on what might happen to them. ('Oh dear!' said the villain in custody, 'What a terrible thing! Who would do a thing like that?') The outcome was that the husband, fearful for his family, declined to testify. He and his wife sold their house and moved away. The burglar went free.

No doubt cases like that were exceptional and many petty criminals were convicted and sentenced. But it sounded as if rich and powerful professional criminals could often get away with their crimes, and that the police could spend years unsuccessfully trying to get them and, indeed, with similar lack of success, could spend years trying to bring to justice those defence lawyers whom they suspected of systematically perverting the course of justice.

It was only when I had a son involved in the system that I reflected that, while one part of our culture is the detective story, in which the good detective is out to catch the bad criminal, another part of our culture is the television drama in which the noble defence lawyer shows that the accused is innocent and that the police and the prosecution lawyers are the villains. It is very unusual indeed for the prosecuting lawyer to be the hero of a story.

Eventually, in 1999, the year in which I retired, Piers, now a Senior Prosecutor, moved to London, where he was again able to live in the flat at the Angel, Islington, which we had bought a decade earlier. At first he was working at the Horseferry Road office, and it sounded to me like hard work. Sometimes, after appearing in court all day, he would go back to the office and pick up fifty files for the next day. After skimming through them to find the serious cases, perhaps a murder, a rape and a grievous bodily harm, he might spot a case where custody time was running out. So he would ring the prison governor to make sure that the prisoner was released before the allotted time ran out, but also ring the police in case they wanted to re-arrest the prisoner.

After that he would go out to the local Turkish restaurant for a meal, and when he got back to the flat would do any necessary work on the serious cases. As for the minor offences, he would hope to be able to deal with them off the cuff when in court. The following day each of the accused would be represented by both defence counsel and a solicitor, and Piers would go from one case to another, sometimes trying the patience of the court as he sorted through his files trying to extract the one that was now needed.

Meanwhile James, once he had settled into his job at the *Universidad Alfonso Decimo, el Sabio,* decided that property in Madrid was a better insurance against old age than a pension plan with a bank, so he sold his share of the London flat to Piers, and with some help from me bought himself a flat in the middle of Madrid, in *La Latina*, the nearest equivalent in Madrid to Soho in London. Later he bought another flat in the suburbs to rent out, then another at *El Escorial* to refurbish and rent out, and more and more it seemed as if he was well settled in Spain, with a job he liked at the university and with his income supplemented by rents from the flats he owned.

Meanwhile Piers had been able to buy my share of the flat at the Angel as well as James's share, and thus they both had somewhere secure to live. Kate, however, after separating from Andrew Savage and moving to London, worked in various different jobs and moved from one rented room to another. I wanted her, like them, to have a place of her own. It felt, somehow, as if it was a duty I owed her mother. But it was far more difficult than when we had bought the house in Wright Street in Southport. The prices of houses and flats had continued to rise and London was more expensive than Southport. All the same, a solution presented itself in 1997.

Twenty years earlier, shortly after I took over as headmaster of King George V School, I had gone to a summer conference of the Secondary Heads' Association, where at supper I found myself sitting next to an elderly retired headmistress. We got on well and it turned out that she was Florence Kirkby, who for many years was the Treasurer of the SHA. In the middle of the meal she said to me, 'You sound to me like the sort of young man who would not have thought to buy back his past added years.' 'What is that?' I asked. 'It's the time' she replied, 'from your twentieth birthday until the date at which you started teaching, which is pensionable only if you have made the appropriate contributions.'

She went on to ask a number of questions. 'What age are you?' 'Did you do National Service?' 'At what age did you start teaching?' 'Are you married?' And when she had got the answers and worked out that the extra time which could be pensionable from my twentieth birthday until two months short of my 24ᵗʰ was three years and 304 days, she said, 'You need to write to the Department of Education at Mowden Hall, Darlington, giving them your date of birth and DES reference number, and tell them that you want to buy back your past added years under scheme 3 at 5% over ten years.'

'Just a moment', I said, 'Could you say that again more slowly?' I wrote it down on the back of my menu card. Later that night, and before I went to bed, I wrote out the letter. The DES replied that they would make the necessary deductions from my pay, and the effect of that was that by the time I reached the age of sixty, my pensionable service was calculated as forty years, and since one's pension was worked out by multiplying one's final salary by the number of years' service and then dividing by eighty, I was already entitled to retire on half pay.

It was, however, perfectly possible to continue working until the end of the academic year in which one reached the age of 65, when the maximum permissible pension was 45 eightieths of one's final salary, and since I enjoyed my work and found it rewarding in itself, there was no reason why I should not do that. The government always took 9% of every teacher's pay as a contribution towards their eventual pension, and for ten years there had been a further deduction of the 5% required to buy back my 'past added years.' After that I paid a regular Additional Voluntary Contribution of 6% each month to the Prudential, bringing my total monthly pensionable deductions to the maximum allowed, i.e. 15% of my salary. The effect of this was that by about the age of 63 I would have reached my maximum permissible pension level.

At that point I had a bright idea. Perhaps I could retire as a teacher on 31st August 1997, at the end of the academic year in which I would reach my 63rd birthday (1st November 1996), but continue working as the Principal of Collyer's, paid at the top of the support staff scale, roughly half of my then salary, for the next two years. I would be getting my pension (45 eightieths of my pay) plus pay at the top of the support staff scale and would be doing rather better than if I simply continued on my present pay scale for the next two years. The college would save about £75,000 – roughly half of my pay for two years plus the extra 15% they would no longer have to pay in National Insurance and pension contributions.

I put the idea to the Remuneration Committee of the Governing Body, and they received it enthusiastically. I told them that I needed to clear it in advance with our auditors, with Teachers' Pensions, with the Inland Revenue and with the Sixth Form Colleges' Employers' Forum to ensure that there was nothing improper about it. That was done, and rather to my surprise there was no difficulty. On the contrary, I was told that it was far simpler and more straightforward than the arrangements being made at that time for various college principals who were needing to retire early. I stressed that all the governors and staff of the college needed to know what was happening. It would not do for there to be any suggestion of secrecy or of an arrangement which could somehow be seen as underhand.

The deal went ahead. Sometime in the following year the *Times Educational Supplement* published a double page spread giving the salaries of all the six hundred or so principals in the Further Education sector, starting with the very highest paid, at about £100,000, and ending with the lowest paid, the Principal of the College of Richard Collyer in Horsham, at not much more than

£30,000. That had an asterisk by it and an explanation that the circumstances were unusual, but it did not reveal what was unusual about them.

The effect of the deal was that, although I continued as Principal of Collyer's until the summer of 1999 (the end of the academic year in which I reached my 65th birthday on 1st November 1998), I retired as a schoolmaster in the summer of 1997 and started to get my pension. Apart from the annual pension I also, like all retiring teachers, got a lump sum of three times the annual pension.

When the system started that lump sum was an amount which would have enabled a teacher, perhaps after years of living in a school house, to buy a house of his or her own. Even in 1997, with a lump sum in excess of £90,000, it was enough for me to buy something which would provide a home for Kate, and the following year, with her agreement, I spent £65,000 on a two-bedroom former council flat in Hoxton, just across the Grand Union Canal from Islington and within easy walking distance of Piers's flat at the Angel.

Remembering the experience of buying (and later selling) the house in Wright Street in Southport, I proposed to her a different way of dealing with this. She could live in it rent-free and gradually buy it with regular contributions over the next decade or so. If at any time she wanted to leave, she could have back what she had paid and put that towards buying a house or flat somewhere else. Effectively it was an interest-free mortgage so long as she wished to continue with the arrangement, but with the option of getting out whenever she liked.

We agreed that for the first three months she should live there without paying anything, to allow time to get her financial affairs and the flat sorted out. I provided the furniture and fittings, bought beds and bedding, put up curtains and ensured that the flat was well decorated and in good repair. Then in January 1999, three and a half months after moving in, she started paying £500 a month, which was roughly what she was paying in rent for a bed-sitter at the time. If she went on doing that for nearly eleven years, towards the end of 2009, by which time she would be 48, she would own the flat outright.

I put the arrangement in writing, stressed that she was under no obligation to stay there, and pointed out that it was something I only had the opportunity to do once in a lifetime – i.e. on receiving the lump sum related to my pension. She need not be concerned about my being able to repay her if she decided to leave. In the last resort I would always have the resale price of the flat.

It seemed a good arrangement. I would be retiring at the end of August 1999 with the reassurance that all three of my children had somewhere secure to live, James in Madrid, Piers at the Angel, Islington, and Kate in Hoxton, where she was in a position to get an income from letting out one or even two rooms and devote herself to things she enjoyed: amateur acting, painting and drawing, at all of which she was talented. Perhaps she could even supplement her income by selling her paintings. Then in January 1999, the same month that Kate started buying the flat in Hoxton and seven months before I was due to retire, Cathy and I moved half a mile nearer the centre of Horsham, from our house in Wimblehurst Road to Springfield Park.

74. Springfield Park

I first encountered Springfield Park, where we have now (in 2018) lived for nearly twenty years, when I went to Horsham thirty-five years earlier in 1983. Springfield Park House, which had been built in the eighteenth century by a prosperous Horsham merchant, Samuel Blunt, was by then an independent school, providing schooling for girls up to the age of sixteen. It was to the north of the town centre and across North Parade from Horsham Park, which had at one time been the estate of the Hurst family, while Springfield Park had been the estate of the Blunt family. Since Springfield Park School did not have a sixth form, many of its girls, after taking O level, came on to Collyer's to take an A level course, and the year after I arrived in Horsham I was invited to go there at the end of the Summer Term to give the prizes away.

It was a memorable occasion at which the headmistress, in the manner typical of head teachers throughout the country, spoke at Prizegiving about the various achievements of the pupils and then, again in a manner typical of head teachers, ended her speech with some high-minded thoughts with which to send her pupils home at the end of term. I was sitting next to her on the stage with piles of books waiting on a table to be given out as prizes, and a couple of yards in front of me was a row of sixteen-year old girls, some of whom would be my students the following term, all wearing their smart school uniforms.

The headmistress reached the end of her speech with a peroration about how important it was for all the girls to be helpful at home and care for their pets. 'So girls', she concluded, 'I want you all to go home and stroke your pussies.' The girls in front of me struggled to prevent themselves from laughing. I sat there with a straight face, went on to provide them with another high-minded speech, and gave away the prizes.

A few years later the school ran into financial difficulties which caused it to close. The main building stood empty and unused for a few years, then some vandals lit a fire in it and gutted the interior of what had been perhaps the most splendid house in Horsham, and after that it stood unused and derelict for a few more years. Eventually a building firm called Berkeley Homes did a deal with the trustees of the estate, the Horsham District Council and English Heritage to restore the house, and in return they were given planning permission to convert it into seven apartments and build another forty-one houses in what was left of the grounds.

By the summer of 1998, a year before I was due to retire, we had lived in Wimblehurst Road for thirteen years. We liked our house there and we liked the garden and it was only five minutes' walk from Collyer's. Only once had we even thought of moving, when I had seen a seventeenth century house for sale in the Causeway, the road which leads down from the Carfax to the medieval parish church of St Mary-the-Virgin, and beyond the churchyard to the River Arun, Denne Hill and the Sussex countryside. But Cathy liked neither the house nor the thought of living in the Causeway, where she felt she might be expected to behave like one of the worthies of Horsham. So we stayed in Wimblehurst Road.

Then in the summer of 1998 Cathy saw a large poster with a question mark on it in the grounds of Springfield Park. It suggested that something was going on there, so she investigated and one Saturday morning took me to see it. Work had begun on Springfield Park House, and even the Horsham stone roof was being replaced. At the same time the foundations were being laid for the forty-one new houses to be built in a style compatible with the great house. Some were conversions of the old stable block, but most were entirely new.

It looked as if it would be an attractive place to live, with its own trees and shrubs, just across the road from Horsham Park, and only ten minutes' walk to the Carfax, which was still the 'centre' of the town. It was a similarly short walk to Collyer's, to the

Horsham Hospital and to the Capitol, the local theatre and cinema. It was not much further to Horsham Station or to the parish church.

Meanwhile the house in Wimblehurst Road had become too big for us and the garden would also eventually be too big for me to cope with easily. So we got an agent to show us round the Springfield Park site. We looked at one of the projected houses; its kitchen was too small. We looked at another; the arrangements for garaging and parking two cars were inconvenient. The agent who was showing us round listened to our comments and said she might have just what we wanted. She did. Opposite a wooded area, in which was both garaging and parking spaces, and in the middle of a terrace of seven houses, there was a good sized house which exactly suited what we wanted. We decided to buy it.

The estate agent responsible for selling the houses in Springfield Park asked if we would like him to come and look at our present house with a view to selling it. He came on the Monday, sent someone round to measure up and take pictures on the Tuesday, rang on the Wednesday to ask if a client could come round that evening, rang on Thursday to say they were happy to pay the asking price, and then, when I walked out of the front door on Friday to go to work, I saw a SOLD notice already in place. The purchasers agreed to wait until our new house in Springfield Park was built, so when it was completed, in January of 1999, we moved in.

Each of the houses in Springfield Park was purchased freehold, so each of the residents owned his or her own house, garden, garage and parking space. But there were substantial communal areas as well: a considerable woodland area and smaller garden areas, as well as an external stone wall, internal roads, three gates, a few parking spaces for visitors and two stores for communal refuse bins.

All of that needed to be looked after, so once Berkeley Homes had completed all the building work and before they withdrew from the site, a management company was set up and we were asked if we were prepared to act as directors of the company. Several of us were, and before long we were engaged in a succession of meetings in each other's houses to consider how to organise things.

Eventually, in the summer of 2000, nearly a year after I had retired, we had to have our first Annual General Meeting, and George Yuill, one of the other directors, who was himself a company secretary, suggested that, since I had been a headmaster, I might as well chair it. Before long it was clear that we needed a chairman from one day to the next, rather than just for an annual meeting. Someone had to decide what to do if residents parked in the visitors' parking spaces, or if the gates were not working properly or if the bin stores were untidy. So I found myself taking on the role of chairman and doing it for the next four years, until the summer of 2004.

During the years that I was the chairman we agreed on a managing agent to deal with day-to-day maintenance and I got an arboriculturalist to draw up a plan for the care of the grounds, and in particular the trees. I presided over the monthly directors' meetings and established a newsletter, which was produced regularly by Sally Neely, a retired doctor, who took on the job of secretary. But mostly being the chairman of the Springfield Park Management Company meant that when there was a complaint about someone parking in the wrong place I would need to speak to the offender (who was invariably pleasant, polite and apologetic), when the gates failed to work I needed to get out a screwdriver and fix them open until they could be properly repaired, and when the bin store was untidy I needed to get out a broom and sweep it clear.

We had moved to Springfield Park at the end of January 1999, seven months before I retired on 31st August. I had no particular wish to retire. I enjoyed my job. But I had known for the last forty-two years that I would need to retire at the end of the academic year in which I reached my 65th birthday, and I had reached that at the beginning of the previous November. So I was looking forward to having time to read and write.

I did some gardening, went to the theatre with Cathy, both in London and in Guildford, took exercise by going to a gym and by walking in the local countryside, visited long-neglected friends and relations, and watched films on television in the evenings without feeling that I ought to be doing something else. Above all I relished the opportunity to indulge for several hours at a time in the luxury of reading - getting down to Gibbon's *Decline and Fall of the Roman Empire*, which I had bought some years earlier but had not yet started, and going through all the novels of Patrick O'Brien about sea-faring life in the early nineteenth century.

I was able to indulge my taste for poetry, but found increasingly that I was inclined not so much to read new poetry as to go back over what I knew already and learn it, so that I could recite it to myself. Eventually I photocopied the poems I liked most and arranged them in sections in a ring-binder: sonnets, psalms and canticles, love poems, war poetry, comic verse, poems about human emotions, narrative verse, hymns, and other poetry which could not easily be categorised.

My taste in poetry is, I suppose, like my taste in music, what might be called the popular classics. But whereas music is something I like to have in the background but relatively seldom concentrate on, I like to have poetry readily available in my mind, so that I can recite it and think about it at any time, when standing in a queue, sitting in a waiting room, or going for a walk.

The habit of learning poetry went back to the time in my first year at Christ's Hospital when the whole school marched the three miles into Horsham to the Odeon Cinema to see the 1944 film of Shakespeare's play *Henry V*. It felt to me as if Shakespeare had foreseen the twentieth century clash between England and Nazi Germany and provided a medieval representation of it. After getting back to the house I started at the beginning learning the Prologue ('Oh for a Muse of fire...'), the speech before Harfleur ('Once more unto the breach, dear friends, once more...') and the speech before Agincourt ('Who's he that wishes so? My cousin

Westmoreland...'). Seventy years later I can still recite them to myself when walking across Horsham Park or driving up a motorway.

As for music, I am just as content when reading to sit in the garden with birdsong around me as to sit in my study playing Vaughan Williams's *Fantasia on a Theme of Thomas Tallis* on a record player – and of all the records I ever heard on *Desert Island Discs*, the one which moved me most was that chosen by the Indian novelist, Vikram Seth, of the sound of a nightingale in full song in a Surrey wood in 1942, rising above the hum of the engines of Lancaster bombers on their way to a raid on Germany, gradually growing louder as they came from the West and then dying away in the East.

For some years after coming to Horsham I kept up the practice of running round the park early each morning, but in the 1990s I did that less frequently and after I retired took to going to a gym instead, usually three times a week. The thing I particularly liked at the gym was using the rowing machine, both for long stretches of, say, half an hour and for short sprints of only a minute. But then I bought a rowing machine of my own and Cathy got herself a cycling machine, and since then we have used them at the same time as each other up in the box room on the top floor of the house.

Strangely enough the exercise and the poetry I learnt got intermingled. At one time I had learnt a dozen psalms with a view to saying two of them each day: 1 and 8 on Mondays, 15 and 23 on Tuesdays, 46 and 84 on Wednesdays, 95 and 100 on Thursdays, 121 and 130 on Fridays and 137 and 150 on Saturdays. But when rowing I would occupy my mind by running through all twelve of them, together with the *Magnificat*, the *Nunc Dimittis* and the *Te Deum*. Then on another day I would start with all the sonnets I knew, or three of Keats's Odes, or a couple of narrative poems, and so on, and decide what to go on to recite according to how much longer I was intending to go on using the rowing machine.

Poetry remains important to me. Learning it helps with understanding it, and in whatever circumstances I find myself I can always find a sonnet or a psalm or something from Browning or Burns or Kipling or Keats to keep me company.

CH again (from 1990)

75. Governor

◇◇◇◇◇◇◇◇◇◇◇◇◇◇◇◇◇◇◇◇◇◇◇◇◇◇◇◇◇◇◇◇

In November of 1990 Eddie Ashby, the Head of Technology at Collyer's, was killed by a drunken driver. He had first come to Collyer's in 1963 as an eleven year old schoolboy and twenty years later, in September 1983, as I took over as Principal, he returned as a member of staff. He had been a boy at Collyer's for seven years and he was a member of the teaching staff for just over another seven years. Then, one morning in November 1990, a man who had been drinking far too much had a row with his wife and left home in his car and in a rage. She rang the police. A few minutes later his car hit Eddie Ashby, and by the time two police cars arrived on the scene Eddie was dead. He was 38.

He left a widow, Heather, in her mid-thirties, and a small son, Christian, who was only seven. When I went to see them Christian was working on the lights for their Christmas tree, designing a programme, as he had been taught by his father, to get them to come on and go off intermittently. He was clearly a very bright little boy. I talked with Heather about how they were going to cope, and what emerged was her hope that Christian might one day go to Christ's Hospital. I said I would investigate the possibilities.

One of the ways in which a child could be admitted to Christ's Hospital was an arrangement whereby a person who made a donation of a specified amount to the foundation was elected to the Court of Governors with the right to present a child in need. At that time the amount was £5,775 and the intention was that the newly elected governor should find a child in need who would benefit from a boarding education at Christ's Hospital and be capable of coping with what was essentially a grammar school curriculum.

There were five or six hundred Donation Governors, most of them Old Blues, i.e. former pupils, but some as representatives of, for

571

example, London livery companies. At each Leaving Service throughout our years at school we had heard the Headmaster read the Charge, exhorting us never to forget the great benefits we had received and charging us in time to come, according to our means, to enable others to enjoy the same advantages. Most of those who joined the Court of Governors did so when the main expenses of bringing up their own children were behind them and they had some spare money. At fifty-seven I was fairly typical.

The members of the Mercers' Company on the Governing Body of Collyer's were sympathetic about the death of Eddie Ashby and were anxious to do whatever they could to help. They explained that the Company would pay a third of Christian's fees at a prep school and contribute towards the cost of his uniform. But he was not at a prep school, his primary school did not charge fees, and he did not need any school uniform. Thus the Company found it difficult to help because it was used to providing its charity to the sort of child who went to an independent school. I told them that it would be immensely helpful if they could arrange for Christian to go to Christ's Hospital, but that would have involved them in the cost of a presentation, which was a step too far.

The outcome was that I became a Governor in my own right and in September of 1994, fifty years after I had gone to Christ's Hospital myself, Christian started there. He did very well at both O and A level, developed his talent for setting up and operating lighting systems by doing the lighting for school plays, and in the autumn of 2001 went up to Christ's College, Cambridge, to read Natural Sciences. A couple of years later I was able to go to his graduation ceremony and shortly afterwards to his wedding. His talents lay in the relatively new area of computer technology and after coming down he set up his own very successful information technology company.

In 1991, shortly after I became a Governor, Mike Pearey, the Clerk of Christ's Hospital, asked me to join a working party looking at the issue of 'Need.' I had known Mike since we had been at school and played rugby football together. He was an out-standing scrum half who had played in the Christ's Hospital seven-a-side team which won the Public Schools' Sevens Competition in 1951. After retiring from the Royal Navy as a captain he had returned to Christ's Hospital as Clerk, the chief executive of the foundation which supported and financed the school, and as Clerk he was responsible to the Council of Almoners, whose chairman was the Treasurer of the hospital. The names are confusing to anyone not well acquainted with the place, but for these purposes it is worth remembering that the Headmaster ran the school, the Clerk was the chief executive of the foundation and the Treasurer was the Chairman of the Council of Almoners, which governed both the school and the foundation.

The reason for setting up a working party on 'Need' was that the needs of earlier centuries, such as a lack of the basic necessities of life, had been replaced by other needs, such as those arising from the death or illness of a parent or their divorce. There continued to be a need for a caring, sustaining, school community. Those of us who formed the working party took the view that, although 'Need' was difficult to define, it could often be recognised. Those applying for a child to be offered a place had to understand that the child's ability would be assessed with a view to judging how far he or she was likely to benefit from an education at Christ's Hospital and how far he or she was likely to contribute something of benefit to others.

It also needed to be clear that, while the hospital existed to look after children in need, it was also looking for children of ability or talent from families without sufficient income to pay for boarding education in any other independent school. I put our conclusions onto one side of A4 paper, and Mike Pearey, who was responsible for admissions, made good use of them. Other than that my obligations as a governor usually went no further than taking an interest in how Christian was getting on and turning up to two meetings a year – one at the school and the other in the Mansion House in the City.

Then in 1998 Susan Mitchell, the first female Treasurer of Christ's Hospital in more than four and a half centuries, decided to hold a conference and Mike Pearey invited me to speak and give free rein to my ideas about the future of the hospital. Remembering the principle that one should 'think the unthinkable, but always express it wearing a dark suit', I took care to wear a dark suit for the occasion.

I reminded the conference that Christ's Hospital was not a public school, as that term is generally understood, but rather a charity, the product of a *'dede of pittie.'* It existed to provide for children in need - those who came from homes with a low income and would benefit from what Christ's Hospital had to offer. To do that the hospital needed a very substantial income, and it needed to spend it economically. Expenses were going up. The annual cost of providing for each child was now £11,675, whereas it had been only £203 for a boy and £171 for a girl fifty years earlier when I was at the school. Meanwhile pay expenditure was rising and the refurbishment and development of the buildings could cost millions. It was necessary to look carefully at both capital and recurrent expenditure.

While expenses were going up, income was being threatened. The phasing out of the assisted places scheme by the Labour Government which had just taken office would soon reduce the foundation's income by half a million a year, and the government had tax plans which could reduce it even further. My view was that while the Council of Almoners could hope for a bright future with the value of its property and investments increasing, it should plan for the worst, recognising that both its property and its investments might decline in value, and looking for ways to reduce recurrent expenditure so that it could always pay for it out of income and not by reducing capital.

Another problem was a change in the intake. Back in the middle of the twentieth century the former London County Council had given clever working-class boys and girls who did well in the eleven-plus examination the opportunity of going to Christ's Hospital, and many had had their lives transformed – in the case of the boys by marching, chapel, Greek grammar, rugby football, madrigals, sleeping on boards, nose-blowing by numbers, and the aspiration to be entitled to walk along the Grecians' path. The only league tables in those days gave the number of Oxbridge open awards, and only a few schools, such as Manchester Grammar School or Winchester, ever got more awards than Christ's Hospital.

But when the Inner London Education Authority was formed in 1965 it wanted clever working-class boys and girls to go to comprehensive schools, so it broke the relationship with Christ's Hospital and once the hospital had fewer working-class boys from London getting Oxbridge scholarships, the school came to be perceived as academically weaker. Any independent school which charges low fees and is thought to have relatively low academic standards begins to look like a second-rate public school. That was how the school was coming to be widely regarded, and it was a potential disaster. What was needed was the re-establishment in public perception of the idea that Christ's Hospital was a first-rate charitable institution rather than a second rate public school.

Meanwhile it was threatened by three developments in the second half of the twentieth century. The first was that the introduction of free secondary education for all in by the 1944 Education Act had undermined its status as a charitable institution. Before the Second World War only 2% of the population got free secondary education and the benefit of an education at Christ's Hospital was incalculable. Since the implementation of the 1944 Act in 1947 there had been free secondary education for all, and the existence of a fee structure at Christ's Hospital could now make the claim to be a charitable institution look absurd. The ideal solution was to charge no fees.

The second way in which circumstances had changed was that boarding was no longer as popular as in the past. More mothers who wanted their children at home had the self-confidence to say so. Fathers no longer felt the same social pressure to send their sons away at the age of seven. Boarding was increasingly seen as an outworn, socially exclusive, expensive, unnecessary and anachronistic practice. So my second proposal was that Christ's Hospital should become a day school, which would, of course, be far cheaper to run than providing boarding education. Even if it spent twice or three times as much per pupil as a typical state school, it could cut recurrent expenditure by half, avoid charging any fees, and still have a well-paid, well qualified staff providing substantial individual attention to the children.

But as a day school for children in need Christ's Hospital was in the wrong place, since Horsham is in a particularly prosperous area. To fulfil its mission effectively it would need to move back to London to a site accessible to children from some of the poorer districts of London. My preferred site was the old Stratford marshalling yards, south-east of the Hackney marshes, within easy reach of playing fields on the edge of the marsh, and with good public transport in all directions. It was a large and largely derelict area which would be readily accessible to children living in deprived areas of London, and many years later it was bought up and redeveloped for the Olympics of 2012. Back in 1998 I had suggested that we should aim to redevelop the area with a grand Palladian school building which would compete with Greenwich Hospital or even Buckingham Palace as a tourist attraction and whose outward magnificence would be an expression of the educational excellence within.

There would be fewer staff and thus a significant reduction in the payroll cost, and although the capital cost of new buildings would be vast, that is a one-off expenditure and in terms of long-term planning not comparable with recurrent payroll costs. Another benefit would be a reduction in the amount of staff time and energy spent on disciplinary matters. As anyone who has worked in both a boarding school and a day school will know, the overwhelming majority of serious disciplinary issues arise outside normal teaching hours.

Next it seemed necessary to tackle the issue of the criteria by which children would be selected for admission, which was necessarily a difficult problem because of the tension between the desirability of running a school with high standards of achievement and the mission of providing for children in need. To put it bluntly, there are children with high levels of ability who are not in real need, and there are children in need who have low levels of ability. There is no guaranteed correlation between need and ability. Statistically there is probably an inverse correlation between them. So we had to face the problem that we wanted two different things which did not sit easily together: provision for children in need, the essential reason for the hospital's existence, and high levels of achievement, which were important if parents were to want to send their children there and if teachers were to want to teach there.

I suggested resolving that problem by having two separate modes of entry. First, the school could require no more than the ability to cope with what was essentially a grammar school curriculum in the case of a child in need presented by a governor. The second aim, of attracting clever and talented children from low income families could be met by means of a competitive examination open to anyone whose parental income was below a level published openly beforehand. The same examination could be used in four different ways: first, for the selection of children to be awarded places by open competition; secondly, for the selection of children applying for entry under all the various historical and geographic categories; thirdly, to provide information about academic performance to any governor uncertain about which child to present; and finally, after children were admitted, for determining the classes in which to place them.

Meanwhile there was a national need for more housing and the West Sussex Council plan for the period up to 2011 projected nearly 38,000 new houses. The Almoners of Christ's Hospital needed to be able to present the planning authorities with an attractive, practical solution for the future of the Horsham site, which could become the pedestrianised centre of a thriving community of well-tended and largely lease-hold properties, whose ground rents would be payable to the Almoners of Christ's Hospital. The school chapel could be the parish church. The former boarding houses could be converted into expensive apartment blocks, and on the other side of the avenue a range of new smaller houses could fill in the spaces between the larger ones surviving from the days of the school. A splendid library was already in place, as were excellent recreational facilities, including a Sports Hall, a swimming pool and an Arts Centre.

While the site near Horsham would be at the centre of a flourishing new community, the Christ's Hospital of the future would rise out of the former Stratford marshalling yards, and just as the school had flourished in Sussex during the twentieth century on the proceeds of the increment of land and property values in London, in the twenty-first century Christ's Hospital might be able to flourish again in London on the proceeds of the increment of land and property values in Sussex.

So in summary my proposal was that the hospital should above all keep to its original mission of caring for children in need, that it should charge no fees and that it should become a London day school. Its admissions policy should be to attract able children from families with low incomes, so that it could transform the lives of clever Bangladeshi girls and talented Afro-Caribbean boys as it had transformed so many of our lives in the past. In concluding I acknowledged that it was reasonable to assume that most Old Blues would prefer things to remain like the best of what we remembered. But, as Tancredi says in Giuseppe di Lampedusa's novel *The Leopard,* 'If we want things to stay as they are, things will have to change.'

76. Preaching in Chapel

In the autumn of 1999, shortly after I had retired and two years after Peter Southern had taken over at Christ's Hospital as Head Master, I was asked to preach at the Remembrance Day Service.

Fifty-five years earlier, on Remembrance Sunday 1944, just after 1st Airborne Division's attack at Arnhem had been defeated with heavy casualties, I had been sitting just inside chapel, in the bottom row, because I was in my first term in the school, as the Old Blues killed in both World Wars were remembered. I explained that and went on to ask why we were now engaged in an Act of Remembrance, more than half a century after the Second World War and more than eighty years after the first, when none of us knew any of those who were killed. What or whom were we remembering? And why were we doing it in chapel?

I went on to suggest that Remembrance is not quite the same thing as 'remembering' and pointed to the parallel with the Christian practice of engaging each Sunday in an act of remembrance of Jesus in the service of Holy Communion. Bread and wine serve as a memorial of the body and blood of Jesus. Past and present are mingled. The intention is for the past to be made effective in the present.

So it is with Remembrance Sunday. It is a deliberate affirmation about the past. For many it has something to do with the idea that such things as heroism and the defence of freedom should be seen as part of our national identity. But it certainly should not involve a glorification of war, which, however much it may be necessary, remains a symbol of Man's corruption of his God-given potential for good. Still less should it be a celebration of victory.

It is, I suggested, first of all an occasion when we can hold up in remembrance those who lost their lives fighting, for example, in the Battle of Britain, the Battle of the Atlantic, in the Western Desert, in Burma or across the Lüneburg Heath, so that we might live in freedom. Secondly, remembering Jesus's command to his followers that they should love their enemies, we should spare some thought for our former enemies and their suffering. Thirdly, remembering the command to comfort widows and orphans in their distress, we should hold up before God in prayer the widows and orphans of war - of whatever nationality.

I spoke of the difficulty of embracing in one's imagination all the millions killed in two World Wars, or even as many as the 578 Old Blues killed in those wars. But I suggested that it was worth reflecting that it was roughly one in ten of all the boys who went through the school in the first forty years of the century. Take any day in that forty years and you could assume that two or three in each form, or five or six in each house, would be killed off - eighty out of the whole school assembled in chapel on any day.

As for the second point, about sparing some thought for our former enemies, I quoted the example of Warden Spooner of New College, Oxford, who put up a plaque in the college chapel just after the First World War commemorating three German New College men who had been killed in the First World War. He faced considerable opposition, but it had seemed to me when I first saw it as an undergraduate that it was to his eternal credit that he insisted and that it was done.

As for remembering the widows and orphans of war, I gave the very personal example that my sister-in-law, married to my twin brother, also an Old Blue, had no memory of her father. He had been a music master in a German *Gymnasium*, or grammar school, in the 1930s and was killed fighting on the Russian front in 1944. His wife was a widow for fifty years and had died only five years earlier.

All over the world there were women who had lost husbands, sons and others they had loved in wars fought in Europe, in Asia, in Africa and at sea. I knew an elderly lady in Horsham whose husband was killed in the R.A.F., and she had now been a widow for fifty-six years. There were Argentinean mothers and fathers mourning their sons lost in the Falkland Islands. There were Iraqi women mourning a husband killed in the desert. On Remembrance Sunday we should reach out to embrace them all. Of course it was right to start by holding in remembrance our own dead, especially members of our own families or the 578 Old Blues who had been killed in the two World Wars. But if possible we should then widen our sympathies.

I finished with the poem *Vergissmeinicht*, which in English means 'Forget-me-not', by an Old Blue, Keith Douglas, who was killed by a shell splinter at the age of 24, four days after the Normandy landings, just a few weeks before I joined the school as a little boy in 1944. The poem had been written a year earlier, at Homs in Tripolitania in the Western Desert, and it encapsulated what I had been talking about. It was written by someone none of us knew, it reached out in sympathy to a dead enemy, and by referring to the photograph of a German girl who had written '*Steffi, Vergissmeinicht* in a copybook gothic script', it led on to cause us to think of those who mourn their loved ones. That German girl in the photograph could well have still been alive, in her seventies, and still remembering the dead, as were we.

Two years later, in 2001, when the chaplain, Munna Mitra, arranged a series of sermons on the theme of *The Word and the World*, he asked me to preach in chapel again. I said I would try to tackle the topic of *The Word* and leave *The World* to others.

I recalled that about half a century earlier, when I was a History Grecian, the then Head Master spent the whole of the Michaelmas Term, one double period a week for each of twelve weeks, expounding the first eighteen verses of St John's Gospel to some thirty or forty of the most senior boys in the school. That's an at average rate of about an hour for each verse, and I'm not sure that I understood very much more at the end than I did at the beginning.

But however little I understood at the time of what Flecker was getting at, on reflection I am inclined to feel that at least he got his priorities right, because the first eighteen verses of St John's gospel (just 252 words in the original Greek) are a brilliant summary of the theological ideas of whoever wrote that gospel. So I went on to try to explain what those opening words were getting at.

Everyone in chapel had heard the first five of those verses read out only a few minutes earlier, so they knew that it began *In the beginning was the Word,* and some may have known that the Greek word here translated as 'Word' is λογος. What they did not necessarily know was that, while the literal translation of λογος is 'word', here it means something closer to 'universal wisdom', or even 'divine wisdom', which some Greek philosophers saw as the origin of all things.

Educated second century Greeks would have understood perfectly well what St John was getting at when he began like this: 'At the beginning of time all that existed was divine wisdom, and that divine wisdom is an essential aspect of what we mean by 'God.' It existed as part of God from the beginning. It was the means whereby all creation took place, and nothing was ever created other than through, or by means of, this 'divine wisdom'. The creative, or life, force was in it, and that life force shone like a light in the darkness of primeval chaos, and the darkness has never been able to put it out.'

That was my own rather literal translation of what is expressed so beautifully, though not necessarily intelligibly, in the King James Bible's version of St John's opening words, and both Susan Mitchell, then the Treasurer, and the Head of Chemistry, Jenny Williams, told me afterwards that it was the first time they had ever felt that they understood it. Where St John must have astonished his readers is when he goes on to identify the λογος, the source of all creation, with Jesus. He was suggesting that the man Jesus was also divine wisdom in human form. And in those 252 words John sets out what became the essence of Christian teaching about how the eternal Word (the λογος) took human form as a manifestation of God on earth.

The main point I wanted to make in the sermon was that if Christians see Jesus as the Word, the expression of divine wisdom on Earth, then it is worth looking at what he said. And it is worth noticing that he did not tell his followers what they should believe. Instead he told them to follow him and he tried to convey something about a new way of looking at things and about how that should affect the way we behave. When he was asked questions he never replied with definitions. Instead he told stories to illustrate what he was getting at and he provoked his listeners to think for themselves.

His teaching combined practical good sense with limitless aspirations. Thus if he told us to love our neighbours as ourselves, he was starting from the recognition that we are naturally self-centred, but at the same time was suggesting that as we go through life we should seek to escape our natural self-centredness and enter into a sympathetic understanding of those around us. Start by loving your brother whom you have seen, and you may eventually get round to loving God whom you have not seen. Jesus was not requiring his listeners to believe anything. He was giving them guidance on how to live.

His teaching was paradoxical and sometimes contradictory. It was often ambiguous but always illuminating, and it throws the moral responsibility back on the listener or the reader. As a guide for living it is, I suggested, usually better to ask yourself what Jesus would have done than appeal to principles.

I ended by explaining that as a teenager I had encountered Christianity at Christ's Hospital, just after the Second World War, a time when life there harsh and brutal and bullying was rife. A group of senior boys, moved by the teaching and spirit of Christ, treated others, including the young, with respect and even sympathy and kindness, and in so doing helped to make the school a better place.

Conversion to following Christ is for most people, I suggested, not a sudden dramatic experience such as that experienced by St Paul on the road to Damascus. It may begin simply with the recognition that Jesus had something to say worth considering. That in turn should lead to humility, uncertainty and the recognition that one is an infant in the faith and may have many years ahead in which to grow and hope to be gradually converted nearer to the image of Christ, whose spirit and ideas can still influence us. The best way of starting is to look in the gospels at what he said and see if you can recognise the λογος, the divine wisdom, in his words.

After another couple of years, in 2003, I was asked to preach in chapel again – this time on the anniversary of the birth of King Edward VI, on 12th October 1537, and 450 years after his death at the age of fifteen, on 6th July 1553, just ten days after signing the charter of Christ's Hospital on 26th June. I began with that information, and went on tell them how, rather more than half a century ago, when I was a little boy in the school, I was told that Edward VI, as he lay dying, signed the charter of the hospital, saying 'I thank God that he has given me life thus long to perform this good work' and promptly expired.

The story is not literally true. After all, it was ten days after signing the charter that the young king died. But literal truth and factual accuracy are often less important than understanding, and great truths can be revealed in stories which are neither factually accurate nor in any literal sense true. The various dates I had quoted when I began speaking were historically accurate but entirely unimportant, whereas the story of the young king signing the charter had something worthwhile to tell us about a 'deede of pitie.'

The stories which Jesus told, and which we get in profusion in the gospels, were also not literally true but were intended to illustrate truths about how people should live. The stories of the Good Samaritan and of the Prodigal Son were made up to illustrate great moral truths, and there was no one, clear, simple message in them. Their significance can depend on the circumstances in which you read them.

What is true of the stories Jesus told is also true of many of the stories told about him. St Luke tells us that after Jesus's birth angels appeared in the sky singing 'Glory to God in the highest and on earth peace to men of goodwill.' That is not a statement of historical accuracy. It was St Luke's way of proclaiming to the world that the birth of Jesus was an event of immense significance - that something wonderful had happened.

The first three gospels include many of the stories Jesus told to illustrate his attitude to how we should try to live. The fourth of them, St John's Gospel, includes none of Jesus's parables and is more concerned to explain to us the significance of his life and ministry. The stories St John tells us about Jesus go further than those in the other gospels and are particularly rich in symbolism. In St Mark's gospel we find Jesus feeding a great multitude when only five loaves and two small fishes seemed to be available. By St John's gospel he is turning water into wine. St Mark tells us how Jesus drove out evil spirits and cured lepers and the blind, the deaf and the dumb. By St John's gospel he is raising Lazarus from the dead.

It is at least questionable whether it is sensible to take St John's stories literally, and one of the dangers of doing so is that we may then miss their significance. The point of the story of turning water into wine is that Jesus has the power to transform things. Follow him. Turn to him as your guide through life and you may well find that your life is transformed. The point of the story about raising Lazarus from the dead is that Jesus can give us new life. Turn to him as the Light of the World, as the Way, the Truth and the Life (I am using all those words metaphorically, of course, not literally) and your life will be renewed.

Origen, one of the early fathers of the Christian Church, writing in the first half of the third century, argued that the purpose of the scriptures was to raise Man from the world of the senses to the world of the spirit and convey eternal truth. Whether something was factually true or not, he said, it was the spiritual point of the story, not the factual content, which mattered, and he applied this approach even to the account of the Resurrection.

So it was not some new-fangled, liberal, watered-down version of the Christian tradition I was offering. It was a view which has in various ways survived down the centuries but has too often lost out to two tendencies which are characteristic of the failings of human nature. One is the tendency to be dependent on superstitious mumbo-jumbo and ritualistic expressions of religion - something Jesus condemned frequently. The other is the tendency to turn to literal interpretations of the Bible as an alternative to thinking about the real significance of the Christian story and the real significance of Christ's teaching.

Christian faith is not about what you believe, and it is not about factual accuracy – however desirable that is when you are writing History essays. Jesus didn't go around telling his disciples which historical facts they should believe. Nor did he require them to give assent to particular theological propositions. He told them to follow him and he told them stories to illustrate how they should think and how they should live. They should praise God. They should give thanks for all the benefits they had received. They should care for others. They should be ready to forgive those who do them harm....and so on. Ideally by following him they would be transformed into the likeness of God.

I concluded with a quotation from the school's Foundation Hymn: 'Best with righteous living shall our grateful thanks be paid, lifting up with hearts forgiving holy prayer in duty made. Praise we thus the God of heaven, Christ our saviour and our host, with the Lord of spirits seven, Father, Son, and Holy Ghost.'

77. Almoner

◇◇◇◇◇◇◇◇◇◇◇◇◇◇◇◇◇◇◇◇◇◇◇◇◇

Several of those at the Treasurer's Conference back in 1998 had told me that they had enjoyed my talk. But no-one took seriously my suggestion that the school should return to London, become a day school for talented children from homes with little money, and charge no fees. One or two said that they assumed I had my tongue in my cheek. 'No', I replied, 'I was entirely serious, though I expect Council will try to put it off for another fifty years.' Shortly afterwards the Almoners debated the idea, but I was not surprised to hear that they had dismissed it and confirmed their intention for the school to remain on the Horsham site.

Instead Council made a firm commitment to a long-term future on the Horsham site and had a masterplan drawn up setting out its vision for the development of the buildings. The first element of this plan was the construction of separate boarding houses for the Grecians, a term now applied to all the boys and girls in their A level year. Next was a programme of refurbishment of all sixteen of the other boarding houses, and the intention was to build a number of high quality and substantial houses for the members of staff in charge of the boarding houses. It all looked very promising. The new building works would be expensive, but once completed the campus would be magnificent.

Some time in 2001 two of my contemporaries from school, Peter Birkett and Peter Bloomfield, both of whom were, like me, members of the Court of Governors, suggested that I should stand for election to the Council of Almoners. Peter Birkett had been the Senior Grecian (the head boy) in my last year at school. He had met his wife, Ursula, while they were both up at Cambridge, and they got married just before he went out with her to Tanganyika as a colonial officer in 1957, expecting to spend his life in the colonial service. But 'the wind of change' which Harold

Macmillan was to speak about in 1960 was already blowing through Africa, and some time before Tanganyika became independent in 1961 (it did not unite with Zanzibar to become Tanzania until 1964), Peter and Ursula were already back in England. Later he became one of Her Majesty's Inspectors of Taxes.

Peter Bloomfield had left Christ's Hospital a year before us to go to Sandhurst, after which he was commissioned into the RASC. He left the army while still a captain and set up his own public relations firm. By 2001 he had already been on Council for six years and was embarking on a second six year term. He and Peter Birkett proposed me for election, pointing out that now that Peter Attenborough, the former Headmaster of Charterhouse, was stepping down, it would be useful to replace him on Council with someone else who knew about schools, and that since I lived in Horsham, I would be in a good position to play an active part in the affairs of the hospital. I needed to submit a statement to the electors, who were all the other Governors, and shortly afterwards was elected to serve as an Almoner for the six years from the beginning of 2002 until the end of 2007.

The Council of Almoners, often referred to simply as Council, was the body responsible for the charitable foundation which funded Christ's Hospital and was able to do so largely because of the increasing value over the centuries of the extensive property it owned in London. It was made up of some twenty-three Almoners, with about a third appointed by the City of London, another third elected by the Court of Governors and the rest representing a variety of bodies such as the Royal Navy and the universities of Oxford and Cambridge. Over the centuries they had maintained the foundation's purpose and had from time to time made significant strategic decisions, such deciding in the eighteenth century to educate the girls separately in Hertford, and deciding at the beginning of the twentieth century to move the boys' school to Horsham.

At the time I was a pupil in the school most boys were required to leave at or fairly soon after the school leaving age and were found jobs in the City in banking and shipping and insurance. The principal exceptions were those who were seen as likely to win open awards to either Oxford or Cambridge and were encouraged to look forward to a life in the ordained ministry, or teaching in universities and schools, or serving in the home civil service or the colonial service. Other exceptions included those who were preparing for admission to Sandhurst or to go to one of the teaching hospitals. There was no careers advice, but there was a clear assumption that the ablest children should be guided towards 'the honourable and poorly paid professions' and that the others should be found jobs in the City.

That gradually changed in the second half of the twentieth century, as secondary education developed throughout the country. It became more and more usual for teenagers to stay at school until they had taken A level and leave at the age of eighteen. Council left the running of the school to the Head Master and sought to increase its annual income and ensure a rise in the capital value of the foundation's resources by investing in the stock market and buying and selling property. It also retained responsibility for new building work and any other capital expenditure.

In two areas it seemed that for the last hundred years, ever since the school had been moved to Horsham, it had neither taken direct responsibility itself nor delegated it to anyone else. One of those areas was the maintenance of the buildings. They had been well constructed at the beginning of the twentieth century and had survived throughout that century. If there was a leak in the chapel roof, one of the grounds staff would go up a ladder and try to repair it. If something needed re-painting, one of the grounds staff would get out a paint brush. But there was no long term maintenance programme and after a hundred years some buildings were very much in need of care and attention. The other area in which Council seems never to have given serious thought to its responsibilities was regular annual expenditure by the school. The Head Master in Horsham and the Headmistress in Hertford would would indicate each year how much money they needed in the light of rising pay expenditure and other costs, and Council would provide it.

Meanwhile Council had set up an extraordinarily large and complicated structure of committees and sub-committees. There were Governance, Planning, Finance, Audit, Health and Safety, Disciplinary, Treasures and Education committees, together with innumerable sub-committees, each operating on its own, most of them meeting once a term, and with none of them knowing what the others were doing. The Education Committee was in appearance something like a school governing body, but in practice was little more than a discussion group.

This lack of an effective governing body for the school had mattered relatively little for centuries. Both the girls' school in Hertford and the boys' school in Horsham attracted high quality staff and there was little need for the Almoners to interfere. Council provided the money; the schools looked after themselves – at least until there was a serious disagreement over policy. But in the second half of the twentieth century, although the foundation was still immensely rich (it was in fact the richest school in the country – and needed to be because of its charitable mission), it was being affected by inflation. Costs were rising and in the 1970s Council was gradually and reluctantly driven to accept that it could not afford to fund both a boys' and a girls' school. It could, of course, have decided to close one of them, but instead it began to discuss the possibility of amalgamating them.

That led to a serious clash with the then Head Master, David Newsome, a former Cambridge don who could not stomach the idea of co-education. In 1979 he left to be the Headmaster of Wellington College and the following year Council formally resolved 'to bring together the boys and girls of the Foundation on one site at Horsham.' They sold the Hertford site. David Newsome was replaced by Derek Baker, a former History Grecian, whom I had known both at school and at Oxford, and who came to the headship of Christ's Hospital from being a lecturer at Edinburgh University.

He presided over the amalgamation of the two schools, but after some years Council managed to clash with him as well, and just as David Newsome had left under a cloud of disagreement, so did Derek Baker – in 1985. No reason was ever given publicly and, although I knew many of the people involved, I was never clear about what had gone wrong. My impression was that Derek had been frustrated by indecisiveness on Council and had made his own decisions about the deployment of money, and that in turn had led to indignation among the Almoners about the ways in which he had used the money. While David Newsome left for another headship, Derek Baker took up a post as Professor of Medieval History at the University of West Texas.

By the time I became a governor in 1991 the Head Master was Richard Poulton, another historian, who had come to Christ's Hospital from the headship of Wycliffe College, a small public school in Gloucestershire, and whose amiable personality was a considerable asset after some years of difficulty and division. The school flourished under him for ten years and then from 1997 had another ten years under another excellent head, Peter Southern. Peter was the son of the distinguished medieval historian, Sir Richard Southern, whose writing on *The Making of the Middle Ages* and on *St Anselm and his Biographer* I had found inspirational, and he came to Christ's Hospital from teaching at Westminster and Dulwich and from the headship of Bancroft's School in Woodford Green.

When I joined Council at the beginning of 2002, in the middle of Peter's headship, both the school and the foundation which funded it seemed to be flourishing. Prospects for a substantial and reliable income from property rents and from investments seemed good, and it also looked as if there was a reasonable prospect of being able to sell some of the 1,200 acres of agricultural land owned locally if it was re-designated for house building and the value then increased significantly. So bright were the prospects for the future that there was even talk of the possibility of building another school across Big Side, perhaps in association with the government, so that the surplus funds of the foundation should not stand idle.

Shortly after I joined Susan Mitchell came to the end of her time as Treasurer and a new Treasurer took over. I was appointed to serve on the Education Committee and on the Premises Sub-committee of the Finance Committee and was struck by the difference between the two groups. The Education Committee was a large body including all the Almoners who were not on the Finance Committee and a few other individuals. It met once a term, approved the minutes of its previous meeting, which set out in detail who had said what, engaged in low level discussion of what I suppose were intended to be educational issues, and decided little or nothing of any relevance to the affairs of the school. It seemed to me that it was little more than a dumping ground for those Almoners whom the Treasurer did not want on the Finance Committee.

The Premises Sub-committee of the Finance Committee, by contrast, was a small group of professionals who had recently made a start on assessing what needed doing to get the buildings of Christ's Hospital into a good state of repair. I was the only Almoner on it and little more than an observer, so it seemed that my main function was to report back to Council on what was being proposed. But in the devious way in which the affairs of Council worked, the Chairman of the Premises Sub-committee would submit a written report to the Chairman of the Finance Committee, which in turn would discuss the report and decide whether or not to accept what was proposed. After that both the discussions and recommendations of the Finance Committee were recorded in minutes which would be received by each of the Almoners shortly before their next termly meeting, so any report back by me was superfluous.

I found myself increasingly out of sympathy with the whole way Council operated. There were far too many committees and sub-committees. They met infrequently and usually knew little or nothing of what the others were discussing or deciding. It seemed to me that what was needed was something like a Finance and General Purposes Committee, which would meet at least once a month in order to keep the business of the foundation moving. I also wanted clear rules about such things as when the agenda of a meeting should be sent out and I wanted the minutes of meetings to record decisions and recommendations rather than discussions. Too often we were sent dozens of pages of minutes of several committees and sub-committees shortly before a meeting, and usually the minutes described discussions in detail while failing to indicate whether or not a decision had been reached, and if so, what it was. Once there were over two hundred pages of papers received just a few days before a meeting of Council - all to be 'received' or 'approved'.

There was much to admire in the operation of bodies such as the Premises Sub-committee and other sub-committees dealing with such things as investments or the property portfolio, and Christ's Hospital was clearly still a remarkable school, with good teaching and admirable arrangements for the care of its pupils, but Council seemed to me dysfunctional and its meetings virtually superfluous. There was a lack of clarity about Almoners' responsibilities and about what was required of them. We were in danger of simply turning up once a term to a meeting to approve the minutes of the last meeting, pass motions congratulating our colleagues on such distinctions as becoming an Alderman of the City of London, give assent to administrative trivia which did not need to concern us at all, note and comment on information placed before us, listen to statements by the various chairmen of committees and sub-committees, receive reports and statistics from the Head Master and the Clerk, and do little or nothing that was at all related to our real obligations.

When the Almoners were considering investment strategy or how far to use leverage to extend the property portfolio, I realised that I was an amateur in the presence of professionals and I did not interfere. When we discussed anything to do with the running of a

school, I knew that I was a professional in the presence of amateurs, many of whom, despite their ignorance, mistakenly assumed
that they knew what they were talking about

The level at which matters to do with the running of a school were
discussed was sometimes embarrassingly low. When there was
talk of the school taking serious cuts (though in reality the so-
called cuts were no more than a slowing up of the rate of increase
in expenditure) one of the City Almoners, faced with a proposal
for a pay rise in line with the national figure of 3%, suggested that
in a time of such financial difficulty the Christ's Hospital staff
might have to accept that they would not get a rise. I made the
point that to break away like that from the national pay award
would have damaging long-term consequences, and most
Almoners saw the point.

A few minutes later we were faced with approving a similar percentage increase in total employment costs. Now I argued for a
lower increase. That was treated with a supercilious laugh by the
Treasurer, who pointed out that I was the person who only ten
minutes earlier had insisted on the importance of keeping in line
with national pay awards. It seemed to me ludicrous to have to
explain to City financiers that pay rises and pay expenditure were
two different things. As levels of pay rose while funding was
reduced, one would have to face cutting the total number of staff.
But that was not an issue they were prepared to face, and one of
the City Almoners, on his way to being Lord Mayor, commented
that the affairs of Christ's Hospital were not the same as those of
'the comp. down the road.'

78. Money Matters

◇◇

Although I was not a member of the Finance Committee I was increasingly concerned about the way financial matters were dealt with. Over a period of less than a year five serious problems arose for which no budget provision had been made, and each of them was dealt with by spending hundreds of thousands of pounds of accumulated capital. A break-in to a boarding house revealed the need for expensive security arrangements. Asbestos was found in several buildings and had to be removed. High level repairs were needed to the roofs of buildings whose maintenance had been neglected for a century. The front of Dining Hall was in danger of falling down. The government was projecting increased employer's contributions to National Insurance.

The simple solution to each of these problems was simply to deal with them and pay whatever it cost. Thus the Treasurer proposed that better security should be put in place in all the boarding houses 'regardless of cost', and that was agreed. My view was that the issue should have been brought to Council only at the point at which there was some idea of the approximate cost and of where the money was going to come from. It might have been found, for example, from a capital equipment budget or a long-term maintenance budget, or some from one and some from the other. Perhaps the cost could have been spread over two or three years. But under no circumstances should it have been undertaken 'regardless of cost', with no idea of how much money was needed or where it would come from. Much the same applied to each of the other issues.

At the same time I was critical of the way the capital equipment budget submitted by the school was dealt with. No figure for expenditure on capital equipment had been given to the school. The Head Master simply submitted a shopping list of everything required, and the Almoners looked through the list. One asked if the Music Department really needed a new euphonium. The Head Master assured us that it did and that was agreed. Another asked if the infirmary really needed a new dentist's chair. Again the Headmaster assured us that it did and that was agreed as well. Eventually the whole list was agreed. My view was that Council should not have been concerned with those details, but should have set a budget limit, within which the Head Master could make his decisions.

I put both of these issues to the new Treasurer but achieved nothing other than to irritate him. His reply was that I should leave these things to people who understood them – that is, the members of the Finance Committee. The only explanation I could think of for this apparently casual and, as I thought, irresponsible approach to expenditure was that Council was used to the idea that the foundation was so rich that it had no need to bother either about spending a few hundreds of thousands of pounds on anything which clearly needed doing, or about placing a limit on the school's annual expenditure.

Before long I was able to look at the foundation's long term financial forecast. There was a healthy closing balance surplus of nearly £4,000,000 in the current financial year, but Council was projecting an average capital spend of over £5,000,000 in each of the next five years, and it was also expecting in each of the same five years to spend on the school over £2,000,000 more than it was getting in income. The excess of projected expenditure over income during those five years was approaching £40,000,000. No wonder that, even with a projection of extra income, the forecast showed an accumulated deficit of nearly £30,000,000 by the end of the decade! If, as the Principal of Collyer's, I had ever projected a deficit of three thousand pounds, let alone thirty million, I would have been sent back to think again and would probably have lost my job. Even a projected deficit of £30 would have been unacceptable.

Not surprisingly the largest element of Christ's Hospital's revenue expenditure was employment costs. At the time I joined Council it employed over three hundred people – roughly two and a half for every child in the school, nearly a third of them teachers but also teaching support staff, cleaners, grounds and catering staff and those employed in the Counting House on such things as accounts and servicing the various committees and sub-committees of Council. Again, and not surprisingly, total employment costs were forecast to rise each year more than income, so that by the end of the decade they were expected to rise from just under two-thirds to more than three-quarters of income. If we carried on at that rate, in less than twenty years annual pay expenditure alone would exceed annual income.

I saw the forecast as a warning and believed that the problems it revealed needed to be tackled as a matter of urgency – before the budget for 2003-4 was agreed. It would be painful. But every year we put it off the worse the problem would get and the more difficult to solve. At the moment we were still in a position to say with a clear conscience that we reacted to the problem as soon as it became apparent. That would not be so in a few months' time if we failed to get to grips with it now.

If we merely insisted that total employment costs must not rise beyond the current level of approximately 64% of total income, the foundation's financial position would still get worse. But if we reduced annual employment costs by 1% a year, getting them down to 60% by 2007-8, and if they were then kept at that level, that would result in a small annual surplus by the end of the decade. It was, I believed, the duty of Council to set financial limits of that sort. Then it would be the duty of the Headmaster (responsible for the teaching staff), the Bursar (responsible for the grounds, cleaning and catering staff) and the Clerk (responsible for the Counting House staff) to operate within the limits set by Council.

As it happened I had considerable experience (too much!) of tackling this problem from the other side. I was something of an expert on ensuring high standards in an educational institution with ever decreasing income, and I would willingly have helped if the Head Master or the Bursar or the Clerk had asked me to do so as someone who happened to have experience of these matters. But my function as an Almoner was simply to join with the others in setting financial limits. Council's responsibility was for setting budgetary limits. Instead the Treasurer, on behalf of Council, simply asked the Head Master to be as economical as possible, and at the same time declared that nothing should be done which would damage the education of the children. The deficit continued to rise every year.

There were three obvious ways of solving Christ's Hospital's financial problems. The first and most attractive was to increase income from donations and legacies, but there was a limit to how much could be achieved that way. The second was to increase income from parental contributions. That was the worst solution, because it was a move towards betraying the purpose of providing for children in need and instead selling the benefits of Christ's Hospital to those who could afford to pay. The third was to exercise a tight control of expenditure. That could not only provide a way out of financial difficulties; it could also generate creative solutions to the problems which would inevitably arise, and it might even give the school a new lease of life. There was no sign that that would happen, and the Treasurer would not even allow discussion in Council of how to reduce expenditure. Financial matters were for the Finance Committee.

The Finance Committee was largely made up of Almoners who worked in the City of London – investment bankers, solicitors, insurance men, pension advisers, stockbrokers and suchlike. They were almost all people who did very well financially when their clients were doing well and pretty well when their clients were doing badly, and their communal view of the financial position was clear. Of course there were some immediate concerns, but the stock market would eventually pick up, so would the property market, and there was the prospect of a vast increase in income when the agriultural land around the school grounds was re-classified as building land. Fund-raising would produce even more money, and meanwhile we could get on with spending £2,000,000 a year more than the foundation's income on running the school and at the same time plan for large-scale capital expenditure.

My view was entirely opposed to that. Although things might get better, until they did we ought to be planning realistically in the light of the present financial situation. Above all we needed to balance the Income and Expenditure Account, which would only be possible if we limited the rate of increase of employment costs. It was a view dismissed as irritatingly irrelevant to the affairs of the hospital. Christ's Hospital had survived for four and a half centuries, the Treasurer pointed out, and it would continue to do so. Temporary problems were there to be overcome and the Finance Committee could be relied on to overcome them. Peter Bloomfield mentioned that the King Edward VII Hospital in Midhurst was in imminent danger of closing because it was spending more than its income. That was dismissed as an irritating irrelevance as well. The Treasurer's view was that we should leave these thing to the Finance Committee and not make economies which would damage the education of the children in our care.

I was increasingly frustrated by what I saw as the irresponsibility of Council in this matter. I formed the view that many of its members were impressively professional in their approach to generating income, whether through investments or property leverage, but amateur when it came to controlling expenditure – so much so that they were likely to dissipate in uncontrolled expenditure any increases they generated in income. In May 2003 I put my views in writing. It was, I believed, a mistake to assume that cuts were the main threat to the nature of Christ's Hospital as a charitable institution. On the contrary, the most obvious direct threat at that time was the one posed by solving immediate financial difficulties by increasing parental contributions, refusing entry to children in need and offering places to children whose parents could afford to pay.

The ability and willingness of parents to pay the fees was, for most of the country's leading independent schools, the first and essential criterion when offering places; the child's ability to reach a required level in an entrance examination came second. That was not so for Christ's Hospital. In the past children had been disqualified from entry quite simply by the fact that their parents could have afforded to pay for them. Once that principle was abandoned we would be abandoning the very purpose for which the hospital existed.

We might not be able to balance our budget in the coming year, I accepted, but we should aim to do so as soon as was reasonably possible, and it was clear that we needed to reduce expenditure, which, as it happens, would not be particularly difficult, because Christ's Hospital's annual level of expenditure per pupil was so high that there was plenty of scope for making savings. Of course it needed a higher level of expenditure per pupil than the average school or college maintained out of the public purse, but spending about six times as much on those in their late teens as would be spent on them in the maintained sector, and nearly twenty times as much in the case of the youngest pupils, was excessive.

I was not proposing specific solutions, because that, I believed, was a matter for the school. I was arguing that Council should set financial limits which would inevitably lead to pressure on staffing, which in turn would generate thought about how best to rearrange things. I also believed that these were not matters to be dealt with quickly. Any headmaster faced with managing a significant reduction in funding was going to need more than a year in which to achieve it. Few things could be more damaging to the personal relationships and loyalty on which any school depends than sudden and large-scale redundancies.

I also believed that, while employment costs, which were the largest element in each year's revenue expenditure, needed to be reduced, provision for contingencies, which was the smallest element, needed to be increased. The provision for unexpected, and therefore unbudgeted, contingencies was less than 1% of income, so there was not much more than £100,000 available for dealing with such things. But the costs involved in setting up new security arrangements, removing asbestos, repairing roofs, securing the front of Dining Hall, and planning for increased employer's contributions to National Insurance had been more than ten times the amount of the contingency budget.

That lack of budget provision had not mattered when there was a substantial cash surplus. But this was the last year in which the financial forecast was predicting a surplus, and we had clear evidence that we were moving towards a deficit of about thirty million pounds by the end of the decade. That was bad enough in itself; it was all the worse if there was no adequate provision for contingencies.

My disapproval of what seemed to me the mismanagement by Council of the financial affairs of Christ's Hospital led to a succession of clashes. Once when we met at the Guildhall to approve financial arrangements which were presented as substantial cuts (though in reality they were no more than a reduction in the rate at which expenditure was increasing) a City Alderman indicated that he could only agree to 'these swingeing cuts' if he could have an assurance from the Head Master that he agreed with Council policy and accepted the reductions. I responded with some heat. That was the last thing we should expect of the Head Master. He needed to be able to go back and assure his colleagues that he had vigorously opposed the cuts on which Council was insisting, and that he now needed the help of his colleagues in deciding how best to manage.

On another occasion an Almoner questioned whether we should really be permitting a rugby tour of Australia by the 1st XV and a visit to the USA by the band to play in the Rose Bowl in Texas. Yet another was concerned about the large expenditure on peripatetic music teachers and on musical instruments. My view was that such decisions were for the Head Master. If we allowed him so much money that he could pay for trips abroad and for a large number of peripatetic music teachers, there was no reason why he should not do so. The question members of Council should be asking themselves was whether we should provide such lavish funding.

Peter Southern could always provide a persuasive justification for such expenditure when asked to do so. He ran the school well and the performance of the 1st XV, of the band and of many musicians was impressive. He knew what he was talking about and he made good use of the funding with which he was provided. He would have made a similarly good job of economising if he had been required to do that. He could run rings round the Education Committee. When its Chairman wanted a Development Plan, Peter put it off as long as possible. Then, when pressed, he produced a weighty document setting out all the desirable and expensive changes wanted by every department in the school, though with no indication of what was intended to happen, who would do it, or by when. Every member of the Education Committee received a copy, the Head Master was thanked and we moved on to the next item on the agenda.

It was of interest to me, because as Chairman of the Human Resources Sub-committee I had had a Development Plan drawn up and was making regular use of it. We had as a committee decided to create a comprehensive loose-leaf Staff Manual, setting out the whole range of the hospital's policies, and with a copy in each of five specified places, so that anyone could check it. The other members of the sub-committee were all very competent employees of the foundation, and each of them contributed something of value to the manual. The Development Plan specified who was going to do what, the time by which they were expected to complete it and who was responsible for ensuring that they did.

As for the school's Development Plan, nothing happened, and when asked at a Council meeting a year later how it was getting on, Peter explained that in the present difficult financial climate it had been necessary to put it aside. That was the end of it.

79. Day Pupils and Full Fee Payers

Whether one took the view that economies were needed or that in the course of times the markets would pick up and the hospital's financial problems would be solved, it was clear that at the moment expenditure was outstripping income. Some increase in income was clearly desirable, and in 2004 Peter Southern presented Council with a strong and well-reasoned case for Christ's Hospital starting to take fee-paying day pupils. They could be fitted into existing teaching groups, would involve relatively little extra expenditure and their parents would provide a welcome injection of cash.

The issue was put on the agenda to be debated in Council, and I was given the job of making out the case against it. I began by accepting that the case in favour looked strong. It was potentially an effective way of making money and avoiding significant expenditure cuts. There was nothing in the foundation's constitution to preclude it, and there was a large potential market of rich parents in what is one of the most prosperous areas in England. I could well believe that there would enough who could afford the fees to meet the numbers Peter was projecting.

Nor did I see a problem with combining boarders with day pupils. My experience of that at Clifton had been that many prosperous citizens of Bristol chose to have their sons educated as day boys, and the town houses had competed successfully in every way with the boarding houses. The practicalities of the Christ's Hospital scheme had been well worked out and I did not doubt that the Headmaster and his team could operate it successfully. So what possible objection could there be?

The first objection was the danger that local people in Horsham would see Christ's Hospital even more as a posh school for rich kids than they did already - though this, of course, was something which might seem desirable as a way of appealing to rich parents in the area. The next objection was the effect on the perception of the school by our traditional supporters – Old Blues and the City. Why should anyone find the money for Donation Governorships and why should anyone leave a legacy to the foundation if the school was going to sell its heritage to those who could afford to pay, while refusing places to talented and academically bright children from poor homes?

The trouble with these perceptions was that they were so close to reality. Our mission was 'to have regard especially to children of families in social, financial and other need.' Each one of us had a duty to ensure that the charity remained focused on its core objective: the care of children in need. We were expected to 'abide by the fundamental values that underpin all the activities of the organisation' and everything we did should 'stand the test of scrutiny.' All that, of course, was open to interpretation, but it seemed to me that it would be difficult to justify taking fee-paying day pupils if faced with criticism from an aggressive radio journalist.

What is more, once we had started in the direction of solving financial problems by taking children because their parents could afford to pay, after 450 years of not doing that, we were in danger of sliding further and further down the slippery slope from charitable institution to being one more expensive public school, and it was an extraordinary slope to be sliding down at just the time when so many of the best and most expensive independent schools were making a real effort to clamber up the slope the other way, provide some 'public benefit', and be seen to do so.

Peter Southern asked what alternative there was. My answer was that we should continue much as at present but with less money and fewer members of staff. It would be painful. But pain is not the same thing as damage, and if the Headmaster, the Clerk and the Bursar all had to make cuts on a larger scale than anything the school had yet faced, it could, I had already pointed out, produce a re-thinking of policy, a re-organisation of activities, some re-arrangement of teaching spaces and certainly a re-structuring of the staff – not only the teaching staff and their support staff, but the Bursar's staff and the Counting House staff as well.

The Head Master might well find, I suggested, that the school would emerge from the process leaner and fitter, with high morale among those members of staff who knew that they had been chosen to engage in a tough and difficult undertaking. Of course it would not only be some of the dead wood that would have to go (there is usually some in any school), but also some of the healthy branches, some really valuable members of staff, but my experience was that such people usually went off to good jobs elsewhere.

If it turned out that it really was impossible to maintain effective teaching and pastoral care on a significantly reduced budget, then it could be necessary to reduce pupil numbers, and as pupil numbers dropped it would be necessary to reduce staffing even further. But that, I believed, would be better than to give places on the basis of ability to pay. As it happens, my belief was that for some years the school would find it relatively easy to make significant savings without resorting to any very drastic measures.

In the debate which followed Peter Bloomfield, supporting me, painted a memorable picture of children from London housing estates looking out of the windows of the boarding houses each morning as yummy mummies in their 4x4s drove up to off-load their offspring dressed in Tudor fancy dress to join in for the day in what had once been a charitable institution, until the cars arrived to take them back to their plushy homes in the Sussex countryside. He understood very well that the Head Master had thrown us a life-line, a way of avoiding making cuts, but he and I both believed that taking fee-paying day pupils was incompatible with our mission of caring for children in need.

Discussions such as this raised in an acute form the problem that continually faced Council. On the one hand we needed to keep to the hospital's mission and be aware of the need to care for future generations of children. On the other hand we needed to have a care for the well-being of the school as it was at the present time. Those two things pulled in opposite directions. The first required us to cut funding. The second caused us to want to increase it. So the sooner the two functions were separated the better. Council could then concentrate on maximising the funds of the endowment and on deciding how much to allocate to the school and how much to building and maintenance work. A separate body, the Governing Body of the school, would then need to do the best it could with what limited funds were available.

As it happens the issue of separating the school from the foundation was already being worked on for legal reasons to do with protecting the foundation's resources from the danger of litigation against the school. Similarly it was for legal reasons that the Court of Governors was that afternoon being asked to hand over its residual powers as trustees to Council, and before doing so the Governors wanted an assurance that Council could be relied on to keep to the mission. It would scarcely have made sense to have given that assurance while at the same time announcing a new policy of giving day places to rich local kids whose parents could afford to pay. So for the moment the day pupil issue was shelved.

It was also in 2004 that I re-established contact with John Whitehead, with whom I had not been in touch for over a quarter of a century. We had been good friends at school, and Oriel and I had seen something of him and Carolyn, whom he had married in 1964, while he was working at the Foreign Office in London after tours in Washington and Tokyo, and while we were at Stowe. But after 1976, when he went to West Germany as Head of Chancery, the ambassador's right hand man in Bonn, the same year that I went as Headmaster to King George V School in Southport, we both led very busy lives, were a long way apart and lost touch. He spent four years in Bonn, another four in Tokyo, then two in London as Chief Clerk, the Deputy Under-Secretary responsible for the running of the Foreign Office, and in 1986 went back to

Japan as ambassador, Sir John Whitehead, KCMG, for the last six years of his Foreign Office career, retiring in 1992, at the age of sixty.

By 2004 he was well established in a very successful second career, with a number of leading businesses finding his knowledge of Japan, Japanese people and Japanese commerce so valuable that they invited him onto their boards. He had recently become a Donation Governor and I wrote to him to say that I thought it good of him to have given money to the school when it had not treated him very well. A while after we were in touch again I suggested that his talents might be useful to Christ's Hospital and that he should stand for election to the Council of Almoners. So Peter Bloomfield and I proposed him and he was duly elected. He could only do three years (2005/6/7) because Almoners had to retire at the end of the calendar year in which they became 75. As it happens my six year period also finished at the end of 2007, so we spent our last three years on Council together.

This was the time when Council was facing the issue of how to separate the foundation and the school as two different charities. It would be possible for the foundation to own the land, buildings and investments, lease such land and buildings as was needed to the school, and provide the school with an annual income. That was an issue I probably knew more about than anyone else on Council because for sixteen years I had been the principal of a college whose land, buildings and other assets were owned by the Trustees of the Collyer Foundation, while the governance of the college was in the hands of the Governing Body. It was directly analogous to the proposed arrangements for Christ's Hospital. But my relations with the Treasurer were by then seriously strained and he was not going to consult me on any such matter.

John Whitehead, however, was new to Council, had not been involved in any of the previous discussions, and had all the prestige associated with his distinguished careers in the Diplomatic Service and in the City. He was given the task of advising on how responsibilities should be divided between Head Master and Clerk once the school and the foundation were legally separated. He worked at it, made his recommendations and at the same time pointed out that any arrangement was only going to work well with goodwill on both sides and a firm intention to co-operate.

Meanwhile Council policy continued to be that no economies should be allowed to damage the education of the children and that we should await an upturn in the markets and a brighter financial future, but it was now suggested that we could seek to close 'the funding gap' between income and expenditure by increasing parental contributions and taking more full fee payers. At the time there was a limit of 6% on the number of full fee payers, most of whom were parents whose income had increased significantly since their child joined the school. Now it was proposed that 6% should be a target rather than a limit and that before long the target could be raised.

In February 2007, early in the last year in which John Whitehead and I were still members of the Council of Almoners, we met at the Guildhall and considered a proposal from the Chairman of the Education Committee that in future Christ's Hospital should aim to close 'the funding gap' that way. We should market the school to those with a high income and let those conducting the admissions process have the relevant information about parental income, with a view to admitting a specified number of pupils from families with a high income. The rich could help pay for the poor.

In the subsequent debate John Whitehead made out the case against the proposal very effectively. As for the rights and wrongs of it, he pointed out, members of Council had already made up their own minds one way or another. What they should now consider was that, while we already had a limit of 6% on the number of full fee payers, that limit was never approached. There simply had not been the demand from wealthy parents. If we were to turn the 6% into a target and market the school vigorously to the rich, there was no guarantee that such parents would wish to opt for Christ's Hospital rather than one of the many other prestigious independent schools in the south of England. Lacking enough full fee payers, we would need to increase fees for others, and the more children we took from relatively rich families, the more we would have to exclude those in need.

If the school did not attract enough children from rich families, then the temptation would be to spend ever more money in improving the facilities and the staff:pupil ratio to make Christ's Hospital more competitive with leading independent schools in the south-east, and that would widen the so-called 'funding gap' even further. Meanwhile, because this approach would be unacceptable to some of the hospital's closest supporters, we would probably lose in donations and legacies more than we gained by charging higher fees. At just the time when some of the country's most prestigious independent schools were giving bursaries to poorer children, Christ's Hospital would be moving in the opposite direction.

John Whitehead ended by saying that the key to ordering our affairs well was to do only that which is affordable. If that meant doing less for the same number of pupils, or maintaining much the same level of activity for a smaller number, so be it. That, of course, was what I had been arguing unsuccessfully for the previous five years, and five years had been lost with disastrous consequences. Both because the financial position was now even worse and because the inner circle of City Almoners respected the views of a former ambassador more than those of a schoolmaster, his argument carried weight. He also had the support of those of us whom the Chairman of the Education Committee referred to as 'the slash and burn brigade.'

During the debate the Chairman of the Education Committee, when arguing the case for increasing the number of full fee-payers, had said that major savings could only sensibly be achieved by taking a whole accommodation block out of use. I pointed out that he was wrong. It would, for example, be possible to take 18 fewer pupils one year and have one pupil fewer in each of the eighteen houses, which would be neither here nor there as far as the house was concerned but would enable the Director of Studies to have one fewer class that year, with all the consequent knock-on effects. Do that for a few years running and it would produce massive savings.

I was not advocating that particular approach. I only offered it as an example to illustrate the point that the Almoners should set funding limits and not get involved in how the savings should be made. That was a job for the Headmaster, and the Almoners needed to understand this sort of thing before stepping onto the slippery slope of turning Christ's Hospital into a posh school for rich kids. I had nothing against posh schools for rich kids and remained attached to Stowe, which was a very model of such a school. But Christ's Hospital was not that sort of school. It was a charitable institution which existed to look after children in need. It would be tragic if it were to become one more expensive and prestigious independent school.

Instead Council needed to learn how to control expenditure, the school needed to learn how to make its budget after being allocated a specific sum, and a future Governing Body ought to oversee the difficult process of living with a reduced level of recurrent funding. As with the issue of day pupils, 'the slash and burn brigade' had the advantage that Council always found it difficult to make any decisions other than on those matters which could be nodded through. So it usually avoided change and, at least for the moment, the proposal for deliberately seeking full fee-paying boarders, like that for taking fee-paying day pupils, was defeated.

80. The New Dispensation

◇◇◇

During 2007, my last year on Council, there was a change of
Treasurer, Clerk and Head Master – all three within a few months
of each other. I was only peripherally involved, meeting the candidates short-listed for the headship but not taking any part in the
decision-making. The new Treasurer was General Sir Garry
Johnson, recently retired, who had been a junior boy in the school
C.C.F. when I was one of the two sergeants-major. Some years
earlier he had visited the school and gone to see his housemaster,
who, remembering that he had gone into the army, had asked
'Well, Johnson, have you made general yet?' The answer was
'Yes, sir.' The new Headmaster, John Franklin, an Australian, had
previously been the Headmaster of Ardingly and, when interviewed, clearly favoured boosting the school's finances by getting
full fee-paying pupils from abroad – the children of German
industrialists, Russian oligarchs, the Chinese new rich and
Japanese bankers.

As I left Council at the end of 2007 it seemed to me that we had
left them with a terrible inheritance, every year spending millions
of pounds more than our income while City Almoners assured us
that things would improve. In the event the stock market did not
pick up; nor did the property market; West Sussex did not desig-
nate land belonging to Christ's Hospital for new building; donations and legacies were not filling 'the funding gap.' Then in 2008
came the banking crisis, and instead of things getting better, they
got even worse. The new Treasurer, Clerk and Head Master had
to cope as best they could.

The Treasurer reduced the size of Council to make it a more effective decision-making body, slimmed down the committee structure, and adopted the long-overdue reform of specifying each year
what funding the foundation was prepared to provide to the

school. Thus far I approved of the changes, but I was no longer directly involved and my opinion mattered even less than when I was an Almoner.

About the next steps I was more critical. For four and a half centuries admissions had been the responsibility of the foundation. The general principle was that Council decided which children should be admitted and when they should leave, and between arriving and leaving they were in the care of the Head Master. Now decisions about whom to admit were handed over entirely to the school, while at the same time the Head Master was told that, if the funding provided by the foundation was inadequate for the school's needs, he was free to make up the difference in whatever way he could. Understandably his solution was to start taking fee-paying day pupils and to seek to attract boarding pupils whose parents would pay full fees. Those of us who had fought off both of those devices for making money had at the time won the battles, but we had lost the war.

The new policies were explained to the Court of Governors, which no longer had even a residual role as trustees of the hospital's mission, and were commended to them as having not only the benefit of bringing in much needed cash but also of widening the social and ethnic mix of the children. Many of the great and the good, even among Old Blues, saw it as a sensible solution. 'It is the only way forward' was the widespread opinion.

Not everyone agreed. Peter Birkett, Senior Grecian in my last year at school and a devoted supporter of the hospital who had in his time presented four children and who had proposed me to serve on the Council of Almoners, resigned from the group of Old Blues who had undertaken to leave a legacy to the hospital. So did I. Heather Goodare, née Young, Head Girl in 1948-49, wrote a devastating criticism of a prospectus produced in 2012 which was clearly aimed at the rich, pointed out how conveniently near to Gatwick the school was for international pupils, spoke proudly of the Tudor uniform, but neglected to point out that the school existed to care for children in need. Richard Poulton, Head Master from 1987 until 1997, who became a Governor after retiring, was shocked to find that a child he had presented was told that there were plenty of full fee-payers lined up waiting to take his place if he was required to leave. My brother saw the change of policy as profoundly immoral - selling the inheritance of the poor to the rich.

There was a fairly clear dividing line between those who accepted the change of direction and those who disapproved of it. The former thought of Christ's Hospital as an outstandingly good school which had the great merit of providing substantial bursaries to talented children whose parents could not afford full independent school fees. The latter saw it as above all a charitable institution whose mission was to provide for children in need. If you thought of it principally as a school, you were likely to accept the change of policy as necessary for survival. If you thought of it as above all a charitable institution, then the change in admissions policy was worse than a mistake; it was a betrayal of the very nature of the institution.

Those whose priority was ensuring that the hospital could match the provision of the leading independent schools assumed that the extra money from fees was needed because employment costs would 'inevitably' go on rising. But a rise in a school's pay expenditure is no more inevitable than a rise in a family's expenditure. If a family's income is reduced, it may be necessary to cut out the summer holiday, sell a car and even move to a smaller house. The solution is not to go on building up debts on the grounds that nothing should be done to reduce the family's quality of life. It is the same for schools. They need to spend only what they can afford.

If the Head Master had been faced with a steady reduction in funding rather than regular annual increases, he would soon have found that the only way to reduce expenditure was by reducing the total number of members of staff. That in turn would probably result in a decision to increase the average size of teaching groups. If one has a year group of 120 pupils in their early teens, they can as well be taught in five groups of 24 as in six groups of 20. Come to that, they could if necessary be taught in four groups of thirty and thus need only four members of staff rather than six. I had taught O level groups of thirty-four when at Quintin School. The principal consideration is not any idea of the ideal size of a class but rather how many members of staff the school can afford. Much the same applies at every level. A level groups of 18 or 20 require half as many staff as groups of nine or ten.

A gradual reduction of the teaching staff could eventually necessitate reduced pupil numbers. As pupil numbers decreased it would have been possible to convert the relatively recently built Grecians' houses into accommodation for younger members of staff. The accommodation they provided was already significantly better than many young members of staff would have encountered at university, and if provided free would have made a job at Christ's Hospital all the more attractive.

The various problems which would face the Head Master would be inter-related. He was likely to have to reduce total pay expenditure, operate on a tougher pupil:staff ratio, raise the average size of teaching groups, perhaps make some increase in the average number of periods taught by members of staff and possibly decrease a little the total curricular provision to the pupils. Each one of these things has an effect on the others, and doing it well requires the co-operation of the very people who are going to be affected by it.

As Christ's Hospital adjusted to changes such as these there would be a range of consequences, some good and some bad. It would not need so much staff housing, so the sale of houses off the school campus could help reduce the immediate financial problem. It might be possible to provide every member of the teaching staff with free accommodation within the grounds. Before long the demolition of surplus buildings could produce savings on maintenance costs. The important thing would be to turn the problems into opportunities.

Meanwhile a reduction in the number of committees and sub-committees of Council would lead to a reduction in the Counting House staff. At the same time, by going back to the system of pupils doing 'trades', as they had half a century earlier, it would have been possible to reduce the number of cleaners. But that would have been seen as inappropriate for the children of parents paying full fees, and every device for reducing expenditure was distasteful to those whose aim was that rich parents should choose Christ's Hospital rather than Charterhouse or Cranleigh or Lancing.

If Council had acted responsibly in the early twenty-first century, setting the school a clear budget and indicating what the budget was likely to be in a few years' time, then few of these economies would have been needed, and my hope had been that Christ's Hospital would emerge from the financial problems of the early years of the twenty-first century able to continue as a charitable institution providing a first-rate education to clever and talented children from families with incomes too low to be able to afford the fees at any independent school.

The parents in such families might be teachers, nurses, social workers, struggling professional musicians, clergy, distressed gentlefolk or simply members of what used to be called the working class. The foundation could have operated as it had seventy years earlier, setting an income bar on admission, so that no child could enter the school unless his or her parents' income was low enough for them not to be able to afford any contribution towards the cost of maintaining the child at the school. Some, as their financial circumstances improved, might be able to make a contribution later. That had happened in my own case more than half a century earlier. In the last year that John and I were at school my parents paid twelve pounds towards our education, just before the school gave each of us a hundred pounds for clothing and twenty pounds for books before we went up to university.

The longer Christ's Hospital went on spending millions of pounds each year beyond its income, the more likely it was that it would change from a charitable institution into a posh Sussex public school - not as successful academically as Brighton College, nothing like as acceptable socially as Lancing, still less Charterhouse across the border in Surrey, but perhaps able to compete success-fully for full fee-payers with Hurstpierpoint and Ardingly. It was still a very good school, and when inspected in 2012 it was graded 'excellent' on every aspect. But concern among Old Blues about the way it was changing had the effect that in that same year Susan Mitchell started a fund to raise money to pay the cost of sending a child in need to the school, and many of us subscribed to that rather than continuing to give directly to the foundation.

Concern among Old Blues that the percentage of full fee-payers being admitted (26% drawn from the richest 2% of the popula-tion) led in 2015 to a petition being drawn up by a retired Professor of Engineering, David Taplin, living on Vancouver Island in Canada. It was signed by more than a thousand Old Blues. In March 2016 a small group of us led by Professor Keith Bowen, a Fellow of the Royal Society, was deputed to represent the petitioners at a meeting at the Middle Temple with the Treasurer and the Clerk.

Keith spoke of the need to turn away from taking ever more full fee-payers and of the damage of that policy to fund-raising. My brother spoke of the moral imperative to keep to the mission of caring for those in need. Heather Goodare spoke of the desirabil-ity of taking in refugees rather than the children of the super-rich. I commented on the need to cut expenditure and publicise the pain of that in order to encourage donations and legacies. Richard Poulton spoke of the contrast between the time when he was head (1987-96), when Council controlled expenditure and he cared for the staff and the pupils, and the present situation, with the Head Master expected to be a money-making chief executive.

We were received sympathetically, but I fear that neither the peti-tion nor our meeting made any significant difference to Council policy. I remembered how, nearly twenty years earlier, back in 1998, I had recommended that the hospital should keep scrupulously to its mission of caring for children in need, become a London day school, and charge no fees, while transforming the lives of children from homes with low incomes as it had transformed so many of our lives in the past. But I feared that things had gone too far towards turning it into a posh school for rich kids for that to be a possibility.

I encouraged a talented boy living locally, who got grade 8 on both the French horn and the piano at the age of fifteen, to apply to go there for the two A level years. He was given a place and a substantial bursary, but his mother, looking after two children on her own on a very limited income, was still expected to pay £3,000 a year and, like a number of other prospective parents, thought she would have to refuse the place because she could not afford the fees. So in this case I tried to fulfil the obligation to enable others to enjoy the benefits we had ourselves received by paying his fees rather than by giving any more money to the hospital. Two years later, when Tim Duerden got an A* in Music A level and grade A in Chemistry and Biology, and then went on to read Veterinary Science at university, it felt like money well spent.

By 2014 the number of pupils whose parents paid nothing was the same percentage as the number of those whose parents paid full fees. Another quarter of families were paying more than £7,000. The really significant change was that Christ's Hospital was now an independent school charging high fees but offering substantial 'bursaries', rather than a charitable institution providing free education, but expecting a contribution from those parents whose financial circumstances improved.

The scale of its bursaries was impressive. In 2014 all 274 HMC schools between them provided about £60,000,000 worth of bursaries to high-performing children who were thus enabled to escape from their local comprehensive school to a good independent school. More than a quarter of that sum came from Christ's Hospital. Time would tell if it could continue like that.

In 2017 there was a further change when Simon Reid, who had taught English at Christ's Hospital from 1993 until 2004 and had been a very successful housemaster, returned as Head Master. I had met his wife at Stowe back in the summer of 1993, nearly a quarter of a century earlier, when visiting old friends. David Lennard and I were walking through the main building when he pointed out an attractive young woman coming towards us and, knowing where I had been to school, said, 'You must meet Michèle. Her husband has just got a job at Christ's Hospital.'

He introduced us. Michèle was French by origin, born in Madagascar and with a degree in Psychology from Witwatersrand University in South Africa. She was teaching French at Stowe and would, of course, have to give up her job there and look for another post in the Horsham area when Simon moved to Christ's Hospital. I had the staffing needs of Collyer's fairly clear in my head and asked if she could teach both French and Psychology to A level. She could. Before I left we had agreed that she would take up a part-time post in September. In the event she stayed at Collyer's for eleven years, five of them after I retired, until in 2004 Simon went to be the Deputy Head of Worksop College. After seven years there, and another six during which he was the Principal of Gordonstoun, they returned to Christ's Hospital in 2017 when Simon was appointed Head Master.

Several Old Blues who were concerned about the future of the hospital asked me if this would mark a significant change of direction, back towards being a charitable institution rather than an expensive public school. I could not be especially encouraging. It was not Simon's fault, and at the end of his first term in December 2017 he spoke excellently well at the Governors' Meeting at the Mansion House about his educational ideals and his attachment to the charitable nature of the hospital. But the Head Master's job is to run the school and care for the education and welfare of the children within the context of policies determined by the Council of Almoners. There is a limit to how much he can do to influence those policies. Things had gone a very long way in the direction of spending millions of pounds so as to compete in the provision of lavish facilities with the most prestigious schools in the country. In order to balance the books it was still necessary to attract a large number of full fee-payers, and it was still necessary to bring in the money which came from fee-paying day pupils. I doubted if there was now any way back.

Retirement
(1999 onwards)

81. Adjusting to Retirement

◇◇

By the time I retired in 1999 at the age of 65 I had spent fifty years in secondary schools. That was my whole life after the age of ten other than two years in the army and three at Oxford. I had been a schoolboy at Christ's Hospital for eight years and I was a schoolmaster for forty-two: three at Clifton learning my trade, sixteen as a head of history, first at Quintin and then at Stowe, and after that twenty-three years as a headmaster or principal, at KGV and at Collyer's. In the first half of my career I was in schools in which all the pupils were boys. In the second half I presided over two sixth form colleges which had more or less equal numbers of girls and boys.

Throughout the forty-two years that I was a schoolmaster I knew that my latest date for retirement was the end of the academic year in which I reached my sixty-fifth birthday, so when that time came, in the summer of 1999, it was no surprise. I worked until the very end. The A level and GCSE results arrived as usual, producing the same flurry of activity as in every other year. Then at the end of August I removed my books from the shelves in my study and went through files throwing away as much as possible and leaving what I thought might be useful to my successor. On the evening of 31st August 1999 I tidied up my desk and at about 10.30 at night left work for the last time, locked up, posted the keys back through the door and went home. I was free to do whatever I liked for the rest of my life – and get paid a pension for doing it.

As it happens, a decision I had made back in 1984 to require all members of the teaching staff and all the students to be computer literate had an unexpected delayed outcome. For some time before I retired I had been the only member of the teaching staff who was not computer literate, since I had the luxury of a secretary to type things for me. So my colleagues gave me a computer and a printer as a leaving present and Dorothy Boyle, the Head of Business Studies, gave me a disk she had produced for teaching people to type.

I made good use of them. I signed on for an evening class on basic computer literacy at Collyer's during the Autumn Term of 1999, and for some time each day regularly sat at my keyboard in front of the computer screen learning to type using all my fingers. I would, for example, type DCE time after time with the middle finger of my left hand, then CDE and EDC and DEC and ECD, until that finger got used to where the letters were and could type them automatically. Over the next few years I made daily use of the computer, principally as a word processor but also for sending and receiving emails.

Catherine was still teaching at Storrington. She had always done most of the housework: washing and ironing, cooking and cleaning. I tried to be helpful but cannot pretend that I shared at all equally in household tasks. I got up each morning to make a cup of tea and was pleased to make another cup of tea whenever she might want one. I cleared the table after meals and washed up. I did the gardening, put out the rubbish, fed the cats and replenished the birdseed, water, nuts and raisins in the containers just outside the kitchen window. From time to time I would polish the brass or move some furniture and sweep a floor.

But none of that altered the fact that Catherine still did most of the housework, and while I was genuinely grateful for all she did, and did well, I was also aware that while I was now retired and could in a sense indulge in a life of leisure, she, after teaching all day and then getting our supper, would settle down in the evenings not only to preparing the next day's lessons but also to getting ready for all the moderations, assessments, inspections and other devices by which succeeding governments sought to drive up standards of literacy and numeracy in primary schools.

There was no need for her to work if she did not wish to do so. My pension was sufficient for the sort of life we led. So I was delighted when she decided in 2002 to stop full-time teaching and look for an alternative part-time job. After twelve years at Storrington she retired, but she was only fifty-one, still had nine years still to go until she qualified for her pension, and had no wish to give up working completely. So for the time being she was on the West Sussex supply list, able to choose if and when she would substitute for another teacher who was away, and in practice most of her supply work was back in Storrington, where they were pleased to have her fill in for any temporary vacancy. It also had the advantage that she acquired experience of teaching children of other ages than the seven and eight year olds with whom she had mostly worked.

I had been looking forward to having more time to read and write. While I was still working I had avoided much involvement in the affairs of the Horsham parish on the grounds that I was fully occupied with my job. Similarly I had turned down invitations such as one to join the committee of the West Sussex Philharmonic Choir. But once I was retired I no longer had that excuse, so four months after my retirement and throughout 2000 I found myself engaged, at the request of the Vicar, Derek Tansill, on the series of lectures on the history of the Christian Church which were later published as *In the Context of Eternity*. That summer I became the chairman of the management company of Springfield Park, and before long I was co-opted onto the committee of the choir. To begin with I had the not particularly onerous task of collecting Gift Aid on the subscriptions of most of the members, but then, when I failed to turn up to a committee meeting, I found that in my absence I had been made the Deputy Chairman.

At the beginning of 2002 I began my six year term as an Almoner of Christ's Hospital, and, quite apart from meetings of Council, I needed to turn up to meetings of the Education Committee and the Premises Sub-committee and act as Chairman of the Human Resources Sub-committee. In the spring of 2004 I became a Parish

Warden, and all the various commitments related to Springfield Park, the West Sussex Philharmonic Choir, the Horsham Parish and Christ's Hospital, some of them trivial in themselves, added up to a more or less full- time job.

In May of 2004, the month after I had taken on the duties of a Parish Warden, Cathy found a part-time job which gave her immense satisfaction for the rest of her working life. She was appointed to be the West Sussex Education Adviser for the RSPCA (the Royal Society for the Prevention of Cruelty to Animals) and for four days a week during term time she visited schools all over West Sussex teaching model lessons and providing teachers with materials for topics relevant to the care of animals, from mini-beasts to the macro-environment, which they could then them-selves teach. The work took her into primary and secondary schools, independent as well as maintained, and also into universi-ties. Eventually she had taught almost every age group, from nursery school children to graduate students on a PGCE (Post-graduate Certificate of Education) course.

She was also busy in a range of other ways. During the first half of 2005 she joined me working to re-furbish Kate's flat in London. She did most of the planning and preparation for James's marriage in August to Begoña who, we were pleased to discover, saw England as a sort of paradise and wanted to settle here, and in 2006 she was similarly involved in the preparations for the wedding of her daughter, Helen, to Brendan Streeter, who had been Helen's boss when she worked in Southwater and with whom she had for some time shared the car journey back and forth to Brighton, where each of them had a flat.

During 2005 I had had a succession of tests which ended with a diagnosis of prostate cancer, and after I had an operation at the end of October to remove the prostate gland, Cathy had a lot to do looking after me. Afterwards I needed to have a blood test every six months as a check against any recurrence of the cancer and the need for further treatment, but within a few weeks of the operation I was able to carry on as usual. Cathy also carried on with and enjoyed her work as an Education Adviser for the RSPCA.

A couple of years later I was able to have what was in a sense a second retirement. At the end of 2007 I completed my six years as an Almoner of Christ's Hospital and the following April resigned as a Parish Warden. I had already given up the Chairmanship of Springfield Park in 2004 but had remained as one of the directors; in May of 2008 I gave that up as well. In October I resigned from being the Deputy Chairman of the West Sussex Philharmonic Choir. Thus during 2008 I shed all my varied accumulated responsibilities and was able to enjoy what I thought of as my second retirement. I spent some time getting my work on the history of the Christian Church ready for publication by Darton, Longman, Todd, whose editorial director was enthusiastic about publishing it, but by the end of 2009 I had to face the fact that the bankers' crisis had seriously affected the publishing industry and that my book was one of the many casualties.

Cathy's work was also affected by the bankers' crisis. In 2009, as a result of that crisis, which had begun the previous year, less and less money was given to charities and the RSPCA did not just run out of money; it found itself with a deficit of about £7,000,000. As part of the attempt to cope with that and repair its finances, all of its education advisers throughout the country were made redundant. No doubt that helped to restore the financial stability of the organisation, but I could not help but reflect that the total annual pay expenditure on all thirty-six of them was less than some of the individual bonuses still being paid to themselves by bankers presiding over the disasters they had caused. Meanwhile invaluable work educating the next generation about animal welfare was lost.

While the government used public money to rescue the banks because they were too big to be allowed to fail, and senior bankers paid themselves large bonuses, any number of individuals suffered from the knock-on effects of the crash. For those RSPCA Education Advisers who were aged about forty it was something of a personal disaster, and they were just a few among the many thousands whose lives were seriously damaged by the greed and gambling of investment bankers. Catherine, however, had expected to retire after her sixtieth birthday in December 2010, so for her it simply meant that she stopped work a year earlier, at the end of 2009, and for the first six months of 2010 she, like the others, continued to receive her pay as part of the redundancy arrangements.

It meant that she had more time for other things, and in the event the time was needed. In the first place Cathy's mother, Eileen, was becoming increasingly frail and forgetful and in need of care. Already back in the summer of 2001, when she was eighty, she had had a serious fall, breaking one of her hips, and had had to go into hospital. Then in 2008, after another fall and another period in hospital, she stayed with us for three months and it became increasingly clear that she was losing her memory. I first noticed it after I had gone in to see her early one day, had said, 'Good Morning, Eileen' and had given her a kiss. She turned to Cathy and said, 'Who's that nice young man? He reminds me of my son-in-law.'

We realised that it was going to be impossible for her to live on her own in her house, even though it was only half a mile up the road from us. But it might be possible for her to continue living there with a full-time carer. So Cathy started investigating that, and at the same time we did a considerable amount of work on the house to make it as easy as possible for an elderly, frail and forgetful lady to live in it. While we did that we arranged for Eileen to spend a couple of weeks in a retirement home. It was as good a place as one could reasonably expect, but it was soon clear that it would not be a happy long-term solution, so we were immensely grateful and relieved when a splendid Ghanaian girl called Cynthia Botchway came from an organisation called *Helping Hands* and stayed with Eileen for the next four years, looking after her in every way.

It was also useful to Cathy to have the free time which came from being made redundant because her daughter, Helen, had a baby daughter shortly after she and her husband, Brendan, had moved into a Victorian terraced house in Hove. Her waters broke on 10th October 2010, she had a difficult labour until eventually Maisie was born by Caesarean section two days later (if she had been born swiftly the date of her birthday would have been 10.10.10). From then on Cathy devoted herself to being both a good mother and a good grandmother.

Looking after her mother, her daughter, her granddaughter and me still left her time, now she was no longer working for the RSPCA, for her favourite relaxation, which was walking, sometimes with me but more often with one or other of a number of friends. One of those friends was Margaret King, wife of James King, a former colleague of mine; another was Jebs Bridgewater, wife of our new Vicar. With Margaret Cathy did the Moonwalk in London in 2006 to raise money for cancer charities, and since it was the length of a marathon, they had to do plenty of other long walks as they trained for it. With Jebs she walked the South Downs Way in stages in 2009, all the way from Eastbourne to Winchester, to raise money for the refurbishment of St Leonard's Church in the eastern part of Horsham. But with both Margaret and Jebs she mostly just went walking over Denne Hill and off into the Sussex countryside, getting away to walk and talk.

82. The Next Generation

◇◇◇

At the time I retired in 1999 Kate was working as a receptionist for a firm which trained young men as motor cycle couriers and she was living in the flat I had found for her in Hoxton, only a few minutes' walk from Piers's flat near the Angel. He had returned to live there when he transferred to London, still working for the Crown Prosecution Service but now at the Horseferry Road branch. James was in Spain, where he had been for the last ten years and where he was working for the *Universidad Alfonso Decimo, el Sabio*. He reached his thirty-sixth birthday a few days after I retired. Kate was thirty-eight and Piers thirty-four. None of them was married. Kate had been, but the marriage had broken down and it was after that that she had moved to London. Cathy's daughter, Helen, meanwhile, was just coming up to twenty and was starting her second year at the Epsom College of Art and Design.

Kate found the problems of life in the flat in Hoxton beyond her. She seldom found satisfactory tenants for the rooms she wanted to rent out, and those she did find did not always pay their rent. For a couple of years she fairly regularly made the monthly payments towards buying the flat, but they then became erratic and she clearly did not feel the same obligation to keep the payments up-to-date as if she had been paying rent to a landlord. Meanwhile the firm she was working for was found to be raking in money from a government scheme to provide the unemployed with a New Start but was doing relatively little to justify its income. The firm folded up and she lost her job. Shortly afterwards she was suffering from depression, probably far more seriously than I realised, and was living in the flat with neither job nor income, with accumulating rubbish and with one thing after another breaking down: washing machine, television, boiler and plumbing.

Putting those things right was expensive and time-consuming, and on top of that I found that every so often I was having to pay the service charge and council tax, the electricity and water bills, pay off overdrafts accumulated at the bank and at a building society, pay off bailiffs when they were threatening to distrain all her furniture, pay a fine for not having a television license and, when the Waltham Forest Council caught up with her from the time she had lived in a bed-sitter in Leytonstone, pay both the council tax and the fine for non-payment.

Usually she left these problems until the last minute and would then ring me to say that she was getting 'silly letters' and needed help. What was particularly sad about it for me was that her reaction afterwards was to say that I had only helped her in order to humiliate her, and anyway, she would say, she had never wanted to live there and would rather have gone on living in a bed-sitter and paying the rent. To that I could only reply that she was free to go whenever she wanted and that I would repay her everything she had paid, less the numerous payments I had had to make on her behalf.

I kept a detailed account of what it was all costing and subtracted it from such payments as she made. By 2005 the expense of keeping her in the flat was threatening to overtake the payments she had made. Cathy and I spent some weeks clearing rubbish, cleaning, repairing and redecorating, but to no avail. That summer Kate moved out, with not much more than £5,000 of the money she had contributed towards buying it while living there rent-free. I then sold the flat.

I told her that I would still do whatever I could to help her find a permanent place to live, but the initiative would now have to come from her. Shortly afterwards she found a job as a warden at the National Gallery, looking after the pictures. It had the advantage that she was genuinely appreciative of the paintings she was guarding. It had the disadvantage that she could spend all day indoors doing little other than feeling miserable. She gradually used up the £5,000 which I was looking after for her as she moved from one address to another. After it was gone she had less and less contact with James or Piers or me. We sent her Christmas and birthday cards and presents, but seldom got an answer. She told us that her counsellor had said that contact with her family was bad for her. It was very sad, but there was no obvious solution.

James was still in Spain. He clearly loved life in Madrid and it looked as if he was going to stay there for ever. But when he met a Spanish girl, Maria Begoña Serna Cebrian, and they decided to get married, he brought her over to meet his family. She decided that England was a sort of paradise and in the end they not only came to England for their wedding in 2005, but also decided to stay here and live in Southport. Begoña, usually known in England as Begonia, had a flat of her own in Madrid, and she and James were lucky to sell their four flats near the peak of the Spanish property market before coming to live in England. On the other hand they were unlucky that, after transferring their money from euros to sterling, they lost quite a lot because, as a result of the bankers' crash, sterling rapidly declined in value against the euro.

James got a job teaching English for Academic Purposes at Salford University, to which he commuted by train. Large numbers of young men (and some women) from Middle Eastern countries, such as Iraq and Saudi Arabia, wanted to come to England to study. Universities got substantial income from charging high fees, and the government encouraged that because it made it easier to cut university funding. Many of the foreign students already had a degree in, for example, Engineering or Physics or Economics in their own country, but they wanted an English degree which had international status. It was James's job to teach them enough English for them to be able to embark on an English degree course. In particular they needed to be able to make use of phrases such as, 'In the light of recent research it is possible that...' !

It was similar to what he had been doing in Spain for many years, but with the difference that most of his students at Salford had little or no English when they started, and it is more difficult to learn English when one's mother tongue is Arabic than when it is Spanish. It was made even more difficult for them in that they were housed in hostels with their fellow-countrymen, and James

James and Begoña after their wedding in 2005.
They are standing in the cloisters at Christ's Hospital,
outside the Court Room, where the reception was held.

could not persuade the university authorities that they needed
to be found lodgings with English families. On 19ᵗʰ July 2009
Begoña had a baby son, Bobby, and shortly afterwards she and
James bought a particularly attractive house in York Road,
Birkdale, just round the corner from where we had lived from
1976 until 1983.

In 2001, when he was thirty-six, Piers was promoted to be the
Head of the West London CJU, or Criminal Justice Unit, with a
team of lawyers doing the sort of work he had himself been doing
for the last seven years. But he did not enjoy being a manager.
Too much of his time, he felt, was spent drinking coffee at meetings with government ministers who wanted to promote new initiatives - action against domestic violence one week, action against
street crime the next. He came to feel that his main job was protecting his team from all these initiatives, so that they could get on

with the real work of prosecuting the criminals the police had arrested and securing convictions.

He did not have a high view of the way the CPS was run. It was clearly despised by the members of the criminal bar, who, if they were successful, were highly paid out of the proceeds of crime and contemptuous of the prosecutors, and if they were unsuccessful were resentful of what they saw as the relatively secure lives and incomes of those who worked for the CPS. The head of the CPS, the Director of Public Prosecutions, was usually someone whose reputation had been made defending criminals rather than prosecuting them and, after a stint at the CPS, would go on to be a judge. The senior managers were so concerned with developing anti-racist and anti-sexist policies and promoting the latest government initiatives that they often seemed to forget that their core business was prosecuting criminals and securing the conviction of the guilty.

By 2004 Piers felt that he had had more than enough and moved to a job with the Nurses' and Midwives' Council, where he liked the people he was working with but found that most of his work involved constructing cases against nurses and midwives who had made tragic mistakes. An exhausted and overworked young woman might kill a patient by giving him 1,000 milligrams of something instead of 100. An experienced psychiatric nurse might make the mistake of falling in love with one of her patients, wrecking her marriage and tearing her family apart. Now Piers had the job of destroying their careers.

It was not real crime, he felt. It was professional misconduct, and usually sad rather than wicked. Time and again he found that his sympathies were with the person against whom he had to construct a case. So in 2007, when he heard of an opening in the antiterrorist division of the CPS, he returned to the organisation he had left three years earlier, on the same pay scale as he had been on when he had been the head of the West London CJU, but now working for the specialist anti-terrorist division.

Kate, James and Piers after James's wedding,
standing in the main quadrangle at Christ's Hospital.

He was still living in his flat at the Angel, Islington, and each morning he walked two miles or so to the offices of the Crown Prosecution Service near London Bridge and at the end of the day walked back again. Work was now strikingly different from when he had first worked for the CPS. No longer was he picking up fifty files for one day's work. Now he could have just one case for more than a year when, for example, several young men plotted to commit a terrorist attack and they needed to be arrested before they could carry it out. He was going to need to prove their intention to commit the terrorist offence, which is far more difficult than proving an offence after it is committed.

It was particularly difficult because much of the evidence the police had would not be admissible in court. They might have first heard about it when someone overheard and then reported what was being planned. But hearsay is not admissible in court as evidence. Nor were most intercepted telephone conversations, though those picked up by a bug placed, for example, in the suspect's bedroom were admissible. After months of hard work, both before and after the suspects were arrested, it was possible to construct a case, and eventually a case so watertight that the accused saw no alternative to pleading guilty. One important part of the work was ensuring that all appropriate material was disclosed to the defence, for if it was not, then a prosecution which was successful in court could subsequently be lost on appeal.

There were plenty of problems along the way. One day, when he had to appear in court to get an extension of custody and fix a date for the next hearing of nine young men accused of planning serious and highly publicised terrorist offences, he was faced with about three dozen defence lawyers. Each of the nine accused had a legal team led by a Queen's Counsel, with all three dozen of the defence lawyers paid out of Legal Aid. The judge took the view that at the next hearing Piers, instead of dealing with it on his own, was going to need extra legal and administrative support. So when he got back to the office he explained that. The response was that he knew perfectly well that their budget had been cut and he would have to cope alone.

In the event the case was won, with each of the defendants pleading guilty. Piers had a high opinion of the persistent and very hard work of the police involved. He had a similarly high opinion of the Treasury Counsel who would have led the prosecution in the High Court if the case had come to trial, and also of the judge who grasped the issues swiftly and made sentencing decisions which showed how well he understood the case. But his relations with his own manager had broken down so badly that he requested a move to another unit, and the experience of finding his own organisation more of a problem than the criminals he was prosecuting had taken a lot out of him. He was glad to move in 2012 from anti-terrorism to special crimes.

From time to time he would come down to Horsham for the weekend and it was always a pleasure to see him. We would go for a long walk in the Sussex countryside, sometimes with Cathy and sometimes just the two of us. Cathy always fed him particularly well, and although he and I no longer played chess together, since he would now always beat me fairly easily, we would sometimes play through the remarkable chess match played in 1858, when the American chess master, Paul Morphy, took on the Duke of Brunswick and Count Isouard in a box at the Paris Opera House. Morphy's opponents were both considerable amateur players, and it is difficult to fault their play. But Paul Morphy developed his pieces rapidly and at the end of the game sacrificed a rook, a knight, a bishop and eventually his queen to get check mate with his other rook, protected by his other bishop. It is widely seen as the most beautiful chess game ever played. Piers remembered all the moves.

Meanwhile, back in 2000, early in the last year of her degree course, Cathy's daughter, Helen, had reached the age of twenty-one and come into the money from a trust fund set up for her by Mervyn and Eileen, her maternal grandparents, when she was a baby. She immediately knew exactly what she wanted to do with it: buy a flat in Fulham, where, apparently, 'it' was all 'at.' So we went up to Fulham, she found the flat she wanted, and with the trust fund, her mother's savings, some help from her grandmother and from me, and as large a mortgage as possible, she became a property owner and installed a couple of her friends from Collyer's to pay rent, with which she was able to pay off the mortgage. Then, at the end of her degree course, she went to live there herself and look for a job.

Before long she was the assistant to the editor of a new magazine, *Fashionline*. Two months later she was the Assistant Editor and after six months, shortly before the first issue came out, she was the Editor. I still have a copy of each of the first two issues, but no more, because at that stage the company responsible for the magazine collapsed, and after her rapid rise there came an even swifter fall. She was out of a job. But it was all useful experience. After a brief stint designing web-sites, she decided to leave Fulham, made a fifty thousand pound profit selling the flat, and went to live in Brighton, where, as colleagues at Collyer's had told me, 'it' was even more 'at.'

Helen now found a job at *Disctronics* in Southwater, where she worked at putting things onto CDs. One evening I asked her what she had been doing that afternoon and she said she had arranged to have 50,000 copies of the Bible run off. I thought of medieval monks who sometimes spent their whole life writing out one copy of the Bible, and she had run off 50,000 in an afternoon. It was while at *Disctronics* that she cadged a lift most days from Brighton to Southwater and back with her line manager, Brendan Streeter, and though after a while she severed her connection with *Disctronics* and went to work for a public relations firm in Worthing, she did not sever her connection with Brendan. Instead they got married in June of 2006, bought their house in Hove in 2008, had their first child, Maisie, in 2010, moved to a detached house in Hassocks in 2012, and had their second child, Bruno, in 2013.

Kate was still in living London, working as a warden at the National Gallery, but seldom in touch with the rest of the family. James was living in Birkdale with Begoña and Bobby, and was commuting each day to Salford University. Piers was still living at the Angel and walking to and from work at the CPS headquarters near London Bridge. Helen, together with Brendan and Maisie and Bruno, was only forty minutes' drive away from us in Hassocks.

Cathy at fifty-six at the wedding of her daughter

83. Cousins, Nieces and Nephews

<><><><><><><><><><><><><><><><><><><><><><><><><><><><><><><><><><><><><><><><>

As as John and I approached our seventieth birthdays on 1st November 2003, Cathy and Anneliese arranged a splendid 140th birthday party for us and invited all our close relations to lunch at Amberley Castle, the thirteenth century castle of the Bishops of Chichester, now turned into a hotel. They came from all over the place, Margaret and her daughter Cate from Gloucestershire, Beverley and Johnny from Winchmore Hill, Jill and Peter from Rottingdean, and Pamela and Sandra all the way from Cape Cod in Massachusets. Christian turned up from the South coast with Sally and a revised version of *Can't Smile Without You*, a song he had written a quarter of a century earlier and which had gone to No 1 in the USA when it was sung by Barry Manilow in 1978. He had provided alternative words relating it to John and to me: *'the head and the dean, y' know what I mean.'*

Christian had been writing songs, together with two friends, ever since he came down from Cambridge in 1963 with a degree in Classics. He taught in a prep school and combined that and writing pop songs with playing rugby fives at a high level, though he only got round to winning a national championship when playing as a veteran at over the age of forty. His first musical success was with a song called *In Thoughts of You*, sung by Billy Fury, and other songs which he and his friends wrote were performed by Cliff Richard, Cilla Black, Frank Ifield and Helen Shapiro.

Then in 1970, when they could not think who was a suitable performer for a new song they had written, *Don't You Know, She Said 'Hello'*, they recorded it themselves, and since they needed a name for the performers, one of them, sitting on an Underground train with a packet of butterscotch in his hands, suggested the name *Butterscotch*. The song was so popular and was played so much on the radio that they got a number of invitations to perform it at concerts, or 'gigs.' But none of them had ever performed in public, so they sent polite replies explaining that they were already booked, until eventually they received an invitation to appear on *Top of the Pops* and decided to accept. I saw Christian at a family occasion a week before he appeared on television. He was trying to grow his hair a bit longer (usually it was 'short, back and sides'), and a few days earlier he had been out with his mother, Syd's Ivy, to buy a pair of purple, flared trousers and a psychedelic shirt.

Don't You Know, She Said 'Hello' was popular across the Atlantic as well, and the American record company, RCA Records, asked them for an album. Christian and his friends were paid to go on a trip round American radio and television stations promoting it, and while they did that they met Elvis Presley. Some years later Christian was called on to give a different sort of public performance, when Belmont School in Mill Hill, the preparatory school where he had taught for eighteen years, invited him back as the principal guest on Speech Day for the school's Centenary. He had written the words and music of the school song, and now he composed another verse for the occasion and sang it to them. He asked me what sort of thing one should talk about on such an occasion, and I suggested that he should tell the children about meeting Elvis Presley. Both the singing of the extra verse and the talk went down well.

The way the record industry developed in the second half of the twentieth century made it difficult to live off royalties, since it was so easy for people to get copies of popular music without paying for a record. But when *The Association of Massachusetts Dentists* adopted *Can't Smile Without You* as a tune to be played with all their advertisements, Pamela and Sandra on Cape Cod made sure that Christian got the appropriate royalties. Of all the cousins they were the ones who had far the longest distance to come to our 140th lunch party, so it was a particular pleasure to see them.

All three of my own children came to our 140th celebrations, and all of John's three came as well. The oldest of his three was

Frances, who was a year younger than James and a year older than Piers. She was in the middle of a three year course from 2001 till 2004 at Westcott House in Cambridge, where her father had trained forty years earlier, and was acquiring an M.A. in Theology as well as the General Ordination Certificate. In 2004 she was ordained deacon at St Alban's Cathedral and spent three years as a curate before taking an administrative post as the executive officer for the House of Bishops at Church House, Westminster. She stayed there for five years until in 2013 she was 'inducted, installed and collated' as the Vicar of Great St Mary's, Sawbridgeworth, and moved into a large Vicarage.

Her younger sister, Miriam, born in 1972, and thus the youngest by some years of John and Anneliese's children, was the first to get married. While studying at University College, London, she had stayed at the International Lutheran Student Centre in Thanet Street in Bloomsbury. A few years after getting her degree and training in Business Management, she returned as the Assistant Warden, met a tall ice-hockey playing Canadian called Jason Campbell who worked for a law firm in the city, and in 2001 married him in a splendid ceremony conducted by her father in Durham Cathedral. She and Jason then squeezed into her tiny flat at the Lutheran Centre, had a baby son, Jude, in 2004 and just managed to squeeze his cot in as well. Eventually, in 2013, when Miriam became the Manager of the Centre, she acquired a much larger flat and they were able to live in relative luxury.

Her brother, Matthew, who was a few months younger than Piers but quite a lot taller, had always been a kindly and loving older brother to Miriam. Thus, when Miriam was a teenager in the 1980s living in Rochester and she wanted to go to some such event as a pop concert with her friend, Louise, Matthew would take them. In 1989 Miriam, like Frances, had gone north to live in Durham with her parents, while Matthew was still working and living in the south. Miriam always kept in touch with Louise, so when she and Jason got married, she asked Louise to be one of her bridesmaids, while, since their father was the priest conducting the service, it fell to Matthew to fulfil many of the functions of the bride's father. He did so in an impressive fashion. He now met Louise again, no longer the child he had taken to concerts with his little sister, but a young woman, and before long they were engaged. While Miriam and Jason had been married in Durham Cathedral in 2001, Matthew and Louise were married in Rochester Cathedral in 2003. John again officiated.

Matthew, of course, had an English father and a German mother and like his sisters could speak German fluently. Louise, it turned out, had an English grandmother and a German grandfather. Her grandmother had as a girl lived in Kent, but when her widowed mother married a German in the 1930s, they went to live in Hamburg. Thus during the Second World War she was a teenage English girl in Germany, eventually being bombed by the R.A.F. At the end of the war, her step-father now dead, she and her mother returned to England and to Kent.

Louise's grandfather, Georg, another teenager during the war, joined the German army, was captured and, as a prisoner-of-war of the British, was set to work on a farm in Kent. In the summer of 1945, with the war recently over, he was returning from his day's work with the other p-o-ws and with his pitchfork over his shoulder. They passed a couple of English girls, he shouted something out at them in German and was surprised when one of them replied in his own language. Before long they were married and he never returned to Germany – at least, only for the occasional holiday, when, he told me more than sixty years later, he was amused to have a German shopkeeper say to him, *Sie sprechen sehr gut Deutsch für ein Ausländer* (You speak very good German for a foreigner).

I met Georg at Matthew's and Louise's wedding and we reminisced about our very different experiences of serving in an army - he in a war, with his whole life transformed as a result, and I in peacetime in the occupying army in the British zone of Germany, where, in the officers' mess at Fallingbostel, I had learnt the

German marching song, *Wir fahren gegen England*, from our mess waiters, and had sung it with a fellow subaltern at a regimental dinner night. Georg, of course, had sung it on the march, and in the reception after Matthew's and Louise's wedding, as the young people danced, we sat on a sofa singing it together. It is a tender, sentimental song with a twist at the end, and loosely translated it goes like this:

We need to sing a song today and drink the cool, white wine,
The clinking of our glasses marks a parting – yours and mine.
Oh! Fare you well, my love, farewell. Give me your fair white hand,
For we must march away today. We march against England.

The original compares rather favourably with the equivalent English marching song of the time: *Roll out the barrel.*

Two others whom we were delighted to welcome to the birthday party at Amberley Castle on 1ˢᵗ November 2003 were June's daughters, Linda and Vicky – Linda with her husband, Nick Collier. At the time Linda was radiant with vitality and apparently in perfect health. But during December she felt unwell, saw a doctor and was told shortly before Christmas that she might have cancer. A surgeon would investigate and, if necessary, operate early in the New Year. Meanwhile, she and the rest of the family should try to have a good Christmas. They went to their house at Walcott in Norfolk and in rapid succession celebrated Christmas, then Nick's birthday and then the New Year, with Linda at the heart of the celebrations. Once it was all over she and Nick drove the children back to Barnes. After the journey she was breathless and increasingly unwell, so at nine o'clock Nick drove her to hospital. In the early hours of the morning she died. She was forty-three.

While she still looked like a bright young girl, full of promise for the future and full of energy, she had matured into a full-grown human being, cultivating the promise in her children, valuing the companionship of her sister, providing love and support to her husband, sharing with him the dream of creating a country home

A family photograph: Helen, Cathy and my nieces
Vicky and Linda, who is carrying her first child, Chloë,
to whom Cathy is godmother.

in Norfolk surrounded by trees, and able to relax there and read. She had many talents, as a mathematician, an oarswoman, a corporate financier and increasingly as a pianist (she was working towards her LRAM), and was determined to cram as much as possible into her life. But in her last two years much of her time was spent looking after her second child, Imogen, or Immy, who was suffering from and being cured of leukemia, and there was too little time for enjoying family life.

In 2008 her younger sister, Vicky, returned to Cambridge to Darwin College to do a doctorate on 'The Expressible Past: Discursive Modes in *Íslendinga saga.*' She met an American academic, Paul Gazzoli, who despite his nationality and his name, cultivated the appearance and manner of an English country gentleman of the 1920s and was a member of the Oxford and Cambridge Club in Pall Mall, where we sometimes met and which he encouraged me to join. Once he had completed his doctorate on Anglo-Danish relations in the late eleventh century, he went on to further research on Bishop Anscar, a missionary of the same period, while teaching the Anglo-Saxon, Old Norse and Celtic course to undergraduates at both Corpus Christi and Selwyn colleges in Cambridge. His tastes and Vicky's were similar, they got on very well, and they settled down in an attractive house in Argyle Street in Cambridge, he teaching and doing research, she translating Icelandic books into English. Early in 2017 Cathy and I went up to Cambridge to be the witnesses at their wedding.

I had reached an age at which I was trying to off-load a lifetime's collection of books to good homes. I gave books on modern history to James and books on philosophy and anything to do with classical antiquity to Piers. Similarly I was able to give a large number of books on medieval history, as well as chronicles and collections of documents, to Vicky and Paul, who would both make good use of them. Vicky became the leading translator of Icelandic books into English, and later in 2017 went to Iceland to receive a grant from the Icelandic government and be presented with an award by the Icelandic president for producing translations of such high quality that they had brought Icelandic culture to international attention.

My children's other cousins on their mother's side were unable to come. Oriel's brother, Michael, his wife Anne and their two sons, Christopher and Peter, were on the far side of the world in Australia. Fiona, the only daughter of Oriel's twin sister, Chloë, could not come either. She had by then married David Pullen and had three children, Benjamin, Toby and Chloë, and it was a pleasure to be able to visit them in the autumn of 2013, when Toby and Chloë were at home from school at Worth Abbey, even though Benjamin was away at Exeter University.

In November of that year, when John and I could have had a 160th birthday party, it was difficult to arrange anything of the sort because in the intervening ten years six small children of the next generation had been born in our immediate families. First was a little boy, Jude, to Miriam and Jason, then two girls, Olivia and Rachael, to Matthew and Louise. A boy, Bobby, the only male of that generation to have the surname Arnold, was born to James and Begoña, and both a girl and a boy, Maisie and Bruno, were born to Helen and Brendan. The practicalities of travel and child care made a party like that of 2003 impracticable. So we celebrated our birthday quietly. At Christmas time, when Pamela and Sandra came over from Cape Cod to stay, and Beverley, by then a widow, stayed as well, we had a sort of Cousins' Convention, with John from Canterbury (sadly alone, because Anneliese was unwell at the time), Christian and Sally from Chichester, and Jill and Peter from Brighton.

84. *'In the Context of Eternity'*

◇◇◇

Some time during the autumn of 1999, a few weeks after I retired, Derek Tansill, Vicar of Horsham, Canon of Chichester Cathedral, and *ex officio* a member of the Governing Body of Collyer's, came to see me to suggest that during the coming year, the last of the second millennium, I should do a series of talks on the history of the Christian Church. By then I had known him for about fifteen years, ever since he had come to Horsham as Vicar of the parish, three years after I arrived at Collyer's. He was an amiable bachelor who regularly and effectively in his sermons on Sundays related the readings to ordinary life and showed how the scriptures gave useful guidance on how to live and how to look at things.

Once, at a Collyer's Founder's Day service, he told the story of the eighteenth camel, which had been useful for solving a problem. An Arab had provided in his will for half his camels to go to his eldest son, a third to his other son, and just a sixth to a daughter who was already married and well provided for. When he died he left seventeen camels and the sums did not work. His children took the problem to a wise old man of the village who, being good at arithmetic as well as wise, lent them an extra camel, telling them to bring it back once the problem was solved. They soon found that the arithmetic now worked: the elder son had nine camels, the other had six, and the daughter had two. Everything was in accordance with their father's will, and the eighteenth camel was left over. They took it back with thanks.

It was a good story to tell in an educational institution to illustrate the point that anyone seeking to resolve a problem (and there are lots of personal problems to be resolved in any educational institution) needs to back off once the problem is dealt with. A teacher might need to deal with a student's difficulties with his or her parents, but it will not do for the teacher to take over as a sort of surrogate parent. The task is reconciliation. It was a good point to make, and perhaps even more valuable for members of staff than for most students. It was typical of Derek that the story he told about the eighteenth camel made the point memorable.

He had tried, unsuccessfully, as had his predecessor, to get me to become a Reader and preach regularly in church, but I had always replied that I was a teacher rather than a preacher, so instead he got me to do short courses for a few parishioners on topics such as *The Reformation in England* – something I was pleased to do if only to get over the point that the Church of England was not founded by Henry VIII. He would also get me to preach at Holy Communion on particular occasions, such as the beginning of a mission week, when I preached on Samuel Crossman's great hymn, *My song is love unknown*, and later he got me to give a series of sermons at Evensong on *Four Great Reformers: Erasmus, Luther, Calvin and Cranmer.*

He had a demanding job, leading a team of eight full-time clergy in a parish with five churches. The parish church of St Mary-the-Virgin was fairly mainstream in its churchmanship; Holy Trinity was high church, St Leonard's low, St Mark's evangelical and St John's, Broadbridge Heath, charismatic. None of those definitions is either adequate or accurate, but they give some idea of the problem, and it was to Derek's credit that he managed to maintain a happy and co-operative team, with clergy whose views on matters theological and liturgical differed widely while they co-existed equably.

He was also a good trainer of a succession of curates, mostly intelligent young men who needed to continue their studies while carrying a substantial load of work in the parish, but, when they started, were usually inexperienced at speaking in public. So Derek used to get me to listen critically to their sermons and offer constructive criticism. It was something I found worthwhile. The gulf between good sermons and bad ones is wide, and guidance on how to preach a good sermon is not unlike guidance on how to write a good history essay.

Now that I was retired, Derek was proposing something substantial for me to do. He suggested that I could provide a year-long course on the history of the church. I suspect that part of his motivation was the feeling that now that I was retired, after years of working hard, I probably needed something worthwhile to do, and he was right. As it happens, the history of the church was something I had long been interested in, so it was not as if I was starting from scratch.

If I was to do this, I wanted to make it clear that the two thousand years in which the Christian Church had existed was but a brief moment in the context of the two and a half million years in which mankind had walked the earth and the even longer period of anything up to four thousand million years in which the planet we live on has sustained life. At the same time I was interested not only in the way the Church had developed but also in its relationship with the societies within which it existed, and I wanted to tackle the history of the Church throughout the world and not just in England.

I thought it important to pay some attention to the historical context in which Jesus and his disciples lived: the past history of the Jewish people, the Greek intellectual climate in which the *New Testament* was written, and the expansion of the power of Rome to embrace all the land around the Mediterranean. I wanted to make it clear that much of the development of the Church, both its ideas and its structures, happened in the Eastern Mediterranean, where the Roman Empire survived a thousand years longer than in the barbarian West. Above all I wanted to give just as much attention to events in the relatively distant past as to those of more recent times.

It is characteristic of historical writing about the history of the Christian church that authors usually concentrate on the lives and teaching of both Jesus and St Paul and then skip rapidly through the next thousand and a half years, reaching the Renaissance popes a quarter of the way through the book, after which they go into great detail about everything from the Protestant Reformation onwards.

The tendency to neglect the so-called Middle Ages is true of a widely popular view of history. At one time, it is suggested, there were the ancient civilisations of Greece and Rome. Some time later there came into existence the modern world in which we live. In between was a period of history in which nothing of any significance happened and which, for want of a better name, is called the Middle Ages. That view of things is profoundly misleading in relation to history in general and is particularly misleading in relation to the history of the Christian Church.

During the year 2000 I produced twenty-five talks, one a fortnight all the way until Christmas, covering the whole history of the church, and gave as much attention to the sixth and seventh centuries as to the sixteenth and seventeenth. The talks were welcomed by the forty to fifty members of the congregation who turned up, and as others heard of them I was encouraged to repeat them in the autumn of 2002 at Collyer's as an evening class. That in turn led to a book, which I called *In the Context of Eternity*, and sent to Hodder and Stoughton in 2004. They were the publishing firm which had bought up Edward Arnold, who had published my previous book, *Britain, Europe and the World*, nearly forty years earlier, and that seemed a good reason to approach them.

Their history editor was initially encouraging, but eventually wrote to explain that although *In the Context of Eternity* 'reads well, is of great interest, and in its equal attention to each period of history, also fulfils a need which existing texts have failed to satisfactorily address', they were primarily an academic publisher and it was 'probably that bit too populist (and footnote-free) for our list.' He felt sure that 'several other publishers would be interested' and wished me success in finding it 'a more appropriate home.'

In the event I put off contacting other publishers, partly because I was heavily involved for some years in the affairs of both Christ's

Hospital and the Horsham parish, partly because I was far more motivated to write something than to contact publishers about it, and finally because I thought it worth finding the time to revise it to the point at which it was twenty chapters, each of ten pages. The first chapter was a prologue on *Israelites, Jews and Greeks*. Then the first millennium was divided into three sections, each with three chapters, and the second millennium was similarly divided. The final chapter of the book was an epilogue on *The Dawn of a New Millennium*.

My former tutor at Oxford, Colin Morris, now retired as Professor of Medieval History at Southampton University, read through the medieval sections, and an old friend, Peter Newman Brooks, now retired from teaching at Cambridge University, read the section on the Reformation period. My brother John, also retired and now living in Canterbury, and another old friend, Christopher Holdsworth, the retired Professor of Medieval History at Exeter University, both read the whole thing. All four gave helpful advice.

In 2008 I wrote to a number of publishing houses. Academic publishers suggested that I needed to approach more general publishing houses. General publishers suggested that the book was more appropriate for specifically Christian publishing houses. But Christian publishing houses did not even want to read a specimen chapter. SCM Canterbury Press said that their focus was on text books and reference books for undergraduate courses, so my proposal did not fit the specific aims of their present publishing programme. SPCK, the Society for Promoting Christian Knowledge, simply said that they had found that ecclesiastical history did not sell well for them. No wonder! Most ecclesiastical history was entirely unsuited to intelligent general readers and even to the clergy. It usually neglected the historical background to the rise of the Christian Church, it neglected the churches of the East and it neglected the Middle Ages, and what was written was usually far too detailed, even to the point of unintelligibility.

The one editorial director who replied that he not only liked what he had seen but would also consider publishing it was Brendan

Walsh of Darton, Longman, Todd, a publishing house whose website said that they were 'the UK's leading publisher of high quality books on spirituality, religion and theology', and stressed that they were not particularly 'Catholic, Protestant or Anglican, traditional or progressive, conservative or liberal.' Since I was above all concerned with providing an explanation, intelligible to ordinary people, of how the Christian Church had developed, that suited me very well.

Brendan saw the rest of the book, responded with enthusiasm and said that the next step was for him to find an American publisher willing to bring it out in the USA at the same time as DLT published it in England. He wrote to a number of American publishing houses and told them that *In the Context of Eternity* was 'a lively, and readable one-volume history of Christianity that tells the story of how the church developed the way it did, how Christians developed their beliefs and organisational structures, how they came to disagree with each other over a variety of issues and how the church influenced and was influenced by the societies within which it developed.' He described it as 'an exciting and fresh account of how the modern world, the world of scientific revolution, of capitalism, and of the liberal democracy of the United States of America across the Atlantic all emerged out of the interaction of Christianity and Barbarism on the ruins of the Roman Empire in the West.'

Not long afterwards he was writing to say that there was 'blood all over the boardroom carpets' in America. Publishers were in the hands of the bankers and the bankers were in the middle of a banking crisis. We might have to 'go it alone' in England. So we carried on, looking at such issues as how many copies one should produce at a first printing, what sort of a cover the book should have, and whether one should start with a hardback and go on to paperback or begin with a paperback version.

Then at the beginning of September 2009 he wrote to say, 'We're very close in our thoughts about the book, the look and design of it, so we'll work through all these issues together....I will have costs for our new plan soon and will put my formal proposal to colleagues in three weeks.' He went on to say, 'The big 1 volume McCullough history is due soon. We'll blow it out of the water.' The book he was referring to, *A History of Christianity - The First Three Thousand Years,* was published a few weeks later. It avoided most of the failings of ecclesiastical history and was remarkably well-balanced, but it was very big indeed, roughly five times as long as what I had written, and more a book for scholars than for general readers.

Only a month later Brendan Walsh wrote again, this time apologetically to say that his sales and marketing department felt it would be difficult to sell the book in the current climate and he could not go against their decision. It was very disappointing and I felt disinclined to put more effort into something which seemed unpublishable. I wrote to two or three other publishers. But none was prepared to face what they obviously saw as an unprofitable venture. One editor wrote to say that he admired 'the easy erudition with which you have mastered such a mass of information', but explained that his publishing house served 'the evangelical end of the ecclesiastical spectrum' and so was the wrong vehicle for me.

I got the impression that evangelicals wanted evangelical propaganda, catholics wanted devotional works, and both thought that ecclesiastical history was not something the reading public was likely to buy. It was, I decided, necessary to think about getting it published privately, and I was fortunate to find a publishing house, Grosvenor House, which did a very good job of it and brought it out in 2015. Before long it was receiving commendations from a range of distinguished academics and senior clergy.

Henry Mayr-Harting, the Emeritus Regius Professor of Ecclesiastical History at Oxford, whom I had known when we studied the *St Bernard* special subject together as undergraduates, wrote to say that it was 'a marvellous book. It is always clear, sympathetic, and fair-minded. In fact it is in the best sense very Anglican.'

It was a particular pleasure to get commendations from a Roman Catholic and a Lutheran on the same day. One of my former pupils, David McDonough, had given a copy to Michael Brockie, a Roman Catholic priest and canon lawyer who was the Provost of the House of Canons of the Archdiocese of Westminster, and David wrote to tell me that Canon Brockie had described it to him as 'a delight, a veritable *tour de force*' and had added, 'I wish I had had a copy when I was a young seminarian.' By the same post I heard from my brother that Jaako Rusama, a Lutheran Professor of Theology at the University of Helsinki, had written to him to say that he intended to make use of it in his lectures, 'because the way the faith developed is not always sufficiently understood by many theologians and priests.'

John had also recommended it to a retired American publisher, Norman Hjelm, who in turn recommended an American publisher, Wipf and Stock, to me, and in 2017, two years after it had been published in England, it came out in the USA as well.

85. Parish Warden

◇◇

The Vicars of Horsham are Vicars rather than Rectors because in the Middle Ages they held the living not in their own right, but as deputies, or vicars, of the abbess of a local nunnery, and the title of Vicar continued after the Dissolution of the Monasteries. Roger of Wallingford is the first to be recorded, in the thirteenth century, though the parish had existed for centuries before that. The main structure of the parish church of St Mary-the-Virgin also dates from the thirteenth century, and in relatively recent times the parish has built four more churches in different parts of the town, so that by the end of the twentieth century it had five churches, eight full-time clergy, and a varying number of part-time and retired clergy.

Rather unusually Horsham has had three, rather than two, Parish Wardens ever since the Middle Ages, and early in 2004 Derek Tansill came to see Cathy and me to ask if I would to be one of them and if she would be happy about that. It should not, he suggested, be too onerous. There would be a regular meeting at the Vicarage once a fortnight and the various responsibilities for the parish's buildings, finances and other affairs would be shared with the other two wardens.

I had no aspiration to become a warden. Indeed, it was something I had never thought of, and I knew neither who the other wardens were nor what their responsibilities might be. But it was pleasant to be asked and given the impression that I could be of use, and I felt some obligation in retirement to try to be of use. I was also fond of Derek and admired the way in which he ran the parish, relying very largely on the goodwill of volunteers. In running a sixth form college I had always been able to rely on the paid teaching and support staff, and I was well aware how much more difficult, indeed impossible, it would have been if I had had to depend on unpaid volunteers.

So although I preferred to serve the church as a teacher, giving a talk, for example, to *The Friends of St Mary's Church* on the change in architectural style from Romanesque to Gothic or to a house group on how the Doctrine of the Trinity had developed, I agreed to take the job on. The other two wardens, already in post and therefore senior to me, were Myra Ansell, who had responsibility for the St Mary's Almshouses, ten small self-contained flats in buildings immediately to the East of St Mary's Church, and Robin Pilbeam, who was responsible for the Church Centre in the Causeway, where were to be found the parish office, meeting rooms, kitchen and toilets, a house for the Verger and a substantial car park. My predecessor had been responsible for the church itself, so that was the responsibility I undertook.

I inherited a number of problems from the past, such as an on-going argument about payment for recent archaeological work in the churchyard, and the need to get what was known as a 'faculty' to authorise the installation of a triptych and a prayer globe in the church. The triptych had been obtained from another church and the large, iron prayer globe had been made, but they could not be officially installed without a 'faculty', acquiring which involved the completion of a long and complicated document of thirty-six pages on which one had to answer questions about such things as whether or not there were bats in the church and what steps were being taken to ensure that they were not disturbed.

The document then had to go to the Diocesan Advisory Committee, to the Chancellor of the diocese and eventually to the Archdeacon, and I had to write a number of letters explaining why the faculty had not been obtained before the triptych and the prayer globe had been acquired. The level of bureaucracy seemed even higher than in education, but it helped to explain why English churches and cathedrals are so much better looked after than many of the run-down and neglected churches and cathedrals on the continent.

An immediate problem was that the heating system was breaking down and the boiler was not working. Getting the boiler working and getting the nineteenth century radiators cleaned, repainted or, in some cases, replaced, hiring temporary heaters while the work was done, and at the same time planning for a new lighting control system, was immensely time-consuming. I could not help but reflect that they were the sort of thing for which I had had a bursar and a premises manager in the past. It was not my favourite way of spending my time, but it needed doing, so I got on with it and gradually became something of an expert on heating and lighting and sound systems and on devices for gaining access to the highest corners of a church.

Requests for changes and improvements came from all directions. The Archdeacon's Quinquennial Inspection led to the need to repair part of the roof and replace some guttering. Then, since there were fewer infant baptisms than in the past but more adult baptisms, the Vicar asked me to plan for the installation of a total immersion font which could be made available to Christians of all denominations in the town. One of the curates asked me to visit a couple whose daughter had died and discuss with them an appropriate memorial for her. Three members of the congregation wanted benches in the churchyard, inscribed in memory of a close relation who had died.

Once the heating system was working effectively, it had the effect of drying out the organ, and the organist then explained that he needed a humidifier to keep the organ in tune. Installing the humidifier led to the clearing of decades of accumulated rubbish out of the small crypt. The boiler room flooded, and after that the Verger understandably wanted some plumbing work done to avoid a repetition. Several members of the congregation wanted the acoustics of a meeting room improved. Others wanted it well decorated. It was suggested that for reasons to do with health and safety we needed a number of ramps and the removal of some pews to accommodate wheel chairs. A neighbour wanted a fence replaced. Another complained about the noise of the church bells when the bell-ringers were practising, and I arranged for the installation of a device which could be used to muffle the sound.

It was widely assumed that I not only had responsibility for these things but also the authority to get them done and pay for them. I did not. Instead I was very largely in a position of having responsibility without power - the opposite of the position of those press barons described by Stanley Baldwin in 1931 as wanting power without responsibility, 'the prerogative of the harlot through the ages.' I lacked authorisation for doing almost anything and various processes of consultation were needed. In principle I approved of consultation, but I had always seen it as something to be undertaken by a person responsible for making a decision.

As a warden I would consult as required with the Vicar, the other wardens, the other clergy, the Church Committee, the parish's Standing Committee, the Parochial Church Council, the church architect, the contractors, the Archdeacon, the Diocesan Advisory Committee, any individuals involved in a particular project, and quite possibly the District Council, the Friends of St Mary's Church, English Heritage, the Archbishops' Council for the Care of Churches, and so on, and then the project would be abandoned, because as time had passed priorities had changed.

When work was needed on the path through the churchyard I discovered that the churchyard itself, being closed to further burials, was the responsibility of the Horsham District Council, the path through it was the responsibility of the West Sussex Highways Authority and the whole area was under the jurisdiction of the Chancellor of the diocese of Chichester, whose authority might or might not have been delegated to the Archdeacon. The work eventually got done, but then the church architect complained that the wrong sort of grouting had been used.

Not only did I as a warden lack the authority to do anything. I also lacked a budget to pay for anything if a project was approved. I sometimes spent months (even years) in negotiations with one group after another, seeking agreement on issues which in my working life I would have expected to decide after a few moments' thought, or would have delegated to someone else. I saw worthwhile projects founder on a whim, and I wrote innumerable letters of apology and made innumerable apologetic telephone calls to contractors, professional advisers and so on about delays and changes in decisions. I needed to apologise to them when they were blamed for things which were our responsibility. I saw thousands of pounds wasted on professional plans and designs for projects which never came to fruition.

The church was a splendid building, but it needed constant attention and in particular it needed an effective lighting control system, if possible integrated with a sound control system, as and when the money was available. It also needed repainting. Just before I took over as a warden nearly half a million pounds had been spent on a new building attached to the church, which provided toilets, meeting rooms and a kitchen, accommodation for the choir and for the flower arrangers. It was a valuable facility. But it was furnished and decorated like a low grade canteen, and it was difficult to get agreement on what should be done.

Much of this took place after Derek's retirement, for in 2005, shortly after I had been a warden for just over a year, Derek indicated that he would shortly be retiring and that the responsibility for running the parish would devolve during the vacancy on the wardens. He had been a benevolent despot, and was benevolent enough to get away with being despotic. I entirely approved of his benevolent approach to things and took the view that few things matter more in the operation of a parish than getting the ethos right, cultivating an environment in which it is acceptable to make mistakes and in which blaming others for their mistakes is a more serious offence than the original mistake.

The residual problem, however, was that as soon as he left a variety of underlying divisions and aspirations among the clergy were quick to emerge. There was a meeting of the team vicars responsible for Holy Trinity, St Mark's, St John's and St Leonard's churches with the three parish wardens, who spent the whole meeting trying to reassure them that we had no intention of interfering with the way they ran their own churches and were only too pleased to leave it to them.

As the churchwarden responsible for the parish church perhaps the only thing done on my own initiative was the repair and restoration of the statues surrounding the pulpit. That was not because I did not want to do anything else. My natural inclination was to take action, but there were so many requests from others that my time was spent responding to those requests, and then trying to overcome the obstacles to effective action.

Similarly there was little or nothing done on my own initiative when I was acting as a warden responsible for the affairs of the parish as a whole, rather than just St Mary's. Myra and Robin would ask me to tackle matters such as the revision of the constitution of the Standing Committee or revision of the financial regulations. They were both highly competent and dealt with their own responsibilities effectively. But they saw such things as the drawing up of regulations and the drafting of letters as appropriate for someone with my past experience. I suspect that Derek Tansill had thought much the same when asking me to become a warden shortly before he retired.

The vacancy lasted for about a year and a half. In theory a time-lag like that avoids the problem of a new incumbent taking over immediately from a much loved predecessor and facing unfavourable comparison. It also saves the diocese the incumbent's salary for that period. The process of appointment is a strange one, and it involves the writing of a Parish Profile, so that those who might consider the job can read in some detail about the parish. The job of writing the profile was given to me, and I dealt with that by getting a range of people to write their own section. Each of the team vicars, for example, wrote about his own church. I undertook the editorial task of keeping each of them to one page, while in each case leaving space for a picture.

661

Much of it went smoothly. There was a page for the administration of the parish, a page on finance and, very importantly, a page on the Vicarage. But some interesting problems arose. I wrote a section on Horsham and the surrounding area and mentioned that there were numerous other places of worship in the town apart from the five Anglican churches. I listed them in alphabetical order, beginning with the Baptists and ending with the Unitarians and the United Reformed Church. The member of the clergy who was most strongly evangelical objected, saying that the Unitarians ought not to be included because they denied the Doctrine of the Trinity. I pointed out that I had only listed them as having a place of worship. If there had been a mosque or a synagogue in the town, I would have included them. But that carried no weight. He (and the other clergy supported him) did not want Unitarians mentioned in the same sentence as what they saw as acceptable Christian denominations.

As it happens I knew from my brother that in 1942, when Archbishop Temple inaugurated the British Council of Churches, he had faced the problem of whether or not the Unitarians should be included and had given three reasons why they should. The Council was intended to be inclusive rather than exclusive; there were parts of England, notably the Midlands, where the Unitarians were so widely and deeply entrenched that people would simply not understand it if they were excluded; and thirdly, no-one had suggested excluding the Quakers, or Society of Friends. It would, he suggested, be strange to include a body which had no doctrine of the Godhead, while excluding another because it had a mistaken doctrine.

But that was more than half a century earlier, and neither the Quakers nor the Unitarians were now represented on the body purporting to represent all the Christian churches in Horsham. So I had to re-write that section. Following a sentence about the Anglican congregations valuing a co-operative spirit among the Christian denominations and hoping that the new Vicar of Horsham would be ecumenically minded, there was now a separate sentence saying that there was also a Unitarian chapel and a Friends Meeting House in the town and that plans were in hand for building a mosque.

The new Vicar was eventually appointed in the summer of 2007, and before long he indicated that he wanted to do a review both of the affairs of St Mary's and of the parish as a whole. Until then the wardens at St Mary's had automatically been the parish wardens. But being a church warden and being a parish warden were two different things and there was no reason in principle why someone from one of the other four churches in the parish should not be a parish warden. The issue of what responsibilities should be held by church and parish wardens was ideally something which would be settled in the coming review, and it seemed to me desirable that my position should be available. I indicated that I would resign the following spring, at the end of a four year period, and I did.

It was a good thing that I had, because shortly afterwards all members of the congregation were asked to complete a questionnaire citing three thing they liked and three things they did not like about the church. The former was easy. The music, for example, was impressive. The latter was more difficult. I did not want to put my criticisms into a document which might be seen by anyone, so I wrote them in a letter to the Vicar.

I was critical of the preaching, which now too often took the form of vague exhortations to holiness rather than the expounding of the scriptures. I was critical of the public prayer, which too often seemed like messages to God telling Him what to do. I was critical of the lack of good teaching. My letter did not get a reply. Perhaps foolishly I had seen it as constructive criticism. It clearly did not seem like that to the Vicar. Any conversation about such matters was clearly taboo, and ever afterwards I felt that I was perceived as being not quite the right sort of Christian, too conservative and probably too 'liberal.'

The Horsham parish church, which had been known as the church of St Mary the Virgin for more than half a millennium, changed to be 'St Mary's, a church inspired by God's passion for the world', anything such as my involvement as a parish church representative on Horsham Churches Together was cancelled without telling me, and I began to feel like an outsider in a church where I had previously felt at home for twenty years.

86. Old Friends

◇◇◇◇◇◇◇◇◇◇◇◇◇◇◇◇◇◇◇◇◇◇◇◇◇◇◇◇◇◇◇◇◇◇

The first of my old friends to die was Peter Prescott, the other history scholar of my year at Pembroke. He died suddenly at the age of sixty-nine in 2005, and on 6th April 2006, which would have been his seventieth birthday, I spoke at his memorial service at St James's, Piccadilly. I remembered him looking striking in his 1st VIII scarf and scholar's gown and talking of a 'magic evening when we rowed down the setting sun.' I spoke of his career in the British Council, promoting all things British, from string quartets to sausages, to the rest of the world, and how he accompanied Mrs Thatcher to Uzbekistan. I spoke of his spiritual journey, which sometimes led him away from the Church (he was by upbringing a Roman Catholic), but which never diverted him from seeking further understanding, however elusive that might be.

Five years later, in June of 2010, George Bell, who with his wife Helen had been a good friend to both Oriel and me in Southport, died on Shetland after some years of illness. He was released from pain and distress, while his family mourned his loss. It was perhaps the first of a succession of events which ensured that I saw the point of the hymn in which St Francis, encouraging the sun, moon, wind and water to join in praising God, also invites 'most kind and gentle death, waiting to hush our latest breath', to join them. He had appreciated that death could sometimes be not so much an enemy as a kindly deliverer.

In February of 2013 I drove to Buckingham to see my old friend and colleague at Stowe, Charlie Macdonald, who, after an operation which had lasted fourteen hours, was now in a nursing home, unable to move by himself and seriously confused. In March I drove to Leicestershire to see my old friend from Pembroke, Martin Henry, who was suffering from bowel cancer. He told me what a wonderful holiday he had had recently out in India with two of his daughters, Clare and Oriole, spoke about how lucky he was that his son, Sean, was living next door with his family, and that his other daughter, Vicky, had come down from Nottingham to look after him. He had decided not to have any more chemotherapy and had morphine to relieve the pain. Two days later he died.

Meanwhile Cathy's mother was in a specialist dementia nursing home, where she seemed contented but could no longer remember anything and no longer recognised us. On Monday 22nd April I went to Charlie Macdonald's funeral in Stowe Church and saw his coffin lowered into the ground in Stowe churchyard before driving home. The next day Cathy had a call from the nursing home to say that her mother was suddenly seriously ill. We arrived at about the same time as the ambulance. A couple of days later I saw Eileen in hospital before driving up to Leicestershire for a celebration of Martin's life arranged by his four children and attended by many of his old friends.

While I was there Cathy telephoned me to say that her mother had died, and on Sunday 28th I went to a memorial service at Christ's Hospital for Harry Spurrier, who had arrived as a young History master at the beginning of my last year at school, stayed all his working life, and died at the age of 87. All of them had had worthwhile lives, but now 'most kind and friendly death' had freed them from pain and suffering. It was also in 2013, but much later, in November, that John Whitehead, whom I had known well at school and then when we were both Almoners of Christ's Hospital, died at the age of eighty-one. Then another friend from my schooldays, Derek Baker, who had returned to Christ's Hospital as Head Master for six years, died in the summer of 2015 at the age of eighty-four.

2016 saw the deaths of four more friends. In June Vivian Burchill died at the age of ninety. He and his wife, Cathy, had been friends with whom Oriel and I had frequently had meals together when we were living in Strawberry Hill, and later I taught their son,

Chris, at Stowe, so I was glad to see him and Cathy at Vivian's funeral. A few days later Julian Neely died at eighty-two. He was a surgeon whom Cathy and I had only met, together with his wife, Sally, when Cathy and I moved to Springfield Park, but by now we had been friends for ten years or more. We were away at the time of his funeral, but later I was able to recite the Russian Contakion for the Departed over the spot in the Slinfold churchyard where his ashes had been laid.

Two months later, in August, my friend Michael West, who was a mining engineer and also a non-stipendiary clergyman, died at the age of eighty-three. At his funeral I read the passage from St John's gospel where Thomas asks Jesus the way to the place where he is going and gets the answer that Jesus himself is the way and the truth and the life. Then in December Peter Kolter, the husband of my cousin Jill died after a long illness which he had borne with courage and without complaint. I saw him the day before he died and Jill and their two sons, Giles and Luke, were all with him when he died. At his funeral Giles and Luke spoke movingly about their father, who had been born in May 1939 and as a child was living in a displaced persons' camp somewhere in Nazi occupied Austria. He always remembered a farmer who, despite instructions not to feed the displaced persons, put hot baked potatoes into his pigs' troughs just before the children passed by. Peter had been ill for the last fourteen years, and W.E.Henley's poem *Invictus*, or 'Unconquered', which Jill asked me to read, seemed particularly appropriate. It includes the line, 'My head is bloody but unbowed.'

It was also in 2016 that Janet Lawley, my former Vice-Principal at King George V College, who had gone on to be the Headmistress of the Bury High School for Girls, told me of the death of her partner, Kerry, with whom she had been together for forty years. They had always been energetic travelers and theatre-goers, but in retirement ill health limited what they could do. Kerry suffered from an inherited condition which now confined her to a wheelchair. Janet was a large woman whose mobility was restricted by arthritis, but she was able to push Kerry in it and they had a vehicle specially converted to take the wheelchair. They had appeared to be coping well, but now Kerry had suddenly died. I caught the train from Horsham to London, on to Manchester, and from there to Bury, where Janet and I went out to lunch together and she told me what had happened.

A few weeks earlier Kerry had caught an infection and had been taken into hospital. It had been dealt with effectively, but it was thought desirable to send her to a nursing home to recuperate before going home. Janet visited her there. Her mind was as active as ever even though her body was weak. She was looking forward to being able to come home shortly. A couple of days later, when Janet spoke to one of the nursing home staff about visiting her again, she was told that that was difficult because Kerry was being 'fast-tracked.' At first she thought that that meant that Kerry would be home almost at once. No, she was told, Kerry was being 'fast-tracked' to death. It was as abrupt as that. She got to the nursing home as soon as possible. Kerry was dead. It appeared that she had caught the virulent infection MRSA, which is resistant to most anti-biotics, and it had killed her.

Of course, such things happen and it is sad. But it was worse than that. When some time later Janet saw the death certificate, she was shocked to find that it gave the causes of death as alcoholism and dementia. It was ludicrous. Although they both quite often had a glass of wine with their evening meal, they had no more than that, and since Kerry had been confined to a wheelchair for the last few years, there was no way she could have had access to alcohol without Janet knowing. What is more, Janet had seen her only a couple of days before she died, with her mind active and without the slightest sign of dementia.

Janet asked the opinion of the solicitor who was dealing with Kerry's estate. He said that she could take it up with the nursing home, but he would expect them to be defensive and that any suggestion that the death certificate was wrong would be contested by a team of lawyers. The problem was that the nursing home was subject to a financial penalty if a patient contracted an infection while with them, and to a double penalty if the patient had contracted MRSA, against which they were required to take careful precautions. They preferred to specify some other cause of death and avoid the financial penalties.

No-one else would see the certificate other than a statistician compiling statistics about how deaths from MRSA were declining as a result of the care now being taken. Janet, he suggested, should save herself the added grief which tackling the problem would bring. He was quite prepared to take the case on if she really wanted to go ahead, but he warned her that it would be expensive and that there was no guarantee of winning against a relatively powerful organization. His advice was to do nothing. At any other stage of her life Janet would have taken the case on, but not now, while vulnerable after the death of her partner, so she left it. No doubt the nursing home had relied on that.

In the New Year of 2017 I found that the annual dinner of the Old Georgians' Society, for former pupils and students of KGV, was to be on Saturday 29th April. I decided to go to Southport by train, go to the dinner, and if possible travel over to Bury on the Sunday to take Janet out to lunch again. I tried to contact her, but neither email nor telephone call nor letter received any reply. Eventually I telephoned the Bury Girls' Grammar School, where they undertook to find out what had happened. They discovered that she was in hospital. For some reason they did not understand she was not allowed any visitors, but they could pass on any letter I sent, so I wrote to her via the school.

A week or so later the telephone rang and it was Janet, able to tell me for herself what had happened to her over the last three months. She was still in hospital, but was now getting better and was even hoping to be home by the time I had proposed visiting her. She told me the whole sorry story. I had thought that what had happened to Kerry was one of the worst things that had happened to anyone known to me. This was worse, though it was possible to hope that it would have a happy ending.

In early January Janet had woken one Sunday morning to find that she was unable to get up and could hardly move. She was able to use her mobile 'phone, and an ambulance took her to hospital. There she was treated as a difficult woman who didn't know what real pain was. They tried to get her to sit up, but she found it impossible. She was told that a lot of people have to put up with a bit of back pain and she would have to live with it. She tried to explain that she knew what pain was, since she had suffered from arthritis for some years, but this was entirely different.

Those who were meant to be looking after her decided that there was nothing they could do, so they sent her to a nursing home. There it was still impossible for her to get up or even sit up. The pain was intense and led on to a state of disorientation. She did not any longer know who she was. She was hallucinating, soiling herself, making a noise all through the day and the night which disturbed the other residents. The staff at the nursing home could not cope and arranged for her to be sent to another hospital.

In this next hospital she found herself in a large ward with alcoholics and drug addicts, many of whom were suffering from some form of dementia. The staff seemed to assume that she was a drug addict, probably a former prostitute who had been sleeping rough, and they wanted to know where on her body she was secreting her drugs. She had no clothes other than the nightdress she had been wearing when first taken into hospital. No-one now knew who she was or where she lived, and she was in such a state that she could not tell them herself. By then she did not even know her own name. Thus it continued for some time, though she could not tell for how long.

One day in the first half of February a young doctor came to see her, told her that he was a specialist in acute infections and believed from what he had been told of her condition that she was suffering from an acute infection of the spinal cord, and hence the confusion, disorientation and hallucinations. If it was what he thought, then the infected state of the spine would have damaging consequences for the rest of the body, including the brain, which could not function properly until the infected spine was healthy again. He needed to give her antibiotics which were about two hundred times more powerful than anything normally prescribed by a GP.

Thus began two months in a room on her own with a treatment which would inevitably kill not only the bad bacteria infecting the spine but also many of the good bacteria which guard against infection. Hence the need to be isolated in a room where she could be protected against all the possible infections to which she would have little or no immunity. She was without books, radio or television - not that she was in a state to read books, listen to the radio or watch television if they had been available. But gradually she was returning to a world in which at least she knew who she was and could understand what was happening.

One day, when one of the staff spoke about the nearby children's hospital, Janet mentioned that she used to be one of its trustees. It had a transforming effect. Suddenly she was perceived as someone who might have a house (she did), might have relatives (she had a sister who had been ill for some time and one extra sadness in this story is that her sister died while all this was going on), and might have neighbours (she did, and once they knew where she was they brought fresh clothing and took away the laundry).

She was told that it was unlikely that she would ever walk again, but attempts were made to get her a bit more mobile and she asked if she could at least try to see if she could lift herself up using a zimmer frame. They brought one, she counted to three and heaved herself onto her feet. She counted to three again and managed to stand upright. 'Well,' she was told, 'we'll go on from there.' It had been three months since she was first taken into hospital and two months since the treatment had begun. Now she was told that it was possible that she would be able to go home before the end of the month.

It was just then that my letter arrived proposing that I come to see her on Sunday 30th April. She was able to ring me and tell me what had happened. We planned my next visit, when I would bring something for lunch instead of trying to go out, which would have been too much for her. At the end of April I booked into the Ramada Hotel in Southport for three nights. On the Friday evening I went to the Old Georgians' Annual Dinner and met a number of former colleagues. I spent the Saturday with Hilary Anslow, who had been the Principal of King George V College from 1992 until 2010, and with her husband, John, at their beautiful home in Walton-le-Dale in Lancashire, with its vast garden sloping down to the River Ribble, and with a wonderful view of the Ribble Valley. Then on the Sunday I was able to go over to Bury and see Janet again, have lunch with her and rejoice that she was living in her own house after the trauma of the last four months.

As I travelled home I reflected on how many women were left as widows. Eileen had been a widow for thirteen years before she died. Among all the others of whom I have written in this chapter Gilly Prescott, Helen Bell, Gillian Macdonald, Bridget Spurrier, Carolyn Whitehead, Jean Baker, Cathy Burchill, Sally Neely, Florence West, Jill Kolter and Janet Lawley were all left bereaved. Martin Henry's wife, Margaret, had died shortly before he did.

87. Joint Retirement

◇◇

From the beginning of 2010 Cathy and I were both retired. I was seventy-six and she fifty-nine. She had just been made redundant by the RSPCA when they decided that they needed to make the whole of their education department redundant after the bankers' crash had drastically reduced their income. In Cathy's case it had the effect that she was available to go and see her mother every day, while Eileen was still able to recognise her, and she was also available to help her daughter when Helen had her first baby in October of that year.

For three years, from near the end of 2008, Eileen had lived happily in her own home with Cynthia Botchway looking after her, and during 2010 and 2011 Cathy was able to see her almost every day. Eileen and Cynthia were fond of each other, and every Sunday they came to church with me and then came back to a Sunday lunch cooked by Cathy. But towards the end of 2011 Eileen, now aged ninety, had another fall. Either the fall caused her leg to break or a frail and brittle bone in her leg snapped and caused the fall. Whichever it was, she needed to be taken into Worthing Hospital to have it repaired as much as was possible.

It was soon clear that she would never be able to walk again, and what was even more significant was that she was now finding it difficult to remember anything. One day, as she struggled to work out who Cathy was, Cathy assured her that she was her daughter. 'Oh! So was I married then?' 'Yes, you were married to Mervyn for nearly forty-five years.' 'Was he a nice man?' 'Yes, he was lovely. You were very happily married.' 'Oh! Good.'

It was clearly not possible for Eileen to return home, even with Cynthia to look after her. Two people were now needed to lift her and another to adjust clothing or bedding. So while she recuperated in the Horsham Hospital from the operation in Worthing we looked for a suitable nursing home and found a specialist BUPA dementia unit, Oakhill House, on the other side of Horsham. There, for a year and a half, she slept in her own room, was got up, washed and dressed by the staff, was lifted in a hoist into a wheelchair and thence into a chair in the sitting room or to a meal, apparently unaware of anything around her, but always well-dressed and looking amiable and smiling, and, quite extraordinarily, still able to play the piano. Cathy went to see her three times a week and I always went after church on Sunday mornings. At times I would recite something like *Jabberwocky* or *The Owl and the Pussycat* to her. She seemed to recognise them and enjoy them, but I could not be sure.

Towards the end of April 2013 Eileen died, and in May her funeral took place in the crematorium at Worth. My brother, John, took the service according to *The Order for the Burial of the Dead* in *The Book of Common Prayer*. The introductory music was, appropriately, *Elegy,* a piece for two pianos composed by Eileen's husband, Mervyn. Cathy gave a beautiful and moving tribute to her mother, and when we got to the Committal, we heard the opening bars of Chopin's *Nocturne (Op.9 No.2)* being played on a recording by Eileen. As she played John spoke the words set out by Archbishop Cranmer in the sixteenth century: 'Man that is born of woman hath but a short time to live....In the midst of life we are in death....' and eventually, as he spoke of committing her body to be burnt, the curtains around the coffin closed, he finished the words of the Committal, and for another minute or so Eileen was still playing the last, exquisitely beautiful bars of the *Nocturne*.

We had taken great care over the timing of everything, for we had just forty-five minutes. So, for example, we limited the number of verses of each of the hymns, *The day thou gavest, Lord, is ended*, *Dear Lord and Father of mankind* and *Guide me, O thou great Jehovah*. Then, once John had said the Blessing and the Dismissal, we listened to a recording of Eileen playing Chopin's *Fantasie Impromptu (Op. 66)*. It finished two minutes short of our allotted time, ending an extraordinarily beautiful and moving occasion.

Cathy had not only gone regularly to be with her mother. She also regularly went on Wednesdays to see her daughter and grand-daughter and she kept in touch with friends. She and a childhood friend, Jackie Platt, who now lived in Frome, used to meet every few months halfway at Stockbridge in Hampshire. Similarly she would go to see Chris Bassett, who had once been her next-door neighbour, Evelyn Elliott, whom she had met when they were both training to teach for the National Childbirth Trust, Rosemary Graham, who had been her teacher tutor when she was doing the PGCE course, and Rowenna Maunder, a former colleague at Storrington.

She regularly saw two former colleagues from the RSPCA. With one, Jennifer Jones, who lived in London, she would go to the Chelsea Flower Show or the Country Living Exhibition, and Jennifer's partner, Roy Blackwell, would then take them to dinner at the Goring Hotel. On Cathy's sixtieth birthday he and Jennifer gave us dinner at the Athenaeum, of which he was a member. The other of her RSPCA friends was Nikki Sanger, who was younger than Cathy and a single parent on a low income, living in Hurstpierpoint and combining part-time teaching with looking after two young children. She and Cathy would go for long, strenuous walks over the South Downs.

Increasingly I was occupied either with writing talks to give at evening classes or with writing for publication. Sometimes the two things overlapped. A number of requests to repeat the talks I had given on the history of the Christian Church back in 2000 led to my sending an email to the Vicar suggesting it. The suggestion was met with silence. At first, when I had had no answer to previous communications, I had thought that he was both busy and not very good at answering emails. But by now I had come to the conclusion, rightly or wrongly, that this was his way of avoiding contact with someone who was not the right sort of evangelical Christian. I did the talks as an evening class at Collyer's instead, with an audience now wider than the congregation of the parish church.

Later I went on year by year to do other evening classes at Collyer's, and Paul Clarke, Head of English when I arrived at Collyer's and later a particularly good Senior Tutor, presided over the meetings, ensuring that everyone took part in the discussions following the talks. The first series was on *Problems with Christianity and how to resolve them*. It dealt with doctrines, such as the Trinity and Atonement, with the attitude of the Church to topics such as Science or Sex, with its relationship with Politics, and with Prayer. In every case it was largely a matter of showing how the teaching of Jesus and of other Christian thinkers made more sense than much of what was widely assumed to be the Christian position, and that it was possible to be both a Christian and a rational human being.

The second series was on *Christian Thinking Down the Ages*. Again it involved showing how the teaching of Jesus and St Paul, and the ideas of some of the early fathers of the Church, of medieval and Reformation thinkers, and of many modern scholars, can be helpful in looking at the way we should live our lives. A recurring theme was that what matters is not being right about theological propositions or about statements of what happened in the past, but rather seeking to follow the teaching and example of Christ and working towards some greater understanding which, however limited, may influence the way we live for the better.

Meanwhile I was getting on with writing this autobiography, and as I went through my life, with fifty years of it spent in six secondary schools, with three of them now charging fees of over £30,000 and the other three forbidden by law from charging anything, I found myself writing about how this bizarre situation had come about. Cathy, when reading it, suggested that, however interesting I might find the history of secondary education, it was not really relevant to my own autobiography, so before long I was writing a separate book, *Education and Politics, a history of unintended consequences and the case for change*, which is now about to be published in 2018.

Like *Problems with Christianity and how to resolve them* and *Christian Thinking Down the Ages,* it began life as a series of talks followed by discussion in an evening class at Collyer's. When later I knocked it into shape for publication, I had much the same problem as I had had with *In the Context of Eternity.* Routledge said that it was 'incredibly interesting' but lacked the footnotes and scholarly apparatus which they require. Sage were also very complimentary but said that their focus was on course-supporting textbooks rather than on anything more general. Bloomsbury said that it was interesting but 'did not fit with their list.' They all politely wished me well with other publishers. This time I turned to Melrose Books in Ely, who expect the author to share the cost of publication but provide the marketing which is so necessary for getting a book on the shelves of bookshops.

In the summer of 2016, when I had finished *Education and Politics,* I sat in the garden, relaxed and reflected that three of my former colleagues at Collyer's, Paul Clarke, Head of English and then Senior Tutor, Nick Robins, Head of Maths, and Jonathan Simons, Head of Information Technology, were retiring at the end of that term, and Ed Tattersall, Head of Classics, would be retiring a year later. So I wrote to the West Sussex County Times, which published a letter in which I pointed out that all four of them had been appointed in the 1970s and that between them they had served the college and its students for a hundred and fifty-seven years - an average of nearly forty years each. Each of them had served under five different principals, seven prime ministers and seventeen secretaries of state for education.

It was also at that time that I discovered Daphne du Maurier. Many years earlier I had seen the film of *Rebecca.* Now I read *Jamaica Inn* and then went on to *My Cousin Rachel.* It was, I felt, one of the very best novels I had ever read. I was entirely capti-vated by the heroine, if that is the right word for her, since throughout du Maurier's novel there is a tension between the way in which both of Rachel's cousins, first Ambrose and later Philip, find Rachel overwhelmingly attractive but at the same time come to be suspicious of her behaviour, her motives and her intentions, and the reader is encouraged to share their suspicions.

I quite simply found myself in sympathy with her all through the book, finding explanations for why she behaved the way she did and wondering what it was in her early life which might provide a clue to her behaviour. Sitting in a deckchair in the garden I started writing the story from Rachel's viewpoint. *Rachel's Story*, or *My Ashley Cousins*, is a short novel of just under 45,000 words. Where it overlaps with the story told by Philip Ashley in du Maurier's book I keep scrupulously to the events and even to the dialogue of the original.

In my version the tension about what Rachel is up to, which is such an important aspect of Daphne du Maurier's book, is gone, since we know what she is thinking and why she behaves as she does. But there is a different problem. When she was a teenager she had thought it improper for her mother to consider marrying a much younger man, Count Cosimo Sangalletti. Instead she had made herself attractive to Cosimo, married money and a title and in effect destroyed her mother. Now she is herself in love with a younger man, and besides that cannot give him a child. Her conscience tells her that she must give him up. But shame at her past behaviour prevents her from explaining it. He does not understand and the outcome is disaster.

Right from the start there was the obvious problem that any thought of publishing it would run up against the copyright held by the executors of Daphne du Maurier's estate. My publisher at Melrose Books thought it would be worth checking, as she would have liked to publish it, so I asked the executors. The reply was clear and unequivocal: 'As My Cousin Rachel is still in copyright you will not, under any circumstances, be able to publish your own retelling of the work. To do so would be a breach of copyright and, as a result, you may face legal action.' The copyright runs out in 2039, fifty years after Daphne du Maurier's death, by which time I will be long dead. But I rather hope that someone will think it worth publishing then.

Shortly after I had finished writing *Rachel's Story* in 2017 *My Cousin Rachel* was made into a particularly good film with Rachel Weisz ideally cast in the title role. I like to think that if my own book should ever be published, it would have a picture of her on the cover. I also wonder if I might be able to photocopy a few copies for private consumption by close friends and relations without infringing the copyright laws, but I do not yet know the answer to that.

It was many years since I had been the chairman of the Springfield Park management company, and most of the other directors from the early years had one by one either moved or left the committee. Eventually the new directors managed to fall out among themselves and a new start was needed. In 2012 Sally Neely, who was quietly efficient, was persuaded to return as Chairman and she in turn persuaded a number of others, including Cathy, to join her. George Yuill came back to draw up new *Articles of Association* aimed at avoiding the issues over which the recent directors had quarrelled.

Others included Ray Stamp, an elderly businessman who had run his own company and could be relied on to sort out any practical matters himself or else knew someone else who would be able to do so. Cathy took over as secretary, produced the minutes of meetings and the newsletter, and eventually in 2014 took over as chairman. She was outstandingly successful. Day to day matters she dealt with efficiently. Problems she handled with unfailing calm and charm. I sat back and did nothing except feel proud of her. When I wrote the first draft of this in 2017 she was still the chairman and wondering how to hand the job on. Now, as I go over it in the spring of 2018, she has told the other directors that, after four years in the job, she is resigning. She, of course, is no more indispensable than anyone else, the others are highly competent, so no doubt they will carry on effectively.

Cathy has plenty else to occupy her and is particularly good at maintaining contact with both friends and relations. Recently she has just completed an account of her father's life as a musician for a book on the Roberts family, and regularly on Wednesdays she is on what we refer to as 'grandma duty', giving Helen some help and support down in Hassocks and collecting Maisie and Bruno from school. While she is on 'grandma duty' or walking with one of her friends I get on with writing this and look forward to her coming back and to the evenings.

Sometimes we drive over to Guildford to go to a play at the Yvonne Arnaud Theatre, or we walk across the Horsham Park to an opera beamed in from the Met in New York, to a play beamed in from Stratford-on-Avon, or to see a film. Occasionally we go out to an evening meal. But most evenings we have a meal together in the kitchen, afterwards go through to the sitting room, choose something from among the various television programmes we have videoed, watch the News at ten o'clock, and so to bed.

88. The Advance of Age

Most of my life I was blessed with good health. I had all the child-hood illnesses which were still common in the 1930s and 40s: mumps, measles, whooping cough, chicken pox and tonsillitis. In those days, in the case of most of those diseases, if one child in the road had it, the other mothers would bring their children round to catch it, since it was well known that it was better to get them over with while young and acquire immunity. Getting them in adult life could be serious. We were immunized against small-pox, which had more or less been wiped out in England but was still remembered with fear, and we drank pasteurised milk as a precaution against TB, or tuberculosis, another disease which had been a widespread killer but was now far less prevalent than a generation earlier.

I may have had poliomyelitis (commonly known as infantile paralysis) as well, but only the first stage, which was no worse than the common cold, but still provided immunity against getting it later. John was less fortunate, and it left him with the muscles of his left leg somewhat wasted above the knee. But he was well looked after at the German Hospital in Hackney and later at the Lord Mayor Treloar's Home in Alton, and he came home aged two, after eighteen months away, with remarkably little damage. He wore a splint for some months, but once it was removed he could walk without any limp. One effect was that it caused him to hold himself more erect than I did when walking. Our mother pointed out more than once that he did not have my inclination to slouch.

I suppose I caught influenza two or three times during my working life, but the days I ever had off because of illness could be counted on the fingers of two hands. In the summer of 1985, during the holidays and when I was fifty-one, I suffered a hernia as a result of throwing my step-daughter aged five up in the air and catching her. Repair was a simple surgical procedure which was carried out in the small Horsham Hospital, but after two days in hospital it then took another two or three weeks to recover, gradually walking a few yards more every day. Some years later, doing some heavy lifting in the garden, I had a second hernia, on the other side of the body. But by then surgical procedures had advanced so far that I went into hospital one morning, had the operation at midday, and that same afternoon, after being collected by Cathy in her car, was able to walk up the garden path home.

The next time I went into hospital it was for something more serious. When I was about seventy I noticed that I was passing water more frequently than in the past. It was not particularly inconvenient, except when going on a long train or car journey, but in the summer of 2004 I told my doctor, Simon Dean, who gave me some pills to take when going on a journey. They did not make much difference, so in March 2005 I mentioned it again. This time he arranged for me to have a blood test, and when I saw him again in mid-April it appeared that my PSA count of 8.6 was rather high for someone of my age, now 71. The level of PSA, or prostate specific antigens, in the blood might be expected to be about 3 or 4 if nothing was wrong. At 8.6 it was worth investigating, so he arranged for me to be seen by someone at the East Surrey Hospital in Redhill at the end of May. That led to a biopsy at the end of June, and when I was seen about the outcome at the end of July it turned out that I appeared to have moderately aggressive prostate cancer and would need an MRI scan once a machine was available. The scan was on 15th September, just six months after Simon Dean had suggested having a blood test.

Paul Miller, the consultant urologist at East Surrey (Mr Miller for professional purposes, because he was a surgeon – not Dr Miller) arranged to see me early in October and explained that it was possible to treat it with radiotherapy, chemotherapy or hormone therapy, or, if one was fit enough to stand up to surgery, he could cut it out and ideally get rid of the problem completely. He had wanted to see me to assess whether or not, at my age, that might be the best way to proceed. He thought that I seemed fit enough, so he arranged to have me into hospital the following week. 'I'm used to doing this', he said, 'I do about one a week', and he performed the operation, a radical prostatectomy, on 31st October, the day before my seventy-second birthday.

Everything went well and when a couple of days later I asked Cathy to bring me David McCullough's biography of Harry S. Truman to read, Paul Miller told her that that was a good sign. I was fortunate both in my surgeon and in being looked after in Buckland Ward, which was a model of efficiency. I had to wear a catheter for a month or so after the operation, and then, when it was removed, had to learn to control my bladder with a significant part of my plumbing removed. There was no immediate need for further treatment. I simply had a blood test about once every six months and would then go for an appointment at the hospital, where Mr Miller's registrar would tell me that the PSA was somewhere between 0 and 0.1, which, he pointed out, was an excellent outcome.

In 2009 I was very briefly in a hospital again, though for an entirely different reason. We had decided to go on a cruise through the Baltic, visiting Helsingborg (Hamlet's Elsinore) and Gdansk (or Danzig) on the way to St Petersburg. We were in St Petersburg on 19th June, the day my grandson Bobby was born, so I bought him a collection of wooden Russian dolls, eight altogether, one inside the other, as a birthday present. Then, on the way back in the middle of the Baltic the ship ran into a force 12 gale, and as I was, rather foolishly under the circumstances, walking round the upper deck, I was caught by a particularly fierce gust of wind, fell and dislocated my right shoulder.

The shoulder remained out of its socket for the next twenty-four hours. I was strapped up and given pain-killers, which were not very effective, until we put into harbour at Copenhagen. There a Danish ambulance collected me and a Danish orthopaedic surgeon took hold of my right hand, put his foot under my shoulder socket and wrenched the arm back into position. The pain stopped. There was no charge and no need for any documentation. All medical care in Denmark was free, and free to everyone of whatever nationality. They delivered me back to the cruise ship with a few hours to spare, and the long process of recovering the use of the arm began.

Meanwhile my eyesight was deteriorating and in 2010 my local optician referred me to a consultant, who recommended the removal of the cataracts which were developing in both eyes. The operations, a few weeks apart, were swift, efficient and very effective. In this case a local anaesthetic in the eye was all that was needed and I was awake throughout. At the point at which the consultant, a Mr Wilson, said that he was about to begin, I started reciting Keats's *Ode on a Grecian Urn* to myself, and as I came to the end and in my mind was saying 'Beauty is truth, truth beauty....', Mr Wilson announced that he had finished and I could get up.

The next operation, a few weeks later, took longer. Again I recited the *Ode on a Grecian Urn* to myself, then Coleridge's *Kubla Khan*, and I was just deciding what to recite next as the operation ended. Each time, when the patch over my eyes was removed, I found that I could see better than since my early teens. I no longer needed spectacles, except for reading, and when I went for an eye test some months later I found that I could read even the bottom line of the eye chart.

At about the same time I had my hearing tested. I was not aware of any problem, but Cathy said that I too often asked her to repeat things, and when I had a hearing test it emerged that there was moderate hearing loss on one side and a little on the other. Wearing hearing aids was recommended, so at about the same time that I stopped wearing spectacles I started wearing hearing aids. I tried to hide them by growing my sideburns longer.

The psalmist, writing about three thousand years ago, suggested in what we know as psalm 90, (*Domine, refugium*), that the natural duration of a man's life was 'threescore years and ten', and he went on to say that 'though men be so strong that they come to fourscore years, yet is their strength then but labour and sorrow.' But of course there have been considerable advances in medical science since then, particularly over the last century, and I had benefited from them. In particular the development of anaesthetics had made a range of surgical procedures possible. My life would have been far less pleasant in my seventies if I had had to live with a double hernia, a seriously cancerous prostate, cataracts in both eyes and gradually deteriorating hearing. As it was, I was still enjoying life and have been glad to be able to go on enjoying it into my eighties, playing in 'extra time' rather than in 'injury time.'

In the summer of 2010 my PSA reading, which had been somewhere between 0 and 0.1 for nearly five years, was 0.1, and by November it had gone to 0.2. A few months later it was 0.4 and by October 2011 it had risen to 0.8. Those are very low readings. But what troubled the doctors was that it was doubling every few months. A microscopic bit of cancerous tissue, invisible for years to any test known to medical science, was growing inside me in the prostate bed, and one does not have to be much of a mathematician to work out that if it continued doubling in size, the PSA score could reach about 12 in another couple of years and something like 200 two years after that, by which time one might be dead.

Some intervention was needed, and this time I was seen by a consultant oncologist, Dr Julian Money-Kyrle, who arranged for me to have a course of radiotherapy at the St Luke's Cancer Centre at the Royal Surrey Hospital in Guildford. 'Little and often' was the approach, so from the middle of January until the end of February of 2012 I drove over to Guildford and back regularly, five times a week. The times of appointments varied, but on a typical day the treatment might be at 11.00 a.m., so I would leave home at 9.00, arrive before 10.00, spend anything up to half an hour queuing for a parking space and then get undressed and drink three tumblers of water half an hour before my appointment so that my bladder was full.

While the patients waited for their daily treatment, and after they had drunk the prescribed amount of water, the main topic of conversation was parking. The hospital was getting bigger and bigger. It was catering for more and more patients, and it wanted and needed more parking spaces. But the local authority had its own reasons for refusing planning permission and took the view that the hospital should not expand beyond the space available. As a result the parking issue seemed to dominate all else in the affairs of the hospital. They could only provide more spaces for patients by reducing the number for members of staff, and then the staff could not get to work. While I was going there in January and February of 2012 there was no solution and no obvious prospect of one.

It was while waiting for the treatment each day that I started writing in a notebook the early chapters of this book, beginning with an account of when I was born and a description of my parents and their families. Then I would lie still for three or four minutes while being zapped (noiselessly and painlessly) by the radiotherapy machine, get dressed and drive home, arriving back after a total of nearly four hours. It was a bit like commuting to work and back. After lunch I usually found that I needed to go to sleep in the afternoon. The radiographer explained that, although nothing appeared to be happening when one was having the treatment, something was going on inside the body, and it needed a bit of rest and recovery time each day.

During the next year or so, as I approached my eightieth birthday, I felt fit and well. While Cathy frequently used a cycling machine in the early morning, I would use my rowing machine, and while rowing for about half an hour would keep my mind occupied by reciting poetry to myself: psalms and canticles one day, sonnets another, narrative poems another, and so on. The main exercise I got other than that was walking, and I frequently walked into town and back, to church or the bank or to choir practice or the shops. There was, of course, nothing remarkable in that, but a number of my friends and contemporaries were now suffering from arthritis or back problems, so instead of assuming that it was in the nature of things that one could walk, I was thankful that in my case it was still possible, and that the walk across the Horsham Park was such a pleasant one.

It was, I appreciated, time to recognise that eventually one had to die. As a child growing up in a war I had scarcely thought of death. The only deaths I saw were at a distance in the sky, as airplanes were shot down, or on newsreels at the cinema. My first direct contact with it was in the train crash of April of 1953, which left me very conscious of my good fortune in surviving. Chloë's death from cancer back in 1966 left me similarly grateful that Oriel was still alive. Then my father died (too young, it seemed to me) in the autumn of 1977, and at the beginning of the 1980s death loomed large: Oriel's elder sister, June, died in August of 1981 and my mother in September, Oriel herself in September 1982 and Nora, with all three of her daughters having predeceased her, less than a year later.

At that stage death seemed to me unspeakably cruel – the last great enemy. But I saw enough of illness, dementia and suffering among my friends and relations in the twenty-first century to recognise that death can eventually be a welcome release from a life which has run its course, and it is of course in the nature of life that whatever is living has to die. The only things which never die are those which never lived. Meanwhile I am enjoying life and counting the years after the age of seventy as a bonus.

The worst thing I had ever experienced was the death of Oriel when I was still forty-eight, and it was not just that I missed her, but that I felt that I faced the prospect of a lifetime of loneliness. Awareness that vast numbers of people have to deal with that did not make it any easier. So I count myself extremely fortunate to have met and then married Cathy, and while I was married to Oriel for just over twenty-three years, I have now, in 2018, been married to Cathy for over thirty-three, and at the age of eighty-four view her not just with love but also with gratitude.

At 84.

89. Politics

◇◇◇◇◇◇◇◇◇◇◇◇◇◇◇◇◇◇◇◇◇◇◇◇

My earliest recollection of anything which could be called 'political' is finding when I got back to Woodford Bridge at the age of six in the summer of 1940, after some months of evacuation, that our Member of Parliament, Mr Churchill, was now Prime Minister. It was a matter of considerable pride. What is more, it seemed that he had been against the bad things for which the Conservative Party had been responsible, such as the depression and appeasement, and although I did not know what those words meant, I did understand that the Labour Party was now supporting him against Hitler, so we were going to win the war, and afterwards everything would be better.

The Labour Party, as I understood it, stood for fairness and equality and looked after the workers, while the Conservative Party looked after the interests of the bosses, who treated the workers badly, had more money than was good for them and probably indulged in unmentionable vices. Everyone I knew supported the Labour Party. Why Mr Churchill was a Conservative was a puzzle I could not resolve.

The first general election I remember was in 1945, by which time I was eleven and had been at Christ's Hospital for a year. I was enthusiastic about the idea of a Labour victory. A Labour government would set up a National Health Service and a system of National Insurance. There would be unemployment pay for those who needed it and retirement pensions for all. They would build council houses and provide free schooling. The major industries would all be nationalised and owned by the people. There would be no need for strikes. The government would tax the rich, redistribute wealth to the poor and give everyone a better life.

The Conservatives apparently took the view that people should either own their own home or rent from a private landlord.

689

People should pay for doctors and hospitals as the need arose, save for their pensions, and send their children to public schools if they could afford it. Private enterprise and competition would produce prosperity; welfare for the poor was an unfortunate necessity. At eleven I preferred the vision of a Socialist Utopia. But the Labour victory in 1945 was followed by years of post-war austerity, after which the country benefited from a gradual return to prosperity during the years from 1951 onwards, when Churchill led a Conservative peacetime government. When he resigned in 1955, the new Prime Minister, Sir Anthony Eden, was in a good position to win another general election.

At the time of that election I was up at Oxford, and although I was now twenty-one and qualified to vote, my name was not on the electoral roll, so I was unable to do so. That resolved a potential problem. I still wanted a Labour victory, but my own MP was still Winston Churchill (Sir Winston instead of Mr Churchill since the coronation year of 1953) and he was an object of admiration, affection and veneration. I did not want to vote against him. My parents sent me his electoral address, written by the leader of the local Conservative Association. It ended like this: 'We all know that when we have a problem, we take it to a neighbouring MP, but it would be a sad day for Woodford and a sad day for the country if Sir Winston Churchill, who has chosen to end his days as the member of parliament for this constituency rather than as a peer of the realm should not be allowed to do so.' On that ticket he was re-elected.

By the election of 1959 Oriel and I were recently married and living in Bristol. Now it was her name that was not on the electoral roll, so since she would have voted Conservative while I voted Labour, we agreed that a good solution was for me to vote Liberal. Thus it was not until the general election of 1964 that I eventually voted for a Labour candidate in a general election, and by then I was a signed up member of the Labour Party, even if neither very active nor reliable.

During the 1960s, when teaching modern history at Quintin School, I found myself explaining to my pupils what the Liberals and the Conservatives had stood for in the nineteenth century. The Liberals, I would explain, had believed that society worked best when all men (though not necessarily women) are free. They believed in freedom for men to speak, worship, and even be ruled as they wished, so they advocated religious toleration at home and opposed the subjugation of native peoples overseas. They believed that the law of supply and demand was the best way to produce a prosperous economy, and thus they were against both tariffs and regulations controlling industry. Governments, they believed, should interfere as little as possible.

The principal characteristic of their opponents, the Conservatives, was the belief that society should conserve and pass on to the next generation those things of value which had been inherited from the past, whether institutions such as the Monarchy, the House of Lords, and the Church of England or, for example, the hedges and ditches which represented rural life. Conservatives were suspicious of ideology, looked for practical solutions to whatever problems came to hand and preferred common sense to clever ideas.

They took the view that Liberalism carried seeds of disaster if taken to its logical conclusion. It could lead to self-government by Hottentots or Irishmen, the destruction of agriculture or industry by cheap foreign imports, and the exploitation of the working class by a grasping and irresponsible capitalist middle class. The Conservatives did not want any more 'dark satanic mills' built in 'England's green and pleasant land.' Instead they wanted to weld all classes into one nation, maintain the union of the United Kingdom and push out wider still and wider the bounds of the British Empire, so that more and more of the world would have the benefit of sound, practical, British rule.

As it happens, the Irish issue, the growth of Empire and eventually the First World War, diverted the Conservative Party away from the social reform which had been one of the characteristics of its opposition to Liberalism, and a necessary consequence of that was the rise of a working class movement and the creation of a Labour Party. The Liberal Party disintegrated as the intellectual certainties of the nineteenth century gave place to a whole range of disagreements, and as it declined the Labour Party grew, so that by the second half of the twentieth century the two main political parties were Conservative and Labour.

I had grown up in an environment in which not only the Labour Party but also the trade unions were seen by most people I knew as admirable organisations defending the interests of working men and women against the greed of unscrupulous employers. But during the decades after the Second World War the trade unions increasingly seemed to be pursuing their own selfish interests against the interests of society as a whole, with their leaders as much corrupted by power as they claimed was the case with the industrialists whom they opposed. I was increasingly disillusioned with the approach of trade unionists such as the miners' leader, Arthur Scargill, who would publicly proclaim support for a 7% pay rise for nurses while at the same time demanding a 30% pay rise for his own members.

That sense of disillusionment came to a head when I was in my mid-forties in 1979. The Labour prime minister from 1976 until 1979, James Callaghan, and his Chancellor of the Exchequer, Denis Healey, had managed to limit inflation in 1978 by keeping pay rises down to 10%. Now they wanted to keep them down to 5%. But the trade union leaders said they wanted 'free collective bargaining' for their members. The relatively new leader of the Conservative Party, Margaret Thatcher, responded by saying that she was also in favour of 'a free market economy.' Essentially she was suggesting that if the electorate voted Conservative, then the captains of industry could fight it out with the trade unions and see who won. The trade union leaders, by their opposition to pay restraint, ensured that Labour lost the election, and over the next eighteen years they lived to regret it.

At local level union and professional association members were often far more sensible and co-operative than one would have expected from the public image projected by their leaders, and my own experience was entirely positive. When the caretaker of King George V School, Ken Miller, was required by his union, the GMB (now known as UNISON), to go on strike in the so-called 'winter of discontent' of 1978-9, he made sure that I had any keys I might need and assured me that I could telephone him in the event of a problem.

When the Assistant Masters' and Mistresses' Association (AMMA) instructed its members to 'withdraw their goodwill' over a dispute with the government about lunch-time supervision, the staff of KGV, who got a free lunch in return for supervising in the lunch hour, solved the problem of what they should do by carrying on as usual but paying for their lunches so that they would not be deemed to be supervising.

Then in the 1990s the NAS/UWT (the National Association of Schoolmasters and Union of Women Teachers (two bodies unwillingly united by equal opportunities legislation) called on its members to disrupt the running of schools by short, irregular strike action: Tuesday morning and Friday afternoon one week, Monday afternoon and Thursday morning a couple of weeks later. Their representative at Collyer's, Steve Gilham, gave me a list of who was going on strike and at what times, so that appropriate deductions could be made from their pay, but assured me that they would all set work for their students to do while they were away and that there would be no noticeable disruption.

Similarly local union officers were helpful and co-operative. When we ran a *Challenge of Industry Conference* at King George V College, one after another of the firms that were invited wrote patronisingly to say how much they approved of a college taking an interest in industry but that they could not spare anyone to speak at it, while the Transport and General Workers' Union immediately agreed to send one of its officials to take part. Then, when the West Sussex education authority refused to accept that there was a problem with a long-standing member of staff at Collyer's, but later, accepting that there was a problem, wanted him dismissed with no income until he reached retirement age, it was an official of his professional association who suggested the solution of redundancy.

Thus throughout twenty-three years as a headmaster or college principal I experienced only helpful co-operation from union and professional association members, whether it was the GMB or the TGWU, AMMA or the NAS/UWT. There was general recognition that we would all have to work together once any dispute was over and that no-one should behave in a way which would imperil that. Whatever was happening at national or local authority level, we in our own small corner of the world needed to treat each other with respect and understanding.

During those years leading Tory politicians, not least the prime minister, would lecture the public sector about the merits of the world of business and how schools could learn from the management techniques practised in industry. I sometimes thought they might have done well to encourage industry and the world of business to see the way we did things in grammar schools and sixth form colleges as a model for good industrial relations.

There was a down side, of course, to such a co-operative approach. Politicians were able to push the pay and conditions of teachers in sixth form colleges below the levels of those in primary schools, and the pay and conditions of university lecturers were made even worse, with low pay going alongside short-term contracts and job insecurity. Of course it was a free market, so a dissatisfied mathematics teacher in a sixth form college could look for a job as a City trader and a dissatisfied Biology lecturer at a university could always retrain as a plumber. Some did.

One aspect of the free market economy became particularly evident when large businesses were required to publish information about the remuneration of their senior staff. Two of the members of the Governing Body of Collyer's were chief executives of large business organisations. Roger Taylor, the Chief Executive of Royal and Sun Alliance, whose daughter had been a student at Collyer's, and Tim Walker, an Old Collyerian who was the Chief Executive of Caradon plc, were both likeable and admirable men and assets to the Governing Body, though neither of them had the qualifications which would have been necessary for them to be considered for appointment to the teaching staff.

Between them they earned more in one year in pay, bonuses and share options than the college's total pay expenditure, including such things as National Insurance and pension contributions. On the one hand I did not begrudge them their wealth. They had chosen to go into occupations in which high pay was the reward for success, and both had been very successful. On the other hand, it could not help but seem disproportionate as our funding was reduced year after year.

The Conservatives, whose government was responsible for that steady reduction in funding, had gone through a strange change. In the nineteenth century they had believed that the stability of society was threatened by an excess of Liberty and had opposed doctrinaire Liberalism. By the middle of the twentieth century circumstances had changed round them, so that by then they believed that individual liberty was threatened by an excess of state control. Now they were opposing doctrinaire Socialism and facing in the opposite direction politically from a century earlier.

After the neo-Liberal Conservatives had dismantled the nationalised industries and sold them off to private ownership, the Labour Party called itself New Labour, abandoned Socialism and turned itself into something more like an old Conservative Party, looking for practical solutions to problems and filling the space in the moderate centre of British politics which the Conservatives had abandoned. The Liberals, such as were left of them, adopted a reforming and non-doctrinaire posture, apparently somewhere to the left of Labour.

I had as time had gone by acquired a measure of sympathy with a range of political attitudes. I was a Liberal in the sense that I believed that people should be allowed as far as possible to live their own lives in their own way and give expression freely to their thoughts and beliefs. But I was opposed to economic liberalism if it meant that the rich were free to get richer while the poor got poorer. I was a Conservative in the sense that I believed in preserving what was valuable in our institutions and our way of life, but I also believed that that was best achieved by piecemeal reform rather than by opposing all change. I wanted a Labour government to redistribute wealth and I sometimes justified voting Labour on the essentially conservative grounds that reform would prevent unrest and even revolution. So I was a member of the Labour Party in the 1960s, a disillusioned Socialist in the 1970s, a member of the Social Democratic Party in the 1980s, a member of the Labour Party again in the 1990s, but no longer a member of any party by the end of the millennium.

In 2010, when the Conservatives and Liberal Democrats formed a Coalition government, they indicated that their highest priority was to reduce the very large budget deficit. I wrote to my local M.P., Francis Maude, to make a suggestion. Ministers had already reduced their own pay by 5%. If Members of Parliament did the same, they could then go on to legislate to cut the pay and pensions of all public employees by the same 5% and that would enable them to reduce funding on public services by the same amount. It was, I suggested, an approach which was demonstrably fair and also easy for people to understand. Someone with a comfortable pension of £100,000 would lose £5,000. Someone with a small pension of only £1,000 would lose £50. The national deficit would be massively reduced, while front line services would be protected. But it needed to be done quickly if they were to get away with it.

Francis Maude's replied in his own handwriting: 'Much in what you say – but it would be tough to do!' In the event it was too tough, and the government tried to cut the deficit by a combination of cuts in public services and increases in indirect taxes, such as VAT, which hit the poor harder than the rich. Within a few years the richest 10% of the population were paying no more than 35% of their total income in taxation, while the poorest 10%, so long as you take indirect taxes into account, were paying 47%. By 2014 the relatively new Archbishop of Canterbury, Justin Welby, was saying publicly that it is a disgrace to have so many poor people in such a rich country. It remains a disgrace.

In 2015 I was saddened by the government's decision to decide whether or not Great Britain should remain in the European community by a referendum, which I saw as a form of mob rule. I was even more saddened by the outcome of the referendum. So by the general election of 2017 I was entirely out of sympathy with the Conservative government's policy. Nevertheless, because I knew our fairly recently adopted Conservative candidate, Jeremy Quin, and liked him, I broke the habit of a lifetime and voted for a Conservative.

90. Religion

◇◇◇◇◇◇◇◇◇◇◇◇◇◇◇◇◇◇◇◇◇◇◇◇◇◇◇

I am not at all sure if my brother and I grew up in a Christian household. We were never taken to church, and if my parents ever spoke about religion, I do not remember it. But somehow I picked up that we lived in a Christian country and that Christianity had something to do with, for example, Noah's Ark, Moses in the bulrushes, Samson and Delilah, King Solomon and Jesus. Perhaps we had a book of *Stories from the Bible*, but I don't remember it the way I remember *Lamb's Tales from Shakespeare*.

With hindsight it is clear that the moral assumptions we lived with were, in a sense, Puritan. There was no alcohol in the house, nor did our parents ever go in a pub, though at Christmas, when my father's brothers and his sister gathered together with their families, both my mother and father would happily drink a glass of sherry and my mother would play popular tunes on the piano. We never played card games, and betting, whether on horses or the dogs, was clearly seen as something only done by men who were, if not wicked, at least irresponsible.

There was a clear difference between Right and Wrong. Swearing, lying and greed, for example, were all wrong, while kindliness and helping others was good. The idea that 'Cleanliness is next to Godliness' probably introduced the concept of God to me, but any idea I had about God at that stage in my life was no more than that He was a being who in some undefined way presided over everything, was on our side against the Germans and the Japanese, and could also be assumed to be on the side of the workers and against the bosses. If God was ever mentioned at my elementary school, Ray Lodge, again I have no memory of it.

It was not until I went away to school at Christ's Hospital at the age of ten that I encountered regular and repeated teaching about

Christianity. We went to chapel every morning, and every day there was a reading – usually from one of the gospels. We had house prayers every evening, and at those we had a range of readings selected by senior boys over the years and kept in a ring binder: stories from the *Old Testament* (I particularly liked the *Book of Ruth*, though I had no idea of its significance) and uplifting passages from writers such as St Thomas à Kempis. I was struck by the contrast between the noble ideas I encountered in chapel and at house prayers and the frequently unpleasant behaviour of many of those around me. Ideal and reality were a long way apart.

We sang the *Magnificat* in chapel most Sundays and I especially liked the bit about putting down the mighty from their seat, filling the hungry with good things and sending the rich empty away. It seemed to lend authority to the idea that God and His angels were on the side of the workers. I was impressed by the stories, or parables, that Jesus was reported to have told, and in my early teens I decided that I was a Christian. At the age of fourteen I was baptised. John took much the same view of things, so over a period of three days we were baptised on Friday, with our housemaster, Eric Littlefield, as our godfather, confirmed on Saturday, and then went to Holy Communion for the first time on Sunday.

I enjoyed singing hymns, and among all those I sang, at least one every day during term time for eight years, the one which had the most influence on my thinking was Francis Thompson's *In No Strange Land*, in which he asks if it makes sense to look for God up in the heavens and turns instead to the here and now and ends with the image of 'Christ walking on the waters not of Gennesareth but Thames.'

In my teens I had various problems with the gospels. The birth narratives told by Matthew and Luke and the stories of the passion, crucifixion and resurrection in all four gospels did not present me with a problem. But I could not see why Jesus told a crowd of devils, or unclean spirits, to enter into a herd of swine, which then got drowned, or why on earth he cursed a fig tree. One solution was to skip these passages, and that is what I did at first. The other, which I adopted later, was to recognise that they are parts of an oral tradition written down a few decades after the stories were first told, and that the men who told them had a cast of mind very different from the way we think two thousand years later. What is strange is not so much that there are parts of the gospels which are difficult, or even impossible, to understand or believe, but rather that so much speaks so directly and clearly to us.

I had something of a crisis of conscience in my last year at school when a boy I knew in another house suddenly disappeared. He had been expelled for some unmentioned, apparently unmentionable, but implicitly homosexual, offence. I only knew that much because I persisted in asking about it. I then went to see the school chaplain and quoted the story of the woman taken in adultery. He replied by explaining that that story did not appear in the oldest manuscripts of St John's gospel, and I need not let it concern me. I was shocked. After all, the early church had thought the story important enough as an illustration of how Jesus thought to include it in St John's gospel. As for whether the authorities at school had good reason for acting as they did, I had no way of knowing. But I was quite sure that the chaplain's reaction to my concerns was inappropriate. I was in no danger thereafter in believing in the infallibility of the clergy.

What influenced me above all were the stories Jesus told, such as those of the Good Samaritan, the Prodigal Son and the two men who went up to the temple to pray. I admired the way he was reported to have replied to questions, such as what was the greatest commandment in the Law and whether or not it was right to pay taxes to Caesar, and impressed by the way he reacted to situations such as being faced with the woman taken in adultery.

Up at Oxford I encountered theology and by the time I was studying *St Bernard* as a special subject I found myself writing essays on such topics as whether Peter Abelard or Gilbert de la Porée strayed further into heresy when writing about the Doctrine of the Trinity. The answer appeared to be that Abelard was the better scholar, but his relationship with Heloise got his name into the Sunday papers, so it was his work that was condemned rather than Gilbert's. Such things interested me, but getting one's theological ideas right always seemed to me far less important than understanding what Jesus was teaching and trying to follow him.

At Pembroke we were all required to attend chapel at least three times a week. The services were attended even by Roman Catholics, who, no doubt, like Naaman the Syrian, bowed their heads in the house of Rimmon while thinking of the Lord God of Israel, and then on Sundays would go off to the Roman Catholic Chaplaincy. They were also attended by evangelicals, who on Sundays would go off to the nearby church of St Ebbe's, where they would receive the sacrament from someone other than the college chaplain, Colin Morris, who had not experienced a dramatic Pauline conversion and was therefore seen by them as not a proper Christian.

I saw the Roman Catholics as too sure that the Church had the right answer to everything and the evangelicals as too sure that the Bible had the right answer to everything. I was less sure about right answers, but I went every day to the brief service of Matins, immediately before breakfast. It was in line with the practice of regular public worship that I had got used to in eight years at Christ's Hospital.

Some of my best friends were Roman Catholics, notably Peter Prescott, the other history scholar of my year, and Peter Glazebrook, another history scholar, who came up the following year to read Law and who later, when a Fellow of Jesus College, Cambridge, arranged for me to spend a term there as a Fellow Commoner. One week-end during the summer vacation, and while I was studying medieval monasticism, he took me to stay at Belmont Abbey, where he had been at school, for the very valuable and enjoyable experience of encountering Benedictine monasticism at first hand.

Another of my friends, and another of the scholars of my year, Robin Ellis, was an Anglo-Catholic. That is, he was attached to that part of the Church of England which emphasised the importance of the ancient beliefs and practices of the universal, or catholic, church, while not accepting the authority of the pope. Anglo-Catholicism was what George Orwell, in his 1940 essay *Inside the Whale* refers to as 'the ecclesiastical equivalent of Trotskyism.' Another of the Pembroke history scholars, Ted Barnes, this time, like Peter Glazebrook, from the year after me, was also an Anglo-Catholic, and many years later, in 2011, he and Robin both joined the Ordinariate, an organisation set up by Pope Benedict XVI to provide a refuge in the bosom of Rome from the synodical storms of the Church of England, in which modern evangelicals were taking over and they felt increasingly uncomfortable. By then Ted Barnes was retired from presiding over the diocese of Richborough as one of the so-called 'flying bishops', who were appointed in 1995 to care for those parishes in the Church of England which had a large number of members strongly opposed to the ordination of women, and Robin was the retired Archdeacon of Plymouth.

I did not number any strong evangelicals among my friends. Undergraduates of that persuasion were inclined to accost strangers in the Porter's Lodge with questions such as, 'How are you with Jesus?', and they tended to produce knock-down arguments such as that since Jesus was neither mad nor bad, he must have been the Son of God, or similarly that, since he was neither sick nor thick, it followed as a matter of ineluctable logical necessity that he must have been divine. Their favourite verse in the whole Bible appeared to be the sixth verse of the fourteenth chapter of St John's gospel, when Jesus answers a question from Thomas by saying, 'I am the way, the truth and the life. No one comes to the Father except through me.' He was using vivid imagery to impress on Thomas that what really matters is following him rather than paying scrupulous attention to the Law. He was not condemning all Buddhists, Hindus and other non-Christians to exclusion from the love of God. Like so much else in the Bible, it needs to be seen in context and understood, rather than being used as a weapon to exclude others.

I found that I could discuss things with Roman Catholics and with Anglo-Catholics. We could understand each other and agree on where we differed. With evangelicals it was more difficult. They apparently needed to avoid the contamination of anyone who disagreed with them and they gave the impression that they would go away and pray that I might see the light and be converted to being a proper Christian.

I was interested in theological issues such as the Doctrine of Atonement, Eucharistic Theology and even the question of whether or not the *filioque* clause should or should not be included in the Creed. But it never seemed to me to be important to be right about such things. Jesus did not go around requiring people to give assent to theological propositions. But he did expect those who had an excessively legalistic view of things to alter the way they thought, to 'repent', and to consider what really mattered.

Many years later I came across the writings of Erasmus, who argued in the early sixteenth century that it should be possible to have fellowship with the Father, Son and Holy Spirit without being able to explain philosophically the distinction between them. What mattered was that Christians should live at peace with one another, and he believed that that would only be possible if 'we define as little as possible.' I was instinctively in sympathy with him, but I could not go all the way. The danger with abandoning all theology is that it leaves the way open for extremists of one sort or another to assert their own views as something both 'right' and 'required for salvation.'

Some, who see themselves as 'Catholics', will assert that it is 'altogether necessary for salvation' to believe in the Infallibility of the Pope and the Immaculate Conception and the Bodily Assumption of the Blessed Virgin Mary – all of them relatively recent requirements of the Roman Catholic Church, dating respectively from 1870, 1854 and 1950. Others, who call themselves 'Evangelicals',

RETIREMENT (1999 ONWARDS)

require belief in a statement drawn up at a Bible Conference at Niagara in 1895 setting out 'five fundamentals of the Christian religion': the Bible is the Word of God and cannot err; Jesus is God; he was born of a virgin; he suffered and was punished on the cross as a substitute for sinful mankind; Christians should expect his imminent return in glory to bring about the bodily resurrection of those of the dead who have been saved.

Both of these movements, whether the authoritarianism of modern Catholicism (both the Roman Catholic and Anglo-Catholic versions) or the ideological certainties of 'Evangelicals' and 'Fundamentalists', are reactions against the eighteenth century Enlightenment. Instead of welcoming scientific discoveries and the new insights into Christianity which came from such things as biblical criticism and the study of ecclesiastical history, they reacted defensively, as if any advance in knowledge or understanding was necessarily a threat to the faith.

As a schoolmaster at Clifton I regularly went to chapel each day and to communion on Sundays. While teaching at Quintin School I went to Assembly each day and to communion in the Twickenham Parish Church on those Sundays when we were not visiting either my parents or Oriel's. At Stowe I again went regularly to chapel each day and to communion on Sundays. I sometimes took what was known as 'lay chapel' on Thursdays, I encouraged the members of my History Sixth to listen critically to the sermons they heard on Sundays, and I was strongly opposed to the wish of an evangelical chaplain to make the brief daily service voluntary, so that only committed Christians would go to it. I saw the regular daily service as an opportunity to educate the boys about Christianity, whether they were 'committed' or not. I most certainly did not want it to be a self-selecting gathering of particularly holy boys, separating themselves off from those they saw as heathens.

I believed that the young needed to be taught about Christianity, and that the Christian life should be an attempt to follow the example and teaching of Jesus, who seemed to have an extraordinary capacity for entering into a sympathetic understanding of those whom he met – except, rather strikingly, those who were self-satisfied and religious. It was also important to recognise that the core of St Paul's teaching was that Jesus had freed mankind from slavish obedience to laws, so that they could be free to live life fully, and that the core of St John's teaching was that what mattered was loving one another.

My position as a traditional, middle-of-the-road Anglican, interested in both theology and church history, but with no certainty about what one should believe, was established while I was still a young man. On All Saints' Day 1961, our joint 28th birthday, my brother John, by then a clergyman and a curate in Sheffield, gave me a copy of a little book by Archbishop Michael Ramsey, *Introducing the Christian Faith*, in which on the first page the archbishop described himself as 'a Christian humanist.' I found his view of things comforting, and came to think of myself as a Christian agnostic, or preferably 'an agnostic Christian.'

When *Honest to God*, by the then Bishop of Woolwich, John Robinson, was published in 1963, I was entirely in sympathy with his views, such as that heaven and hell should not be seen as physical places. Much later the wife of a Conservative county councillor said to me that, while she was not a Christian herself, she felt that bishops should not undermine the faith of ordinary people. She was thinking particularly of David Jenkins, Bishop of Durham, who had said that the Resurrection was not just a conjuring trick with bones. I, on the other hand, felt that the views of both John Robinson and David Jenkins were reassuring and did much to make sense of Christianity.

Many who believed far more than I did and were far more confident in their beliefs were disillusioned later in life, and I knew several clergymen who lost their faith and worked later as schoolmasters or psychotherapists or in careers guidance. Perhaps because I was not committed to any particular theological ideas nor to confident assertions about past events, there was nothing to be disillusioned about and my Christian faith, in the sense of trusting in the teaching and example of Jesus, was able to survive.

91. Changing Times

◇◇

Much had changed in my lifetime. I grew up in the 1930s and 40s in the Essex village of Woodford Bridge while it was turning into a London commuter suburb. The tradesmen all had horses and carts and much of the while their horses roamed freely on the marsh between our house and the River Roding. The smithy half way up the hill had a chestnut tree outside, under whose spreading branches one could stand and watch the horses being shod. There was a metropolitan drinking fountain with a trough from which the horses could drink, and at the end of it children could get drinking water to squirt out by pressing a button. What made it 'metropolitan' I never knew, but it seemed to give it a certain status.

There must have been some cars, because the Clatworthys' garage on the corner of Waltham Road, where we lived, could not have existed for no purpose. But the only person I can remember having a car was the local doctor, Dr Roberts, and even the newest built houses, such as ours, did not have a garage. Anyway, during the war petrol was a limited and rationed luxury and even people who owned a car could not usually use it. Our road, when we moved there, was only a mud track, but later I watched with fascination as a concrete surface was laid.

In the early 1950s, when I was in the army and shortly after I had learnt to drive, my father acquired a car. Some ten years or so later, when I was over thirty, I got one of my own. Now they seem to be everywhere and Woodford Bridge, where I lived for twenty years, is no longer in Essex but in the Greater London Borough of Redbridge, a rather run-down suburb oppressed by the maze of roads which form the beginning of the M11.

If during my childhood someone wanted to make a telephone call, it was necessary to go to the telephone box along the road and round the corner. Later my parents had a 'phone in the house, and now, with mobile 'phones proliferating, the telephone boxes of my childhood have been first vandalised and then removed. Back before the Second World War it was far more usual to communicate by letter and it was still possible for someone, arriving at his office in the City and finding a meeting arranged for the end of the working day, to write a letter to his wife warning her that he would be late for supper, and the letter would be delivered by the afternoon post. Today it is an occasional pleasure to get a letter written in ink by a friend, but more usually my friends and I communicate by email.

At Ray Lodge Elementary School in Woodford Bridge we had ink wells in our desks, filled by the ink monitor from a brass ink pot with a very long spout, and we dipped the brass nibs of our wooden pens into them and also used pencils. 'The pencil is mightier than the pen', wisely observed Robert M. Pirsig, the author of *Zen and the Art of Motorcycle Maintenance*, though the quotation comes from his less well-known book, *Lila*. After all, it is easier to rub out and make corrections. Similarly, half a century later, the word-processor is mightier than the typewriter – for much the same reason.

During the years 1944 until 1952, while I was at Christ's Hospital, ballpoint pens, invented in 1938 by a Hungarian journalist, László Bíró, were more and more widely used. But not by us. It was forbidden. Somehow, being new, they were seen as not quite decent or proper, so to this day I retain the feeling (It is a feeling and not a rational decision) that, however much I use a biro when writing something for myself, it would not be right to write a letter using one. I use a biro for postcards but not for letters.

When I was teaching at Clifton I found a biro particularly useful. There was no convenient way of duplicating an examination paper, so when I had to set one, I could write it out using a biro and four or five sheets of carbon paper. It was an immense improvement on writing each one out separately. Then at Quintin School in the 1960s we had a spirit duplicator, or 'Banda' machine, which would run off any number of copies. At some stage in the

1970s Stowe acquired a photocopier, which was another important step forward.

When I went to King George V School in 1976 my secretary was still using a typewriter, but before long she had an electric typewriter and not long after that all the office staff had electronic typewriters. Before I left Collyer's every student and every member of the teaching and support staff (except me) could use a computer as a word-processor. Hence my leaving present of a computer and a printer, both of which, together with a disk for learning how to type, proved invaluable.

Back in my childhood telegrams were still a means of urgent communication. But every word, including the address, cost money, so I was impressed to learn that Lord Cranborne, heir of the Marquess of Salisbury, once wrote a telegram which is a model of economy and conciseness to his father at Cranborne House near Salisbury, to let him know that he would be arriving at Salisbury station at six o'clock later that day. It read: SALISBURY, CRANBORNE. ARRIVING SALISBURY SIX, CRANBORNE. Telegrams, of course, like letters, have been superseded by the 'phone and now seem to survive only as a traditional form of greeting at weddings from those unable to attend.

One of the great luxuries of my childhood was the wireless. The apparatus for receiving radio signals through the air had only been invented at the beginning of the century and it was in order to sell wireless sets that a British Broadcasting Company had been formed in 1922 to make and transmit programmes, so that there was something to listen to. It had been transformed in 1926 into a public corporation financed by the revenue from wireless licences and with a monopoly of broadcasting. To my parents it was a wonderful innovation. I cannot remember life without it, and every day (or at any rate it now seems as if it was every day) John and I would listen to *Children's Hour*, with its enthralling *Stories for Younger Listeners*.

Of television I knew nothing, though the British Broadcasting Corporation began transmitting the first public television service

in the world on 2nd November 1936, the day after my third birthday, from Alexandra Palace in North London near where my
mother's Aunt Nell and Uncle Ernie lived at Muswell Hill. The
first time I looked at a television screen was on the day of the new
queen's coronation in 1953, when, in the British zone of Germany,
after parading with my platoon, firing a salute with Lee Enfield
rifles and marching past in review order, I repaired to the Officers'
Mess at Campbell Barracks, Bielefeld, where a REME officer had
set up a television receiver. But we could see nothing but a blur.
In those days the pictures had to cross the North Sea, and by the
time they reached Germany we could not tell if the image on the
screen was the queen or a coach or the Household Cavalry. Only
some years later were television pictures beamed up to a satellite
in space, from which they could then be beamed down to another
part of Earth.

A decade later, when teaching at Quintin School in London and
living at Strawberry Hill, I used to watch television while baby-
sitting for friends and always enjoyed it. But we did not get a television set of our own until Oriel's parents gave us their black and
white one when they got a new colour television set at the time we
moved to Stowe in 1967. We then watched the impressive twenty-
six week series *The Forsyte Saga* and every Sunday afternoon sat
with the children and a large plate of sandwiches to watch the
latest series for children: *Anne of Green Gables, Tom Brown's
Schooldays* and *The Last of the Mohicans*. The quality of programmes on both the BBC and ITV, the alternative independent
channel, seemed to me high.

Half a century later I am far more critical. The quality of the pictures is better - and we acquired a colour set of our own when we
went to live in Southport in 1976. The proliferation of channels is
vast. But much of what is provided is so excruciatingly bad that it
would be embarrassing to admit to having ever watched it. On
the other hand, Cathy and I now have a device known as a PVR, a
personal video recorder, so that it is possible to record any programme one wants to watch, play it at one's leisure and, if it is on
ITV, skip fast forward through the advertisements. We frequently

have our supper, then look at the time, decide to watch an hour-long episode of a series, and click a button. Perhaps in another three-quarters of a century, or sooner, that will seem as primitive as early wirelesses do now.

The thing which has changed most dramatically over the last three-quarters of a century is the value of money. In 1935 my father, with an income of £3 a week, or £156 a year, was able to buy an end-of-terrace house for £485, putting down a deposit of £30, which it had taken years to save. Eighty years later a house like that might cost anything up to a thousand times as much. Similarly the fried fish and chips which we could buy at the end of the war for tuppence-happeny from *Roberts, Wet, Dried and Fried, Fishmongers*, on the other corner of our road from the Clatworthys' garage, might well now cost anything up to £10, which is also a thousand times as much.

The main meal of the day in my childhood was 'dinner' in the middle of the day: roast meat (beef or lamb or pork) on Sundays, cold meat on Mondays, which was washday, probably bubble-and-squeak on Tuesday, stew on Wednesday, perhaps sausages and mash on Thursday, fish on Friday and something special on Saturdays, when we might also have Spam (until Lease-Lend ended with the ending of the war) at what was called 'high tea.' In the years of austerity after the war we might still have tinned salmon for tea on Saturday or winkles, which one bought by the pint from the fish shop and ate by winkling them out of their shells with a pin. I kept the pin permanently in the collar of my jacket against the possibility of getting some winkles to eat. We never went hungry, except during the period of austerity after the war, when both bread and potatoes were rationed.

In the twenty-first century, now that both chicken and salmon are farmed on an industrial scale, we probably have both of them about once a week. In the 1930s and the 1940s, when beef, lamb and pork were relatively cheap by comparison with now, we had a chicken only once a year, on Christmas Day, as a great luxury. Salmon was something which came in a tin. Fresh salmon was

something caught with a rod and line by members of the aristocracy with the help of a gillie, so I never tasted fresh salmon, or
trout, come to that, until some time in the 1960s.

Over the last thirty or more years life has become more settled than
in the same period of time before I moved to Horsham in 1983. In
the period from December 1951, when I met Oriel, until she died in
September 1982, I moved from one place to another: from school at
Christ's Hospital to the army, stationed successively in Aldershot,
Bielefeld and Fallingbostel, then on to Oxford, Clifton, Stowe and
finally to Southport. But for all of the last thirty-five years Cathy
and I have lived in Horsham, for fourteen of them in Wimblehurst
Road, whence I walked into Collyer's each working day, and for
nearly twenty in retirement in Springfield Park.

Holidays abroad were impossible in my childhood because of the
war, and for obvious reasons even the English coast was inaccessible. It was still difficult to go abroad in the immediate post-war
years because of the financial restrictions on taking money out of
the country (£50 a year per person), because holidays abroad were
in effect an import at a time when we needed to 'Export or Die.'

In the more prosperous years of the sixties, by which time Oriel
and I were married, we were able regularly to take the children on
holiday at the end of the summer term, usually to somewhere
around the coast of England: to Sherringham, Bexhill, Camber
Sands, Minehead and Aldeburgh, and later as far as Anglesey and
the Scilly Isles. But it was not until the Easter holidays of 1982,
six months before she died, that Oriel went abroad for the first
time since arriving in England from India nearly forty years earlier.
We spent a week together in Paris at the time of the Falklands War.

After Cathy and I were married, however, we quite frequently
went on holiday overseas, mostly to a whole range of islands:
Minorca, Malta, Crete, Rhodes, Cyprus, the various Canary
Islands, Madeira and St Lucia, as well as to Shetland to see Helen
and George Bell, to the Isle of Wight to see Liz and Brian Mead,
and to Jersey, Guernsey and the Orkney Islands. Most recently we

On holiday in Minorca with Helen,
fairly soon after we were married.

On holiday in St Lucia about ten years later.
Cathy had often ridden a horse before. It was my first time.

have been on holiday in Sicily, more than seventy years after George Wakefield was wounded and captured in the battle for the Primosole Bridge in July 1943.

Occasionally we have been to the mainland of Europe, in France to Normandy, the Auvergne, Provence and the Dordogne, and in Italy to the Amalfi and Ligurian coasts, to Rome, Sienna, Florence, Venice, Verona, Lucca and Pisa. We stayed in the Austrian Alps and crossed into Bavaria, where I revisited and Cathy saw for the first time the castles built by King Ludwig II: *Neuschwanstein* and *Hohenschwangau*, *Linderhof* and *Herrenchiemsee*, which I had first seen when I stayed in Munich with the Curtius family in my teens.

Once we got as far east as Jordan, where we visited Petra and, following in the footsteps of Lawrence of Arabia, went from Wadi Rum to Aqaba. Another time we went on a cruise, across the North Sea, which turned out to be far bigger than I had realised, and through the Baltic as far as St Petersburg. Later still we crossed the Atlantic and visited Boston and stayed at the Little Inn on Pleasant Bay on Cape Cod with my cousins Pamela and Sandra, and then in 2017 to New York, where Sandra has an apartment overlooking Central Park.

Shortly before that we had been to the Italian lakes and stayed at a hotel on the bank of Lake Como. From there we went on a trip into Switzerland and visited Lake Lugano, which had an impressive mountain towering over it, whose summit could be reached by a funicular railway. All my life, if I saw a hill, my inclination had been to climb it. If I saw a cathedral or a castle, it seemed that it was there to be visited. If I encountered a water slide, I slid down it. So now Cathy and I took the train to the top and decided to walk down. There was a path, though a very rocky one which was steep in places, the views were beautiful and the sun shone through the trees. After an hour I was saying how wonderful it was and that this was the best part of the holiday. After two hours my legs were giving way and eventually I fell. Cathy got me down, but I realised that at the age of eighty-three I needed to be a bit more careful about what I tackled.

By comparison with those who have travelled to the Great Wall of China, gone by boat up the Amazon or sailed to the Galapagos Islands, our travels have been limited. But by comparison with most people I knew of my parents' generation they are extensive. That generation went abroad to run the empire or to fight in a war but seldom on holiday. My mother and father went abroad just once in their lives, on a package holiday to Benidorm on the east coast of Spain. Oriel's father spent his working life in India, but once he had returned to England with his family he never again went abroad. Cathy's parents were unusual in that they ventured on holiday as far as France, Italy, Spain, Switzerland, Norway and even Canada.

92. Epilogue

◇◇◇◇◇◇◇◇◇◇◇◇◇◇◇◇◇◇◇◇◇◇◇◇◇◇◇◇◇◇◇

It was not only such things as transport and communications, what we ate and where we went on holiday which changed in my lifetime. Attitudes changed as well. As a child I grew up with casually held assumptions of the racial superiority of the British. The Chinese were Chinks, the Japanese Nips, the French Frogs, the Italians Wops and any other Mediterranean people (not that one had ever met any) were dagoes, probably quick-tempered, dark-skinned and likely to carry a knife. Africans, Indians and people even further afield were natives. The Germans were the Huns. To the previous generation they had been the Boches and by the time I was in the army they were the Krauts. I heard when I was a child that they regarded themselves as the master race, and my objection to that was not so much that it smacked of arrogance as that it was foolish of them to make such a claim when it was the British who were superior.

In April 1945, at the age of eleven, I was profoundly shocked by the pictures which came out of Belsen when British troops liberated the camp, and I was horrified that the Nazis should have sought to exterminate the Jews because they saw them as racially inferior. But at the same time I was reading books by writers such as G.A.Henty or Captain Marryat, in which the villain of a story was likely to be a half-breed. The stories would feature clear-eyed, clean-limbed Englishmen fighting their traditional enemy, the French, and they would be assisted by noble savages in the form of Red Indians. But the villain would be someone of mixed race, the product of a union between a white man and an Indian squaw, and therefore sure to be congenitally deceitful and untrustworthy. It was years before I realised how very unpleasant that view of things was and even longer before I realised that the science of Genetics indicates that mixing the races tends to have beneficial rather than harmful effects.

While I assumed in some vague way the racial superiority of the white man, I also as a teenager came to assume that that carried with it a moral obligation to care for 'the lesser breeds without the law.' Similarly I assumed that men had a responsibility to care for 'the weaker sex' and the rich a responsibility to care for the poor. But assumptions of racial superiority, male superiority and social superiority can all too easily lead not to care for but instead to maltreatment of those of a different race, the abuse of women and contempt for and neglect of the poor and unemployed.

People can comfort themselves by telling jokes about those whom they wish to see as inferior. Thus the English told jokes about the Irish ('What is written on the bottom of Irish milk bottles?' Answer: 'Please open at other end.') Such jokes may be objectionable, but they are nothing like as objectionable as the reality of notices saying, *Room to let. No blacks. No Irish. No dogs.* I never saw such a notice, but I was assured that they had been common in London in my childhood and had been seen as acceptable.

Physical chastisement of some form or another as a correction to poor behaviour was common both in schools and in the home. Hanging was the penalty for murder. The hunting of foxes with dogs by men and women on horseback was widespread in the English countryside, and was engaged in by people of all classes. All this changed as attitudes changed and people were required to behave both publicly and in private in a gentler way than had been usual.

The Plowden Report of 1967 on primary education, with its gentle, comforting message that 'at the heart of education lies the child', had a massive impact on approaches to teaching in primary schools, though by 1981 the Department of Education and Science was issuing a publication with the very different message that 'the curriculum is at the heart of education.' Capital punishment for murder was abolished in 1965, corporal punishment in any school funded out of the public purse was made illegal in 1987 and in independent schools in 1998. Fox hunting was made illegal in

2004. Early in the twenty-first century there was even a move towards making it illegal for parents to slap their child.

The way things had changed can be illustrated by a couple of letters I received from two Old Collyerians shortly before I retired. The first enclosed a magazine article extracted from the autobiography of another Old Collyerian who was describing life at Collyer's in the late 1950s. The author came in each day by bus with five other boys from the village of Cuckfield. One day a boy from another school shot a pea from a pea shooter at an elderly lady and hit her. She assumed it was a Collyer's boy and telephoned the headmaster to complain. He sent for all six of the Collyerians who came from Cuckfield, announced that he was going to beat all of them, since they were communally responsible for each other's behaviour, and proceeded to do so until the blood seeped through their trousers, where it congealed. Did I, I was asked, think that a response was required? I replied that I thought it better not to respond, as any reply would only stir up the issue. We would do better to ignore it.

A couple of days later I had a letter was from another Old Collyerian in more or less these words: 'Dear Headmaster, As I drive along Hurst Road I am shocked to see your students swarming across the road like a crowd of Bosnian refugees, entirely disregarding the traffic and the designated crossing place.' I reflected that if I saw one of my students crossing the road without regard for the traffic, sent her to my study and beat her until the blood seeped into her skirt and congealed, I would be charged with assault and 'actual bodily harm' and would be sent to prison. Times had changed, and not entirely for the worse.

Public attitudes to sex had changed as well. When I was a child the very word 'sex' was never mentioned and one was left to discover its power as one grew up. It became socially acceptable when one got married, as Oriel and I did in 1959, and some time after that Philip Larkin famously wrote that 'sexual intercourse began in 1963 (which was rather late for me) - between the end of the Chatterley ban and the Beatles first LP.' The 'Chatterley ban' had ended in November 1960 with the acquittal of Penguin Books Ltd after prosecution under the Obscene Publications Act for publishing D.H.Lawrence's book *Lady Chatterley's Lover*. The verdict was widely seen later as marking the beginning of the permissive society. The Beatles' first long-playing record, *Please Please Me*, was released in March 1963.

It was a time when some young girls followed pop musicians around offering themselves for sex, and many pop stars, disc jockeys and television presenters saw sex with teenage girls as the prize they had won for their celebrity. At the time any criticism of their behaviour was seen as 'Victorian prudery.' The dividing line between sexual liberty and license to rape and abuse was not clear and half century later elderly celebrities were being accused, and sometimes convicted, of sexual offences back in the 1960s.

In my youth it was entirely usual for two young men or two young women to share a flat together. After all, homosexuality was not something anyone would talk about in polite society, male homosexual acts were illegal and female homosexual acts unthinkable. At the same time it was scandalous for a young man and a young woman to share a flat when unmarried. Then in 1967 private sexual acts between men over twenty-one were no longer a criminal offence, it became more acceptable for a young man and a young woman to live together without being married, and gradually assumptions about co-habitation changed and even seemed to go into reverse.

One way in which my own attitude changed in later life was as a result of a conversation with Penelope Maynard, at one time Head of English and later one of the Senior Tutors at Collyer's. I had for most of my adult life taken the view that what the Christian Church calls Original Sin could in a modern world be more helpfully expressed as Natural Self-centredness, and that a measure of self-centredness was needed by primitive human beings in order to survive in a dangerous world. The problem with that is that so many men are inclined to assert their own selfish interests against the interests of others. It was entirely desirable that a man's sympathies should expand to embrace his family, eventually his tribe and even a whole nation, but in each case he was liable to promote those interests at the expense of others and might see a neighbouring family, tribe or nation as an enemy to be attacked and exploited.

When one looks at the history of mankind in that way, Jesus's command not just to love God but also our neighbours looks like advice to seek to overcome one's natural self-centredness and develop some sympathetic understanding of others. But it assumes that one starts from a position of self-satisfaction. What Penelope pointed out to me was that many girls grew up without a sense of self-worth and were conditioned to be self-deprecating and submissive. Under those circumstances what was needed was not to overcome one's natural self-centredness but rather to learn to appreciate oneself and acquire a capacity for assertiveness – not aggressiveness, but the confidence to give expression to one's own opinions. It was a lesson worth learning, even quite late in life.

My own attitudes had changed in other ways. At eighty I had more sympathy with the policy of Appeasement in the 1930s than I had had when I was twenty or thirty. St Augustine had believed that an essential qualification for martyrdom was that one should have tried to avoid it, and similarly I had come to believe that an essential qualification for going to war was that one should demonstrably have done everything possible to avoid it. One benefit of the policy of Appeasement in the 1930s was that no reasonable person could possibly have thought that the British government wanted war in 1939. In the late twentieth and early twenty-first centuries it seemed to me that we went to war too easily, in Bosnia, Iraq and Afghanistan, and looking back I felt that Harold Wilson's greatest achievement as prime minister had probably been that he had, with some difficulty, kept Great Britain out of the Vietnam War.

In my youth I had assumed that the essential tasks of government were defence against foreign enemies and maintaining law and order at home, and that its next two most important tasks were the provision of a stable currency and the redistribution of wealth from the rich to the poor. Within that context there was scope for very different political approaches, and in my lifetime there were two great political revolutions in England. In both cases what seems extraordinary when one looks back is that the main opposition parties at the time accepted what their political opponents had done and sought to assure the electorate that they could do it better.

The first was the creation of the Welfare State and the nationalisation of much of heavy industry and transport by Clement Attlee's Labour government of 1945-51. The Conservatives who followed them in government from 1951 until 1964, accepted what had been done and argued that they could run the Welfare State and the nationalised industries more efficiently. The Conservative Party, they argued, was the 'natural party of power' and for some years from the 1950s until the 1970s the political and economic policies pursued by both Conservative and Labour governments could be described as Butskellism, a term derived from conflating together the names of the conservative Chancellor of the Exchequer, R.A.Butler, and the Labour Chancellor of the Exchequer, Hugh Gaitskell.

It was not until Margaret Thatcher came to power in 1979 that there was the next great political revolution, involving the dismantling of much of the Welfare State and the privatisation of industry in the name of promoting a free market economy. After that the New Labour government of Tony Blair from 1997 onwards accepted most of what the Tories had done and suggested that they could run a free market better. As Great Britain moved into the twenty-first century neither the Conservative nor the Labour Party was obviously committed to ideals of Social Justice. Still less did politicians appear to believe that it should be a function of government to re-distribute wealth. Meanwhile, as the natural consequence of a free market economy, the rich got richer and the poor got poorer.

For my own part, I am aware of having much for which to be thankful, and I now look back at the age of eighty-four aware that I need to find some point at which to bring this autobiography to an end. It is possible that I will live for many more years, but it is more or less thirteen years since I was diagnosed with prostate cancer, and although the National Health Service has not only kept me alive but also has also enabled me to be fit and active, I appreciate that I cannot go on for ever. So, for no better reason than that 84 divides into twelve lots of seven, I will look back over my life until now, seeing where I was at the end of each stretch of seven years.

At seven I was recently back from evacuation, had just watched some of the Battle of Britain, and was sleeping in an Anderson shelter during the Blitz. At fourteen I was in the Great Erasmus year at Christ's Hospital and preparing to take School Certificate in the summer of 1948. At twenty-one, with two years' National Service behind me, I had just gone up to Oxford to read History, and at twenty-eight I had been married to Oriel for two years and had moved from my first job at Clifton to be the Head of History at a London grammar school. We were living in Strawberry Hill and had a daughter a few months old.

When I was thirty-five we had been at Stowe for two and a half years and had three children: Kate, James and Piers. My first book was published and was selling well. At forty-two I moved to be the headmaster of King George V School in Southport and we lived in Birkdale. Then, a few weeks before my forty-ninth birthday, Oriel died. She was just forty-seven and we had been married for twenty-three years. The children were 21, 19 and 17. I moved to Horsham to be the principal of Collyer's and when I reached the age of fifty-six I had been there for six years and had been married to Cathy for five of them.

At sixty-three, with forty years as a schoolmaster behind me, I was nearing retirement. At seventy, some years retired, I was fully occupied with being an Almoner of Christ's Hospital, a Parish

Warden and the Chairman of the Springfield Park Management Company. By the time I was seventy-seven I had put all those jobs behind me, had acquired a grandson, Bobby, and had settled down to regular writing. Now that I am eighty-four *In the Context of Eternity* has been published both in England and the USA, *Education and Politics* is due to be published in a few weeks' time, and this autobiography is nearly ready for publication. There are at least three other books I would like to produce if I live long enough.

Bobby shortly after his second birthday,
and in March 2018 at the age of eight.

The problem with ending an autobiography is that, if one is still writing it, the story has clearly not yet finished. But some ending is needed, so I will finish with a statement of the faith which has sustained me through a long, happy and fulfilled life. I continue to believe in God the Father as what St Anselm described as *aliquid quod major nihil cogitari potest* – 'that than which nothing greater can be thought' and I recognise how immeasurably far I am from any understanding of what that is. I believe in God the Son as the person we know from the Gospels as Jesus of Nazareth, who taught about how to live and how to look at things, and that what matters is love and reconciliation and relationships, but I also know that his teaching can be and is interpreted in many different ways. I believe in God the Holy Ghost as the inner voice in all of us which guides us about right and wrong, and I recognise that it is easy to be mistaken and that the biggest mistake is to be too sure that one is right about things.

As for what happens when we die, I only know that we cannot know. But I am satisfied with Jesus's comment that there are plenty of resting places in his Father's house, and I like the answer which David Jenkins, the former Bishop of Durham, gave when asked what he thought would happen to him when he died. He replied, speaking metaphorically of course, 'I shall fall into the loving arms of my Saviour.'

Index

Most of the index entries begin with a surname; some begin with a forename. Thus 'Marilyn Monroe', but 'Olivier, Sir Lawrence'. The decision on which way to do it is in each case arbitrary.

Education and Politics

a History of Unintended Consequences and the Case for Change

David Arnold

A history of secondary education, written with the aim of showing why there is so much dissatisfaction with things as they are today, how the present confusion developed, and how there could be a way out. Labour and Liberal, Conservative and Coalition governments are all criticised by an historian who spent his working life as a schoolmaster and now advocates a fundamental re-appraisal of how English education should be organised.

PRICE: £9.99 (Paperback) ISBN No: 978-1-912333-06-6

For further information on this and other Melrose Books titles please contact our Sales & Marketing Department:
Phone: +44 (0)1353 646608 Fax: +44 (0)1353 646601
E-mail: sales@melrosebooks.co.uk
www.melrosebooks.co.uk

Melrose Books

MELROSE BOOKS
ORDER FORM

CALL +44 (0) 1353 646608

POST
Melrose Books
St Thomas Place
Ely, Cambridgeshire
CB7 4GG, UK

FAX
+44 (0) 1353 646601

EMAIL
 sales@melrosebooks.co.uk

INTERNET
www.melrosebooks.co.uk

ORDERING

QUANTITY	TITLE	ISBN	PRICE	TOTAL
	Education and Politics	978-1-912333-06-6	£9.99	

POSTAGE RATES

UK	£3.75 per book	plus £1.00 for each additional copy	
Europe	£7.00 per book	plus £3.00 for each additional copy	
USA/Rest of the World	£10.00	plus £5.00 for each additional copy	

POSTAGE £ :

GRAND TOTAL £ :

PERSONAL DETAILS

Title: Surname: First Name:

Organisation:

Address:

Country: Tel:

Fax: Email:

PAYMENT DETAILS

SELECT PAYMENT METHOD

☐ **CHEQUE** payable to Melrose Books for the amount of : *(For international convenience all credit card charges will be made in Sterling)*

CREDIT CARD ☐   **VISA** ☐   **AMEX** ☐   **MASTERCARD** ☐   **SWITCH** ☐   **ISSUE NO** ☐

3 digit Card security No.

START DATE (SWITCH ONLY) /

EXPIRY DATE /

SIGNATURE

DATE / /

PLEASE KEEP ME INFORMED OF ALL NEW TITLES BY MELROSE BOOKS:

BY POST ☐   BY EMAIL

PLEASE KEEP ME INFORMED OF NEW TITLES IN ONLY THIS GENRE BY MELROSE BOOKS:

BY POST ☐   BY EMAIL

37, Springfield Park, North Parade
Horsham. West Sussex. RH12 2BF.
27th September 2018

Dear Hilary,

It was never my intention to send Christmas letters,
partly, no doubt, because though most of my working
life I was busy with such things as keep fits and
carol services and end of term entertainments. But
now I am aiming to make up for that by sending
you a whole autobiography. Early it 2012 I
began at the beginning while commuting each day
to the hospital it Guildford for a course of radio-
-therapy; and it grew from there until now it is
rather long and dreary.

Later I started working on a history of
secondary education in England with a view to
showing how we have got into the present muddle
and going on to argue that if only politicians,
all persuasions would give up their entrenched if
out of date attitudes, it could be possible to

national system, end the divide between the independent and maintained sectors, and provide teenagers with a curriculum which could for many of them be both more useful and more interesting than what they have at present.

By an extraordinary coincidence the very first copies of both books were delivered to me from two different publishers on the same day and at the same time, and I have taken the liberty of enclosing a flyer for Education and Flexibilities, a history of unintended consequences and the case for change, in the hope that you may find it of interest. I don't expect many people to agree with my particular solution to our educational problems but I do hope to get them to recognise that there is a problem and start talking about it. With best wishes,

David.